This volume provides a broad overview of current theory and research in the field of nonverbal behavior and details the major contemporary research areas within it. The contributions, written by some of the most prominent researchers in this area of study, consider nonverbal behavior from a broad perspective, focusing on the fundamental psychological processes that underlie it.

Readers will find several approaches to nonverbal behavior used throughout the volume, and the contributors' work represents a variety of research traditions and methodologies. What unites the contributions is the shared conviction that nonverbal behavior is an important phenomenon with implications both for people's understanding of their own phenomenological and emotional worlds and for the nature of their social interactions with others.

Fundamentals of Nonverbal Behavior is a comprehensive and up-to-date resource, acquainting readers with research on nonverbal behavior being conducted around the world. Apart from its appeal to psychologists working on nonverbal behavior, readers in the broader field of psychology and specialists in communication, linguistics, ethology, and neuroscience will find this important volume of interest.

Studies in Emotion and Social Interaction

Paul Ekman
University of California, San Francisco

Klaus R. Scherer
Université de Genève

General Editors

Fundamentals of nonverbal behavior

Studies in Emotion and Social Interaction

This series is jointly published by the Cambridge University Press and the Editions de la Maison des Sciences de l'Homme, as part of the joint publishing agreement established in 1977 between the Fondation de la Maison des Sciences de l'Homme and the Syndics of the Cambridge University Press.

Cette collection est publiée co-édition par Cambridge University Press et les Editions de la Maison des Sciences de l'Homme. Elle s'intègre dans le programme de co-édition établi en 1977 par la Fondation de la Maison des Sciences de l'Homme et les Syndics de Cambridge University Press.

Fundamentals of nonverbal behavior

Edited by

Robert S. Feldman
University of Massachusetts at Amherst

Bernard Rimé
Université de Louvain

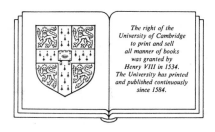

The right of the
University of Cambridge
to print and sell
all manner of books
was granted by
Henry VIII in 1534.
The University has printed
and published continuously
since 1584.

Cambridge University Press

Cambridge
New York   Port Chester   Melbourne   Sydney

Editions de la Maison des Sciences de l'Homme

Paris

Published by the Press Syndicate of the University of Cambridge
The Pitt Building, Trumpington Street, Cambridge CB2 1RP
40 West 20th Street, New York, NY 10011, USA
10 Stamford Road, Oakleigh, Melbourne 3166, Australia
and
Editions de la Maison des Sciences de l'Homme
54 Boulevard Raspail, 75270 Paris, Cedex 06

© Maison des Sciences de l'Homme and Cambridge University Press 1991

Printed in the United States of America

Library of Congress Cataloging-in-Publication Data
Fundamentals of nonverbal behavior / edited by Robert S. Feldman
and Bernard Rimé.
  p. cm. – (Studies in emotion and social interaction)
ISBN 0-521-36388-8. – ISBN 0-521-36700-X (pbk.)
1. Nonverbal communication (Psychology)
I. Feldman, Robert S. (*Robert Stephen*), 1947–
II. Rimé, Bernard. III. Series.
BF637.N66F87 1991
153.6'9 – dc20   90–45314

British Library Cataloguing-in-Publication Data
Fundamentals of nonverbal behavior. – (Studies in emotion and social
interaction)
I. Feldman, Robert S. (*Robert Stephen*) II. Rimé, Bernard
III. Series
153.69

ISBN 0-521-36388-8 (hardback)
ISBN 0-521-36700-X (paperback)
ISBN 2-7351-0398-6 (hardback France only)
ISBN 2-7351-0399-4 (paperback France only)

Contents

Preface

Since 1980, the relative trickle of research that marked the nascence of the study of nonverbal behavior has become a surging – and mature – tide. Investigators in a variety of fields, holding divergent perspectives, have made important strides in discovering the origins of nonverbal behavior and elucidating the functions and consequences of nonverbal behavior in other behavioral domains.

Such growth has led to a good deal of intellectual excitement and fomentation, not only in psychology (in which much of the work has been carried out) but also in such related areas as anthropology, communication, ethology, and neuroscience. However, at the same time, this interest in nonverbal behavior has resulted in an area that defies easy summarization and classification and that could well be considered fragmented.

Precisely because the work on nonverbal behavior is so diverse, it is difficult to do justice to the breadth and scope of the area. Consequently, this volume provides both a broad overview of the current foundations of the field and a selective view of the most noteworthy areas of study, carried out by the most prominent researchers in the field of nonverbal behavior.

Fundamentals of Nonverbal Behavior was written with several goals in mind. First, it reviews current theory and research, with an emphasis on providing broad coverage of the field and focusing on the principal psychological processes that underlie nonverbal behavior. Second, the book draws on the major researchers in the field, showing how their own (and others') research programs fit into the general field of nonverbal behavior and psychology. Finally, the book is comprehensive, acquainting readers with work on nonverbal behavior in laboratories around the world.

This last goal differentiates this book from other collections of work on nonverbal behavior. The authors represented here were chosen from a global arena using several criteria: (1) They have made important and continuing contributions to the area of nonverbal behavior; (2) their work is of the highest quality; (3) they were able to consider the field of nonverbal behavior from a wide perspective and not just in terms of their own area.

Consistent with the diversity of the field, we have not constrained our contributors by adopting a single definition of nonverbal behavior, and so readers will find several meanings of the term employed. Likewise, our contributors come from several different research traditions and use a variety of methodologies in their research programs. What unites these researchers is the shared conviction that nonverbal behavior is an important phenomenon with implications for both people's understanding of their own phenomenological and emotional worlds and their social interactions with others.

In sum, we have tried to produce a volume that transcends a mere collection of isolated chapters and provides a broad, comprehensive, current, and practical resource – for readers who wish to learn about nonverbal behavior as well as for those interested in current research trends in the field.

Organization and major themes

Fundamentals of Nonverbal Behavior moves from the molecular level of behavior – considering the neuropsychological foundations of nonverbal behavior – to the molar level, in which the functions of nonverbal behavior on the regulation of interpersonal interaction are considered. In moving between these extremes, the chapters cover the range of methodologies, types of nonverbal behavior (e.g., facial expressions, gestures, and tones of voice), and general approaches to the field.

In Part I, "Biological Approaches to Nonverbal Behavior," Rinn (Chapter 1) reviews the neuropsychology of facial expression, summarizing the neuromechanisms that produce specific kinds of facial expression. His presentation is informed by his research on the blind and the differences from sighted individuals that they display in their facial expressivity. Rinn argues that the neural underpinnings of facial expressions represent an ideal focus for the interaction of several disparate disciplines, including social psychology, clinical–behavioral psychology, and neuropsychology.

Feyereisen (Chapter 2) traces some of the ways in which the focus of neuropsychologists has shifted. For example, the early assumption that there is a one-to-one correspondence between brain structure and particular nonverbal behaviors now is viewed by neuropsychologists as overly simplistic. Drawing on work with brain-damaged patients, Feyereisen points out the necessity of fine-grained analyses based on descriptions of particular nonverbal behaviors and the psychological processes that underlie them.

In Part II, "Sociodevelopmental Approaches to Nonverbal Behavior," two chapters consider the ways in which nonverbal behavior develops. In Chapter 3, Camras, Malatesta, and Izard present evidence concerning the ways in which the expression of several primary emotions develop during infancy. Drawing both on ethological and more experimentally oriented literature, they consider the distinction between the observation of particular facial expression patterns and the affective meaning of the expression.

Halberstadt, in contrast, takes a life-span view of the development of nonverbal behavior, considering the socialization processes that form a person's general emotional expressivity (Chapter 4). She illustrates how the expressiveness of one's family is related to later skill at decoding and encoding nonverbal communications, and she constructs a general model that summarizes the full range of socialization factors that influence nonverbal expressivity.

Part III, "Affective and Cognitive Processes," begins with Ekman and O'Sullivan's (Chapter 5) review and summary of some of the primary issues relating to facial expression. They compare measurement systems for assessing facial expression, question how universal facial expressions of emotion are, and consider the degree of accuracy in judging facial expressions of emotion. Finally, they discuss the current status of the facial feedback hypothesis, which suggests that proprioceptive feedback from muscle activity is related to the way in which emotions are experienced.

Chapter 6, by Kappas, Hess, and Scherer, shifts the focus to the relation between emotion and tone of voice. After summarizing the basic physiological processes producing speech, the authors describe the current work on tone of voice and emotion and discuss the importance of linking theories of emotion with psychophysiological research and work on vocal behavior – a linkage that is currently missing.

Finally, in Chapter 7, Rimé and Schiaratura examine the function of gestural motor activity during speech. After reviewing the literature, their own research, and the problem of the classification of hand gestures, they conclude that gestures are inextricably linked to verbal encoding processes.

Part IV, "Individual Differences and Social Adaptation," considers nonverbal behavior from an idiographic perspective and social adaptation framework. In Chapter 8, Manstead reviews several basic individual differences in facial expressivity, including race, socioeconomic status, culture and nationality, and gender, and considers the correlates of facial expressiveness and autonomic activity.

Chapter 9, by Feldman, Philippot, and Custrini, discusses nonverbal behavioral skill in the context of broader social competence. These researchers have found that abilities in sending and receiving facial nonverbal behaviors are related to overall social success during childhood.

Finally, DePaulo's contribution (Chapter 10) is an overview of the way in which nonverbal behavior is used during self-presentation. She shows how the voluntary control over nonverbal expressive behavior develops with age and permits (or impedes) successful social interaction.

In the fifth and final part of the book, "Interpersonal Processes," three chapters discuss the role of nonverbal behavior in interpersonal interaction. Bernieri and Rosenthal (Chapter 11) explore how the nonverbal behavior displayed by two individuals is coordinated during a social encounter. In Chapter 12, Ricci Bitti and Poggi describe the functions of specific gestures during social interaction, not in terms of their intra-individual effects (as in Rimé and Schiaratura's chapter), but vis-à-vis their symbolic referents in social discourse.

Chapter 13 completes the volume with Patterson's description of a broad functional model of interactive nonverbal behavior. He examines the coordination of nonverbal behaviors across various communication channels and the role such coordination plays in interactive behavior.

As is clear from the range of topics covered in this volume, our contributors have addressed the breadth of the field of nonverbal behavior. It is equally clear, however, that at this juncture in the field's development, total inclusivity is too ambitious an undertaking for a single volume. What this book does do, though, is provide a sense of the considerable advances made by researchers and theoreticians in the field and suggest that substantial developments lie ahead.

We are grateful, of course, to the chapter authors, who produced first-rate chapters. Much of the editing was done under the auspices of a grant, #IA AEGH-G6192688, from the United States Information Agency, which provided funds to facilitate travel between the United States and Belgium. In addition, indirect support was provided by the U.S. National Institute of Disabilities and Rehabilitation Research and the Belgian FNRS (#1.5.410.86F) and the Belgian Ministère de l'Education Nationale (FRSFC; #IM-787-205). We also are grateful to our respective universities, which supported the Bitnet communications network that facilitated communication between the two countries. Finally, we thank our ever-encouraging and patient families, who helped this endeavor in untold ways.

Robert S. Feldman
Amherst, Massachusetts

Bernard Rimé
Louvain-la-Neuve

Contributors

Frank J. Bernieri
Department of Psychology
Oregon State University

Linda A. Camras
Department of Psychology
Depaul University

Robert J. Custrini
Department of Psychology
University of Massachusetts,
Amherst

Bella M. DePaulo
Department of Psychology
University of Virginia

Paul Ekman
Human Interaction Laboratory
University of California,
San Francisco

Robert S. Feldman
Department of Psychology
University of Massachusetts,
Amherst

Pierre Feyereisen
Faculté de Psychologie
Université de Louvain, Belgium

Amy G. Halberstadt
Department of Psychology
North Carolina State University

Ursula Hess
Faculté de Psychologie
Université de Genève

Carroll E. Izard
Department of Psychology
University of Delaware

Arvid Kappas
Faculté de Psychologie
Université de Genève

Carol Malatesta
Department of Psychology
Long Island University

Antony S. R. Manstead
Department of Psychology
University of Manchester

Maureen O'Sullivan
Department of Psychology
University of San Francisco

Miles L. Patterson
Department of Psychology
University of Missouri, St. Louis

Pierre Philippot
Department of Psychology
University of Massachusetts,
Amherst

Isabella Poggi
Department of Sciences
of Languages
University of Rome
"La Sapienza"

Pio Enrico Ricci Bitti
Department of Psychology
University of Bologna

Bernard Rimé
Faculté de Psychologie
Université de Louvain, Belgium

William E. Rinn
Harvard Medical School and
Spaulding Rehabilitation
Hospital
Boston, Massachusetts

Robert Rosenthal
Department of Psychology
Harvard University

Klaus R. Scherer
Faculté de Psychologie
Université de Genève

Loris Schiaratura
Faculté de Psychologie
Université de Louvain, Belgium

PART I

Biological approaches to nonverbal behavior

1. Neuropsychology of facial expression

WILLIAM E. RINN

Overview

The human face has an alluring quality that has drawn the attention of artists and scholars for centuries. So central is its behavior to social interaction that the recognition of faces and the imitation of facial behaviors are among the first perceptual and motor skills that human infants learn. Facial appearance is the primary means by which persons identify and distinguish one another. It is the place on the body where the emotions are most clearly visible and most distinguishable, and it is the principal center of communication and social interaction, both verbal and nonverbal.

The behavior of the face also provides an unusually clear window into the workings of the nervous system. The range of behavior of which the face is capable is broad indeed, and each behavior reflects the workings of a particular group of neural circuits. The rapid and highly precise movements of the lips during speech, the facial reactions to taste and smell, the knit brow of puzzlement, the elevation of the brows during greeting or startle and orienting, the squinting in bright sunlight, the blinking from hyperarousal or corneal irritation, the movements of the brows to punctuate speech, the manipulation of the lips and cheeks during chewing, the facial contortions of sneezing and gagging, and, of course, the expressions of the various emotions all reflect the workings of different combinations of neural circuits.

Neuromechanisms of facial behavior

Facial expressions have their origin in patterns of contractions of the facial muscles. These muscles move the facial skin and connective tis-

The author wishes to thank the New York Association for the Blind, the Industrial Home for the Blind, and the State University of New York at Stony Brook for their help and support in conducting the research described in this chapter.

3

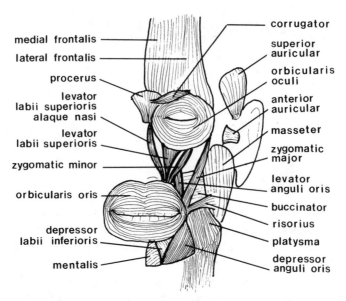

medial frontalis

lateral frontalis

procerus

levator
labii superioris
alaque nasi

levator
labii superioris

zygomatic minor

orbicularis oris

depressor
labii inferioris

mentalis

corrugator

superior
auricular

orbicularis
oculi

anterior
auricular

masseter

zygomatic
major

levator
anguli oris

buccinator

risorius

platysma

depressor
anguli oris

Figure 1.1. Muscles of facial expression. (From Rinn, 1984. Copyright 1984 by the American Psychological Association. Reprinted by permission of the publisher.)

sue, creating folds, lines, and wrinkles and moving the facial landmarks into the various stereotyped configurations that we know as the emotional expressions (Figure 1.1).

The facial muscles are stimulated to action by impulses carried through the nerves. Anatomists distinguish between *sensory* nerves, which carry sensory information to the brain from peripheral receptors, and *motor* nerves, which carry motor impulses from the brain to the muscles. They further distinguish two types of motor nerve: *Upper motor neurons* carry impulses from motor centers in the brain to nuclei in the brain stem or spinal cord. *Lower motor neurons* carry the motor impulses from the nuclei in the brain stem or cord out to the muscles themselves. The lower motor neuron circuit that stimulates the muscles of facial expression is called the seventh cranial nerve; it is the seventh of the 12 major peripheral nerve tracts that emanate from the brain stem. It is also called the *facial nerve*.

A few aspects of facial expression are controlled by the other cranial nerve tracts. The third cranial nerve, called the *oculomotor nerve*, innervates the levator palpebrae muscle, which elevates the eyelid in expressions of surprise. Note, however, that the eye is opened even wider by

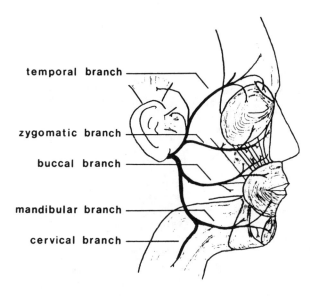

temporal branch

zygomatic branch

buccal branch

mandibular branch

cervical branch

Figure 1.2. The facial nerve. (From Rinn, 1984. Copyright 1984 by the American Psychological Association. Reprinted by permission of the publisher.)

the action of the frontalis muscle, which raises the brow and lifts the eye cover fold. Also, the eye is closed by means of the orbicularis occuli muscle. Both the frontalis and the orbicularis oculi are innervated by the facial nerve. The third cranial nerve also carries autonomic nervous system fibers that govern pupil diameter, which can vary with the person's emotional state, although it has minimal influence on the overall facial expression. The third, fourth, and sixth cranial nerves govern movements of the eyeball that may play a part in some facial expressions. The fifth cranial nerve, called the *trigeminal nerve,* innervates the muscles that manipulate the mandibles during chewing. It is also responsible for clenching the jaw in anger. However, this by itself has an almost imperceptible effect on facial expression. In fact, the facial nerve is by far the most important cranial nerve for the muscles of facial expression, and it will be the focus of most of the following discussion.

The facial nerve tract (usually referred to simply as the facial nerve) is a collection of neurons whose cell bodies are clustered together in the brain stem, forming the facial nerve nucleus, and whose axons are bundled together from their brain stem origin until they emerge onto the face just below the ear. At that point they split into two main divisions, eventually forming five main branches (Figure 1.2).

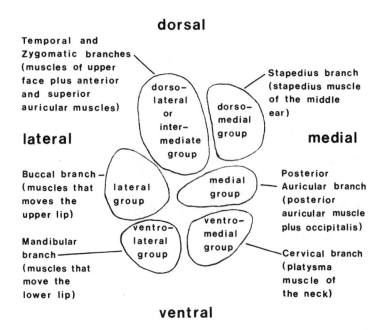

dorsal

Temporal and
Zygomatic branches
(muscles of upper
face plus anterior
and superior
auricular muscles)

lateral

Buccal branch
(muscles that
moves the
upper lip)

Mandibular
branch
(muscles that
move the
lower lip)

dorso-
lateral
or
inter-
mediate
group

lateral
group

ventro-
lateral
group

dorso-
medial
group

medial
group

ventro-
medial
group

Stapedius branch
(stapedius muscle
of the middle
ear)

medial

Posterior
Auricular branch
(posterior
auricular muscle
plus occipitalis)

Cervical branch
(platysma
muscle of
the neck)

ventral

Figure 1.3. The facial nerve nucleus. This is a schematic composite of a horizontal cross section of the facial nerve nucleus, based on drawings culled from various studies. (From Rinn, 1984. Copyright 1984 by the American Psychological Association. Reprinted with permission of the publisher.)

We generally speak of the facial nerve as though it were singular. But actually there are two facial nerves, one for each side of the face, with each having its own separate brain stem nucleus of cell bodies. The axons of the various end branches of the facial nerve do not cross the midline of the face. Muscles on the left side of the face are supplied only by the left facial nerve; muscles on the right side are supplied only by the right nerve. For muscles that traverse the midline (such as the orbicularis oris that encircles the mouth), the left side of the muscle is supplied by the left nerve, and the right side is supplied by the right nerve.

As we already noted, the cell bodies of these axons are clustered together in the brain stem, to form the facial nerve nucleus. The topographical organization of these cell bodies is not random; indeed, their spatial arrangement is highly specific and orderly (Figure 1.3). Cell bodies in the dorsal region of the nucleus (facing the back of the head) send their axons to the upper face branches of the facial nerve. Laterally situated cell bodies map to the midface branches of the nerve. Cells in the ventral aspects of the nucleus (facing the front of the head) send their axons to the branches that supply the lower face. Medially situated cells (facing the center of the brain stem) map to the muscles of the neck and the auricular muscles that move the ears, which is an important part of the orienting response in lower animals.

The facial nerve nucleus receives its own input from a number of upper motor neuron circuits. The pattern in which the various cell bodies are stimulated from above determines which muscles will contract and which will not. If only the cell bodies that map to the forehead muscles are stimulated, then only the the eyebrows will move. If only those cell bodies that map to the depressor anguli oris are stimulated, an isolated downward movement of the lip corners can be expected. Facial expressions require complex patterns of stimulation of the cell body groups to move the muscles in various stereotyped configurations.

The left and right facial nerves do not communicate directly with each other. That is, the brain stem nucleus of the left facial nerve does not send fibers directly over to the right facial nerve, and vice versa. When the two sides of the face behave similarly, it is because both facial nerve nuclei have received similar signals from upper motor neuron circuits. When the two sides of the face behave dissimilarly, it is because they have received dissimilar signals from upper motor neuron circuits.

The cortical motor system

For heuristic purposes, upper motor neuron circuits that supply neural impulses to the facial nerve nucleus and to other lower motor neuron nuclei may be divided into two classes: *cortical* and *subcortical*. The cortical motor system is centered in the anterior lip of the central sulcus of the cerebral cortex in an area called the *motor strip*. The organization of the neural cells in this region is highly systematic and forms a sort of "map" of the muscles of the body (Figure 1.4). The portions of the motor strip that are situated on the medial aspects of the hemisphere are neurally connected to the contralateral foot and ankle. The cortical representation of the contralateral calf, thigh, buttock, belly and back, shoulders, arms, hands and fingers, neck, and face are successively laid out across the lateral surface of the hemisphere. Electrical stimulation of any region of the motor cortex produces almost instantaneous contraction of the corresponding muscle on the side contralateral to stimulation. Surgical

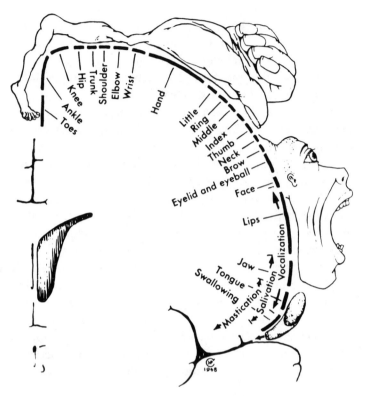

Figure 1.4. The cortical motor strip. This drawing schematically shows the somatotopic organization of the motor strip, as depicted through a vertical cross section of the left frontal lobe. (Reprinted with permission of Macmillan Publishing Company, a division of Macmillan, Inc., from *The Cerebral Cortex in Man*, by W. Penfield and T. Rasmussen. Copyright 1950 by Macmillan Publishing Company Inc., renewed 1978 by Theodore Rasmussen.)

ablation of any portion of the motor strip usually produces a total paralysis of the corresponding muscles on the side contralateral to the ablation.

The cortical representation of the face has a number of interesting features. Like the hand, the face representation is larger than the cortical representation of the rest of the body. The hand and the face together occupy approximately two thirds of the entire cortical motor strip, with the rest of the body squeezed into the remaining space. This disproportionate representation reflects the importance of the cortex in the control of the hands and face. The representation of the lower face is substantially larger than that of the upper face, again reflecting the greater importance of the cortex for the behavior of the lower face than for the forehead.

Axons extending from the motor strip form the *pyramidal tract*, which extends down through the brain stem, after which most of the fibers cross the midline to the other side of the brain and descend farther, finally forming synapses with the various lower motor neuron nuclei in the spinal cord. In its course through the brain stem, before it crosses the midline, the pyramidal tract gives off various branches to innervate some of the 12 cranial nerves (those that are motoric rather than sensory in nature), including the facial nerve. Axons extending from the face portion of the motor strip travel with the rest of the pyramidal tract and descend deep into the brain stem to the region known as the *pons*. There, the fibers from the face representation break away from the rest of the pyramidal tract. Most of these fibers cross the midline and synapse on the cell bodies of the facial nerve nucleus on the contralateral side, but some do not cross the midline and, instead, synapse on the cell bodies of the ipsilateral facial nucleus. Thus each facial nerve nucleus receives many fibers from the contralateral pyramidal tract and some from the ipsilateral pyramidal tract.

The cell bodies of the facial nerve nucleus that map to the lower face receive virtually all of their cortical input from the contralateral cortex through pyramidal fibers that crossed the midline. However, the cell bodies that map to the midregion of the face receive only 75% of their cortical input from the contralateral side, whereas 25% of the input comes from the ipsilateral cortex, through fibers that did not cross the midline. For the uppermost region of the face, the ipsilateral fibers are even more abundant, with 50% of fibers coming from ipsilateral and 50% from contralateral cortex.

In general, muscles of the body that are innervated exclusively from the contralateral cortex (primarily the hands and lower face) have the highest degree of fine motor control, and they tend to be involved in learned, skilled, voluntarily induced movements and delicate motor operations. These contralaterally controlled muscles are also usually bilaterally independent, so that the left side of the body can be moved independently of the right side. In contrast, muscles that receive much of their cortical input from the ipsilateral hemisphere (e.g., muscles of the trunk of the body) usually are poorly controlled and are involved in nonskilled and even nonvoluntary behaviors such as automatic postural adjustments. They also tend to have a lesser degree of bilateral independence. Thus it is difficult to contract only one side of the stomach muscles, and it is unthinkable that the two sides could be engaged in different behaviors.

This pattern is very much in evidence in the muscles of the face. The muscles of the lower face, with their strictly contralateral innervation, are capable of exceedingly delicate motor operations and are importantly involved in learned, skilled, volitionally induced behaviors, most notably speech. Both sides of the lower face are capable of independent movement, without mirror movement of the opposite side. In contrast, the facial muscles that surround the eyes, with their 25% ipsilateral innervation, are much less involved in skilled activities, and unilateral movements are much more difficult. For example, most young children and some adults are unable to close just one eye without mirror closing of the other eye. Still higher on the face, the muscles that elevate the brows receive half of their cortical innervation from ipsilateral and half from contralateral cortex. Finely controlled movements of the brows are very difficult, and they play little or no role in learned skilled behaviors. Most persons have great difficulty with unilateral elevation of the brows, without a mirror elevation of the other brow. Some persons can raise just the left or just the right, but few can raise both unilaterally.

Voluntary versus spontaneous movements

A fascinating fact of the neuropsychology of facial behavior is that the cortical motor system is specialized for learned, skilled, volitionally induced facial behaviors but not for emotionally induced, nonvolitional facial behaviors. Persons with lesions of the face representation in the cortical motor strip may have complete paralysis of the contralateral side of the face and be unable to retract the mouth corners on command, but they may have normal smiles on the paralyzed side if something strikes them as amusing (Figure 1.5). Indeed, the smile is sometimes more pronounced on the paralyzed side, probably because of insufficient cortical inhibition on that side. In contrast, persons with lesions in certain subcortical areas (e.g., the globus pallidus) may have normal ability to move the face on command but may lack spontaneous expressive facial movements on the affected side. These common neurological findings establish clearly that the cortex handles volitional facial movements but that emotional expressions are organized elsewhere.

The subcortical motor system

The subcortical motor system is not actually a unitary system at all but a collection of highly interactive brain nuclei and neural circuits, each of

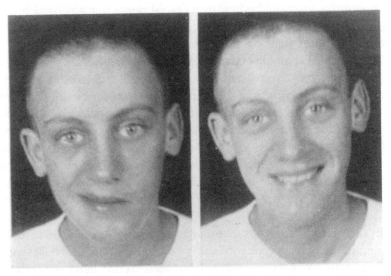

Figure 1.5. Example of paralysis of volitional facial movement, with spar-ing of emotional facial movement. This patient has a tumor in the face region of the right motor strip. In attempting to retract volitionally both mouth corners, a dense left-side paralysis is evident. However, his genu-ine emotional smile produces normal movement on the paralyzed side. (From *The Neurologic Examination,* by R. N. DeJong. New York: Hoeber Medical Division, Harper & Row, 1967. Reprinted by permission of J. B. Lippincott.)

which contributes its own specialized influence to the final motor re-sponse. It includes the classically defined "extrapyramidal" system (the basal ganglia and other major subcortical motor structures of the di-encephalon, midbrain, pons, and medulla). The subcortical system, as the term is used in this discussion, also includes spinal and brain stem reflex circuits, plus some nuclei of the hypothalamus, as well as motor aspects of the autonomic nervous system, and some limbic structures that when electrically stimulated or surgically destroyed affect motor be-havior. These subcortical motor structures carry their influences to the lower motor neuron nuclei, including the facial nerve nucleus, through a number of pathways, but they do not generally utilize the pyramidal tract. A few of these structures have direct connections with the facial nerve nucleus (e.g., the red nucleus sends impulses directly to the up-per face portion of the facial nerve nucleus). However, most of these structures influence facial behavior by sending their influences first to the reticular formation, which is a very large network of richly intercon-nected neurons in the brain stem. Neurons in the reticular formation then stimulate the cell bodies of the facial nerve nucleus (which is anatomically located within the reticular formation). Thus most subcortical motor influences follow a circuitous route to the facial nerve.

The subcortical motor systems are phylogenically older than the cortical motor system. Spinal and brain stem reflex circuits represent the most archaic means of motor control and are present in all vertebrates. In fish, these reflex circuits are supplemented by a *paleostriatum*, consisting of a rudimentary globus pallidus and a hypothalamus. In birds, other structures are added, and rudimentary basal ganglia (called the *corpus striatum*) are evident. In mammals, the basal ganglia are more fully developed, and a well-organized cerebral cortex is evident. But the cortical motor structures, and the frontal lobes in general, are fully elaborated only in humans.

In fish, birds, and most mammals, the most highly developed extrapyramidal structures (paleostriatum, corpus striatum, and basal ganglia) are centrally involved in complex but stereotyped behaviors related to the reduction of drive states, for example, mating, eating, fighting, and fleeing. In birds, reptiles, and lower mammals, such behaviors are destroyed by lesions of the extrapyramidal structures, whereas lesions of the primitive cortex have little effect.

Many subcortically organized motor behaviors are organized into *fixed-action patterns* – relatively invariant sequences of muscle contractions that are called up as a group, rather like a subroutine in a computer program. They are evident in such motor behaviors as sneezing or gagging, in which the movements are highly stereotyped and the sequence, once started, is nearly always carried through to completion.

The motor aspects of emotional facial expressions are organized similarly to fixed-action patterns, that is, as relatively invariant sequences of muscle actions that can be called up as a group. Persons with bilateral supranuclear lesions of the pyramidal tract (lesions of the pyramidal tract above the level of the facial nerve nucleus) often develop a syndrome known as *pseudobulbar palsy*, which frequently includes episodes of involuntary laughing or crying in the absence of the congruent emotional experience (Figure 1.6). These episodes are essentially indistinguishable from normal emotional laughing and crying: They have the same respiratory, secretory, vocal, vascular, and facial muscular sequences, but the patient reports no emotional experience or even an emotion that is dyscongruent with the motor response. The patient is typically unable to inhibit the laughing or crying and must simply endure it until it abates on its own. This well-documented clinical phenom-

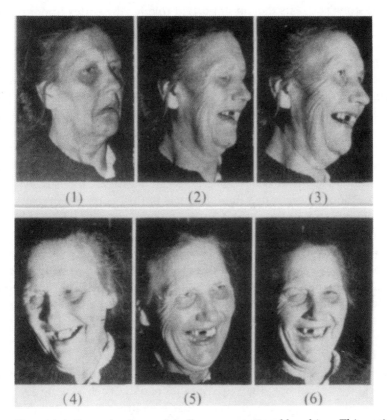

Figure 1.6. Example of pseudobulbar nonemotional laughing. This patient with amyotrophic lateral sclerosis is shown in successive stages of involuntary nonemotional laughing. The patient was not feeling mirthful when these pictures were taken and in fact was struggling to suppress the behavior because it was painful to her. (From "Pathophysiology of emotional disorders associated with brain damage" by K. Poeck, in P. J. Vinken and G. W. Bruyn [Eds.], *Handbook of clinical neurology* [Vol. 3]. New York: American Elsevier, 1969. Reprinted by permission.)

enon suggests several conclusions: that the circuits for the motor expression of emotion are separate from the circuits that produce the emotional experience and that the motor presentation of the emotions (at least laughing and crying) are fixed-action patterns, each of which can be triggered in its entirety by some internal signal. It is noteworthy that this phenomenon is associated with a lesion of the pyramidal tract, the circuit through which the cortex exercises volitional control over the face. The fact that persons with pseudobulbar palsy cannot inhibit these expressions suggests that an important role for the cortex under normal circumstances is the inhibition of emotional expression.

In general, it may be said that the cortical system mediates volitional or "instrumental" behaviors, that is, behaviors that are under the control of their expected consequences. Such behaviors can be shaped by operant conditioning techniques. The subcortical system mediates non-volitional or "respondent" behaviors, that is, behaviors that are under the control of antecedent events. These behaviors can be made to occur in response to new eliciting stimuli through classical conditioning techniques, but they cannot be operantly conditioned through reward and punishment. Cortical behaviors tend to be learned responses, whereas subcortical behaviors are innate. Because of this, cortical behaviors vary widely from culture to culture (e.g., language), but subcortical behaviors are universal across cultures (e.g., emotional expressions). We usually have a conscious awareness of cortically mediated behaviors and can readily produce or inhibit them at will. But we often are unaware of subcortically mediated behaviors (e.g., pupil dilation), cannot adequately produce them volitionally (although approximations are sometimes possible), and have difficulty inhibiting them when they occur spontaneously. The cortex may often be centrally involved in the inhibition of subcortically generated behaviors.

The cortical and subcortical circuits of the brain do not take turns issuing responses. Rather, they act simultaneously, each leaving its influence on the final pattern of facial muscle contraction. Thus it does not strictly make sense to speak of a given facial gestalt as being of cortical or subcortical origin. One might better speak of cortical or subcortical influences affecting various dimensions of the final product – the facial expression.

One probable role of the cortical motor system in everyday facial behavior is the social regulation of the face through the implementation of display rules. *Display rules* are socially learned prescriptions and prohibitions that define appropriate facial behavior (Ekman & Friesen, 1975). The implementation of display rules may involve exaggerating the expression of a genuinely felt emotion or the muting or inhibiting of a genuinely felt emotion. It can also involve feigning an emotion not felt or masking a felt emotion with a more socially appropriate one. In practice, this may amount to smiling as you greet guests in a reception line, feigning a look of interest in what someone is saying, inhibiting a giggle or a cry, or masking an expression of fear with a "brave smile."

The facial behaviors prescribed by display rules have much more in common with cortically, than with subcortically, mediated behaviors. Display rules are not evident in infants but are learned throughout childhood and are operantly conditioned through reward and punishment. The facial behaviors mandated by display rules can be produced or inhibited at will. In contrast, genuine emotional expressions are present very early in life and are not learned. They can only be approximated on command and are difficult to inhibit when they occur spontaneously.

Some facial behaviors do not fall neatly into the categories of cortical or subcortical. An example is the abrupt movements of the eyebrows that often accompany speech. These have been dubbed "punctuation movements" by Ekman and Friesen (1975) because they seem to reflect the intonation contours of the voice and add emphasis to certain points. Punctuation movements occur in the context of speech, which is itself a manifestly volitional and cortically mediated activity. But the speaker is generally unaware of the movements, and most persons cannot adequately reproduce the movements on verbal command. (Volitional attempts result in much slower movements, incorrectly lateralized movements, or no movement at all.) Lack of awareness and poor volitional control are characteristics of subcortically mediated behaviors. In addition, punctuation movements are a product of the upper part of the face, where cortical influences are much less pronounced.

Current research

There is evidence that persons born blind or blinded very early in life do not have good cortical control of the face. A handful of studies in the last 50 years have found that although congenitally blind subjects have recognizable and seemingly normal facial expressions when faced with an emotion-evoking situation (Goodenough, 1932; Thompson, 1941), they cannot adequately pose expressions of emotions not felt. For example, one study found that when these subjects attempted to portray anger expressions, they did such things as squint their eyes or elevate their brows, but they did not draw their brows down and together, which is the most prominent feature of a genuine anger expression (Webb, 1974). Other posed emotions were similarly impaired. Similar results have been obtained by other researchers (Dumas, 1932; Fulcher, 1942; Mischenko, 1935, 1936). Impaired volitional control of the face but with normal spontaneous expressions suggests a malfunctioning of the face's cortical regulation.

The conversational expressions of the congenitally blind have been described as anomalous. During conversation, their faces are said to be "blank," expressionless (Harper, 1978; May, 1977; Thompson, 1941; Webb, 1974). This abnormality is not present in infancy, and its development reportedly parallels the development in sighted children of the ability to pose expressions properly in social situations (Freedman, 1964; Thompson, 1941). Without the ability to learn display rules by means of visual imitation, it seemingly would be quite difficult to acquire these learned skills. And without the ability to pose expressions, the implementation of display rules would be impossible. This blank-face phenomenon has been mentioned by several authors on the subject of congenital blindness, and it is widely acknowledged to be a stigmatizing factor that can reduce employability and social adjustment and can even lead to misdiagnoses of mental retardation or emotional illness.

Such findings are relevant for clinical reasons as well as having implications for the social psychology of nonverbal communication. They also are important to our understanding of the neuropsychology of facial expression. Yet this subject has been systematically explored by only a very few investigators.

With the assistance of two local agencies for the blind in New York, I set out to replicate and expand the findings just described. I found 20 adults (mean age 37) who were born blind or blinded very early in life and who were otherwise normal (no other impairments, no retardation – in fact, many had advanced degrees). Eleven of them were victims of retrolenticular fibroplasia, a condition associated with the overoxygenation of premature infants. The other causes of blindness included retinoblastoma (two cases), optic atrophy (three cases), glaucoma (one case), and head trauma (one case). For two of the subjects, the cause of the blindness was unknown.

Posed emotional expressions

I videotaped these 20 congenitally blind subjects and 20 sighted subjects while they attempted to pose expressions of common emotions (fear, anger, surprise, disgust, and humor). Each emotion was verbally identified, and a scene was described in which that emotion might be experienced. I asked the subjects to pose the facial expression that would go with that emotion and to portray the emotion very strongly. I stood behind the subject so as not to unconsciously model the expression in question for the sighted subjects. The tapes of these sessions were subsequently analyzed by two research assistants who did not know the hypotheses being addressed.

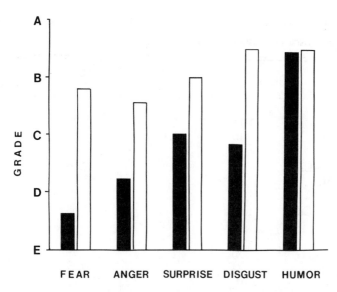

Figure 1.7. Mean grades given to the posed emotional expressions. Dark bars represent blind subjects, and white bars represent sighted subjects.

The videotapes of the posed expression were analyzed in several ways. The simplest was having the two scorers rate the overall adequacy of the expressions, giving them a letter grade of A for excellent, B for good, C for average, D for poor, and E for expressions that were judged to be wholly inadequate. Figure 1.7 shows the results of these ratings. With the exception of the humor expression (a smile), the blind subjects' posed expressions were judged to be inferior to those of the sighted subjects. The blind-versus-sighted differences were statistically significant ($p = .000$) in each case, except humor.

We also analyzed the posed expressions using the Facial Action Coding System (FACS), which is a catalog of all possible facial movements and the visual appearance and muscular basis of each (Ekman & Friesen, 1978). In the FACS, each discrete movement of part of the face is called an *action unit (AU)*. For example, AU-4 is scored when the brows are drawn downward and together, owing to a contraction of the corrugator muscle. AU-12 is scored when movement of the facial landmarks indicates a contraction of the zygomatic muscle (which elevates the lip corners, raises the cheeks, increases the depth and angles of the nasolabial folds, etc.). To simplify the scoring, some AUs that are difficult to distinguish from one another were combined. For example, AU-1,

Table 1.1. *Mean amplitude of expression-appropriate and expression-irrelevant action units for posed emotional expressions*

Expression	Blind mean	Sighted mean	t test (df = 38)	Signif. level[a]
Fear				
Appropriate AUs	.71	1.19	2.28	.015
Irrelevant AUs	.10	.15	0.52	.609
Anger				
Appropriate AUs	.56	.88	2.10	.022
Irrelevant AUs	.48	.03	−5.03	.000
Surprise				
Appropriate AUs	1.60	2.07	1.68	.051
Irrelevant AUs	.22	.28	.60	.555
Disgust				
Appropriate AUs	.70	1.63	5.55	.000
Irrelevant AUs	.24	.22	−0.25	.804
Humor				
Appropriate AUs	2.75	2.81	0.30	.385
Irrelevant AUs	.20	.24	0.50	.621

[a]One-tailed probability levels are used for expression-appropriate AUs because of a priori predictions of poorer posing by blind than sighted subjects. Group comparisons of expression-irrelevant AUs use two-tailed significance tests, as no prediction was made regarding the direction in which the groups would differ.

which elevates the medial part of the brow, and AU-2, which elevates the temporal part of the brow, were combined into AU-1, 2 which was scored whenever any elevation of the brow was detected.

For each expression, the scorers rated the amplitude of each of nine AUs, using the convention of 0 = absent, 1 = trace, 2 = subtle, 3 = fully developed, and 4 = maximum possible amplitude. For each posed expression, Table 1.1 lists the mean amplitude score for the AUs appropriate to the expression and the AUs irrelevant to the expression. An AU was considered appropriate to an expression if it were listed as a component of that expression in the FACS or in Ekman and Friesen's earlier (1975) treatment of the subject. Again, with the exception of the humor expression, the blind subjects showed less inclination to produce the correct AUs at adequate amplitude. For the fear expression, the blind subjects failed to open their eyes wide or drop their jaw adequately. For anger, they did not knit their brows and, instead, tended to raise them and to lower their mouth corners, thereby yielding an expression that bore little resemblance to anger. For surprise, they failed to open their eyes sufficiently wide. And for the disgust expression, the blind subjects had inadequate brow knitting, squinting, nose wrinkling, and lip-corner depressing.

Instructed nonemotional facial movements

The findings of previous researchers were thus replicated and documented with improved methods of measurement. With the exception of a smile, the congenitally blind cannot adequately pose expressions of emotions not felt. But is this due to unfamiliarity with the facial appearance of these emotions or to an impairment of volitional control of the face? To test this, the posing task was simplified. After having them pose the emotional expressions, all subjects were asked to perform separately each of the nine action units on verbal command (e.g., "Raise your eyebrows," "Squint yours eyes"). If they were deficient in volitionally inducing these simple and nonmeaningful facial movements, that would indicate an impairment of the face's cortical motor control.

The tapes were scored by the same two raters. For each instructed facial movement, the raters judged the amplitude (0 through 4) of the action unit that corresponded to the instructed movement as well as the amplitude of the other eight AUs, which were considered irrelevant to the intended movement. As shown in Table 1.2, the blind subjects generally did less well than did the sighted subjects; that is, they did not perform the intended movements with as much intensity as did the sighted subjects. The group differences were statistically significant for five of the nine instructed movements and also when data were collapsed across all nine instructed movements. For some instructed movements, the blind subjects also had excessive amplitude on irrelevant movements, but this was not a general characteristic of the findings. Overall, the impaired ability of the blind to perform these simple facial movements on command supports the position that the blind have impaired cortical motor control over the facial musculature.

Associated and mirror movements

Another way to assess cortical control of the face is to assess volitionally induced unilateral facial movements, by examining them for associated movements or mirror movements. Associated movements are movements

Table 1.2. *Mean amplitude of appropriate and irrelevant facial action units generated for each instructed facial movement*

Command and action unit	Blind mean	Sighted mean	t-test (df = 38)	Signif. level[a]
Raise brows (AU-1,2)				
Appropriate AUs	2.40	3.25	2.65	.006
Irrelevant AUs	.28	.31	.53	.602
Lower brows (AU-4)				
Appropriate AUs	1.45	3.00	4.36	.000
Irrelevant AUs	.34	.27	.83	.413
Open eyes wide (AU-5)				
Appropriate AUs	2.08	3.13	4.36	.000
Irrelevant AUs	.43	.31	2.25	.030
Squint eyes (AU-6,7)				
Appropriate AUs	1.93	2.85	2.98	.003
Irrelevant AUs	.33	.54	1.82	.077
Wrinkle up nose (AU-9,10)				
Appropriate AUs	2.05	2.53	1.29	.103
Irrelevant AUs	.76	.94	1.96	.057
Lip corners up (AU-12,13)				
Appropriate AUs	2.13	2.63	1.28	.105
Irrelevant AUs	.36	.43	.79	.437
Lip corners down (AU-15)				
Appropriate AUs	1.10	2.05	2.44	.010
Irrelevant AUs	.19	.22	.29	.776
Press lips (AU-23,24)				
Appropriate AUs	3.03	3.10	0.38	.354
Irrelevant AUs	.16	.16	0.00	1.000
Let jaw drop (AU-26)				
Appropriate AUs	2.75	2.98	1.15	.128
Irrelevant AUs	.06	.03	.41	.681
Across all movements				
Appropriate AUs	2.10	2.83	6.51	.000
Irrelevant AUs	.32	.36	0.71	.482

[a] Based on one-tailed probability for appropriate AUs and on two-tailed probability for irrelevant AUs.

that accompany an intended movement but are unnecessary for the performance of the intended movement. The presence of associated movements indicates a lack of discrete control of the muscles involved in the intended movement and suggests a compromise of cortical motor function.

Table 1.3. *Criteria for assessing the adequacy of volitional unilateral facial movements*

Amplitude:
    4.00   Intended movement is of normal amplitude.
    2.67   Intended movement has distinctly low amplitude.
    1.33   Intended movement is of only trace amplitude.
    0.00   Intended movement has amplitude of zero.

Unilaterality (absence of mirror movements):
    4   Unilateral, correct side.
    3   Bilateral, but stronger on the intended side.
    2   Bilaterally even.
    1   Bilateral, but stronger on the unintended side.
    0   Movement on the unintended side only.

Discreteness (absence of associated movements, other than mirror movements):
    4   No associated movements.
    2   Slight associated movements.
    0   Much associated movements.

Mirror movements are a particular kind of associated movement. They are identical to an intended movement (although usually of lesser amplitude) but occur on the opposite side of the body. Mirror movements are normal in regard to the muscles that are innervated by both hemispheres (e.g., the muscles along the trunk of the body). In young children, these movements are common even in those muscles that receive exclusive contralateral innervation (e.g., the hands and lower face). However in adults, such movements suggest compromise of the cortical motor system (Abercrombie, Lindon, & Tyson, 1964; Connolly & Stratton, 1968; Fog & Fog, 1963; Green, 1967).

I surveyed facial associated movements and facial mirror movements in the blind and sighted subjects by having them attempt unilateral elevation of the left and right brow, unilateral closure of the left and right eye, and unilateral retraction of the left and right lip corners. I judged the adequacy of these unilateral movements in terms of the amplitude of intended movements, the degree of unilaterality (i.e., the absence of mirror movements), and the degree of discreteness (i.e., the absence of other associated movements). The measurements were based on the criteria indicated in Table 1.3. Note that all measures are adjusted so that the scores have a possible range of 0 through 4. This permits easy comparison of the effects of amplitude, unilaterality, and discreteness. In each case, the subject's right-side score was added to his or her left-

Table 1.4. *Adequacy of volitional unilateral facial movements*[a]

	Blind	Sighted	t	One-tailed p
Amplitude				
Raise brow	4.49	6.33	2.02	< .025
Close eye	6.81	7.54	1.05	not signif.
Retract lip corner	5.13	7.55	3.40	< .001
Unilaterality (absence of mirror movements)				
Raise brow	5.32	4.70	−1.14	not signif.
Close eye	4.78	6.95	5.35	< .0005
Retract lip corner	6.68	7.90	3.19	< .055
Discreteness (absence of associated movements)				
Raise brow	6.95	7.00	0.08	not signif.
Close eye	6.67	6.40	−0.32	not signif.
Retract lip corner	6.11	7.70	2.07	< .025

[a]Each score can range between 0 and 8 and is the sum of the individual scores for the right and left side of the face.

side score in order to obtain a combined measure of the adequacy of these unilateral movements. These summary scores could range between 0 (if a score of 0 were obtained for both sides) and 8 (if a score of 4 were obtained from each side).

The blind subjects generally performed these unilateral movements very poorly, often generating no movement at all or movement of only the wrong side of the face. Table 1.4 shows that the blind subjects produced these unilateral movements at a reduced amplitude in both the upper and lower face. The blind also had less adequate unilaterality (more mirror movements) and less adequate discreteness (more associated movements) than did the sighted subjects, but this was true only for the lower face. Both the blind and the sighted subjects produced numerous mirror and associated movements in attempting unilateral movements of the eyebrows. However, the striking inadequacy of mid- and lower face unilateral movements in blind subjects (especially the severity of the associated and mirror movements) strongly suggests an impairment of cortical motor functioning in congenitally blind persons.

Conversational expressions

Recall that the congenitally blind are said to have an absence of facial movements (i.e., a "blank" expression) during social interaction, pre-

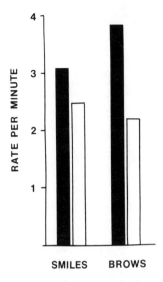

Figure 1.8. Rate per minute of conversational smiles and eyebrow punctuation movements for blind and sighted subjects during a structured interview. Dark bars represent blind subjects, and white bars represent sighted subjects.

sumably due to an absence of the learned, social modulation of the face. To determine this, I engaged blind and sighted subjects in a structured interview while videotaping their faces. The control group was expanded to 34 sighted persons for this part of the procedure. The interview consisted of asking each person to interpret each of 20 old sayings. This procedure had been successful in previous research in producing numerous conversational smiles and punctuation movements of the brows in sighted subjects. The tapes of these sessions were analyzed by research assistants that did not know the hypotheses being considered.

The tapes were reviewed twice by each scorer: once to assess the eyebrow movements during speech and once to assess the smiles. Both events were scored for amplitude, based on FACS criteria and using the same 0-through-4 amplitude scale as in scoring the posed expressions.

As I mentioned earlier, I have interpreted punctuation movements of the brows as being of subcortical origin. Thus, I anticipated that the impaired cortical regulation of the face in the blind would have no effect on these movements, and I predicted that punctuation movements would occur with equal frequency in both blind and sighted subjects. This was confirmed (Figure 1.8). In fact, these movements narrowly

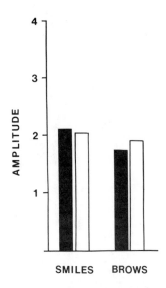

Figure 1.9. Mean amplitude of conversational smiles and eyebrow punctuation movements for blind and sighted subjects during a structured interview. Dark bars represent blind subjects, and white bars represent sighted subjects.

missed being significantly more common (more punctuation movements per minute of conversation) in the blind than in the sighted subjects. The amplitude of these events was very nearly equal for the two groups (Figure 1.9), which strongly supports the position that these movements are of subcortical origin.

I had predicted that conversational smiles (seemingly the premier example of the face's social regulation) would be less common and of lower amplitude in blind than in sighted subjects, but this was not confirmed (Figure 1.8). Indeed, the *rate* of smiles per minute of conversation was substantially higher for the blind than the sighted subjects, with the difference narrowly missing being statistically significant in the direction opposite my prediction. And the mean *amplitudes* of blind and sighted subjects' smiles were almost identical (Figure 1.9).

Given the finding that congenitally blind subjects have impaired cortical control of the face, one might interpret the normalcy of the conversational smiles as an indication that such smiles are not of cortical origin, that is, that they are products of the subcortical system – perhaps expressions of genuine enjoyment or mirth. Recall, however, that the single emotional expression that the blind subjects had no difficulty volitionally (cortically) posing was a smile. Thus it cannot be ruled out that their conversational smiles were part of the learned, instrumental (i.e., cortical) regulation of the face.

Discussion

These findings clearly show that the congenitally blind have generally poor quality of volitionally induced facial movements, both during the posing of emotional expressions and during volitionally induced non-emotional facial movements (e.g., raising the eyebrows). I have interpreted this as indicating a compromise of the cortical motor regulation of the face in the blind subjects. Skeptics might propose another explanation: Perhaps the blind simply have reduced facial motility; that is, perhaps for some reason, their facial muscles have a more rigid tone and are thus less given to extensive variations in degree of contraction. However, this interpretation is inconsistent with the findings of normally expressive facial movements by blind subjects during conversation. Indeed, the unusually high motility of the faces of blind subjects during conversation contrasts sharply with the lack of movement of the same muscles during volitionally induced facial movements. In addition, the sharp differences between blind and sighted subjects in the degree of associated movements and mirror movements during attempts at unilateral movements provides compelling clinical evidence of impaired cortical motor functioning.

Smiles are different

Recall that the only posed expression in which the blind subjects showed no deficit was a smile. All other expressions were significantly impaired in the blind subjects, but the smile was posed very well by both blind and sighted subjects. There are two possible interpretations of this finding. The first is that the cortical impairment of the blind in posing emotional expressions does not extend to smiles; that is, the cortex can manage posed smiles quite well, even though virtually all other expressions are impaired. The second explanation is that these volitionally induced smiles are of subcortical origin. Perhaps the cortex produces volitional smiles by triggering some subcortical circuit that, in turn, stimulates the facial nerve nucleus in the pattern necessary to produce the muscle contractions of a smile. In either case, it is evident that the neural organization of smiles is different from the other expressions.

That conclusion is also in line with the observations of other authors on the subject. Etcoff (1986), for example, proposed that smiles serve as symbolic gestures much more commonly than do the other emotional expressions.

The blank-face phenomenon

Many authorities have described the faces of congenitally blind persons as "blank" or "expressionless," and this is generally considered to be a significant stigmatizing factor for them. Yet I found virtually no examples of inexpressiveness among the blind subjects. The intensity of their smiles and brow movements matched those of the sighted subjects, and these movements occurred with markedly greater frequency (greater rate per minute) in blind than in sighted subjects, although the differences did not quite reach statistical significance. Indeed, several blind subjects showed somewhat extreme amounts of brow punctuation movements during speech. Six of the 20 blind subjects (30%) produced 5 or more brow movements per minute of conversation, and their scores ranged as high as 12.7 per minute. These always occurred in the context of speech and were not simply facial twitches or ticks. Only one of the 34 sighted subjects (2.9%) produced brow movements at a rate as high as 5 per minute. This probably reflects an absence of normal cortical inhibition of these movements in the blind subjects. In any case, it is clear that the blind subjects in this study produced nothing comparable to a blank-face phenomenon.

My study was restricted to observations of smiles and speech-punctuating movements of the eyebrows during a question-and-answer interview. It is therefore possible that in a different type of social context, sighted subjects would have produced a broader array of social expressions (e.g., interest, puzzlement, disapproval, contempt, incredulity, sarcasm) and that blind-versus-sighted differences would have emerged; that is, the blind subjects might have lacked these expressions.

It is also possible that reports of a blank-face phenomenon reflect a misinterpretation of something else. Congenitally blind subjects may have many other defects of nonverbal communication that, in the observer's mind, merge with deficits of expressiveness, although they do not actually involve the muscles of facial expression. Many of the interactional aspects of nonverbal communication are usually lacking in congenitally blind subjects, for example, occasionally looking away from the listener while talking, looking directly at the speaker while listening, nodding to indicate comprehension, emitting nonverbal cues of a desire to interrupt the speaker, and responding appropriately to similar non-verbal cues of the sighted speaker or listener. In addition, most of the blind subjects in my study had defects of nonverbal communication that involved the eyes. For many, the eyes were wholly or partially closed throughout the procedure, and a few had almost continuous rapid jerky eye movements (the so-called searching nystagmus that is often seen in the congenitally blind). And, of course, in most cases eye contact was extremely poor. All of these factors can interfere with the many mes-sages that are communicated with the face. It is possible that the inex-pressiveness or noncommunicativeness of the eyes, or the absence of nonverbal interactional cues, leaves many sighted observers feeling that the circle of communication is incomplete, and they may interpret this as general facial inexpressiveness on the part of the blind subjects.

Why are there motor impairments in blindness?

It is at first curious that a purely sensory deficit such as blindness should be associated with impairment of motor control. However, the fact is that motor systems of the brain are nearly always integrated with sen-sory systems. For example, targeted movements of the hand require that the subject have continuous feedback of the current position of the hand so that course corrections can be made as the movement is exe-cuted. The position information is provided by both visual feedback and proprioceptive feedback, that is, feedback of the tension in the various muscles of the arm.

The sense organs for muscle tension are called *muscle spindles.* Muscles that move skeletal structures around and work against resistance (e.g., muscles of the arms and hands, jaw muscles) are richly supplied with spindles. But in the muscles of facial expression, which move no skeletal structures and do not work against significant resistance, scarcely any muscle spindles have been found (Brodal, 1981; Olkowski & Manocha, 1973). The limited amount of position sense that we do have regarding our facial landmarks probably comes from mechanoreceptors in the fa-cial skin. Thus we must rely on visual feedback to augment this som-esthetic feedback, especially during childhood when the subtleties of volitional facial communication are being learned.

The importance of visual feedback of the face (through reflected im-ages) for the motor control of the face can be demonstrated by its role in the control of the upper face, which is usually poor. Most persons cannot perform very well unilateral elevations of the brows. Asked to raise just one brow, many people raise the opposite one or else lower the one they intended to raise. And they often believe that they are performing the action correctly until they are shown their own reflected image in a mirror. Then, after some practice with a mirror, many people can improve their control over their eyebrows.

For sighted persons, visual feedback of the position of the various facial landmarks probably is important to the development of social–volitional control over the face. It is likely that, as children, we use visual feedback to learn good visual control over the lower face, and that the absence of vision during childhood leaves the congenitally blind without the feedback necessary to learn the kind of volitional control over the face that is necessary to pose expressions or appropriately modulate the face's natural (subcortically mediated) expressiveness.

Stated in oversimplified terms, people born blind cannot pose emotional expressions for the same reason that persons born deaf cannot easily learn to sing. They lack the particular kind of feedback necessary to know whether they are doing it right.

Conclusions

It is clear that there is much we can learn from the microobservation of persons blinded early in life. Such studies can provide information about brain–behavior relationships, as well as about the structure of social interaction and the role of nonverbal behavior. There is also considerable clinical value in such studies, as they help pinpoint areas of communication of which the congenitally blind need to be aware. The 20 blind subjects who participated in my study uniformly found it interesting and useful. Other investigators should be encouraged to explore these issues from the clinical perspective, with an eye toward remediation.

More broadly, it can be very profitable to examine the neural underpinnings of nonverbal behaviors in general. Such studies can provide valuable insight into a variety of clinical phenomena that seem to be derangements of nonverbal behavior. Examples include autistic head banging and related self-stimulating behaviors, the repetitive "checking" and "cleaning" behaviors associated with obsessive–compulsive disorder, nail biting, thumb sucking, teeth grinding, and the facial twitches and vocal expletives associated with Tourette's syndrome. Exploring the neural basis of normal nonverbal behaviors has also been shown to be highly rewarding in regard to gestures, intonations, contours of speech, and gaze shifts associated with cognitive processes.

With a few exceptions, the neural underpinnings of nonverbal behavior have been explored in only a cursory way, but it is an ideal focus for the interaction of social psychology, clinical–behavioral psychology, and neuropsychology. The collaborative efforts of these disciplines can be expected to yield findings that will have utility in all three spheres and beyond.

References

Abercrombie, M. J., Lindon, R. L., & Tyson, M. C. (1964). Associated movements in normal and physically handicapped children. *Developmental Medicine and Child Neurology, 6,* 573–577.

Brodal, A. (1981). *Neurological anatomy: In relation to clinical medicine.* New York: Oxford University Press.

Connolly, K., & Stratton, P. (1968). Developmental changes in associated movements. *Developmental Medicine and Child Neurology, 10,* 49–56.

Courville, J. (1966). Rubrobulbar fibers to the facial nucleus and lateral reticular nucleus (nucleus of the lateral funiculus). *Brain Research, 1,* 317–337.

DeJong, R. N. (1979). *The neurologic examination.* Hagerstown, MD: Harper & Row.

Dumas, G. (1932). La mimique des aveugles. *Bulletin de L'Academie de Medicine, 107,* 607–610.

Ekman, P., & Friesen, W. V. (1975). *Unmasking the face.* Englewood Cliffs, NJ: Prentice-Hall.

(1978). *The Facial Action Coding System.* Palo Alto, CA: Consulting Psychologists Press.

Etcoff, N. L. (1986). The neuropsychology of emotional expression. In G. Goldstein & R. Tarter (Eds.), *Advances in clinical neuropsychology* (pp. 127–179). New York: Plenum.

Fog, E., & Fog, M. (1963). Cerebral inhibition examined by associated movements. In M. Bax and R. MacKeith (Eds.), *Minimal cerebral dysfunction* (pp.52–62). London: Spastic Society and H. Heinemann.

Freedman, D. G. (1964). Smiling in blind infants and the issue of innate vs acquired. *Journal of Child Pyschology and Psychiatry, 5,* 171–184.

Fulcher, J. S. (1942). "Voluntary" facial expression in blind and seeing children. *Archives of Psychology,* no. 272, pp. 1–49.

Goodenough, F. L. (1932). Expression of the emotions in a blind–deaf child. *Journal of Abnormal and Social Psychology, 27,* 328–333.

Green, J. B. (1967). An electromyographic study of mirror movements. *Neurology, 17,* 91–94.

Harper, F. W. (1978). Gestures of the blind. *Education of the Visually Handicapped,* Spring, pp. 14–20.

May, M. (1977). *AFB Practice Report: Nonverbal communication and the congenitally blind: A subject bibliography of print and non-print materials for the development of training programs.* New York: American Foundation for the Blind.

Mishchenko, M. N. (1935). [Peculiarities of voluntary movements of the facial muscles in blind people.] *Sovetsk. Nevropat.*, no. 7, 121–132. (Abstract only) (1936). [Quint's method of the investigation of the facial motor phenomena of blind children and youth.] *Nevropat. i Psikhiat.*, 5, 1379–1386. (Abstract only)

Olkowski, Z., & Manocha, S. L. (1973). Muscle spindles. In G. H. Bourne (Ed.), *The structure and function of muscle* (2nd ed., pp. 365–482). New York: Plenum.

Penfield, W., & Rasmussen, T. (1950). *The cerebral cortex of man.* New York: Macmillan.

Poeck, K. (1969). Pathophysiology of emotional disorders associated with brain damage. In P. J. Vinken & G. W. Bruyn (Eds.), *Handbook of clinical neurology* (Vol. 3, pp. 343–367). New York: American Elsevier.

Rinn, W. (1984). The neuropsychology of facial expression: A review of the neurological and psychological mechanisms for producing facial expressions. *Psychological Bulletin, 95* (1), 52–77.

Thompson, J. (1941). Development of facial expression of emotion in blind and seeing children. *Archives of Psychology*, no. 264, pp. 1–47.

Webb, N. C. (1974). The use of myoelectric feedback in teaching facial expression to the blind. *Research Bulletin: American Foundation for the Blind, 27*, 231–262.

2. Brain pathology, lateralization, and nonverbal behavior

PIERRE FEYEREISEN

Introduction to the neuropsychology of nonverbal behavior

Neuropsychologists probably do not consider the expression *nonverbal behavior* in the same way that other psychologists do. Psychology is multidimensional, and each approach stresses different aspects of behavior: cognitive, developmental, social, pathological, and so on. Therefore, to enable specialists to communicate with one another and to assess the contribution of neuropsychology to the study of nonverbal behavior, we first have to define our terms: How does neuropsychology see nonverbal behavior? What perspective does this discipline have?

Nonverbal behavior

Verbal and nonverbal impairments have been observed in the behavior of brain-damaged patients since the beginning of clinical neuropsychology (Hécaen & Albert, 1978). Various disorders have been described in regard to walking, dressing, drawing, orienting attention to environmental features, performing gestures on request, and recognizing objects from vision. Formally speaking, all these activities – to the extent that they do not involve a linguistic code – may be called nonverbal. Of course, there is no general explanation for such a heterogeneous set of phenomena: Science cannot describe ill-defined objects, and the first objective is to formulate manageable problems. In the general meaning of the term, no study of "nonverbal behavior" is possible because the topic is too broad. Neuropsychologists therefore usually prefer to speak about more restricted issues in nonverbal behavior, like motor planning, face recognition, and space representation. A subset is selected of what peo-

The author is supported as a Research Associate by the National Fund for Scientific Research (Belgium).

31

ple can do besides using language, and specific problems are studied within this domain. This chapter is devoted to expressive and receptive gestures and facial and vocal cues of emotion as studied by neuropsychology. It will not be an exhaustive review; rather, we shall discuss the main preoccupations of the field and some current representative studies.

The aims and methods of neuropsychology in the study of nonverbal behavior

Neuropsychology formulates questions about nonverbal behavior within a specific perspective and devises original methods to answer them. In this domain, as in others, it uses properties of the central nervous system in order to study psychological functions. From this viewpoint, the most relevant characteristic of the brain is its architecture: All things are not done in the same place at the same time. Some structures may be extremely specialized, with cells or modules coding defined events of the environment. Other parts of the neuronal tissue might be of more general use. Cross-modal transfer relies on what we call *associative structures*. An analogy with the working memory of a computer may also help clarify the logic of some distributed organizations (i.e., inconsistent localizations). The ultimate goal of neuropsychology may be the perfect mapping of psychological states on cerebral states. Indeed, speaking, listening, moving, and perceiving bodily, facial, and vocal cues imply the activation of different brain areas. Thus, the first studies attempted to "localize" in the brain those functions underlying nonverbal behavior. However, the problems encountered in this enterprise required changes in orientation.

The localization of brain functions. A great deal of information has been gathered about the locus and the anatomy of brain structures in which lesions disrupt visuogestural, visuofacial, and auditory–vocal processing (Kolb & Whishaw, 1985). But the more such information accumulates, the more difficult it is to synthesize it. Indeed, the lesions resulting in nonverbal impairments cover large areas, and generalizations are allowed only in terms of gross distinctions between the right and left hemispheres or among the frontal, parietal, temporal, and occipital lobes. These densely interconnected areas encompass different structures and do not constitute the precise localization that a neuropsychologist hopes to have. Animal experimentation may permit finer specification, but ethics and human complexity do not, and so we are left with approximations. Thus, several left-hemiphere sites, cortical and subcortical, have been found to be involved in the production of symbolic gestures (Agostini, Coletti, Orlando, & Tredici, 1983; Basso, Luzzatti, & Spinnler, 1980; De Renzi, Faglioni, Lodesani, & Vecchi, 1983; Heilman, Rothi, & Kertesz, 1983; Jason, 1985; Kertesz & Ferro, 1984; Paillard, 1982). Similarly, the comprehension of pantomimic gestures and of nonverbal sounds may be disrupted by very different left-hemisphere lesions (Ferro, Martins, Mariano, & Castro-Caldas, 1983; Varney & Damasio, 1987; Varney, Damasio, & Adler, 1989). Emotional processing also relies on several structures that interact within the limbic system but whose specific functions remain largely unknown (Damasio & Van Hoesen, 1983; LeDoux, 1986; Panksepp, 1986). Brain damage that elicits pathological outbursts of laughing, for instance, may have diverse localizations (Poeck, 1969).

This complexity relates to our current knowledge of the brain mechanisms of motor control and visual perception (see, e.g., Phillips, Zeki, & Barlow, 1984). A product of a long phylogenesis, the central nervous system processes information on several levels. The facial musculature, for example, is under the direct control of facial nuclei in the brain stem, and these neurons receive signals from basal ganglia and the motor cortex (Rinn, 1984). The cells that command motor activity are themselves activated by other neurons related to perceptual and motivational mechanisms. Thus, facial expression may be impaired by damage to these structures or by interruptions of their connections. Clinicians have the difficult task of uncovering the distinctive features of the different pathological outcomes. To be guided in that research, they need a model of the hidden operations resulting in motor output. Using a "black box," which may be legitimate in other fields of psychology, is not permissible here. Thus, brain functions cannot be precisely located if the behavioral categories are too large (Posner, Petersen, Fox, & Raichle, 1988). Global terms like *gesture production* or *emotional processing* cover a diversity of processes and are not useful for understanding the brain code. Refined descriptions of mental functioning are required to build testable hypotheses about the mapping of behavioral processes in the nervous tissue. Accordingly, with the current state of knowledge, localization of function is, at the very least, premature. We shall have to wait to see whether the assumption of a one-to-one correspondence between elementary psychological input–output functions and neuronal activity is realistic or whether more distributed organizations (i.e., many-to-many correspondences) is more accurate.

Toward a taxonomy of mental functions. Neuropsychology may, nevertheless, pursue a more reasonable objective than localizations. Together with other psychological approaches, it can help describe the architecture underlying nonverbal behavior.

The information-processing models provide a framework for a taxonomic analysis of mental functions. These models have been developed mainly with regard to word, face, and object recognition and probably originate from a common source in reaction-time analysis that distinguishes different stages: (1) stimulus identification, (2) response selection, and (3) response programmation (Sanders, 1980; for recent discussions, see, e.g., Meyer, Irwin, Osman, & Kounios, 1988; Miller, 1988). For instance, it is assumed that a task like object naming involves different, partially parallel, processes: first, a visual analysis leading to a structural description that is independent of the viewer's perspective and of the object peculiarities; second, a semantic description leading to the selection of a lexical entry; and third, a phonological description addressing the articulatory programs (Humphreys, Riddoch, & Quinlan, 1988). Some independent variables may selectively affect one of these processes. Similarly, brain lesions may disturb one operation while sparing the others. Thus, there is converging evidence for the distinctions drawn from experimental analysis of normal subjects. It also follows that brain functions cannot be localized before the elementary operations underlying complex performances like naming or gesturing are identified. Studies of the reception and production of vocal and facial signals of emotion may be conducted using the same rationale.

From such an information-processing perspective, modality specificity is assumed for input and output components: Sense organs code information in different formats. Moreover, these sensory codes are assumed to be addressed to specific recognition devices. In the visual modality, for instance, there are specialized processing units for written words, faces, pictures, and so on. According to the input modality, different kinds of information are available from these early stages. For example, phonological information is more readily extracted from written words than from pictures, and so oral naming responses are faster or more accurate for words than for pictures. Inversely, some functional or affective features might be more easily activated from nonverbal than from verbal input. The question then arises as to whether the central "semantic" component is amodal or whether it is still shaped by modality-specific properties. If so, a verbal and visual (nonverbal) long-term memory should be distinguished (Shallice, 1987, 1988, chap. 12). Some reactions may also bypass this central stage and be said to be automatic; in these cases, direct connections from stimulus identification to response programmation are assumed.

Other taxonomies of psychological functions are drawn from the analysis of memory tasks. In this domain, neuropsychology also intends to examine the relevance of the distinctions drawn from experimental data in cognitive psychology (articulatory loop versus visuospatial sketch, declarative versus procedural memory, etc.; see, e.g., Baddeley, 1986; Squire, 1986). These studies, however, pertain to aspects of nonverbal behavior other than those selected for this chapter.

Methods. Neuropsychological research mainly uses three kinds of method (Hannay, 1986; Jeeves & Baumgartner, 1986). Historically, the first was the study of brain-damaged people, one major result being the uncovering of functional asymmetries. Second, procedures were devised to compare left and right hemispheres in normal subjects. Third, and more recently, noninvasive medical imagery techniques like electroencephalography, cerebral blood flow analysis, and positron emission tomography have provided descriptions of brain activity during mental functioning. Some of these techniques are still in their infancy and have yet to be used to dissociate components of nonverbal behavior as defined in this chapter. Others are better developed but raise specific methodological problems that will not be discussed here (see, e.g., Brandeis & Lehmann 1986 regarding event-related potentials). Thus, our focus will be on the first two methods, analysis of pathology and laterality studies. Illustrations will be provided from studies on nonverbal behavior.

INFERENCES FROM BRAIN LESIONS

Double dissociations. Observing the behavior of brain-damaged people shows dissociations between components that are closely related in normal functioning. For example, some aphasics (i.e., subjects suffering from various kinds of language impairments as a result of focal cerebral lesions) may pantomime the function of an object they cannot name (Feyereisen, Barter, Goossens, & Clerebaut, 1988). These data could provide evidence for the functional independence of two communicative modalities in the late response stages. However, an alternative account may be simply that one task, gesturing, is easier than another, naming. The single processor underlying speech and gestures would show impairment only in the most demanding conditions (assumed to be the verbal ones) because the most complex processes are also the most prone to disruption by brain lesions. Thus, in order to demonstrate a separation of the verbal and nonverbal communication processes, it is necessary to find other subjects without a language deficit who are impaired in the nonverbal task (Shallice, 1988, chap. 10). In this way, the description of the reverse dissociation, or the analysis of task requirements in normal subjects, can rule out the interpretation in terms of processing demands. If this cannot be demonstrated, a single component will be assumed, and its functioning can be described to account for the observed impairment. Aphasics have been shown, for instance, to learn some types of gestures more easily than others (Coelho & Duffy, 1986; Daniloff, Fritelli, Buckingham, Hoffman, & Daniloff, 1986). It is unlikely that specific brain areas code different kinds of gestures (Amerind, American Sign Language, etc.) and that patients with inverse performances can be found. A better research strategy is to identify the variables that influence sign learnability, such as motor complexity, iconicity, and concreteness of the referent.

Group- versus single-case comparisons. When the task of neuropsychology was seeking localizations, large groups of patients were used in order to reduce the weight of interindividual differences and measurement errors. Group studies were also conducted to compare the consequences of right- and left-hemisphere anterior and posterior lesions. These data are relevant to the assessment of general probabilistic propositions like this one: "Impairments of symbolic gesture comprehension more likely follow left-hemisphere damage than right-hemisphere damage." But group studies are inadequate when a finer description of the cerebral architecture is needed, largely because of the great heterogeneity of the pathological population (Caramazza, 1986; McCloskey & Caramazza, 1988). Consider a question like this: Does the comprehension of pantomimes relate to that of nonverbal sounds (Varney, 1982)? In a sample of 44 aphasics, performances in two tasks, gesture-to-picture and sound-to-picture matching, were significantly associated. Only five subjects behaved normally in the first task but were impaired in the second, whereas four other subjects showed the reverse dissociation. If a cerebral lesion may affect one result and not the other, the processes must be independent, despite statistical analysis showing a significant association. The observation of one exception is enough to disqualify a general rule. Similar examples are the production and comprehension of symbolic gestures, which are generally associated in the aphasic population, but there also are cases of impaired comprehension not accompanied by expressive disorders (Gainotti & Lemmo, 1976; Rothi, Mack, & Heilman, 1986). If the objective is not to assess the risk of associated disorders but to describe dissociations of functions, answers cannot be found at the group level.

Careful case studies have now become the standard of research in neuropsychology. The instructions to authors for *Cognitive Neuropsychology* (1987, vol. 4, p. 110) state:

> In reports of group studies, criteria for selecting and for grouping patients must be detailed and explicit. . . . The designation of a group of patients simply as Broca's aphasics, for example, would not be sufficient. A set of patients classified as Broca's aphasics can be extremely heterogeneous, and any conclusions reached in such a study may, in fact, be true for only a few of the patients in this group. One way around this problem is to treat each patient as an individual, i.e., carry out single-case studies. Another is to provide explicit evidence of homogeneity.

A case study here consists of a series of experiments in which different tasks relying on different input or output components of the cognitive architecture are compared. In a case of naming disorders, for example, the subject may be required to pantomime the use of a visually presented object in addition to the main naming task. This condition involves object recognition from visual analysis, recall of functional semantic features, and programming of a manual response. If the gesture is normally performed, it will be concluded that naming disorders do not result from impaired object recognition, the operation shared by naming and gesturing (Riddoch & Humphreys, 1987). In this case, impairment could be due to defective retrieval of a phonological form without a semantic deficit or to impaired access to the meaning of a word from visual information. These hypotheses can be tested with a spoken word-to-picture matching task, yes–no questions about semantic features of the object, and the like.

Methodological problems remain, however, the most serious, owing to the necessity of ruling out alternative accounts in terms of task demands (Shallice, 1988, chap. 10). To avoid ad hoc interpretations, neuropsychology must rely on external evidence and the theoretical justification of assumed dissociations. Series of case studies also must be devised to demonstrate reproducibility.

LATERALITY EFFECTS. Another method used in neuropsychology to disentangle mental processes relies on the observation of lateral differences in normal subjects. Dissociations are shown by finding task–hemisphere interactions (Hellige, 1983; Kinsbourne & Hiscock, 1983). At the expressive level, the comparison of hand performances is straightforward. If task A gives an advantage to the right hand and task B to the left, it will be concluded that different processes are involved. For example, if most right-handed subjects use principally their right hand in speech-related gestures but show no hand preference in body touching, one might suppose that the two kinds of gesture rely on different mechanisms (Kimura, 1973). This line of reasoning is followed in the search for more subtle lateral differences in facial or ocular motility (Campbell, 1986; Hiscock, 1986). At the receptive level, in the auditory modality, the comparison concerns performances when two different stimuli are simultaneously presented to each ear (dichotic listening paradigm). An advantage of one ear – for example, a right-ear superiority in speech processing – is interpreted as a consequence of the specialization of the contralateral hemisphere in the task. In the visual modality, information from the periphery of the right visual field is received in the nasal part of the right retina and the temporal part of the left; this signal is first represented in the left visual cortex. As a central presentation activates both hemispheres, short exposure durations – durations shorter than the reaction time of eye movements (estimated 200 msec) – are required in laterality studies. These special conditions for vision raise interpretation problems. Sergent (1983, 1984) suggested that the right hemisphere was favored in the processing of degraded signals, so that left-visual-field advantages are expected in simple discrimination tasks of stimuli rapidly presented in the periphery. Task–hemisphere interactions are also difficult to interpret when floor levels of processing are reached (Hellige, 1983; for further discussion, see Hellige & Sergent 1986; Sergent & Hellige, 1986).

Conclusions concerning the aims and methods of neuropsychology. Today, laterality studies are not intended to describe the global functioning of the right and the left hemispheres, and observations of clinical populations are not intended to locate brain structures underlying behavior. Instead, they offer an original way of assessing the relevance of psychological distinctions drawn from other sources. Thus, research in neuropsychology should be examined in relation to proposed behavior taxonomies. In the next two sections, we shall discuss data on very simple dichotomies comparing verbal and nonverbal behavior and emotion and cognition. Until recently, these distinctions inspired a major part of the work on gestural, facial, and vocal behavior, inside and outside neuropsychology. In the last section, finer distinctions in the nonverbal domain will be proposed, and advances in the description of mental architecture may be expected from these more detailed functional subdivisions.

The verbal–nonverbal dichotomy

Labeling some instances of behavior *nonverbal* orients the inquiry along particular lines. What animals do is usually not described under the heading of *nonverbal behavior* (no animal data are examined in this chapter). Of all the possible meanings of the term, a restricted sense is intended here. Typically, this shorthand label stands for a longer description of the relations between the verbal and nonverbal components of complex processing. There are several reasons that one of the main problems in psychology concerns the role of language in other human activities: First, language use often influences nonverbal behavior, for example, facing a conversational partner or looking at surrounding features. Second, seemingly nonverbal activity implying silent thought, like the attribution of mental states to other persons, may be accompanied by covert verbal representations. Third, many operations have both verbal and nonverbal aspects: Matching facial expressions and emotion names, for instance, requires both face categorization and word comprehension. A special case is provided by speech-related movements that cross the line between the verbal and nonverbal. Fourth, verbal and nonverbal behavior may, to some extent, serve similar functions: One may refer to objects by means of words or gestures and express feelings in sentences or bodily movements. These modalities may be compared to emphasize similarities and differences or to identify the common path in verbal and nonverbal processes. Neuropsychology has a special role to play in this kind of research (Feyereisen, 1988).

Are verbal and nonverbal behavior independent? From a neuropsychological perspective, this question may be answered by describing aphasic brain-damaged patients without nonverbal impairments and other patients without language disorders who display abnormal nonverbal behavior. In parallel, experimental studies of normal subjects may demonstrate interactions between laterality effects and the verbal or nonverbal nature of the task. If these attempts fail, it can be concluded that verbal and nonverbal behavior share fundamental properties or that another kind of distinction is needed.

The left-hemisphere superiority in verbal tasks has been known since the earliest descriptions of aphasia, and, during the first half of the 20th century, the role of the right (no longer called minor) hemisphere was described in nonverbal, mainly visuospatial, tasks. Accordingly, the first studies of nonverbal behavior in neuropsychology concerned the nature of hemispheric differences, which were easily observed but still poorly understood. The verbal–nonverbal distinction was superimposed on the left–right distinction. Then the question arose as to whether cerebral asymmetries relate to the specificity of language processing, such as the unilateral representation of phonology and syntax in the left (verbal) hemisphere. Or on the contrary, is the verbal–nonverbal dichotomy only a consequence of more fundamental specializations? Three explanations questioned the specificity of left-hemisphere linguistic competence and challenged the verbal–nonverbal distinction: That is, the left-hemisphere verbal superiority could result from the asymmetry of (1) symbolic functioning, (2) motor control, or (3) analytic versus holistic processing. Until recently, these three explanations constituted the main framework for the analysis of lateral differences and the study of the nonverbal behavior of brain-damaged subjects, especially left-hemisphere–damaged aphasic subjects (Christopoulou & Bonvillian, 1985; Feyereisen & Seron, 1982; Peterson & Kirshner, 1981). We shall now examine these three alternative accounts of hemispheric specialization.

Symbolic–nonsymbolic behavior

Language may be viewed as just one manifestation of the symbolic function, which includes the use of representational gestures. Accordingly, it was suggested as early as 1870, when Finkelnburg introduced the notion of "asymbolia," that the language disorders observed after left-hemisphere damage are only some of the many possible impairments of symbolic functioning (Duffy & Liles, 1979). Neuropsychology now has specific terms for these nonverbal disorders on the expressive and receptive levels. The idea remains, however, that left-hemisphere specialization is not restricted to verbal processes but also concerns the use of nonverbal symbols (Bates, Bretherton, Shore, & McNew, 1983; Duffy & Duffy, 1981; Kendon, 1983).

Difficulties in making the conventional gestures called *emblems* and in pantomiming objects are well established in the population of left-hemisphere–damaged subjects. These problems might be explained by impairments in understanding verbal instructions, but they also are present in imitation tasks (e.g., De Renzi, 1985) or may arise in the absence of auditory comprehension disorders. Similarly, on the receptive level, aphasic subjects are, statistically speaking, more impaired than are other brain-damaged control subjects in gesture-to-picture matching tasks (see Feyereisen, 1988, for a review). Comparable deficits are described in senile dementia of the Alzheimer type (de Ajuriaguerra, Richard, Rodriguez, & Tissot, 1966; Kempler, 1988; Rapcsak, Croswell, & Rubens, 1989; see also Ska & Nespoulous, 1987). But although the existence of nonverbal disorders after left-hemisphere damage is not disputed, the problem of identifying the impaired mechanism remains.

Similar to the "asymbolia hypothesis" is the assumption of a "central communication system," which relies on the description of parallel changes, after brain lesions, in verbal and nonverbal behavior in more interactive situations like interviews or referential communication tasks (Duffy, Duffy, & Mercaitis, 1984; Glosser, Wiener, & Kaplan, 1986, 1988). The more or less spontaneous gestures made by aphasics may not depend on a separate "nonverbal communication system" but, rather, may originate with words in a single computational stage (Mc-Neill, 1985).

Empirical support was found for this position in a study that described parallels in the communicative content of gesture and speech (Cicone, Wapner, Foldi, Zurif, & Gardner, 1979). Two patients had difficulties in using function words: They used a kind of "telegraphic" speech, and the majority of their gestures (80%) were informative. Two other patients used few content words, and their empty speech was accompanied by nonrepresentational gestures (but still in the same proportion of about 50% as in normal production). The results are somewhat difficult to interpret because the reason that aphasics sometimes can and sometimes cannot compensate for word-finding difficulties by means of gestures remains unknown (Behrmann & Penn, 1984; Feyereisen et al., 1988; Herrmann, Reichle, Lucius-Hoene, Wallesch, & Johannsen-Horbach, 1988).

The study of Cicone et al. also showed a relation between gestural and verbal fluency: The two subjects with a speech rate (number of words per minute) below normal made fewer gestures than did the two subjects with word-finding difficulties but a normal speech tempo. However, this result was contradicted by other studies in which the rate of gesture production was not related to speech fluency (Feyereisen, 1983; Feyereisen, Bouchat, Déry, & Ruiz, 1990; LeMay, David, & Thomas, 1988; Smith 1987a,b). Furthermore, contrary conclusions were reached when other indices were used to assess gestural and verbal performance.

The discrepancies between observations seem mainly due to interindividual variability in such unconstrained communicative situations. Normal people often speak without gesturing, even though they have the capacity to make gestures. One range of questions concerns the cognitive conditions for being able to find adequate nonverbal substitutes for unavailable word forms (as most aphasics sometimes do); another concerns the pragmatic reasons for performing gestures in conversation. Gross generalizations like those favored by the asymbolia hypothesis are now untenable in a cognitive neuropsychology in search of the elementary operations underlying observable behavior. The hypothesis of a general communication disorder should also be rejected on the basis of the pragmatic appropriateness of aphasic behavior in interactive situations (Foldi, Cicone, & Gardner, 1983; Prutting & Kirchner, 1987).

Temporal–spatial organization in motor control

Speech and gestures may also be considered skilled motor performances. A general inability to control the sequences of movements results in verbal and nonverbal deficits. Thus, an alternative to the asymbolia hypothesis is to interpret the association of verbal and gestural disorders in aphasia as a result of a left-hemisphere dominance in the temporal organization of sequential movements (Kimura, 1976). The main argument in support of this hypothesis is that copying meaningless hand movements is as impaired as is imitating symbolic gestures (see also De Renzi, Motti, & Nichelli, 1980; Lehmkuhl, Poeck, & Willmes, 1983). The nature of the mental representations underlying motor behavior was not precisely described in this context, but several hypotheses were proposed to identify the process for which the left hemisphere showed superiority: controlling rapid changes in the speech apparatus or in hand positions (Kimura, 1982), activating visuokinetic formulas in the memory for both static positions and movement sequences (Jason, 1983; Rothi & Heilman, 1984), and performing movements without visual feedback (Haaland, Harrington, & Yeo, 1987). These hypotheses address various aspects of motor control, and all should be supported by appropriate case studies if the lesions have different consequences according to the site and the subject (Hécaen, 1978; Heilman, Rothi, & Valenstein, 1982).

A motor-control hypothesis has been proposed to account for lateral differences in gesture production by normal subjects (see review in Feyereisen, 1986a). Left-hemisphere involvement in nonspeech movement was assumed from right-hand preference in gestural activity by right-handers (Dalby, Gibson, Grossi, & Schneider, 1980; Kimura, 1973; Sousa-Posa, Rohrberg, & Mercure, 1979). In self-touching behavior, no consistent asymmetry was observed, and preferences changed according to the nature of the concurrent task (Hatta & Dimond, 1984; Kimura, 1973). Thus, these two kinds of movements seem to rely on different cerebral mechanisms. Two interpretations of lateral differences remain plausible. First, Kimura (1976) related right-hand preference to right-hand ability and left-hemisphere motor competence. The flexion–extension and pronation–supination components of spontaneous gestures were recorded, and the right-hand movements were found to be more complex than those of the left hand; that is, the right-hand gestures required more changes (Kimura & Humphrys, 1981). Assumed, but not recorded, hemispheric activation was checked by comparing lateral differences in three verbal tasks: The subjects had to describe their daily activity (neutral condition), to comment on a favorite book (verbal condition), and to explain the way to reach a given place (spatial condition). Hand choice was not influenced by the conversation topic (Lavergne & Kimura, 1987). Second, Kinsbourne (1986) suggested explaining manual preference in gesturing in the same way as for lateral eye movements. Left-hemisphere involvement in verbal tasks would induce biases in favor of using the right hand and looking to the right, whereas right involvement in visuospatial tasks would have the opposite effect. The interpretation of lateral eye movements is still disputed, and no clear conclusion emerges from this abundant literature (Ehrlichman & Weinberger, 1978; Hiscock, 1986). But the motor complexity of eye movements to the right or to the left should not differ, and so other variables are expected to influence lateral bias. Asymmetry in mouth opening was also analyzed in this context: Lateral differences were shown to vary with the task and the subject's characteristics (Graves, 1983; Graves, Goodglass, & Landis, 1982; Graves, Landis, & Simpson, 1985; Hager & Van Gelder, 1985; Wyler, Graves, & Landis, 1987). The aperture may vary with the activation of the controlateral hemisphere, but some data also support the alternative interpretation of a left-hemisphere superiority in the control of verbal and nonverbal oral movement sequences (Goodale, 1988; Wolf & Goodale, 1987).

Similar discussions have been held in regard to other lateral differences in nonverbal behavior. When the hand movements were analyzed in block manipulations during problem-solving tasks (Hampson & Kimura, 1984), manual preference interacted with the nature of the problems, verbal (e.g., crossword puzzles) versus nonverbal (e.g., jigsaw puzzles). Actually, such preferences do not relate to performance (in other words, one hand is not always chosen for higher efficiency). Thus, it is very unlikely that complexity in motor control is the sole factor determining hand choice in this case and, more generally, explaining handedness (Annett, 1985; Fennell, 1986; Morgan & McManus, 1988).

In summary, studies of hemispheric differences in motor control were successful in dismissing the verbal–nonverbal dichotomy, but they failed to isolate the critical variables explaining motor impairments after left-hemisphere damage or manual preference and dexterity in right-handers.

Analytic versus holistic perceptual processes

Does verbal and nonverbal behavior dissociate at the receptive level because speech perception and recognition of vocal, facial, or gestural signals rely on specific processes? For instance, in the same visuofacial modality, are impairments in lipreading and face recognition independent of each other (Campbell, Landis & Regard, 1986)? As was the case at the expressive level with the motor-control hypothesis, the verbal–nonverbal dichotomy in describing cerebral asymmetry can be criticized in regard to perceptual processes.

In normal subjects, lateral differences in the visual, auditory, or tactile modalities did not relate to the verbal or symbolic nature of the input (Bradshaw, Burden, & Nettleton, 1986; Davidoff, 1982). Some processing of verbal information may give rise to a right-hemisphere advantage or to the absence of a laterality effect. This is the case with Japanese *kanji* characters or with gestural signs (Lambert, 1982; Poizner & Battison, 1980). Inversely, some experimental conditions favor the left hemisphere for processing nonverbal musical information (Peretz, 1985). Left-hemisphere–damaged subjects are impaired in recognizing meaningless shapes or in discriminating nonverbal sounds presented in rapid succession (Bisiach, Nichelli, & Sala, 1979; Tallal & Newcombe, 1978). Accordingly, it has been suggested that the verbal–nonverbal dichotomy be abandoned, and it is instead theorized that the left hemisphere specializes in the analytic-processing mode and the right hemisphere in the holistic-processing mode (Bradshaw & Nettleton, 1981; Cohen, 1982). Nonverbal receptive disorders in aphasics, as revealed in gesture-to-picture or sound-to-picture matching tasks, might relate to this con-tribution of the left hemisphere to perceptual processing. For example, the performances of such subjects improve when verbal cues focus on the relevant dimensions of the pictures (Koemeda-Lutz, Cohen, & Meier, 1987).

However, the analytic–holistic distinction has drawn criticism. First, it has been noted that the processes for which one hemisphere is advan-taged are very diverse and that thus it is meaningless to look for a single label to describe multidimensional performances (Bertelson, 1982). The circularity of the argument has also been denounced: As no external criterion allows for an a priori distinction between analytic and holistic processes, there is a tendency to call a task holistic when a right-hemi-sphere advantage is observed and analytic when the inverse result is found (Sergent, 1983). Sergent's alternative interpretation (1983) is that lateral differences depend on the physical properties (luminance, spatial frequency, etc.) of the input in relation to task demands (discrimination, identification, etc.). Another solution is to call holistic the processing of structural or configurational properties and analytic the processing of local information (Morais, 1982). The behavior of brain-damaged pa-tients or lateral differences in processing gestural, facial, or vocal signals has not yet been studied from these perspectives.

Conclusions

Many brain lesions cause simultaneous verbal and nonverbal impair-ments. Moreover, lateral differences have been observed across a wide range of mental tasks and do not fit the verbal–nonverbal dichotomy. Incidentally, many confounding variables in the proposed distinction have been identified: Verbal behavior, like some aspects of nonverbal behavior, is also symbolic and sequentially organized and relies on ana-lytic processes. Thus, the brain structures that are believed to underlie specific linguistic functions might also be used for nonverbal behavior and relate to more general purposes: communication, motor control, or fine-grained perceptual processes. Nevertheless, the search for global characterizations of hemispheric specialization with alternative dichoto-mies has flawed the reasoning with a selective reading of the observa-tions. Only supportive evidence has been examined, and data showing dissociations between verbal and nonverbal impairments were disre-garded as statistically nonsignificant. Group studies from this period of research provided the main body of knowledge on nonverbal behavior but are representative of the approach that is now highly criticized by cognitive neuropsychologists.

Before we examine the finer distinctions in the nonverbal domain, in an attempt to identify elementary operations resulting in overt behavior, we must discuss another influential hypothesis that assumes a separation of affective and cognitive processes. Do the neuropsychological data show the independence of two modes of processing information?

Emotion–cognition dichotomy

A great impetus for neuropsychological research on nonverbal behavior was the suggestion that affect relies on specific brain mechanisms and more particularly that the right hemisphere plays a dominant role in various emotional processes. Observations of brain-damaged subjects and analysis of lateral differences in normal subjects provided converging evidence for a cerebral asymmetry in the processing of facial and vocal information at the expressive and receptive levels. (For some recent reviews, see Davidson, 1984; Gainotti, 1984, 1989; Heilman, Watson & Bowers, 1983; Kinsbourne & Bemporad, 1984; Leventhal & Tomarken, 1986; Silberman & Weingartner, 1986).

These data have been used to support distinctions within the psychological domain. Zajonc (1984) cited the review of Tucker (1981) to argue for the separation of cognitive and affective modes of processing information. According to Leventhal (1984) and Buck (1985), however, right-hemisphere involvement in emotion might be only a particular instantiation of the holistic processes for which it is assumed to be specialized. Thus, it would be worthwhile to compare emotional and nonemotional aspects of nonverbal behavior in order to test the relevance of the emotion–cognition dichotomy from a neuropsychological point of view (Feyereisen, 1989). This section will discuss, first, data on facial behavior and, second, data on vocal behavior. In each case, emotional expression will be distinguished from the reception of emotional cues, and laterality studies from impairment analysis in brain-damaged subjects.

The production of facial movements

Faces can express affective states, but frowning, cheek bulging, or lip pressing may also be used with other communicative purposes in diverse emblems. Moreover, signals like yawning or lip licking may serve physiological functions. Are facial lateral differences influenced by the emotional nature of the movement?

Facial asymmetry. Motor asymmetry may be studied in normal subjects by means of the technique of "chimeric" faces: From a normal and a mirror-reversed photograph, two facelike composites may be constructed, one with two originally right parts and one with two left. The two stimuli may be compared on scales rating expressivity or intensity. The left hemiface, which is under the direct control of the right hemisphere, is usually rated as more expressive than the right is. The interpretation of this asymmetry is still disputed, however (for reviews, see Borod & Koff, 1984; Campbell, 1986; Hager 1982; Sackeim & Gur, 1983; Thomson, 1985).

The hypothesis of separation between cognition and emotion gained support from such discussions. First, the expected task–hemisphere interaction was found significant in a study comparing the intensity of sad and thoughtful expressions in right and left composites (Cacioppo & Petty, 1981). Second, resting faces were not found to be asymmetric, which provides control for some bias in judging expressivity (Sackeim, 1985). Some problems remain, however. First, facial asymmetry might be due to a greater mobility of the left hemiface (Koff, Borod, & White, 1981). Accordingly, realization of emotional and nonemotional movements resulted in similar lateral differences (Alford & Alford, 1981; Alford, 1983; Borod & Koff, 1983; Campbell, 1982). Second, the issue of asymmetry in spontaneous expressions is controversial. Ekman, Hager, and Friesen (1981) claimed that lateral differences exist only in posed expressions, although, some authors report asymmetry in spontaneous expressions (Borod, Koff, & White, 1983; Dopson, Beckwith, Tucker, & Bullard-Bates, 1984; Tucker, Beckwith, Dopson, & Bullard-Bates, 1985). In their own subsequent study, Hager and Ekman (1985) found most posed expressions to be symmetric. Third, another controversy involves the role of emotional valence in facial asymmetry. For example, a smile was sometimes found to be symmetric, whereas a sad expression favored the left hemiface (e.g., Sackeim & Grega, 1987). Right-hemisphere superiority was assumed for negative emotion only (see Davidson, 1984, for a review), but other studies have reported left-hemiface superiority in spontaneous smiles (Wylie & Goodale, 1988), right-hemiface superiority in expressing sadness (Braun, Baribeau, Ethier, Guérette, & Proulx, 1988), and the absence of a valence–hemiface interaction in posed expressions (Borod, Kent, Koff, Martin, & Alpert, 1988).

In conclusion, the hemispheric contribution to facial expression of emotion and to facial motor control is not completely understood. Lateral differences appear to vary with task demands, but the factors underlying right- or left-hemiface advantages remain unknown. Problems also stem from the functional interpretation of facial asymmetry: Does greater expressivity demonstrate an advantage or a handicap? Does asymmetry depend on the greater activation of one hemisphere or on the greater inhibitory influence of the other (Rinn, 1984)? Comparison of right- and left-brain–damaged subjects should tell us whether unilateral lesions result in a loss of activation (reduced expressivity of the contralateral hemiface) or a disinhibition (increased expressivity of the ipsilateral hemiface).

Facial expression after unilateral brain damage. Reduced facial expressivity in right-hemisphere–damaged patients has been shown in the slide-viewing paradigm (Borod, Koff, Perlman-Lorch, & Nicholas, 1986; Buck & Duffy, 1980). Posing upon verbal request or imitation also resulted in movements of lower intensity for this group than for a left-hemisphere–damaged group (Borod, Koff, Perlman-Lorch, Nicholas, & Welkowitz, 1988). This attenuation of spontaneous and posed facial movements did not relate to other impairments in the production of nonemotional facial movements, although other studies found no group difference in facial expression (Kolb & Milner, 1981; Mammucari et al., 1988; Pizzamiglio, Caltagirone, Mammucari, Ekman, & Friesen, 1987; Pizzamiglio & Mammucari, 1989; Walker-Batson, Barton, Wendt, & Reynolds, 1987). Facial asymmetry in aphasic subjects depended on task requirements: Smiling, singing, and counting up to ten are left sided, whereas spontaneous speech, naming, and repetition are right sided (Graves & Landis, 1985). In poses for negative emotions, asymmetries resulted from mild motor impairments on the side corresponding to the damaged hemisphere, right or left, but smiles remained symmetrical (Bruyer, 1981). These data demonstrate that both hemispheres are involved in the control of facial motility. Further studies are needed to identify the influence of diverse movement characteristics on laterality: emotional or nonemotional, spontaneous and posed, upper or lower part of the face mobilized, or complexity of the movement realization.

The interpretation of facial cues

Facial processings may also be compared on the receptive level. Faces provide information not only about emotional state but also about identity, age, gender, and so forth. Does emotion recognition relate to identity recognition? Evidence from normal subjects favors the hypothesis of independence (Ley & Strauss, 1986). Left-hemifield advantages are found in the two tasks, but covariance analysis has shown that lateral differences are not related on any single factor (Pizzamiglio, Zoccolotti, Mammucari, & Cesaroni, 1983). Similarly, subject gender and stimulus similarity did not affect lateral differences in the same way when the perception of facial expression and perception of facial identity was compared (Strauss & Moscovitch, 1981).

The behavior of brain-damaged subjects also shows dissociations between emotional and nonemotional processes, even if both depend on an intact right hemisphere (for a review, see Feyereisen, 1986b). In a covariance analysis, equalizing groups of right- and left-hemisphere–damaged subjects in facial-identity processing did not eliminate differences in processing emotion (Bowers, Bauer, Coslett, & Heilman, 1985). Some patients with unilateral or bilateral lesions can recognize identity but not emotion (Bowers & Heilman, 1984; Etcoff, 1984b), and others show the reverse impairment (Bruyer et al., 1983; Tranel, Damasio, & Damasio, 1988). Right-hemisphere–damaged patients had less success in identifying facial emotion than in giving the meaning of conventional facial gestures, whereas aphasics performed similarly in the two conditions (Goldblum, 1980). Thus, difficulties in processing facial expressions of emotion did not arise from general visual impairments.

A difficulty remains, however, in relating these results to the possibility of right-hemisphere specialization in emotional processing. Does matching faces or judging similarity on the basis of expressed emotions require affective processes? Do lateral differences depend on the emotional nature of the input? As was the case in studies of the expressive side, the possible influence of emotional valence on laterality effects has also been discussed (Manning, 1986; Pizzamiglio et al., 1983; Reuter-Lorenz & Davidson, 1981; Strauss & Moscovitch, 1981). In this domain, input quality and task demands can be confounding variables, but this problem has been overcome through some elegant experimental procedures. For example, McKeever and Dixon (1981) instructed their subjects to learn faces for further recognition. The faces were actually neutral but were described in emotional terms in one condition and in neutral terms in the other. The left-visual-field advantage in recognition was observed only in female subjects in the emotional condition. In another study by McLaren and Bryson (1987), two faces were simultaneously presented, with the task being to decide which one was the happier (or the sadder in another condition). The happy face was paired with either a neutral face or a sad one (there were similarly sad–neutral and sad–happy contrasts in the other condition). A left-hemifield advantage was observed for emotional faces and a right-hemifield advantage for neutral faces. In this case, the perceptual contrast was reduced, and so the task was more difficult (the reaction times were slower). Thus, the results may be interpreted as showing different perceptual competence of the cerebral hemispheres. Finally, Gage and Safer (1985) examined the influence of mood context on facial expression recognition: No lateral differences were observed when the learning and recognition contexts were congruent. This result again precludes identifying lateral differences with a simple emotion–cognition dichotomy.

Expressive use of intonation

Like the face, the voice can be used for expressing emotion or for non-emotional purposes. Indeed, some aspects of prosody are determined by linguistic constraints, such as an interrogative rising tone or a stress as a mark of emphasis. As yet, neuropsychology has no way of studying these vocal productions in normal subjects, and so the only information is from observing brain-damaged subjects. Hemispheric or subcortical lesions impair vocal production, and acoustical analysis of amplitude and fundamental frequency have shown more monotony, higher pitch, and increased variability as compared with normal subjects (Ross, Edmondson, Seibert, & Homan, 1988; Shapiro & Danly, 1985). Analyses of the lateral differences in relation to the emotional or the linguistic nature of the production remain disputed. Some authors assume a right-hemisphere involvement in any processing of prosody, but others do not find its contribution to the execution of linguistic prosody to be significant (Emmorey, 1987; Ross, 1984, 1988; Ryalls & Behrens, 1988).

The interpretation of vocal cues

Many neuropsychological studies of the reception of vocal cues were also conducted under the hypothesis of a right-hemisphere dominance in emotional processing. Is the emotion–cognition dichotomy supported in this domain?

In normal subjects, the use of the dichotic listening procedure does not yield unambiguous conclusions. Although a left-ear advantage has been observed in processing emotional intonation (Bryden, Ley, & Sugarman, 1982; Ley & Bryden, 1982), similar lateral differences have been found in recognizing nonemotional sounds like coughing or sneezing, in identifying a speaker's age or gender, and in processing linguistic stress contrast (e.g., Blumstein & Cooper, 1974; Carmon & Nachshon, 1973; King & Kimura, 1972). Furthermore, laterality effects partially depend on attentional strategies (Mahoney & Sainsbury, 1987). Both hemispheres seem to be involved in the emotional processing of verbal material. No left-ear advantage is observed when subjects have to judge the emotional tone of words that have an emotional meaning (Morais & Ladavas, 1987) or when the task is to process the emotional content of words monaurally presented (Safer & Leventhal, 1977).

No clearer dissociation of emotional and nonemotional processes was revealed in observations of brain-damaged subjects. Right-hemisphere – lesioned subjects may be hampered in making emotional attributions from prosody (Heilman, Scholes & Watson, 1975; Tucker, Watson, & Heilman, 1977), but they also are impaired in recognizing voices (Assal, Aubert, & Buttet, 1981; Van Lancker & Canter, 1982) and perceiving linguistic stress (Weintraub, Mesulam, & Kramer, 1981) or interrogation marks (Heilman, Bowers, Speedie, & Coslett, 1984).

Moreover, some left-hemisphere damage also impairs the emotional processing of the prosody of neutral sentences, often in relation to disorders in spoken-language comprehension (Schlanger, Schlanger, & Gertsman, 1976; Tompkins & Flowers, 1985). When the verbal content itself transmits emotional information, both groups of patients, right- and left-hemisphere damaged, will perform better if intonation and meaning are congruent and worse when the message is incongruent (Bowers, Coslett, Bauer, Speedie, & Heilman, 1987; Seron, Van der Kaa, Van der Linden, Remits, & Feyereisen, 1982; Tompkins & Flowers, 1987). These data converge with the results of dichotic listening studies to show that both hemispheres are involved in processing prosody (Hartje, Willmes, & Weniger, 1985).

Conclusions

The question of whether hemispheric specialization relates to the distinction between emotional and cognitive processing or to other dimensions cannot be answered clearly if it is cast in general terms. Indeed, different conclusions can be reached from a literature review in regard to diverse aspects of nonverbal emotional behavior, and it remains to be demonstrated whether facial motor asymmetry or lateral differences in processing prosody depend on the differential involvement of the cerebral hemispheres in emotion. The comprehension of facial expression of emotion is clearly dissociated from the recognition of facial identity, but it may also rely on perceptual competence in processing faces in non-emotional dimensions. Thus, little support is found in contemporary neuropsychology for general dichotomies between cognition and emotion or between analytic and holistic modes of processing, but attention is being paid to different task requirements in order to discover more refined distinctions.

Another problem in the study of the dissociation between emotion and cognition is raised by the notion that true emotional reactions are automatically triggered and that they occur when motor- and perceptual-controlled processes fail (Leventhal, 1984; Oatley & Johnson-Laird, 1987). Studies of brain pathology have shown that spontaneous facial expressions of emotion rely on mechanisms other than the voluntary production of face movements in experimental situations, even if some lesions may impair both kinds of behavior or if similar lateral differences are observed in posed and spontaneous facial expressions (Borod et al., 1983, 1986; Pizzamiglio & Mammucari, 1989; Rinn, 1984). Similarly, after right-hemisphere damage, impairments in the recognition of facial expression of emotion may dissociate from reduced autonomic responding (Caltagirone, Zoccolotti, Originale, Daniele, & Mammucari, 1989). These dissociations raise doubt about the relevance of a good deal of neuropsychological data to the study of emotion, because automatic processes are less often elicited than are controlled ones. For instance, neuropsychologists have yet to study the unintended motor mimicry of facial expressions of emotion as recorded by electromyography, conditioning to facial stimuli, and preattentive discrimination of some facial expressions.

Automatic processes refer to autonomous modules that are specialized in some input–output transfer functions. It is assumed that apart from a "semantic" route linking input to output via propositional representations, some direct routes also exist outside the subject's control. Thus, a description of automatic emotional reactions relies on the identification of these various components, which may function without the influence of the cognitive system. From such a perspective, specialized recognition devices and autonomous response mechanisms should be described and further subdivisions drawn in the information-processing architecture. These expected advances in the neuropsychology of nonverbal behavior are anticipated by some preliminary results that we now shall examine in more detail.

The fractionation of nonverbal behavior

Although the first approaches to nonverbal behavior in neuropsychology – relying on simple dichotomies like verbal–nonverbal (visuospatial) codes or emotion–cognition – were unable to support such global distinctions, the results suggested that finer dissociations were possible. Similarly, the cognitive neuropsychology of language, motor control, and visual perception progressed by abandoning unspecific labels – aphasia, apraxia, visual agnosia, and the like – and by attempting to identify the underlying elementary operations. These lines converge for a deeper analysis of the processes of producing and understanding facial, vocal, and gestural signals. Until now, the main body of neuropsychological evidence for the fractionation of nonverbal behavior has been provided by the study of brain-damaged patients.

Emotional processing of facial and vocal information

A comparison of production and comprehension. At first sight, manifesting emotion and perceiving emotions in others are very different, and it is unlikely that one would find similar impairments of these processes after brain lesions. Expressive and receptive disorders have been shown to dissociate in the processing of prosody (Gorelick & Ross, 1987; Ross, 1981; Speedie, Coslett, & Heilman, 1984). In a group study by Borod et al. (1986), performances in the production and comprehension of emotional facial expression were not correlated. With covariance analysis, Zoccolotti, Scabini, and Violani (1982) demonstrated the independence between electrodermal reactivity and the ability to interpret facial expressions of emotion. And it has often been stressed that the emotional brain differentiates along the anteroposterior or the dorsoventral axis as well as on the lateral dimension (Bear, 1983; Davidson, 1984; Kinsbourne & Bemporad, 1984). Distinguishing between perceptual and motor components is the first step in identifying emotional processes.

A comparison of verbal, vocal, and facial modalities. Other studies show dissociations among different input modalities. Some lesions of the right hemisphere disturb emotional processing in the visual modality only (Habib, 1986). For example, a patient examined by Bowers and Heilman (1984) was unable to match facial expressions and emotional names but showed no impairments in processing prosody. Similar cases, or inverse dissociations, can be found in the series of Benowitz et al. (1983). In the

single-case study by Rapcsak, Kaszmiak, and Rubens (1989), the patient
was impaired in naming emotional faces and in pointing to named facial
expressions, but discriminination of emotional faces and matching faces
to prosody and to scenes were correct. Other patients were impaired in
processing facial expressions of emotions but performed normally when
presented with emotional words or sentences (Etcoff, 1984a; Kolb &
Taylor, 1981). In a pilot study, left- and right-hemisphere–damaged patients were compared in two similar tasks: pointing in an array of three
responses to the face corresponding to a target facial expression of emotion and finding, out of three, the synonymous word for the name of
an emotion (Feyereisen, 1989). Right-hemisphere–damaged subjects had
superior scores in the verbal task. In a second experiment, matching
a facial expression to its emotion was not found to be easier than matching a facial expression to a pictured scene. Thus, extracting invariant
information from two different faces was as difficult as was making an
emotional attribution from a situation and selecting the appropriate facial expression. Some right-hemisphere–damaged patients, but no left-
hemisphere–damaged patients, also showed impairments in facial
matching in a third experiment in which the correct response and the
target face were two identical photographs. Further studies should identify more precisely the defective functions in these cases of brain
damage.

In regard to response modalities, some right-hemisphere lesions were
found to impair vocal and facial but not verbal expression of emotion
(Borod, Koff, Perlman-Lorch, & Nicholas, 1985). Verbal reports also con-
tradict the nonverbal expressions of emotion in the complaints of some
patients who are unable to express vocally the emotions they experience
(Ross, 1981) and in others who have uncontrollable outbursts of laughing or crying without feeling happy or sad (Poeck, 1969). These pathologies should be the object of more systematic observations, as they relate
to dissociations assumed in some models of emotional processing between nonverbal expression and verbal reports. The possibility of supra-
modal disorders – for instance, from impaired evaluations of pleasantness (indifference, anhedonia) or from inability to infer emotional states
in others from situational and nonverbal cues – should also be investigated.

Gestural behavior

Theoretical perspectives on manual activity during speaking. Previously neuropsychological observations of manual preferences in normal subjects

and of gestural behavior in aphasics generally used the hypothesis of common mechanisms underlying verbal and nonverbal behavior. Left-hemisphere involvement was assumed for symbolic function, communication, or motor control. These studies deviate somewhat from the general aim of neuropsychology to identify dissociations, but they can be read with renewed interest when searching for evidence of the separation of gesture and speech and for dissociations within gestural processing. There is no reason, indeed, that nonverbal behavior should be assumed to be simple and unstructured when the diversity of aphasic pathologies shows that verbal behavior can be subdivided into multiple components: Global explanations cannot be true in one domain but simplistic in another.

Interest in gestures in contemporary neuropsychology stems from the opportunity they offer of using other input and output to study mental functions. For example, in the study of picture-naming impairments, it is assumed that the lesion has spared the early processes if the patient can gesture the use of an object he or she cannot name; that is, the impairment may be an inability to access the phonological word form from visual or semantic information (Butterworth, Swallow, & Grimston 1981; Riddoch & Humphreys, 1987). Drawings from memory (Gainotti, Silveri, Villa, & Caltagirone, 1984) also address the semantic system, but this behavior is less spontaneous than are gestures in normal subjects and is less readily elicited in aphasic subjects.

The cognitive neuropsychology approach stresses the specificity of the different communicative modalities. If some aphasics can produce gestures in relation to pictures they cannot name, the verbal and the nonverbal responses must differ in some unknown respect. Different hypotheses may be proposed: Information extracted from a picture can be used to program a gesture, but it does not suffice to activate the phonological store. As there are more words than plans for action, a response is more difficult to select in the verbal modality, and motor programs for gestures are less demanding than are those for words.

Experimental psychology proposes a more dynamic view of the relationships between gesture and speech conceived as concurrent activities. During the preparation phase, manual and oral movements compete for common resource and exchange information (Levelt, Richardson, & La Heij, 1985), and during execution, they may be finely coordinated (Chang & Hammond, 1987; Smith, McFarland, & Weber, 1986). These mutual influences probably do not rely on symbolic representations of oral and manual movements in central "programs" coding the communication intents; rather, they might be described as transfers of information between autonomous peripheral processors, separate from top–down control (Kelso & Tuller, 1984; Kelso, Tuller, & Harris, 1983). Aphasic behavior has not yet been analyzed from such a perspective, although, Hadar, Steiner, and Rose (1984) suggested that speech-related head movements be studied for their possible role in speech-production mechanisms and especially for the distribution of stress in sentences. Of course, stress relates to the semantic, lexical, and syntactic aspects of an utterance, but low-level constraints in motor control may also contribute to shaping the relationships between gesture and speech, together with more abstract representations in message conceptualization (Feyereisen, 1987).

The influence of gestural context on auditory comprehension. Only two studies have experimentally examined the clinical intuition that gestural cues facilitate auditory comprehension in aphasia beyond the frequent observation that imitation of action is less impaired than is the execution of verbal commands. Venus and Canter (1987) studied a group of 16 subjects with comprehension disorders. They did not find different performances in matching spoken words to pictures between two conditions: word alone or word plus gestural cue. Performances in the gesture-alone condition were inferior, as Duffy and Watkins (1984) also reported. These results are not conclusive, however, because of the heterogeneity of the aphasic population: By accepting the null hypothesis of absence of effect, one runs the risk of missing possible facilitatory effects of gestural context in specific cases.

In the other study, greater attention was paid to the description of comprehension disorders in the individual aphasic subjects (Feyereisen & Hazan, 1987). A group of 16 subjects was given pretests to examine phonological discrimination in words and nonwords, word recognition, and semantic relatedness judgments. It was hypothesized that gestures facilitate comprehension in the case of defective phonological processing or that of dissociation between phonological and semantic processing, but not in the case of semantic disorders. Thus, a critical observation for the hypothesis concerned the use of gestural cues by subjects with pure word deafness (impaired auditory comprehension with correct understanding of written material). This pathology is very uncommon, however, and there were no cases in the group of dissociation between written and auditory comprehension. It remained possible, however, that the disorders of the subjects showing impaired comprehension resulted from a defective access to semantic information from word recognition with spared access from nonverbal input. Indeed, a pictorial context was found to facilitate sentence comprehension in some cases of aphasia (Nicholas & Brookshire, 1981; Pierce & Beekman, 1985). Next, a word-to-picture matching task was devised to compare three conditions: a target word presented in isolation (e.g., "a glass"), with a gesture, or with a verbal qualification ("a glass of milk"). Three subjects made more than 25% errors in the verbal condition (respectively, 30%, 45%, and 55%). Two performed better when a gestural cue was added (5% and 15% errors), but one showed similar impairment (55%). A verbal qualification did not improve performances to the same extent. The subjects' characteristics accounting for differences in facilitation by context were not identified.

Progress in the neuropsychological analysis of gesture comprehension can be expected from detailed single-case studies (see Humphreys & Riddoch, 1987, for insightful analogies with related phenomena). The specificity of gestural processing is suggested by impaired discrimination and comprehension of gestures in left-hemisphere–damaged subjects without an auditory comprehension deficit, and their performances in a gesture imitation task were also within the normal range, and thus receptive disorders did not result from visual impairment (Rothi et al., 1986). The nature of these nonverbal comprehension deficits, however, is difficult to specify given our current state of knowledge about gesture perception, a neglected field in cognitive psychology. What kind of semantic information do gestures transmit? Can they be compared with pictures, or are they formed from another subset of semantic features? Should different categories of gestures be distinguished on the basis of the stressed dimension of the referent (shape, distinctive part, function, dynamic property, etc.)? Or do gestures, like prosody, relate to nonfigurative dimensions of speech (emphasis, metalinguistic comments, socioaffective expressions)? Gestural impairments can be identified only in comparison with normal functioning, and the possible role of gesture in speech perception can be identified only in the light of a model of language processing.

Conclusions

The neuropsychology of nonverbal behavior has long been influenced by the study of simple questions: Is aphasia a specific language impairment or the consequence of a more general disorder? Is there a right-hemisphere dominance in emotional processing? But even naive approaches may be fruitful, and the pioneering studies have yielded clues to the complexity of mental functioning. The next step is to delineate the architecture of nonverbal behavior by distinguishing between input and output processes and searching for the specificity of the different perceptual and expressive modalities. These distinctions, however, represent only preliminary stages in the understanding of nonverbal behavior.

First, a better description of the assumed operations is needed. If, for instance, there is a special recognition device for facial expressions of emotion, what are the specific input for and output of this module? Is the process specialized in the integration of local information like mouth shape or eyebrow movements, or is it sensitive to configurational properties like signs of tension or relaxation? Does context exert influences before recognition or in a later stage of cognitive interpretation? How are blended expressions processed? Second, the nature of the relations between the different processes should be identified. Does the system function on the basis of representations and rules using if–then instructions, or can it be described as the propagation of activation along a set of excitatory and inhibitory connections? Can discrete stages be identified, or is information continuously processed until a threshold for a response decision is reached? Third, what sort of constraints are described in the architecture underlying nonverbal behavior? Many kinds of distinctions could be justified by neuropsychological observation, and analysis should focus on convergent evidence from experimental psychology so as to avoid ad hoc explanations. Thus, many important points are missing from the description of the mental operations producing nonverbal behavior.

Some of the problems delaying progress in the field arise from a lack of communication among subdomains. The study of gesture production and comprehension was disconnected from the psychology of language, and the study of facial expression from that of face recognition. Many conclusions of social psychological experiments have not yet been examined from a neuropsychological perspective. More particularly, the issue of automaticity in nonverbal expression or in the processing of emotional cues has been neglected. Inversely, the psychology of "nonverbal communication" uncritically uses global notions like coding, decoding, sensitivity, and cognitive styles, whereas the cognitive approach in neuropsychology suggests that producing and interpreting nonverbal signals result from several separate operations. It is the objective of general reviews like this one to bring together such disparate pieces of knowledge.

References

Agostoni, E., Coletti, A., Orlando, G., & Tredici, G. (1983). Apraxia in deep cerebral lesions. *Journal of Neurology, Neurosurgery, and Psychiatry, 46*, 804–808.

Alford, R. D. (1983). Sex differences in lateral facial facility: The effects of habitual facial concealment. *Neuropsychologia, 21*, 567–570.

Alford, R. D., & Alford, K. F. (1981). Sex differences in asymmetry in the facial expressions of emotion. *Neuropsychologia, 19*, 605–608.

Annett, M. (1985). *Left, right, hand and brain: The right shift theory.* Hillsdale, NJ: Erlbaum.

Assal, G., Aubert, C., & Buttet, J. (1981). Asymétrie cérébrale et reconnaissance de la voix. *Revue Neurologique, 137*, 255–268.

Baddeley, A. (1986). *Working memory.* Oxford: Claredon Press.

Basso, A., Luzzatti, C., & Spinnler, H. (1980). Is ideomotor apraxia the outcome of damage to well-defined regions of the left hemisphere? Neuropsychological study of CAT correlations. *Journal of Neurology, Neurosurgery, and Psychiatry, 43*, 118–126.

Bates, E., Bretherton, I., Shore, C., & McNew, S. (1983). Names, gestures, and objects: Symbolization in infancy and aphasia. In K. E. Nelson (Ed.). *Children's language* (Vol. 4, pp. 59–123). Hillsdale, NJ: Erlbaum.

Bear, D. M. (1983). Hemispheric specialization and the neurology of emotion. *Archives of Neurology, 40*, 195–202.

Behrmann, M., & Penn, C. (1984). Nonverbal communication of aphasic patients. *British Journal of Disorders of Communication, 19*, 155–168.

Benowitz, L. I., Bear, D. M., Rosenthal, R., Mesulam, M. M., Zaidel, E., & Sperry, R. W. (1983). Hemispheric specialization in nonverbal communication. *Cortex, 19*, 5–11.

Bertelson, P. (1982). Lateral differences in normal man and lateralization of brain function. *International Journal of Psychology, 17*, 173–210.

Bisiach, E., Nichelli, P., & Sala, C. (1979). Recognition of random shapes in unilateral brain damaged patients: A re-appraisal. *Cortex, 15*, 491–499.

Blumstein, S., & Cooper, W. E. (1974). Hemispheric processing of intonation contour. *Cortex, 10*, 146–158.

Borod, J. C., Kent J., Koff, E., Martin, C., & Alpert, M. (1988). Facial asymmetry while posing positive and negative emotions: Support for the right hemisphere hypothesis. *Neuropsychologia, 26*, 759–764.

Borod, J. C., & Koff, E. (1983). Hemiface mobility and facial expression asymmetry. *Cortex, 19*, 327–332.

(1984). Asymmetries in affective facial expression: Behavior and anatomy. In N. Fox & R. Davidson (Eds.)., *The psychobiology of affective development* (pp. 293–323). Hillsdale, NJ: Erlbaum.

Borod, J. C., Koff, E., Perlman-Lorch, M., & Nicholas, M. (1985). Channels of emotional expressions in patients with unilateral brain damage. *Archives of Neurology, 42*, 345–348.

(1986). The expression and perception of facial emotion in brain-damaged patients. *Neuropsychologia, 24*, 169–180.

60   Pierre Feyereisen

Borod, J. C., Koff, E., Perlman-Lorch, M., Nicholas, M., & Welkowitz, J. (1988). Emotional and non-emotional facial behaviour in patients with unilateral brain damage. *Journal of Neurology, Neurosurgery, and Psychiatry, 51*, 826–832.

Borod, J. C., Koff, E., & White, B. (1983). Facial asymmetry in posed and spontaneous expressions of emotions. *Brain and Cognition, 2*, 165–175.

Bowers, D., Bauer, R. M., Coslett, H. B., & Heilman, K. M. (1985). Processing of faces by patients with unilateral hemisphere lesions. I. Dissociation between judgments of facial affect and facial identity. *Brain and Cognition, 4*, 258–272.

Bowers, D., Coslett, H. B., Bauer, R. M., Speedie, L. J., & Heilman, K. M. (1987). Comprehension of emotional prosody following unilateral hemispheric lesions: Processing defect versus distraction defect. *Neuropsychologia, 25*, 317–328.

Bowers, D., & Heilman, K. M. (1984). Dissociation between the processing of affective and nonaffective faces: A case study. *Journal of Clinical Neuropsychology, 6*, 367–379.

Bradshaw, J. L., Burden, V., & Nettleton, N. C. (1986). Dichotic and dichoptic techniques. *Neuropsychologia, 24*, 79–90.

Bradshaw, J. L., & Nettleton, N. C. (1981). The nature of hemispheric specialization in man. *Behavioral and Brain Sciences, 4*, 51–91.

Brandeis, D., & Lehmann, D. (1986). Event-related potentials in the brain and cognitive processes: Approaches and applications. *Neuropsychologia, 24*, 151–168.

Braun, C. M. J., Baribeau, J. M. C., Ethier, M., Guérette, R., & Proulx, R. (1988). Emotional facial expressive and discriminative performance and lateralization in normal young adults. *Cortex, 24*, 77–90.

Bruyer, R. (1981). Asymmetry of facial expression in brain damaged subjects. *Neuropsychologia, 19*, 615–624.

Bruyer, R., Laterre, C., Seron, X., Feyereisen, P., Strypstein, E., Pierrard, E., & Rectem, D. (1983). A case of prosopagnosia with some preserved covert remembrance of familiar faces. *Brain and Cognition, 2*, 257–284.

Bryden, M. P., Ley, R. G., & Sugarman, J. H., (1982). A left-ear advantage for identifying the emotional quality of tonal sequences. *Neuropsychologia, 20*, 83–87.

Buck, R. (1985). Prime theory: An integrated view of motivation and emotion. *Psychological Review, 92*, 349–413.

Buck, R., & Duffy, R. J. (1980). Nonverbal communication of affect in brain damaged patients. *Cortex, 16*, 351–362.

Butterworth, B., Swallow, J., & Grimston, M. (1981). Gestures and lexical processes in jargonaphasia. In J. Brown (Ed.), *Jargonaphasia* (pp. 113–124). New York: Academic Press.

Cacioppo, J. T., & Petty, R. E. (1981). Lateral asymmetry in the expression of cognition and emotion. *Journal of Experimental Psychology: Human Perception and Performance, 7*, 333–341.

Caltagirone, C., Zoccolotti, P., Originale, G., Daniele, A., & Mammucari, A. (1989). Autonomic reactivity and facial expression of emotion in brain damaged patients. In G. Gainotti & C. Caltagirone (Eds.), *Emotion and the dual brain* (pp. 204–221). Berlin: Springer-Verlag.

Campbell, R. (1982). Asymmetries in moving faces. *British Journal of Psychology, 73*, 95–103.

(1986). Asymmetries of facial action: Some facts and fancies of normal face movement. In R. Bruyer (Ed.), *The neuropsychology of face perception and facial expression* (pp. 247–267). Hillsdale, NJ: Erlbaum.

Campbell, R., Landis, T., & Regard, M. (1986). Face recognition and lipreading: A neurological dissociation. *Brain, 109,* 509–521.

Caramazza, A. (1986). On drawing inferences about the structure of normal cognitive systems from the analysis of patterns of impaired performances: The case for single patient studies. *Brain and Cognition, 5,* 41–66.

Carmon, A., & Nachshon, I. (1973). Ear asymmetry in perception of emotional nonverbal stimuli. *Acta Psychologica, 37,* 351–357.

Chang, P., & Hammond, G. R. (1987). Mutual interactions between speech and finger movements. *Journal of Motor Behavior, 19,* 265–274.

Christopoulou, C., & Bonvillian, J. D. (1985). Sign language, pantomime, and gestural processing in aphasic persons: A review. *Journal of Communication Disorders, 18,* 1–20.

Cicone, M., Wapner, W., Foldi, N., Zurif, E., & Gardner, H. (1979). The relation between gesture and language in aphasic communication. *Brain and Language, 8,* 324–349.

Coelho, C. A., & Duffy, R. J. (1986). Effects of iconicity, motoric complexity, and linguistic function on sign acquisition in severe aphasia. *Perceptual and Motor Skills, 63,* 519–530.

Cohen, G. (1982). Theoretical interpretations of lateral asymmetries. In J. G. Beaumont (Ed.), *Divided visual field studies of cerebral organization* (pp. 87–111). New York: Academic Press.

Dalby, J. T., Gibson, D., Grossi, V., & Schneider, R. D. (1980). Lateralized hand gesture during speech. *Journal of Motor Behavior, 12,* 292–297.

Damasio, A. R., & Van Hoesen, G. W. (1983). Emotional disturbances associated with focal lesions of the limbic frontal lobe. In K. M. Heilman & P. Satz (Eds.), *Neuropsychology of human emotion* (pp. 85–110). New York: Guilford Press.

Daniloff, J. K., Fritelli, G., Buckingham, H. G., Hoffman, P. R., & Daniloff, R. G. (1986). Amer-Ind versus ASL: Recognition and imitation in aphasic subjects. *Brain and Language, 28,* 95–113.

Davidoff, J. (1982). Studies with non-verbal stimuli. In J. G. Beaumont (Ed.), *Divided visual field studies of cerebral organization* (pp. 29–55). New York: Academic Press.

Davidson, R. J. (1984). Affect, cognition, and hemispheric specialization. In C. E. Izard, J. Kagan, & R. B. Zajonc (Eds.), *Emotion, cognition, and behavior* (pp. 320–365). Cambridge: Cambridge University Press.

de Ajuriaguerra, J., Richard, J., Rodriguez, R., & Tissot, R. (1966). Quelques aspects de la désintégration des praxies idéomotrices dans les démences du grand âge. *Cortex, 2,* 438–662.

De Renzi, E. (1985). Methods of limb apraxia examination and their bearing on the interpretation of the disorders. In E. A. Roy (Ed.), *Neuropsychological studies of apraxia and related disorders* (pp. 45–64). Amsterdam: North Holland.

De Renzi, E., Faglioni, P., Lodesani, M., & Vecchi, A. (1983). Performance of left brain damaged patients on imitation of single movements and motor sequences. Frontal and parietal-injured patients compared. *Cortex, 19,* 333–343.

De Renzi, E., Motti, F., & Nichelli, P. (1980). Imitating gestures: A quantitative approach to ideomotor apraxia. *Archives of Neurology, 37,* 6–10.

Dopson, W. G., Beckwith, B. E., Tucker, D. M., & Bullard-Bates, P. C. (1984). Asymmetry of facial expression in spontaneous emotion. *Cortex, 20,* 243–251.

Duffy, J. R., & Watkins, L. B. (1984). The effect of response choice relatedness on pantomime and verbal recognition ability in aphasic patients. *Brain and Language, 21,* 291–306.

Duffy, R. J., & Duffy, J. R. (1981). Three studies of deficits in pantomimic expression and pantomimic recognition in aphasia. *Journal of Speech and Hearing Research, 24,* 70–84.

Duffy, R. J., Duffy, J. R., & Mercaitis, P. A. (1984). Comparison of the performances of a fluent and a nonfluent aphasic on a pantomimic referential task. *Brain and Language, 21,* 260–273.

Duffy, R. J., & Liles, B. Z. (1979). A translation of Finkelnburg's (1870) lecture on aphasia as "asymbolia" with commentary. *Journal of Speech and Hearing Disorders, 44,* 156–168.

Ehrlichman, H., & Weinberger, A. (1978). Lateral eye movements and hemispheric asymmetry: A critical review. *Psychological Bulletin, 85,* 1080–1101.

Ekman, P., Hager, J., & Friesen, W. V. (1981). The symmetry of emotional and deliberate facial actions. *Psychophysiology, 18,* 101–106.

Emmorey, K. O. (1987). The neurological substrates for prosodic aspects of speech. *Brain and Language, 30,* 305–320.

Etcoff, N. L. (1984a). Perceptual and conceptual organization of facial emotions: Hemispheric differences. *Brain and Cognition, 3,* 385–412.

(1984b). Selective attention to facial identity and facial emotion. *Neuropsychologia, 22,* 281–295.

Fennel, E. B. (1986). Handedness in neuropsychological research. In H. J. Hannay (Ed.), *Experimental techniques in human neuropsychology* (pp. 15–44). New York: Oxford University Press.

Ferro, J. M., Martins, I. P., Mariano, G., & Castro-Caldas, A. (1983). CT scan correlates of gesture recognition. *Journal of Neurology, Neurosurgery, and Psychiatry, 46,* 943–952.

Feyereisen, P. (1983). Manual activity during speaking in aphasic subjects. *International Journal of Psychology, 18,* 545–556.

(1986a). Lateral differences in gesture production. In J. L. Nespoulous, P. Perron, & A. R. Lecours (Eds.), *The biological foundations of gestures: Motor and semiotic aspects* (pp. 77–94). Hillsdale, NJ: Erlbaum.

(1986b). Production and comprehension of emotional facial expressions in brain-damaged patients. In R. Bruyer (Ed.), *The neuropsychology of face perception and facial expression* (pp. 221–245). Hillsdale, NJ: Erlbaum.

(1987). Gestures and speech, interactions and separations: A reply to McNeill (1985). *Psychological Review, 94,* 493–498.

(1988). Nonverbal communication. In F. C. Rose, R. Whurr, & M. A. Wyke (Eds.), *Aphasia* (pp. 46–81). London: Whurr.

(1989). What can be learned from lateral differences in emotional processing? In G. Gainotti & C. Caltagirone (Eds.), *Emotions and the dual brain* (pp. 121–146). Berlin: Springer-Verlag.

Feyereisen, P., Barter, D., Goossens, M., & Clerebaut, N. (1988). Gestures and speech in referential communication by aphasic subjects: Channel use and efficiency. *Aphasiology, 2,* 21–32.

Feyereisen, P., Bouchat, M. P., Déry, D., & Ruiz, M. (1990). The concomitance of speech and manual gesture in aphasic subjects. In G. R. Hammond (Ed.), *Cerebral control of speech and limb movements* (pp. 279–301). Amsterdam: North Holland.

Feyereisen, P., & Hazan, K. (1987). *Les gestes facilitent-ils la compréhension auditive des mots chez les patients aphasiques?* Unpublished manuscript.

Feyereisen, P., & Lignian, A. (1981). La direction du regard chez les aphasiques en conversation: Une observation pilote. *Cahiers de Psychologie Cognitive, 1,* 287–298.

Feyereisen, P., & Seron, X. (1982). Nonverbal communication and aphasia, a review: I. Comprehension. II. Expression. *Brain and Language, 16,* 191–212 & 213–236.

Foldi, N. S., Cicone, M., & Gardner, H. (1983). Pragmatic aspects of communication in brain-damaged patients. In S. J. Segalowitz (Ed.), *Language functions and brain organization* (pp. 51–85). New York: Academic Press.

Gage, D. F., & Safer, M. A. (1985). Hemisphere differences in the mood state-dependent effect for recognition of emotional faces. *Journal of Experimental Psychology: Learning, Memory, and Cognition, 11,* 752–763.

Gainotti, G. (1984). Some methodological problems in the study of the relationships between emotion and cerebral dominance. *Journal of Clinical Neuropsychology, 6,* 111–121.

(1989). Disorders of emotions and affect in patients with unilateral brain damage. In F. Boller & J. Grafman (Eds.), *Handbook of neuropsychology* (pp. 345–361). Amsterdam: Elsevier.

Gainotti, G., & Lemmo, M. A. (1976). Comprehension of symbolic gestures in aphasia. *Brain and Language, 3,* 451–460.

Gainotti, G., Silveri, C., Villa, G., & Caltagirone, C. (1984). Drawing objects from memory in aphasia. *Brain, 106,* 613–622.

Glosser, G., Wiener, M., & Kaplan, E. (1986). Communicative gestures in aphasia. *Brain and Language, 27,* 345–359.

(1988). Variations in aphasic language behaviors. *Journal of Speech and Hearing Disorders, 53,* 115–124.

Goldblum, M. C. (1980). La reconnaissance des expressions faciales émotionnelles et conventionnelles au cours des lésions cérébrales. *Revue Neurologique, 136,* 711–719.

Goodale, M. A. (1988). Hemispheric differences in motor control. *Behavioral Brain Research, 30,* 203–214.

Gorelick, P. B., & Ross, E. D. (1987). The aprosodias: Further functional–anatomical evidence for the organisation of affective language in the right hemisphere. *Journal of Neurology, Neurosurgery, and Psychiatry, 50,* 553–560.

Graves, R. (1983). Mouth asymmetry, dichotic ear advantage, and tachistoscopic visual field advantage as measures of language lateralization. *Neuropsychologia, 21,* 641–649.

Graves, R., Goodglass, H., & Landis, T. (1982). Mouth asymmetry during spontaneous speech. *Neuropsychologia, 20,* 371–381.

Graves, R., & Landis, T. (1985). Hemispheric control of speech expression in aphasia: A mouth asymmetry study. *Archives of Neurology, 42,* 249–251.

Graves, R., Landis, C., & Simpson, C. (1985). On the interpretation of mouth asymmetry. *Neuropsychologia, 23,* 121–122.

Haaland, K. Y., Harrington, D. L., & Yeo, R. (1987). The effects of task complexity on motor performance in left and right CVA patients. *Neuropsychologia, 25,* 783–794.

Habib, M. (1986). Visual hypoemotionality and prosopagnosia associated with right temporal lobe isolation. *Neuropsychologia, 24,* 577–582.

Hadar, U., Steiner T. J., & Rose, F. C. (1984). Involvement of head movement in speech production and its implications for language pathology. In F. C. Rose (Ed.), *Advances in neurology.* Vol. 42: *Progress in aphasiology* (pp. 247–261). New York: Raven Press.

64   Pierre Feyereisen

Hager, J. C. (1982). Asymmetries in facial expression. In P. Ekman (Ed.), *Emotion in the human face* (2nd ed., pp. 318–352). Cambridge: Cambridge University Press.

Hager, J. C., & Ekman, P. (1985). The asymmetry of facial actions is inconsistent with models of hemispheric specialization. *Psychophysiology, 22,* 307–318.

Hager, J., & Van Gelder, R. (1985). Asymmetry of speech action. *Neuropsychologia, 23,* 119–120.

Hampson, E., & Kimura, D. (1984). Hand movement asymmetries during verbal and nonverbal tasks. *Canadian Journal of Psychology, 38,* 102–125.

Hannay, H. J. (Ed.). (1986). *Experimental techniques in human neuropsychology.* New York: Oxford University Press.

Hartje, W., Willmes, K., & Weniger, D. (1985). Is there parallel and independent hemispheric processing of intonational and phonetic components of dichotic speech stimuli? *Brain and Language, 24,* 83–99.

Hatta, T., & Dimond, S. J. (1984). Differences in face touching by Japanese and British people. *Neuropsychologia, 22,* 531–534.

Hécaen, H. (1978). Les apraxies idéomotrices: Essai de dissociation. In H. Hécaen & M. Jeannerod (Eds.), *Du contrôle moteur à l'organisation du geste* (pp. 343–358). Paris: Masson.

Hécaen, H., & Albert, M. L. (1978). *Human neuropsychology.* New York: Wiley.

Heilman, K. M., Bowers, D., Speedie, L., & Coslett, H. B. (1984). Comprehension of affective and nonaffective prosody. *Neurology, 34,* 917–921.

Heilman, K. M., Rothi, L., & Kertesz, A. (1983). Localization of apraxia-producing lesions. In A. Kertesz (Ed.), *Localization in neuropsychology* (pp. 371–392). New York: Academic Press.

Heilman, K. M., Rothi, L., & Valenstein, E. (1982). Two forms of ideomotor apraxia. *Neurology, 32,* 342–346.

Heilman, K. M., Scholes, R., & Watson, R. T. (1975). Auditory affective agnosia. Disturbed comprehension of affective speech. *Journal of Neurology, Neurosurgery, and Psychiatry, 38,* 69–72.

Heilman, K. M., Watson, R. T., & Bowers, D. (1983). Affective disorders associated with hemispheric disease. In K. M. Heilman & P. Satz (Eds.), *Neuropsychology of human emotion* (pp. 45–64). New York: Guilford Press.

Hellige, J. B. (1983). Hemisphere x task interaction and the study of laterality. In J. B. Hellige (Ed.), *Cerebral hemisphere asymmetry: Method, theory, and application* (pp. 411–443). New York: Praeger.

Hellige, J. B., & Sergent, J. (1986). Role of task factors in visual field asymmetries. *Brain and Cognition, 5,* 200–222.

Herrmann, M., Reichle, T., Lucius-Hoene, G., Wallesch, C. W., & Johannsen-Horbach, H. (1988). Nonverbal communication as a compensative strategy for severely nonfluent aphasics? A quantitative approach. *Brain and Language, 33,* 41–54.

Hiscock, M. (1986). Lateral eye movements and dual-task performance. In H. J. Hannay (Ed.), *Experimental techniques in human neuropsychology* (pp. 264–308). New York: Oxford University Press.

Humphreys, G. W., & Riddoch, M. J. (1987). The fractionation of visual agnosia. In G. W. Humphreys & M. J. Riddoch (Eds.), *Visual object processing, a cognitive neuropsychological approach* (pp. 281–306). Hillsdale, NJ: Erlbaum.

Humphreys, G. W., Riddoch, M. J., & Quinlan, P. T. (1988). Cascade processes in picture identification. *Cognitive Neuropsychology, 5,* 67–103.

Jason, G. W. (1983). Hemispheric asymmetries in motor function: I. Left-hemisphere specialization for memory but not performance. II. Ordering does not contribute to left-hemisphere specialization. *Neuropsychologia, 21,* 35–45 & 47–58.

(1985). Gesture fluency after focal cortical lesions. *Neuropsychologia, 23,* 463–481.

Jeeves, M. A., & Baumgartner, G. (Eds.). (1986). *Methods of investigation in neuropsychology.* Oxford: Pergamon (reprint of *Neuropsychologia,* 24[1], special issue).

Kelso, J. A. S., & Tuller, B. (1984). Converging evidence in support of common dynamical principles for speech and movement coordination. *American Journal of Physiology: Regulatory, Integrative, and Comparative Physiology, 15,* R928–R935.

Kelso, J. A. S., Tuller B., & Harris, K. S. (1983). A "dynamic pattern" perspective on the control and coordination of movement. In P. F. MacNeilage (Ed.), *The production of speech* (pp. 137–153). New York: Springer-Verlag.

Kempler, D. (1988). Lexical and pantomime abilities in Alzheimer's disease. *Aphasiology, 2,* 147–159.

Kendon, A. (1983). Gesture and speech: How they interact. In J. M. Wiemann & R. P. Harrison (Eds.), *Nonverbal interaction* (pp. 13–45). *Sage Annual Reviews of Communication Research* (Vol. 11). Beverly Hills, CA: Sage.

Kertesz, A. (1985). Apraxia and aphasia: Anatomical and clinical relationships. In E. A. Roy (Ed.), *Neuropsychological studies of apraxia and related disorders* (pp. 163–178). Amsterdam: North Holland.

Kertesz, A., & Ferro, J. M. (1984). Lesion size and location in ideomotor apraxia. *Brain, 107,* 921–933.

Kimura, D. (1973). Manual activity during speaking. I. Right-handers. II. Left-handers. *Neuropsychologia, 11,* 45–50 & 51–55.

(1976). The neural basis of language qua gesture. In H. Whitaker & H. A. Whitaker (Eds.), *Studies in neurolinguistics* (Vol. 2, pp. 145–156). New York: Academic Press.

(1982). Left-hemisphere control of oral and brachial movements and their relation to communication. *Philosophical Transactions of the Royal Society of London, Series B, 298,* 135–149.

Kimura, D., & Humphrys, C. A. (1981). A comparison of left- and right-arm movements during speaking. *Neuropsychologia, 19,* 807–812.

King, F. L., & Kimura, D. (1972). Left-ear superiority in dichotic perception of vocal nonverbal sounds. *Canadian Journal of Psychology, 26,* 111–116.

Kinsbourne, M. (1986). Brain organization underlying orientation and gestures: Normal and pathological cases. In J. L. Nespoulous, P. Perron, & A. R. Lecours (Eds.), *The biological foundations of gestures: Motor and semiotic aspects* (pp. 65–76). Hillsdale, NJ: Erlbaum.

Kinsbourne, M., & Bemporad, B. (1984). Lateralization of emotion: A model and the evidence. In N. A. Fox & R. J. Davidson (Eds.), *The psychobiology of affective development* (pp. 259–291). Hillsdale, NJ: Erlbaum.

Kinsbourne, M., & Hiscock, M. (1983). Asymmetries of dual-task performances. In J. B. Hellige (Ed.), *Cerebral hemisphere asymmetry: Method, theory, and application* (pp. 255–334). New York: Praeger.

Koemeda-Lutz, M., Cohen, R., & Meier, E. (1987). Organization of and access to semantic memory in aphasia. *Brain and Language, 30,* 321–337.

Koff, E., Borod, J. C., & White, B. (1981). Asymmetries for hemiface size and mobility. *Neuropsychologia, 19,* 825–830.

Kolb, B., & Milner, B. (1981). Observations of spontaneous facial expression after cerebral excisions and after intracarotid injection of sodium amytal. *Neuropsychologia, 19*, 505–514.

Kolb, B., & Taylor, L. (1981). Affective behavior in patients with localized cortical excisions: Role of lesion side and site. *Science, 214*, 89–91.

Kolb, B., & Whishaw, I. Q. (1985). *Fundamentals of human neuropsychology.* New York: Freeman.

Lambert, A. J. (1982). Right hemisphere language ability: 2. Evidence from normal subjects. *Current Psychological Reviews, 2*, 139–152.

Lavergne, J., & Kimura, D. (1987). Hand movement asymmetry during speech: No effect of speaking topic. *Neuropsychologia, 25*, 689–693.

LeDoux, J. E. (1986). The neurobiology of emotion. In J. E. LeDoux & W. Hirst (Eds.), *Mind and brain: Dialogues in cognitive neuroscience* (pp. 301–354). Cambridge: Cambridge University Press.

Lehmkuhl, G., Poeck, K., & Willmes, K. (1983). Ideomotor apraxia and aphasia: An examination of types and manifestations of apraxic symptoms. *Neuropsychologia, 21*, 199–212.

LeMay, A., David, R., & Thomas, A. P. (1988). The use of spontaneous gesture by aphasic patients. *Aphasiology, 2*, 137–145.

Levelt, W. J. M., Richardson, G., & LaHeij, W. (1985). Pointing and voicing in deictic expressions. *Journal of Memory and Language, 24*, 133–164.

Leventhal, H. (1984). A perceptual-motor theory of emotion. In L. Berkowitz (Ed.), *Advances in experimental social psychology* (Vol. 17, pp. 117–182). New York: Academic Press.

Leventhal, H., & Tomarken, A. J. (1986). Emotion: Today's problems. *Annual Review of Psychology*, pp. 565–610.

Ley, R. G., & Bryden, M. P. (1982). A dissociation of right and left hemispheric effects for recognizing emotional tone and verbal content. *Brain and Cognition, 1*, 3–9.

Ley, R. G., & Strauss, E. (1986). Hemispheric asymmetries in the perception of facial expressions by normals. In R. Bruyer (Ed.), *The neuropsychology of face perception and facial expression* (pp. 269–289). Hillsdale, NJ: Erlbaum.

McCloskey, M., & Caramazza, A. (1988). Theory and methodology in cognitive neuropsychology: A response to our critics. *Cognitive Neuropsychology, 5*, 583–623.

McKeever, W. F., & Dixon, M. S. (1981). Right hemisphere superiority for discriminating memorized from non-memorized faces: Affective imagery, sex, and perceived emotionality effects. *Brain and Language, 12*, 246–260.

McLaren, J., & Bryson, S. E. (1987). Hemispheric asymmetries in the perception of emotional and neutral faces. *Cortex, 23*, 645–654.

McNeill, D. (1985). So you think gestures are nonverbal? *Psychological Review, 92*, 350–371.

Mahoney, A. M., & Sainsbury, R. S. (1987). Hemispheric asymmetry in the perception of emotional sounds. *Brain and Cognition, 6*, 216–233.

Mammucari, A., Caltagirone, C., Ekman, P., Friesen, W., Gainotti, G., Pizzamiglio, L., & Zocolotti, P. (1988). Spontaneous facial expression of emotions in brain damaged patients. *Cortex, 24*, 521–533.

Manning, L. (1986). Interhemispheric asymmetry in facial expression recognition: Relationship to field-dependence. *Cortex, 22*, 601–610.

Meyer, D. E., Irwin, D. E., Osman, A. M., & Kounios, J. (1988). The dynamics of cognition and action: Mental processes inferred from speed–accuracy decomposition. *Psychological Review, 95*, 183–237.

Miller, J. (1988). Discrete and continuous models of human information processing: Theoretical distinctions and empirical results. *Acta Psychologica, 67,* 191–257.

Morais, J. (1982). The two sides of cognition. In J. Mehler, M. Garrett, & E. Walkes (Eds.), *Perspectives in mental representations* (pp. 277–309). Hillsdale, NJ: Erlbaum.

Morais, J., & Ladavas, E. (1987). Hemispheric interactions in the recognition of words and emotional intonations. *Cognition and Emotion, 1,* 89–100.

Morgan, M. J., & McManus, I. C. (1988). The relationship between brainedness and handedness. In F. C. Rose, R. Whurr, & M. A. Wyke (Eds.), *Aphasia* (pp. 85–130). London: Whurr.

Nicholas, L. E., & Brookshire, R. H. (1981). Effects of pictures and picturability on sentence verification by aphasic and nonaphasic subjects. *Journal of Speech and Hearing Research, 24,* 292–298.

Oatley, K., & Johnson-Laird, P. N. (1987). Towards a cognitive theory of emotions. *Cognition and Emotion, 1,* 29–50.

Paillard, J. (1982). Apraxia and the neurophysiology of motor control. *Philosophical Transactions of the Royal Society of London, Series B, 298,* 111–134.

Panksepp, J. (1986). The anatomy of emotions. In R. Plutchik & H. Kellerman (Eds.), *Emotion: Theory, research, and experience: Vol. 3. Biological foundations of emotion* (pp. 91–124). Orlando, FL: Academic Press.

Peretz, I. (1985). Les différences hémisphériques dans la perception des stimuli musicaux chez le sujet normal: I. Les sons isolés. II. Les sons simultanés. *L'Année Psychologique, 85,* 429–440 & 567–576.

Peterson, L. N., & Kirshner, H. S. (1981). Gestural impairment and gestural ability in aphasia: A review. *Brain and Language, 14,* 333–348.

Phillips, C. G., Zeki, S., & Barlow, H. B. (1984). Localization of function in the cerebral cortex. *Brain, 107,* 329–361.

Pierce, R. S., & Beekman, L. A. (1985). Effects of linguistic and extralinguistic context on semantic and syntactic processing in aphasia. *Journal of Speech and Hearing Research, 28,* 250–254.

Pizzamiglio, L., Caltagirone, C., Mammucari, A., Ekman, P., & Friesen, W. V. (1987). Imitation of facial movements in brain damaged patients. *Cortex, 23,* 207–221.

Pizzamiglio, L., & Mammucari, A. (1989). Disorders in facial expression of emotions in brain-damaged patients. In G. Gainotti & C. Caltagirone (Eds.), *Emotion and the dual brain* (pp. 187–203). Berlin: Springer-Verlag.

Pizzamiglio, L., Zoccolotti, P., Mammucari, A., & Cesaroni, R. (1983). The independence of face identity and facial expression recognition mechanisms: Relationship to sex and cognitive style. *Brain and Cognition, 2,* 176–188.

Poeck, K. (1969). Pathophysiology of emotional disorders associated with brain damage. In P. J. Vincken & G. N. Bruyn (Eds.), *Handbook of clinical neurology: Vol. 3. Disorders of higher nervous activity* (pp. 343–367). Amsterdam: North Holland.

Poizner, H., & Battison, R. (1980). Cerebral asymmetry for sign language: Clinical and experimental evidence. In H. Lane & F. Grosjean (Eds.), *Recent perspectives on American Sign Language* (pp. 79–101). Hillsdale, NJ: Erlbaum.

Posner, M. I., Petersen, S. E., Fox, P. T., & Raichle, M. E. (1988). Localization of cognitive operations in the human brain. *Science, 240,* 1627–1631.

Prutting, C. A., & Kirchner, D. M. (1987). A clinical appraisal of the pragmatic aspects of language. *Journal of Speech and Hearing Disorders, 52,* 105–119.

Rapcsak, S. Z., Croswell S. C., & Rubens, A. B. (1989). Apraxia in Alzheimer's disease. *Neurology, 39,* 664–668.

Rapcsak, S. Z., Kaszniak, A. W., & Rubens, A. B. (1989). Anomia for facial expressions: Evidence for a category-specific visual–verbal disconnection syndrome. *Neuropsychologia, 27,* 1031–1041.

Reuter-Lorenz, P., & Davidson, R. J. (1981). Differential contributions of the two cerebral hemispheres to the perception of happy and sad faces. *Neuropsychologia, 19,* 609–613.

Riddoch, M. J., & Humphreys, G. W. (1987). Visual object processing in optic aphasia: A case of semantic access agnosia. *Cognitive Neuropsychology, 4,* 131–185.

Riddoch, M. J., Humphreys, G. W., Coltheart, M., & Funnell, E. (1988). Semantic systems or system? Neuropsychological evidence re-examined. *Cognitive Neuropsychology, 5,* 3–25.

Rinn, W. E. (1984). The neuropsychology of facial expression: A review of the neurological and psychological mechanisms for producing facial expressions. *Psychological Bulletin, 95,* 52–77.

Ross, E. D. (1981). The aprosodias: Functional–anatomic organization of the affective components of language in the right hemisphere. *Archives of Neurology, 38,* 561–569.

(1984). Right hemisphere in language, affective behavior and emotion. *Trends in Neurosciences, 7,* 342–346.

(1988). Prosody and brain lateralization: Fact vs fancy or is it all just semantics? *Archives of Neurology, 45,* 338–339.

Ross, E. D., Edmondson, J. A., Seibert, G. B., & Homan, R. W. (1988). Acoustic analysis of affective prosody during right-sided Wada test: A within subjects verification of the right hemisphere's role in language. *Brain and Language, 33,* 128–145.

Rothi, L. J. G., & Heilman, K. M. (1984). Acquisition and retention of gestures by apraxic patients. *Brain and Cognition, 3,* 426–437.

Rothi, L. J. G., Mack, L., & Heilman, K. M. (1986). Pantomime agnosia. *Journal of Neurology, Neurosurgery, and Psychiatry, 49,* 451–454.

Ryalls, J. H., & Behrens, S. J. (1988). An overview of changes in fundamental frequency associated with cortical insult. *Aphasiology, 2,* 107–115.

Sackeim, H. A. (1985). Morphologic asymmetries of the face: A review. *Brain and Cognition, 4,* 296–312.

Sackeim, H. A., & Grega, D. M. (1987). Perceiver bias in the processing of deliberately asymmetric emotional expression. *Brain and Cognition, 6,* 464–473.

Sackeim, H. A., & Gur, R. C. (1983). Facial asymmetry and the communication of emotion. In J. T. Cacioppo & R. E. Petty (Eds.), *Social psychophysiology* (pp. 307–352). New York: Guilford Press.

Safer, M. A., & Leventhal, H. (1977). Ear differences in evaluating emotional tones of voice and verbal content. *Journal of Experimental Psychology: Human Perception and Performance, 3,* 75–82.

Sanders, A. F. (1980). Stage analysis of reaction processes. In G. E. Stelmach & J. Requin (Eds.), *Tutorials in motor behavior* (pp. 331–354). Amsterdam: North Holland.

Schlanger, B. B., Schlanger, P., & Gerstman, L. J. (1976). The perception of emotionally toned sentences by right-hemisphere-damaged and aphasic subjects. *Brain and Language, 3,* 396–403.

Sergent, J. (1983). The role of the input in visual hemispheric asymmetries. *Psychological Bulletin, 93,* 481–514.

(1984). Inferences from unilateral brain damage about normal hemispheric functions in visual pattern recognition. *Psychological Bulletin, 96,* 99–115.

Sergent, J., & Hellige, J. B. (1986). Role of input factors in visual-field asymmetries. *Brain and Cognition, 5,* 174–199.

Seron, X., Van der Kaa, M. A., Vanderlinden, M., Remits, A., & Feyereisen, P. (1982). Decoding paralinguistic signals: Effect of semantic and prosodic cues on aphasic comprehension. *Journal of Communication Disorders, 15,* 223–231.

Shallice, T. (1987). Impairments of semantic processing: Multiple dissociations. In M. Coltheart, G. Sartori, & R. Job (Eds.), *The cognitive neuropsychology of language* (pp. 111–127). Hillsdale, NJ: Erlbaum.

(1988). *From neuropsychology to mental structure.* Cambridge: Cambridge University Press.

Shapiro, B. E., & Danly, M. (1985). The role of the right hemisphere in the control of speech prosody in propositional and affective contexts. *Brain and Language, 25,* 19–36.

Silberman, E. K., & Weingartner, H. (1986). Hemispheric lateralization of functions related to emotion. *Brain and Cognition, 5,* 322–353.

Ska, B., & Nespoulous, J. L. (1987). Pantomimes and aging. *Journal of Clinical and Experimental Neuropsychology, 9,* 754–766.

Smith, A., McFarland, D. H., & Weber, C. M. (1986). Interactions between speech and finger movements: An exploration of the dynamic pattern perspective. *Journal of Speech and Hearing Research, 29,* 471–480.

Smith, L. (1987a). Fluency and severity of aphasia and non-verbal competency. *Aphasiology, 1,* 291–295.

(1987b). Nonverbal competency in aphasic stroke patients' conversation. *Aphasiology, 1,* 127–139.

Sousa-Poza, J. F., Rohrberg, R., & Mercure, A. (1979). Effects of type of information (abstract–concrete) and field dependence on asymmetry of hand movements during speech. *Perceptual and Motor Skills, 48,* 1223–1230.

Speedie, L. J., Coslett, H. B., & Heilman, K. M. (1984). Repetition of affective prosody in mixed transcortical aphasia. *Archives of Neurology, 41,* 268–270.

Squire, L. R. (1986). Mechanisms of memory. *Science, 232,* 1612–1619.

Strauss, E., & Moscovitch, M. (1981). Perception of facial expressions. *Brain and Language, 13,* 308–332.

Tallal, P., & Newcombe, F. (1978). Impairment of auditory perception and language comprehension in dysphasia. *Brain and Language, 5,* 13–24.

Thomson, J. K. (1985). Right brain, left brain; left face, right face: Hemisphericity and the expression of facial emotion. *Cortex, 21,* 281–289.

Tompkins, C. A., & Flowers, C. R. (1985). Perception of emotional intonation by brain-damaged adults: The influence of task processing levels. *Journal of Speech and Hearing Research, 28,* 527–538.

(1987). Contextual mood priming following left and right hemisphere damage. *Brain and Cognition, 6,* 361–376.

Tranel, D., Damasio, A. R., & Damasio, H. (1988). Intact recognition of facial expression, gender, and age in patients with impaired recognition of facial identity. *Neurology, 38,* 690–696.

Tucker, D. M. (1981). Lateral brain function, emotion, and conceptualization. *Psychological Bulletin, 89,* 19–46.

Tucker, D. M., Beckwith, B. E., Dopson, W. G., & Bullard-Bates, P. C. (1985). Asymmetrical facial expression indeed: A reply to Dave and Thomson. *Cortex, 21,* 305–307.

Tucker, D. M., Watson, R. T., & Heilman, K. M. (1977). Discrimination and evocation of affectively intoned speech in patients with right parietal disease. *Neurology, 27,* 947–950.

Van Lancker, D. R., & Canter, G. J. (1982). Impairment of voice and face recognition in patients with hemispheric damage. *Brain and Cognition, 1,* 185–195.

Varney, N. R. (1982). Pantomime recognition defect in aphasia: Implications for the concept of asymbolia. *Brain and Language, 15,* 32–39.

Varney, N. R., & Damasio, H. (1987). Locus of lesion in impaired pantomime recognition. *Cortex, 23,* 699–703.

Varney, N. R., Damasio, H., & Adler, S. (1989). The role of individual difference in determining the nature of comprehension defects in aphasia. *Cortex, 25,* 47–55.

Venus, C. A., & Canter, G. J. (1987). The effect of redundant cues on comprehension of spoken messages by aphasic adults. *Journal of Communication Disorders, 20,* 477–491.

Walker-Batson, D., Barton, M. M., Wendt, J. S., & Reynolds, S. (1987). Symbolic and affective non-verbal deficits in left- and right-hemisphere injured adults. *Aphasiology, 1,* 257–262.

Weintraub, S., Mesulam, M. M., & Kramer, C. (1981). Disturbances in prosody: A right hemisphere contribution to language. *Archives of Neurology, 38,* 742–744.

Wolf, M. E., & Goodale, M. A. (1987). Oral asymmetries during verbal and non-verbal movements of the mouth. *Neuropsychologia, 25,* 375–396.

Wyler, F., Graves, R., & Landis, T. (1987). Cognitive task influence on relative hemispheric motor control: Mouth asymmetry and lateral eye movements. *Journal of Clinical and Experimental Neuropsychology, 9,* 105–116.

Wylie, D. R., & Goodale, M. A. (1988). Left-sided oral asymmetries in spontaneous but not posed smiles. *Neuropsychologia, 26,* 823–832.

Zajonc, R. B. (1984). On the primacy of affect. *American Psychologist, 39,* 117–123.

Zoccolotti, P., Scabini, D., & Violani, C. (1982). Electrodermal responses in patients with unilateral brain damage. *Journal of Clinical Neuropsychology, 4,* 143–150.

PART II

Sociodevelopmental approaches to nonverbal behavior

3. The development of facial expressions in infancy

LINDA A. CAMRAS, CAROL MALATESTA, AND CARROLL E. IZARD

I at once commenced to make notes on the first dawn of the various expressions which he exhibited, for I felt convinced, even at this early period, that the most complex and fine shades of expression must have had a gradual and natural origin.
– Charles Darwin (1887/1969)

Like many of us today, Charles Darwin sought to understand human emotional expressions by observing their development in infancy. Darwin kept a diary of his first child's expressive behavior and used this record in both his seminal volume, *The Expression of Emotions in Man and Animals* (1872/1965), and his later essay, *A Biographical Sketch of an Infant* (1877). In these works, he described facial and bodily displays of pain–discomfort, anger–rage, sadness and grief, determination, disgust, surprise–astonishment, fear, and a variety of other affective states. Darwin detailed the morphology of many facial expressions, often indicating their anatomical (muscular) basis. In addition, he reported eliciting stimuli associated with each emotional expression and with some of their constituent facial movements. To help explain their evolutionary origin, Darwin presented hypotheses regarding the adaptive function of some components of emotional expressions. For example, he suggested that raising the upper lip in disgust may serve to exclude or expel an offensive odor. Based on his observations of infant expressions as well as on other forms of evidence, Darwin concluded that human facial expressions are characteristic of the species and thus provide evidence for the common ancestry of racial groups and the evolution of humans.

For almost a century, Darwin's conclusions regarding the phylogeny and ontogeny of human facial expressions were largely ignored or rejected. Since 1970, however, there has been renewed interest in emotional expressions, largely owing to an impressive body of research

73

demonstrating cross-cultural consistency in the labeling of a number of facial expressions according to their corresponding emotion. This research has set the stage for substantial advances in both theory and methodology, culminating in the recent development of anatomically based systems for coding facial expressions and their application to studies of adults, children, and infants (Ekman & Friesen, 1978; Friesen & Ekman, 1984; Izard, 1979; Izard, Dougherty, & Hembree, 1983).

In this chapter, we shall focus on the development of infant facial expressions as mainly elucidated in studies using objective or anatomically based coding systems. We shall begin by briefly reviewing the current views of infants' facial expressions and their relationship to emotion, as well as strategies and criteria for inferring the motivational basis or emotion meaning of infants' facial expressions. Here we shall draw on the ethological literature in regard to the similar motivational basis of nonverbal animal displays. Then we shall look at empirical studies of facial expression patterns describing the emotions in infants of enjoyment, interest, surprise, disgust, fear, distress–pain, anger, and sadness, in which we shall distinguish between the data produced in these studies and the inferences regarding emotion that can be drawn from the data. Alternative hypotheses concerning the affective meaning of an expression will be offered for several facial patterns. In the final section of the chapter, we shall summarize our knowledge of the development of infants' facial behavior, indicate some gaps in our current understanding, and point to directions for future research.

Current views of infant facial expression and emotions

Differential emotions theory

Differential emotions theory (Izard, 1971, 1977) is a broad conceptual framework that describes the structure and functions of discrete emotions. These emotions and their interrelations are viewed as the emotions system, the primary motivational system for cognition and action. The theory regards each fundamental or basic emotion as having distinct neural substrates and distinct expressive and experiential components. Thus each emotion is a system or subsystem of interacting components. A central premise of this theory is that each emotion has adaptive, organizational, and motivational functions.

Differential emotions theory has been extended to the domain of development (Izard & Malatesta, 1987), and several of the theoretical principles pertain to the emotion expressions. First, in both the general theory and the developmental theory, emotion expressions are seen as (1) contributing to the activation and regulation of emotion experiences (feelings), (2) communicating something about internal states and intentions, and (3) evoking responses in others. Although the face has been the focus of most of the empirical research on expression, the theory recognizes that vocal, postural, and other voluntary bodily movements may subserve all of these functions.

Differential emotions theory holds that emotion expressions provide an excellent window on early mental and social development, as they are seen as a bridge between underlying neural processes and inner experiences–feelings on the one hand and individual–environment relations on the other. The theory maintains that there are innate emotion-specific neuromuscular patterns (facial expressions) for each of several basic emotions, that these expressions are preadapted to serve the functions described earlier, and that biological and social forces mediate developmental changes in expressive behavior. Basically, the changes are from instinctlike expressions to more restricted and controlled emotion signals. Through maturation and learning, expressions may become fragmented, miniaturized, exaggerated, or idiosyncratically modified. In relation to the corresponding feelings, they may become inhibited or completely disassociated. Because the theory maintains that there is an innate expression–feeling concordance, it proposes that the socialization and self-regulation of emotion expressions contribute to the regulation of emotion experiences and feelings (see Izard & Malatesta, 1987, for a review of the relevant evidence).

The aspect of differential emotions theory that we shall examine here is the notion that innate configurations of facial movements can be reliably identified as signals of discrete emotions. This hypothesis of innateness does not imply that all the basic expressions are present at birth or that each expression emerges full blown. Rather, as in other domains of development, genetic programs may unfold at different ages. The theory predicts that a particular family of elicitors will be more closely associated with certain emotion expressions than others will. The identity of a band of elicitors can be detected by looking at the types of emotion they elicit and by considering their functional significance for self-regulation and for recruitment of motivation in others. An emotion expression can be micromomentary or protracted and intense, and in either case the expression may disappear before the accompanying feeling subsides.

The best basis for inferring a relation between an expression and an underlying feeling or motivational state in preverbal infants is coherence among individual traits (emotion responsiveness, physiological reactivity, temperament), stimulus event or context, and subsequent behaviors of infant and caregiver. Few, if any, studies of expression–feeling relations have taken into account all these variables. Another basis for inferring a relation between expression and feeling is evidence of stability or continuity of expressive behaviors in the same situations (or in different situations that are conceptually and functionally similar) at different ages (Izard, Hembree, & Huebner, 1987; Hyson & Izard, 1985; Stenberg, Campos, & Emde, 1983).

Alternative views

In contrast with differential emotions theory, several versions of a differentiation theory of emotional development have been proposed (Bridges, 1932; Ekman & Oster, 1982; Fridlund, Ekman, & Oster, 1987; Sroufe, 1979). Differentiation theories may take many forms, but all include the notion that there are fewer emotion states in infancy than in adulthood and that early emotions differentiate into later ones. Theories may vary, however, in the number and identity of initial emotion states as well as the exact differentiation processes that occur during development.

Analogous to embryonic differentiation, emotional differentiation might involve structural changes in the components of emotion (e.g., the emergence of new facial expressions) and/or changes in the organization of components (e.g., the relationship between facial expression and feeling state). Differentiation theories need not hold that early emotional responding is entirely diffuse and unorganized, just as differentiation theories of cell development do not imply that cells are initially unorganized. However, most germane to this chapter, such theories do allow that a developmentally invariant concordance between expression and emotion may not initially exist. Thus, some facial expressions (e.g., smiles) may emerge early as completely nonemotional responses but may become integrated into an emotion system later in development. Alternatively, some facial expressions may initially be tied to affective states, but these states may differ from those associated with the expression in adulthood. A third possibility is that the facial expressions themselves may differentiate so that early expressive responses may be "blends" or combinations of components that later are produced separately as discrete emotional facial expressions.

These many possibilities suggest that empirical research is necessary to clarify the relationship between infants' facial expressions and emotions. We shall now turn to the ethological literature for guidelines as to how such research might be conducted.

Ethology and the motivational analysis of expressive behavior

In their early classic studies of animal communication, ethologists (e.g., Lorenz, 1950, 1965; Tinbergen, 1952, 1953, 1969) frequently were confronted with nonverbal acts whose motivational basis they wished to determine. To obtain evidence regarding the motivational basis of such acts, investigators typically looked at (1) the morphology or form of the behavior, (2) the situational contexts in which the act occurs, and (3) the concomitant and subsequent behaviors of the individual producing the target action (Hinde, 1970, 1974; Moynihan, 1955a, 1955b; Tinbergen, 1959). We shall consider each of these as it relates to infants' facial expressions. Then we shall consider a fourth factor that has not been used by ethologists but has played a critical role in debates about emotion in human infants: the cognitive status of the expresser.

Morphology

To determine the motivational basis of a signal, ethologists often look for a structural resemblance between the signal and some behavior whose motivational basis is already known or can be assumed. This related behavior might be an instrumental action, as animal displays often include a ritualization or formalization of instrumental behaviors (Daanje, 1950). For example, some threat displays involving bared teeth are considered to be ritualized versions of biting. The related behavior also might be another communicative act (e.g., one already known to be a threat display).

In general, investigators of infants' facial expressions have looked for morphologically related signals to support their interpretations of infants' facial behaviors. Their strategy has been to identify infants' facial expressions that are structurally similar to expressions considered to be emotion signals in adults. For many investigators, such formal resemblance has been considered sufficient to establish that the infant expression is indeed an expression of emotion. But other forms of converging evidence may be required if subtle differences in morphology exist and/or if there are indications from nonmorphological sources that an emotion inference may not be appropriate.

Concomitant and subsequent behaviors

According to ethological theorists, a second form of evidence for a signal's motivational basis is temporal association between the signal and another behavior whose motivational basis is known. For example, if a display is associated with an increased probability of attack by the displaying individual, it is considered to reflect some degree of underlying aggressive motivation. If a display occurs in exclusive association with other displays known to be threats, it too is considered a threat display.

Regarding infants' emotional facial expressions, some investigators have similarly examined nonfacial behaviors accompanying the putative emotional facial expression. This can strengthen inferences regarding an expression's emotional basis to the extent that infants produce nonfacial actions whose emotion relevance is admitted by most observers. But considering the limited behavioral capacities of infants during their first few months, it is not surprising that a consensus regarding the emotion relevance of nonfacial infant behavior is sometimes difficult to obtain. Thus additional sources of evidence must be sought.

Situational context and presumed eliciting stimuli

Ethologists will often use situational context and/or apparent eliciting factors to make inferences regarding the motivational basis of a signal. For example, if a display occurs when two males confront each other at a territorial border, it may be hypothesized to be a threat display. This inference, however, is tempered by the fact that some signals produced during territorial encounters convey other information. Thus, to strengthen their inference, investigators ideally attempt to identify all contexts in which the signal is produced, and inferences about the signal's motivational basis are dependent on this entire range. Thus, if a display is produced exclusively in situations of actual conflict and/or other situations in which aggression might reasonably occur (e.g., male–male encounters at territorial borders), then ethologists will consider the target signal to be a threat display.

Regarding infants' facial expressions, the eliciting situation has been used as a critical source of evidence regarding emotions during the first few months, as infants are limited in their ability to produce emotion-appropriate concomitant nonfacial behavior. Thus it may crucial to observe the full range of contexts in which infants produce particular facial expressions in order to strengthen inferences regarding their emotion meaning at early ages. At the same time, we must recognize that few stimuli will always elicit the same emotions in all individuals at any age. Thus it also is important to look for coherent relations among facial expressions, subsequent behaviors, and eliciting conditions in order to strengthen inferences regarding the significance of the expressions and their relations to underlying experiential phenomena or motivational states.

Cognitive status

Although not considered by ethologists, the cognitive status of the expresser has been used by some investigators to make judgments about infant emotions. This approach is derived from adult emotion theories that view affect as being dependent on cognitive analysis (Lazarus, Kanner, & Folkman, 1980; Mandler, 1984; Schachter & Singer, 1962). According to these theories, specific emotions are the precipitates of specific forms of information processing, meaning analysis, and/or appraisal. For example, fear is the apprehension of an undesired future state and thus should not occur until the infant is capable of such apprehension.

Investigators who take this position hold that emotional expressions would not be seen before the infant is capable of performing the necessary informational analysis. The earlier appearance of such expressions generally might be handled in one of two ways. The first is limited capitulation. That is, one might admit a limited set of "natural" or "sensory" elicitors (e.g., loud noise for fear) that can elicit the emotion without requiring the typical process of meaning analysis (e.g., see Bowlby's, 1973, discussion of "natural clues to danger"). The second approach has been to deny that an emotion has actually been produced. As part of this second approach, two alternative interpretations for emotional expressions generally are offered. One asserts that the expression reflects an emotion precursor but not an emotion (e.g., Sroufe, 1984). Thus the fear expression reflects a negative hedonic state but not the emotion of fear. Similarly, neonatal smiles have been said to reflect a positive hedonic state but not the emotion of enjoyment or joy. The second interpretation denies the presence of any affective underpinnings whatsoever. Thus neonatal smiles are "reflexive" responses produced during states of REM sleep, and no affective state can be inferred (e.g., Campos & Barrett, 1984; Wolff, 1987).

Next, we shall review studies of infants' facial expressions highlighting the evidence produced in these studies regarding their phenomenological and motivational basis, that is, their status as expressions of emotion. To emphasize our commitment to separating description from inference, we shall avoid the term *emotional expression* and instead refer to facial expressions or facial patterns. Those facial patterns described in Izard's AFFEX-coding system provide a focus for our review. In particular, we shall consider the AFFEX-described patterns for the seven emotions that have been most widely studied during the first year of life: enjoyment, interest, surprise, disgust, fear, distress–pain, anger, and sadness. In order to ensure comparability among the studies to be reviewed, we shall discuss only those investigations that used an anatomically based coding system or provided objective descriptions of the facial expressions under consideration.

In the course of our review unresolved issues will be highlighted. As will be seen, resolution of some issues might be achieved by acquiring further data from domains of evidence that were not thoroughly examined in previous studies. However, in some cases, disagreements among investigators are grounded in fundamental differences in the types of inferences they are willing to make based on the data that have been acquired. In these cases, a theoretical consensus probably cannot be achieved at this time. Instead, we shall propose that investigators aim to make explicit the criteria underlying their assertions about emotional and expressive development. Thus the basis for disagreements will be clear even if the controversies themselves must remain unresolved.

Smiling and the inference of enjoyment in infants

Infant smiling provides a good illustration of the complexities encountered in the study of expressive development. Although smiling can be observed at birth, some investigators have been reluctant to attribute the emotion of happiness to newborns (Campos & Barrett, 1984; Emde, Gaensbauer, & Harmon, 1976; Wolff, 1987) or even to infants under 3 months of age (Sroufe, 1979, 1984). Here we shall examine investigators' arguments and positions in regard to the preceding ethological and cognitive criteria for inferring emotion.

In regard to morphology, no study of infant smiling has systematically examined its development using an anatomically based coding system, although several investigators have reported informal observations of developmental changes in the morphology of infants' smiles. The most detailed description can be found in an early report by Wolff (1963), who saw the smiles of neonates as involving a slight contraction of m. zygomatic major, producing a slight upward movement of the mouth corners. Because neonatal smiles occur during REM sleep, the infants' eyes are closed, and there is no accompanying contraction of m. orbicularis oculi, the muscle encircling the eye. By the second week, smiling sometimes occurs when the eyes are open, but the infant's gaze is glassy and unfocused. In the third week, infants produce some focused, bright-eyed smiles accompanied by the action of m. orbicularis oculi.

With reference to the morphology of adult smiles, Ekman and his associates (Ekman & Friesen, 1982; Ekman, Friesen, & O'Sullivan, 1988) proposed that genuine smiles of happiness (which they term *Duchenne smiles*) involve the contraction of m. orbicularis oculi, whereas nongenuine (e.g., deliberately produced) smiles do not. Consistent with this hypothesis, Fox and Davidson (1988) found that 10-month-old infants produce more Duchenne smiles with their mothers than with strangers. Furthermore, only Duchenne smiles were associated with left frontal EEG activity, hypothesized to be an approach-related pattern. Thus if future studies of smiles in younger infants confirm that the contraction of m. orbicularis oculi begins in the third week, then some might argue on morphological grounds that smiles become emotional at that time. But morphology alone may not provide sufficient evidence for inferring the emotion status of smiles or other facial expressions.

Most studies of older infants' smiling have been principally concerned with determining the stimulus conditions eliciting this expression (Emde, Gaensbauer, & Harmon, 1976; Emde & Harmon, 1972; Sroufe, 1979; Sroufe & Waters, 1976; Wolff, 1963, 1987). During the first week, neonatal smiles occur spontaneously during REM sleep, and then these endogenous (internally generated) smiles gradually decrease over the next several months. Starting at the end of the first month, exogenous (i.e., externally elicited) smiles begin to be seen. During the next several weeks, exogenous smiles can be elicited by mild to moderate stimulation of various sorts: auditory, tactile, kinesthetic, and visual; social and nonsocial. These early smiles are thought to be produced by fluctuations in tension or arousal level produced by the mild stimulation (Sroufe, 1984; Sroufe & Waters, 1976).

Preferential smiling to social over nonsocial stimuli also develops between 6 and 12 weeks, and by 12 weeks, infants have begun to smile selectively to familiar persons and during newly mastered activities (e.g., Lewis, Sullivan, & Brooks-Gunn, 1985). These smiles of mastery and recognition are also thought to be associated with fluctuations in arousal (i.e., mild increases followed by a decrease accompanying recognition or successful performance). Here, however, the fluctuations in arousal result from the infant's imposition of a primitive form of meaning (e.g., familiar vs. unfamiliar) on the environment.

Interestingly, the elicitors of smiling in infants have not generally been described in evaluative terms (e.g., as desirable or undesirable in themselves). Several investigators (Campos & Barrett, 1984; Emde & Harmon, 1972; Wolff, 1987) appear to accept infants' exogenous (externally stimulated), but not endogenous (internally stimulated), smiles as expressing a pleasurable response. This may reflect the implicit use of two of the ethological criteria just described: morphology and eliciting situation. Exogenous smiles are reported to begin at the same age at which Wolff (1963) described focused, open-eyed (i.e., mature-looking) smiles to be first produced (i.e., around 3 weeks). Thus, exogenous smiles could be accepted as indicating pleasurable responses because they meet some "minimum plausibility" criterion for eliciting stimulus and also bear a close morphological resemblance to adult smiles. Whether this pleasurable response is a true emotion or an emotion precursor has been the subject of some debate, but there at least is agreement regarding the general hedonic tone accompanying post-neonatal smiles.

Considering that infants' smiles are often produced in response to stimuli that would not necessarily elicit emotion in adults (e.g., a bull's eye target; Emde & Harmon, 1972), arguments regarding their emotion meaning might be strengthened by a look at concomitant nonfacial behaviors. Along these lines, Weinberg, Gianino, and Tronick (1989) found a relationship between smiling and sustained social play in 6-month-old infants, and again, Fox and Davidson (1988) found an association between Duchenne smiles and left frontal EEG activity in 10-month-old infants. Data on nonfacial concomitants of smiling have not been gathered for younger infants. Given the infrequency of their smiling and their limited behavioral capacities, convincing nonfacial evidence of enjoyment or joy might be difficult to obtain for younger infants. Nevertheless, information about the concomitants of infant smiles (and in particular, neonatal smiles) could contribute to our understanding of their emotion status.

Although not considered by ethologists, several researchers have used the fourth criterion – cognitive engagement – as a primary basis for inferring the motivational underpinnings of infants' smiles. For example, Sroufe (1979, 1984) argued that true emotions must involve the imposition of meaning on a stimulus, and so smiles do not reflect the emotion of joy in infants until they are elicited in recognition or mastery situations, that is, at around 3 months of age. Before that time, smiles are considered to reflect a positive hedonic state, which is considered a precursor to emotion. In contrast, differential emotion theory does not define emotion in terms of cognitive variables. Rather, emotions are feeling states that may result from direct transformations of sensory data or the detection of certain physical features of the stimulus as well as from cognitive appraisal or meaning imposition. Thus, emotion status is not assigned to infant smiles according to the infant's cognitive abilities. Although cognitive analysis may usually be part of the elicitation of joy or enjoyment in older infants and in children and adults, it is not a prerequisite for an emotional response.

To summarize, smiling has probably been the most widely studied of all infant facial expressions. Investigators concur that this expression signals enjoyment for infants over 3 months of age, but they do not agree about the emotion status of smiles in younger infants. Depending on the criteria used, investigators may draw substantially different conclusions about the developmental relationship between smiling and joy or enjoyment. Perhaps because smiling has received so much attention, arguments about its emotion status have been relatively well articulated, which is not true for most other emotions. Nonetheless, those arguments used in the debate about smiling apply also to other emotions and facial patterns.

Interest

Several distinct facial patterns are presented in AFFEX as expressions of interest. Described in nonanatomical terms, these are (1) brows drawn together and slightly lowered; (2) brows raised, thereby widening the eyes; (3) lips pursed; (4) eyes narrowed by contraction of m. orbicularis oculi; and (5) cheeks raised by contraction of m. orbicularis oculi. These may be produced alone or in combination with (6) mouth open and relaxed or (7) mouth open and relaxed with tongue forward. In addition, a face that appears alert and attentive but with no facial movements may be coded as "hypothesized" interest.

In regard to morphology, these same facial patterns are hypothesized by differential emotions theory to be adult expressions of interest, although their status is the subject of some debate among emotion theorists. For example, Ekman's (1972, 1982) neurocultural theory does not currently recognize interest as a primary emotion, and so there may be no adult morphological standard with which infants' expressive patterns can be compared.

Considered as a homogeneous group, the various facial patterns described for the emotion of interest have been investigated in several laboratory studies. For example, Langsdorf, Izard, Rayias, and Hembree (1983) found relationships among the interest facial patterns, duration of visual fixation, and heart rate deceleration in 2- to 8-month-old infants. Fox and Davidson (1985) observed expressions of interest and disgust in 2- to 3-day-old infants presented with sucrose and citric acid solutions. With respect to interest, the infants produced substantial durations of this expression in both conditions but displayed significantly more interest in the sucrose. The infants also showed more left-frontal EEG activity in response to sucrose as opposed to citric acid, a pattern hypothesized to be associated with approach as opposed to withdrawal. More information about the particular interest patterns shown in response to sucrose versus citric acid might be useful for interpreting their study. For example, data reported in a similar study by Rosenstein and Oster (1988) suggest that the "pursed lips" interest pattern is shown to citric acid and the "open mouth with tongue forward" pattern is the response to sucrose. Although both facial expressions are coded as interest according to AFFEX, Rosenstein and Oster view them as indicating differential responses to the two taste stimuli.

Departing from the usual coding procedures, Sullivan and Lewis distinguished among interest patterns recorded in their studies of contingency learning by infants. For example, in a study of 4- and 6-month-olds, these investigators (Sullivan & Lewis, 1989) separated the lowered-brows interest pattern (which they termed *excitement*) from all other patterns (which they termed *interest*). Although their findings were complex, we shall touch on several of their results: First, those subjects who learned the contingency showed more lowered brows throughout the procedure than did the noncontingent subjects. The other interest configurations showed a different pattern, occurring most often during baseline and decreasing thereafter more for contingent subjects than for noncontingent subjects. These data suggest that the several interest expression patterns may not be equivalent and may be related to other undiscovered factors operating during the procedure.

Interest expression patterns have also been reported in a variety of other studies. For example, a number of investigators (e.g., Fox & Gelles, 1984; Haynes, Izard, & Slomine, 1989; Malatesta & Haviland, 1982) found them to occur during mother–infant interactions. Although analyses of their data suggest that mothers attend to these configurations, their specific elicitors and concomitants within the interaction have not been described.

Surprisingly, interest configurations are often the most common expression observed in studies designed to investigate other emotion responses. For example, in a study by Hyson and Izard (1985), interest was the predominant emotion coded during brief separations in a strange situation procedure. In a study of facial responses to pain stimuli, interest expressions were observed for about 14% of the soothing interval following a DPT inoculation (Izard, Hembree, & Huebner, 1987). Although it may be argued that interest is an emotion that occurs in a wide range of eliciting circumstances, alternative explanations should be considered for the many interest expressions observed in both positive and negative emotion settings.

One alternative is a partial reinterpretation of these expression patterns along lines suggested by the Austrian physiologist Albrecht Peiper. According to Peiper (1963), many facial behaviors can be explained as sensory reactions serving to increase or decrease receptivity to a stimulus. Muscles that radiate from a sensory organ (e.g., the eye) can be contracted to increase stimulus reception, whereas muscles that encircle an organ can be contracted to decrease receptivity. Furthermore, reactions can spread from an organ that is directly stimulated to an organ that is not stimulated. For example, a bright light may cause an infant to close tightly both its eyes and its mouth. Peiper thus proposed that facial expressions may serve a direct function for the infant expresser.

According to Peiper, in regard to the several interest expression patterns, some would be considered to increase stimulation. For example, Peiper described a spreading reaction during attentive observation in which the brows are raised and the eyes and mouth are opened. If the infant is looking up, the brows will also be raised as part of an "ocular–frontalis" reflex. According to the AFFEX system, these brow and mouth movements are considered variants of interest.

Peiper also described a defensive facial reaction to negative stimuli that included narrow (or closed) eyes and contracted and/or lowered brows. This defensive brow movement is similar to the knitted brow variant of interest, both being attributed principally to the action of m. corrugator supercilli. But according to AFFEX, the knitted brow of interest may not be lowered and, in any case, is not sufficiently intense to decrease visual input substantially.

Peiper's description of the functional properties of interest-related expressions is similar to proposals made by several other investigators. For example, Darwin (1872/1965) and Ekman (1979) both argued that raised brows could serve to increase one's range of vision and that contracted and/or lowered brows could decrease glare from intense light. These two facial movements may now be completely "emancipated" from these original causal factors and viewed as expressions reflecting the operation of a generalized interest program. However, alternative possibilities along the lines just suggested also must be considered.

First, raised (and possibly knitted) brows may sometimes retain their instrumental function and thus may sometimes occur in noninterest situations (e.g., facing a bright light, glancing upward). Second, in the domain of interest situations, raised and knitted brows (as well as other interest patterns) may be only partially emancipated from their original instrumental functions. For example, Darwin contended that "contracted" brows originally served as an instrumental means of coping with certain difficulties in vision but then evolved into an expression of concentration or determination in the face of any difficulty "encountered in a train of thought or action" (Darwin, 1872/1965, p. 222). Thus in modern humans, knitted brows more generally express a state of mind associated with difficulties of any sort. Similarly, raised brows began as a means for increasing visual input but evolved into a general expression of attention, again, an associated state of mind. Determination and attention both may be considered forms of interest, but they are not completely equivalent psychological states. From this perspective, one might argue that raised and knitted brows should not be considered equivalent expressions of a unitary primary emotion (see Hinde, 1960).

As we indicated, few studies have explored the individual patterns currently regarded as interest expressions; however, several reports consistent with the views of Peiper, Darwin, and others can be found in the literature. For example, Oster (1978) contended that 3-month-old infants sometimes produce knitted (but not raised) brows during the recognitory assimilation preceding smiles of mastery or recognition. Similarly, in her naturalistic study of older infants and toddlers, Demos (1982) observed instances of lowered brows occurring in association with exertion and effort (i.e., difficulties), and raised brows occurring in the context of questioning or "flirtation" (i.e., attentiveness).

Further studies are needed to explore the distributional patterns of occurrence for raised and knitted brows as well as the other individual facial patterns currently seen as interest expressions. In particular, investigations comparing responses to visual and nonvisual (e.g., auditory) interest elicitors might prove useful in explaining the heterogeneity of movement patterns described for the emotion. Further studies might also explore the broad range of eliciting circumstances for each of the expression patterns as well as their nonfacial behavioral concomitants. Thus, using the ethologists' guidelines, we might more completely analyze these facial patterns and resolve some important questions regarding their motivational–phenomenological basis.

Surprise

According to AFFEX, the surprise expression features raised brows (which widen the eyes) and an open rounded or oval mouth. This pattern has also been described for adults, although a more stereotyped version includes raised upper eyelids (Darwin, 1872/1965; Ekman & Friesen, 1975). As we indicated, the raised brows of the surprise pattern are also a version of the interest expression described by AFFEX. The mouth, however, is opened more widely in the surprise configuration than in the interest pattern and is rounded or oval.

In regard to situation elicitors, infants' surprise expressions have proved difficult to produce in the laboratory. Although numerous studies have used surprise reactions to index perceptual and cognitive development, the AFFEX stereotypical facial expression is not usually seen. For example, in one of the best controlled studies, Hiatt, Campos, and Emde (1979) presented 10- to 12-month-old infants with two surprise elicitors: a vanishing object and a covert toy switch. Although visual search measures indicated that the infants were indeed surprised by the manipulations, only 25% of them showed elements of the surprise configuration. Furthermore, they showed these surprise elements equally often in the surprise and nonsurprise experimental conditions. Because the raised brow component of the surprise pattern is coded as interest when it appears in isolation, a straight AFFEX coding of the data may have indicated that this interest pattern was being produced in both surprise- and nonsurprise-eliciting situations.

Several investigations of the surprise expression pattern have involved presentation of unusual masks to infants, although these are sometimes difficult to evaluate because of the lack of manipulation checks, that is, a confirmation of a surprise reaction using nonfacial behavior indicators. The exact incidence of AFFEX-codable expressions is sometimes difficult to infer from the reported data. For example, Vaughn and Sroufe (1976) observed infants' facial responses to a peek-a-boo hiding game during which the mothers unexpectedly donned a mask before reappearing before their infants. Like Hiatt, Campos, and Emde, these investigators reported elements of surprise rather than complete expressions. Whereas half of the 8- and 10-month-old infants showed some elements of surprise, only 30% of the 12-month-olds and 20% of the 16-month-olds did so. Of additional note, surprise elements were not the infant's immediate response to the unexpected event but, instead, followed an initial sobering of expression. Furthermore, as in the case of Hiatt, Campos, and Emde, the surprise elements reported in their study might themselves be coded as expressions of interest using the AFFEX system. Indeed, using a different procedure involving the presentation of masks, Schwartz, Izard, and Ansul (1982) found interest to be the most frequently coded emotional expression patterns. Virtually no surprise was shown, although the investigators report observing behavioral indications that infants had noticed some discrepancies.

One possible interpretation of these findings is that surprise was not really evoked in the eliciting situations used in these studies. However, this would conflict with most persons' conceptions of surprise, including those of the investigators. Furthermore, nonfacial behavioral concomitants consistent with a surprise interpretation have been reported in some investigations.

A second possibility is to reinterpret the surprise expression patterns along lines suggested by Peiper. As we indicated, Peiper described a spreading reaction in which the brows are raised and the mouth and eyes are opened during attentive observation. Depending on the degree and contour of mouth opening, such an expression would be coded as either interest or surprise according to the AFFEX system. Thus, the surprise expression pattern might reflect intense visual attention to the environment. Consistent with this interpretation, in their studies of contingency learning, Sullivan and Lewis (1989) found surprise expressions to increase for contingent subjects during the period preceding peak responding.

Also consistent with this interpretation are a number of observations made by Camras (1988) in a naturalistic study of her daughter Justine's expressive development. Starting with her daughter's birth, Camras kept a diary in which she recorded the circumstances in which Justine produced seven of AFFEX's emotional expression patterns: happiness, surprise, disgust, fear, anger, sadness, and distress–pain. In addition, starting in her daughter's fourth week, Camras videotaped her in order to obtain a verifiable record of her infant's facial responses to the presumed eliciting situations and to a broad range of routine daily activities such as bathing, feeding, diaper changing, and face-to-face play. These tapes are currently being coded by research assistants trained to use both Ekman and Friesen's (1978) Facial Action Coding System (FACS), Izard's MAX (1979) and AFFEX (1983) systems for coding facial expressions.

In regard to the surprise expression pattern, this configuration was occasionally produced during the first two months when the infant raised her brows while opening her mouth to take the nipple during feeding. But, starting at about 8 weeks of age, Justine showed the surprise pattern quite frequently during bouts of excited attention to the environment. During these bouts, Camras's daughter would also wave her arms in the general direction of her gaze and produce soft panting vocalizations. In subsequent months, the pattern came to be seen quite often as the infant reached, grabbed, and mouthed an object. These observations suggest that the surprise expression pattern may be an intense form of the attentive facial response that Peiper described and also may be closely related to some of the interest patterns that AFFEX described. This facial response may sometimes occur when the infant encounters a surprising event (see Demos, 1982, for a possible naturally occurring example). The results obtained thus far in laboratory studies of surprise show that a less intense version of this expression – codable as interest by AFFEX – may be the more usual response in many surprising situations.

Further research is required to clarify the relationship between the surprise and interest patterns and to determine whether or not they are expressions of qualitatively different emotions. Toward this end, additional information about situational elicitors and the concomitant behaviors for these expression patterns would be useful. At this point, the observed elicitors and concomitants for the surprise pattern, as well as its morphological resemblance to some interest configurations, indicate that during the first few months of life this facial expression may not represent surprise as a discrete emotion.

Disgust

As described by AFFEX, the disgust expression in infants is lowered brows, wrinkled nose, and an open, angular mouth with slight protrusion of the lower lip and protrusion of the tongue beyond the gum line. This expression is morphologically similar to, but more extreme than, the disgust expressions usually described for adults (Ekman & Friesen, 1975; Izard, 1977; Tomkins, 1963). Adult expressions are typically described as wrinkling the nose or lifting the upper lip. The tongue is protruded only in extreme cases or when a substance is actually ejected from the mouth. As we shall see, an adultlike wrinkled nose and lifted upper lip (as well as the AFFEX-codable disgust expression patterns) all are observable in infants. Examining the circumstances under which they occur will highlight some of the problems that may arise when morphology alone is used as a basis for drawing emotion inferences.

In regard to situational elicitors, studies of infants' responses to taste stimuli (Cowart, 1981; Ganchrow, Steiner, & Daher, 1983; Steiner, 1973) have provided considerable information about the development of disgust-related facial patterns. Using Ekman & Friesen's (1978) comprehensive Facial Action Coding System, Rosenstein and Oster (1988) conducted the most detailed study yet of neonatal facial responses to bitter, sour, salty, and sweet tastes. They found that responses to all taste stimuli typically were a wrinkled nose and/or a lifted upper lip along with raised cheeks (by contraction of m. orbicularis oculi). For the sweet stimulus, these responses were transitory reactions to the insertion of the stimulus-delivering pipette and were quickly followed by facial relaxation. Virtually no smiling was observed in response to the sweet taste. Responses to the sour and bitter tastes included the negative midface actions just described and also the frequent presence of pursed lips in response to the sour taste and a gaping mouth for the bitter taste. No distinctive mouth actions were found in response to the salty taste.

Although relevant to our notions of disgust, there has been little research on infants' facial responses to odors. Steiner (1979) reported that pleasant and unpleasant odors (e.g., vanilla vs. rotten eggs) elicit facial reactions similar to those he identified for sweet versus bitter tastes. However, according to both Chiva (1987) and Peiper (1963), negative responses occur only when the trigeminal nerve is stimulated along with the olfactory nerve. Thus there is virtually no current evidence for disgust responses in infants to odors per se.

These studies used coding procedures that did not enable a direct determination of whether the AFFEX disgust expressions occurred frequently. Using the AFFEX system directly, Fox and Davidson (1985) found both neonates and 8-week-old infants to show disgust expressions in response to citric acid. Consistent with their report, Camras observed in her daughter such disgust configurations in response to the taste of a sour vitamin solution. These observations indicate that the AFFEX disgust pattern occurs in response to at least some taste stimuli that adults might consider appropriate elicitors of disgust.

Further observations by Camras indicate that disgust expressions also sometimes occur in response to nontaste stimuli. In her study, she coded such expressions in a number of situations, including washing her infant's face and pouring water over her body during a bath, restraining her head, and aspirating her nostrils with a syringe (to clear them when she had a cold). These observations indicate that AFFEX-codable disgust configurations occurred in response to a variety of intrusive stimuli, although not all emotion theorists would consider some of these elicitors appropriate to disgust.

Camras's study – as well as data reported by Rosenstein and Oster (1988) and Demos (1982) – also showed that the simple wrinkled nose and lifted upper lip described as disgust expressions for adults can be observed in infants and in situations that involve intrusive but not necessarily disgusting stimuli. As we indicated, in their taste study, Rosenstein and Oster observed these facial movements in response to the insertion of the stimulus-delivering pipette. Demos (1982) reported seeing an example during an episode of face washing. Camras observed wrinkled noses and lifted upper lips in all of the situations listed above as elicitors of AFFEX-codable disgust patterns. In addition, Camras frequently observed lifted upper lips when her daughter was pulled from a lying to a sitting position. Thus these simpler disgust expressions also occur in situations that some investigators might not consider as eliciting disgust.

In the face of such ambiguous situational data, information about concomitant (nonfacial) behaviors might prove useful in attempting to draw inferences about the presence of disgust as an emotion. Unfortunately, there is little information at this point regarding the concomitants of either simple or complex disgust expressions in various situations. A few early studies (Canestrini, 1913, cited in Cowart, 1981; Shirley, 1933) reported ANS (autonomic nervous system) and/or behavioral responses to sour or bitter tastes, including irregularities in pulse rate and respiration, motor restlessness, and disruption of sucking. These reports have not yet been confirmed in modern studies measuring facial behavior. More recently, Fox and Davidson (1985) reported suppression of the right-frontal EEG in response to citric acid. According to their theory, this is associated with withdrawal rather than approach emotions. They did not, however, examine any other indicators of avoidance or withdrawal.

Several researchers have noted that the disgust expression itself contains movements that may serve to reduce contact with the stimulus. For example, a protruded tongue may function to eject the undesirable tastant, and a wrinkled nose may serve to reduce contact between airborne molecules and the olfactory receptors (Andrew, 1963; Darwin, 1872/1965; Peiper, 1963; Rosenstein & Oster, 1988). Investigators with a cognitive orientation prefer to consider these facial responses of avoidance to be sensory reactions rather than expressions of disgust as an emotion. Thus, in the cases of both disgust and smiling, there may be fundamental disagreement about the criteria used to establish the presence of emotion in infancy.

Fear

The expression of fear as described by AFFEX is raising and drawing the brows together, widening the eyes by raising the upper lids, and opening and retracting the corners of the mouth. This expression has also been described for adults (Darwin, 1872/1965; Friesen & Ekman, 1984; Izard, 1977), although a more extreme version includes tensed lower eyelids (Ekman & Friesen, 1975; Izard, 1977). For infants, configurations not including widened eyes may also be coded by AFFEX as fear.

The fear expression pattern has not often been observed in laboratory studies designed to elicit fear responses in infants. For example, Hiatt, Campos, and Emde (1979) presented 10- to 12-month infants with two fear elicitors (stranger approach, visual cliff) and found only 6% to show any components of the fear expression in response to the stranger and only 15% to show components of the fear expression in response to the visual cliff. Other studies of infants' facial responses to "fear of strangers" paradigms also have reported few or no instances of the stereotyped fear facial configuration (Fox & Davidson, 1987; Sroufe, 1979; Waters, Matas, & Sroufe, 1975). In both stranger approach and visual cliff studies, nonfacial indicators of fear (i.e., avoidance of the stranger, refusal to cross the cliff) have been produced.

Perhaps surprisingly, similarly low frequencies of fear expression patterns have been observed in several studies designed to elicit other emotions. For example, Sullivan and Lewis (1989; Sullivan, personal communication, 1988) reported that 10- to 24-week-old infants show fear configurations during their contingency learning procedure. Schwartz, Izard, and Ansul (1982) found that some 7- and 13-month-old infants showed the fear pattern in response to unusual three-dimensional clay masks. Although interest and anger were the most common expression patterns, 17.6% of the infants (3 out of 17) did show a fear configuration. Displays of pure fear were fleeting and invariably accompanied by interest–fear, sadness–fear, and/or anger–fear blends.

The results reported by Schwartz et al. are consistent with Camras's observations of the fear expression pattern in her daughter. The coded videotapes thus far have revealed examples of this pattern as early as the seventh month. Like Schwartz et al., Camras observed these expressions to cooccur with other emotion configurations, usually interest, anger, and sadness. The fear and fear blend patterns were observed in several situations that might be predicted to produce fear (as well as other negative emotions). These included limb restraint, a loud noise (produced by clashing metal pot covers), and anticipation of a loud noise (i.e., the sight of the metal pot covers). However, fear configurations and blends were also produced in other circumstances that were not related to fear. For example, at 10 months of age, Camras's daughter produced a brief fear configuration and extended fear–anger blends while protesting being fed. Although Justine clearly objected to the eliciting situation (i.e., her mother's attempts to get her to eat), it seems unlikely that she experienced fear under these circumstances.

These observations suggest that our interpretation of the fear configuration requires further consideration. To clarify the meaning of this expression pattern, data on its nonfacial concomitants seem particularly germane. In addition, examining the morphological details of AFFEX-codable fear configurations produced in fear-appropriate versus fear-inappropriate circumstances might also improve our understanding of this pattern. For example, eye widening may occur only in the fear-appropriate situations. Until more fear configurations are observed in such situations, our understanding of this expression pattern must be considered incomplete.

Distress–pain and anger

We shall discuss the distress–pain and anger expression patterns to-gether because of their significant relationships in morphology and con-texts of occurrence. The AFFEX facial pattern for distress–pain is low-ered brows, tightly closed eyes, raised cheeks, and a squared open mouth. Morphologically, this pattern is identical to the principal expres-sion that AFFEX described for anger, except that the eyes are narrowed but open for anger, whereas they are closed for distress–pain. Adults have an expression similar to the AFFEX anger expression (Ekman & Friesen, 1975), but without the raised cheeks. Pain expressions found in adults (Craig & Patrick, 1985; LeResche, 1982; Leventhal & Sharp, 1965; Prkachin & Mercer, 1989) have been similar, but often not identical, to the AFFEX infant expression.

In neonates, facial responses to pain stimuli (i.e., a heel lance; Grunau & Craig, 1987) have been shown to vary with the infant's initial behav-ioral state. Quiet but alert infants appear to show the AFFEX pain ex-pression, but quiet and sleepy infants do not produce the squared, open-mouthed component, possibly because of a less intense pain reac-tion. These findings indicate that prior state may be an important yet rarely considered factor affecting infants' facial responses to an elicitor.

Older infants' responses to pain stimuli were studied most thoroughly in Izard's investigations of facial reactions to DPT inoculations (Izard, Hembree, Dougherty, and Spizzirri, 1983; Izard, Hembree, & Hueb-ner, 1987). At 2, 6, 12, and 18 months, infants were videotaped as they received the inoculation and during the subsequent 10 seconds (postinoculation soothing interval). Data analysis (Izard et al., 1987) showed that the distress–pain facial pattern is the predominant facial response at 2 months and is displayed for 41% of the postinoculation soothing interval. However, the anger facial pattern is also shown for virtually the same proportion of time at 2 months of age (38%), and in older infants, the anger pattern assumes quantitative predominance. By 18 months, infants display the distress–pain and anger patterns for 13% and 54% of the soothing interval, respectively. At all ages, the sequence of facial responses to the inoculation tends to be distress–pain followed by anger.

Although distress–pain expressions have not been widely studied, considerably more attention has been paid to the development of anger expressions. In several investigations designed to elicit this emotion, Campos and his colleagues examined infants' production of the anger expression pattern or its individual elements. For example, Stenberg, Campos, and Emde (1983) studied 7-month-old infants in frustration situations involving the repeated presentation and removal of a teething biscuit. They found that 66% of their infants showed one or more components of the anger expression.

In a later study, Stenberg and Campos (1988) examined the responses of 1-, 4-, and 7-month-old infants to nonpainful arm restraint. At both 4 and 7 months, 9 out of 16 infants (56%) showed AFFEX-codable complete expressions of anger. In contrast, only a single 1-month-old displayed the complete anger expression pattern. Inspection of the data figures, however, shows that over 80% of the infants of all ages produced the brow, cheek, and mouth actions characteristic of both anger and distress–pain. In addition, the tightly closed eyes of distress–pain were scored for over 80% of the infants at 1 month of age, and the open but narrowed eyes of the anger pattern were scored for over 80% of the 4- and 7-month-olds. These data suggest that the facial responses of infants at all ages were substantially the same, except that 1-month-olds tended to keep their eyes closed, thus showing the distress–pain pattern – whereas older infants tended to keep their eyes open – thus being scored as showing anger.

Although a direct coding of the distress–pain pattern would be required to confirm this interpretation of Stenberg's study, the proposal carries with it the implication of significant similarities in infants' facial responses to both nonpainful arm restraint and the DPT inoculations observed in Izard's studies. That is, in both situations, the younger infants (1- and 2-month-olds, respectively) may have responded with predominantly the distress–pain pattern, and the older infants tended toward the anger pattern. This developmental change in the coded facial response might reflect changes in the infants' tendency to keep their eyes open, owing to a general development of alertness. In addition, greater eye opening in older infants might be due to a decrease in the spreading reaction to negative stimulation as proposed by Peiper (1963). This decrease would be expected both as age increased and intensity of stimulation decreased. Consistent with this interpretation is the observation that in Izard's inoculation study, the distress–pain pattern at all ages tended to be followed by the anger pattern, possibly as the infant opened its eyes while recovering from a pain stimulus. In any event, if 1-month-old infants show the distress–pain pattern in response to nonpainful arm restraint, the pattern should no longer be considered a specific pain response. Instead, given their morphological similarity, one might hypothesize that the distress–pain and anger patterns reflect quantitative rather than qualitative differences in emotional response. Infants' tendency to show one or the other pattern could reflect age, alertness, and/or intensity of response rather than qualitative differences in the elicited emotion. Whether this response should be considered anger or some more general form of negative affect (i.e., distress) depends on one's theoretical perspective and the criteria used to attribute specific emotions to infants.

Consistent with the proposal that the distress–pain and anger patterns are expressions of qualitatively similar affects are Camras's observations of her daughter's expressive development. One noteworthy finding was that the distress–pain pattern frequently was observed during the first nine weeks in response to both painful and nonpainful stimuli (e.g., aspirating the infant's nostrils with a syringe, pouring water on her during her bath). Even more significant, the distress–pain pattern was sometimes seen upon termination of a pleasant stimulus (e.g., termination of physical contact with mother). Although it is possible that internally generated physical discomfort occurred at these times and thus elicited the distress–pain facial response, such a possibility is an unlikely explanation for the many instances in which this expression pattern was seen during the first months of life.

Observations at later ages in both this and other studies are also consistent with the proposed reinterpretation of the distress–pain and anger expression patterns. For example, Matias, Cohn, and Ross (1989) observed distress–pain expressions during face-to-face interactions between mothers and their 4-month-old infants. Camras occasionally observed and videotaped the distress–pain configuration along with anger responses following the termination of a desirable stimulus when Justine was 10 months old and thus past the age when much internally generated discomfort is suspected to occur. Even at 2 years of age, Justine was observed to produce this expression when crying intensely after being forbidden to open a medicine cabinet. Thus distress–pain configurations have been seen in a number of situations that clearly entailed no physical pain or discomfort.

A second type of observation that Camras made also indicates that the distress–pain and anger patterns may represent quantitative differences in negative emotion rather than qualitatively different affective responses. After 1 month of age, Camras observed that her daughter often produced both the distress–pain and anger facial patterns during a single bout of crying. Before 1 month, the anger facial pattern was not observed, as the infant spent relatively little time in an alert open-eyed state and correspondingly spent no time crying with her eyes open. During the second month, Justine kept her eyes open for gradually longer periods of time and similarly sometimes opened her eyes during a bout of crying. Thus the anger pattern as well as the distress–pain pattern was coded at this age.

A third observation consistent with the proposed reinterpretation of the distress–pain and anger patterns is the extensive overlap in situation elicitors for these expressions. In Camras's study, 18 situational elicitors were identified for distress–pain configurations produced during the first nine weeks of life. For 13 of these situational categories, the anger pattern was also recorded as occurring at one time or another. For 5 situational categories, the distress–pain pattern was observed, but the pattern for anger was not. Interestingly enough, 4 of these circumstances were among the least likely to cause physical pain: sleep, gentle bouncing (as a soothing attempt), water poured on the body during a bath, and refusing the pacifier. Even more significant, no situational circumstance was identified that elicited the anger pattern without also eliciting at some time the expression pattern of distress–pain. Thus the similarities observed in morphology and contextual occurrence suggest that the distress–pain and anger patterns may not reflect discrete, qualitatively different emotions, at least during the first months of life. The current data are not conclusive, however, and additional systematic studies are needed to test the alternative hypotheses.

In regard to laboratory studies of older infants, anger expressions have also been observed in several investigations using Ainsworth's strange situation procedure. For example, Hyson and Izard (1985) videotaped 13- and 18-month-old infants in a separation episode, during which the infant is left alone in an unfamiliar room. Overall, anger was the predominant negative facial response and was displayed for 42% of the coding interval at 13 months and 29% at 18 months.

In a second study, Shiller, Izard, and Hembree (1986) also found that anger was the predominant negative affect pattern coded for a sample of 13-month-old infants, and, individual differences among infants were also observed. Infants classified as insecure–ambivalent in their attachment (Ainsworth, Blehar, Waters, & Wall, 1978) displayed a sadness expression pattern for a substantial length of time (20 to 27% of the coding interval), although the anger pattern was still predominant for these infants (38 to 40%). For a larger sample that included the infants described by Shiller et al., McGinnes, Izard, and Phillips (1984) reported anger for 41.5%, sadness for 8.1%, and distress–pain for 0.4% of the codable record. Fox and Davidson (1987) also found that 10-month-old infants displayed the anger and sadness patterns when briefly separated from their mothers. In addition, 32% of these infants displayed anger and/or sadness patterns during a stranger approach sequence, but only 10% showed a fear response.

Anger patterns have also been observed infrequently in studies designed to elicit nonnegative emotions such as enjoyment, surprise, and interest. For example, low frequencies of anger were coded by Sullivan and Lewis (1989) and tended to occur along with sad configurations and fussing at the end of their contingency learning procedure. The anger pattern was also the predominant negative pattern coded in Schwartz et al.'s (1982) study of infants' responses to unusual masks. It was shown by approximately 15% and 18% of their 7- and 13-month-old subjects.

In conclusion, current studies indicate that infants over 2 months of age display an anger pattern as their principal facial response to a variety of negative elicitors: inoculation, arm restraint, and separation from mother. In fact, no study thus far has found any other negative facial pattern to be shown more frequently by infants older than 1 or 2 months. These observations, along with the morphological similarity between the distress–pain and anger patterns and the contextual data we presented, suggest that the two patterns may represent quantitative rather than qualitative differences in affective response and that, in older babies, the anger facial pattern replaces the distress–pain pattern shown at younger ages. Further research is necessary to delineate the development of these facial patterns and their relationship to specific emotions. Toward this end, additional information about the situational elicitors and behavioral concomitants that may differentiate them from one another and from other negative facial patterns would be useful.

Sadness

The sadness facial pattern is oblique brows (i.e., inner corners raised), narrowed eyes, raised cheeks, and mouth corners drawn downward. The lower lip may also be pushed up by contraction of the chin muscle.

Although no investigation has produced sadness as the principal facial response, the sad facial pattern has been observed infrequently in a number of studies involving negative elicitors. For example, in Izard's inoculation studies, the sadness configuration was shown for about 3%

of the soothing interval at all ages, with a slight tendency to increase as the postinoculation time was lengthened. In Shiller et al.'s (1986) strange situation study, a minority of infants (those classified as having insecure–ambivalent attachments; see Ainsworth et al., 1978) displayed substantial amounts of sadness (20 to 27%), although on the average this facial pattern was shown for only 11% of the coded record. Fox and Davidson (1987) also coded at least one sad expression for 37% of their infants during a brief separation procedure (although anger was the more common response, shown by 58% of their infants). In addition, Fox and Davidson observed both sadness and anger patterns in 37% of their subjects during a stranger approach sequence. Finally, sadness configurations (along with anger and fussing) also were infrequently shown toward the end of Sullivan and Lewis's (1989) contingency-learning procedure. Thus, when they have been observed in laboratory studies, sadness expression patterns have invariably been mixed with distress–pain and/or anger patterns.

Sadness configurations also have been observed in naturalistic studies of infant expressive behavior. Both Camras and Demos (1982, 1986) found the sadness pattern to occur under the same circumstances in which distress–pain and/or anger patterns are produced. In Camras's study, these included aspirating the infant's nostrils with a syringe, moving her suddenly, administering a sour vitamin, bathing her, removing her pacifier, and terminating physical contact with her mother. As in the case of the distress–pain patterns, some of these circumstances do not seem consistent with any current theoretical proposals regarding the elicitation of sadness as an emotion (Ekman, 1984; Plutchik, 1980; Stein & Jewett, 1986).

Camras found a possible clue to interpreting the sadness pattern while coding facial behavior produced during bouts of crying in response to the aforementioned elicitors. During a crying bout, the sadness patterns were displayed during brief lulls as the infant closed her mouth, opened her eyes, and lowered the intensity of her crying vocalizations. Thus sadness configurations alternated with expressions of distress–pain and anger, which themselves occurred as the infant opened her mouth and intensified her crying. This patterning suggests that the sadness configuration is associated with a relatively low intensity of negative affect (e.g., distress or anger) or with the reduction or inhibition of such negative affect. Similar interpretations of the sadness mouth and brow configurations have been offered by Oster (1982) and Darwin (1872/1965), respectively. In addition, this interpretation is consistent with Fox and Davidson's (1988) failure to find differences in EEG associated with anger versus sad expressions in 10-month-old infants. Such differences are theoretically predicted from their model, which depicts anger as an approach emotion and sadness as a withdrawal emotion. If the anger and sadness facial patterns do not reflect these qualitatively discrete emotions in young infants, concomitant approach versus avoidance differences in EEG would not be expected.

Summary and conclusion

As demonstrated in this review, considerable data on infant facial expressions have been acquired since 1970. Although much of this information is consistent with the current formulation of differential emotions theory, some studies have generated new hypotheses regarding infant facial expressions, their origins, development, and motivational–phenomenological basis. Whether these hypotheses will be confirmed in future systematic investigations remains to be seen, although there clearly are a number of exciting avenues to be investigated.

In this chapter we outlined several kinds of evidence relevant to understanding infants' facial expressions: morphology, eliciting circumstances, and concomitant and/or subsequent behaviors. In regard to morphology, the AFFEX-specified emotional expression patterns for infants are similar to those described for adults, although there may be subtle but possibly important differences in morphological detail for some expressions (e.g., neonatal smiles, anger expressions; see Oster & Hegley, 1989) that could prove significant in future studies. In regard to eliciting circumstances, some studies have demonstrated that infants show facial responses consistent with the emotions believed to be elicited in the incentive procedure, although some expressions (e.g., surprise, fear) have not always been observed in such circumstances. In addition, the elicitors for several negative emotions have not yet been differentiated. Relatively few studies have examined nonfacial behavior concomitant with or subsequent to the production of an emotional expression pattern. Such data might prove particularly useful in evaluating hypotheses based on differential emotions theory as well as some of the alternative possibilities we discussed.

Although future research will contribute to our understanding of infants' emotional facial expressions, the resolution of some issues also will depend on our interpretations of or inferences drawn from our data. For example, it is quite likely that future studies will demonstrate some systematic differences in the cry vocalizations accompanying the distress–pain, anger, and sadness expression patterns. Investigators may disagree as to whether these differences indicate separate emotions or merely quantitative differences in distress. Such divergences in interpretation will rest in part on differences of opinion about necessary and sufficient evidence for attributing emotion to infants and inferring the phenomenological and motivation underpinnings of their expressive behavior. We recognize that at this time there is no consensus on the issue of adequate evidence. We believe, however, that its absence behooves investigators to maintain the separation of data and inference and clarify their own criteria for judging the meaning of infants' facial expression. In this way, we will be able to pursue both provocative and profitable research on emotional and expressive development.

References

Ainsworth, M., Blehar, M., Waters, E., & Wall, S. (1978). *Patterns of attachment: A psychological study of the strange situation*. Hillsdale, NJ: Erlbaum.

Andrew, R. J. (1963). The origins and evolution of the calls and facial expressions of the primates. *Behavior, 20*, 1–109.

Bowlby, J. (1973). *Attachment and loss. Vol. 2. Separation*. New York: Basic Books.

Bridges, K. M. B. (1932). Emotional development in early infancy. *Child Development, 3*, 324–341.

Campos, W., & Barrett, K. (1984). Toward a new understanding of emotions and their development. In C. E. Izard, J. Kagan, & R. Zajonc (Eds.), *Emotions, cognition, and behavior* (pp. 229–263). Cambridge: Cambridge University Press.

Camras, L. A. (1980). Animal threat displays and children's facial expressions: A comparison. In D. Omark, F. Strayer, & D. Freedman (Eds.), *Dominance relations: An ethological view of human conflict and social interaction* (pp. 121–136). New York: Garland STPM Press.

(1982). Ethological approaches to nonverbal communication. In R. S. Feldman (Ed.), *Development of nonverbal communication* (pp. 3–28). New York: Springer-Verlag.

(1988). *Darwin revisited: An infant's first emotional facial expressions*. Paper presented at the International Conference on Infant Studies, Washington, DC.

Chiva, M. (1987). Comment. Presented at the Meeting of the International Society for Research on Emotion, Worcester, MA, August.

Cowart, B. (1981). Development of taste perception in humans: Sensitivity and preference throughout the lifespan. *Psychological Bulletin, 90*(1), 43–73.

Craig, K., & Patrick, C. (1985). Facial expression during induced pain. *Journal of Personality and Social Psychology, 48*,(4), 1080–1091.

Daanje, A. (1950). On the locomotory movements in birds and the intention movements derived from them. *Behavior, 3*, 48–98.

(1877). A biological sketch of an infant. *Mind, 7*, 285–294.

Darwin, C. (1872). *The expression of the emotions in man and animals*. London: John Murray. (Reprint, Chicago: University of Chicago Press, 1965)

(1887). *The autobiography of Charles Darwin*. London: John Murray. (Reprint, New York: Norton, 1969)

Demos, V. (1982). Facial expressions of infants and toddlers. In T. Field & A. Fogel (Eds.), *Emotion and early interaction (pp. 127–160)*. Hillsdale, NJ: Erlbaum.

(1986). Crying in early infancy. In T. B. Brazelton & M. M. Yogman (Eds.), *Affective development in early infancy* (pp. 39–74). New York: Ablex.

Ekman, P. (1972). Universals and cultural differences in facial expressions of emotion. In J. Cole (Ed.), *Nebraska Symposium on Motivation* (pp. 207–283). Lincoln: University of Nebraska Press.

(1979). About brows: Emotional and conversational signals. In J. Aschoff, M. von Cranach, K. Foppa, W. Lepenies, & D. Ploog (Eds.), *Human ethology* (pp. 169–202). Cambridge: Cambridge University Press.

(1984). Expression and the nature of emotion. In K. R. Scherer and P. Ekman (Eds.), *Approaches to emotion* (pp. 319–343). Hillsdale, NJ: Erlbaum.

Ekman, P., & Friesen, W. V. (1971). Constants across cultures in the face and emotion. *Journal of Personality and Social Psychology, 17*(2), 124–129.

(1975). *Unmasking the face*. Englewood Cliffs, NJ: Prentice-Hall.

(1978). *The facial action coding system*. Palo Alto, CA: Consulting Psychologists Press.

(1982). Felt, false and miserable smiles. *Journal of Nonverbal Behavior, 6*(4), 238–252.

Ekman, P., Friesen, W. V., & O'Sullivan, M. (1988). Smiles when lying. *Journal of Personality and Social Psychology, 54*(3), 414–420.

Ekman, P., Oster, H. (1982). Review of research, 1970–1980. In P. Ekman (Ed.), *Emotion in the human face* (2nd ed., pp. 147–173). Cambridge: Cambridge University Press.

Emde, R., Gaensbauer, T., & Harmon, R. J. (1976). Emotional expression in infancy: A biobehavioral study. *Psychological Issues Monographs, 10*(37), 1–189.

Emde, R., & Harmon, R. (1972). Endogenous and exogenous smiling systems in early infancy. *Journal of Child Psychiatry, 11*(2), 177–200.

Emde, R., & Koenig, K. (1969). Neonatal smiling and rapid eye movement states. *American Academy of Child Psychiatry, 8*, 57–67.

Fox, N., & Davidson, R. (1985). Sweet/sour – interest/disgust: The role of approach-withdrawal in the development of emotions. In T. Field & N. Fox (Eds.), *Social perception in infants* (pp. 53–71). Norwood, NJ: Ablex.

(1987). Electroencephalogram asymmetry in response to the approach of a stranger and maternal separation in 10 month old infants. *Developmental Psychology, 23*, 233–240.

(1988). Patterns of brain electrical activity during facial signs of emotion in 10 month old infants. *Developmental Psychology, 24*(2), 230–236.

Fox, N., & Gelles, M. (1984). Face-to-face interaction in term and preterm infants. *Infant Mental Health Journal, 5*(4), 192–205.

Fridlund, A., Ekman, P., & Oster, H. (1987). Facial expressions of emotion. In A. Siegman & S. Feldstein (Eds.), *Nonverbal behavior and communication* (2nd ed., pp. 143–224). Hillsdale, NJ: Erlbaum.

Friesen, W. V., & Ekman, P. (1984). *EMFACS: Emotion Facial Action Coding System*. (Available from W. V. Friesen, Department of Psychiatry, University of California, San Francisco)

Ganchrow, J., Steiner, J., & Daher, M. (1983). Neonatal facial expressions in response to different qualities and intensities of gustatory stimuli. *Infant Behavior and Development, 6,* 473–484.

Grunan, R., & Craig, K. (1987). Pain expression in neonates: Facial action and cry. *Pain, 28,* 395–410.

Haynes, O. M., Izard, C., & Slomine, B. (1989). *Infants' full-face expressions, partial expressions, and expressive blends during playful and stressful interactions with their mothers.* Unpublished manuscript.

Hiatt, S., Campos, J., & Emde, R. (1979). Facial patterning and infant emotional expression: Happiness, surprise, and fear. *Child Development, 50,* 1020–1035.

Hinde, R. A. (1960). Unitary drives. *Animal Behavior, 7* (3–4), 131–141.

(1970). *Animal behavior: A synthesis of ethology and comparative psychology* (2nd ed.). New York: McGraw-Hill.

(1974). *Biological bases of human social behavior.* New York: McGraw-Hill.

Hyson, M., & Izard, C. E. (1985). Continuities and changes in emotion expressions during brief separations at 13 and 18 months. *Developmental Psychology, 21*(6), 1165–1170.

Izard, C. E. (1971). *The face of emotion.* New York: Appleton-Century-Crofts.

(1977). *Human emotions.* New York: Plenum.

(1979). *The maximally discriminative facial movement coding system (MAX).* Newark, DE: Instructional Resources Center, University of Delaware, Newark, 19711.

Izard, C. E., Dougherty, L., & Hembree, E. (1983). *A system for identifying affect expressions by holistic judgments (AFFEX).* Newark, DE: Instructional Resources Center, University of Delaware, Newark, 19711.

Izard, C. E., Hembree, E., Dougherty, L., & Spizzirri, C. (1983). Changes in 2- to 19-month-old infants' facial expressions following acute pain. *Developmental Psychology, 19*(3), 418–426.

Izard, C. E., Hembree, E., & Huebner, R. (1987). Infants' emotional expressions to acute pain: Developmental changes and stability of individual differences. *Developmental Psychology, 23,* 105–113.

Izard, C. E., & Malatesta, C. (1987). Perspectives on emotional development I: Differential emotions theory of early emotional development. In J. D. Osofsky (Ed.), *Handbook of infant development* (pp. 494–554). New York: Wiley.

Langsdorf, P., Izard, C., Rayias, M., & Hembree, E. (1983). Interest expression, visual fixation and heart rate changes in 2- to 8-month-old infants. *Developmental Psychology, 19*(3), 375–386.

Lazarus, R., Kanner, A., & Folkman, S. (1980). Emotions: A cognitive–phenomenological analysis. In R. Plutchik & H. Kellerman (Eds.), *Emotions: Theory, research and experience* (pp. 189–218). New York: Academic Press.

LeResche, L. (1982). Facial expression in pain: A study of candid photographs. *Journal of Nonverbal Behavior, 7,* 46–56.

Leventhal, H., & Sharp, E. (1965). Facial expressions as indicators of distress. In S. S. Tomkins & C. Izard (Eds.), *Affect, cognition and personality* (pp. 296–318). New York: Springer-Verlag.

Lewis, M., Sullivan, M., & Brooks-Gunn, J. (1985). Emotional behavior during the learning of a contingency in early infancy. *British Journal of Developmental Psychology, 3,* 307–316.

Lorenz, K. (1950). The comparative method in studying innate behavior patterns. *Symposia of the Society of Experimental Biology, 4,* 221–268.

(1965). *Evolution and modification of behavior.* Chicago: University of Chicago Press.

104   Linda A. Camras, Carol Malatesta, and Carroll E. Izard

McGinnes, G., Izard, C., & Phillips, R. (1984). *Anxiety, distress or protest?: Infants' emotion expression during brief separation.* Unpublished manuscript.
Malatesta, C., & Haviland, J. (1982). Learning display rules: The socialization of emotion expression in infancy. *Child Development, 53*(4), 991–1003.
Mandler, G. (1984). *Mind and body.* New York: Norton.
Matias, R., Cohn, J., & Ross, S. (1989). A comparison of two systems that code infant affective expression. *Developmental Psychology, 25*(4), 483–489.
Moynihan, M. (1955a). Some aspects of the reproductive behavior in the black-headed gull *(Larus ridibundus L.)* and related species. *Behavior 4* (Suppl.), 1–201.
(1955b). Types of hostile displays. *Auk, 72,* 247–259.
Oster, H. (1978). Facial expression and affect development. In M. Lewis & L. Rosenblum (Eds.), *The development of affect* (pp. 43–76). New York: Plenum.
(1982). *Pouts and horseshoe-mouth faces: Their determinants, affective meaning and signal value in infants.* Paper presented at the International Conference on Infant Studies, Austin, TX.
Oster, H., & Hegley, D. (1989). *Adult judgments of infant facial expressions: Evidence for developmental changes in expressions of negative emotions.* Paper presented at the meeting of the American Association for the Advancement of Science, San Francisco, January.
Peiper, A. (1963). *Cerebral function in infancy and childhood.* (B. Nagler & H. Nagler, Trans.). New York: Consultants Bureau.
Plutchik, R. (1980). *Emotion: A psychoevolutionary synthesis.* New York: Harper & Row.
Prkachin, K., & Mercer, S. (1989). *Pain expression in patients with shoulder pathology: Validity, properties and relations to sickness impact.* Manuscript submitted for publication.
Rosenstein, D., & Oster, H. (1988). Differential facial response to four basic tastes in newborns. *Child Development, 59*(6), 1555–1568.
Schachter, S., & Singer, J. (1962). Cognitive, social and physiological determinants of emotional state. *Psychological Review, 69,* 379–399.
Schwartz, G., Izard, C. E., & Ansul, S. (1982). *Heart rate and facial response to novelty in 7- and 13-month-old infants.* Paper presented at the International Conference on Infant Studies, Austin, TX.
Shiller, V., Izard, C. E., & Hembree, E. (1986). Patterns of emotion expression during separation in the strange-situation. *Developmental Psychology, 22*(3), 378–383.
Shirley, M. (1933) *The first two years: A study of 25 babies: Vol. 2. Intellectual development.* Minneapolis: University of Minnesota Press.
Sroufe, L. A. (1979). Socioemotional development. In J. Osofsky (Ed.), *Handbook of infant development* (pp. 462–516). New York: Wiley.
(1984). The organization of emotional development. In K. R. Scherer & P. Ekman (Eds.), *Approaches to emotion* (pp. 109–128). Hillsdale, NJ: Erlbaum.
Sroufe, L. A., & Waters, E. (1976). The ontogenesis of smiling and laughter: A perspective on the organization of development in infancy. *Psychological Review, 83*(3), 173–189.
Stein, N., and Jewett, J. (1986). A conceptual analysis of the meaning of negative emotions: Implications for a theory of development. In C. E. Izard (Ed.), *Measuring emotions in infants and children,* vol. 2. Cambridge: Cambridge University Press.
Steiner, J. (1973). The gustofacial response: Observation on normal and anencephalic newborn infants. In J. Bosma (Ed.), *Fourth Symposium on Oral Sensa-*

tion and Perception (pp. 254–278). Bethesda, MD: U.S. Department of Health, Education and Welfare.

(1979). Human facial expression in response to taste and smell stimulation. In H. Reese & L. Lipsitt (Eds.), *Advances in child development and behavior.* (Vol. 13, pp. 257–295). New York: Academic Press.

Stenberg, C., & Campos, J. (1988). *The development of anger expressions in infancy.* Unpublished manuscript.

Stenberg, C., Campos, J., & Emde, R. (1983). The facial expression of anger in seven month old infants. *Child Development, 54,* 178–184.

Sullivan, M., & Lewis, M. (1989). Emotion and cognition in infancy: Facial expressions during contingency learning. *International Journal of Behavioral Development, 12*(2), 221–237.

Tinbergen, N. (1952). Derived activities. *Quarterly Review of Biology. 27,* 1–32.

Tinbergen (1953). *Social behavior in animals.* London: Chapman & Hall.

(1959). Comparative studies of the behavior of gulls (*Laridae*). *Behavior, 15,* 1–70.

(1963). On the aims and methods of ethology. *Zeitschrift für Tier Psychologie, 20,* 410–429.

(1969). *The study of instinct* (2nd ed.). New York: Oxford University Press.

Tomkins, S. (1963). *Affect, imagery and consciousness.* New York: Springer.

Vaughn, B., & Sroufe, L. A. (1976). *The face of surprise in infants.* Paper presented at the meeting of the Animal Behavior Society, Boulder, CO.

Waters, E., Matas, L., & Sroufe, L. A. (1975). Infant reactions to an approaching stranger: Description, validation and functional significance of wariness. *Child Development, 46,* 348–356.

Weinberg, K., Gianino, A., & Tronick, E. (1989). *Facial expressions of emotion and social and object oriented behavior are specifically related in 6 month old infants.* Poster presented at the meeting of the Society for Research in Child Development, Kansas City, MO.

Wolff, P. (1963). Observations on the early development of smiling. In B. Foss (Ed.), *Determinants of infant behavior, II* (pp. 113–138). New York: Wiley.

(1987). *The development of behavioral states and the expression of emotions in early infancy.* Chicago: University of Chicago Press.

4. Toward an ecology of expressiveness: Family socialization in particular and a model in general

AMY G. HALBERSTADT

In this chapter I begin with a major influence on expressiveness – the socialization of emotion expression in the family – and summarize some of the research that I and others have been doing in this area. It appears that individual differences in expressiveness emerge almost immediately from birth (Field, 1982, 1985) and that these differences may be mediated by socialization as early as the first half year of life (Malatesta & Haviland, 1982). The influence of family socialization seems persistent, continuing well into adulthood (Balswick & Avertt, 1977; Burrowes & Halberstadt, 1987; Gallegos & Friedman, 1989; Halberstadt, 1986). Second, I report on some of the consequences of experiencing different kinds of communication styles in one's family. Specifically, the expressiveness style experienced within the family seems to be associated with one's skill at judging and sending nonverbal communications (Halberstadt, 1983, 1986) and with success in social interaction (Cassidy & Parke, 1989; Halberstadt, 1984; Halberstadt, Hoeft, & Tesh, 1990). In the third section, I develop an ecological model that includes societal, familial, and peer socialization influences as well as a variety of self-factors (e.g., constitutional, affective, motivational, cognitive, and personality characteristics) and some of the interactions among these various types of influences.

First, what is expressiveness, and why is it important? To define expressiveness, we need to distinguish between an emotion expression as a discrete behavioral event and expressiveness as a persistent individual difference in behavioral style. *Emotion expressions* are nonverbal or verbal behaviors that suggest that a person is experiencing one or more affec-

This research was supported by grants from the National Institute of Mental Health (MH42425) and the National Institute of Child Health and Human Development (HD22367). I thank Howard Friedman and A. S. R. Manstead for reading and commenting on selected portions of the manuscript.

tive or evaluative states. Smiling, nose wrinkling, or saying "Thank you" all are emotion expressions. These emotion expressions are consciously or unconsciously emitted via one or more channels, such as the face, voice, body, and words. Expressions include both spontaneous, unfeigned behavior and learned behavior that has been modified by socialization experiences (Buck, 1982, 1984; Lewis & Michalson, 1983; Zivin, 1986). Our emotion expressions occur most frequently in the presence of other people but also occur, albeit less frequently, when we are alone (Buck, 1984; Kraut & Johnston, 1979). We can measure expressions in at least six different ways: the affective valence (assessed either dimensionally, e.g., on a scale ranging from positive to negative affect, or categorically, e.g., as a discrete emotion such as fear, anger, or happiness), the frequency of occurrence, the intensity when occurring, the duration of expression, the purity versus affective mixture of expression, and the changeability across affective valences or in speed of onset.

Expressiveness is a persistent pattern of exhibiting emotional expressions in a variety of socioemotional situations, and our judgments about a person's style of expressiveness are based on aggregates of that individual's emotion expressions over time and across situations. Research on emotion expressions shows that people vary their expressions considerably depending on their specific feelings and the rules embedded in the social event, whereas research on expressiveness shows that people also show consistency in their responses across situations.

People themselves are aware of their own expressiveness styles in comparison with others' styles, which can be recognized and measured by family, friends, and researchers (e.g., Burrowes & Halberstadt, 1987; Friedman, Prince, Riggio, & DiMatteo, 1980; Notarius & Levenson, 1979). For example, a colleague may begin to gesticulate as soon as he begins to talk, whether teaching in class or talking on the telephone with his romantic other, and his face may be constantly active, evoking images of sunshine and clouds moving rapidly across a sky. Another colleague may have a "deadpan" face, which she changes very little whether during conversation, at parties, or at comedy movies. These reliable and stable behavior patterns allow us to develop expectations and make predictions about people's expressiveness across situations. Thus, expressiveness research focuses on these persistent individual styles and their antecedents and consequences, for example, how early experiences (e.g., family socialization) affect individuals' expressiveness styles or how individuals vary along other factors (e.g., popularity) as a possible consequence of their own level of expressiveness. Although expressiveness can be evaluated when people are alone and outside a social context, this chapter will concentrate primarily on expressiveness in social situations.

Many studies have found expressiveness to be associated with a host of other factors, including people's occupational interests (Friedman et al., 1980), physicians' success at recruiting patients (DiMatteo, Hays, & Prince, 1986; Friedman et al., 1980), mothers' effective interactions with their infants and the infants' subsequent positive outcomes (Diskin & Heinicke, 1986), lack of loneliness in males (Christian & Worell, 1989), popularity and friendship (Buck, 1975; Riggio, 1986), and mood contagion to others (Friedman & Riggio, 1981). Thus, expressiveness appears to be an important aspect of individuals' socioemotional composition, and the development of expressiveness styles in individuals over their life span appears well worth further exploration.

Before we begin, however, we must distinguish three different perspectives associated with the concept of expressiveness. In this chapter, expressiveness is considered to be a communication style that a person adapts from the social interaction norms and values of his or her referent group. This view suggests that an individual's communication style is strongly influenced by socialization, although constitutional variables also clearly are important and interact with socialization processes.

This view can be distinguished from a perspective that considers expressiveness to be a reflection of emotional experience and thus a fairly isomorphic reproduction of internal state, and from another perspective that treats expressiveness as a personality characteristic. Both of these latter perspectives emphasize constitutional variables that imply more of an underlying, persistent organization than does the more socialization-oriented communication style perspective.

Clearly, the latter two perspectives are valid at least to some degree: The "reflection" hypothesis is right in that observable expressions do indeed reflect underlying emotion states at least occasionally, and the personality hypothesis is right in that pervasive expressive patterns may reflect or be associated with personality characteristics in some individuals, as will be described in later sections. But this is not the whole story. In the case of the reflection hypothesis, we know that we do not always show what we feel, nor do we always feel what we show. In the case of the personality hypothesis, people's stereotypes regarding expressive and inexpressive individuals are fairly strong; for example, expressive people are perceived as extroverted, impulsive, warm, and outgoing, and nonexpressive people as introverted, calm, cool, and reserved. When these stereotypes are tested, however, in multimethod research that removes the covariance of similar methods, some personality variables continue to distinguish expressiveness as measured behaviorally, but not all that strongly (Halberstadt, 1984). Further, the hypothesis that personality causes a particular expressive style needs to be tested. And finally, at least some theorists believe that personality is also largely constructed during socialization, too.

Thus, we need a perspective that considers expressiveness as a communication style. This perspective is informed by socialization theory and research on socioemotional development. It recognizes that in infancy, emotion experience and expression appear to be almost or entirely identical (e.g., Bridges, 1932; Izard, 1971, 1977; Izard & Malatesta, 1987; Zivin, 1982) and that it is during this developmental period that the "reflection" hypothesis is most often valid. With time, however, children in our culture become able to disengage emotional experience from expression, so that sometimes emotional states occur without being expressed, and other times emotional states are expressed without actually occurring (see Lewis & Michalson, 1983, for a curvilinear hypothesis that suggests that a period of independence between facial expression and internal state precedes the synchrony of later infancy and early childhood, and see Rosaldo, 1984, for evidence of cultural variation in the degree of feeling–expression disengagement). Almost all theories of emotion development note this developing dissynchrony of affect and expression, and the increasing ability of children to modulate their emotional expression in order to fit cultural expectations regarding their own behavior and in order to help regulate the affective experience itself. Many consider this separation between emotional experience and expression to be an important aspect of social development (e.g., Lewis & Michalson, 1983; Malatesta & Haviland, 1985; Saarni, 1982; Tomkins, 1962).

The distinction between internal experience and outward expression is clearest in adulthood, when the understanding and use of display rules are well-developed and important regulators of expressiveness. Thus, the view that expressiveness is a communication style emphasizes the socialization models over the hydraulic models (i.e., that emotions must build up and eventually surface) assumed in the reflection perspective and the temperament models emphasized in the personality perspective. The communication-style perspective is also strongly interactionist and developmental, in that in this view, an individual's style develops over time, based on (1) the social context, (2) the person's bio-logical givens interacting with the requirements and expectations of the social context, and (3) the person's motivations and values in response to the biological and social forces. Finally, the communication-style per-spective recognizes the importance of expressiveness as a powerful reg-ulator of social interaction (Barrett & Campos, 1987; Campos & Barrett, 1984; Ekman & Oster, 1979; Frodi, Lamb, Leavitt, & Donovan, 1978; Klinnert, 1984) and as "a form of social communication that demands a response" (Harkness & Super, 1985, p. 25). Expressions are perceived as meaningful communications from infancy through adulthood and, as such, are subject to others' interpretations. These interpretations may be based not only on the expressions themselves in a particular context and on the expresser's individual expressiveness history but also on the interpreter's own expressiveness and experiences. Thus, one's style of expressiveness may influence how others perceive one's own emotional states, and it may also influence one's perceptions of others' emotional states.

Family socialization of expressiveness

First I shall chronicle the relation between family socialization processes for emotion expression and people's own emotion expressiveness through their life span. I shall concentrate on family norms for emotion expression for two reasons: It is in family situations that we initially attempt to communicate our needs and desires. And whereas family differences might develop as a consequence of our cultural context, we are more likely to tap precise differences by focusing on family norms.[1]

The basic and not too surprising hypothesis is that when the family environment is high in expressiveness, younger family members also develop similarly high expressiveness, and when the family environ-ment is low in expressiveness, younger family members develop simi-larly low expressiveness. This simple formulation emerges out of the social learning tradition, which hypothesizes that children observe the behavior of their parents and siblings and model those behaviors ac-cordingly. As active participants in this process, children may note dif-ferences in communication styles between parents and may choose to model their same-sex parent or powerful, similar, or nurturant family members (e.g., Bandura, 1969; Bandura, Ross, & Ross, 1961).[2]

Family members are also active participants in this process, channel-ing children into appropriate settings and experiences, encouraging or punishing certain behaviors, actively coaching their children with non-verbal examples or verbal descriptions of appropriate behavior, and labeling children's behavior as appropriate, inappropriate, and/or typical for that child. These specific socialization techniques are discussed in greater detail in the third section of the chapter; for now it is important to note that social learning and socialization theories, in general, suggest that children tend to adopt the communication styles found in their family settings.

This hypothesis has been tested in over a dozen studies that assessed the expressiveness styles of mothers and their offspring. Other studies investigated paternal expressive styles, and it is hoped that future research will include other family members (e.g., grandparents, stepparents, siblings).

In a very young sample, Malatesta and Haviland (1982) found similarities in both facial muscle use and some discrete facial emotional expressions in 3- and 6-month-old infants and their mothers during play interactions and a reunion following the mother's absence. A developmental trend for expressiveness suggested that the older infants were more like their mothers than were the younger infants.

Field and her colleagues (Field et al., 1988) found that 3- to 6-month-old infants of depressed mothers show a persistent, depressed interaction style. Although this supports the hypothesis that infants and their mothers share expressiveness styles, the similarity in expressiveness may be more a consequence of shared emotion states or of the infants' giving up trying to signal their nonresponsive mothers (e.g., Tronick & Gianino, 1986). Alternatively, the depressed style may be a function of either intrauterine experience or genetic inheritance, as even neonates of depressed mothers appear depressed (Field et al., 1985).

In a comprehensive study of mothers' expressiveness styles during pregnancy and of infant behavior and mother–infant interactions in the infants' first two years of life, Diskin and Heinicke (1986) found long-term stability in the mothers' expressiveness styles and many associations between prebirth maternal expressive style and subsequent infant development. These relationships were significant even after other maternal variables were included in the analyses.

In an observational study of toddlers having a doctor's examination and lunch in the presence of their mothers, Denham (1989, 1990) found that the mothers' happy displays were positively related to the children's happy displays and were negatively related to the children's sad and angry expressions. The mothers' angry displays were negatively related to children's happy displays and positively related to the children's sad, afraid, and angry expressions. Camras et al. (1990) also observed similar rates of happy expressions and smiling in 3- to 7-year-old children and their mothers during toy play in the lab, and similar negative lower-face expressions and smiling during extended home visits. In a self-report study, Brody and Landau (1984) found that mothers' reports of their happy expressiveness were significantly related to their children's separately obtained predictions of their own emotions.

This study, and to some degree the two studies preceding it, assessed children's expressiveness independently of their mothers' presence or when their mothers were not part of the observed interactions. Thus, at least some of the mother–child commonalities in expressiveness styles could not have been simply due to the children's immediate imitation of their mothers' expressiveness. Rather, these studies suggest that the parent–child commonalities are the results of young children's successful internalization of maternal expression styles and associated values for expressiveness. All of the observational studies that we shall consider used independent measures of parents' and children's expressiveness and support the notion that expressiveness styles are internalized rather than simply imitated.

In a study of kindergarten children, mothers' expressiveness, as measured by self-report, was differentially associated with their children's positive and negative expressiveness in a variety of emotion-eliciting situations (Halberstadt & Fox, 1990; Halberstadt, Fox, & Aaron, 1990). Children whose mothers were high expressive were relatively more expressive of negative affect than were children whose mothers were low expressive, but these latter children showed significantly more positive affect than did children whose mothers were high expressive.

These results suggest several interesting possibilities, all of which require further testing. First, as a consequence of the family value for inexpressiveness, children from low-expressive homes may be socialized to mask their negative expressions more successfully than are children from high-expressive homes, whereas making positive expression may not be important, even in low-expressive homes. Second, the parents' expressiveness may influence their children's belief systems concerning the acceptability and reasonableness of emotionality. Because young children do not seem to distinguish between the expression of emotion and the actual emotionality (i.e., they apply the reflection hypothesis), children might model parental expressions and then internalize them as emotional experiences, or they might construct feeling rules (Hochschild, 1979) that they later activate in similar situations. For example, in homes where anger expression is abundant, children may not only perceive that anger expression is acceptable but also that feeling angry is acceptable and even appropriate as well. As a consequence, children may not only be more expressive of anger but may also experience greater anger. Third, parents' negative expressiveness may be inherently disturbing to children and may dampen or overwhelm their positive emotions and consequently their positive expressiveness (see also Denham, 1989). Research evidence for the first part of this third hypothesis is accumulating: (1) Infants as young as 10 weeks are disturbed by their mothers' anger expressions (Haviland & Lelwica, 1987); (2) toddlers and preschoolers are distressed by anger expression, even when the anger is not directed at them (Cummings, 1987; Cummings, Iannotti, & Zahn-Waxler, 1985); and (3) toddlers become increasingly distressed with repeated exposure to adults' verbal arguments (Cummings, Zahn-Waxler, & Radke-Yarrow, 1981). Further, the physically aggressive responses that children enact following their observations of angry encounters are not imitations of the angry adults' behavior, thus suggesting some type of contagion effect and/or a disinhibition of previously restrained aggressiveness (Cummings et al., 1985), both of which can reduce the children's opportunities for expressing positive affect.

One might think that family socialization influences would dissipate over time, as peer and school influences become more important in children's lives, but the connection between family expressiveness and self-expressiveness continues with some strength through the college years. Four questionnaire studies support this hypothesis (Balswick & Avertt, 1977; Gallegos & Friedman, 1989; Halberstadt, 1986; Halberstadt, Tesh, & Hoeft, 1989), and another questionnaire study indicates that family expressiveness is negatively related to ambivalence to expressed emotion (King & Emmons, 1990).

In addition, observational research with college students supports this hypothesis (Halberstadt, 1986). In this research, students were chosen according to their high or low scores on the 40-item Family Expressiveness Questionnaire (FEQ; Halberstadt, 1986).[3] The students were unobtrusively videotaped while getting acquainted and conversing for 5 minutes about happy and about sad topics of their own choosing. Raters later determined whether the students were telling happy or sad stories by judging videotape segments without sound or voice tone segments with the tape electronically filtered so that the words could not be understood.

As predicted, students from high-expressive families were more facially expressive when sharing emotional experiences than were those from low-expressive families. Students from more expressive families also smiled more often and for longer. When voice tone and facial sending were combined, a three-way interaction indicated that individuals from more-expressive families were more-expressive senders in channels that were relatively more difficult for judges to recognize (sad–negative for females, happy–positive for males) compared with those from less-expressive families. Thus, family expressiveness is related to self-expressiveness in facial sending and may also have an impact on self-expressiveness in voice tone.

Finally, the relationship between family expressiveness and self-expressiveness has been supported for anger expression in college students and in adults (Burrowes & Halberstadt, 1987). In this study, the participants filled out questionnaires on family expressiveness (Halberstadt, 1986), self-expressiveness (slightly lengthened from Friedman et al., 1980), and anger in social situations (adapted from Averill, 1982). They also solicited a family member, spouse, or close friend to fill out shortened questionnaires about the participant.

Family expressiveness of negative affect was significantly related to the subjects' own expression and experience of anger, whether measured by the subject or the nominated family member, spouse, or friend. Specifically, subjects from families that were more apt to express negative emotion reported more actual expression of their anger and more intense and more enduring experiences of anger, during which time they had less control over their anger experience and expression, compared with subjects from families that less often expressed negative emotion.

These relationships between families' expressiveness and individuals' anger experiences held even when the subjects' self-expressiveness was partialed out, and they were equally strong in the samples of college students and of older adults when examined separately. We might wonder, though, whether these results are the result of the greater willingness of people from more-expressive homes – than that of people from less-expressive homes – to report more intense experiences. If so, the correlations between family expressiveness and anger may merely be due to the greater willingness of subjects from more-expressive families to describe more intensely angering experiences. However, when we partialed out the reported intensity of the experience from the correlations between negative family expressiveness and the anger variables, these relationships were just as strong, indicating that negative family expressiveness is related to the subjects' present-day expressions of anger and also possibly to their anger experiences as well.

Summary

The socialization process for expressiveness may yield returns as early as 3 months of life. Neonatal imitation may be the beginning of the socialization process: Field, Woodson, Greenberg, and Cohen (1982) found that infants imitate models' facial behavior almost immediately after birth. Thus, parents' styles and their relatively expressive or inexpressive play may expand and intensify or may channel and restrict the neonate's repertoire. This socialization process may be similar to that of learning language; just as certain babbling sounds drop out as an infant learns a language without need for those sounds, so may emotional expression be channeled or modified. Despite the diversity of methods and measures, the relationship between parents' expressiveness styles and children's expressiveness found in infancy consistently appears throughout childhood and, indeed, is maintained well into adulthood.

Two questions about the causality of this relationship: I have consistently posited that the socialization process is a major causal influence for this relationship, but other influences must also be relevant. For example, similar family styles may be influenced by genetic material that family members share, as suggested for some personality or temperament characteristics (e.g., Eysenck, 1967; Gray, 1971; Plomin, Pedersen, McClearn, Nesselroade, & Bergeman, 1988). Also, we know that individual differences in expressiveness styles appear at birth (Field, 1982, 1985), and these are certainly not the consequence of socialization experiences (but see Field, 1987, for nongenetic, in vitro possibilities).

Even if there is shown initially to be a constitutional similarity in parent–child expressiveness, socialization processes will, however, play some role in the family–child relationship. For example, Shields and Stern (1979) found that mothers and their 7-to-10-year-old children reported similar physiological responses to anxious situations, although fathers and their children did not. Because fathers contribute the same amount of genetic information as do mothers, the different relationships are not likely due to genetic influence. Thus, the similarity between mothers and children may be based on the mothers' labeling of her own states being imitated during development and internalized by her child.

A second question concerns the assumption in these studies that the parents' expressiveness influences the developing children's expressiveness. This assumption is not at the expense of recognizing that infants and children influence their parents' behavior. Of course, either direction accepts socialization as a valid explanation. Children may certainly influence family communication styles, and developmental theory has increasingly emphasized the bidirectionality of social-interaction influence. A growing literature indicates that parents are responsive to infants' and children's signals, and the studies described in this chapter suggest that parents have a range within which to respond to infants: Some parents are at the high-expressive end of the range, and others are at the low-expressive end. Thus, infants make demands on their parents' responding styles and guide their interactions with their parents, but parents also guide their interactions with their infants.

Family expressiveness and social consequences

I shall now discuss the various ways in which family expressiveness styles are associated with persons' communication skills and social outcomes.

Communication skills

Sending. To be successful communicators, we need to know when to send which messages, and then we need to have the skill to carry out our intentions. The former knowledge is discussed later (see "Knowledge of display rules"); it is the latter skill which I consider now. We have seen that individuals from high-expressive families are themselves more spontaneously expressive. However, as defined earlier, expressiveness is a style, not a skill. Clearly, it is not always socially wise to be expressive and to reveal everything that one is thinking or feeling. Likewise, it is not always adaptive to inhibit the expression of what one is feeling and thinking. Thus, one's level of expressiveness – no matter what it is – as a general persistent pattern does not necessarily indicate skill or lack of skill in sending messages. Sending skill is the ability to send relevant messages clearly when a social situation requires it, and not just whatever or whenever one is feeling or thinking about something in particular. In the studies described next, the subjects were tested for their ability to communicate a specific message clearly. Indeed, sometimes sending ability may involve suppressing other feelings and thoughts in order to communicate the intended message.

The predictions were that individuals from high-expressive families would be more skilled at posed sending, simply because they would have had so much practice in their families at expressing themselves in general. The first study of college students' vocal encoding supported this hypothesis, as two measures of family expressiveness were positively related with sending skill (Halberstadt, 1983).

In the second study, using the Family Expressiveness Questionnaire and visual as well as vocal posed encoding, there was no overall difference, but those subjects from high-expressive families had a greater relative advantage at sending the more difficult items, compared with the subjects from low-expressive families who more accurately sent the easier items (Halberstadt, 1986). These results required rethinking the relationship between family expressiveness and sending skill. First, simply because individuals from high-expressive homes are themselves more expressive – and so have more experience at facially, vocally, and bodily expressing themselves than do individuals from low-expressive homes – they may not be able to turn those expressive experiences to advantage. Further, sending skill may be composed of several kinds of skill. First, individuals may need to inhibit feelings that are not relevant to the message to be communicated. Second, they may need to simulate the feelings that they do wish to communicate, whether or not those feelings are actually felt (Ekman, 1972; Ekman & Friesen, 1969; Shennum & Bugental, 1982). We are currently testing these hypotheses, observing children's ability to inhibit emotion expression, to simulate emotion expression, and to do both simultaneously when masking felt emotions with simulated expressions.

Judging. It seems that when the family environment is low in expressiveness, persons should become sensitive to the most subtle displays of emotion in order to relate effectively to other family members. When the family environment is high in expressiveness, however, persons might not have to work as hard to perceive their family members' emotional states. Therefore, the predictions were that individuals from low-expressive families may be acquiring a great deal more practice at judging than were individuals from high-expressive families. Thus, individuals from low-expressive families should become more skilled in perceiving emotion, whereas individuals from high-expressive families may never develop as much skill in perceiving emotion in others. There is some evidence for this in repeated-measures designs in which the subjects practice over time. In these studies, practice alone improves juding skill even without any feedback (e.g., DePaulo, Rosenthal, Eisenstat, Rogers, & Finkelstein, 1978; Rosenthal, Hall, DiMatteo, Rogers, & Archer, 1979). The studies described next test the adage "practice makes perfect" in between-subjects designs that can consider the importance of family-expressiveness background.

Three studies tested nonverbal judging skill or related abilities with children in association with their mothers' expressiveness. Daly, Abramovitch, and Pliner (1980) found that 5-year-old children of accurately expressive mothers were better decoders than were children of less accurately expressive mothers, especially for slides of good senders. Denham and Couchoud (1988) found that mothers' reports of their own expressiveness were associated with their preschoolers' knowledge of emotion display rules, which may be related to nonverbal judging skill. Camras and her colleagues (Camras et al., 1988, 1990) compared the understanding of emotion labels of 3- to 7-year old children whose abusing or nonabusing mothers varied in their posed sending accuracy and in overall expressiveness during laboratory play and extended home observations. The children's emotion knowledge was positively associated with both their mothers' sending skill and general expressiveness, especially with their mothers' negative facial expressions (regardless of mothers' abuse classification). This research is the closest test of the hypothesis and suggests that judging skill in children is positively related to their expressive environment.

Children from low-expressive homes, however, may have only an initial disadvantage at recognizing emotional communications. In such homes, parental expressions may be more subtle, blended, or incomplete or may entail greater masking. Precisely because their families are less expressive, it may take these children longer to begin developing their judging skill, but they may also be more motivated to become more proficient.

The judging hypothesis has also been tested in six small studies with college students (total $N = 233$) (Halberstadt, 1984). Socialization of emotional expression was measured by the subjects' reports of family expressiveness, generally with the Family Expressiveness Questionnaire (FEQ) or some modified version of it. Judging skill was measured by the subjects' ability to identify others' emotions via voice tone, face, or face and body on slides, film, or videotape. In each study, the relationship between family expressiveness and judging was negative, and the combined effect was highly significant. Individuals growing up in less-expressive families were more skilled at recognizing emotional communications that were individuals from more-expressive families. The advantage for subjects from low-expressive families may develop because skill in recognizing subtle emotional communications becomes more important to "survival" in their families than in more-expressive families in which emotional expression is abundant, and practice is not necessary.

The research with children indicates a positive relationship, whereas the research with college students suggests a negative relationship. With age, a crossover effect may emerge such that children from less-expressive homes become more skilled than children from more-expressive homes. Children from high-expressive families may have more practice initially at labeling emotion expressions and may also have more prototypical displays available to them for learning emotion expression categories. Children from low-expressive families may have fewer examples of emotion expressions available from which to learn, and those expressions may be miniaturized or incomplete, without all the display markings readily apparent. Thus, skill in low-expressive families may be initially slowed compared with that of high-expressive families, but over time, learning in low-expressive families continues so that the developing individual acquires skill in both obvious prototypical displays as well as more subtle displays in which the expression is miniaturized or only partially enacted. This hypothesis needs to be tested, and ideal studies would include a longitudinal or cross-sequential design that measured judging of miniaturized and partial expressions as well as prototypical expressions.

Successful social interactions

Two kinds of questions can be addressed regarding social interactions. First, is there any overall effect on people's social functioning as a consequence of family styles of expressiveness? Second, do individuals from similarly expressive backgrounds flock together?

Overall influence of family expressiveness. A positive relationship between family expressiveness and successful social interactions is suggested, for two reasons. First, based on the findings just reported, it appears that children adopt at least partially the parental styles of expressiveness that they observe and experience. Thus, individuals from more-expressive families are themselves likely to be more expressive and consequently perceived as warm, friendly, and outgoing (Halberstadt, 1984) as well as extroverted and sociable. On the down side of expressiveness, more expressive individuals have also been occasionally described as more impulsive, hostile, and neurotic, although impulsive could also be described as "spontaneous," and the latter two characteristics are not predominant aspects of the stereotype. Individuals from less-expressive families are themselves likely to be less expressive and consequently perceived as quiet, mild mannered, and calm (Halberstadt, 1984) but also introverted, controlled, inhibited, and nondominant. The warmth, friendliness, and sociability generally associated with the expressive stereotype may make expressive individuals popular choices for social interactions, particularly among children or during the early stages of friendship, before the impulsive, excitable, and dominant aspects of the expressive profile become evident to the other participant.

Second, although I discussed earlier the possibility that children from more negatively expressive homes may themselves feel anger more and may certainly express more anger, other outcomes are possible. For example, as a consequence of parents' willingness to deal with open conflict, children may learn social skills for negotiation and conflict resolution that they can apply to classroom situations (Cassidy & Parke, 1989). Cummings and his colleagues (Cummings et al., 1981; Cummings, Zahn-Waxler, & Radke-Yarrow, 1984) reported that children whose parents openly expressed conflict did show prosocial attempts to mediate between, reconcile, and distract their parents. Thus, even if children are feeling and expressing greater aggression as an immediate consequence of observing angry encounters (e.g., Cummings, et al., 1985), a long-term consequence may be to work harder and more successfully at enunciating one's needs and desires and at resolving conflict when it does occur.

Work with children supports the hypothesis that family expressiveness is associated with successful social interactions: Kindergarteners' and first graders' popularity, as measured by their peers, was positively related to their parents' expressiveness, especially their same-sex parent (Cassidy & Parke, 1989). The parents' expressiveness was also associated with the children's expressive behavior, as measured by peer and teacher ratings reflecting classroom behavior. These findings tended to hold for both positive and negative parental expressiveness unless otherwise indicated. Boys from more-expressive families were less shy, and boys whose fathers were more negatively expressive tended to be less aggressive and more prosocial, compared with boys whose fathers were less negatively expressive. Girls from more-expressive families were more prosocial and less disruptive, and girls whose fathers were more negatively expressive were also less aggressive, compared with girls whose fathers were less negatively expressive. The children's popularity and behavior may be interrelated, but it is unlikely that either of these variables is somehow influencing the parents' expressiveness.

Even during the college years, family expressiveness styles and popularity may be related, at least in first impressions. In a social interaction study, college students filled out a 22-item evaluation of their discussions about personally happy or sad experiences and about their partner during the discussions (Halberstadt, 1984). The four-item scale of greatest interest to us is the subject's liking for and perceived reciprocity of that feeling from his or her partner. The analysis of that scale indicated that subjects from more-expressive families reported a greater liking of and reciprocity of that feeling from their partners, compared with subjects from less-expressive families. These results are intriguing and need to be replicated, both in this type of first-impression situation and in more enduring social relationships, such as those measured by Cassidy and Parke (1989).

Interactions with others from similar and different expressive backgrounds. It seems likely that people do not easily understand messages communicated by individuals with different expressiveness styles, and thus they behave differently toward those individuals. Differences between ourselves and others in nonverbal communication are not often consciously noted, and when they are, the concept of different styles is not usually invoked as an explanation. Rather, our explanations of others often involve attributions about their personalities (only some of which may be accurate), and these attributions, in turn, affect our interactions with them, thus beginning a self-fulfilling cycle of behavior. If people from different backgrounds misperceive one another, based on their expectations of "appropriate" styles of communication, then it follows that people will find it easier to understand individuals from a similar background as well as to find them more interpersonally agreeable. The predictions were that individuals prefer interactions with others from similarly expressive backgrounds. This was tested in two ways: first, by considering first impressions of college students from similar or dissimilar backgrounds and, second, by examining whether college students chose as their friends those who had similarly expressive family backgrounds.

The first study included the college students described earlier (Halberstadt, 1984, 1986). To determine whether similar versus different levels of family expressiveness affected the subjects' and their partners' first impressions of each other, the same four-item evaluative scale was used, and an ANOVA including the subjects' and their partners' family expressiveness as factors was conducted. The significant interaction between the subjects' and their partners' family expressiveness indicated that the subjects reported greater liking for and perceived liking by their partners from similar expressive backgrounds, compared with partners from dissimilar expressive backgrounds. Although these data were gathered after only a 15-minute encounter, the results revealed that social interactions have a greater probability of success when occurring with individuals of similar family backgrounds.

Two more studies investigating college students' social interactions assessed longer-term friendship patterns (Halberstadt, Hoeft, & Tesh, 1990). If individuals prefer interactions with others from similar expressive backgrounds, then one's family's expressiveness may be influential in at least two ways when making friends. First, family expressiveness may be relevant to the choices that an individual makes when seeking out particular persons as friends. For example, people may simply feel more comfortable with others who are similar to their own family, and so they may choose a friend based on that individual's similarity to their family.

Second, family expressiveness may influence who accepts an offer of a friendship. It is likely that people use interaction styles with unrelated others that are similar to the interaction styles that they use with their families, whether or not they intend to develop long-term friendships with those others. Based on their own family experiences, some interaction partners appreciate that style of interaction and are likely to respond positively to initial overtures, thereby encouraging further acquaintance. But others do not appreciate that style of interaction and so are more likely to reject initial advances, thereby halting the friendship process early on. Thus, family expressiveness may be influential in both the choice of specific people as friends and the fostering of a positive atmosphere conducive to exploring similar values and interests from which a friendship can develop.

In the first study, college students who scored above the median and the mean on both the positive and the negative scales of the FEQ (Halberstadt, 1986) filled out two more questionnaires, one on self-expressiveness (lengthened from Friedman et al., 1980) and one on affect intensity (the intensity or magnitude of emotional experience, shortened from Larsen & Diener, 1987; Larsen, Diener, & Emmons, 1986). One of each subject's close friends agreed to participate by filling out a questionnaire about his or her own expressiveness style. The subjects' family expressiveness and their friends' self-expressiveness were significantly related for positive expression and overall expressiveness, but the relationship was not significant for negative expression (Halberstadt et al., 1989).

In the second study, college students filled out the FEQ and the same self-expressiveness and affect intensity questionnaires, and the close friends were also asked to fill out all three questionnaires about themselves (Halberstadt, Hoeft, & Tesh, 1990). Again, the subjects' family expressiveness and their friends' self-expressiveness were significantly related for positive expression and overall expressiveness, but the relationship was not significant for negative expression. These correlations held even when the subjects' self-expressiveness was partialed out. Of course, self-expressiveness and affect intensity are also related to both family expressiveness and the friends' self-expressiveness, so multiple regressions were conducted to determine which questionnaire or combination of questionnaires would be most successful in predicting the friends' self-expressiveness. Although reports of self-expressiveness and affect intensity yielded significant equations when they were fitted by themselves, the best-fitting model contained only family expressiveness. Considering that there are many other influences in choosing a close friend, it is noteworthy that the subjects' family expressiveness accounted for a quarter of the variance in the chosen friend's self-expressiveness. These results suggest that friendship choices may be influenced by expressiveness styles as emergent from families, and also that people may seek out others whose expressiveness styles resemble their family styles.

Summary

It appears that (1) subjects from more-expressive homes may be better at sending relatively difficult emotional communications, although future research should subdivide general sending skills into subskills that may relate differently to family socialization of expressiveness; (2) children from low-expressive homes may have an initial disadvantage at recognizing others' emotional communications in early childhood, but by college age, they are more skilled at judging nonverbal communications than are subjects from high-expressive homes; (3) children from high-expressive homes are more popular, less aggressive, and more prosocial than are children from less-expressive homes; and (4) both initial and longer-term social interaction preferences seem to be for those with similar expressive family backgrounds.

It seems clear that parental expressiveness styles have a variety of impacts on the developing individual. We have discovered a great deal about family expressiveness styles and influences on expressivness as a communication style, but there is much more yet to find out.[4]

An ecological model describing the development of expressiveness

As mentioned earlier, family socialization is not the only process determining how individuals come to have particular styles of expressiveness. First, there are many socialization influences on the developing individual. Some of these are broadly based, such as societal influences, and others are closer to home, such as peer influences and the family influences just described. Second, there are many internal state self-factors that help determine expressiveness, such as physiological, affective motivational, cognitive, and personality factors. Finally, there are self-mediators that affect individuals' expressiveness levels by mediating the influence of socializing agents and modulating the influence of internal states.

The model presented in Figure 4.1 does not seek to explain any one event of expression but, rather, indicates how individual differences in expressiveness may emerge over time. Thus, only those variables that distinguish among individuals – as opposed to situations or qualities in elicitors – are identified.[5] The model includes three socialization influences that are separate but overlapping; these are represented in Figure 4.1 by the ellipses for societal, peer, and family expressiveness.

That the ellipse representing societal norms and values for expressiveness encompasses the other ellipses shows that the individual's own norms and values for expressiveness are affected directly by societal patterns for expression communicated via the media, school, and other institutionalized structures, as well as indirectly by societal patterns for expression communicated via the family and peer norms, values, and behaviors, which have an influence all their own. The family expressiveness and peer expressiveness ellipses also overlap, suggesting that they may be mutually influential and possibly interactive in their effect on self-expression.

The model also identifies self-factors that influence expressiveness; these include physiological, affective, motivational, cognitive, and personality variables. These are represented in the rectangle in the lower part of the model. The self-factors are also partially encompassed by the societal expressiveness ellipse, in order to show that some of the self-factors develop within, and thus are influenced by, a societal context. The self-factors are probably affected by family and peer socialization processes as well – hence the overlap and permeable boundaries with the other two socialization ellipses.

Finally, other self-factors affect people's expressiveness levels by mediating the influence of socializing agents and modulating the influence of internal states. These are call self-mediators and are represented as the closest area encircling self-expressiveness.

Figure 4.2 shows the more complex version of the model. Again, the model suggests that an individual's self-expressiveness is influenced by societal, family, and peer expressiveness. Cultural and class norms and values are included under societal expressiveness, and four general socialization processes are included under family and peer influences; these four processes probably hold for societal influences as well. Again, the socialization influences are mediated by individual characteristics, now identified as autonomy, need for approval, and awareness of socialization contingencies. That is, the values and behaviors of society, family, and peers influence a person only to the degree that he or she is receptive to those messages.

As in Figure 4.1, the rectangle in the lower part of the model represents some of the stable individual characteristics that directly influence an individual's expressiveness. Self-expressiveness is influenced by physical factors such as gender, age, and physiological arousal, as well as fairly stable psychological characteristics, such as pervasive emotion states (e.g., depression), motivational and cognitive factors (the ability to self-regulate, self-values for expression, knowledge of display rules, and appraisal of the socioemotional situation), and personality characteristics (e.g., extroversion). At least some of these influences moderate one another; gender, for example, may moderate the influence of age and vice versa, and knowledge of display rules may influence one's value for expression and vice versa. The self-factors are also mediated

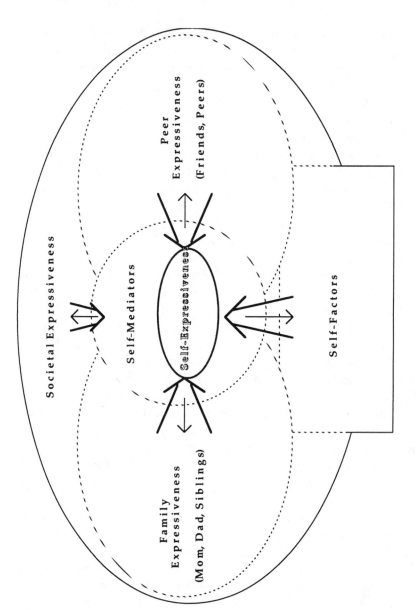

Figure 4.1. A simple model of the development of expressiveness.

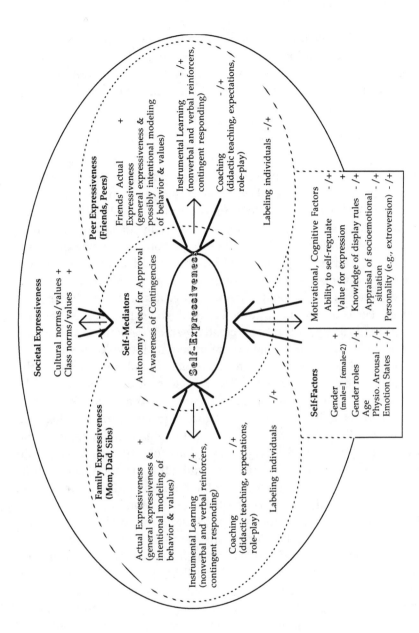

Figure 4.2. A more complex model of the development of expressiveness.

by the individual characteristics of autonomy, need for approval, and awareness of socialization contingencies. For example, the ability to self-regulate one's expressiveness style may not be activated unless one is interested in obtaining approval from socializing others.

Societal expressiveness

Culture. Much evidence has accumulated to indicate the universality of meaning of at least some facial expressions (e.g., Ekman, 1972; Ekman & Friesen, 1971); however, this does not preclude the probability of strong societal influences on expressiveness, especially in social situations. That cultural norms and values influence persons' styles of expressiveness is not a surprising hypothesis: Cultural and ethnic groups that value expressiveness should be composed of people who are more expressive compared with people in cultural groups that devalue expressiveness. For example, in cultures in which the expression of emotion is identified as an opportunity for creative self-expression, as a cleansing process, or as a useful social communication, individuals should be more expressive, compared with individuals in cultures in which the expression of emotion is identified as reflecting an immature or "weak" personality, as an opportunity for evil spirits to expand their domain of influence, or as an inadvisable disturbance of group harmony. Three anthropological investigations that examined expressiveness suggest that societies vary in (1) their socialization goals for expression, based on their values for emotion expression, and (2) their socialization time lines, based on their beliefs about when infants and toddlers are capable of learning and achieving those goals for expression.[6]

In Utku Eskimo society, for example, infants and toddlers are expressive and "spoiled" by other Americans' standards; that is, the Utku do not expect babies to be able to control their desires, and the adults delight in fulfilling the babies' every whim (Briggs, 1970). When, however, a sibling is born several years later, toddlers are expected to develop restraint and emotional self-control. Thus, young Utku toddlers are at least as expressive of anger as are other American toddlers, but Utku children seem calmer and less reactive to frustrating situations than other American children are. By early adulthood, Utku expressions of anger or hostility are extremely rare (Briggs, 1970).

The Javanese socialization of expression appears in several ways similar to that of the Utku Eskimos. The Javanese also attempt to fulfill their infants' every need. They, too, consider infants as unsocializable, though their fulfillment of their infants' needs is carried out in a gentle yet unemotional manner. They do not expect any self-control from their toddlers until they understand simple language, at which time restraint is suggested and teaching commences. By age 5, Javanese children are expected to adopt a quiet, controlled, and formal demeanor, and this demeanor and the avoidance of strong expression of emotion are continued throughout adulthood (Geertz, 1959).

The Gusii people of Southwest Kenya believe that intense expression of emotion is disruptive to social interaction, possibly dangerous to the individual, and certainly to be avoided (Dixon, Tronick, Keefer, & Brazelton, 1981). Observations of their behavior indicate that these values regarding emotion are immediately reflected in caregiving strategies. Gusii mothers rarely play with their infants in face-to-face situations, and when they were asked to (for the sake of studying those interactions), mothers of 2- to 24-week-old infants engaged in brief face-to-face play encounters, and averted their gaze from the infants, more than did American mothers. Dixon et al. (1981) suggest that the Gusii mothers are as responsive and sensitive to their infants' behaviors as are American mothers but that their goals are different. Whereas American mothers seek to increase positive affect and thus create play sequences characterized by peaks of intense excitement, Gusii mothers create even, gentle, modulated interactions with their infants that dampen or diffuse their infants' affective responses.[7]

The Utku, Javanese, and Gusii all share values for inhibition of emotion expression. In contrast, although most Americans do not encourage negative expression in their young (see Miller & Sperry, 1987, for a possible exception), American mother–infant play is characterized by peaks of positive excitement and the mothers' amplification of positive affect and expression in their infants (Dixon et al., 1981). Regarding socialization time lines, the Utku and the Javanese believe that infants are incapable of being socialized immediately and that certain milestones must be achieved before socialization can commence. In contrast, the Gusii and Americans begin socializing their babies very early in infancy. Thus, the anthropological data indicate that a person's expressiveness is very much influenced by his or her cultural norms and values regarding expressiveness.

Besides these anthropological accounts, there are three questionnaire reports of cultural similarities and differences in expressiveness, each focusing on a different aspect of expressiveness. One 10-nation study investigated cultural and ethnic differences in parents' tolerant versus restrictive responses to their children's anger expression (Lambert, Hamers, & Frasure-Smith, 1979). Several group differences emerged: For example, Italian and English parents were more tolerant of anger expression than French-Belgian and English-Canadian parents were. Another study investigated emotional expressiveness and experiences reported by college students from four different cultural groups (Sommers, 1984). The Americans were more interested in inhibiting expressions of anger than the West Indians, Chinese, or Greeks were (although it was the West Indians who were more concerned than any other group about *not feeling* anger). Also, the West Indians and Chinese were more concerned about concealing expressions of love than were the Greeks or Americans (although it was the West Indians and Americans who were most interested in *feeling* love). A third study investigated nonverbal reactions to emotional experience in college students from eight nations (Wallbott, Ricci Bitti, & Banninger-Huber, 1986). Across emotions, the Italian, Swiss, and German students reported the most vocal responses, whereas the British and Israeli students reported the fewest. The British, French, and Israeli students reported the most facial responses, whereas the Spanish students reported the fewest. Although the British and French reported many facial reactions, they also were the subjects reporting the most intense attempts at self-control.

Some ethnic differences have also been found. Three general reports describe black culture as valuing and engaging in expressiveness more than white mainstream culture did (Hanna, 1984; Kochman, 1981; Lewis, 1975), though only some observational studies of specific behaviors have revealed differences. A metaanalysis indicates that blacks express themselves with touching more than whites do (Halberstadt, 1985), although Smith (1983) found no differences in the overall rates of smiling, eye gaze, and leaning between black female and white female dyads. Interestingly, Halberstadt and Saitta (1987) found that blacks are portrayed in the media (newspaper photographs and advertisements) as tilting their head and body and smiling relatively more than whites do, but in observations of actual behavior in public settings, blacks were observed enacting relatively fewer of these behaviors than whites did. Hispanic- and Anglo-Americans reported themselves to be similarly expressive (Gallegos & Friedman, 1989).

Some cultural differences are occasionally interactive with gender, whereas white males are less expressive than white females are (Hall,

1984), and Javanese males are less expressive than Javanese females are (Geertz, 1959). Black males and females are similarly expressive (Lewis, 1975), and Chinese males (from both mainland China and Taiwan) may be slightly more expressive than Chinese females are (Buck & Teng, 1987).

Class. There are few studies of class influences on expressiveness. The 10-nation study reporting cultural differences also found large and persistent class differences in 9 of the 10 cultures studied: For example, working-class parents were more restrictive of their children's anger expression than middle-class parents were (Lambert et al., 1979). A summary of studies of touching behavior suggests that lower-class children and mothers express themselves with touch more than middle-class children and mothers do (Halberstadt, 1985). Regarding class differences in smiling, Bugental, Love, and Gianetto (1971) reported anecdotally that lower-class mothers did not smile in a clinic waiting room with their children, whereas middle-class mothers did. But Landau (1977), in observations during one typical day, found that lower-class Israeli infants smiled more than middle-class Israeli infants did in the presence of their mothers, and Anisfeld (1982) found an earlier onset of smiling in lower-class Sephardic Israeli infants than in middle-class Ashkenazic Israeli infants. These differences, however, may be due to ethnicity, parent education, caregiving styles, and/or family structural differences, as well as class, and in at least one of these studies, they may also be a consequence of genetic differences. Finally, not all of these studies clearly reported their actual measure(s) for class, and operational definitions of class were not always similar across studies that did report their measures (Halberstadt, 1985).

Summary. Cultural and class expressiveness appear to affect people's own levels of expressiveness. Sometimes the influence is global (as in norms for overall expression or inhibition), and sometimes it is behavior specific (as in anger expression or frequency of touch). Although some cultural differences may be due to constitutional differences among groups, socialization appears as a powerful influence.

Although there is no direct evidence, it seems likely that the influence of expressiveness may be bidirectional, with societal values changing in response to individuals' behaviors, for example, particularly powerful or charismatic individuals. To wit, American society has been moving toward more frequent and intense smiling in public settings and official photographs. Indeed, this trend may have affected Jimmy Carter's understanding of the value of a smile, or at least his willingness to grin publicly from ear to ear in his bid for the 1976 presidency. His broad smile in the early years of his presidency may have, in turn, prompted greater smiling by others in public settings and photographs from 1976 to the present. In the model in Figure 4.2, this proposed bidirectionality between individual and societal expressiveness is reflected in the dotted lines between the ellipses for societal, family, peer, and self-expressiveness. The dotted lines suggest the permeability of the boundaries: Societal expressiveness influences individuals and also families and peers, but individuals also have some corresponding influence on societal (and family and peer) norms, values, and mean rates of behaviors.

Self-factors

Gender. Hall (1984) summarized gender differences in expressiveness in several metaanalyses and found that women are more facially expressive than men are, that women smile more than men do, and that women are more bodily expressive in terms of hand, head, and body movement and touch others more than men do. Buck and his colleagues found that women are not only more expressive than men in general are but that women's expressiveness also appears relatively more "meaningful" to observers (Buck, Baron, & Barrette, 1982; Buck, Baron, Goodman, & Shapiro, 1980; see also Manstead, Chapter 8 in this volume, for a more detailed discussion). On the other hand, men exhibit both more bodily restlessness and bodily relaxation and also more speech errors than women do.

Women and men may receive different feedback regarding their use of expression channels: Facial expressiveness in terms of changeability seems associated with positive impressions of women, whereas speech fluency, body movements, and smiling are associated with positive impressions of men (Buck et al., 1980; Bugental, Kaswan, & Love, 1970; Noller, 1982; Shrout & Fiske, 1981). Thus, not only do men and women differ in their expressiveness styles, but they also may be rewarded differently for their nonverbal behavior.

These gender differences were noted not only for expressiveness overall and for channel (e.g., facial expression vers‑‑ speech errors) but also for emotion. Women tend to be more emotionally expressive than men are, with some exceptions for negative emotions, especially anger (e.g., Allen & Haccoun, 1976; Birnbaum & Croll, 1984; Brody, 1985; Fuchs & Thelen, 1988). Brody (1985), however, cautioned that at least some of these emotion expression differences have been studied in only one or a few situations, and thus these gender differences need to be investigated further across contexts.

Gender role characteristics also seem associated with expressiveness, as measured by smiling and frowning (Halberstadt, Hayes, & Pike, 1988; Klions, Sanders, Hudak, Dale, & Klions, 1987; LaFrance & Carmen, 1980; but see also Zuckerman, DeFrank, Spiegel, & Larrance, 1982, Study 2), walking style (Frable, 1987), and body cues (Lippa, 1978); these differences occasionally interact with gender but do not always account for the larger gender differences (Halberstadt et al., 1988). Thus, gender differences in quantity and quality of expressiveness are abundant, though not easily organized into a coherent scheme without some post hoc shuffling.

Developmental research on facial expressiveness, smiling, and touching indicates very few gender differences in early childhood, suggesting that such differences in expressiveness emerge after the preschool years and may well be the consequence of parental and peer socialization of appropriate gender role behaviors and the children's own adoption of gender role behaviors as they learn the rules of their culture (Brody, 1985; Buck, 1977; Hall, 1984). Some data reveal that girls may actually experience a more emotionally expressive environment than do boys while they are growing up. For example, it seems that mothers exhibit greater positive expressiveness toward female infants than toward male infants (Fogel, Toda, & Kawai, 1988); mothers and older siblings make more frequent references to feeling states to girl toddlers than to boy toddlers (Dunn, Bretherton, & Munn, 1987); fathers (but not mothers) are more affectionately expressive toward their preschool daughters than their sons (Noller, 1978); fathers (but not mothers) tend to mention emotions more often to their daughters than to their preschool-aged sons when reading a picture book with them (Grief, Alvarez, & Ulman, 1981); and in families with adolescent daughters there is greater nonverbal expressiveness than in families with adolescent sons, which appears primarily due to the fathers' differential behavior (Noller & Callan, 1989). Also, children seem to be aware of their differentially expressive experiences: Female college students report slightly more expressiveness in their family life than do male college students (Halberstadt, 1981).

One might wonder about the causal direction of these findings. For example, parents' greater expressiveness might be a response to their daughters' expressiveness rather than a cause. In the Noller and Callan study, however, the fathers' greater nonverbal expressiveness with their daughters was not a matching response, at least during the study, as the daughters were no more expressive than the sons were then.

Parents may also differentially encourage or discourage general or specific emotion expressiveness with their reinforcement practices. For at least some emotion expressions, mothers of male infants may give more contingent or matching responses than do mothers of female infants (Malatesta, Grigoryev, Lamb, Albin, & Culver, 1986; Malatesta & Haviland, 1982), and by the time babies are 1- to 2-years-old, mothers seem less responsive to their male baby's cries than to their female baby's cries (Lewis & Michalson, 1983). Boys' expressions of anger may be more acceptable than girls' expressions, especially among working-class versus middle-class parents, and girls' fear expressions may be more acceptable than boys' fear expressions in both classes (Birnbaum & Croll, 1984). Also, boys may expect more positive parental responses to their anger than girls do, who may expect more positive parental responses to their sadness than boys do (Fuchs & Thelen, 1988). In addition, two broad developmental reviews of gender differences in emotion expressiveness indicate that male infants are initially more expressive than female infants are, but by school age, there is a crossover, with boys inhibiting affect expression to a greater degree than girls do (Brody, 1985; Haviland & Malatesta, 1981). Another study suggests that this pattern occurs slightly later, during elementary school (Fuchs & Thelen, 1988). It does seem likely that parents' expressiveness in regard to their children's gender affects their children's developing expressiveness.

Age. Several theorists have hypothesized that emotion expressiveness is inhibited with age, primarily as a consequence of socialization (e.g., Jones, 1950, 1960; Izard, 1971; Tomkins, 1962, 1963, 1979), and indeed, overall expressiveness does seem to be attenuated during early development. In play interactions with their mothers, 6-month-old infants changed their facial expressions less frequently than did 3-month-old infants (Malatesta & Haviland, 1982). Similar results were obtained in an infant longitudinal study, although by $7\frac{1}{2}$ months, infants became more positively expressive (Malatesta et al., 1986). In a longitudinal diary study, mothers reported that their children were more expressive when observing angry or affectionate situations as toddlers than at 6 years of age (Cummings et al., 1984). In laboratory play and home activity, both happy and sad facial expressions were produced more often by 3- to 7-year-old children than by their mothers (Camras et al., 1990). While watching a videotape about children injured in a car accident, second graders were more negatively expressive than fifth graders were (Fabes, Eisenberg, & Miller, 1989). And in a series of studies, Eisenberg, Fabes, Schaller, and Miller (1989) also found sad facial reactions decreasing with age, especially for males. Finally, first graders reported greater expressiveness of negative emotions than did fourth and sixth graders (Fuchs & Thelen, 1988). Some of these age differences, however, may reflect emotional considerations as well as expressive differences, and the participants' activities may have also varied by age. No one has yet systematically controlled for emotion experience while measuring expressiveness.

Besides an overall reduction in expressiveness, particular types of expressions may become partially expressed or miniaturized later in the life span. For example, "plus" and "minus" faces expressed during conflict become abbreviated and only partially represented during the school years (Zivin, 1982). Also, in a study in which adult women reported similar levels of emotional experience, the older women's negative facial expressions were more fragmented or only partially represented (the mean ages for the two age groups were 55 and 69 years), compared with the negative facial expressions of the younger middle-aged women (the mean age was 33 years). The older women also masked negative emotions more often than did the younger women (Malatesta & Izard, 1984). All these studies examined facial expressions, but one questionnaire study suggests an exception to the reduced expressiveness with age (Malatesta & Kalnock, 1984). In this study, the older people (mean age was 66 years) reported being as expressive of their feelings as the younger and middle-aged individuals did (mean ages were 26 and 47 years, respectively). Although the older subjects felt that people their age should be less expressive of their emotions than the younger or middle-aged individuals did, their self-reports of how much emotion they actually expressed and their verbal expressiveness in written descriptions of emotion experiences were similar to those of the younger groups.

These intriguing cross-sectional studies suggest that facial expressiveness is fragmented or miniaturized with age but that expressiveness in other forms is maintained or increased, though this needs to be tested in multichannel investigations of various emotion experiences. The studies also suggest a hydraulic model of emotion experience: When certain expressive channels become restricted over time (e.g., face), other means of expression may evolve (e.g., verbal communication). Further, in a culture in which emotionality and age are not respected but words are, older people may discover that verbal communications of their feelings are more successful than facial or vocal "emotional" expressions are. Finally, these age effects may be interactive with gender differences, as described in regard to gender differences.

A different type of expressiveness effect may also come with age, when pervasive moods and personality characteristics are reflected in more permanent facial features that then influence momentary expressions. When Malatesta and Fiore (1985) examined senior citizens' sending of facial communications, they found systematic affective errors that corresponded to the subjects' self-reports of personality and pervasive mood characteristics, suggesting a "crystallized affect" (Haviland, personal communication in Malatesta, 1981) in their expressiveness styles. This is especially interesting in light of the hypothesized disengagement between feeling and expression in early childhood and throughout adulthood (e.g., Lewis & Michalson, 1983). Perhaps in later adulthood there is a returning correspondence of expressiveness to internal state.

Physiological arousal. The relationship between physiological arousal and expressiveness has been debated for over a century, resulting in three general types of hypotheses. The facial feedback hypotheses posit that facial expressiveness directs physiological activity in the direction of the emotion being posed (e.g., Ekman, 1972; Ekman, Levenson, & Friesen, 1983; Izard, 1977, Tomkins 1962, 1979; Zuckerman, Klorman, Larrance, & Spiegel, 1981).

The internalizer–externalizer hypotheses suggest a negative association between physiological arousal and expressiveness, but the causal path of the association is not clear (e.g., Buck, 1984; Buck, Savin, Miller, & Caul, 1972; Eysenck, 1967; Gray, 1971; Jones, 1950, 1960; Lanzetta & Kleck, 1970; Notarius & Levenson, 1979; see also Manstead, 1988, and Chapter 8 in this volume for a more detailed discussion). Whereas Jones (1950, 1960) suggested that the overt expression of an emotion is associated with less internal arousal and that the inhibition of expression increases internal arousal, Eysenck (1967) and Gray (1971) believe that it is physiological responsivity that determines how sensitive an individual is to socialization pressures and, therefore, whether a person will express emotion overtly, thus allowing it to pass out of the nervous system. Notice that the internalizer–externalizer hypothesis generally assumes a hydraulic model of emotion; that is, eventually an emotion is likely to be expressed overtly in some form or another in order to get it out of the system. Also, both Jones and Gray assume that socialization influence is unidirectional; that is, the goal of socialization is always to punish expressiveness and therefore inhibit expressive behavior.

A third type of hypothesis uses specific physiological measures such as heart rate and heart rate variability as indicators of individual differences in reactivity and central nervous system organization (Porges, 1974, 1983). Using these measures, researchers have found a relationship between physiological reactivity and emotional expression in infants. For example, Field (1982) found lower mean heart rates and greater heart rate variability in high-expressive infants compared with low-expressive infants. Fox and Gelles (1984) reported greater short-term heart rate variability in infants with more enduring expressions of interest, and Stifter, Fox, and Porges (1985) found higher vagal tone and greater short-term and greater long-term heart rate variability in more-expressive, compared with less-expressive, 5- and 10-month-olds. Halberstadt, Fox, and Aaron (1990) found no relationship between heart rate variability and expressiveness in their study of 6-year-olds.[8] These results suggest that heart rate variability appears to reflect individual differences in emotional expressiveness very early in life but may become disengaged from displays of expressiveness as children learn and adopt the display rules of their family and culture.

Thus, facial feedback hypotheses suggest that overt expressiveness positively affects internal arousal; internalizer–externalizer hypotheses state that expression and arousal are negatively related; and at least some psychophysiological hypotheses propose that the system's physiological responsivity directs overt expressiveness. Evidence has actually been accumulating for all three hypotheses. Rather than serve as a battleground for these hypotheses, this chapter merely recognizes, in Figure 4.2 with bidirectional arrows, the probable mutual influence of physiological and overt expression.

Pervasive emotion states. Emotion must determine expressiveness to some degree, and this model does not deny the importance of emotional experience to expressiveness. Specific emotion experiences certainly influence the affective valence of an expression, as well as the frequency, intensity, duration, purity, and changeability of the expression. However, it is only when a mood state is persistent and enduring that an individual's style of expressiveness may be affected. For example, a persistent state of depression might lead to a sad expressiveness style or at least to the attenuation of overall expressiveness. Few studies, however, link the influence on pervasive mood states to styles of expressiveness. Ellgring (1986) found that smiling, gazing, and speech and facial activity generally increase as patients become less depressed during therapy. Also, two studies using a variation of Buck's (1984) slide-viewing paradigm found that depressed females were less accurately expressive than were nondepressed females, and, in one of those studies, depressed females were also less accurately expressive than were other female patients in a psychiatric control group (Gerson & Perlman, 1979; Prkachin, Craig, Papageorgis, & Reith, 1977). Chronic loneliness also seems to influence expressive accuracy (Gerson & Perlman, 1979). Although sending skill and expressiveness are somewhat confounded, these results suggest that depression and certain types of loneliness may be associated with a lack of facial responsivity or at least some facial ambiguity. Other persistent influences that may be due to pervasive mood states include crystallization of affect (Haviland in Malatesta, 1981; Malatesta & Fiore, 1985) and demeanor effects (DePaulo, Chapter 10 in this volume; Zuckerman, Larrance, Hall, DeFrank, & Rosenthal, 1979).

Motivational–cognitive factors. This grab bag of influences is meant to describe the motivation, knowledge, and ability to moderate one's behavior in the face of internal and external stimulation. It includes a large number of influences, only four of which are named here. Although at least some of these factors have been widely studied in their own right, there has been little or no research on expressiveness. The following discussion is therefore offered in a generative spirit.

SELF-REGULATION. Most definitions of self-regulation highlight the role of parental socialization as well as maturational and experiential processes in helping the individual develop internal control. The construct is complex, however, with meanings differing according to the researchers' goals, perspectives, and focus in the life span. As a consequence, self-regulation has been defined as the ability "to initiate and cease activities according to situational demands," "to modulate the intensity, frequency, and duration of verbal and motor acts," and "to generate socially approved behavior in the absence of external monitors" (Kopp, 1982, p. 199). The definition that seems most relevant to a discussion of self-expressiveness is being able to modulate physiological arousal and/or overt expressiveness in response to internal or external elicitors (Kopp, 1982). Although self-regulation is generally thought to be an inhibitory mechanism to reduce arousal, it may also be an enhancing function for responsiveness toward certain elicitors and thus may be guided by values for both emotional experience and expressiveness. Also, self-regulation of emotion states may sometimes be best achieved by expressing that state. For example, "slumping" rather than a proud, upright posture following a failure experience may actually help an individual to strive harder on a second task (Riskind, 1984).

VALUES FOR SELF-EXPRESSION. Again, based on cultural, family, peer, and personal influences, each of us has established a set of values for self-expressiveness across situations. Although knowledge of the display rules of one's culture carries some normative force and although each person absorbs at least some of the culture's values, the diversity of rules and values available (e.g., by means of ethnicity, gender, age) requires each individual to create consciously or nonconsciously his or her own value system. Note that a person's values and behaviors may not necessarily correspond immediately or even over relatively long periods of time. Self-regulation is one way to achieve that correspondence, based also on the interaction with our emotional experience.

KNOWLEDGE OF DISPLAY RULES. (Ekman, 1972; Ekman & Friesen, 1969). Display rules are the "cultural standards about the quality and intensity of emotions that can be expressed in different contexts" (Brody, 1985, p. 114) and the "societal rules for appropriate type and intensity of expressive behaviors in particular situations by individuals of specific social categories" (Zivin, 1986, p. 123). Several studies report a better understanding of these rules with age (e.g., Saarni, 1979, 1982) and a greater use of the rules in expressive situations with age and by gender (Buck, 1977; Feldman, Jenkins, & Poopola, 1979; Feldman & White, 1980; Shennum & Bugental, 1982). Knowledge of the cultural standards for expression is obtained from peers, family, and culture, but the actual corpus of knowledge rests within the individual and is organized and structured in ways unique to each person. For example, information about display rules may be imperfectly transmitted (e.g., by depressed, neglectful, or abusive parents) or imperfectly understood, and of course, peers, families, and cultures vary in their guidelines for appropriate expression rules.

APPRAISAL OF THE SOCIOEMOTIONAL SITUATION. Although the term *appraisal of the socioemotional situation* has many meanings for cognitive and emotion theorists (e.g., see Campos & Stenberg, 1981; Zivin, 1986), in this chapter, appraisal of the situation means identifying others' values for expressiveness, their expectations for one's own behavior, one's own interpersonal goals, and one's own value for expression within the particular situation. Some self-monitoring processes can be included here, but the notion of appraisal covers a larger domain of social evaluation. The importance of this factor is its more conscious cognitive assessment of expressiveness as a social communication and one's choice to regulate the social interaction. Given this sociocognitive assessment, appraisal allows for the application of display-rule knowledge, using self-regulation and in accordance with one's values for expressiveness.

Personality factors. A case was made in the 1930s for a relationship between personality characteristics and expressiveness as a style of communication (e.g., Allport & Cantril, 1934). Since then, a relationship has been identified for several personality characteristics. Extroversion, as measured by four different questionnaires and by teacher ratings, appears related to expressiveness whether measured by self-report, judges' ratings, or communication accuracy or pleasantness (Allport & Cantril, 1934; Buck, 1975, 1977; Buck, Miller, & Caul, 1974; Buck, Savin, Miller, & Caul, 1972; Cunningham, 1977; Field & Walden, 1982; Friedman et al., 1980; Miller-Herringer & Friedman, 1989; Riggio, 1986; Riggio & Friedman, 1982, 1986; Scherer, 1978; but see also Harper, Wiens, & Matarazzo, 1979; Lippa, 1977; Notarius & Levenson, 1979). Impulsivity, emotionality, hostility, neuroticism, sociability, self-esteem, field-dependence, dominance, empathy, inhibitedness, and shyness have also been found to be related to expressiveness (Buck 1975; Buck, Miller, & Caul, 1974; Cunningham, 1977; Estes, 1938; Friedman et al., 1980; Kagan, Reznick, & Snidman, 1987; Kagan, Reznick, Snidman, Gibbons, & Johnson, 1988; Miller-Herringer & Friedman, 1989; Notarius & Levenson, 1979; Riggio, 1986; Sabatelli, Dreyer, & Buck, 1979). Thus, personality characteristics have some relationship to persons' expressiveness styles, during both childhood and adulthood. Other variables that may be found to relate to expressiveness include one's emotional range (e.g., Sommers, 1981; Sommers & Scioli, 1986) and one's affect intensity (Larsen & Diener, 1987; Larsen et al., 1986).

Some personality variables affect expressiveness only in certain situations. For example, repressers during anxious conditions appear more expressive than do other low- or high-anxious subjects (Asendorpf & Scherer, 1983). Also, although self-monitoring seems to be associated with greater expressiveness overall, cross-channel and cross-situational consistency in expressiveness is also influenced by self-monitoring

(Lippa, 1977). Finally, high self-monitors conceal their victory displays when in the presence of their opponent more than when they are alone, compared with low self-monitors (Miller-Herringer & Friedman, 1989).[9]

Summary. Numerous self-factors can be hypothesized to affect expressiveness. Whereas some of these factors have received substantial attention (e.g., gender, personality), others have not (e.g., age, values for expression). These self-factors also interact with one another and with socialization factors. Finally, the evidence supporting constitutional origins for some of these factors varies in strength; evidence supporting socialization influences in directing or creating these factors as differentiating expressiveness is generally strong.

Family expressiveness factors

Family socialization of children is an exceedingly complex, multifaceted process, during which family members are not always aware of their own goals, or the methods they use to socialize others. In an earlier section of this chapter, I chronicled the research showing that parental expressiveness affects children's expressiveness. In this section, I describe how this socialization process may occur and shall suggest four methods: modeling, reinforcement, coaching, and labeling.[10]

Modeling. Family styles of expressiveness help determine children's own style of expressiveness in three ways: First, children imitate the normal day-to-day behavior of respected, similar, or nurturing others, and this, of course, is the basic tenet of social learning theory (e.g., Bandura, 1969; Bandura, Ross, & Ross, 1961). We know that this imitative process begins in the neonatal stage within hours after birth (Field et al., 1982), and during just the third through sixth months of life alone, the average infant is exposed to over 30,000 facial expressions (Malatesta & Haviland, 1985) so that he or she has ample opportunity to learn an expressiveness style via imitation (e.g., Malatesta et al., 1986; Malatesta & Haviland, 1982). Although some observation and modeling occur out of context, for instance, during play, most observations are in context. Imitation can be an immediate process, such as in social referencing (Campos & Stenberg, 1981), during which the child turns to a respected adult for immediate guidance in defining and acting in a situation and takes on the expression (and emotion) modeled by the adult. Imitation can also be a longer-range project, in which children observe their parents arguing and store that information until much later, when they apply those styles of expression to arguments with their own spouse. This type of influence involves children's active attempts to understand the world around them and then to imitate behaviors that they identify as appropriate and desirable.

So far, we have described children as the active participants, with the parents constantly and primarily nonconsciously providing data on expressiveness in their every action. But parents can also be active participants, and a second means of influence may be the family members' specific attempts to model behavior for the children. Sometimes parents consciously model particular kinds of expressive behavior for their children, for example, in situations in which they or their children are not sure of the appropriate behavior or in unusual situations that are perceived as important learning grounds for children. And family members also occasionally model their attitudes toward expressiveness, for instance, admiring or denigrating certain kinds of expressive behavior, such as kissing in public ("sweet" or "shocking") or weeping at a funeral ("honest" or "embarrassing"). Whether children distinguish between family members' normal patterns and the behaviors or attitudes specifically modeled (and probably exaggerated) for their benefit is not known. Also, what children learn from both of these types of encounters is not only specific behaviors that can be imitated immediately or much later but also working models of the world, which children then activate in similar situations so as to interpret and respond appropriately.

A third type of influence actually involves what is not available for imitation: When older family members have homogeneous expressiveness styles, children observe a limited range of behaviors. Also, if people of similar expressiveness styles flock together, as suggested in the second section ("Family expressiveness and social consequences"), then children have little opportunity to see different styles in others. Thus, their experience of emotion expression is channeled, in that they may not become aware that other ways of expressing oneself are even possible. Whiting (1980) and Harkness and Super (1983) explained this process as assigning children to specific settings. Once the children are placed in a particular setting, only experiences characteristic of that setting are available to them.

Instrumental learning. Family members may try to control children's expressiveness by verbal and nonverbal reinforcers and punishments and by contingent responding, for example: "I know that injection probably hurt, and I am very proud that you hardly cried at all," or "I am tired of all those complaining, pouty faces that you make!" Family members' responses can be verbal, as in the examples just given, or they can be nonverbal, such as the corresponding rewarding or punishing faces that parents and siblings can make, the sudden movement or increasing tension in their bodies, and their tone of voice. Or family members may also choose to ignore behavior and not provide any ostensible response at all.

When family members do respond, the speed of response may indicate the intensity necessary to get attention, and it may also indicate an attitude toward the emotion being experienced. For example, the Kipsigis mothers of Kenya, who try to reduce crying as a social communication, wait for their tearful children to come to them before they attempt to distract them from their distress; American mothers respond more quickly to their children, going directly to the child, labeling crying events as emotional experiences, and working through the underlying causes for the behavior (Harkness & Super, 1985). It may be that low-expressive mothers act to sooth their children more quickly than do high-expressive mothers, who encourage more intense levels of arousal.

I know of no observational studies assessing family reinforcement of expressive behavior. However, Saarni's (1985) questionnaire on parental attitudes toward control of children's expressiveness (PACES) may be useful in assessing parents' reinforcement techniques and their consequences for children's expressiveness. In a study of empathy and facial expressiveness, parental control as measured on a subscale of the PACES was associated with less facial expressiveness in elementary school–aged boys (Fabes, Eisenberg, Miller, & Fultz, 1988).

Coaching. Family members may coach children in three different ways. The most obvious technique is didactic (Lewis & Saarni, 1985), in which reinforcement principles are coupled with exact instructions for the appropriate behavior ("Now remember, put a big smile on your face; say 'Thank you *very* much'; and say it as though you mean it"; or "Don't be such a namby-pamby – tell him right back what you think about that!"). Thus, children are guided with scripts that they consciously attempt to follow and for which they are reinforced, depending on their ability to enact the role. Family members may also convey more subtle expectations to children regarding what they might express and feel in particular circumstances (Saarni, 1985). Finally, parents may also create situations in which children can practice their expressiveness styles, for example, teasing one's daughter in order to give her an opportunity to practice fighting back (Miller & Sperry, 1987).

Labeling. Parents may label a child as "the expressive one" or the "inexpressive one." Such labels help the child internalize both the rules of appropriately expressive behavior and his or her role in the family for enacting particular forms and levels of expressiveness. These labels are also duly noted by other family members and friends. Then, once a child is identified in a particular way, others may tend to act in ways that will confirm the label, and the child may accept the label and seek to fulfill its meaning as well. Labels may be especially powerful when the behaviors are perceived to be unique to the child or as a consequence of his or her choices (Baumeister & Cooper, 1981; Saarni, 1985). Also, labels have their greatest impact when applied to the child, but they may also affect a child's expressiveness when applied to other individuals. For example, if a sibling is labeled the "expressive one" or the "inexpressive one," then other children in the family may understand that, conversely, they are not of that style.

Instrumental learning, coaching, and labeling may be especially prevalent in families for which behavior and values for expressiveness do not coincide. For example, parents may value certain kinds of accents other than their own, or they may value not gesticulating with one's hands while talking yet be unable to restrain their own hands from moving during a conversation. Or very high expressive parents may wish that their children are less expressive (or vice versa). In such cases, children's styles may be less stable and may follow a different developmental course as they come to understand the differences between their parents' values and behavior and as they incorporate these values into their own value system and behavioral styles.

Peer expressiveness factors

As can be seen in the model, the processes by which peers influence individuals' expressiveness are posited to be very similar to the processes by which the family influences expressiveness. The content of peer influence may agree with the family's influence, may provide different information, or may conflict with lessons learned from the family (Hartup, 1981). Further, peer impact may be greater or lesser depending on the individual's self-mediators (autonomy, need for approval, awareness of contingencies), his or her own values and/or behavior, and relative to the agreement, independence, or conflict with parental influence. There are very few studies, however, of peer influences on expressiveness, and thus I shall rely primarily on anecdotes to suggest the processes that I see as most relevant and in need of investigation.

Modeling. It is clear from many studies that children use peers' expressions to guide their own behavior (e.g, Camras, 1977; Zivin, 1982). It is likely that children also learn from those experiences that certain kinds of expressions are appropriate to, or at least successful in, certain kinds of social situations. Children may immediately adapt those expressions or may modulate their own to be more concordant with their friends' (Foot, Chapman, & Smith, 1977; Smith, Foot, & Chapman, 1977), or children may remember their friends' responses and defer imitating their peers' expressiveness styles until a later time (Hartup, 1983). Because children engage in different kinds of experiences with their peers, compared with their parents, they may see certain expressions much more frequently with their peers than their parents (e.g., guilt or shame). In their peer interactions, children may also see the presence or absence of expressions coupled with different kinds of eliciting situations (Camras, 1985). Also, children may guide one another toward different cultures with different messages about expressiveness (e.g., by watching MTV instead of the "Bill Cosby" show). Thus, children may learn new styles of and values for expressiveness in their peer niche.

Instrumental learning. Peer reinforcement and punishment has been identified for a wide variety of social behaviors, including aggression (Patterson, Littman, & Bricker, 1967) and sex-appropriate play (Fagot, 1977; Fagot & Patterson, 1969; Lamb & Roopnarine, 1979). Hartup (1983) suggests that peer reinforcement begins fairly early in life and that children's deliberate use of these techniques increases with age. That these findings generalize to expressiveness behavior can, at present, be supported only by anecdotal evidence: John, a toddler, came home one day and reported about his best friend, "Max won't let me kiss him anymore." When a motivational inquiry was made, John replied, "I guess Max thinks only his parents should kiss him." Further interactions during the week revealed that Max still wanted to play with John and to be his friend but that he no longer wanted to be kissed by his peers. Now that John has learned that Max reacts very negatively to being kissed, he can (1) chance jeopardizing the friendship by continuing to kiss Max (an unlikely choice); (2) try to identify another means of expressing affection (possible); (3) reduce his displays of affection (likely); or (4) drop Max from his play list altogether (unlikely). In addition, John may now imitate Max by not kissing his peers either. If he does, he will provide a different sort of model for other children. Further, he may now differentially reinforce his own peers' behavior and, as he gets older, possibly coach them as well.

Coaching. Although didactic teaching and role play experiences with peers are probably rare, expectations may be more common (Saarni, 1985). Children do seem to have many expectations about how others ought to behave and may well make suggestions regarding how they might express themselves in certain situations in which they are not involved. Although I am not aware of any research on this topic, recent programs in mediation techniques at the primary and secondary school level might allow opportunities for such investigations.

Labeling. As with families, being identified as the "loud one" or the "quiet one" in the group may have a powerful impact on a child's behavior with his or her peers. Also, recognizing another member of the group as "loud" or "quiet" can help the child identify his or her own style as different.

Summary. Though few studies have examined peers' influences on individuals' expressive styles, peer influence using the four socialization methods seems probable. This area is rich in research possibilities in terms of direct peer influence on children's values for, appraisals of, and actual behavioral expressiveness and in terms of the interactions among peer, family, and societal influences and self-factors.

Self-mediators

All of these socialization processes are from the perspective of the socializer, but children's understanding and willingness to be influenced by these processes are relevant as well. For example, social learning theory clearly suggests the importance of parental modeling of expressive behaviors and also children's subsequent choices to imitate those behaviors. Ultimately, the internalization of values for expressive behavior and the adoption of actual behaviors are consequences of the children's choices. That is, children decide which individuals to imitate and which behaviors to adopt. The effects of instrumental learning and coaching are also clearly demonstrated, but individual differences in learning contingencies and in willingness to engage in behaviors on partial reinforcement schedules probably varies as a function of children's autonomy seeking, need for approval, and the degree to which the child understands that the behaviors are being similarly or differentially reinforced within the three socialization ellipses and for that child's self-factors (e.g., sex and age). Thus, children's willingness to be acted upon affects how well he or she learns the lesson. Finally, in regard to labeling, the degree to which children's behavior is influenced at least partially depends on the children's accepting the labels. Saarni (1985) made a similar point in her discussion of expectation, suggestion, and expectancy in acquiring emotions. Parents, peers, and others may have expectations that they may or may not convey to their children. If the child processes the expectation as a meaningful communication, then the expectation will become a suggestion that the child must evaluate and accept, resist, or reject. An accepted suggestion becomes internalized as an expectancy. The acceptance of labels and suggestions may depend on how well they fit with a child's already developing self-concept (see Swann, 1987, for a review). Thus, four kinds of socializing processes can influence a child, but in turn he or she must accept and internalize them. Finally, although our discussion has focused on children as the individuals to be socialized, these socialization processes and agents are influential throughout the life span.

Summary

In the first part of this chapter, I chronicled the evidence for a relationship between family styles of expressiveness and individuals' own personal styles of expressiveness. It appears that the process by which infants come to share the expressiveness styles of their families begins very early (e.g., Field et al., 1982; Malatesta & Haviland, 1982) and continues well into adulthood (e.g., Burrowes & Halberstadt, 1987; Gallegos & Friedman, 1989). Then, I discussed nonverbal communication skill and successful social interactions as two probable types of consequences associated with family expressiveness styles. Finally, I developed a more comprehensive model of expressiveness, which includes a wide range of socialization influences and some constitutional variables as well. This model emphasizes socialization as a major influence on individuals' expressiveness styles and describes socialization as composed of many processes with several sources that are successful only when an individual is receptive to them. These socialization processes are usually nonverbal, usually subtle, and often involve respected or loved individuals. There is now a great deal of evidence that many of the sources identified in the model are successful at socializing individuals, although much work needs to be done regarding peer influences and in assessing the validity and frequency of the processes by which family and peer socialization occur.

Notes

1. In at least some families, it is likely that individuals vary from one another in their expressiveness levels; that the expressiveness levels of individuals, and thus of the family as a whole, may vary over time; and that there may be milestones that affect the family's expressiveness. Nevertheless, reports of family expressiveness indicate that subjects can provide averaged estimates of the expressiveness of their families, and these reports indicate a substantial amount of temporal stability (Halberstadt, 1986).
2. Children may also influence family communication styles as well as be influenced by them, and developmental theory has increasingly emphasized the dual direction of social interaction influence. Research, however, has lagged behind theory, and few reports on children's influence on the expressive tenor of the home are available.
3. This questionnaire is the most frequently used measure of family styles of expressiveness in the research reported in this chapter. For 40 items, subjects report the frequency of events like "Expressing exhilaration after an unexpected triumph" and "Telling a family member how hurt you are" in their family while the subject was growing up, using 9-point Likert scales. Positive items are summed into one scale, and negative items are summed into another. The questionnaire is internally consistent and reliable over time (Halberstadt, 1983), and parents and college-age students agree on their family expressiveness while the students were growing up (Burrowes & Halberstadt, 1987). Correlations between family expressiveness and shyness, self-monitoring, and self-expressiveness are low to moderate, suggesting good discriminant validity (Burrowes & Halberstadt, 1987; Gallegos & Friedman, 1989; Halberstadt, 1986). Finally, the network of relationships found in research with the questionnaire indicates good construct validity for the FEQ.
4. Another hypothesis that could be tested is whether the relationship between expressiveness and social interaction is differently affected by family socialization. For example, individuals from more-expressive homes might become more expressive in the presence of others than while alone, relative to individuals from less-expressive homes. And individuals from less-expressive homes might be less expressive in the presence of others than while alone. Of course, such interaction would also depend on the kind of social interaction and emotion being experienced.
    Another issue regarding the consequences of parental expressiveness styles is the influence of parental consistency and inconsistency across channels and across affects on children's affective and expressive develop-

ment. In his "double-bind" theory of schizophrenia, Bateson hypothesized that inconsistent (incongruent) communications cause affective childhood disturbances (Bateson, Jackson, Haley, & Weakland, 1956). Although today there are few adherents to the double-bind theory, some studies suggest that certain types of socioemotional problems are associated with parents' inconsistent communication styles (e.g., Bugental, Love, Kaswan, & April, 1971). Other studies, however, indicate that positive outcomes are associated with at least certain kinds of incongruent or "diverse" communications relative to congruent or "redundant" communications (Beakel & Mehrabian, 1969; Hall, Roter, & Rand, 1981; Lessin & Jacob, 1984; Woolfolk, 1978). No studies specifically address the consequences of inconsistent ("diverse") communications for children's expressiveness styles, although hypotheses can easily be generated.

5. Another model for the development of expressive behavior, based on a six-component framework using a computer analog and 17 processes, was constructed by Zivin (1986). Her comprehensive framework organizes five major theories of emotion and emotion expression and seeks a synthesis in a fragmented area in socioemotional development. Zivin identified areas of consensus regarding normative emotion expression development and delineated the process by which an emotion expression occurs. Because these theorists' perspective is the reflection hypothesis and because my model evolves from a communication perspective, I seek my own path, a path biased in favor of socialization processes and individual differences.

In this chapter, I focus on expressiveness of emotion, but many aspects of this model are important in describing how individuals come to experience emotion as well as express it. Although it is often difficult to disentangle individuals' experiences and expressions of emotion (see Sommers, 1984, for a successful example of distinguishing between the two), I shall concentrate on the expression of emotion.

6. Harkness and Super (1983, 1985) discuss two other dimensions in socialization. One is the set of typical physical and social settings (or "niche") in which children develop, and the other is the issue of who is in charge. When infants and toddlers are not perceived as having achieved reason or restraint (e.g., Utku and Javanese cultures), then it is clear that parents must manage their children's affective and physical states. However, societies that identify infants as socializable may be distinguished according to whether they place responsibility for socialization solely on the caretaker or on the infant and the caretaker as the two parties negotiate a mutually acceptable balance of power. Caretaking in the United States and Europe, especially among the middle and upper classes, might be characterized at the shared responsibility end of the spectrum, based on the negotiations that occur even during infancy and the acceptance of individual differences in willfulness.

7. In a somewhat related study on caretaking styles, Caudill and Weinstein (1969) distinguished between American mothers' more active, stimulating style of caretaking and Japanese mothers' more passive, soothing style. Other studies of American and Japanese mothers replicate some of these findings and identify other differences (e.g., Fogel, Joda & Kawai, 1988; Kanaya, Nakamura, & Miyake, 1987–1988; Otaki, Durrett, Richards, Nyquist, & Pennebaker, 1986). Although group constitutional differences have been noted in infants (e.g., Freedman, 1979, 1984), these caretaking differences appear to be influenced by socialization norms and goals as

much as by any genetic variation. Given an identical infant state, American and Japanese mothers respond quite differently (e.g., American mothers chat with an alert baby, whereas Japanese mothers lull an alert baby), and they use the same mothering behavior in response to different infant states (e.g., American mothers chat to happy infant vocalizing, whereas Japanese mothers chat to unhappy infant vocalizing). These caretaking differences may affect expressiveness in children by establishing different contingencies in infancy.

8. These results bear some resemblance to those evaluating the relationship between the dimension of inhibitedness and heart rate variability (Kagan, Reznick, Clarke, Snidman, & Garcia-Coll, 1984; Kagan, Reznick, & Gibbons, 1989; Kagan et al., 1987, 1988). The inhibitedness construct is distinct from expressiveness, however, in that it (1) was developed based on a variety of behaviors, of which only some relate to expressiveness, (2) is occasionally described as the personality trait of shyness, and (3) relies on the concept of psychological uncertainty as well as physiological arousal.

9. These findings provide the substance for the personality hypothesis that I outlined in the introduction. Although personality variables may influence expressiveness, expressiveness styles may also affect attributions regarding people's underlying nature. The causal relationships are not clear, and the size of the correlations suggests that many additional factors are at work in influencing expressiveness styles.

10. The socialization process has also been described as including direct processes (instrumental learning, classical conditioning, and didactic teaching) and indirect processes (identification, imitation, and social learning) (e.g., Lewis, 1987; Lewis & Saarni, 1985). The distinction that seems most relevant is the agency of the actor, that is, who is doing the work.

References

Allen, J. G., & Haccoun, D. M. (1976). Sex differences in emotionality: A multidimensional approach. *Human Relations, 29,* 711–722.

Allport, G. W., & Cantril, H. (1934). Judging personality from voice. *Journal of Social Psychology, 5,* 37–54.

Anisfeld, E. (1982). The onset of social smiling in preterm and full-term infants from two ethnic backgrounds. *Infant Behavior and Development, 5,* 387–395.

Asendorpf, J. B., & Scherer, K. R. (1983). The discrepant repressor: Differentiation between low anxiety, high anxiety, and repression of anxiety by autonomic–facial–verbal patterns of behavior. *Journal of Personality and Social Psychology, 45,* 1334–1346.

Averill, J. R. (1982). *Anger & aggression: An essay on emotion.* New York: Springer-Verlag.

Balswick, J., & Avertt, C. P. (1977). Differences in expressiveness: Gender, interpersonal orientation, and perceived parental expressiveness as contributing factors. *Journal of Marriage and the Family, 39,* 121–127.

Bandura, A. (1969). Social-learning theory of identificatory processes. In D. A. Goslin (Ed.), *Handbook of socialization theory and research* (pp. 213–262). Chicago: Rand-McNally.

Bandura, A., Ross, D., & Ross, S. A. (1961). Transmission of aggression through imitation of aggressive models. *Journal of Abnormal and Social Psychology, 63,* 575–582.

Barrett, K. C., & Campos, J. J. (1987). Perspectives on emotional development II: A functionalist approach to emotions. In J. D. Osofsky (Ed.), *Handbook of infant development* (2nd ed., pp. 555–578). New York: Wiley.

Bateson, G., Jackson, D. D., Haley, J., & Weakland, J. (1956). Toward a theory of schizophrenia. *Behavior Science, 1*, 251–264.

Baumeister, R. F., & Cooper, J. (1981). Can the public expectation of emotion cause that emotion? *Journal of Personality, 49*, 49–59.

Beakel, N. G., & Mehrabian, A. (1969). Inconsistent communications and psychopathology. *Journal of Abnormal Psychology, 74*, 126–130.

Birnbaum, D. W., & Croll, W. L. (1984). The etiology of children's stereotypes about sex differences in emotionality. *Sex Roles, 10*, 677–691.

Blanck, P., Zuckerman, M., DePaulo, B., & Rosenthal, R. (1980). Sibling resemblances in nonverbal skill and style. *Journal of Nonverbal Behavior, 4*, 219–226.

Bridges, K. M. B. (1932). Emotional development in early infancy. *Child Development, 3*, 324–341.

Briggs, J. L. (1970). *Never in anger.* Cambridge, MA: Harvard University Press.

Brody, L. R. (1985). Gender differences in emotional development: A review of theories and research. *Journal of Personality, 53*, 102–149.

Brody, L. R., & Landau, L. B. (1984, August). *Mothers' emotional styles and preschoolers' emotional attributions.* Paper presented at the meeting of the American Psychological Association, Toronto.

Buck, R. (1975). Nonverbal communication of affect in children. *Journal of Personality and Social Psychology, 31*, 644–653.

(1977). Nonverbal communication of affect in preschool children: Relationships with personality and skin conductance. *Journal of Personality and Social Psychology, 35*, 225–236.

(1982). Spontaneous and symbolic nonverbal behavior and the ontogeny of communication. In R. S. Feldman (Ed.), *Development of nonverbal behavior in children* (pp. 29–62). New York: Springer-Verlag.

(1984). *The communication of emotion.* New York: Guilford Press.

Buck, R., Baron, R., & Barrette, D. (1982). Temporal organization of spontaneous nonverbal expression: A segmentation analysis. *Journal of Personality and Social Psychology, 42*, 506–517.

Buck, R., Baron, R., Goodman, N., & Shapiro, B. (1980). Unitization of spontaneous nonverbal behavior in the study of emotion communication. *Journal of Personality and Social Psychology, 39*, 522–529.

Buck, R., Miller, R. E., & Caul, W. F. (1974). Sex, personality, and physiological variables in the communication of affect via facial expression. *Journal of Personality and Social Psychology, 30*, 587–596.

Buck, R. W., Savin, V. J., Miller, R. E., & Caul, W. F. (1972). Nonverbal communication of affect through facial expressions in humans. *Journal of Personality and Social Psychology, 23*, 362–371.

Buck, R., & Teng, W. (1987, August). Spontaneous emotional communication and social biofeedback: A cross-cultural study of emotional expression and communication in Chinese and Taiwanese students. In A. G. Halberstadt (Chair), *Social and biological influences on expressivity.* Symposium conducted at the meeting of the American Psychological Association, New York City.

Bugental, D. E., Kaswan, J. W., & Love, L. R. (1970). Perception of contradictory meanings conveyed by verbal and nonverbal channels. *Journal of Personality and Social Psychology, 16*, 645–655.

Bugental, D. E., Love, L. R., & Gianetto, R. M. (1971). Perfidious feminine faces. *Journal of Personality and Social Psychology, 17*, 314–318.

Bugental, D. E., Love, L. R., Kaswan, J. W., & April, C. (1971). Verbal–nonverbal conflict in parental messages to normal and disturbed children. *Journal of Abnormal Psychology, 77,* 6–10.

Burrowes, B. D., & Halberstadt, A. G. (1987). Self- and family-expressiveness styles in the experience and expression of anger. *Journal of Nonverbal Behavior, 11,* 254–268.

Campos, J. J., & Barrett, K. C. (1984). Toward a new understanding of emotions and their development. In C. E. Izard, J. Kagan, & R. B. Zajonc (Eds.), *Emotions, cognition, and behavior* (pp. 273–314). Cambridge: Cambridge University Press.

Campos, J. J., & Stenberg, C. R. (1981). Perception, appraisal and emotion: The onset of social referencing. In M. E. Lamb & L. R. Sherrod (Eds.), *Infant social cognition: Empirical and theoretical considerations* (pp. 273–314). Hillsdale, NJ: Erlbaum.

Camras, L. A., (1977). Facial expressions used by children in a conflict situation. *Child Development, 48,* 1431–1435.

(1985). Socialization of affect communication. In M. Lewis & C. Saarni (Eds.), *The socialization of emotions* (pp. 141–160). New York: Plenum.

Camras, L. A., Ribordy, S., Hill, J., Martino, S., Sachs, V., Spaccarelli, S., & Stefani, R. (1990). Maternal facial behavior and the recognition and production of emotional expression by maltreated and nonmaltreated children. *Developmental Psychology, 26,* 304–312.

Camras, L. A., Ribordy, S., Hill, J., Martino, S., Spaccarelli, S., & Stefani, R. (1988). Recognition and posing of emotional expressions by abused children and their mothers. *Developmental Psychology, 24,* 776–781.

Cassidy, J., & Parke, R. D. (1989, April). Family expressiveness and children's social competence. In R. D. Parke (Chair), *Emotional expression in the family.* Symposium conducted at the meeting of the Society for Research in Child Development, Kansas City, Mo.

Caudill, W., & Weinstein, H. (1969). Maternal care and infant behavior in Japan and America. *Psychiatry, 32,* 12–43.

Christian, C., & Worell, J. (1989, May). *Paths to loneliness.* Paper presented at the Nags Head Sex and Gender Conference, Nags Head, NC.

Cummings, E. M. (1987). Coping with background anger in early childhood. *Child Development, 58,* 976–984.

Cummings, E. M., Iannotti, R. J., & Zahn-Waxler, C. (1985). Influence of conflict between adults on the emotions and aggression of young children. *Developmental Psychology, 21,* 495–507.

Cummings, E. M., Zahn-Waxler, C., & Radke-Yarrow, M. (1981). Young children's responses to expressions of anger and affection by others in the family. *Child Development, 52,* 1274–1282.

(1984). Developmental changes in children's reactions to anger in the home. *Journal of Child Psychology and Psychiatry, 25,* 63–74.

Cunningham, M. R. (1977). Personality and the structure of the nonverbal communication of emotion. *Journal of Personality, 45,* 564–584.

Daly, E. M., Abramovitch, R., & Pliner, P. (1980). The relationship between mothers' encoding and their children's decoding of facial expressions of emotion. *Merrill–Palmer Quarterly, 26,* 25–33.

Denham, S. A. (1987, April). *Preschoolers' mothers' expression of and coping with emotion.* Poster presented at the meeting of the Society for Research in Child Development, Baltimore.

(1989). Maternal affect and toddlers' social–emotional competence. *American Journal of Orthopsychiatry, 59,* 368–376.

(1990). *Maternal emotional responsiveness and toddlers' social–emotional competence.* Unpublished manuscript. George Mason University, Fairfax, VA.

Denham, S. A., & Couchoud, E. A. (1988, March). Knowledge about emotions: Relations with socialization and social behavior. In J. Gnepp (Chair), *Emotion knowledge and emotional development.* Symposium conducted at the meeting of the Conference on Human Development, Charleston, SC.

DePaulo, B., Rosenthal, R., Eisenstat, R., Rogers, P., & Finkelstein, S. (1978). Decoding discrepant nonverbal cues. *Journal of Personality and Social Psychology, 36,* 313–323.

DiMatteo, M. R., Hays, R. D., & Prince, L. M. (1986). Relationship of physicians' nonverbal communication skill to patient satisfaction, appointment noncompliance, and physician workload. *Health Psychology, 5,* 581–594.

Diskin, S. D., & Heinicke, C. M. (1986). Maternal style of emotional expression. *Infant Behavior and Development, 9,* 167–187.

Dixon, S., Tronick, E., Keefer, C., & Brazelton, T. B. (1981). Mother–infant interaction among the Gusii of Kenya. In T. M. Field, A. M. Sostek, P. Vietze, & P. H. Leiderman (Eds.), *Culture and early interaction* (pp. 149–168). Hillsdale, NJ: Erlbaum.

Dunn, J., Bretherton, I., & Munn, P. (1987). Conversations about feeling states between mothers and their young children. *Developmental Psychology, 23,* 132–139.

Eisenberg, N., Fabes, R. A., Schaller, M., & Miller, P. A. (1989). Sympathy and personal distress: Development, gender differences, and interrelations of indices. In N. Eisenberg (Ed.), *New Directions in Child Development* (Vol. 44, pp. 107–126). San Francisco: Jossey-Bass.

Ekman, P. (1972). Universals and cultural differences in facial expressions of emotion. In J. K. Cole (Ed.), *Nebraska Symposium on Motivation, 1971* (Vol. 19, pp. 207–283). Lincoln: University of Nebraska Press.

Ekman, P., & Friesen, W. V. (1969). Nonverbal leakage and clues to deception. *Psychiatry, 32,* 88–106.

(1971). Constants across cultures in the face and emotion. *Journal of Personality and Social Psychology, 17,* 124–129.

Ekman, P., Levenson, R. W., & Friesen, W. V. (1983). Autonomic nervous system activity distinguishes among emotions. *Science, 221,* 1208–1210.

Ekman, P., & Oster, H. (1979). Facial expressions of emotion. *Annual Review of Psychology, 30,* 527–554.

Ellgring, H. (1986). Nonverbal expression of psychological states in psychiatric patients. *European Archives of Psychiatry and Neurological Sciences, 236,* 31–34.

Estes, S. G. (1938). Judging personality from expressive behavior. *Journal of Abnormal and Social Psychology, 33,* 217–236.

Eysenck, H. J. (1967). *The biological basis of personality.* Springfield, IL: Thomas.

Fabes, R. A., Eisenberg, N., & Miller, P. (1989). *Maternal correlates of children's empathic responsiveness.* Manuscript submitted for publication.

Fabes, R. A., Eisenberg, N., Miller, P., & Fultz, J. (1988, November). *Mother's attitudes towards emotional expressiveness and children's emotional responsiveness.* Paper presented at the annual meeting of the National Council on Family Relations, Philadelphia.

Fagot, B. I. (1977). Consequences of moderate cross-gender behavior in preschool children. *Child Development, 48,* 902–907.

Fagot, B. I., & Patterson, G. R. (1969). An *in vivo* analysis of reinforcing contingencies for sex-role behaviors in the preschool child. *Developmental Psychology, 1,* 563–568.

Feldman, R. S., Jenkins, L., & Popoola, O. (1979). Detection of deception in adults and children via facial expressions. *Child Development, 50,* 350–355.

Feldman, R. S., & White, J. B. (1980). Detecting deception in children. *Journal of Communication, 30,* 121–128.

Field, T. (1982). Individual differences in the expressivity of neonates and young children. In R. S. Feldman (Ed.), *Development of nonverbal behavior in children* (pp. 279–298). New York: Springer-Verlag.

   (1984). Early interactions between infants and their postpartum depressed mothers. *Infant Behavior and Development, 7,* 19–26.

   (1985). Neonatal perception of people: Maturational and individual differences. In T. Field and N. Fox (Eds.), *Social perception in infants* (pp. 31–52). Norwood, NJ: Ablex.

   (1987). Affective and interactive disturbances in infants. In J. D. Osofsky (Ed.), *Handbook of infant development* (2nd ed., pp. 972–1005). New York: Wiley.

Field, T., Healy, B., Goldstein, S., Perry, S., Schanberg, S., Zimmerman, E. A., & Kuhn, C. (1988). Infants of depressed mothers show "depressed" behavior even with nondepressed adults. *Child Development, 59,* 1569–1579.

Field, T., Sandberg, D., Garcia, R., Vega-Lahr, N., Goldstein, S., & Guy, L. (1985). Pregnancy problems, postpartum depression, and early mother–infant interactions. *Developmental Psychology, 21,* 1152–1156.

Field, T., & Walden, T. A. (1982). Production and perception of facial expressions in infancy and early childhood. In H. W. Reese & L. P. Lipsett (Eds.), *Advances in child development and behavior* (Vol. 16, pp. 169–211). New York: Academic Press.

Field, T. M., Woodson, R., Greenberg, R., & Cohen, D. (1982). Discrimination and imitation of facial expressions by neonates. *Science, 218,* 179–181.

Fogel, A., Toda, S., & Kawai, M. (1988). Mother–infant face-to-face interaction in Japan and the United States: A laboratory comparison using 3-month-old infants. *Developmental Psychology, 24,* 398–406.

Foot, H. C., Chapman, A. J., & Smith, J. R. (1977). Friendship and social responsiveness in boys and girls. *Journal of Personality and Social Psychology, 35,* 401–411.

Fox, N., & Gelles, M. G. (1984). Face-to-face interaction in term and preterm infants. *Infant Mental Health Journal, 5,* 192–205.

Frable, D. E. (1987). Sex-typed execution and perception of expressive movement. *Journal of Personality and Social Psychology, 53,* 391–396.

Freedman, D. G. (1979). *Human sociobiology: A holistic approach.* New York: Free Press.

   (1984). *Human infancy: An evolutionary approach.* Hillsdale, NJ: Erlbaum.

Friedman, H. S., Prince, L. M., Riggio, R. E., & DiMatteo, M. R. (1980). Understanding and assessing nonverbal expressiveness: The Affective Communication Test. *Journal of Personality and Social Psychology, 39,* 333–351.

Friedman, H. S., & Riggio, R. E. (1981). Effect of individual differences in nonverbal expressiveness on transmission of emotion. *Journal of Nonverbal Behavior, 6,* 96–104.

Frodi, A. M., Lamb, M. E., Leavitt, L. A., & Donovan, W. L. (1978). Fathers' and mothers' responses to infant smiles and cries. *Infant Behavior and Development, 1,* 187–198.

Fuchs, D., & Thelen, M. H. (1988). Children's expected interpersonal consequences of communicating their affective state and reported likelihood of expression. *Child Development, 59,* 1314–1322.

Gallegos, P., & Friedman, H. S. (1989). *The influence of family interaction and culture on the development of individual nonverbal expressivity: A focus on Hispanic women.* Manuscript submitted for publication.

Geertz, H. (1959). The vocabulary of emotion. *Psychiatry, 22,* 225–237.

Gerson, A. C., & Perlman, D. (1979). Loneliness and expressive communication. *Journal of Abnormal Psychology, 88,* 258–261.

Gray, J. A. (1971). *The psychology of fear and stress.* New York: McGraw-Hill.

Grief, E. B., Alvarez, M., & Ulman, K. (1981, April). *Recognizing emotions in other people: Sex differences in socialization.* Paper presented at the meeting of the Society for Research in Child Development, Boston.

Halberstadt, A. G. (1981). The relationship between family expressiveness and nonverbal communicative behavior. *Dissertations Abstract International, 42,* 1670B–1671B. (University Microfilms No. 8120025).

(1983). Family expressiveness styles and nonverbal communication skills. *Journal of Nonverbal Behavior, 8,* 14–26.

(1984). Family expression of emotion. In C. Z. Malatesta & C. E. Izard (Eds.), *Emotion in adult development* (pp. 235–252). Beverly Hills, CA: Sage.

(1985). Race, socioeconomic status, and nonverbal behavior. In A. Siegman & S. Feldstein (Eds.), *Nonverbal communication and interpersonal relations* (pp. 227–266). Hillsdale, NJ: Erlbaum.

(1986). Family socialization of emotional expression and nonverbal communication styles and skills. *Journal of Personality and Social Psychology, 51,* 827–836.

Halberstadt, A. G., & Fox, N. (1990, March). *Mothers' and their children's expressiveness and emotionality.* Poster presented at the Conference for Human Development, Richmond, VA.

Halberstadt, A. G., Fox, N., & Aaron, N. (1990). *Do expressive mothers have expressive kids? The role of socialization and physiological factors on children's affect expression.* Unpublished manuscript. North Carolina State University, Raleigh, NC.

Halberstadt, A. G., Hayes, C. W., & Pike, K. M. (1988). Gender and gender role differences in smiling and communication consistency. *Sex Roles, 19,* 589–604.

Halberstadt, A. G., Hoeft, S., & Tesh, M. (1990, March). *Self- and family expressiveness and emotionality correlates in friendship choices.* Poster presented at the Conference for Human Development, Richmond, VA.

Halberstadt, A. G., & Saitta, M. B. (1987). Gender, nonverbal behavior, and dominance: A test of the theory. *Journal of Personality and Social Psychology, 53,* 257–272.

Halberstadt, A. G., Tesh, M., & Hoeft, S. (1989). *Self- and family-expressiveness styles and friendship choices.* Unpublished manuscript. Vassar College, Poughkeepsie, NY.

Hall, J. A. (1984). *Nonverbal sex differences: Communication accuracy and expressive styles.* Baltimore: Johns Hopkins University Press.

Hall, J. A., Roter, D. L., & Rand, C. S. (1981). Communication of affect between patient and physician. *Journal of Health and Social Behavior, 22,* 18–30.

Hanna, J. L. (1984). Black/white nonverbal differences, dance, and dissonance: Implications for desegregation. In A. Wolfgang (Ed.), *Nonverbal behavior: Perspectives, applications, intercultural insights* (pp. 373–409). Lewiston, NY: Hofgrefe.

Harper, R. G., Wiens, A. N., & Matarazzo, J. D. (1979). The relationship between encoding–decoding of visual nonverbal emotional cues. *Semiotica, 28,* 171–192.

Harkness, S., & Super, C. M. (1983). The cultural construction of child development: A framework for the socialization of affect. *Ethos, 11,* 221–231.

(1985). Child–environment interactions in the socialization of affect. In M. Lewis & C. Saarni (Eds.), *The socialization of emotions* (pp. 21–36). New York: Plenum.

Hartup, W. W. (1981). Peer relations and family relations: Two social worlds. In M. Rutter (Ed.), *Scientific foundations of developmental psychiatry* (pp. 280–292). Baltimore: University Park Press.

(1983). Peer relations. In P. H. Mussen & E. M. Hetherington (Eds.), *Handbook of child psychology: Socialization, personality, and social development* (Vol. 4, pp. 103–196). New York: Wiley.

Haviland, J. J., & Malatesta, C. Z. (1981). A description of the development of sex differences in non-verbal signals: Fantasies, fallacies and facts. In C. Mayo & N. Henley (Eds.), *Gender and nonverbal behavior* (pp. 183–208). New York: Springer-Verlag.

Haviland, J. M., & Lelwica, M. (1987). The induced affect response: 10-week-old infants' responses to three emotion expressions. *Developmental Psychology, 23,* 97–104.

Hochschild, A. R. (1979). Emotion work, feeling rules, and social structure. *American Journal of Sociology, 85,* 551–575.

Huston, A. C. (1983). Sex-typing. In P. H. Mussen & E. M. Hetherington (Eds.), *Handbook of child psychology: Socialization, personality, and social development* (Vol. 4, pp. 387–467). New York: Wiley.

Izard, C. E. (1971). *The face of emotion.* New York: Appleton-Century-Crofts.

(1977). *Human emotions.* New York: Plenum.

Izard, C. E., & Malatesta, C. Z. (1987). Perspectives on emotional development I: Differential emotions theory of early emotional development. In J. D. Osofsky (Ed.), *Handbook of infant development* (pp. 494–554). New York: Wiley.

Jones, H. E. (1950). The study of patterns of emotional expression. In M. L. Reymert (Ed.), *Feelings and emotions* (pp. 161–168). New York: McGraw-Hill.

(1960). The longitudinal method in the study of personality. In I. Iscoe and H. W. Stevenson (Eds.), *Personality development in children* (pp. 3–27). Austin: University of Texas Press.

Kagan, J., Reznick, J. S., Clarke, C., Snidman, N., & Garcia-Coll, C. (1984). Behavioral inhibition to the unfamiliar. *Child Development, 55,* 2212–2225.

Kagan, J., Reznick, J. S., & Gibbons, J. (1989). Inhibited and uninhibited types of children. *Child Development, 60,* 838–845.

Kagan, J., Reznick, J. S., & Snidman, N. (1987). The physiology and psychology of behavioral inhibition in children. *Child Development, 58,* 1459–1473.

Kagan, J., Reznick, J. S., Snidman, N., Gibbons, J., & Johnson, M. O. (1988). Childhood derivatives of inhibition and lack of inhibition to the unfamiliar. *Child Development, 59,* 1580–1589.

Kanaya, Y., Nakamura, C., & Miyake, K. (1987–1988). Cross-cultural study of expressive behavior of mothers in response to their 5-month-old infants' different emotion expression. *Research and Clinical Center for Child Development, 11,* 25–31.

King, L. A., & Emmons, R. A. (1990). Conflict over emotional expression: Psychological and physical correlates. *Journal of Personality and Social Psychology, 58,* 864–877.

Klinnert, M. D. (1984). The regulation of infant behavior by maternal facial expression. *Infant Behavior and Development, 7,* 447–465.

Klions, D. E., Sanders, K. S., Hudak, M. A., Dale, J. A., & Klions, H. L. (1987). Facial action patterns, electromyography, and moods in response to an insoluble task as a function of sex and sex-role differences. *Perceptual & Motor Skills, 65,* 495–502.

Kochman, T. (1981). *Black and white styles in conflict.* Chicago: University of Chicago Press.

Kopp, C. B. (1982). Antecedents of self-regulation: A developmental perspective. *Developmental Psychology, 18,* 199–214.

Kraut, R. E., & Johnston, R. E. (1979). Social and emotional messages of smiling: An ethological approach. *Journal of Personality and Social Psychology, 37,* 1539–1553.

LaFrance, M., & Carmen, B. (1980). The nonverbal display of psychological androgyny. *Journal of Personality and Social Psychology, 38,* 36–49.

Lamb, M. E., & Roopnarine, J. L. (1979). Peer influence on sex-role development in preschoolers. *Child Development, 50,* 1219–1222.

Lambert, W. E., Hamers, J. F., & Frasure-Smith, N. (1979). *Child rearing values: A cross-national study.* New York: Praeger.

Landau, R. (1977). Spontaneous and elicited smiles and vocalizations of infants in four Israeli environments. *Developmental Psychology, 13,* 389–400.

Lanzetta, J. T., & Kleck, R. E. (1970). Encoding and decoding of nonverbal affect in humans. *Journal of Personality and Social Psychology, 16,* 12–19.

Larsen, R. J., & Diener, E. (1987). Affect intensity as an individual difference characteristic: A review. *Journal of Research in Personality, 21,* 1–39.

Larsen, R. J., Diener, E., & Emmons, R. A. (1986). Affect intensity and reactions to daily life events. *Journal of Personality and Social Psychology, 51,* 803–814.

Lessin, S., & Jacob, T. (1984). Multichannel communication in normal and delinquent families. *Journal of Abnormal Child Psychology, 12,* 369–384.

Lewis, D. K. (1975). The black family: Socialization and sex roles. *Phylon, 36,* 221–237.

Lewis, M. (1987). Social development in infancy and early childhood. In J. D. Osofsky (Ed.), *Handbook of infant development* (2nd ed., pp. 419–493). New York: Wiley.

Lewis, M., & Michalson, L. (1983). *Children's emotions and moods: Developmental theory and measurement.* New York: Plenum.

Lewis, M., & Saarni, C. (1985). Culture and emotions. In M. Lewis & C. Saarni (Eds.), *The socialization of emotions* (pp. 1–16). New York: Plenum.

Lippa, R. (1977). Expressive control, expressive consistency, and the correspondence between expressive behavior and personality. *Journal of Personality, 46,* 438–461.

——— (1978). The naive perception of masculinity–femininity on the basis of expressive cues. *Journal of Research in Personality, 12,* 1–14.

Maccoby, E. E., & Martin, J. A. (1983). Socialization in the context of the family: Parent–child interaction. In P. H. Mussen & E. M. Hetherington (Eds.), *Handbook of child psychology: Socialization, personality, and social development* (Vol. 4, pp. 1–101). New York: Wiley.

Malatesta, C. Z. (1981). Affective development over the lifespan: Involution or growth? *Merrill–Palmer Quarterly, 27,* 145–173.

Malatesta, C. Z., & Fiore, M. (1985, June). *The meaning of affect in older faces.* Paper presented at the British Psychological Association International Conference, Cardiff, Wales.

Malatesta, C. Z., Grigoryev, P., Lamb, C., Albin, M., & Culver, C. (1986). Emo-

158   Amy G. Halberstadt

tion socialization and expressive development in preterm and full-term infants. *Child Development, 57,* 316–330.
Malatesta, C. Z., & Haviland, J. M. (1982). Learning display rules: The socialization of emotion expression in infancy. *Child Development, 53,* 991–1003.
(1985). Signals, symbols, and socialization: The modification of emotional expression in human development. In M. Lewis & C. Saarni (Eds.), *The socialization of emotions* (pp. 89–116). New York: Plenum.
Malatesta, C. Z., & Izard, C. E. (1984). The facial expression of emotion: Young,
middle-aged, and older adult expressions. In C. Z. Malatesta & C. E. Izard
(Eds.), *Emotion in adult development* (pp. 253–273). Beverly Hills, CA: Sage.
Malatesta, C. Z., & Kalnok, M. (1984). Emotional experience in younger and
older adults. *Journal of Gerontology, 39,* 301–308.
Manstead, A. S. R. (1988). The role of facial movement in emotion. In H. L.
Wagner (Ed.), *Social psychophysiology: Theory & clinical applications* (pp. 105–
129). New York: Wiley.
Miller, P., & Sperry, L. L. (1987). The socialization of anger and aggression.
Merrill–Palmer Quarterly, 33, 1–31.
Miller-Herringer, T., & Friedman, H. S. (1989). *The nonverbal display of emotion in
public and private conditions: Expressive cues, self-monitoring, and personality.*
Manuscript submitted for publication.
Noller, P. (1978). Sex differences in the socialization of affectionate expression.
Developmental Psychology, 14, 317–319.
(1982). Channel consistency and inconsistency in the communications of mar-
ried couples. *Journal of Personality and Social Psychology, 43,* 732–741.
Noller, P., & Callan, V. J. (1989). Nonverbal behavior in families with adoles-
cents. *Journal of Nonverbal Behavior, 13,* 47–64.
Notarius, C. I., & Levenson, R. W. (1979). Expressive tendencies and physiologi-
cal response to stress. *Journal of Personality and Social Psychology, 37,* 1204–1210.
Otaki, M., Durrett, M. E., Richards, P., Nyquist, L., & Pennebaker, J. W. (1986).
Maternal and infant behavior in Japan and America: A partial replication.
Journal of Cross-cultural Psychology, 17, 251–268.
Patterson, G. R., Littman, R. A., & Bricker, W. (1967). Assertive behavior in
children: A step toward a theory of aggression. *Monographs of the Society for
Research in Child Development, 32,* (5, Serial No. 113).
Plomin, R., Pedersen, N. L., McClearn, G. E., Nesselroade, J. R., & Bergeman,
C. S. (1988). EAS temperaments during the last half of the life span: Twins
reared apart and twins reared together. *Psychology and Aging, 3,* 43–50.
Porges, S. W. (1974). Heart rate indices of newborn attentional responsivity.
Merrill–Palmer Quarterly, 20, 231–254.
(1983). Heart rate patterns in neonates: A potential diagnostic window to the
brain. In T. M. Field & A. Sosteck (Eds.), *Infants born at risk: Physiological,
perceptual, and cognitive processes.* New York: Grune & Stratton.
Prkachin, K. M., Craig, K. D., Papageorgis, D., & Reith, G. (1977). Nonverbal
communication deficits and response to performance feedback in depression. *Journal of Abnormal Psychology, 86,* 224–234.
Riggio, R. E. (1986). Assessment of basic social skills. *Journal of Personality and
Social Psychology, 51,* 649–660.
Riggio, R. E., & Friedman, H. S. (1982). The interrelationships of self-monitoring
factors, personality traits, and nonverbal social skills. *Journal of Nonverbal
Behavior, 7,* 33–45.
(1986). Impression formation: The role of expressive behavior. *Journal of Personality and Social Psychology, 50,* 421–427.

Riskind, J. H. (1984). They stoop to conquer: Guiding and self-regulatory functions of physical posture after success and failure. *Journal of Personality and Social Psychology, 47*, 479–493.

Rosaldo, M. Z. (1984). Toward an anthropology of self and feeling. In R. A. Shweder & R. A. LeVine (Eds.), *Culture theory: Essays on mind, self, and emotion* (pp. 137–157). Cambridge: Cambridge University Press.

Rosenthal, R., Hall, J. A., DiMatteo, M. R., Rogers, P. L., & Archer, D. (1979). *Sensitivity to nonverbal communication: The PONS test.* Baltimore: Johns Hopkins University Press.

Saarni, C. (1979). Children's understanding of display rules for expressive behavior. *Developmental Psychology, 15*, 424–429.

(1982). Social and affective functions of nonverbal behavior: Developmental concerns. In R. S. Feldman (Ed.), *Development of nonverbal behavior in children* (pp. 123–147). New York: Springer-Verlag.

(1985). Indirect processes in affect socialization. In M. Lewis & C. Saarni (Eds.), *The socialization of emotions* (pp. 187–209). New York: Plenum.

Sabatelli, R. M., Dreyer, A. S., & Buck, R. (1979). Cognitive style and sending and receiving of facial cues. *Perceptual and Motor Skills, 49*, 203–212.

Scherer, K. R., (1978). Personality inference from voice quality: The loud voice of extroversion. *European Journal of Social Psychology, 8*, 467–487.

Shennum, W. A., & Bugental, D. B. (1982). The development of control over affective expression in nonverbal behavior. In R. S. Feldman (Ed.), *Development of nonverbal behavior in children* (pp. 101–121). New York: Springer-Verlag.

Shields, S. A., & Stern, R. M. (1979). Emotion: The perception of bodily change. In P. Pliner, K. P. Blankstein, & I. M. Spigel (Eds.), *Perception of emotion in self and others* (pp. 85–106). New York: Plenum.

Shrout, P. E., & Fiske, D. W. (1981). Nonverbal behaviors and social evaluation. *Journal of Personality, 49*, 115–128.

Smith, A. (1983). Nonverbal communication among black female dyads: An assessment of intimacy, gender, and race. *Journal of Social Issues, 39*, 55–67.

Smith, J. R., Foot, H. C., & Chapman, A. J. (1977). Nonverbal communication among friends and strangers sharing humor. In A. J. Chapman & H. C. Foot (Eds.), *It's a funny thing humor.* Oxford: Pergamon.

Sommers, S. (1981). Emotionality reconsidered: The role of cognition in emotional responsiveness. *Journal of Personality and Social Psychology, 41*, 553–561.

(1984). Adults evaluating their emotions: A cross-cultural perspective. In C. Z. Malatesta & C. E. Izard (Eds.), *Emotion in adult development* (pp. 319–338). Beverly Hills, CA: Sage.

Sommers, S., & Scioli, A. (1986). Emotional range and value orientation: Toward a cognitive view of emotionality. *Journal of Personality and Social Psychology, 51*, 417–422.

Stifter, C. A., Fox, N., & Parges, S. W. (1989). Facial expressivity and vagal tone in five- and ten-month-old infants. *Infant Behavior and Development, 12*, 127–137.

Swann, W. B., Jr. (1987). Identity negotiation: Where two roads meet. *Journal of Personality and Social Psychology, 53*, 1038–1051.

Tomkins, S. S. (1962). *Affect, imagery, consciousness: Vol. 1. The positive affects.* New York: Springer-Verlag.

(1963). *Affect, imagery, consciousness: Vol. 2. The negative affects.* New York: Springer-Verlag.

(1979). Script theory: Differential magnification of affects. In H. E. Howe, Jr. (Ed.), *Nebraska Symposium of Motivation* (Vol. 26, pp. 201–236). Lincoln: University of Nebraska Press.

Tronick, E. Z., & Gianino, A. F., Jr. (1986). The transmission of maternal disturbance to the infant. In E. Z. Tronick & T. Field (Eds.), *New directions for child development: Vol. 34. Maternal depression and infant disturbance* (pp. 5–11). San Francisco: Jossey-Bass.

Wallbott, H. G., Ricci Bitti, P., & Banninger-Huber, E. (1986). Non-verbal reactions to emotional experiences. In K. R. Scherer, H. G. Wallbott, & A. B. Summerfield (Eds.), *Experiencing emotion: A cross-cultural study* (pp. 98–116). Cambridge: Cambridge University Press.

Whiting, B. B. (1980). Culture and social behavior: A model for the development of social behavior. *Ethos, 8,* 95–116.

Woolfolk, A. (1978). Student learning and performance under varying conditions of teacher verbal and nonverbal evaluative communication. *Journal of Educational Psychology, 70,* 87–94.

Zivin, G. (1982). Watching the sands shift: Conceptualizing development of nonverbal mastery. In R. S. Feldman (Ed.), *Development of nonverbal behavior in children* (pp. 63–98). New York: Springer-Verlag.

(1986). Processes of expressive behavior development. *Merrill–Palmer Quarterly, 32,* 103–140.

Zuckerman, M., DeFrank, R. S., Spiegel, N. H., & Larrance, D. T. (1982). Masculinity–femininity and encoding of nonverbal cues. *Journal of Personality and Social Psychology, 42,* 548–556.

Zuckerman, M., Klorman, R., Larrance, D. T., & Spiegel, N. H. (1981). Facial, autonomic, and subjective components of emotion: The facial feedback hypothesis versus the externalizer–internalizer distinction. *Journal of Personality and Social Psychology, 41,* 929–944.

Zuckerman, M., Larrance, D. T., Hall, J. A., DeFrank, R. S., & Rosenthal, R. (1979). Posed and spontaneous communication of emotion via facial and vocal cues. *Journal of Personality, 47,* 712–733.

PART III

Affective and cognitive processes

5. Facial expression: Methods, means, and moues

PAUL EKMAN AND MAUREEN O'SULLIVAN

. . . so your face bids me, though you say nothing.
                                                    – Fool to King Lear

Introduction

Poets and philosophers often focus on the face as central to human communication, but the interest of psychologists in facial expression has been more episodic. At first, many well-known researchers such as Allport (1924), Landis (1924), Goodenough (1932), Guilford (1929), and Klineberg (1938) studied facial expressions of emotion. Several influential reviewers (Bruner & Tagiuri, 1954; Hunt, 1941; Tagiuri, 1968), however, argued that there were no consistent answers to fundamental questions such as whether information provided by facial expressions was accurate or whether facial expressions of emotion were universal. During the next 20 years there were comparatively few studies of facial expression, with the exception of Schlosberg's reports (1941, 1952, 1954) that categorical judgments of emotion could be ordered in terms of underlying dimensions.

A number of more recent developments have contributed to the resurgence of interest in facial expression, including methodological, theoretical, and technological advancements. Indeed, part of the difficulty in obtaining consistent results in the early facial expression studies was the lack of well-defined, objective methods for describing facial behavior. Since 1970, several reliable facial measurement techniques have been developed, which have allowed greater precision within studies and greater comparability across studies than was possible earlier. This

This chapter incorporates some material from Ekman (1989) and Fridlund, Ekman and Oster (1987). Paul Ekman's work is supported by a Research Scientist Award from the National Institute of Mental Health (MH 06092).

chapter will compare and contrast several different facial measurement techniques. We shall then illustrate the reason for using such time-consuming methods by examining recent findings concerning a specific facial expression: the smile. The exactitude of the current measurement methods permits us to explore subtle differences among smiles that were not possible even 20 years ago.

In addition to advances in measurement techniques, theoretical breakthroughs and empirical findings also have contributed to a resurgence of interest in facial expression. Tomkins (1962, 1963) provided a theoretical rationale for studying the face as a means for learning about personality and emotion. He also showed that observers could obtain very high agreement in judging emotion if the facial expressions were carefully selected to reveal what he believes are the innate facial affects (Tomkins & McCarter, 1964). Tomkins greatly influenced both Ekman and Izard in planning their initial cross-cultural studies of facial expression. The resulting evidence of universality in facial expression also re-kindled interest in this topic.

The evidence for universals in facial expression fits not only with Tomkins's theory but also with the newly emerging interest in applying ethological methods and concepts to human behavior. Interested in the biological bases of behavior, human ethologists welcomed evidence of commonalities in social behavior across cultures, and they provided the first detailed "catalogs" describing naturally occurring facial behavior (Blurton Jones, 1972; Brannigan & Humphries, 1972; Grant, 1969; Mc-Grew, 1972). Because the question of the universality of facial expression is so central to thinking about emotion and nonverbal behavior, we shall review the more recent studies in this area, thereby updating and refining the issues in this domain.

In the 1960s and 1970s, the availability of low-cost photography and videotaping encouraged several researchers to measure the ability to recognize facial expressions (O'Sullivan & Guilford, 1975; Rosenthal, Hall, DiMatteo, Rogers, & Archer, 1979). The question of what kind of information can be conveyed by the face, however, continues to be debated. For this reason, we also shall review the issues to be considered in assessing accuracy in judging facial emotional expressions.

The final topic that we shall address is the role of facial feedback in the phenomenology of emotion. The increasing interest of psychologists in issues pertaining to emotion suggested the facial feedback hypothesis as one with broad appeal.

The topics this chapter will address – facial measurement, universality, accuracy, and facial feedback – were chosen for their importance, both historically and theoretically. Nonetheless, several areas have been excluded from consideration. In recent years, developmental psychologists investigating attachment, mother–infant interaction, and the development of emotion have begun to study facial expression. Because other chapters in this book discuss developmental aspects of nonverbal behavior, it will not be addressed here.

The encoding or expression of individual facial behavior is receiving more and more attention (Rusalova, 1987), with many researchers examining encoding differences among schizophrenics (Garfield, Rogoff, & Steinberg, 1987; Morrison, Bellack, & Mueser, 1988) and brain-damaged individuals (Weddell, Trevarthan, & Miller, 1988). But we shall not review this research or that on the relationship between the face and the autonomic nervous system (Ekman, Levenson, & Friesen, 1983; Levenson, Ekman, & Friesen, in press) and the central nervous system (Davidson, Ekman, Saron, Senulis, & Friesen, 1990), as it is too far afield from the nonverbal behavior emphasis of this book.

For the same reason, research on the words used to describe facial expressions of emotion will not be reviewed. Ekman, Friesen, and Ellsworth (1972) reanalyzed many of the experiments conducted from 1914 to 1970. They found, contrary to Bruner and Tagiuri's assessment (1954), that the data yielded consistent, positive answers to fundamental questions about the language used to describe facial expression, the influence of context on judgments of facial expression, the accuracy of judgments, and similarities across cultures. More recent thinking on the language and labels used to describe facial expressions of emotion includes that of Russell and Fehr (1987) and Ekman and O'Sullivan (1988). Other reviews of facial expression research include Charlesworth and Kreutzer (1973) on infants and children; Chevalier-Skolnikoff (1973) and Redican (1975, 1982) on nonhuman primates; Izard (1977) on theories of emotion; Ekman and Oster (1979) on the face; and Fridlund, Ekman, and Oster (1987) on facial expression of emotion, including developmental and physiological aspects.

Facial measurement

Two major methodologies for studying facial expressions have been developed: the measurement of visible facial actions using facial coding systems and the measurement of electrical discharges from contracting facial muscle tissue (facial electromyography).

Measurement of visible facial action

Since Landis's report in 1924, many systems have been devised to structure and analyze the observation of facial action. Such measurement systems share the following features: (1) They are noninvasive; (2) they offer a permanent visual record (videotape or cinema) that allows slowed playback and/or multiple viewings rather than real-time observation; and (3) they rely on an observer who scores or codes behavior according to a set of predetermined categories or items. Many of these systems were not constructed as independent contributions but, rather, in the course of studying other substantive questions. Typically, the rationale for developing these systems was based on neither sound theoretical argument nor empirical data (see Ekman, 1982, for a detailed comparison of 14 major facial coding systems).

A problem encountered by all researchers trying to understand facial behavior is selecting appropriate behavioral units for dividing the ongoing, complex, and dynamic stream of facial activity. Though this issue is of prime importance, many coding systems have not considered it. As Altmann commented, "What stage in our research could be more crucial than this initial choosing of behavioral units. Upon it rests all of our subsequent records of communication interactions and any conclusions we may draw from them" (Altmann, 1968, p. 501; also see discussions by Buck, Baron, & Barrette, 1982; and Condon & Ogston, 1967a,b).

Two major approaches have been used in constructing facial coding systems: the message judgment approach and the measurement of sign vehicle approach. In the message judgment approach, facial expressions are presented in their entirety, and judgments are solicited from observers. For example, slides of psychiatric patients are shown to judges who must then classify each one as depressed, normal, or schizophrenic. Message judgment approaches either place expressions along emotion scales (e.g., Schlosberg, 1941, 1952, 1954) or in discrete emotion categories (e.g., Izard, 1971, 1972; also see the review of both scaling and categorical approaches by Ekman, Friesen & Ellsworth, 1982b).

In the measurement of sign vehicle approach, slides are examined for particular differences that might differentiate diagnostic categories. For example, depressives might raise their inner eyebrows more than schizophrenics or normals do, and the schizophrenics might show more perioral facial actions.

Both approaches to facial coding have value in certain applications, although the message judgment approach is singularly handicapped: It is impossible in such a system to determine exactly which facial signs result in judgment differences. This liability is particularly pronounced when studying emotional behavior. But an analytic approach that specifies discrete facial actions avoids sloppy inferences regarding critical facial signs of emotion.

Facial unit selection. The choice of behavioral units in facial coding systems has been based on theory (largely ethological formulations), inductive observation, or facial anatomy.

Theory-based selection. Ekman, Friesen, and Tomkins's (1971) Facial Affect Scoring Technique (FAST) specified what they considered, on the basis of their previous research, to be the distinctive components of six universal affect expressions (77 descriptors of the hypothesized facial appearance for happiness, sadness, anger, fear, surprise, and disgust). FAST proved to be useful in studies relating subjects' facial expressions to autonomic responses, experimental conditions, and observers' judgments. But it could not be used to determine whether actions other than those specified were relevant to emotion or to study developmental changes or individual differences in the expression of emotion. No provision was made to code the intensity of the facial behaviors, and facial descriptors were specified as happening in two states, either "on" or "off."

Izard continued working with theoretically based coding systems and produced the Maximally Descriptive Facial Movement Coding System (MAX; Izard, 1979) and the System for Identifying Affect Expression by Holistic Judgment (AFFEX; Izard & Dougherty, 1980). Like FAST, MAX and AFFEX are based on early facial expression recognition studies that established that certain configurations of facial muscle groups are universally judged to be associated with particular emotions. Neither MAX nor AFFEX offers an exhaustive listing of possible facial behaviors; MAX, for example, provides only those 27 descriptors that Izard hypothesized were necessary to form judgments about seven "primary" emotions. No data are provided to show that the facial actions excluded are not part of emotional expression, and thus the "exhaustiveness" of the systems cannot be confirmed or disconfirmed using these systems. No provision is made for encoding response intensity, and like FAST, facial action is seen as either "on" or "off."

MAX and AFFEX were designed primarily for coding emotional expressions in infants. Oster and Rosenstein (1983) pointed out three difficulties inherent in the use of MAX and AFFEX for this purpose. First, when scoring facial behavior one cannot distinguish between organized patterns of facial expression in infants and configurations that coincidentally match adult facial stereotypes. Second, in these systems one can classify infant expressions as "fitting" a particular adult category on the basis of only a few facial actions, occurring in just two of the three areas of the face. The omission of certain facial actions from MAX and AFFEX thus makes it impossible to verify whether infant (or even adult) expressions meeting the coding criteria are the same as their standardized adult counterparts or whether other infant expressions that do not resemble adult stereotypes constitute meaningful communicative signals. Third, and perhaps most serious, is the absence of any independent evidence that the configurations specified in MAX and AFFEX indicate the presence of the corresponding discrete emotional states in infants. This last objection likewise applies to the use of MAX and AFFEX for coding adult expressions.

Inductively based selection. Several overlapping listings of facial actions have been derived by observing spontaneous behavior in infants (Nystrom, 1974; Young & Decarie, 1977), children (Blurton Jones, 1971; Brannigan & Humphries, 1972; Grant, 1969; McGrew, 1972), and normal adults and psychiatric patients (Grant, 1969), which were reviewed in detail by Ekman (1982). The inductively based systems have been useful in generating "ethograms," or catalogs of the salient behaviors in the communications repertoire. Blurton Jones's system has been adopted with some variations by a number of developmental psychologists.

The inductively based facial coding systems cannot be considered as general-purpose facial measurement systems, as the parsing of facial actions is inconsistent – all include both simple actions and complex movements that are not subdivided into components. Behavioral units are occasionally objectively identified but are often given names laden with subjective judgments (e.g., "angry frown"). These terms only complicate inferences about the facial behavior (e.g., whether or not the frown signifies anger). Many behavioral units are vaguely described, so that investigators cannot know whether they are coding the same actions. Descriptions of actions are often not in accord with the underlying facial anatomy. For example, Birdwhistell (1970) attempted to construct a facial measurement system paralleling linguistic units, and Grant (1969) derived measurement units from their ostensible (i.e., unvalidated) "function." Static facial signs (e.g., individual, racial, or age-related differences in physiognomy) make it difficult to identify certain actions in systems in which facial behavior is described in terms of static configurations, for instance, "oblong mouth."

Anatomically based selection. Because every facial movement is the result of muscular action, any complex facial movement can be scored analytically in terms of the minimal muscle actions that collectively produced the movement. Seaford (1976) provided an excellent, detailed critique of the hazards in theoretically and inductively derived systems. In contrast, his description of a regional variation in facial expression showed the advantages of an anatomical approach.

Several investigators have attempted to derive anatomically based systems (Ermiane & Gregarian, 1978; Frois-Wittman, 1930; Fulcher, 1942; Landis, 1924; see Ekman, 1982, for analyses of these systems). Because only anatomically based coding systems offer the possibility of being comprehensive, the extant systems can be evaluated against this standard.

The comprehensiveness of any facial coding system must be assessed according to four criteria. First, all visible facial actions must be included in the system (regardless of theoretical or inductive notions about function or signal value). Second, a provision for coding the intensity of facial actions must be included, as it is particularly important to measure muscular excursions in the left versus the right side of the face and to assess intensity of emotion. Third, a provision for timing the facial actions, with regard to both stimulus situations and the patterning of the facial actions themselves, must be included in a comprehensive system. The response dynamics that must be coded include onset time, apex time, and offset time; these fine-grained dynamics have already been implicated in the discrimination between deceptive and honest expressions (Ekman & Friesen, 1982) and feigned and unfeigned smiles (Ekman, Hager, & Friesen, 1981). Fourth, the behavioral units must be clearly and operationally defined, with high interrater reliabilities and suitable validity data.

Measured according to these criteria, nearly all of the anatomically based systems fall short, as most were devised solely to measure emotion. The systems devised by Frois-Wittman (1930), Fulcher (1942), and Landis (1924) contained only limited subsets of facial actions, and they made no provision for timing actions. Ermiane & Gregarian (1978) offered a system that coded all visible facial actions, including intensity information, but did not code the timing of facial actions. Ermiane and

Gregarian also distinguished the actions of some muscles without data supporting that they operated independently in visible behavior.

Facial Action Coding System: FACS

The Facial Action Coding System (FACS) (Ekman & Friesen, 1976, 1978) was developed to fill the need for a comprehensive, general-purpose system applicable in any context, not just in emotion-related situations. As a prerequisite, Ekman and Friesen sought to discover the precise role of each facial muscle on visible facial expression. In order to do so, they resurrected Duchenne's (1862) method of inserting needle electrodes in individual facial muscles. The muscle activity elicited by electrical stimulation at the electrode tip indicated the effect of each muscle on facial appearance. The facial actions that Ekman and Friesen discerned were found to be in accord with Hjorstjo's (1970) independent anatomical studies of the appearance of single facial muscle actions.

The descriptions of facial actions comprising FACS were based not only on the resulting stimulation data but also on the determination of whether particular muscle combinations produced visibly distinguishable facial actions. Distinct muscles that produced morphologically identical facial actions were combined. But if a single muscle were found to produce two or more visibly distinct actions, two or more facial action units were designated. Ekman and Friesen derived 44 action units (AUs) that can, singly or in combination, account for all visible facial movements. All AUs can be scored according to five-point intensity ratings, and the time of the onset, apex, and offset for each AU can be coded. FACS also offers high interrater reliabilities.

FACS takes considerable time to learn and use, requiring repeated, slow-motion viewing of facial actions. Because slow-motion replay is required, FACS is not suitable for real-time coding. By its nature, FACS includes more distinctions than may be needed for any particular study, which increases the expense and tedium of measurement. However, once meaningful behavioral units are derived empirically (i.e., not from theoretical or inductive assertions), it is possible in a given study to collapse some of the elementary measurement units or to disregard subtle distinctions. This point applies especially to studies of emotion – FACS contains hypotheses about which AUs may, in fact, correlate with specific emotional states.

Although not all of the FACS emotion hypotheses have been tested, there is evidence (reviewed by Ekman, 1982) to support a number of the predictions. Studies of spontaneous emotional expression in which a subjective report was used as a validity criterion have supported predictions of the actions that signal happiness, fear, distress, and disgust. And studies using observers' attributions of emotion as a validity criterion have supported FACS predictions for these emotions as well as for surprise and anger.

EMFACS

Ekman and Friesen wanted to supplement the comprehensive FACS with a standardized alternative that measures broader, emotion-related facial actions. The result, EMFACS, considers only emotional expressions and, among those, only the AUs and AU combinations that are best supported by empirical findings or theory as emotion signals. As such, EMFACS is really a theory-based coding system, but with an important difference. Its systematic derivation from FACS permits confident statements about what was omitted. The solidity of EMFACS as a system with empirical grounding is suggested by several concurrent validation studies with FACS, which resulted in high correlations (in the + .80 range) with emotion ratings obtained with FACS and EMFACS.

Coding time with EMFACS is reduced, albeit at the expense of distinguishing subtler AUs and AU combinations, including those indicative of conversational signals. The precise temporal dynamics of the facial actions are ignored in favor of unitary demarcations of peak actions. To maintain an empirical approach to the measurement procedure, the facial actions are, like FACS, described in terms of numerical codes. The coder is also requested not to interpret the actions as emotion signals until they are later tabulated and classified according to EMFACS criteria.

Other measures of visible facial action. Perhaps the most popular measure of facial activity has been the direction of gaze; yet surprisingly this rarely has been studied in relation to emotion or facial expressions. (Exceptions were provided in research by Graham & Argyle, 1975; Lalljee, 1978; Waters, Matas, & Sroufe, 1975.) Although pupil dilation has been studied in relation to emotion, we know of no study of associated changes in facial expression. Blood flow, skin temperature, electrodermal responding, and coloration changes in the face are other measures that so far remain unexplored.

Facial electromyography

Following earlier work by Malmo and Shagass (1949) and others, the use of facial electromyography (EMG) has been advanced as a putative measure of posed expression and also of mood and emotional states that are not necessarily accompanied by overt facial action. Because facial EMG attempts to measure the activity of specific facial muscles, it can be seen as an example of the measurement of sign vehicle approach.

The use of facial EMG techniques does not relieve investigators of having to define units of measurement and to choose which facial behaviors to observe. They must decide what features of the EMG signal are salient (i.e., what constitutes the EMG "response"). Because of the cost in time and effort of using facial EMG techniques – sampling even a small proportion of facial muscles using EMG-recording electrodes requires a large number of electrodes and an inordinate amount of subject preparation – investigators must decide which facial behaviors will be important. Therefore, all facial EMG–emotion research can be seen as necessarily having a theory-based component.

To date, facial EMG techniques have been used in studies of affective imagery and affective disorder (Brown & Schwartz, 1980; Oliveau & Willmuth, 1979; Schwartz, Brown, & Ahern, 1980; Schwartz, Fair, Salt, Mandel, & Klerman, 1976a,b; Schwartz, Fair, Mandel, Salt, Mieske, & Klerman, 1978; Teasdale & Bancroft, 1977; Teasdale & Rezin, 1978), of posed facial expressions (Rusalova, Izard, & Simonov, 1975; Sumitsuji, Matsumoto, Tanaka, Kashiwagi, & Kaneko, 1967, 1977), and of social interaction and empathy (Cacioppo & Petty, 1981; Englis, Vaughan, & Lanzetta, 1981; Vaughan & Lanzetta, 1980, 1981). (For a critical review of the facial EMG–emotion literature, consult Fridlund & Izard, 1983, and Fridlund, Ekman, & Oster, 1987.)

Facial measurement and the Duchenne smile

The utility of fine-grained measurement of facial behavior has been underscored by research on smiling. Ekman (1985) distinguished 18 theoretically different kinds of smiles, including both voluntary and involuntary ones. One type of involuntary smile is what Ekman and Friesen (1982) originally termed a *felt happiness smile* but have since renamed an *enjoyment smile*. Such smiles include all smiles that occur while the person actually experiences, and presumably would report, a positive emotion. These positive emotions could arise from visual, auditory, gustatory, kinesthetic, or tactile stimulation; amusement and delight; contentment and satisfaction; beatific experiences; relief from pain, pressure, or tension; and enjoyment of another person. They proposed that these enjoyment smiles differ in morphology and timing from more deliberate, voluntary smiles such as social, polite, or masking smiles.

Ekman and Friesen's ideas about morphology were based on their studies of voluntary facial actions and the writings of the French anatomist Duchenne:

> The emotion of frank joy is expressed on the face by the combined contraction of the zygomaticus major muscle and the orbicularis oculi. The first obeys the will but that the second is only put in play by the sweet emotions of the soul; the . . . fake joy, the deceitful laugh, cannot provoke the contraction of this latter muscle. . . . The muscle around the eye does not obey the will; it is only brought into play by a true feeling, by an agreeable emotion. Its inertia, in smiling, unmasks a false friend. (1862/1990, p. 126)

Consistent with Duchenne's description, Ekman, Roper, and Hager (1980) found that most people are unable to contract voluntarily the orbicularis oculi muscle.

Based on these findings and Duchenne's observations, Ekman and Friesen (1982) suggested that the common morphological elements in enjoyment smiles are the action of two muscles: the zygomaticus major muscle pulling the lip corners upward toward the cheek bones, and the portion of orbicularis oculi that raises the cheek and gathers the skin inward from around the eye socket (see Figure 5.1). Ekman (Ekman, Davidson, & Friesen, 1990) proposed calling smiles incorporating both of these elements *Duchenne smiles.*

Seven studies have obtained evidence for distinguishing the Duchenne or enjoyment smile from other forms of smiling. Ekman, Friesen, and Ancoli (1980) found that Duchenne smiles occurred more often than did three other types of smiles when people watched pleasant films and that only Duchenne smiles correlated with the subjective report of happiness. Ekman, Friesen, and O'Sullivan (1988) found that Duchenne smiles occurred more often when people were actually enjoying themselves, as compared with people feigning smiling to conceal negative emotions. Fox and Davidson (1988) found that 10-month-old infants' Duchenne smiles occurred more often in response to their mother's approach, whereas other types of smiling occurred more often in response to approach by a stranger. They also found that only Duchenne smiles were associated with the left-frontal EEG activation, the pattern of cerebral activity repeatedly found in positive affect. Matsumoto (1986) found that depressed patients showed more Duchenne smiles in a discharge interview, as compared with an admission interview, but that there was no difference in the rate of other kinds of smiling.

Steiner (1986) discovers that Duchenne smiles, but not other types of smiles, increased over the course of psychotherapy in European patients who were judged to have improved. Ruch (1987) found that Duchenne smiles were sensitive to the amount of humor felt by German adults when responding to jokes or cartoons. And Schneider (1987) pointed out that in young German children Duchenne smiles revealed whether they had succeeded or failed in a game.

Ekman and Friesen (1982) also proposed that involuntary enjoyment smiles would differ from other smiles in the amount of time it takes for the smile to appear, how long it remains on the face before fading, and in the time required for the smile to disappear. Two studies have shown the utility of these measures of timing, which are, however, much more costly to obtain than is the measurement of which muscles are recruited. Bugental (1986) found that women showed more enjoyment smiles with responsive than with unresponsive children. Weiss, Blum, and Gleberman (1987) discovered that involuntary enjoyment smiles occurred more often during posthypnotically induced positive affect than in deliberately posed positive affect.

Collectively, these studies suggest that smiles should no longer be considered a single category of behavior but can be usefully distinguished by measuring their different facets. Such measurements can be made only with comprehensive coding systems such as those described.

The universality of facial expressions of emotion

Although methodological improvements provide the substrate that supports empirical knowledge, the knowledge itself is the goal. In the area of facial expressions of emotion, no issue is more important than the question of whether facial expressions of emotion are universal across all cultures or are specific to each. This question is significant because it addresses several issues: the basic similarity of human emotional experience, the biological basis for emotion, and the relationship between facial expression and emotion. The history of research on the universality of facial expressions began with social scientists who believed that such expressions were culturally determined. At least five early studies (Dickey & Knower, 1941; Triandis & Lambert, 1958; Vinacke, 1949; Vinacke & Fong, 1955; Winkelmayer, Exline, Gottheil, & Paredes, 1971) attempted to show differences across cultures in the way that observers judge facial expressions. In fact, their findings were either ambiguous or showed similarity across literate cultures.

All five of these studies were undertaken to demonstrate that facial expressions are culturally specific, and yet they found evidence of universality. But each study had major design flaws. Most gave little thought to the necessity of sampling systematically the facial expressions studied. Rather than selecting expressions according to either theory or a representative data base, the stimuli were selected for convenience.

Researchers who have attempted to demonstrate universality have used three different research methods: (1) poses of emotion elicited from members of different cultures, (2) spontaneous expressions compared in two or more cultures, and (3) comparison of judgments of emotions made by observers in different cultures who viewed the same set of facial expressions.

Eliciting poses

Ekman and Friesen (1971) asked members of one culture to show how their face would look if they were the person in each of a number of different emotional contexts (e.g., "you feel sad because your child died," "you are angry and about to fight"). They interpreted their findings as strongly supporting the possibility of universality, as observers in another culture did far better than chance in identifying which emotional contexts the posed expressions were intended to portray. This finding had unusual relevance because the persons displaying the expressions were members of a visually isolated New Guinea culture (the South Fore). The ability of Americans to understand these New Guinean expressions could not be attributed to earlier contact between these groups or to both having learned their expressions from mass media models.

Three problems limit these findings, however. First, there has been only one such study, and it has not been repeated in another preliterate, visually isolated culture, or for that matter in a literate, non-Western, or Western culture. Second, not all six of the emotions portrayed were accurately recognized. Although anger, disgust, happiness, and sadness were distinguished from one another and from fear and surprise, the American observers could not distinguish the New Guineans' portrayals of fear and surprise. Third, the facial expressions were posed, and so Mead (1975) argued that establishing that posed expressions are universal does not mean that spontaneous facial expressions of emotion are universal. Ekman (1977) responded that the most likely explanation of why people can readily interpret and pose facial expressions is that they had seen those same facial expressions and experienced them in everyday social life. Evidence for the spontaneous expression of emotion in different cultures is particularly germane to this argument.

Comparing spontaneous expressions

Ekman and Friesen (1971) compared spontaneous facial expressions by Japanese and American college students. They selected Japan as the comparison culture because of the widely held Western belief in Asian inscrutability. They hoped to show that this stereotype was based on display rules about masking negative affect in the presence of an authority, as suggested by their neurocultural theory of emotion (Ekman & Friesen, 1969). Male college students in Tokyo and in Berkeley, California, came into a laboratory and watched both neutral and stress-inducing films while their skin resistance and heart rate were measured. The videotapes of the facial expressions (filmed with a hidden camera unknown to the subject until after the experiment) were coded by persons who did not know which film was seen when the facial expressions occurred. A correlation greater than .90 was found between the particular facial movements shown by the Japanese and the American students (Ekman, 1973; Friesen, 1972). Virtually the same repertoire of facial movements occurred at the same points in time.

Later in the same experiment a scientist, dressed in a white coat, entered the room and sat with the subject while he watched the stress film. It was predicted that in the presence of an authority figure the display rules for managing facial behavior should operate differently in the two countries; that is, there would be more monitoring of negative facial behavior in Japan than in the United States. Facial measurements were in the predicted direction. The Japanese students showed more raised lip corners (social smiling) than did the Americans (Friesen, 1972). Slow-motion analyses of the facial expressions revealed a sequencing of facial behaviors in which a smiling movement was superimposed on the muscular action of disgust or fear. This was the first study to show how cultural differences in the management of facial expressions (display rules) can mask universal facial expressions.

Two problems, however, limit the findings from this study. Again it is but a single study; no one has yet attempted to replicate it. The second limitation is that the stress-inducing films elicited only two negative emotions (disgust and fear), thereby not allowing determination of whether the full range of emotional expressions is universal. The next type of research met these two criticisms, studying many emotions and with many replications.

Comparing observers' judgments

Typically, in most cross-cultural facial expression studies, the people in each culture are shown still photographs of facial expressions and are asked to select a single emotion word or category from a list of words or categories. Very high agreement was found in the specific emotions attributed to facial expressions across a variety of cultures (five literate cultures, Ekman, 1972; Ekman, Sorenson, & Friesen, 1969; nine literate cultures, Izard, 1971; two literate cultures, Niit & Valsiner, 1977; and one non-Western literate culture, Boucher, 1973; Boucher & Carlson, 1980). The strength of this kind of evidence is its many replications. Unlike the first two kinds of research, this type of study has been repeated in many cultures, by different investigators, using different photographs of facial expression.

These studies have provided consistent evidence for the common recognition of at least six emotions (happiness, anger, fear, sadness, surprise, and disgust). Izard reported agreement also for shame and interest, but there is a question about whether it was facial expression or head position that was the clue to recognizing these emotions. There have been no other cross cultural studies of the facial expressions of shame and interest. Ekman and Friesen (1986) reported agreement across 10 Western and non-Western literate cultures in the identification of a specific expression for contempt (Figure 5.1). Although there is some argument about this (Izard & Hayes, 1988, and reply by Ekman & Friesen, 1988; also P. E. Ricci Bitti, personal communication, 1986), Ekman and Heider (1988) again replicated the recognition of contempt in a non-Western culture.

Six questions can be raised about such judgment studies in which the same set of faces is shown to observers in different cultures. First, establishing agreement across cultures about the recognition and labeling of an emotion does not prove that the emotion is expressed or experienced in the same way across these cultures. This objection seems highly implausible. The recognition of emotion is not a matter that is taught for-

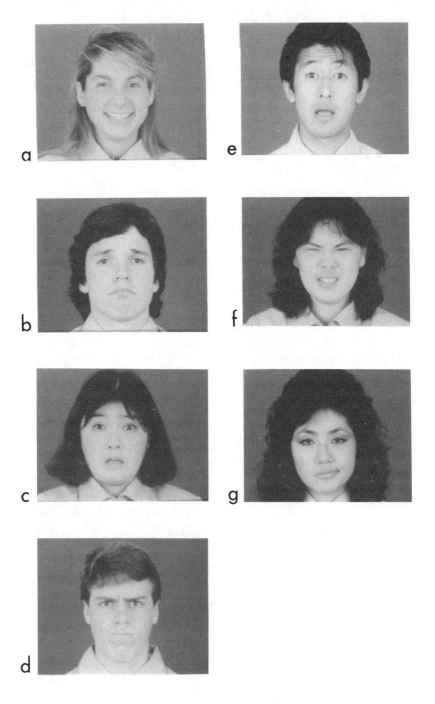

Figure 5.1. Seven basic emotions: (a) happiness, (b) sadness, (c) fear, (d) anger, (e) surprise, (f) disgust, and (g) contempt. (Matsumoto & Ekman, 1989.)

mally but presumably is learned by observing the expressions that actually do occur. (Some have suggested that the recognition of emotion is innate, but whether it is innate or learned is not relevant to this particular point.) If the expression of anger involved a slack jaw and raised brows in culture A and lowered brows and pressed lips in culture B, then the people from those cultures should disagree in their judgments of emotion when viewing photographs of these two different expressions. But this did not happen. People from different cultures agree in attributing anger to photographs showing lowered brows and pressed lips and agree in attributing surprise when the jaw is slackened and the brows are raised (Figure 5.1).

A second objection is that the observers in all these studies were responding to posed, not spontaneous, expressions. It seems far-fetched to propose that these are two unrelated sets of facial expressions, a posed set that for some reason is recognized across cultures and a spontaneous set that is culture specific. Furthermore, the posed expressions are similar in form to the expressions found in the cross-cultural studies of spontaneous expressions. Although such comparisons between spontaneous and posed behavior can be made only for disgust, fear, and happiness (because other emotions have not been elicited in cross-cultural studies of spontaneous expression), there is no reason to expect that such similarity would not be found for other emotions. In Western cultures, such similarities between posed and spontaneous expressions have also been established for anger, surprise, and sadness.

Another answer to this question about whether universality is established if the judged expressions are posed comes from the study of the spontaneous facial behavior of Japanese and American college students described earlier (Ekman, 1973; Friesen, 1972). Japanese and American observers judged whether the facial expressions of Japanese and American students were elicited by watching a stressful or a neutral film. Observers of both cultures were equally accurate whether they judged members of their own or the other culture. Moreover, persons of either culture who were judged correctly by Americans were also judged correctly by Japanese ($r > +.75$).

A third objection is that all the people who were studied shared the same visual or media culture. Perhaps they all learned to recognize emotional expressions, or even to make those expressions, by observing the same models in films, television, and photographs. This criticism is met by a judgment study in a visually isolated, preliterate New Guinea culture, the South Fore (Ekman & Friesen, 1971). (These were the same subjects whose poses of emotion were described at the beginning of this section in regard to the evidence of universality.) The South Fore subjects had seen no movies, television, or photographs. They spoke neither English nor pidgin. They had never worked for a Caucasian or lived in a government settlement. Nearly 10% of the members of this culture were studied. For anger, happiness, sadness, disgust, and surprise (except as distinguished from fear) the faces identified with each emotion were the same as in literate cultures. Karl Heider and Eleanor Rosch were skeptical of these findings, believing that facial expressions are culture specific. In 1970, on a field trip to West Iran, they repeated this study with the Dani, a culture even more remote than the South Fore, and they obtained a nearly perfect replication of Ekman and Friesen's results (reported in Ekman, 1973).

The fourth criticism of the judgment studies is that the judgment tasks that they used might have concealed cultural differences in the perception of secondary blended emotions. Many students of emotion have noted that facial expressions may contain more than one message (Ekman & Friesen, 1969; Izard, 1971; Plutchik, 1962; Tomkins, 1963). The two emotions in a blend may be of similar strength, or one emotion may be primary and much more salient than the other secondary emotion. In earlier cross-cultural studies, the investigators presumed that the expressions they showed displayed a single emotion rather than a blend and therefore did not give those who observed the expressions an opportunity to choose more than one emotion term for each expression. Without such data, however, it is not possible to ascertain whether an expression conveys a single emotion or a blend, and if it is a blend, whether cultures agree in their judgment of the secondary emotion. Earlier evidence of cross-cultural agreement in the judgment of expressions might be limited just to the primary message and not the secondary blended emotions.

A later study by Ekman et al. (1987) resolved this problem. In this study members of 10 literate Western and non-Western cultures were shown a set of Caucasian facial expressions. Instead of being limited to selecting one emotion term or category for each expression, the observers were allowed to indicate both the presence of multiple emotions and the relative intensity of each. There was very high agreement across cultures about the secondary blended emotion signaled by an expression.

The fifth question is whether there is universality not just in which emotion is signaled by an expression but also in the intensity of the perceived emotion. Only two cross-cultural studies (Ekman, 1972; Saha, 1973) obtained intensity judgments, and no differences among cultures were found. But not many cultures were examined in either study. Ekman et al. (1987) addressed this question as well and found cross-cultural agreement about the relative strength of expressions of the same emotion. With few exceptions, the 10 cultures they examined agreed on which of two different expressions of the same emotion was more intense.

Ekman et al. (1987), however, did uncover evidence of cultural differences in the absolute intensity level attributed to an expression. The Asian cultures (Hong Kong, Japan, Sumatra) attributed less-intense emotions to expressions than did the non-Asians. Because all the expressions shown had been of Caucasian faces, it was not possible to know whether this might be caused by the Asians' reluctance to attribute strong emotions to a foreigner. To examine this issue, Matsumoto and Ekman (1989) showed expressions of both Japanese and Americans to observers in both countries. Regardless of the culture or sex of the person they were judging, the Japanese made less intense judgments than did the Americans. Work is now in progress to investigate whether the Japanese make less intense attributions than do Americans when judging other personal characteristics apart from emotion.

Although no one study, or one kind of research, is conclusive, collectively they provide an enormous body of consistent evidence for the universality of at least some facial expressions of emotions. Although the evidence is strong for fear, anger, disgust, sadness, surprise, and happiness, there still are questions about contempt, shame, and interest. Also, there are no data on how many expressions for each emotion are universal. Nor is it known how often these universal expressions of emotion are seen in ordinary social life. And little has yet been documented about cultural differences in facial expression, except for the single study of display rules (Ekman, 1973; Friesen, 1972) discussed earlier and the recent evidence regarding differences in the judgment of emotional intensity (Ekman et al., 1987).

Despite this evidence, it could still be argued that facial expressions of emotion are culturally variable social signals and that the commonality in judgments can be attributed solely to common learning experiences. According to this interpretation, exposure to the same mass media representations of emotional expression might have taught people in each culture how to label facial expressions. But this explanation was invalidated by studies of isolated, preliterate cultures not exposed to the mass media: the South Fore in Papua New Guinea (Ekman & Friesen, 1971), and the Dani in West Iran (Heider & Rosch, reported by Ekman, 1973). Members of these cultures chose the same facial expressions for particular emotions as did members of literate cultures.

A limitation of these cross-cultural experiments is that the facial expressions presented were not genuine but were posed by subjects instructed to show a particular emotion or to move particular facial muscles. One interpreter of this literature (Mead, 1975) suggested that universality in judgments of facial expression might be limited to just such stereotyped, posed expressions. Two experiments, however, argue against this interpretation. Winkelmayer, Exline, Gottheil, and Paredes (1978) chose motion picture samples from interviews with normal and schizophrenic individuals to see whether emotion judgments by members of different cultures would differ when spontaneous rather than posed expressions were shown. There was no overall difference among American, British, and Mexican observers. However, the Mexican observers were less accurate than the others were in judging the facial expressions of normal, but not schizophrenic, subjects. This difference had not been predicted, may have been due to language and/or culture, and has not been replicated.

The evidence strongly supports universality for six or more emotions, which represents only a small percentage of facial behavior. How accurate are people in using facial behavior to infer emotional state in an ongoing social interaction? Is the face used as a source of information in ordinary human relationships?

Accuracy in judging facial expressions of emotion

In determining the accuracy of judgments based on facial expression, a continuing problem has been deciding on a criterion, independent of the face, for establishing which emotion, if any, was experienced at the moment of facial expression. This is especially problematic considering that most facial behavior is probably not related to emotional display; rather, it appears to be punctuative, gestural, self-communicative, or parapractic (Ekman, 1977, 1979).

The problem of an independent criterion, and thus the possibility of validation, has been the greatest obstacle to research on accuracy in judging facial expressions of emotion. A common approach has been to ask subjects to describe their feelings (usually retrospectively) and to see whether their facial expressions differ when reporting emotion A compared with emotion B. Such self-reports are error prone, however, as subjects may fail to remember, or to distinguish among, the emotions experienced, particularly if several minutes elapse before they make the report. For example, a subject who successively felt anger, disgust, and contempt while watching a film might not recall all of these reactions, their exact sequence, or their time of occurrence. This problem can be reduced by limiting self-reports to grosser distinctions (i.e., between pleasant and unpleasant feelings); however, one then cannot determine specifically the relationships between more complex facial behaviors and more differentiated affective states.

A second approach has used elicitors to arouse specific emotions, for example, affectively positive versus negative films or slides; anticipation of an electric shock versus a no-shock trial; or hostile versus friendly remarks made by a confederate. The respondents' facial expressions are then evaluated for variance attributable to the experimental conditions. Because it is unlikely that all subjects experience the same, discrete, sustained emotion during a particular condition, this approach can usually show only that different facial expressions are used in presumably pleasant and unpleasant conditions or that there are overriding commonalities in facial behavior during experimental inductions.

Attempts to predict or "postdict" other information about a subject (e.g., whether he or she has many friends) have also been used to assess accuracy (Archer & Akert, 1977; Cline, 1964). This approach implies, however, that facial expressions can provide information about enduring traits in addition to transient states. Difficulties encountered in the operational definition of traits, in addition to selecting units of facial measurement, encumber this approach.

If particular changes in vocal intensity or prosody, gross body movement, head position, or speech content were infallible indicators of particular emotions, these could serve as accuracy criteria. Unfortunately, there is no evidence that these channels impart any more accurate information about emotional states than do facial expressions. The same difficulties befall investigators who seek unambiguous benchmarks for emotion in the (peripheral) autonomic nervous system or in the central nervous system.

There is, in fact, no single infallible way to determine an individual's "true" emotional state. Multiple convergent measures should be used, such as facial, postural, and psychophysiological, to gain a more reliable indication of the emotions displayed and experienced.

Emotional information in the face

Despite these difficulties, there is evidence that facial expressions of emotion can provide accurate information about the occurrence of pleasant, as compared with unpleasant, emotional states. A reanalysis of studies from 1914 to 1970 concluded that both facial measurement and observers' judgments can accurately distinguish pleasant from unpleasant states (Ekman, Friesen, & Ellsworth, 1972, 1982a). Since then, a number of experiments have replicated these findings but have not extended them to possible distinctions among particular positive and negative emotions. There is little information pinpointing the specific facial actions that differentiate pleasant and unpleasant states. In the vast majority of studies, most investigators have used the message judgment approach, which precludes determining to which configurations the observers were responding. Those who directly measured facial expression have, in large part, failed to report the frequency of specific actions and/or the full-face conformations that provided the pertinent information.

More recent experiments using facial electromyography have produced evidence bearing on the discrimination of pleasant versus unpleasant emotional states. Schwartz, Fair, Salt, Mandel, and Klerman (1976a,b) used an affective-imagery task to induce emotions. They showed that "happy" imagery conditions were separable from negative-affect conditions, largely through the reciprocal activities in EMG sites overlying the corrugator supercilii (which lowers and draws together the brows) and zygomatic major (which raises the lip corners into a smile). Corrugator sites also tend to show EMG activity corresponding to self-reported negative-thought frequency (Teasdale & Rezin, 1978). Fridlund, Schwartz, and Fowler (1984) also reported good discrimination of "happy" from negative-affect imagery trials. In these EMG studies, the imagery trials are presumed to induce "real" emotions. That they may instead induce a type of posed expression was suggested by Ekman, Hager, and Friesen (1981) and later by Fridlund and Izard (1983).

A careful analysis of what responses are being detected in these EMG experiments has yet to be performed. Are subjects in "negative-affect" conditions just frowning more, and in "positive-affect" conditions, smiling more? Or is there other, more tonic muscular activity signifying an index of mood? No definitive data have been provided.

In addition to distinguishing positive from negative emotions, facial expressions seem also to provide accurate information about the intensities of, and distinctions among, several specific negative and positive emotions. Surprisingly, few decoding studies have attempted to categorize seemingly spontaneous facial expressions into a range of emotional categories. Most studies either have used posed expressions as stimuli or have instructed subjects merely to classify facial expressions along a pleasant–unpleasant dimension. Only a few studies offer relevant data.

Ekman, Friesen, and Ancoli (1980) used FACS to study the spontaneous facial expressions that occurred while the subjects watched motion picture films and then reported on their subjective experience. High correlations were found for specific facial actions hypothesized to be signs of positive and negative emotions and for self-reports of the intensity of those positive and negative emotions. Facial actions that reliably distinguished reports of disgust were also isolated.

Several facial EMG studies have tried to discriminate among multiple posed emotional states. Highly patterned, multiple-site EMG activity is found with instructions to pose facial expressions of several emotions (Sumitsuji, Matsumoto, Tanaka, Kashiwagi, & Kaneko, 1967, 1977). Trained actors generate higher-amplitude, more discriminable EMG patterns than do untrained controls (Rusalova, Izard, & Simonov, 1975). Vaughan and Lanzetta (1980) employed a "vicarious classical conditioning" paradigm in which observers are exposed to a model who appears to be experiencing pain. Under these conditions, subjects generate EMG patterns congruent with emotions of "anticipation" and "pain" when models are ostensibly anticipating, and then receiving, noxious stimuli. Finally, Fridlund et al. (1984) showed reliable multivariate classifications of both posed and imagery-related trials across emotional categories of happiness, sadness, anger, and fear.

Paradoxically, the emotional information communicated by the face can be inferred from situations in which the face is used to falsify such information. Facial expressions may not only reflect emotional state but may also (1) feign emotion when none is present (e.g., the social smile), (2) attenuate or dampen the apparent intensity of any felt positive emotion (e.g., the dampening smile), and/or (3) mask the presence of a negative felt emotion with a simulated alternative emotion (e.g., the masking smile). Quite often the literature has obscured these distinctions by using the overinclusive term *deception*. In order to understand by which process the subjects are responding, it is necessary in facial deception studies to sample both facial behavior and other response systems possibly indicative of emotion. Among the dozens of recent experiments on interpersonal deceit, few (e.g., Ekman & Friesen, 1974; Harper, Wiens, & Fujita, 1977; Lanzetta, Cartwright-Smith, & Kleck, 1976; Mehrabian, 1971; Zuckerman, DeFrank, Hall, Larrance, & Rosenthal, 1979) explicitly instructed their subjects to conceal their emotions and also obtained evidence (independent of the face) that the subjects actually experienced some emotion.

These experimental tests of the extent to which the face can be used to deceive have yielded contradictory results, which are most likely due to variations in the strength or number of emotions aroused, the subjects' motivation to deceive, and their prior practice in perpetrating such deception. However, these experiments have also differed in other ways, for example, whether the subjects knew they were being videotaped, whether the observers knew that deception might be involved, whether the observers were trained, and whether channels other than facial expression were available to the observers.

Information from the face versus other nonverbal channels

It is clear that the face provides emotional information. What is less clear is how this information compares with that obtained from the voice, speech, and body movement. A number of studies have compared observers' judgments of an event perceived via different verbal and nonverbal "channels": audiovisual, aural alone, or visual alone. Others have focused on which of several discrepant cues (delivered across channels) are remembered or acted upon. Since the initial findings by Mehrabian and Ferris (1967), most experiments have found that the face is more accurately judged, produces higher agreement, or correlates better with judgments based on full audiovisual input than does speech content or tone of voice; this difference has been termed *video primacy* (Argyle, Alkema, & Gilmour, 1971; Bugental, Kaswan, & Love, 1970; Burns & Beier, 1973; DePaulo, Rosenthal, Eisenstat, Rogers, & Finkelstein, 1978; Zaidel & Mehrabian, 1969). Video primacy is especially apparent when speech content is filtered (Zuckerman, Amidon, Bishop, & Pomerantz, 1982). The results of a few experiments have departed from the Mehrabian and Ferris (1967) findings and have suggested that the face was less important than another channel was (Berman, Shulman, & Marwit, 1976; Shapiro, 1972) or that the channel cue varied with the observer (Van de Creek & Watkins, 1972). The factors accounting for these differences in findings are not yet known.

A study by Ekman, Friesen, O'Sullivan, and Scherer (1980) found that the relative weight given to facial expression, speech, and body cues depended on both the judgment task (e.g., rating the stimulus person's dominance, sociability, or relaxation) and the conditions in which the behavior occurred (whether subjects frankly described positive reactions to a pleasant film or tried to conceal negative feelings aroused by a stressful film). The correlation between judgments made by observers who saw the face with speech were quite low on some scales (e.g., calm–agitated) and quite high on other scales (outgoing–withdrawn).

Krauss, Apple, Morency, Wenzel, and Winton (1981) also published data on the relative weighting of verbal and nonverbal channels. Krauss and his colleagues used judgments from observers of a televised political debate and videotaped samples of interviews with college women, alone and in combination with typescripts and content-filtered speech, and they concluded that there was "no support for the widespread assumption that nonverbal channels . . . form the primary basis for the communication of affect" (Krauss et al., 1981, p. 312). As such, the Krauss et al. findings have been interpreted as corroborating those of Ekman et al. (1980) in negating video primacy. However, O'Sullivan and Ekman (1983) criticized the Krauss et al. findings because (1) no independent evidence was obtained that the videotaped expressers were emotionally aroused, (2) typescripts were selected with bias toward samples rich in verbal content, (3) face and body were not isolated for videotaped presentations, and (4) the rating scales used had low ecological validity. O'Sullivan and Ekman (1983) reemphasized that the Ekman et al. (1980) data did not negate video primacy but, rather, established its dependence on context.

Studies by Bugental and her colleagues suggested that the influence of facial expression, as compared with other sources, depends on the expresser, the perceiver, the message contained in each channel, and previous experience. Children were less influenced than were adults by a smile shown by an adult female when it was accompanied by negative words and voice tone (Bugental, Kaswan, Love, & Fox, 1970). Some experimental grounds for distrusting mothers' smiles was found in a study showing that smiling in mothers (but not fathers) was not related to the positive versus negative content of the simultaneous speech (Bugental, Love, & Gianetto, 1971). Also, mothers (but not fathers) of disturbed children produced more discrepant messages (among face, voice, and words) than did parents of nondisturbed children (Bugental, Love, & Kaswan, 1971).

The whole question of how much information is conveyed by separate channels may have been miscast. There is no evidence that individuals in actual social interactions selectively attend to different channels, although there is speculation that this may be an individual characteristic of interest. There is no evidence that information conveyed to separate channels is merely additive. We believe that it is more likely that different channels contribute differentially depending on the trait or emotion of interest. The expression of some emotions are probably more easily expressed or inhibited in one channel than in another, and observers may prefer a particular channel when all are available but can use information from other channels if forced to do so. We shall now turn from the question of how one person knows the emotional state of another to the question of knowing our own emotional state.

Facial feedback

How can we account for the subjective experience of emotion? The debate over this issue has been dominated by theorists arguing for the primacy of either "peripheral" visceral and striate-muscle responses (James, 1884, 1890; Lange, 1885; Tomkins, 1962, 1963, 1982) or the primacy of "central" cognitive appraisal (e.g., Cannon, 1927, 1931; Lazarus, Averill, & Opton, 1970; Plutchik, 1977; Schachter & Singer, 1962).

Citing Darwin's (1872) classic work on the origins of emotional expressions, Tomkins (1962, 1963, 1982) modified and extended James's theory of emotion, positing that discrete, differentiated emotions derive from feedback from innately patterned facial expressions. Tomkins's assertions set the stage for several experiments designed to test the "facial feedback hypothesis" – that patterned proprioceptive feedback from facial muscle activity (or from integrated facial expressions) is a necessary and/or sufficient determinant of the experience of emotion (see Buck, 1980, for a detailed account of the facial feedback hypothesis and related research).

A variant of the facial feedback hypothesis, set within the framework of self-attribution theory (Bem, 1967; Schachter, 1964), postulates that we can use information from our own facial (and other) behavior to infer what we feel. Laird's original study (1974) provided a model for later facial feedback experiments: The subjects were instructed to contract particular facial muscles, producing – presumably without their awareness – a "happy" or "frowning" expression that they maintained on their faces while viewing slides or cartoons. The face manipulation had a significant, though small, effect (compared with the effect of the slides) on their reported feelings. A subsequent series of experiments found that individual differences on the face manipulation task were related to other indices of an individual's tendency to use "self"- versus "situation"-produced cues (Duncan & Laird, 1977).

Tourangeau and Ellsworth (1979) failed to confirm the strong version of the facial feedback hypothesis, that is, that overt facial expression is both necessary and sufficient for the experience of emotion. Facial manipulations had no significant effect on self-reported emotion and only ambiguous effects on physiological responses. The study was roundly criticized. The criticisms pointed out the difficulties in testing experimentally the facial feedback hypothesis. Hager and Ekman (1981) cited three main shortcomings: (1) The specific requested movements were not valid analogs of emotional expressions; (2) other expressions besides the requested movements may have occurred; and (3) the procedures were subject to contamination by demand characteristics. Izard (1981) asserted that any role that facial feedback might play in emotional experience would be reflexive, nearly immediate, and only a few milliseconds in duration. Tomkins (1981) commented on the artificiality of the expression-manipulation procedure and on the fact that the procedure bypassed the numerous physiological systems normally involved in affect (e.g., respiration and blood flow). In response to these criticisms, Ellsworth and Tourangeau (1981) stated that their experiment disconfirmed the "necessity" version of the facial feedback hypothesis and not the "sufficiency" variant. The criticisms of the Tourangeau and Ellsworth (1979) experiment, and the authors' rebuttal, should be consulted for elaborations of these issues.

Other tests for the facial feedback hypothesis have monitored facial expressivity and other (usually physiological) indices of emotional behavior (e.g., Zuckerman, Klorman, Larrance, & Spiegel, 1981). A positive correlation between magnitudes of within-trial facial expressions and adjunctive indices of emotion is taken as supporting the hypothesis. Buck (1980) schematized the various interpretations and derivatives of the facial feedback hypothesis and the corresponding methods for testing each.

The strongest evidence for a positive link between voluntary facial expression and emotion comes from a series of experiments by Lanzetta, Kleck, and colleagues (Colby, Lanzetta, & Kleck, 1977; Kleck, Vaughan, Cartwright-Smith, Vaughan, Colby, & Lanzetta, 1976; Lanzetta, Cartwright-Smith, & Kleck, 1976), investigating the effect of overt facial expression on the intensity of emotional arousal produced by shock. Attempts to conceal facial signs of pain consistently led to decreases in both skin conductance and subjective ratings of pain, whereas posing the expression of intense shock significantly increased both measures of arousal. When the subjects were told that they were being observed by another person, they showed less intense facial expressions and correspondingly reduced autonomic responses and subjective ratings of pain, even though they received no instructions to inhibit their responses (Kleck et al., 1976).

These findings can be interpreted in various ways (see Lanzetta et al., 1976). Before concluding that facial feedback was directly and causally related to the observed changes in arousal, it would be necessary to rule out the possibility that some other strategy used by the subjects might have affected (or comediated) both their facial expressions and emotional experience. It is also not clear that the effect is specific to facial versus bodily signs of emotion. Nevertheless, these findings suggest that overt facial expression is often correlated with intensity of emotional arousal. Evidence that facial feedback can determine which emotion is experienced is far more tenuous.

There are ample neuromuscular pathways by which facial activity can mediate emotional experience, including exteroceptors in the superficial layers of facial skin, distention and thermoreceptors in the deeper facial skin, and possible spindle organs in facial muscle tissue sensitive to the state of contraction. The studies to date must be seen only as very weak tests of a facial feedback hypothesis. Demand characteristics and possible effects of comediating systems (cognitive or other) for both facial action and ANS measures cannot be discounted. One real test of the facial feedback hypothesis – providing subjects with "simulated" multichannel facial feedback to trigeminal afferent fibers – is technologically unfeasible at this time. Clinical evidence is probably not useful, as studies of changed emotionality in facial hemiparetics are confounded with depressive reactions secondary to disability.

Finally, the studies to date have underestimated the impact of external, social feedback, that is, the micromomentary reactions of conspecifics to an individual's facial displays. From this perspective, the visual, tactile, or auditory feedback from others' reactions may represent an additional basis for the individual's appraisal of emotion or even the principal basis, according to those who emphasize the socialization of emotion (Lewis & Michalson, 1982).

Although other nonverbal channels also communicate emotion and contribute to its experience, the face has a centrality and a universality in this regard that compel our attention – not only as scientists but also as friends, lovers, parents, and casual observers.

References

Allport, F. M. (1924). *Social psychology.* Boston: Houghton Mifflin.

Altmann, S. (1968). Primates. In T. Seboek (Ed.), *Animal communication: Techniques and results of research* (pp. 466–522). Bloomington: Indiana University Press.

Archer, D., & Akert, R. (1977). Words and everything else. Verbal and nonverbal cues in social interpretation. *Journal of Personality and Social Psychology, 35,* 443–449.

Argyle, M., Alkema, F., & Gilmour, R. (1971). The communication of friendly and hostile attitudes by verbal and nonverbal signals. *European Journal of Social Psychology, 1,* 385–402.

Bem, D. J. (1967). Self perception: An alternative interpretation of cognitive dissonance phenomena. *Psychological Review, 74,* 183–200.

Berman, H. J., Shulman, A. D., & Marwit, S. J. (1976). Comparison of multidimensional decoding of affect from audio, video and audiovideo recordings. *Sociometry, 39,* 83–89.

Birdwhistell, R. L. (1970). *Kinesics and context.* Philadelphia: University of Pennsylvania Press.

Blurton Jones, N. G. (1971). Criteria for use in describing facial expression in children. *Human Biology, 41,* 365–413.

(1972). Non-verbal communication in children. In R. A. Hinde (Ed.), *Nonverbal communication* (pp. 271–296). Cambridge: Cambridge University Press.

Boucher, J. D. (1973). *Facial behavior and the perception of emotion: Studies of Malays and Temuan Orang Asli.* Paper presented at the Conference on Psychology Related Disciplines, Kuala Lumpur.

Boucher, J. D., & Carlson, G. E. (1980). Recognition of facial expression in three cultures. *Journal of Cross-Cultural Psychology, 11,* 263–280.

Brannigan, C. R., & Humphries, D. A. (1972). Human nonverbal behavior, a means of communication. In N. G. Blurton Jones (Ed.), *Ethological studies of child behavior* (pp. 37–64). Cambridge: Cambridge University Press.

Brown, S. L., & Schwartz, G. E. (1980). Relationships between facial electromyography and subjective experience during affective imagery. *Biological Psychology, 11,* 49–62.

Bruner, J. S., & Tagiuri, R. (1954). The perception of people. In G. Lindzey (Ed.), *Handbook of social psychology* (Vol. 2, pp. 634–654). Reading, MA: Addison-Wesley.

Buck, R. (1980). Nonverbal behavior and the theory of emotion: The facial feedback hypothesis. *Journal of Personality and Social Psychology, 38,* 811–824.

Buck, R., Baron, R., & Barrette, D. (1982). Temporal organization of spontaneous emotional expression: A segmentation analysis. *Journal of Personality and Social Psychology, 42,* 506–517.

Bugental, D. E. (1986). Unmasking the "polite smile": Situational and personal determinants of managed affect in adult–child interaction. *Personality and Social Psychology Bulletin, 12,* 7–16.

Bugental, D. E., Kaswan, J. W., & Love, L. R. (1970). Perception of contradictory meanings conveyed by verbal and nonverbal channels. *Journal of Personality and Social Psychology, 16,* 647–655.

Bugental, D. E., Kaswan, J., Love, L., & Fox, M. (1970). Child versus adult perception of evaluative messages in verbal, vocal, and visual channels. *Developmental Psychology, 2*, 367–375.

Bugental, D. E., Love, L., & Gianetto, R. (1971). Perfidious feminine faces. *Journal of Personality and Social Psychology, 17*, 314–318.

Bugental, D. E., Love, L., & Kaswan, J. (1971). Verbal–nonverbal conflict in parental messages to normal and disturbed children. *Journal of Abnormal Psychology, 77*, 6–10.

Burns, K. L., & Beier, E. G. (1973). Significance of vocal and visual channels in the decoding of emotional meaning. *Journal of Communications, 23*, 118–130.

Cacioppo, J. T., & Petty, R. E. (1981). Electromyographic specificity during covert information processing. *Psychophysiology, 18*, 518–523.

Cannon, W. B. (1927). The James–Lange theory of emotions: A critical examination and an alternative theory. *American Journal of Psychology, 39*, 106–124.

(1931). Again the James–Lange and the thalamic theory of emotions. *Psychological Review, 38*, 281–295.

Charlesworth, W. R., & Kreutzer, M. A. (1973). Facial expression of infants and children. In P. Ekman (Ed.), *Darwin and facial expression* (pp. 91–168). New York: Academic Press.

Chevalier-Skolnikoff, S. (1973). Facial expression of emotion in non-human primates. In P. Ekman (Ed.), *Darwin and facial expression* (pp. 11–89). New York: Academic Press.

Cline, V. B. (1964). Interpersonal perception. In B. A. Maher (Ed.), *Progress in experimental personality research* (Vol. 1, pp. 221–284). New York: Academic Press.

Colby, C. Z., Lanzetta, J. T., & Kleck, R. E. (1977). Effects of the expression of pain on autonomic and pain tolerance responses to subject-controlled pain. *Psychophysiology, 14*, 537–540.

Condon, W. S., & Ogston, W. D. (1967a). A method of studying animal behavior. *Journal of Auditory Research, 7*, 359–365.

(1967b). A segmentation of behavior. *Journal of Psychiatric Research, 5*, 221–235.

Darwin, C. (1955). *The expression of the emotions in man and animals.* New York: Philosophical Library. (Originally published 1872)

Davidson, R. J., Ekman, P., Saron, C., Senulis., J., & Friesen, W. V. (1990). Approach–withdrawal and cerebral asymmetry: Emotional expression and brain physiology I. *Journal of Personality and Social Psychology, 58*(2), 330–341.

DePaulo, B. M., Rosenthal, R., Eisenstat, R. A., Rogers, P. L., & Finkelstein, S. (1978). Decoding discrepant nonverbal cues. *Journal of Personality and Social Psychology, 36*, 313–323.

Dickey, R. V., & Knower, R. H. (1941). A note on some ethnological differences in recognition of simulated expressions of the emotions. *American Journal of Sociology, 47*, 190–193.

Duchenne, G. B. (1990). *The mechanism of human facial expression.* (R. A. Cuthbertson, Ed. and Trans.). Cambridge: Cambridge University Press. (Original work published 1862)

Duncan, J., & Laird, J. D. (1977). Cross-modality consistencies in individual differences in self-attribution. *Journal of Personality, 45*, 191–206.

Ekman, P. (1972). Universals and cultural differences in facial expressions of emotion. In J. Cole (Ed.), *Nebraska Symposium on Motivation* (pp. 207–283). Lincoln: University of Nebraska Press.

(1973). Cross cultural studies of facial expressions. In P. Ekman (Ed.), *Darwin and facial expression* (pp. 169–229). New York: Academic Press.

(1977). Biological and cultural contributions to body and facial movement. In J. Blacking (Ed.), *The anthropology of the body* (pp. 34–84). London: Academic Press.

(1979). About brows: Emotional and conversational signals. In M. von Cranach, K. Foppa, W. Lepenies, & D. Ploog (Eds.), *Human ethology* (pp. 169–249). Cambridge: Cambridge University Press.

(1982). Methods for measuring facial action. In K. Scherer & P. Ekman (Eds.), *Handbook of methods in nonverbal behavior research* (pp. 45–90). Cambridge: Cambridge University Press.

(1985). *Telling lies*. New York: Norton.

(1989). The argument and evidence about universals in facial expressions of emotion. In H. Wagner and A. Manstead (Eds.), *Handbook of social psychophysiology* (pp. 143–164). Chichester: Wiley.

Ekman, P., Davidson, R. J., & Friesen, W. V. (1990). The Duchenne smile: Emotional expression and brain physiology I. *Journal of Personality and Social Psychology, 58*(2), 342–353.

Ekman, P., & Friesen, W. V. (1969). The repertoire of nonverbal behavior: Categories, origins, usage, and coding. *Semiotica, 1*, 49–98.

(1971). Constants across cultures in the face and emotion. *Journal of Personality and Social Psychology, 17*, 124–129.

(1974). Detecting deception from the body or face. *Journal of Personality and Social Psychology, 29*, 288–298.

(1976). Measuring facial movement. *Journal of Environmental Psychology and Nonverbal Behavior, 1*, 56–75.

(1978). *The Facial Action Coding System*. Palo Alto, CA: Consulting Psychologists Press.

(1982). Felt, false, and miserable smiles. *Journal of Nonverbal Behavior, 6*, 238–252.

(1986). A new pan-cultural expression of emotion. *Motivation and Emotion, 10*, 159–168.

(1988). Who knows what about contempt: A reply to Izard and Haynes. *Motivation and Emotion, 12*, 17–22.

Ekman, P., Friesen, W. V., & Ancoli, S. (1980). Facial signs of emotional experience. *Journal of Personality and Social Psychology, 39*, 1125–1134.

Ekman, P., Friesen, W. V., & Ellsworth, P. (1972). *Emotion in the human face: Guidelines for research and an integration of findings*. Elmsford, NY: Pergamon.

(1982a). What components of facial behavior are related to observers' judgments of emotion? In P. Ekman (Ed.), *Emotion in the human face* (2nd ed., pp. 98–110). Cambridge: Cambridge University Press.

(1982b). What emotion categories or dimensions can observers judge from facial behavior? In P. Ekman (Ed.), *Emotion in the human face* (2nd ed., pp. 39–55). Cambridge: Cambridge University Press.

Ekman, P., Friesen, W. V., & O'Sullivan, M. (1988). Smiles when lying. *Journal of Personality and Social Psychology, 54*, 414–420.

Ekman, P., Friesen, W. V., O'Sullivan, M., Chan, A., Diacoyanni-Tarlatzis, I., Heider, K., Krause, R., LeCompte, W. A., Pitcairn, T., Ricci Bitti, P. E., Scherer, K. R., Tomita, M., & Tzavaras, A., (1987). Universals and cultural differences in the judgments of facial expressions of emotion. *Journal of Personality and Social Psychology, 53*, 712–717.

Ekman, P., Friesen, W. V., O'Sullivan, M., & Scherer, K. (1980). Relative importance of face, body and speech in judgments of personality and affect. *Journal of Personality and Social Psychology, 38*, 270–277.

Ekman, P., & Friesen, W. V., & Tomkins, S. S. (1971). Facial Affect Scoring Technique (FAST): A first validity study. *Semiotica, 3*, 37–38.

Ekman, P., Hager, J. C., & Friesen, W. V. (1981). The symmetry of emotional and deliberate facial actions. *Psychophysiology, 18*, 101–106.

Ekman, P., & Heider, K. (1988). The universality of a contempt expression: A replication. *Motivation and Emotion, 12*(4), 303–308.

Ekman, P., Levenson, R. W., & Friesen, W. V. (1983). Emotions differ in autonomic nervous system activity. *Science, 221*, 1208–1210.

Ekman, P., & Oster, H. (1979). Facial expressions of emotion. *Annual Review of Psychology. 30*, 527–554.

Ekman, P., & O'Sullivan, M. (1988). The role of context in interpreting facial expression: Comment on Russell and Fehr (1987). *Journal of Experimental Psychology, 117*, 86–88.

Ekman, P., Roper, G., & Hager, J. C. (1980). Deliberate facial movement. *Child Development, 51*, 886–891.

Ekman, P., Sorenson, E. R., & Friesen, W. V. (1969). Pan-cultural elements in facial displays of emotions. *Science, 164*, 86–88.

Ellsworth, P., & Tourangeau, R. (1981). On our failure to disconfirm what nobody ever said. *Journal of Personality and Social Psychology, 40*, 363–369.

Englis, B. G., Vaughan, K. B., & Lanzetta, J. T. (1981). Conditioning of counterempathetic emotional responses. *Journal of Experimental Social Psychology, 38*, 375–391.

Ermiane, R., & Gergarian, E. (1978). *Les expressions du visage.* Paris: La Pensée Universelle.

Fox, N. A., & Davidson, R. J. (1988). Patterns of brain electrical activity during facial signs of emotion in 10 month old infants. *Developmental Psychology. 24*, 230–236.

Fridlund, A. J., Ekman, P., & Oster, H. (1987). Facial expression of emotion. In A. Siegman & S. Feldstein (Eds.), *Nonverbal behavior and communication* (pp. 143–224). Hillsdale, NJ: Erlbaum.

Fridlund, A. J., & Izard, C. E. (1983). Electromyographic studies of facial expressions of emotions and patterns of emotions. In J. T. Cacioppo & R. E. Petty (Eds.), *Social psychophysiology: A sourcebook* (pp. 243–286). New York: Guilford Press.

Fridlund, A. J., Schwartz, G. E., & Fowler, S. C. (1984). Pattern recognition of self-reported emotional state from multiple-site facial EMG activity during affective imagery. *Psychophysiology, 21*, 622–637.

Friesen, W. V. (1972). *Cultural differences in facial expressions in a social situation: An experimental test of the concept of display rules.* Unpublished doctoral dissertation, University of California, San Francisco.

Frois-Wittman, J. (1930). The judgment of facial expression. *Journal of Experimental Psychology, 13*, 113–151.

Fulcher, J. S. (1942). "Voluntary" facial expression in blind and seeing children. *Archives of Psychology, 38* (272), 1–49.

Garfield, D. A., Rogoff, M. L., & Steinberg, S. (1987). Affect recognition and self-esteem in schizophrenia. *Psychopathology, 20*(5), 225–233.

Goodenough, F. L. (1932). Expression of the emotions in a blind–deaf child. *Journal of Abnormal Social Psychology, 27*, 328–333.

Graham, J. A., & Argyle, M. (1975). The effects of different patterns of gaze combined with different facial expressions. *Journal of Human Movement Studies, 1*, 178–182.

Grant, N. G. (1969). Human facial expression. *Man, 4*, 525–536.

Guilford, J. P. (1929). An experiment in learning to read facial expression. *Journal of Abnormal and Social Psychology, 24,* 191–202.

Hager, J. C., & Ekman, P. (1981). Methodological problems of Tourangeau and Ellsworth's study of facial expression and experience of emotion. Journal of *Personality and Social Psychology, 40,* 358–362.

Harper, R. G., Wiens, A. N., & Fujita, B. (1977). *Individual differences in encoding–decoding of emotional expression and emotional dissimulation.* Paper presented at the Annual Meeting of the American Psychological Association, San Francisco.

Hjorstjo, C. H. (1970). *Man's face and mimic language.* Lund: Studentliterature.

Hunt, W. A. (1941). Recent developments in the field of emotion. *Psychological Bulletin, 38,* 249–276.

Izard, C. E. (1971). *The face of emotion.* New York: Appleton-Century-Crofts.

(1972). *Patterns of emotion: A new analysis of anxiety and depression.* New York: Academic Press.

(1977). *Human emotions.* New York: Plenum.

(1979). *The maximally discriminative facial movement coding system (MAX).* (Available from Instructional Resources Center, University of Delaware, Newark)

(1981). Differential-emotions theory and the facial feedback hypothesis of emotion activation: Comments on Tourangeau's "The role of facial response in the expression of emotion." *Journal of Personality and Social Psychology, 40,* 350–354.

Izard, C. E., & Dougherty, L. M. (1980). *System for identifying affect expressions by holistic judgment (AFFEX).* Newark: Instructional Resources Center, University of Delaware.

Izard, C. E., & Haynes, O. M. (1988). On the form and universality of the contempt expression: A challenge to Ekman and Friesen's claim of discovery. *Motivation and Emotion, 12,* 1–16.

James, W. (1884). What is an emotion? *Mind, 9,* 188–204.

(1890). *The principles of psychology.* New York: Holt.

Kleck, R. E., Vaughan, R. C., Cartwright-Smith, J., Vaughan, K. B., Colby, C. Z., & Lanzetta, J. T. (1976). Effects of being observed on expressive, subjective, and physiological responses to painful stimuli. *Journal of Personality and Social Psychology, 34,* 1211–1218.

Klineberg, O. (1938). Emotional expression in Chinese literature. *Journal of Abnormal and Social Psychology, 33,* 517–520.

Krauss, R. M., Apple, W., Morency, N., Wenzel, C., & Winton, W. (1981). Verbal, vocal, and visible factors in judgments of another's affect. *Journal of Personality and Social Psychology, 40,* 312–320.

Laird, J. D. (1974). Self-attribution of emotion: The effects of expressive behavior on the quality of emotional experience. *Journal of Personality and Social Psychology, 29,* 475–486.

Lalljee, M. (1978). The role of gaze in the expression of emotion. *Austrian Journal of Psychology, 30,* 59–67.

Landis, C. (1924). Studies of emotional reactions: II. General behavior and facial expression. *Journal of Comparative Psychology, 4,* 447–509.

Lange, C. G. (1885). *Om sindsbevaegelser. et psyko. fysiolog. studie.* Copenhagen: Krønar.

Lanzetta, J. T., Cartwright-Smith, J., & Kleck, R. E. (1976). Effects of nonverbal dissimulation on emotional experience and autonomic arousal. *Journal of Personality and Social Psychology, 33,* 354–370.

Lazarus, R. S., Averill, J. R., & Opton, E. M. (1970). Toward a cognitive theory of emotion. In M. Arnold (Ed.), *Feelings and emotions* (pp. 207–232). New York: Academic Press.

Levenson, R. W., Ekman, P., & Friesen, W. V. (in press). Voluntary facial expression generates emotion-specific nervous system activity. *Psychophysiology*.

Lewis, M., & Michalson, L. (1982). The socialization of emotions. In T. Field & A. Fogel (Eds.), *Emotion and early interaction*. Hillsdale, NJ: Erlbaum.

McGrew, W. C. (1972). *An ethological study of children's behavior*. New York: Academic Press.

Malmo, R. B., & Shagass, C. (1949). Physiologic studies of reaction to stress in anxiety and early schizophrenia. *Psychosomatic Medicine, 11*, 9–24.

Matsumoto, D. (1986). *Cross-cultural communication of emotion*. Unpublished doctoral dissertation. University of California, Berkeley.

Matsumoto, D., & Ekman, P. (1989). *Japanese and Caucasian facial expressions of emotion (JACFEE) and neutral faces (JACNeuF)*. (Available from Dr. David Matsumoto, The Wright Institute, 2728 Durant Ave., Berkeley, CA 94704)

———— (1989). American–Japanese cultural differences in rating the intensity of facial expressions of emotion. *Motivation and Emotion, 13*, 143–157.

Mead, M. (1975). Review of *Darwin and facial expression* (P. Ekman, Ed.). *Journal of Communication, 25*, 209–213.

Mehrabian, A. (1971). Nonverbal betrayal of feeling. *Journal of Experimental Research in Personality, 5*, 64–73.

Mehrabian, A., & Ferris, S. (1967). Inference of attitudes from nonverbal communication in two channels. *Journal of Consulting Psychology, 31*, 248–252.

Morrison, R. L., Bellack, A. S., & Mueser, K. T. (1988). Deficits in facial-affect recognition and schizophrenia. *Schizophrenia Bulletin, 14*,(1), 67–83.

Niit, T., & Valsiner, J. (1977). Recognition of facial expressions: An experimental investigation of Ekman's model. *Tartu Riikliku Ulikooli Toimetised: Trudy po Psikhologii*, No.429, 85–107.

Nystrom, M. (1974). Neonatal facial–postural patterning during sleep: I. Description and reliability of observation. *Psychological Research Bulletin, 14*, 1–16.

Oliveau, D., & Willmuth, R. (1979). Facial muscle electromyography in depressed and nondepressed hospitalized subjects: A partial replication. *American Journal of Psychiatry, 136*, 548–550.

Oster, H., & Rosenstein, D. (1983). *Analyzing facial movement in infants*. Unpublished manuscript.

O'Sullivan, M., & Ekman, P. (1983). *Is the behavior emotional? A reply to "Verbal, vocal and visible factors in judgments of another's affect."* Unpublished manuscript.

O'Sullivan, M., & Guilford, J. P. (1975). Six factors of behavioral cognition: Understanding other people. *Journal of Educational Measurement, 12*(4), 255–271.

Plutchik, R. (1962). *The emotions: Facts, theories and a new model*. New York: Random House.

———— (1977). Cognitions in the service of emotions: An evolutionary perspective. In D. K. Candland, J. P. Fell, E. Keen, A. I. Leshner, R. M. Tarpy, & R. Plutchik (Eds.), *Emotion* (pp. 189–212). Monterey, CA: Brooks/Cole.

Redican, W. K. (1975). Facial expression in nonhuman primates. In L. A. Rosenblum (Ed.), *Primate behavior* ₄Vol. 4, pp. 103–194). New York: Academic Press.

———— (1982). An evolutionary perspective on human facial displays. In P. Ekman (Ed.), *Emotion in the human face* (2nd ed., pp. 212–280). Cambridge: Cambridge University Press.

Rosenthal, R., Hall, J. A., DiMatteo, M. R., Rogers, P. L., & Archer, D. (1979). *Sensitivity to nonverbal communication: The PONS test*. Baltimore: Johns Hopkins University Press.

Ruch, W. (1987, June). *Personality aspects in the psychobiology of humour laughter*. Paper presented at the third meeting of the ISSID, Toronto.

Rusalova, M. N. (1987). Lateralization of voluntary control of facial expression. *Human Physiology, 13*(4), 263–268.

Rusalova, M. N., Izard, C. E., & Simonov, P. V. (1975). Comparative analysis of mimical and autonomic components of man's autonomic state. *Aviation, Space, and Environmental Medicine, 46*, 1132–1134.

Russell, J. A., & Fehr, B. (1987). Relativity in the perception of emotion in facial expression. *Journal of Experimental Psychology, 116*, 233–237.

Saha, G. B. (1973). Judgment of facial expression of emotion – A cross-cultural study. *Journal of Psychological Research, 17*, 59–63.

Schachter, S. (1964). The interaction of cognitive and physiological determinants of emotional states. In L. Berkowitz (Ed.), *Advances in experimental social psychology* (Vol. 1, pp. 49–80). New York: Academic Press.

Schachter, S., & Singer, J. E. (1962). Cognitive, social, and physiological determinants of emotional state. *Psychological Review, 69*, 379–399.

Schlosberg, H. (1941). A scale for the judgment of facial expression. *Journal of Experimental Psychology, 29*, 497–510.

  (1952). The description of facial expressions in terms of two dimensions. *Journal of Experimental Psychology, 44*, 229–237.

  (1954). Three dimensions of emotion. *Psychological Review, 61*, 81–88.

Schneider, K. (1987). Achievement-related emotions in preschoolers. In F. Hahseh & J. Kuhl (Eds.), *Motivation, intention and volition*. Berlin: Springer-Verlag.

Schwartz, G. E., Brown, S. L., & Ahern, G. L. (1980). Facial muscle patterning and subjective experience during affective imagery. *Psychophysiology, 17*, 75–82.

Schwartz, G. E., Fair, P. L., Mandel, M. R., Salt, P., Mieske, M., & Klerman, G. L. (1978). Facial electromyography in the assessment of improvement in depression. *Psychosomatic Medicine, 40*, 355–360.

Schwartz, G. E., Fair, P. L., Salt, P., Mandel, M. R., & Klerman, G. L. (1976a). Facial expression and imagery in depression: An electromyographic study. *Psychosomatic Medicine, 38*, 337–347.

  (1976b). Facial muscle patterning to affective imagery in depressed and nondepressed subjects. *Science, 192*, 489–491.

Seaford, H. W. (1976). *Maximizing replicability in describing facial behavior*. Paper presented at the Annual Meeting of the American Anthropological Association, Washington, DC.

Shapiro, J. G. (1972). Variability and usefulness of facial and bodily cues. *Comparative Group Studies, 3*, 437–442.

Steiner, F. (1986). Differentiating smiles. In E. Branniger-Huber and F. Steiner (Eds.), *FACS in psychotherapy research* (pp. 139–148). Reading, MA: Addison-Wesley.

Sumitsuji, N., Matsumoto, K., Tanaka, M., Kashiwagi, T., & Kaneko, Z. (1967). Electromyographic investigation of the facial muscles. *Electromyography, 7*, 77–96.

  (1977). An attempt to systematize human emotion from EMG study of the facial expression. *Proceedings of the Fourth Congress of the International College of Psychosomatic Medicine*, Kyoto, Japan.

198   Paul Ekman and Maureen O'Sullivan

Tagiuri, R. (1968). Person perception. In G. Lindzey & E. Aronson (Eds.), *Handbook of social psychology* (pp. 395–449). Reading, MA: Addison-Wesley.

Teasdale, J. D., & Bancroft, J. (1977). Manipulation of thought content as a determinant of mood and corrugator activity in depressed patients. *Journal of Abnormal Psychology, 86,* 235–241.

Teasdale, J. D., & Rezin, V. (1978). Effect of thought-stopping on thoughts, mood and corrugator EMG in depressed patients. *Behavior Research and Therapy, 16,* 97–102.

Tomkins, S. S. (1962). *Affect, imagery, consciousness: Vol. 1. The positive affects.* New York: Springer-Verlag.

(1963). *Affect, imagery, consciousness: Vol. 2. The negative affects.* New York: Springer-Verlag.

(1981). The role of facial response in the experience of emotion: A reply to Tourangeau and Ellsworth. *Journal of Personality and Social Psychology, 40,* 355–359.

(1982). *Affect, imagery, consciousness: Vol. 3. Cognition and affect.* New York: Springer-Verlag.

Tomkins, S. S., & McCarter, R. (1964). What and where are the primary affects? Some evidence for a theory. *Perceptual and Motor Skills, 18,* 119–158.

Tourangeau, R., & Ellsworth, P. C. (1979). The role of facial response in the experience of emotion. *Journal of Personality and Social Psychology, 37,* 1519–1531.

Triandis, H. C., & Lambert, W. W. (1958). A restatement and test of Schlosberg's theory of emotion with two kinds of subjects from Greece. *Journal of Abnormal and Social Pschology, 58*(3), 321–328.

Van de Creek, L., & Watkins, J. T. (1972). Responses to incongruent verbal and nonverbal emotional cues. *Journal of Communication, 22,* 311–316.

Vaughan, K. B., & Lanzetta, J. T. (1980). Vicarious instigation and conditioning of facial expressive and autonomic responses to a model's expressive display of pain. *Journal of Personality and Social Psychology, 38,* 909–923.

(1981). The effect of modulation of expressive displays on vicarious emotional arousal. *Journal of Experimental Social Psychology, 17,* 16–30.

Vinacke, W. E. (1949). The judgment of facial expressions by three national–racial groups in Hawaii: I. Caucasian faces. *Journal of Personality, 17,* 407–429.

Vinacke, W. E., & Fong, R. W. (1955). The judgment of facial expressions by three national–racial groups in Hawaii: II. Oriental faces. *Journal of Social Psychology, 41,* 184–195.

Waters, E., Matas, L., & Sroufe, L. (1975). Infants' reaction to an approaching stranger: Description, validation, and functional significance of wariness. *Child Development, 46,* 348–356.

Weddell, R. A., Trevarthen, C., & Miller, J. D. (1988). *Neuropsychologia, 26*(3), 373–385.

Weiss, F., Blum, G. S., & Gleberman, L. (1987). Anatomically based measurement of facial expressions in simulated versus hypnotically induced effect. *Motivation and Emotion, 11,* 67–81.

Winkelmayer, R., Exline, R. V., Gottheil, E., & Paredes, A. (1978). The relative accuracy of U.S., British, and Mexican raters in judging the emotional displays of schizophrenic and normal U.S. women. *Journal of Clinical Psychology, 34,* 600–608.

Young, G., & Decarie, T. G. (1977). An ethology-based catalogue of facial/vocal behaviors in infancy. *Animal Behavior, 25,* 95–107.

Zaidel, S., & Mehrabian, A. (1969). The ability to communicate and infer positive and negative attitudes facially and vocally. *Journal of Experimental Research in Personality, 3,* 233–241.

Zuckerman, M., Amidon, M. D., Bishop, S. E., & Pomerantz, S. D. (1982). Face and tone of voice in the communication of deception. *Journal of Personality and Social Psychology, 43,* 347–357.

Zuckerman, M., DeFrank, R. S., Hall, J. A., Larrance, D. T., & Rosenthal, R. (1979). *Journal of Experimental Social Psychology, 15,* 378–396.

Zuckerman, M., Klorman, R., Larrance, D. T., & Spiegel, N. H. (1981). Facial, autonomic, and subjective components of emotion: The facial feedback hypothesis versus the externalizer–internalizer distinction. *Journal of Personality and Social Psychology, 41,* 929–944.

6. Voice and emotion

ARVID KAPPAS, URSULA HESS, AND KLAUS R. SCHERER

... with many kinds of animals, man included, the vocal organs
are efficient in the highest degree as a means of expression.
— Darwin 1872/1965, p. 83

Approaches to the study of vocal affect communication

In a cross-cultural survey on emotional reactions, with 27 countries on
all five continents, changes in the voice were reported for all the emotions studied (Wallbott & Scherer, 1986b). This finding should come as
no surprise, given Darwin's early claim concerning the importance of
vocal indicators of affective state for the communication of emotion. Yet,
it took decades for the systematic study of human nonverbal vocal communication to emerge, unlike the study of facial expression, which was
already pursued quite intensively at the beginning of this century (see
Ekman, Friesen, & Ellsworth, 1982). Impeding early research on vocal
phenomena was the very nature of vocalization: It is difficult to capture
or to store. Although it has been possible to freeze both facial expressions and posture in paintings and sculptures or by using early photographic techniques, only the invention of phonographic records and
magnetic tape, as well as the development of electroacoustic analysis
facilities (Hollien, 1981), has made research on vocal cues possible at
all. In recent years the development of digital storage and analysis methods have been made feasible through advanced computer technology
(Scherer, 1982; Wolf, 1981).

Apart from the problem of storing the vocal signal, the early research
was hampered by the lack of a concise and reliable terminology to specify the phenomenon. The terms used in everyday language to describe
voice and speech characteristics are frequently confounded with de-

200

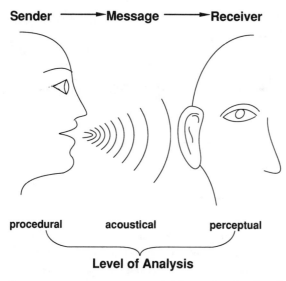

Figure 6.1. The relationship of different levels of analysis of vocal communication to Shannon and Weaver's model of communication.

scriptors of speaker state or are too general to apply to a specific vocal feature. Frequently, the categories used to denote vocal features (e.g., "harsh") refer to a gestalt that cannot be easily characterized in terms of objective acoustic parameters, such as mean fundamental frequency or spectral energy distribution ratios. Although there will be significant differences for some of these parameters between a vocalization that is perceived as harsh and one that is not perceived as such, these might not be solely responsible for the subjective experience of harshness. In outlining the possibilities for the analysis of vocal communication, it is helpful to distinguish among three levels or domains of description (see, e.g., Titze, 1974):

1. The production (procedural) level, referring to the state of the human vocal apparatus at the time an utterance was produced (e.g., subglottal pressure, vocal cord length, vocalis contraction, soft palate position, vocal tract shape).
2. The acoustical level, referring to an objective representation of the voice signal as it travels through air (e.g., sound pressure level, fundamental frequency, glottal pulse shape, formant amplitude ratios, formant frequency ratios).
3. The perceptual level, referring to the descriptions provided by everyday language for the categorization of voices (e.g., loudness, pitch, vibrato, register, ring).

Although these three levels can easily be related to elements of a simple communication model à la Shannon and Weaver (1949; Figure 6.1),

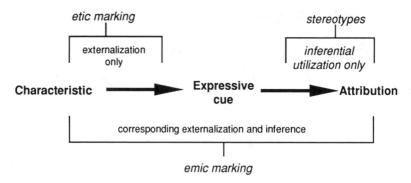

Figure 6.2. Etic and emic markers.

it is more appropriate to regard the sender → message → receiver distinction and the level of analysis as closely related but not identical. For example, it is possible both to perform acoustical analyses on emotional utterances and to relate particular acoustical features to the attribution processes of a receiver, thus remaining within the acoustical level of description yet analyzing sender as well as receiver processes. To clarify the distinction between the two processes and strategies of investigation, the concept of etic and emic markers is helpful (Giles, Scherer & Taylor, 1979; and Figure 6.2). *Emic markers* are behaviors that are both correlated with a particular state and recognized by conspecifics as being correlated with that state. *Etic markers*, on the other hand, while being correlated with an internal state, are not recognized by the interaction partner and therefore are not used in the attribution process. (Obviously, attributions may be based not only on actual markers but also on stereotypes, superstition, misperception, or other factors.)

To highlight the usefulness of this distinction, we shall consider two examples: If we are interested in how we can tell whether our conversation partner on the other end of the telephone is smiling (as we actually can; see Tartter, 1980), we do not need to investigate acoustic features not transmitted over the telephone line (such as energy components above 5 kHz). If, on the other hand, we are interested in using the vocal indicators of the effects of a psychoactive drug treatment as a diagnostic tool, we may not necessarily want to know whether anyone but the computer can tell the difference. Scherer suggested (e.g., 1978, 1982) a modified Brunswikian lens model (Brunswik, 1956) as helpful for separating these two very different classes of studies (Figure 6.3). In its simplest form the lens indicates an encoding process (externalization of a

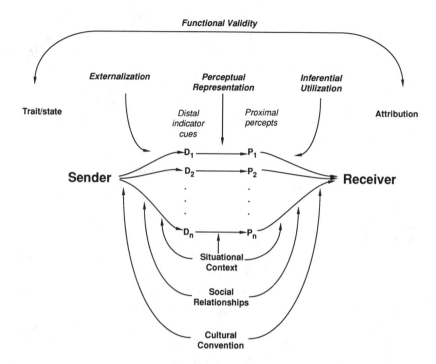

Figure 6.3. Modified version of the Brunswikian lens model.

speaker's state) and a decoding process (attribution of a receiver). Information may be transmitted through more than one channel, sequentially and in parallel, with different levels of redundancy. Indeed, communication is not context free but is embedded in a framework of cultural or social rules and information, shared by the participating individuals. Information transmission may be disturbed at any point of the process through noise. The model can simply be applied as an aid to distinguish conceptually among the processes in (nonverbal) communication and be tested empirically using path analytic methods (Scherer, 1978).

Depending on the level of analysis or description used, researchers have concentrated on particular questions regarding the communication of affective state. The fact that each domain requires a different expertise has discouraged many researchers from investigating the communication process at all three levels of description or at both the sender (encoding) and the receiver (decoding) side. Consequently, a fascinating accumulation of knowledge regarding specific phenomena emerged, but these bits and pieces have not yet been successfully integrated into a theory of the role of vocal parameters in the communication of affect, thus disappointing all those who had hoped for easy answers concerning the relationship of affective state and voice. Harrison and Wiemann described the study of communication in the nonverbal domain as follows: "It appears that the easy findings in nonverbal communication have been skimmed off by early explorers. What lies ahead is a difficult and often tedious task" (1983, pp. 279–280).

In this chapter we shall try to take stock of where we are in the endeavor to add vocal analysis to nonverbal communication research. Our research group, first at the University of Giessen and then at the University of Geneva, has specialized in this research domain over the past 15 years, and this chapter will outline our group's theoretical and methodological development. In addition, we shall review some of the major empirical results obtained in our own and other laboratories. In line with our predominant research concerns, much of our discussion will focus on the vocal communication of emotion. A brief review of the major production mechanisms of vocalization will lead into a summary of the work on vocal affect expression in animals, highlighting the phylogenetic continuity of this mode of communication. We shall then outline the major parameters of vocal analysis and describe the pattern of findings on the encoding or externalization of affect in the voice. Finally, we shall turn to the question of decoding, the ability of naive judges to infer emotion from the voice, with and without additional information from other channels. We shall conclude with an outlook that attempts to specify some of the promising perspectives for future research.

Effects of emotion on the voice

There is considerable evidence that emotional states have a direct impact on the production of both speech and nonspeech vocalization. Scherer (1979a) attempted to show the effects of affect-induced muscle tension changes on vocalization. Similarly, Ohala (1981) mentioned three bodily changes that have an impact on the sounds produced during vocalization:

1. Dryness in the mouth or larynx.
2. Accelerated breathing rate.
3. Muscle tremor.

There is not, as yet, a clear and exhaustive mapping of the bodily changes evoked by emotional states and the resulting vocal changes. Its absence is mainly due to theoretical problems in defining what exactly emotions are and discriminating on a physiological basis among the states that we understand as basic or primary emotions. Although there is a growing consensus that there are physiological differentiations among some affective states (e.g., Campos, 1988; Davidson, 1988; Ekman, 1988; Levenson, 1988), it might not be possible to find autonomic signatures of emotional states as distinct as the facial expressive indicators of affective state. In this chapter, we shall review the evidence available today as well as advance some hypothetical predictions for further research.

To understand the effects of both affective states and voluntary control on vocalizations in humans, it is helpful to understand the nature of the vocalization process. We shall therefore first outline the mechanisms of voice production in humans and subhuman animals.

Mechanisms of voice and speech production

Both speech and non-speech vocalizations are composed of two separate mechanical processes: phonation and articulation. The flow of air through the vocal tract is the basis of all human vocalizations, and *phonation* refers to the production of sound waves, which are then modified or filtered by articulatory processes.

Next we shall describe the relevant mechanical concepts in speech production. A thorough discussion of the central pathways relevant to the control of phonation and articulation would be beyond the scope of this chapter, but interested readers are referred to Ploog (e.g., 1986, 1988) for more detailed information.

Phonation. The larynx functions as a valve regulating the flow of air in and out of the lungs and preventing food and drink from entering the lungs and in addition, it is specially adapted to act as a vibrator "chopping up" the airstream issued from the lungs. These two functions are accomplished by a complex arrangement of cartilages, muscles, and other tissues (Figure 6.4). The larynx is similar in all primates (Ploog, 1988).

The vibrating elements in the larynx are the vocal cords, folds along the lateral walls of the larynx that can be stretched and positioned by several specific muscles within the larynx itself (*intrinsic laryngeal muscles*). Each vocal fold extends between the thyroid cartilage and one of the arytenoid cartilages. Contraction of the posterior cricoarytenoid muscles

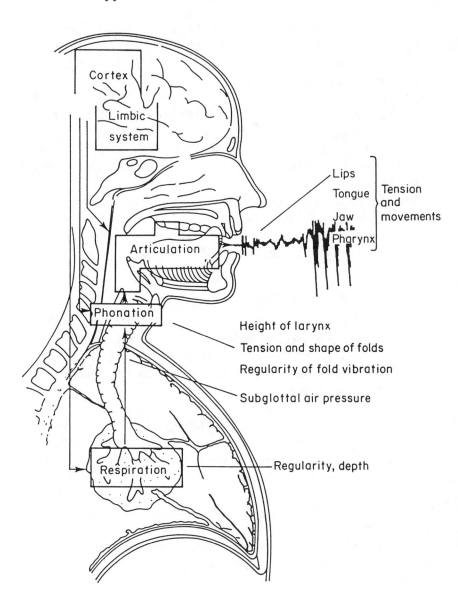

Figure 6.4. Overview of the voice production system and its major determinants (Scherer, 1989).

pulls the arytenoid cartilages away from the thyroid cartilage, thus stretching the vocal folds. The transverse arytenoid muscle pulls the arytenoid cartilages together, approximating the two vocal folds so that they can vibrate in a stream of expired air. Conversely, contraction of the lateral cricoarytenoid muscles pulls the arytenoid cartilages forward and apart to allow normal respiration. The thyroarytenoid muscles are made of groups of small muscle fibers, each controlled separately by different nerve fibers. The muscle fibers adjacent to the wall of the larynx and other individual portions also contract independently of one another.

These contractions control the shape of the vocal folds during the different types of phonation. The folds may be thick or thin or may have sharp or blunt edges. The different shapes and distances between the folds result in various acoustic changes. The use of computer models has helped considerably in estimating the acoustical changes caused by the shape of the vocal folds (e.g., Titze & Talkin, 1979). The farther apart the folds are while vibrating, the more air is allowed to rush through, increasing the amount of noise in the speech signal. The resulting phonation type is described as "whispery" or, in extreme cases, "breathy" (Laver, 1980). If the folds are tensely contracted, the effect is typically perceived as "harsh." If both folds are very close together and only a small part is allowed to vibrate while the other parts are firmly closed, a falsetto phonation results. The shape of the vocal folds during phonation can be studied with a laryngoscope – which in its simplest form is a 45° mirror with a light source attached to it – that can be inserted into the pharynx to allow visual inspection of the larynx.

The rapid opening and closing action of the vocal folds creates a vibratory pattern whose frequency constitutes the fundamental frequency (F_0) of speech. The fundamental frequency is an important aspect of the perception of the pitch of voice and can be changed in at least two very different ways. First, it can be changed by stretching or relaxing the vocal folds either by the mechanism of the intrinsic muscles of the larynx, as described, or by the muscles attached to the external surface of the larynx: These muscles can pull against the cartilages and thereby help stretch or relax the folds. The action of the external laryngeal muscles is usually combined with an upward or downward movement of the larynx to control pitch of voice. The second means for changing fundamental frequency is to change the shape and mass of the vocal fold edges. When very high frequency sounds are emitted, different parts of the thyroarytenoid muscles contract so that the edges of the vocal fold are sharpened and thinned, whereas when lower-frequency sounds are emitted, the thyroarytenoid muscles contract in a different pattern so that broad edges with a large mass are approximated. There has been some debate about the importance of subglottal pressure for determining the fundamental frequency. It seems that although subglottal pressure changes are proportional to fundamental frequency changes, the frequency changes are too small to account for subglottal pressure as a major determinant of pitch variation (Ohala, 1978).

Articulation. The sound impulses emanating from the glottal folds are filtered by the vocal tract which, according to its shape, amplifies certain frequencies (resonance frequencies) and dampens other frequencies. The major organs of articulation are the lips, the tongue, and the soft palate. The resonators include the mouth, the nose and associated nasal sinuses, the pharynx, and the chest cavity itself (Figure 6.4). By changing the position of the articulators, the shape of the vocal tract as a whole changes so that the sound waves, depending on their frequencies, are selectively amplified or attenuated to produce different vowels or are obstructed to produce stops, fricatives, and plosives. It is in the size, shape, and details of the articulators that humans differ from all other primates. In articulation, as in phonation, it is frequently possible to achieve the same acoustical result by employing different means. And it is therefore not commonly possible to decide on the basis of a single acoustical parameter the state of articulators and laryngeal settings.

Vocal expression of affective state in animals

The study of vocalizations in animals is of particular interest for the understanding of vocal nonverbal communication, because it is likely that many of the processes involved are phylogenetically continuous (Darwin, 1872; Ekman, 1973; Ploog, 1986; Scherer, 1979a, 1985). Ample evidence has been collected indicating that most animal vocalizations express the motivational and emotional state of the individual (Dittus, 1988; Eisenberg, 1974, 1976; Green, 1975; Jürgens, 1979, 1982, 1988; Jürgens & Ploog, 1976; Marler, 1984; Marler & Tenaza, 1977; Morton, 1977; Ploog, 1974; Seyfarth & Cheney, 1982; Tembrock, 1971, 1975; Todt, 1988). In a neuroethological approach, vocal behavior patterns are regarded as fixed-action patterns used as signals in social communication (Ploog, 1986). One possible gain from studying vocalizations of nonhuman species is to find cross-species universality and phylogenetic continuity that allow insights into basic biological patterns of affect vocalization. Three notions are of specific interest in this context:

1. Structural continuity in the brain structures involved in vocalizations and affect.
2. Cross-species similarity in acoustic features of vocalizations because of physiological influences on the phonation and articulation mechanisms, given functionally similar antecedent events and consequentially similar behavioral patterns (such as preparatory actions for flight or fight when confronted with a dangerous aggressor).
3. Cross-species similarity of acoustic structures of vocalizations that might have developed as a function of specific ecological "demands" of the natural environment.

Development of control structures. Anatomical studies and studies employing electrical brain stimulation and brain lesions have found evidence for a progression from mostly automatic call productions in lower vertebrates to more voluntary vocal productions in higher vertebrates, particularly subhuman primates and humans (Ploog, 1986, 1988). Although the ability to speak seems to be unique to humans, many relevant structures are homologous in humans and monkeys, except for the direct motor pathway from the laryngeal representation in the primary motor cortex to the laryngeal motor neurons in the medulla, which does not exist in monkeys. On the basis of the neurological evidence Jürgens (e.g., 1988) concluded that monkeys seem to lack the capacity to communicate information unrelated to the momentary motivational state. (There is, however, evidence for representational vocalizations in infrahuman species, such as the alarm calls of vervet monkeys [Marler, 1984; Seyfarth & Cheney 1982; see also Marler & Mitani, 1988]). The final pathway from the motor nuclei to the phonatory muscles is homologous in humans and monkeys (Ploog, 1988), but differences in the shape of the supralaryngeal vocal tract prevent nonhuman species from articulating most of the sounds that are necessary for speech. A summary of the neurobiology and pathology of subhuman vocal communication and human speech may be found in Ploog (1988).

Development of acoustical structures. Although each of many hundred primate species has its own vocal repertoire (Ploog, 1986), physiological factors influencing phonation and articulation under affective arousal might still be similarly structured across different species. Tembrock (1971, 1975) and Morton (1977) studied this notion, and Tembrock (1975) found, based on acoustic analyses of calls across different species, repeated short sounds with low frequencies for calls in the contact range, seemingly concurrent with states of relaxation and contentment (e.g., play calls). Low frequencies were characteristic of threat calls and dominance calls in agonistic encounters, and short calls with a high-amplitude onset and a broad-frequency spectrum were characteristic of defense calls. High frequencies, repeated frequency shifts, and a tendency toward temporal prolongation were found for submission calls. High frequencies and temporal prolongation were characteristic of attraction calls over long distances. Morton (1977) conceptualized the relationship between acoustic structure and affective state with a "motivation-structural rule." According to this rule, low frequency and harsh sounds are used by birds and mammals in hostile contexts, whereas more pure and tonelike sounds are utilized when animals are frightened, appeasing, or approaching in a friendly manner. Backed by a body of empirical data on bird and mammal sounds, Morton proposed a selective value in using these calls, namely, that low-frequency utterances might feign a large body size in combat situations, whereas high-frequency vocalizations might appear more like those of an infant, owing to its smaller resonance body.

Based on this argument and spectrographic studies of acoustical changes as a function of retracting the corners of the mouth, Ohala (1980) hypothesized an acoustical origin of the smile in humans. Ohala's evidence suggests that smiling produces upward shifts in the acoustical structure of vocalizations that are similar to utterances produced with a shorter vocal tract, such as is typical for infants. Ohala's proposal is an example of the creative use of ethological empirical evidence in the framework of human affective displays.

One problem with most studies of vocalization patterns in subhuman animals is the use of various nonstandardized descriptors of call types. The lack of consensual classification systems of acoustic characteristics on one hand and the difficulty to assess the sender's motivational state on the other hand encumber quantitatively sound comparisons across species and frequently within species. Clearly, there is a need for more experimental work both in the field and in the laboratory (see Scherer & Kappas, 1988).

Ecological demands. Regarding environmental influences on the structure of nonhuman vocalizations, there seem to be a variety of instances in which the acoustical pattern of a call is particularly suited to serve a specific function in a specific habitat (e.g., Brown & Waser, 1988). One example is the structure of the loud vocalizations of howling monkeys that seem to regulate intergroup spacing. The barklike structure of these calls is not only particularly well suited to propagate over long distances but also provides very precise information about the distance to the caller, based on reverberation phenomena (Whitehead, 1987) that would not be easy to detect with slow-onset, temporally prolongated vocalizations. It would be beyond the scope of this chapter to discuss this matter in detail, but we shall note that there might be an evolutionary continuity with regard to the use of specific communication channels for particular communicative functions that is easier to understand by studying habitat-related communicative behaviors. For a functional analysis of the use of particular channels, or signs within channels in humans, the study of environmental fits between habitat and sign is of particular interest. It is amusing to note, in concluding this section, that Charles Dickens was convinced that the Americans had such loud voices because of the large distances their voices had to cover on the huge farms.

Acoustical characteristics of affective vocalizations

Parameters of acoustical analysis. A comprehensive analysis of the findings regarding the acoustical signatures of affective vocalizations is difficult because many of the researchers used (trained or untrained) judges and differing sets of scales to assess the vocal parameters in their studies (e.g., Constanzo, Markel, & Constanzo, 1969; Davitz, 1964a,b; Eldred & Price, 1958; Green & Cliff, 1975; Markel, Bein, & Phillis, 1973; Scherer, Koivumaki, & Rosenthal, 1972). On the other hand, studies using objective analyses of fundamental frequency, intonation, loudness, and rate measures frequently have utilized only a subset of measures, of emotions to be compared, or of both. Ideally, the objective acoustical measurement of affective vocalizations is the most promising level of description. Parameters are well defined and can be easily extracted. However, there is some cost involved, in money and time, as well as in acquiring the necessary acoustic–phonetic expertise.

Next we shall describe the acoustic parameters that have been employed and then give an overview of the results accumulated so far. Extensive reviews of studies relating to the acoustic characteristics of discrete emotional states can be found in Scherer (1981a, 1986a) and Bergmann, Goldbeck, and Scherer (1988). For a more detailed description of the parameters typically employed, see Scherer (1982, 1989).

TIME PARAMETERS. The temporal aspects of speech that are usually assessed are speech rate (number of syllables per time unit, including pauses), articulation rate (number of syllables per time unit, excluding pauses), and the frequency and duration of pauses. Another set of measures commonly employed pertains to disturbances of continuity (e.g., Speech Disturbance Ratio, ah-ratio, non-ah-ratio, repeats; see, e.g., Mahl & Schulze, 1964). It would be beyond the scope of this chapter to discuss these in detail, but see Siegman and Feldstein (1987) for a detailed review.

AMPLITUDE PARAMETERS. Amplitude parameters describe in the context of human speech the intensity of the sound pressure of waves as they propagate through air, and the intensity of these pressure waves helps determine our perception of loudness. Although intensity is technically easy to assess, it is very difficult to interpret, as it is dependent not only on vocal effort but also on the distance and orientation of the microphone and speaker. Recordings must be controlled with the utmost care concerning differences in the microphone placement and amplifier (tape recorder) settings between conditions.

FREQUENCY PARAMETERS. The parameter that has probably been used most often is the fundamental frequency of the vocalization (F_0). The *fundamental frequency* is the frequency of glottal vibration and is closely related to the perceived pitch of an utterance. Perceived pitch, however, is also dependent on other factors such as voice quality. Standke, Kappas, and Scherer (1984) found a correlation of .89 between estimated (relative) pitch of voice and mean fundamental frequency. Indeed, changes in fundamental frequency can be so fast that they are not perceived as changes in pitch, but the voice appears to have a harsh character, a phenomenon called *jitter*. Slower variations in F_0 are usually perceived as pitch changes, and variations are referred to as *vibrato*. Over longer periods of time – for example, within a sentence – there will be extensive changes in F_0 that are typically referred to as *intonation contours*. Apart from mean F_0, range and variance have been used as parameters of fundamental frequency.

SPECTRAL PARAMETERS (PARAMETERS OF FREQUENCY AND AMPLITUDE). As we outlined in our description of the articulation process, certain frequencies are amplified, and others are attenuated according to the shape of the vocal tract. For a small number of frequencies, given a specific vocal tract shape, there is resonation. The locations of these resonances are called *formants*. They are described by their frequency, their amplitude at the peak, and their bandwidth, indicating whether the resonance is very much localized on a particular frequency or whether neighboring frequencies are amplified as well. The location of the formants determines the perception of the vocalization's sound quality. Vowels are characterized by a specific pattern of formant locations. Although there are interindividual variations in their formant locations, listeners generally have no difficulty identifying a particular vowel. Formants are commonly extracted from a frequency-by-amplitude display of an acoustic waveform, the *spectrum*. Over shorter periods of time the spectrum is dependent on the particular phonemes uttered. Over a longer period of time (several sentences and/or minutes) the variations due to language average out, and the resulting *long-term spectrum* indicates the speaker's habitual settings. If long-term spectra are compared within a person in differing affective states, the differences in the spectra will reflect the impact of those states on either the habitual articulatory settings or the precision with which those settings are achieved. These comparisons should always be made as within-subject designs, because most of the variation is caused by the particular shape of the individual's vocal tract, and large interindividual differences exist.

Empirical data. As we mentioned earlier (see Scherer, 1979a, 1986a) most of the studies in this area lack theoretical and methodological rigor, and some of the most serious shortcomings are the following: using actor-portrayed emotional utterances, as opposed to naturally occurring emotional vocalizations; not systematically controlling important variables such as the number of speakers, the type of emotions studied, the instructions for portrayal, and the verbal material used; and assessing a very limited number of parameters, often without using the latest technology. Yet the findings often converge. In this section we shall review discrete emotions, emotional disorders (particularly depression), and stress (research summaries are based on a more extensive review in Scherer, 1989).

VOCAL CUES OF DISCRETE EMOTIONS. As shown elsewhere (Scherer, 1986a), it is necessary to distinguish the mild or passive forms of a particular emotion category from the strong and active forms of the same type (e.g., cold anger or irritation vs. hot anger or flaring rage). Because this distinction is rarely made in the literature, the following review in some cases had to be based on educated guesses regarding the particular type of the emotion category studied.

Boredom–indifference. The results generally indicate a decrease in mean F_0 (Davitz, 1964a; Fairbanks & Pronovost, 1939) and mean intensity (Bortz, 1966; Davitz, 1964a; Müller, 1960). Most likely, actors simulate reduced sympathetic arousal.

Displeasure–disgust. Three of the studies (Plaikner, 1970; Scherer, 1979a; Scherer, Wallbott, Tolkmitt, & Bergmann, 1985) found an increase in mean F_0, and two others (Kaiser, 1962; Van Bezooijen, 1984) found a decrease. The discrepancy could be due to differences in the respective induction procedures (viewing of an unpleasant film vs. an actor's portrayal of disgust). It might be necessary to differentiate the nature of the antecedent situation more clearly.

Irritation–cold anger. The relevant findings indicate an increase in mean F_0 (Eldred & Price, 1958; Roessler & Lester, 1976), mean intensity (Constanzo, Markel, & Constanzo, 1969; Eldred & Price, 1958), and high-frequency energy (Kaiser, 1962; Roessler & Lester, 1976) as well as a tendency toward downward-directed intonation contours (Höffe, 1960; Kaiser, 1962).

Rage–hot anger. Similar to the pattern for cold anger, increases in mean F_0 (Davitz, 1964a; Fairbanks & Pronovost, 1939; Fonagy, 1978; Höffe, 1960; Wallbott & Scherer, 1986a; Williams & Stevens, 1969, 1972) and mean intensity (Bortz, 1966; Davitz, 1964a; Höffe, 1960; Kotlyar & Morosov, 1976; Müller, 1960; Williams & Stevens, 1969; Van Bezooijen, 1984) have been reported. The specific cues, probably related to very high sympathetic arousal, are increases in F_0 variability and F_0 range (Fairbanks & Pronovost, 1939; Havrdova & Moravek, 1979; Höffe, 1960; Williams & Stevens, 1969).

Sadness–dejection. Possibly because of a high degree of similarity between eliciting situations (see Scherer, Wallbott, & Summerfield, 1986), the results for this affective state are very consistent: decrease in mean F_0 (Coleman & Williams, 1979; Davitz, 1964a; Eldred & Price, 1958; Fairbanks & Pronovost, 1939; Fonagy, 1978; Kaiser, 1962; Sedlacek & Sychra, 1963; Wallbott & Scherer, 1986a; Williams & Stevens, 1969), and F_0 range (Fairbanks & Pronovost, 1939; Fonagy, 1978; Sedlacek & Sychra, 1963; Van Bezooijen, 1984; Williams & Stevens, 1969; Zuberbier, 1957; Zwirner, 1930) as well as ·downward-directed F_0 contours (Fairbanks & Pronovost, 1939; Kaiser, 1962; Sedlacek & Sychra, 1963; Zwirner, 1930). In addition, mean intensity decreases (Davitz, 1964a; Eldred & Price, 1958; Hargreaves, Starkweather, & Blacker, 1965; Huttar, 1968; Kaiser, 1962; Müller, 1960; Skinner, 1935; Zuberbier, 1957) as does high-frequency energy (Hargreaves, Starkweather, & Blacker, 1965; Kaiser, 1962; Skinner, 1935) and precision of articulation (Van Bezooijen, 1984; Zuberbier, 1957).

Grief–desperation. We believe that one should distinguish between a passive reaction to loss, that is, sadness and dejection, and a more aroused state of desperation or violent grief, because theoretically different acoustic correlates for grief–desperation in relation to sadness–dejection are to be expected. Unfortunately, we have been unable to find any studies of these states.

Worry–anxiety. Although there is a large body of literature on verbal and temporal correlates of anxiety (Siegman & Feldstein, 1987) the vocal parameters we described have been studied only rarely. Several studies (Bonner, 1943; Hicks, 1979; Höffe, 1960; Plaikner, 1970) reported a tendency toward a mean F_0 increase.

Fear–terror. Studies consistently report an increase in mean F_0 (Coleman & Williams, 1979; Duncan, Laver, & Jack, 1983; Fairbanks & Pronovost, 1939; Fonagy, 1978; Höffe, 1960; Kuroda, Fujiwara, Okamura, & Utsuki, 1976; Niwa, 1971; Roessler & Lester, 1976; Sulc, 1977; Utsuki & Okamura, 1976; Williams & Stevens, 1969), F_0 range (Fairbanks & Pronovost, 1939; Utsuki & Okamura, 1976; Williams & Stevens, 1969), F_0 variability (Fairbanks & Pronovost, 1939; Williams & Stevens, 1969), and high-frequency energy (Roessler & Lester, 1976, 1979; Simonov & Frolov, 1973).

Enjoyment–happiness. Because the positive emotions have been generally studied in the form of active joy or elation, we have not been able to find empirical evidence for acoustic cues accompanying this state of peaceful enjoyment.

Joy/elation. There are consistent reports of increases in mean F_0 (Coleman & Williams, 1979; Davitz, 1964a; Fonagy, 1978; Havrdova & Moravek, 1979; Höffe, 1960; Huttar, 1968; Kaiser, 1962; Sedlacek & Sychra, 1963; Skinner, 1935; Van Bezooijen, 1984), F_0 range (Fonagy, 1978; Havrdova & Moravek, 1979; Höffe, 1960; Huttar, 1968; Sedlacek & Sychra, 1963; Skinner, 1935), F_0 variability (Havrdova & Moravek, 1979; Sedlacek & Sychra, 1963; Skinner, 1935), and mean intensity (Davitz, 1964a; Höffe, 1960; Huttar, 1968; Kaiser, 1962; Kotlyar & Morosov, 1976; Müller, 1960; Skinner, 1935; Van Bezooijen, 1984).

As shown earlier (Scherer, 1981a, 1986a) the frequent reports of increases in F_0 and intensity, both mean and variability, may indicate a general sympathetic response syndrome. We believe, however, that it would be wrong to assume that only sympathetic arousal is reflected in the voice and that it is unlikely that differential emotional states can be distinguished via vocal parameters. The major argument for this point is that many different affective states can in fact be recognized by naive judges on the basis of the vocal cues alone. Thus, one must assume the existence of differences in the vocal parameters on the basis of which this differential recognition is possible. We are quite certain that greater vocal differentiation will be found as soon as a more complete range of the aforementioned acoustic parameters are used in the relevant studies. The parameters most closely linked to sympathetic arousal happen to be the ones that are most conveniently measured. In addition, the arousal dimension is probably the most dominant one in terms of overall effect.

VOCAL CUES OF AFFECT DISTURBANCE. We shall restrict our review to studies of depressive patients. As always in studies with clinical populations, a major problem is the difficulty of finding patient groups with homogeneous diagnostic criteria. Indeed, the lack of replication of findings in this area can often be traced back to this very problem. For example, one could scarcely expect similar vocal cues for endogenously depressed patients and biphasic, manic-depressive patients, particularly depending on the phase during which the latter might be studied. This difficulty is even more pronounced for the psychoses and, in particular, schizophrenia.

The literature on vocal cues of depression is quite encouraging, however, showing fairly consistent differences between normal and depressed speech and indices for change after therapy. Depressive patients speak with relatively low intensity (Eldred & Price, 1958; Moses, 1954; Whitman & Flicker, 1966; Zuberbier, 1957) and with reduced dynamic range (Zuberbier, 1957). Conversely, the intensity tends to increase after therapy (Hargreaves & Starkweather, 1964, 1965; Ostwald, 1961, 1963; Tolkmitt, Helfrich, Standke, & Scherer, 1982).

Some studies have reported low mean F_0 for depressives (Bannister, 1972; Eldred & Price, 1958; Moses, 1954; Roessler & Lester, 1976). Yet, F_0 seems to decrease after therapy (Klos, Ellgring, & Scherer, 1987; Tolkmitt et al., 1982), a finding that has been explained by assuming a decrease in general tension in the striated musculature (Scherer, 1979a). It might be that the F_0 level is linked to the severity of the depression (Whitman & Flicker, 1966).

This apparent discrepancy might also be due to a lack of homogeneity in the nosologic criteria or to the difference between objective measures of F_0 and subjective ratings of pitch (pitch judgment being influenced by other acoustic variables, such as energy distribution in the spectrum and variability of pitch). As several authors have discovered a narrow range and restricted variability for F_0/pitch in depressive speech (Bannister, 1972; Hargreaves et al., 1965; Newman & Mather, 1938; Ostwald, 1964; Zuberbier, 1957) it may be that the judges are affected by reduced range and other acoustic factors when rating pitch.

Furthermore, several studies (Moses, 1954; Newman & Mather, 1938; Zwirner, 1930) have shown that depressives tend to employ repeated, downward-directed intonation contours (which are not necessarily flat), which give an impression of monotonousness. There is also evidence that depressives use rather lax, imprecise articulation (as reflected in formant precision) and that the precision of articulation improves after therapy (Tolkmitt et al., 1982; Zuberbier, 1957).

Much of this is still very preliminary evidence and urgently requires replication. And moreover, research in this area should become less atheoretical. A number of concrete hypotheses concerning the vocal changes to be expected for different types of emotional disorders were suggested by Scherer (1987).

VOCAL CUES OF STRESS. "Voice lie detectors" have been highly publicized, and quite a number of expensive units have been sold based on dubious claims concerning the function of certain features (e.g., *microtremor*) as markers of deception. Apart from the obvious ethical problems posed by the surreptitious "assessment" of lying for criminal defendants or employees under suspicion, there is no hard evidence that lying can be detected through simple electroacoustic devices (Hollien, 1981; Hollien, Geison, & Hicks, 1987; Scherer, 1981b). One also needs to distinguish between the detection of lying and the detection of stress. Lying does not necessarily produce stress, and there is no reason that such nonstressful lies should produce specific voice changes, given that presumably no physiological reaction takes place.

The strong sympathetic arousal accompanying stress should clearly influence vocal parameters, and in particular one would expect increases in fundamental frequency and F_0 variability. This theoretical expectation has been confirmed in a large number of studies in which stress was experimentally induced (cf. Ekman, Friesen, & Scherer, 1976; Scherer, 1981b; Streeter, Krauss, Olson, Geller, & Apple, 1977; Williams & Stevens, 1969), although individual differences are often very pronounced (as shown in a high degree of response specificity).

To account for the individual differences, we ran a number of experimental studies using personality variables in the form of coping styles. We found that for both male and female subjects, only those with relatively elevated anxiety scores (regardless of whether they repressed or admitted their anxiety) showed an F_0 increase. Furthermore, our data indicated that a consistent effect for female anxiety-deniers (repressers) is more precise articulation with increasing cognitive stress and decreasing precision with mounting emotional stress (Scherer, Wallbott, Tolkmitt, & Bergmann, 1985). Thus, personality factors, coping style, and type of stress should be systematically varied or at least controlled in further studies. To provide a more extensive theoretical basis, Scherer (1986b) proposed that stress be analyzed within the framework of a general theory of emotion, assuming that stress occurs in cases in which a problem cannot be solved through normal emotional responding (with return to baseline within a standard time frame).

The recognition of affective state from vocal cues

There is ample evidence that the voice carries a wealth of information about the speaker. From nonverbal cues, listeners can determine the speaker's gender (Smith, 1979, 1980), age (Helfrich, 1979), socioeconomic background (Robinson, 1979), ethnic group (Giles, 1979), personality (Scherer & Scherer, 1981), and status in small groups (Scherer, 1979b). From vocal cues, listeners can also determine affective states when presented with only a few sentences or, even more clearly, shouts or cries. Many studies have assessed the ability to identify affective states from voices, typically using recordings. The samples ranged from single words or nonsense syllables (spoken in isolation with different inflections) to paragraphs of texts or whole conversations. Scherer (1981a) showed in a review of studies of the perception of affective states that the recognition of emotions from voice and speech samples is as good or better than the recognition of affect from facial expressions (on average 56% accuracy, compared with 12% expected by chance in 28 studies).

The interpretation of the results of many judgment studies is problematic, owing to the stimulus material's lack of ecological validity. Studies using numbers, letters, nonsense syllables, or isolated words as stimuli may introduce artifacts by inviting speakers to produce stereotypical samples that may lead to overestimating the accuracy of the judgment (Bortz, 1966; Davitz, 1964a; Green & Cliff, 1975; Levin & Lord, 1975; Skinner, 1935). The use of poems or similar material might prompt speakers to use voice settings habitually used for reciting such material (Sedlacek & Sychra, 1963; Zuberbier, 1957). The technique most commonly employed is to inject standard sentences into texts of varying emotional content (e.g., Constanzo, Markel, & Constanzo, 1969; Davitz,

1964a; Fairbanks & Pronovost, 1939; Fairbanks & Hoaglin, 1941). Unfortunately, there is frequently an emotional bias in interpreting these sentences (see Kramer, 1963). Given these problems, it is advisable to pretest the stimulus material extensively and to use more than one stimulus type. In one study Sincoff and Rosenthal (1985) demonstrated using the same encoders, differences in recognition of six emotions, depending on whether the neutral sentence technique or letters of the alphabet were used as the stimulus material.

Another problem pertains to the encoder of the stimulus material. On one hand, students, typically employed as subjects in such studies, may frequently not be able to stage believable vocal affective displays, but the use of professional actors (Scherer, Koivumaki, & Rosenthal, 1972; Wallbott & Scherer, 1986a; Williams & Stevens, 1972), on the other hand, does not guarantee vocal samples that are similar to real emotional vocal expressions. Therefore, more than one speaker should encode the stimulus material, as there is considerable evidence for interindividual differences in the ability to portray emotions vocally (see Wallbott & Scherer, 1986a).

A major difficulty is defining the target emotion to be displayed. Frequently, it is not defined satisfactorily if an encoder (speaker) is to portray, for example, suppressed anger or exploding anger. A better approach is to use an explicit scenario so that the (imaginary) antecedent conditions are similar or the same for different actors (Wallbott & Scherer, 1986a).

A problem that has not been addressed relates to the difference of hearing an encoder for the first time (and for only a few utterances) or judging the effective state of a well-known person. It seems that the variability in encoding might present a baseline problem for the judgment of affect. Cues that might be interpreted as indicators of arousal (e.g., tenseness or a high-pitched voice) might be the habitual vocal setting of a specific speaker. The resulting biases in the attribution of emotions are comparable to biases introduced by the facial furrows of elderly people (Malatesta, Fiore, & Messina, 1987). Familiarity with the encoder is a context variable in the framework of attribution of affective states and should be taken into account as such, as it is otherwise difficult to quantify the impact of the phenomena studied in context-free paradigms on everyday interaction (see also Buck, 1983).

In order to address questions regarding the universality of vocal expressive patterns of affective states, Scherer and colleagues are currently undertaking a multinational research project on emotion recognition from vocal cues using the Vocal Emotion Recognition Test (Scherer & Wallbott, in preparation). The test consists of a set of 30 emotions (joy–happiness, sadness, fear, anger, disgust) portrayed by professional actors. These episodes have been selected from a pool of 80 stimuli used in a pilot study. The episodes were produced using a scenario approach, in which the scenarios were selected from a pool of situation descriptions collected in a large-scale cross-cultural study on antecedents of emotion (Scherer, Wallbott, & Summerfield, 1986). The pseudo-sentences were constructed by a phonetician to represent at least one typical syllable from each of six languages (German, English, French, Italian, Spanish, and Danish). The first data from several countries point toward better-than-chance recognition independent of language or culture.

Summarizing the evidence on recognition of emotions from vocal samples, we conclude that there is ample evidence of the subjects' ability to correctly identify affective states from vocal stimuli. This is especially noteworthy, as an identification of the relevant acoustical parameters has so far been successful only for the dimension of arousal. However, if listeners are able to decode the sender's emotional state from vocal cues, the voice must be carrying that information in its acoustical parameters. Systematic analyses of the acoustical parameters on which listeners base their judgments may guide their exploration. The systematic and rule-based variation of voice parameters using synthetic or resynthetized vocalizations can achieve this end.

Recognition of synthetically produced affective vocalizations

Scherer and colleagues used a Moog synthesizer to manipulate systematically a variety of acoustic cues subjects used to determine a speaker's affective state to investigate the cues (Scherer, 1974; Scherer & Oshinsky, 1977). The researchers synthesized tone sequences modeled after the intonation contour of a short sentence, with differences in pitch, duration, and contour. Tempo and pitch variations were found to have the strongest influence on subjects' ratings. Moderate pitch variation led to an impression of sadness, fear, disgust, and boredom, and extreme pitch variations and a rising contour produced attributions of happiness, interest, and fear.

Although the use of fully synthetic stimuli allows complete control over every acoustic parameter, there are drawbacks to this method: The stimuli may appear artificial and thus elicit judgments with low ecological validity. The subjects' attention may be directed to unrealistic acoustic variations, because the linguistically determined vocal structure of an utterance is not present, giving undue importance to the acoustic variation performed on the stimuli.

If intonation carries emotional information, then the relevant information generally must be laid on top of the linguistically required changes in intonation. For instance, a rising intonation contour is a linguistic feature that signals a question. Knapp (1978) offered five examples of how vocal emphasis modifies the meaning of a message:

1. *He's* giving this money to Herbie. (HE is the one giving the money; nobody else.)
2. He's *giving* this money to Herbie. (He is GIVING, not lending, the money.)
3. He's giving *this* money to Herbie. (The money being exchanged is not from another source; it is THIS particular money.)
4. He's giving this *money* to Herbie. (CASH is being exchanged, not a check.)
5. He's giving this money to *Herbie*. (The recipient is HERBIE, not Eric or Rod.)

Add a final rise of intonation, and you get

6. He's giving this money to *Herbie*? (Why is he giving the money to HERBIE and not Mark?)

Actually, examples 1 through 4 can also be converted into questions by changing the final accent to that of a question.

Scherer and colleagues constructed two models to explain how voice parameters associated with affective states might interact with linguistic parameters (Ladd, Silverman, Tolkmitt, Bergmann, & Scherer, 1985; Scherer, Ladd, & Silverman, 1984). The *covariance model* states independence between the two communicative systems. Information regarding the speaker's internal state is encoded independently of the linguistic meaning. Relevant acoustic parameters vary with the strength of a particular state. The *configuration model,* on the other hand, states that verbal and nonverbal cues exhibit categorical linguistic structures, and different speaker states are conveyed by means of different configurations of categorical variables. The assumption is that speaker states involving more complex cognitive processes are better understood in terms of the configuration model, whereas simpler affective states are better understood in terms of the covariation model.

To evaluate the two models, Scherer and associates performed a series of experiments (Scherer, Ladd, & Silverman, 1984). First, recordings or transcripts of utterances were evaluated on several scales using a between-subjects design. The results showed high interrater agreement for the audio and low interrater agreement for the transcript group. Scherer and colleagues concluded that the nonverbal aspects of the statements, and not the content itself, carried the emotional meaning. For the second experiment the 24 utterances yielding the clearest emotional meaning were submitted to several degradation or masking procedures to identify the acoustical features leading subjects to their judgments. (1) The high-frequency components of the utterances were attenuated, completely masking verbal content, but the intonation contour was left intact (low-pass filtering); (2) the utterances were randomly cut and mixed, removing the temporal organization of the utterances and destroying both content and intonation completely, but the spectral cues to voice quality were not changed (random splicing, Scherer, 1971); and (3) the utterances were played backward to mask the content, but the voice quality was left intact. Together with the original full audio stimuli there were 84 stimuli, which were presented to groups of subjects who evaluated them on a set of scales. The results showed that the evaluations were largely determined by voice quality cues, independent of the presence or the absence of content (text) or gross distortions of F_0 contours. These results are seen as evidence that the affective force of the utterance is encoded independently of the verbal content, as posed by the covariance model.

To test the configuration model a different approach had to be used, as masking techniques do not address the assumption that intonational cues signal affect in conjunction with text. To investigate this assumption, the utterances were classified according to contour type (rise vs. fall), and question type (why vs. yes–no), as well as fundamental frequency range and standard deviation. The subjects' ratings on the scales were analyzed using multiple regression analyses. The results demonstrate interactions between contour type and text in communicating aspects of speaker affect.

To control experimentally the intonational parameters relevant to the configurational model, digital speech resynthesis was employed (Goldbeck, Tolkmitt, & Scherer, 1988; Ladd et al., 1985). Resynthesis allows the modification of systematically varied acoustic features of natural speech, leaving all other cues unchanged. Although there is some loss of tone quality, the subjects usually do not have the impression of artificiality generally associated with synthetic speech. The findings suggest that features of cognitive attitude can be transmitted by linguistically coded aspects of sentence structure, whereas gradations of emotions are conveyed by speech activity as a whole (e.g., fundamental frequency range). The same pattern of results was found across speakers and was independent of verbal content.

Kappas (1986) could show that the intonation contour as a whole may capture the affective valence of ambiguous statements. In this study a set of utterances, judged as neutral in transcript, were spoken by an actor expressing either anger or happiness. The resulting samples were judged on a set of emotion and attitude scales. Samples that clearly elicited positive or negative ratings were submitted to digital analysis. The intonation contours as a whole were then transferred onto neutral samples of the same sentences using digital resynthesis. Rate, loudness, and spectral composition were exactly the same; only intonation was varied. A clear valence difference for the resulting sets of sentences was revealed.

These studies emphasize the necessity of integrating the investigation of affective vocal cues with linguistic approaches to understand the role of specific acoustic features in the attribution of emotional states. The linguistic context thus should be taken into account when interpreting the attribution process regarding the use of vocal cues to affective states.

The recognition of affective state from vocal cues in conjunction with other nonverbal channels

Evidence concerning the recognition of affective state from vocal cues indicates that vocal parameters are a prime candidate for diagnosing affective state in interaction. This knowledge is particularly valuable in situations in which no other communication channels are available, such as communication via radio or telephone. But if information from other communication channels is available, the picture will not be as clear. Generally, if both facial and vocal cues are available, subjects tend to base their attributions regarding the speakers' affective state predominantly on facial cues (e.g., Berman, Shulman, & Marwitt, 1976; Ekman & Friesen, 1969; Graham, Ricci Bitti, & Argyle, 1975; Hess, Kappas, & Scherer, 1988; Levitt, 1964; Mehrabian & Ferris, 1967; Wallbott & Scherer, 1986a; Zaidel & Mehrabian, 1969; for an overview, also see Noller, 1985).

Research on the integration of vocal and other communication channels has been hampered by technical as well as methodological problems that make it difficult to determine the processes of attributing affective state (and attitudes). For instance, the vocal and facial stimuli used could not be produced, and thus controlled independently, leading to confounds. The length of the stimuli and the method of presentation were not adequate for a judgment task because of technological limitations. To address some of these problems, Hess, Kappas, and Scherer (1988) used an actor to display specific facial actions that were previously defined using Ekman and Friesen's (1978) Facial Action Coding System (FACS). Vocal parameters were produced independently and synthesized using digital signal–processing algorithms. The synchronized dubbing of facial and vocal stimuli with information regarding the social context provided a systematic and independent variation of the parameters involved, thereby avoiding the confounds of some earlier studies. The increasing availability of synthetic signal production and modification facilities for audio and video material provides the basis for future studies that may systematically investigate the attribution processes that integrate facial and vocal parameters in a more realistic context, while retaining full experimental control and thus providing a better understanding of humans as "regulated multisensory stations in a transmission system" (Birdwhistell, 1968, quoted in Wallbott, 1979).

Hess, Kappas, and Scherer (1988) suggested an integration model that applies varying weights to the importance of channels according to social context (deception, "normal" social interaction). It seems that it is not sufficient to estimate the relative "merits" of vocal parameters in a contextual void. Rather, one must take into account contextual parameters determining the use of specific vocal (or other nonverbal) cues for the attribution process of emotional state. It is likely that we base our attributions in different circumstances on different cues. There is evidence that the focus on facial cues is reduced if deception is involved or expected (e.g., Noller, 1985). Buck (1983) introduced the concept of decoding rules (analogous to the display rules suggested by Ekman [1972], a phenomenon already described by Wundt, 1903). He defined decoding rules as heuristics guiding attention to specific nonverbal cue complexes, depending on the situational context. This notion is appealing, particularly given the functional advantages of a cue selection heuristic with a view to the sheer volume of information provided in a multichannel interaction situation. The results of the synthetic multichannel study support the context dependency of relative channel importance as a function of channel discrepancy (Hess, Kappas, & Scherer, 1988), as well as a function of intimacy of context (Hess & Kappas, 1985).

Integrating approaches to vocal affect communication in the context of social psychology

Many vocal phenomena fulfill both linguistic and nonlinguistic functions, and frequently the concurrence of both phenomena discourages scientists interested in communication processes. It seems, however, that the multifunctionality of vocal signals indicates their pragmatic significance. In fact, as Karl Bühler (1933) pointed out in his *organon* model of language, most signals serve several functions simultaneously. Scherer (1980) suggested using the semiotic approach (Morris, 1946; Peirce, 1931–1935) to differentiate between semantic functions (i.e., nonverbal signs replacing, amplifying, contradicting, or modifying verbal signs), pragmatic functions (expression of sender state, reactions, and intentions), dialogic functions (relationship between sender and receiver, regulation of interaction), and, in addition, syntactic functions, related to the ordering of signs in their sequential and hierarchical organization. One cannot understand the communicative function of messages, be it vocal, facial, or otherwise without acknowledging these levels of functions. Similarly, the knowledge of the context in which the communication occurs determines the translation of the received message. For instance, Wallbott (1988) showed the importance of context information for the attribution of emotions from facial stimuli. One may therefore assume that context information plays a similar role in the interpretation of vocal signals.

Scherer (1977) and Goffman (1979) suggest that nonspeech vocal interjections such as "oh," "oops," or "ouch" may be used strategically to achieve an impression of genuineness. The actual interpretation of such interjections depends on whether a listener is able to recognize a specific affect (e.g., surprise), but this is only a necessary, not a sufficient, precondition. If the listener knows the speaker well (i.e., if the listener has a baseline), he or she might interpret an occasional "oh" quite differently, depending on the speaker's known habits. It is here that our knowledge regarding the marker function of voices gains importance. There is empirical evidence that information about a speaker's gender, age, socioeconomic status, and may be personality is transmitted through paralinguistic features of speech. Even if the interaction partners do not know each other and the interaction is based solely on audible cues (e.g., during a phone call), these markers provide a context for the attribution of emotional states. It is therefore clear that it does not help to try to discover a set of vocal parameters predicting an attribution of affect, personality, or attitudes if one does not take into account the context information regarding the interaction, the interaction history, the interplay of different communication channels, and the linguistic context.

Scherer repeatedly argued (e.g., 1986a) that an explicit theory is required to integrate the results regarding the impact of affective state on vocalizations. He contended that vocalizations are determined by push

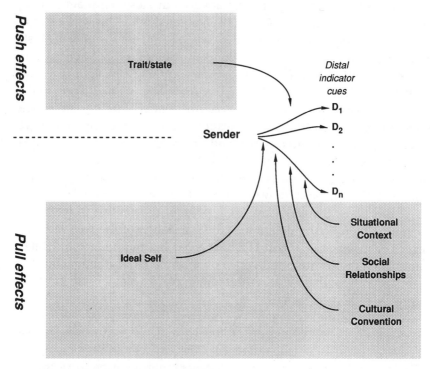

Figure 6.5. Push and pull effects.

and pull factors (Scherer, 1985; Scherer, Helfrich, & Scherer, 1980). Push factors are physically and physiologically linked to internal states such as muscular tension, and pull factors are linked to psychological processes such as display rules (Figure 6.5).

This dichotomy relates to an involuntary–voluntary distinction important to understanding the actual physiological implementation of the production of speech. Knowledge of these factors enables the prediction of specific acoustical changes, given models of speech production. In order to predict push and pull factors, a model that links antecedents to emotional states and the accompanying changes in bodily systems is required. More specifically, we need to explore the physiological mechanisms that underlie the observed correlation between emotional change and change in vocal production, because with the current technology available, we are scarcely able to assess directly the psychophysiological processes accompanying emotional arousal and their effect on voice production. Unfortunately, even on a theoretical level there have been few attempts to predict specific physiological changes in the voice-producing organs as a result of specific emotions. In part, the difficulty stems from the nature of most emotion theories, which have either been too global, for example, in assuming "packaged" neural programs for discrete emotion, or too unspecific, for example, in placing too much emphasis on nonspecific arousal, or too social, for example, by neglecting the psychophysiological underpinnings of the emotional states.

Scherer (1984) proposed a "component process" theory according to which emotional states are produced by the outcomes of a series of five stimulus evaluation checks and that predicts the adaptive effect of the results of these checks on the major subsystems of the organism, including the autonomic nervous system (ANS) and the somatic nervous system (SNS). The componential nature of this approach enables detailed predictions for the emotional impact on voice production. The specific predictions for the acoustic changes as a function of the various emotions just mentioned are shown in Table 6.1. (The procedure used to derive these predictions is outlined in detail in Scherer, 1986a.) We shall give only a brief overview of the theoretical argument.

The subsystem changes (i.e., psychophysiological responses, changes in motor expression, feeling states, or motivational changes) expected as a result of each type of stimulus evaluation check outcome are based on functional considerations with a strong phylogenetic bias. Starting from these assumptions – concerning the need for specific adaptive responses – detailed patterns of predications for voice production are derived from the existing literature on the relationships between ANS and SNS and their effect on the vocal organs (e.g., in relation to vocal cord functioning, tension of the intra- and extralaryngeal musculature, vocal tract wall tension, degree of salivation, articulatory settings). The hypotheses shown in Table 6.1 are derived using standard phonetic assumptions about the effect of such production variables on acoustic parameters.

Although this approach is somewhat speculative, it offers the possibility to link theories of emotion, psychophysiological research, and the acoustic measurement of vocal behavior, particularly insofar as the push effects are concerned. What is still missing and what will constitute the next phase of the theoretical work in our group is a set of predictions concerning the acoustic changes likely to result from pull effects with respect to the emotions (such as sociocultural norms regarding regulation and the control of affect vocalizations, strategic use of vocal emotion display, and accommodation of vocal affect responses). Should this

Table 6.1. Changes predicted for selected acoustic parameters as a function of emotional state

	Parameters											
Voice type	ENJ/HAP	ELA/JOY	DISP/DISG	CON/SCO	SAD/DEJ	GRI/DES	ANX/WOR	FEAR/TER	IRR/COA	RAGE/HOA	BOR/IND	SHA/GUI
F_0												
Perturbation	< =				>	>		>>		>		>
Mean	<	>>	>	<>	<>	>	>	>>	<>	<>	<<	>
Range	< =	>>			<<	>		>>		>>		
Variability	<	>>			<<	>	>	>>	<	>>		>
Contour	<	>			<<	>		>	<	=		>
Shift regularity	=	<						<	<	<		
F_1 mean	<	>	>	>	>	>	>	>	>	>	>	>
F_2 mean			<	<	<	<	<	<	<	<	>	<
F_1 bandwidth	>	<>	<<	>	<>	<	<	<<	<>	<>	<	<
Formant precision		>	>	>	<<	>	>	>	>	>	<	>
Intensity												
Mean	< =	>>	>	>>	<<	>		>	>>	>>	<>	
Range	<	>		>	<			>	>	>		
Variability	<	<			<			>	>	>		
Frequency range	>	>	>	>>	>	>>	>	>>	>	>>	>	
High-frequency energy	<	<>	>	>	<>	>>		>>	>>	>>	<>	>
Spectral noise					>		>					
Speech rate	<	>>			<<	>		>>		>>		
Transition time	>	<			>	<		<		<		

Abbreviations: ANX/WOR, anxiety/worry; BOR/IND, boredom/indifference; CON/SCO, contempt/scorn; DISP/DISG, displeasure/disgust; ELA/JOY, elation/joy; ENJ/HAP, enjoyment/happiness; FEAR/TER, fear/terror; GRI/DES, grief/desperation; IRR/COA, irritation/cold anger; RAGE/HOA, rage/hot anger; SAD/DEJ, sadness/dejection; SHA/GUI, shame/guilt. F_0, fundamental frequency; F_1, first formant; F_2, second formant.

Symbols: >, increase; <, decrease; =, same. Double symbols indicate increased predicted strength of the change. Two symbols pointing in opposite directions refer to cases in which antecedent voice types exert opposing influences.

prove feasible, it would allow us to replace the atheoretical correlational approach that currently prevails in this research domain, as well as to provide links between biological, more specifically psychophysiological, and social–psychological research traditions in the study of communication.

Outlook

The objective analysis of emotional vocalizations might be facilitated by current developments in powerful microcomputers capable of performing complex acoustic analyses at a cost many laboratories can afford. As important as the progress in computer hardware is the development in user-interface technology, making it possible to conduct sophisticated analyses without going through painful programming efforts or long training times. The development of high-density storage devices makes it feasible to store entire discussions, allowing instant access to analyses of any point in the interaction, with pinpoint accuracy and high resolution.

Regarding research centered on the decoding of vocal affective cues, we can expect a simplification of synthesis and resynthesis procedures, allowing the modification and synthesis of speech sequences by rule and permitting the explicit testing of hypotheses without sacrificing the appeal of genuine voice samples. Similarly, the development in the analysis and synthesis of visual material, interactive digital video, and other techniques will allow us to study the interplay of vocal features with facial expression, posture, and gaze.

These technological advances alone, however, will not provide the means for a better understanding of nonverbal vocal communication. We might have to give up the search for a handful of vocal parameters that serve as a "window to our soul" and instead accept the idea that vocal cues to emotion, like the cues that other modalities offer, are deeply embedded in the psychological attribution context. We need powerful attribution models to define the conditions under which parameters have what effect on which decoder.

Our understanding of acoustical characteristics of affective vocalizations can be enhanced only if the necessary theoretical bases are covered. More work on the evolutionary development of affective vocalizations is needed, as is work on human emotion itself. If we do not understand physiological changes as a function of psychological reactions to emotional stimuli (or situations), we will not be able to predict vocal changes, which are, after all, driven by the emotional arousal ("push effects"). At the same time, it is necessary to model the relevant psychological context (e.g., "pull effects," such as vocal display rules). Keys to understanding the psychological context of voice production are studies in the area of development and pathology. Technology has been a decisive factor in the research on voice and emotion. It will remain important, but now, because technology enables the researchers to do what he or she wants, it is the theoretical development that has to follow suit.

References

Bannister, M. L. (1972). *An instrumental and judgmental analysis of voice samples from psychiatrically hospitalized and nonhospitalized adolescents.* Unpublished doctoral dissertion, University of Kansas, Lawrence.

Bergmann, G., Geldbeck, T., & Scherer, K. R. (1988). Emotionale Eindruckswirkung von prosodischen Sprechmerkmalen. *Zeitschrift für experimentelle und angewandte Psychologie, 35,* 167–200.

Berman, H. J., Shulman, A. D., & Marwit, S. J. (1976). Comparison of multidimensional decoding of affect from audio, video, and audiovideo recordings. *Sociometry, 39,* 83–89.

Bonner, M. R. (1943). Changes in the speech pattern under emotional tension. *American Journal of Psychology, 56,* 262–273.

Bortz, J. (1966). *Physikalisch–akustische Korrelate der vokalen Kommunikation.* Arbeiten aus dem physikalischen Institut der Universität Hamburg, 9.

Brown, C. H., & Waser, P. M. (1988). Environmental influences on the structure of primate vocalizations. In D. Todt, P. Goedeking, & D. Symmes (Eds.), *Primate vocal communication* (pp. 51–66). Berlin: Springer-Verlag.

Brunswik, E. (1956). *Perception and the representative design of psychological experiments.* Berkeley and Los Angeles: University of California Press.

Buck, R. (1983). Nonverbal receiving ability. In J. M. Wiemann & R. P. Harrison (Eds.), *Nonverbal interaction* (pp. 209–242). Beverly Hills, CA: Sage.

Bühler, K. (1933). *Ausdruckstheorie.* Jena: Fischer.

Campos, J. J. (1988). Theoretical issues in the psychophysiology of emotion (structured panel discussion). *Psychophysiology, 25,* 422 (abstract).

Coleman, R. F., & Williams, R. (1979). Identification of emotional states using perceptual and acoustic analyses. In V. Lawrence & B. Weinberg (Eds.), *Transcript of the eighth symposium: Care of the professional voice* (Pt. I). New York: Voice Foundation.

Constanzo, F. S., Markel, N. N., & Constanzo, P. R. (1969). Voice quality profile and perceived emotion. *Journal of Counseling Psychology, 16,* 267–270.

Darwin, C. (1872). *The expression of emotions in man and animals.* London: John Murray.

Davidson, R. J. (1988). Theoretical issues in the psychophysiology of emotion (structured panel discussion). *Psychophysiology, 25,* 422 (abstract).

Davitz, J. R. (1964a). Auditory correlates of vocal expressions of emotional meanings. In *The communication of emotional meaning* (pp. 101–112). New York: McGraw-Hill.

(1964b). Personality, perceptual, and cognitive correlates of emotional sensitivity. In *The communication of emotional meaning* (pp. 57–68). New York: McGraw-Hill.

Dittus, W. (1988). An analysis of Toque Macaque cohesion calls from an ecological perspective. In D. Todt, P. Goedeking, & D. Symmes (Eds.), *Primate vocal communication* (pp. 31–50). Berlin: Springer-Verlag.

Duncan, G., Laver, J., & Jack, M. A. (1983). A psycho-acoustic interpretation of variations in divers' voice fundamental frequency in a pressured helium–oxygen environment. *Work in Progress, 16*, 9–16. Edinburgh: University of Edinburgh, Department of Linguistics.

Eisenberg, J. F. (1974). The function and motivational basis of hystericomorph vocalizations. *Symposium of the Zoological Society of London, 34*, 211–247.

(1976). Communication mechanisms and social integration in the black spider monkey *(Ateles fusciceps robustus)* and related species. *Smithsonian Contributions to Zoology, 213*, 1–108.

Ekman, P. (1972). Universals and cultural differences in facial expressions of emotion. In J. R. Cole (Ed.), *Nebraska Symposium on Motivation* (pp. 207–283). Lincoln: University of Nebraska Press.

(1973). *Darwin and facial expression: A century of research in review.* New York: Academic Press.

(1988). Theoretical issues in the psychophysiology of emotion (structured panel discussion). *Psychophysiology, 25*, 422 (abstract).

Ekman, P., & Friesen, W. V. (1969). The repertoire of nonverbal behavior: Categories, origins, usage, and coding. *Semiotica, 1*, 49–98.

(1978). *Facial Action Coding System (FACS): A technique for the measurement of facial action.* Palo Alto, CA: Consulting Psychologists Press.

Ekman, P., Friesen, W. V., & Ellsworth, P. (1982). Conceptual ambiguities. In P. Ekman (Ed.), *Emotion in the human face* (2nd ed., pp. 7–21). Cambridge: Cambridge University Press.

Ekman, P., Friesen, W. V., & Scherer, K. R. (1976). Body movement and voice pitch in deceptive interaction. *Semiotica, 16*, 23–27.

Eldred, S. H., & Price, D. B. (1958). A linguistic evaluation of feeling states in psychotherapy. *Psychiatry, 21*, 11–121.

Fairbanks, G., & Hoaglin, L. W. (1941). An experimental study of the durational characteristics of the voice during the expression of emotion. *Speech Monographs, 8*, 85–90.

Fairbanks, G., & Pronovost, W. (1939). An experimental study of the pitch characteristics of the voice during the expression of emotion. *Speech Monographs, 6*, 87–104.

Fonagy, I. (1978). A new method of investigating the perception of prosodic features. *Language and Speech, 21*, 34–49.

Giles, H. (1979). Ethnicity markers in speech. In K. R. Scherer & H. Giles (Eds.), *Social markers in speech* (pp. 251–289). Cambridge: Cambridge University Press.

Giles, H., Scherer, K. R., & Taylor, D. M. (1979). Speech markers in social interaction. In K. R. Scherer & H. Giles (Eds.), *Social markers in speech* (pp. 343–381). Cambridge: Cambridge University Press.

Goffman, E. (1979). Response cries. In M. von Cranach, E. Foppa, W. Lepenies, & D. Ploog (Eds.), *Human ethology* (pp. 203–249). Cambridge: Cambridge University Press.

Goldbeck, T., Tolkmitt, F., & Scherer, K. R. (1988). Experimental studies on

232   Arvid Kappas, Ursula Hess, and Klaus R. Scherer

vocal affect communication. In K. R. Scherer (Ed.), *Facets of emotion: Recent research* (pp. 119–137). Hillsdale, NJ: Earlbaum.

Graham, J. A., Ricci Bitti, P., & Argyle, M. (1975). A cross-cultural study of the communication of emotion by facial and gestural cues. *International Journal of Psychology, 10,* 57–67.

Green, S. (1975). Variation of vocal pattern with social situation in the Japanese monkey *(Macaca fuscata):* A field study. In L. A. Rosenblum (Ed.), *Primate behavior: Developments in field and laboratory research* (Vol. 4, pp. 2–102). New York: Academic Press.

Green, R. S., & Cliff, N. (1975). Multidimensional comparisons of structures of vocally and facially expressed emotion. *Perception and Psychophysics, 17,* 429–438.

Hargreaves, W. A., & Starkweather, J. A. (1964). Voice quality changes in depression. *Language and Speech, 7* 84–88.

(1965). *Vocal and verbal indicators of depression.* Unpublished manuscript, San Francisco.

Hargreaves, W. A., Starkweather, J. A., & Blacker, K. H. (1965). Voice quality in depression. *Journal of Abnormal Psychology, 70,* 218–220.

Harrison, R. P., & Wiemann, J. M. (1983). The nonverbal domain: Implications for theory, research, and practice. In J. M. Wiemann & R. P. Harrison (Eds.), *Nonverbal interaction* (pp. 271–285). Beverly Hills, CA: Sage.

Havrdova, Z., & Moravek, M. (1979). Changes of the voice expression during suggestively influenced states of experiencing. *Activitas Nervosa Superior, 21,* 33–35.

Helfrich, H. (1979). Age markers in speech. In K. R. Scherer & H. Giles (Eds.), *Social markers in speech* (pp. 63–107). Cambridge: Cambridge University Press.

Hess, U., & Kappas, A. (1985). *Decoding discrepant information in facial and vocal communication channels, with regard to contextual effects.* Paper presented at the Second European Conference on Facial Measurement, Saarbrücken, Germany.

Hess, U., Kappas, A., & Scherer, K. R. (1988). Multichannel communication of emotion: Synthetic signal production. In K. R. Scherer (Ed.), *Facets of emotion: Recent research* (pp. 161–182). Hillsdale, NJ: Erlbaum.

Hicks, J. W. (1979). An acoustical/temporal analysis of emotional stress in speech. *Dissertation Abstracts International, 41,* 417.

Höffe, W. L. (1960). Über Beziehungen von Sprachmelodie und Lautstärke. *Phonetica, 5,* 129–159.

Hollien, H. (1981). Analog instrumentation for acoustic speech analysis. In J. Darby (Ed.), *Speech evaluation in psychiatry* (pp. 79–103). New York: Grune & Stratton.

Hollien, H., Geison, L., & Hicks, J. W., Jr. (1987). Voice stress evaluators and lie detection. *Journal of Forensic Sciences, 32,* 405–418.

Huttar, G. L. (1968). Relations between prosodic variables and emotions in normal American English utterances. *Journal of Speech and Hearing Research, 11,* 481–487.

Jürgens, U. (1979). Vocalization as an emotional indicator. A neuroethological study in the squirrel monkey. *Behaviour, 69,* 88–117.

(1982). A neuroethological approach to the classification of vocalization in the squirrel monkey. In C. T. Snowdon, C. H. Brown, & M. R. Petersen (Eds.), *Primate communication* (pp. 50–62). Cambridge: Cambridge University Press.

(1988). Central control of monkey calls. In D. Todt, P. Goedeking, & D. Symmes (Eds.), *Primate vocal communication* (pp. 162–167). Berlin: Springer-Verlag.

Jürgens, Ü., & Ploog, D. (1976). Zur Evolution der Stimme. *Archiv für Psychiatrice und Nervenkrankheiten, 222,* 117–137.

Kaiser, L. (1962). Communication of affects by single vowels. *Synthese, 14,* 300–319.

Kappas, A. (1986). Der Einfluß von Intonation und Stimmqualität auf die Attribution von Emotionen und Einstellungen. Unpublished master's thesis, University of Giessen, Department of Psychology.

Klos, T. Ellgring, H., & Scherer, K. R. (1987). *Vocal changes in depression.* Manuscript submitted for publication.

Knapp, M. L. (1978). *Nonverbal communication in human interaction* (2nd ed.). New York: Holt, Rinehart and Winston.

Kotlyar, G. M., & Morozov, V. P. (1976). Acoustical correlates of the emotional content of vocalized speech. *Journal of Acoustics of the Academy of Sciences of the USSR, 22,* 208–211.

Kramer, E. (1963). Judgement of personal characteristics and emotions from nonverbal properties of speech. *Psychological Bulletin, 60,* 408–420.

Kuroda, I., Fujiwara, O., Okamura, N., & Utsuki, N. (1976). Method for determining pilot stress through analysis of voice communication. *Aviation, Space, and Environmental Medicine, 47,* 528–533.

Ladd, D. R., Silverman, K. E. A., Tolkmitt, F., Bergmann, G., & Scherer, K. R. (1985). Evidence for the independent function of intonation contour type, voice quality, and F_0 range in signalling speaker affect. *Journal of the Acoustical Society of America, 78,* 435–444.

Laver, J. (1980). *The phonetic description of voice quality.* Cambridge: Cambridge University Press.

Levenson, R. (1988). Theoretical issues in the psychophysiology of emotion (structured panel discussion). *Psychophysiology, 25,* 422–423 (abstract).

Levin, H., & Lord, W. (1975). Speech pitch frequency as an emotional state indicator. *IEEE Transactions on Systems, Man, and Cybernetics, 5,* 259–273.

Levitt, E. A. (1964). The relationships between abilities to express emotional meaning vocally and facially. In J. R. Davitz (Ed.), *The communication of emotional meaning* (pp. 43–55). New York: McGraw-Hill.

Mahl, G. F., & Schulze, G. (1964). Psychological research in the extralinguistic area. In T. A. Sebeok, A. S. Hayes, & M. C. Bateson (Eds.), *Approaches to semiotics* (pp. 51–61). The Hague: Mouton.

Malatesta, C. Z., Fiore, M. J., & Messina, J. J. (1987). Affect, personality, and facial expressive characteristics of older people. *Psychology and Aging, 2,* 64–69.

Markel, N. N., Bein, M. F., & Phillis, J. A. (1973). The relationship between words and tone-of-voice. *Language and Speech, 16,* 15–21.

Marler, P. (1984). Animal communication: Affect or cognition? In K. R. Scherer & P. Ekman (Eds.), *Approaches to emotion* (pp. 345–368). Hillsdale, NJ: Erlbaum.

Marler, P., & Mitani, J. (1988). Vocal communication in primates and birds: Parallels and contrasts. In D. Todt, P. Goedeking, & D. Symmes (Eds.), *Primate vocal communication* (pp. 3–14). Berlin: Springer-Verlag.

Marler, P., & Tenaza, R. (1977). Signalling behavior of apes with special reference to vocalization. In T. A. Seboek (Ed.), *How animals communicate* (pp. 965–1033). Bloomington: Indiana University Press.

234   Arvid Kappas, Ursula Hess, and Klaus R. Scherer

Mehrabian, A., & Ferris, S. (1967). Inference of attitudes from nonverbal communication in two channels. *Journal of Consulting Psychology, 31*, 248–252.
Morris, C. W. (1946). *Signs, language, and behavior.* Englewood Cliffs, NJ: Prentice-Hall.
Morton, E. S. (1977). On the occurrence and significance of motivation-structural rules in some bird and mammal sounds. *American Nature, 111*, 855–869.
Moses, P. J. (1954). *The voice of neurosis.* New York: Grune & Stratton.
Müller, A. L. (1960). *Experimentelle Untersuchungen zur stimmlichen Darstellung von Gefühlen.* Unpublished doctoral dissertation, University of Göttingen.
Newman, S. S., & Mather, V. G. (1938). Analysis of spoken language of patients with affective disorders. *American Journal of Psychiatry, 94*, 913–942.
Niwa, S. (1971). Changes of voice characteristics in urgent situations (2). *Reports of the Aeromedical Laboratory. Japan Air Self Defense Force, 11*, 246–251.
Noller, P. (1985). Video primacy – A further look. *Journal of Nonverbal Behavior, 9*, 28–47.
Ohala, J. J. (1978). Production of tone. In V. A. Fromkin (Ed.), *Tone: A linguistic survey* (pp. 5–39). New York: Academic Press.
   (1980). The acoustic origin of the smile. *Journal of the Acoustical Society of America, 72*, 66 (abstract).
   (1981). The nonlinguistic components of speech. In J. Darby (Ed.), *Speech evaluation in psychiatry* (pp. 39–49). New York: Grune & Stratton.
Ostwald, P. F. (1961). The sound of emotional disturbance. *Archives of General Psychiatry, 5*, 587–592.
   (1963). *Soundmaking: The acoustic communication of emotion.* Springfield, IL: Thomas.
   (1964). Acoustic manifestations of emotional disturbance. *Disorders of Communication – Research Publications, 42*, 450–465.
Peirce, C. S. (1931–1935). Collected papers of Charles Sanders Peirce, 8 vols., C. Hartshorne & P. Weiss (Eds.). Cambridge, MA: Harvard University Press.
Plaikner, D. (1970). *Die Veränderungen der menschlichen Stimme unter dem Einfluß psychischer Belastung.* Unpublished doctoral dissertation, University of Innsbruck.
Ploog, D. (1974). *Die Sprache der Affen und ihre Bedeutung für die Verständigungsweisen des Menschen.* Munich: Kindler.
   (1986). Vocal expressions of emotion. In R. Plutchik & H. Kellerman (Eds.), *Emotion: Theory, research, and experience: Vol. 3. Biological foundations of emotion* (pp. 173–197). Orlando, FL: Academic Press.
   (1988). Neurobiology and pathology of subhuman vocal communication and human speech. In D. Todt, P. Goedeking, & D. Symmes (Eds.), *Primate vocal communication* (pp. 195–212). Berlin: Springer-Verlag.
Robinson, W. P. (1979). Speech markers and social class. In K. R. Scherer & H. Giles (Eds.), *Social markers in speech* (pp. 211–249). Cambridge: Cambridge University Press.
Roessler, R., & Lester, J. W. (1976). Voice predicts affect during psychotherapy. *Journal of Nervous and Mental Disease, 163*, 166–176.
   (1979). Vocal patterns in anxiety. In W. E. Fann, A. D. Pokorny, I. Koracau, & R. L. Williams (Eds.), *Phenomenology and treatment of anxiety* (pp. 225–235). New York: Spectrum.
Scherer, K. R. (1971). Randomized splicing: A note on a simple technique for masking speech content. *Journal of Experimental Research in Personality, 5*, 155–159.
   (1974). Acoustic concomitants of emotional dimensions: Judging affects from

synthesized tone sequences. In S. Weitz (Ed.), *Nonverbal communication* (pp. 105–111). New York: Oxford University Press.

(1977). Affektlaute und vokale Embleme. In R. Posner and H. P. Reinecke (Eds.), *Zeichenprozesse – Semiotische Forschung in den Einzelwissenschaften* (pp. 199–214). Wiesbaden: Athenaion.

(1978). Personality inference from voice quality: The loud voice of extraversion. *European Journal of Social Psychology, 8,* 467–487.

(1979a). Nonlinguistic vocal indicators of emotion and psychopathology. In C. E. Izard (Ed.), *Emotions in personality and psychopathology* (pp. 493–529). New York: Plenum.

(1979b). Voice and speech correlates of perceived social influence. In H. Giles & R. St. Clair (Eds.), *The social psychology of language.* London: Blackwell Publisher.

(1980). Personality, emotion, psychopathology and speech. In H. Giles, W. P. Robinson, & P. M. Smith (Eds.), *Language: Social psychological perspectives* (pp. 233–235). Oxford: Pergamon.

(1981a). Speech and emotional states. In J. Darby (Ed.), *Speech evaluation in psychiatry* (pp. 189–220). New York: Grune & Stratton.

(1981b). Vocal indicators of stress. In J. Darby (Ed.), *Speech evaluation in psychiatry* (pp. 171–187). New York: Grune & Stratton.

(1982). Methods of research on vocal communication: Paradigms and parameters. In K. R. Scherer & P. Ekman (Eds.), *Handbook of methods in nonverbal behavior research* (pp. 136–198). Cambridge: Cambridge University Press.

(1984). On the nature and function of emotion: A component process approach. In K. R. Scherer & P. Ekman (Eds.), *Approaches to emotion* (pp. 293–318). Hillsdale, NJ: Erlbaum.

(1985). Vocal affect signalling: A comparative approach. In J. Rosenblatt, C. Beer, M.-C. Busnel, & P. J. B. Slater (Eds.), *Advances in the study of behavior* (Vol. 15, pp. 189–244). New York: Academic Press.

(1986a). Vocal affect expression: A review and a model for future research. *Psychological Bulletin, 99,* 143–165.

(1986b). Voice, stress, and emotion. In M. H. Appley & R. Trumbull (Eds.), *Dynamics of stress* (pp. 159–181). New York: Plenum.

(1987). Vocal assessment of affective disorders. In D. Kupfer & J. D. Maser (Eds.), *Depression and expressive behavior.* Hillsdale, NJ: Erlbaum.

(1988). Criteria for emotion-antecedent appraisal: A review. In V. Hamilton, G. H. Bower, & N. H. Frijda (Eds.), *Cognitive perspectives on emotion and motivation* (pp. 89–126). Dordrecht: Kluwer Academic Publishers.

(1989). Vocal correlates of emotion. In H. Wagner & A. Manstead (Eds.), *Handbook of psychophysiology: Emotion and social behavior* (pp. 165–197). London: Wiley.

Scherer, U., Helfrich, H., & Scherer, K. R. (1980). Paralinguistic behaviour: Internal push or external pull. In H. Giles, W. P. Robinson, & P. M. Smith (Eds.), *Language: Social psychological perspectives* (pp. 279–282). Oxford: Pergamon.

Scherer, K. R., & Kappas, A. (1988). Primate vocal expression of affective state. In D. Todt, P. Goedeking, & D. Symmes (Eds.), *Primate vocal communication* (pp. 171–194). Berlin: Springer-Verlag.

Scherer, K. R., Koivumaki, J., & Rosenthal, R. (1972). Minimal cues in the vocal communication of affect: Judging emotions from content-masked speech. *Journal of Psycholinguistic Research, 1,* 269–285.

Scherer, K. R., Ladd, D. R., & Silverman, K. E. A. (1984). Vocal cues to speaker affect: Testing two models. *Journal of the Acoustical Society of America, 76,* 1346–1356.

Scherer, K. R., & Oshinsky, J. (1977). Cue utilization in emotion attribution from auditory stimuli. *Motivation and Emotion, 1,* 331–346.

Scherer, K. R., & Scherer, U. (1981). Speech behavior and personality. In J. Darby (Ed.), *Speech evaluation in psychiatry* (pp. 115–135). New York: Grune & Stratton.

Scherer, K. R., & Wallbott, H. G. (in preparation). *Development of a standardized vocal emotion recognition test.*

Scherer, K. R., Wallbott, H. G., & Summerfield, A. B. (Eds.). (1986). *Experiencing emotion: A cross-cultural study.* Cambridge: Cambridge University Press.

Scherer, K. R., Wallbott, H. G., Tolkmitt, F., & Bergmann, G. (1985). *Die Streß-reaktion: Physiologie und Verhalten.* Göttingen: Hogrefe.

Sedlacek, K., & Sychra, A. (1963). Die Melodie als Faktor des emotionellen Ausdrucks. *Folia Phoniatrica, 15,* 89–98.

Seyfarth, R. M., & Cheney, D. L. (1982). How monkeys see the world: A review of recent research on East African vervet monkeys. In C. T. Snowdon, C. H. Brown, & M. R. Petersen (Eds.), *Primate communication* (pp. 239–252). Cambridge: Cambridge University Press.

Shannon, C., & Weaver, W. (1949). *The mathematical theory of communication.* Champaign: University of Illinois Press.

Siegman, A. W., & Feldstein, S. (1987). *Nonverbal behavior and communication* (2nd ed.). Hillsdale, NJ: Erlbaum.

Simonov, P. V., & Frolov, M. V. (1973). Utilization of human voice for estimation of man's emotional stress and state attention. *Aerospace Medicine, 44,* 256–258.

Sincoff, J. B., & Rosenthal, R. (1985). Content-masking methods as determinants of results of studies of nonverbal communication. *Journal of Nonverbal Behavior, 9,* 121–129.

Skinner, R. E. (1935). A calibrated recording and analysis of the pitch, force, and quality of vocal tones expressing happiness and sadness. And a determination of the pitch and force of the subjective concepts of ordinary, soft, and loud tones. *Speech Monographs, 2,* 81–137.

Smith, P. M. (1979). Sex markers in speech. In K. R. Scherer & H. Giles (Eds.), *Social markers in speech* (pp. 109–146). Cambridge: Cambridge University Press.

   (1980). Judging masculine and feminine social identities from content-controlled speech. In H. Giles, W. P. Robinson, & P. M. Smith (Eds.), *Language: Social psychological perspectives* (pp. 121–126). Oxford: Pergamon.

Standke, R., Kappas, A., & Scherer, K. R. (1984). Die Attribution von Stimm und Sprechermerkmalen in Abhängigkeit von Stimmqualität und Kontinuität des Sprechflusses. In A. Schick & K. P. Walcher (Eds.), *Beiträge zur Bedeutungslehre des Schalls* (pp. 389–402). Bern: Lang.

Streeter, L. A., Krauss, R. M., Geller, V., Olson, C., & Apple, W. (1977). Pitch changes during attempted deception. *Journal of Personality and Social Psychology, 35,* 345–350.

Sulc, J. (1977). To the problem of emotional changes in the human voice. *Activitas Nervosa Superior, 19,* 215–216.

Tartter, V. C. (1980). Happy talk: Perceptual and acoustic effects of smiling on speech. *Perception and Psychophysics, 27,* 24–27.

Tembrock, G. (1971). *Biokommunikaton: Informationsübertragung im biologischen Bereich.* Berlin: Akademie-Verlag.

(1975). Die Erforschung des tierlichen Stimmausdruckes (Bioakustik). In F. Trojan (Ed.), *Biophonetik* (pp. 51–68). Mannheim: Bibliographisches Institut.

Titze, I. R. (1974). The human vocal cords: A mathematical model (pt. 2). *Phonetica, 29,* 1–21.

Titze, I. R., & Talkin, D. T. (1979). A theoretical study of the effects of various laryngeal configurations on the acoustics of phonation. *Journal of the Acoustical Society of America, 66,* 60–74.

Todt, D. (1988). Serial calling as a mediator of interaction processes: Crying in primates. In D. Todt, P. Goedeking, & D. Symmes (Eds.), *Primate vocal communication* (pp. 88–107). Berlin: Springer-Verlag.

Tolkmitt, F. J., Helfrich, H., Standke, R., & Scherer, K. R. (1982). Vocal indicators of psychiatric treatment effects in depressives and schizophrenics. *Journal of Communication Disorders, 15,* 209–222.

Tomkins, S. S. (1962). *Affect, imagery, consciousness: Vol. 1. The positive affects.* New York: Springer-Verlag.

Utsuki, N., & Okamura, N. (1976). Relationship between emotional state and fundamental frequency of speech. *Reports of the Aeromedical Laboratory, Japan Air Self Defense Force, 16,* 179–188.

Van Bezooijen, R. (1984). *The characteristics and recognizability of vocal expressions of emotion.* Dordrecht: Foris.

Wallbott, H. G. (1979). Beziehungen zwischen Signalsystemen: Einführung. In K. R. Scherer & H. G. Wallbott (Eds.), *Nonverbale Kommunikation* (pp. 187–192). Weinheim: Beltz.

(1988). Faces in context: The relative importance of facial expression and context information in determining emotion attributions. In K. R. Scherer (Ed.), *Facets of emotion: Recent research* (pp. 139–160). Hillsdale, NJ: Erlbaum.

Wallbott, H. G., & Scherer, K. R. (1986a). Cues and channels in emotion recognition. *Journal of Personality and Social Psychology, 51,* 690–699.

(1986b). How universal and specific is emotional experience? Evidence from 27 countries on five continents. In K. R. Scherer (Ed.), *Facets of emotion: Recent research* (pp. 31–56). Hillsdale, NJ: Erlbaum.

Whitehead, J. M. (1987). Vocally mediated reciprocity between neighbouring groups of mantled howling monkeys *(Alouatta palliata palliata). Animal Behavior, 35,* 1615–1627.

Whitman, E. N., & Flicker, D. J. (1966). A potential new measurement of emotional state: A preliminary report. *Newark Beth Israel Hospital, 17,* 167–172.

Williams, C. E., & Stevens, K. N. (1969). On determining the emotional state of pilots during flight: An exploratory study. *Aerospace Medicine, 40,* 1369–1372.

(1972). Emotions and speech: Some acoustical correlates. *Journal of the Acoustical Society of America, 52,* 1238–1250.

Wolf, J. J. (1981). Acoustic analysis and computer systems. In J. Darby (Ed.), *Speech evaluation in psychiatry* (pp. 105–110). New York: Grune & Stratton.

Wundt, W. (1903). *Grundzüge der physiologischen Psychologie* (Vol. 3). Leipzig: Wilhelm Engelmann.

Zaidel, S., & Mehrabian, A. (1969). The ability to communicate and infer positive and negative attitudes facially and vocally. *Journal of Experimental Research in Psychology, 34,* 966–977.

Zuberbier, E. (1957). Zur Schreib- und Sprechmotorik der Depressiven. *Zeitschrift für Psychotherapie und Medizinische Psychologie, 7,* 239–249.

Zwirner, E. (1930). Beitrag zur Sprache des Depressiven. *Phonometrie III, Spezielle Anwendungen I* (pp. 171–187). Basel: Karger.

7. Gesture and speech

BERNARD RIMÉ AND LORIS SCHIARATURA

Introduction

Some years ago, we instructed volunteer subjects to interact verbally with an experimenter according to two conditions of communication content (Rimé & Gaussin, 1982). The first one simulated a situation of "objective" communication and was presented to the subject as a short-term memory task. It consisted of repeating series of digits enumerated by the experimenter. In the second condition, the subjects were asked to describe to the experimenter noteworthy events that had occurred in their personal life during the preceding week. These interactions were videotaped, and the subjects' nonverbal behaviors were analyzed. The dependent variables were movements of the eyes, head, eyebrows, trunk, and hands. The data showed that the subjects were certainly not immobile when repeating digits during the first condition. Merely pronouncing words thus seems to give rise to some degree of body movement. However, although needed phonation efforts were theoretically exactly the same for repeating digits as for telling personal events, a flow of motor activity occurred in the latter case, with most statistical comparisons between the two conditions resulting in values exceeding the .001 level of significance. The strongest effect actually involved hand gestures.

Why this motor activity of subjects sharing verbally some of their personal representations? Do people perceive their efforts to communicate verbally as insufficient by themselves? Do they consequently try to compensate with attempts at depicting what they mean through nonverbal displays? If this were the case, one would expect nonverbal behaviors

This work was supported by grants 1.5.410.86F from the Fonds de la Recherche Fondamentale Collective (FNRS) and IM-787-205 from the Ministère de l'Education Nationale (FRSFC).

239

to occur less frequently when subjects interact without seeing one another. This issue was examined in a study in which pairs of subjects were asked to hold a conversation about films they saw recently (Rimé, 1982). Half of these dyads interacted with an opaque screen separating the two partners during the conversation. The other half were face to face with no obstacle preventing mutual visibility. These situations were videotaped, and nonverbal behaviors were analyzed. The results showed that compared with subjects who interacted in the face-to-face condition, those who communicated without seeing one another evidenced no decrease in frequency of movements of the trunk, head, eyebrows, or lips. There were only marginally significant differences for movements of the hands and eyes. Overall, among the 15 dependent variables of nonverbal behavior in this study, none was observed to differentiate significantly the two conditions of interaction. At first glance, these data may appear surprising. But anyone who has ever observed the gesturing and facial movement of someone holding a phone conversation would be easily convinced of their ecological validity.

If the amount of nonverbal behavior remains constant when people interact without seeing one another, their function must be other than communicative. Can the display of nonverbal behavior be explained by some increase in the speaker's general arousal level? Indeed, arousal, which happens to be one of the most frequently indexed words in Harper, Wiens, and Matarazzo's (1978) *Nonverbal Communication*, has often been mentioned as an explanatory variable with respect to nonverbal behavior. This arousal explanation of gesturing was tested in an unpublished study by Rimé, Boulanger, and Thomas. Subjects with either a high or a low basal heart rate were selected from among 300 students, and each of them was invited to perform a 150-second biking exercise on a laboratory bicycle. For half of these subjects, the bicycle's resistance was set at a low level, and for the remaining half, the resistance was high. The inducement of either high or low arousal increases was thus achieved, and heart rate measurement confirmed the effectiveness of this manipulation. Immediately after the exercise, the subjects had to hold a conversation with an experimenter so that their speech-accompanying nonverbal behaviors could be monitored. Neither basal arousal nor experimentally induced arousal was found to have a significant effect on these variables. Consequently, the arousal explanation of speech-accompanying gestures was completely unsupported by the facts.

Faced with these negative results, we decided to explore what would happen if subjects were prevented from making the major movements they normally make during a conversation (Rimé, Schiaratura, Hupet, & Ghysselinckx, 1984). Subjects held a 50-minute conversation while sitting in an armchair devised to restrain movements of the head, arms, hands, legs, and feet during part of the experiment. The procedure involved first a 15-minute baseline period with free movements, then a 20-minute period of immobilization, and finally another 15-minute period with free movements. The subjects' nonverbal activity was measured in the body zones that remained free to move during the immobilization, that is, the eyebrows, eyes, mouth, and fingers. The data revealed very strong effects of the immobilization on these variables. Indeed, with respect to base levels, highly significant increases in activity were recorded in all four observed body zones for the immobilization period, with a subsequent return to base levels when free movements were recovered. As these effects were observed only when the subjects were speaking and in no manner when they were listening, the speech processes clearly were included in their elicitation. Any explanation using some arousal consequence of the situations' unusual character seemed unlikely, as temporal analyses failed to detect a habituation effect during the 20-minute immobilization period. These data thus showed that verbal encoding is, at the very least, not dissociable from gesticulation and body movement. But nonverbal channels were not alone in being affected by immobilization. Samples of the dialogues were submitted to a computerized technique of content analysis, and a significant decrease was recorded for vividness of imagery during movement restriction, as compared with baseline and recovery periods. Speech content, then, was also affected by the restriction of the usual speech-accompanying movements.

These data suggest that the gestural motor activity of a speaking person is inextricably linked to his or her verbal encoding activities. This question of the speaking person's motor involvement will be the object of this chapter. Two things in particular have stimulated our scientific curiosity with respect to this phenomenon: First, the speaker's gesticulation is one of the facts to which human beings are most often exposed, as observers as well as actors, and yet it usually goes unnoticed in everyday life. Second, the phenomenon simply cannot be assimilated by current theoretical models in psychology; it even challenges some fundamental distinction usually maintained in this domain. Thus with the gestures and bodily movements of the speaking person, we are faced with embodied thinking. Such a challenge to our respectable conceptual assumptions might offer an opportunity to modify some of our scientific horizons.

To allocate reasonable limits to our enterprise, this chapter will be concerned with only the most typical and most visible manifestations of speech-accompanying nonverbal behaviors, that is, hand gesturing. The topic of speech-accompanying hand gestures has elicited a number of scientific efforts that we shall examine. First, we shall describe the object, by examining a classification of hand gestures.

A classification of speech-related hand movements

Any reader who has ventured into the research literature on hand gestures has been confronted by a jungle of classes of and labels for gestures. Nearly each author invented his or her own solutions to the difficult classification problem raised in this field, so that important obstacles are encountered when communicating ideas and comparing data. Therefore, trying to put some order in the universe of gestures is a reasonable and worthwhile enterprise.

Various classifications have been proposed for speech-related hand movements (Cosnier, 1982; Ekman & Friesen, 1972; Freedman, 1972; McNeill, 1985, 1987a; McNeill & Levy, 1982), although virtually all the gestures considered by these classifications were already mentioned in the system proposed earlier by Efron (1941/1972) in his pioneering work on conversational behaviors among Jewish and Italian immigrants in New York City. Efron himself was partly relying on a classification of gestures introduced by Wundt (1900/1973) at the beginning of this century. We shall review Efron's classes of gestures and compare them with those proposed by later systems. When useful, we shall suggest some extensions or specifications of Efron's categories in order to bring them up to date with respect to related observations by later authors. Next we shall propose amendments to Efron's labels as some of them were far from being self-explanatory. Finally, we shall organize the various categories. The titles and subtitles we use will sometimes not correspond to Efron's labels but, rather, to those we shall propose for the various categories in what might best be considered as a "revised Efron system of gestures" (Schiaratura & Rimé, 1990).

The principal distinction that Efron introduced concerned the referent and was reproduced in every succeeding classification. It assumed that although some hand gestures are obviously related to some external referent – an object or event about which the speaker is talking – others

have their referent within the speaking person's ideational process itself.

Gestures referring to the ideational process

Gestures referring to the ideational process follow the contour of the
speech by marking the speaking person's logical pauses, stresses, and
voice intonations. According to Efron (1941/1972), there are two major
subclasses in this category: speech-marking hand movements and ideographs.

Speech-marking hand movements. This first subclass comprises what Efron
called *batonlike gestures,* which time the successive stages of the referential activity. All the other existing classifications mention categories of
gestures representing some variant of this one:

- Freedman's (1972) *punctuating movements* were described as related to the emphatic aspects of speech, occurring in bursts and in close coordination with
  the rhythmic aspects of speech.
- Freedman's (1972) *minor qualifiers* are movements having some characteristic
  form (e.g., a turning of the wrist), but without being staccatolike. Devoid of
  representational activity, they may be considered stylized accentuation movements.
- McNeill and Levy (1982) and McNeill (1985) distinguished *batonic movements,*
  which they defined as functioning to stress some linguistic item that the
  speaker wishes to emphasize.
- Close to the latter are Ekman and Friesen's (1972) *batons,* which they defined
  as accenting or emphasizing a particular word or phrase.
- McNeill (1987a) also mentioned small uniform movements, which he called
  beats. A typical beat is a simple up-and-down or back-and-forth movement of
  the hand. Such movements are said to appear with clauses that are performing
  an extranarrative role, such as introducing new characters, setting scenes,
  summing up, or anticipating a story.
- Cosnier (1982) gathered under the label *paraverbal* those hand gestures that
  stress speech intonation or emphasis or that mark the major stages of reasoning.

Taken together, these various items argue in favor of a general class of
speech-marking hand movements. The referential correlates of these
speech markers lie within the speech process, and they (1) stress some
elements of the speech for the sake of clarity or emphasis, (2) introduce
some new element into the talk, or (3)"chunk" the sentence according to
the underlying reasoning.

Ideographs. A second class of hand gestures that Efron considered in the broad category of those referring to the ideational process consist of *ideographs,* or logicotopographic gestures. Efron defined ideographs as hand or finger movements sketching in space the logical track followed by the speaker's thinking. In his thinking, Efron was inspired by Gratiolet (1865), a 19th-century French specialist of the study of expression who considered that "when thinking is strongly patterned, while the mind is feeling every bend of it, the raised eye and finger appear as following the thread of some very complicated meander" (p. 322). Although obviously present in everyday life situations, ideographs have less often been isolated than speech markers by later classifications. Nevertheless, Ekman and Friesen (1972) clearly mentioned ideographs under this label and defined them as movements sketching the path or direction of thought. Similarly, McNeill (McNeill, 1985, 1987a; McNeill & Levy, 1982) recognized the existence of ideographs in what he called *metaphoric gestures,* which depict some abstract meaning occurring in the speech (e.g., the logical relation of reciprocity being represented by a hand movement from left to right and from right to left).

With ideographs, we thus have access to hand gestures that have some depictive function. Going one step further, Efron (1941/1972) described other classes of gestures in regard this time not to the speaker's ideation process but, rather, to the object of his or her speech. Some of these gestures still are depictive ones, whereas others are to be considered as evocative ones. We shall examine these two broad classes in the next two sections.

Gestures referring to the object of the speech: Depictive type

Two types of gesture that Efron considered can be placed in this class: *physiographic* and *pantomimic gestures.* As we shall explain later, physiographic gestures will be relabeled as *iconic gestures.*

Iconic gestures. Physiographic gestures are, according to Efron's (1941/1972) definition, hand movements that parallel the speech by presenting some figural representation of the object evoked simultaneously. Gestures of this kind have been mentioned in every existing classification. Freedman (1972) included them under the label of *motor primacy representational movements,* and McNeill (1985, 1987a; McNeill & Levy, 1982) under the label of *iconic hand gestures.* Such gestures were also mentioned by Cosnier (1982) in his class of *illustrative gestures,* as well as by Ekman and Friesen (1972) in their class of *illustrators*. Although often referred to in the research literature, this latter class was too all-encompassing, and so easily led to confusion. Indeed, under this single label of illustrators were grouped together eight different types of gesture. Among them were the aforementioned *batons*, and also the *emblematic gestures* to be described later. Research would likely benefit from more specific categories of gesture.

Various kinds of gestures belonging to the physiographic group have been mentioned by the different proposed classifications, and so we shall examine them further. Basically, three types of physiographic gesture seem to be distinguished with respect to the aspect of the referent being depicted by the speaker's movement. First, the gesture may describe the shape of the referential object, as is the case in the well-known upward spiraling movement of the finger of the person describing a spiral staircase. This type of gesture was called an *iconograph* by Efron (1941/1972), a *pictograph* by Ekman and Friesen (1972), and a *pictomimique* by Cosnier (1982). Second, the gesture may represent some spatial relationship regarding the referent, as in the two open hands placed palm to palm in the person referring to the restaurant located between the bank and the department store. Such gestures were assimilated into the former iconographs by Efron (1941/1972) but were separated from this class or its equivalents by both Ekman and Friesen (1972) and Cosnier (1982). Cosnier labeled them *spatiographic gestures*. Gestures of this kind should not be confounded with ideographs, in which the depicted relationship always is abstract. Third, the gesture may describe some action of the object, as in the ascending movement that accompanies the verbal expression "growing out" or as in the descending one that would parallel some mention of "falling down." These action-depictive gestures were labeled *kinetographs* by Efron (1941/1972) and Ekman and Friesen (1972) and *kinemimic* by Cosnier (1982). A reasonable standardization of the various labels proposed for these three types of physiographic gesture would result in, respectively, *pictographic, spatiographic,* and *kinetographic*. The general label of *iconographic* or, more simply, *iconic gestures,* as introduced by McNeill and Levy (1982), better fits the class as a whole than does the label *physiographic* originally proposed by Efron. The latter appeared as poorly evocative, as suggested by the very loose way in which it is used in the literature.

Pantomimic gestures. Pantomimic gestures are another category that Efron proposed (1941/1972). These and the iconic gestures were distinguished nicely by McNeill and Levy (1982), who referred to Werner and Kaplan's (1963) criterion of the level of differentiation between a gesture and the referred object. At the lower level of this differentiation, the hands of the gesturing person are playing their own role, illustrating their function of manipulating objects. In this case, the referred object of the speech is some acting person, and the described actions are imitated by the speaker's hands. For instance, to illustrate the words "he grasped the box," the speaker's hands shape an imaginary box. This type of hand gesture must be distinguished from those in which the hands play a more abstract role in the representational process, as when the sentence "he swallowed it" is accompanied with a movement of the left hand "swallowing" the right fist. Here, there is a marked differentiation between the referent and the symbol (McNeill and Levy, 1982). Although this second case clearly exemplifies a spatiographic hand gesture, that is, a subclass of iconic gestures, the first one with the lower symbol–referent differentiation introduces us to *pantomimic gestures*, which consist of true mimetic actions. Although pantomimes may be restricted to the activity of the hands, they are often likely to engage the whole body, so that the speaker also becomes an actor. In their strongest form, pantomimes do not need to be accompanied by speech and instead may become autonomous, constituting a conversation in themselves. This is the lowest level of symbol–referent differentiation (see Rimé, 1983).

Gestures referring to the object of the speech: Evocative type

The last two classes of gesture that Efron considered may be grouped in a category referring to their evocative aspect. By this we mean that these gestures no longer depict the referent, as was the case for the iconic and pantomimic gestures. Rather, they simply evoke this referent by some action likely to elicit its presence in the common mental space created between the speaker and the listener. The two types of gesture in this category were labeled by Efron (1941/1972) as, respectively, *deictic* and as *symbolic* or *emblematic gestures*.

Deictic gestures. Deictic gestures, also called *pointing* in lay language, consist of hand or finger gestures directed toward some visually or symbolically present object that is simultaneously referred to in the speech. This object might be a place or an event. Such gestures have been considered by every existing classification. For instance, McNeill (1987a) argued that deictics represent an abstract form of iconic gestures and that they are in fact the first form of iconic gestures displayed by children.

Symbolic gestures. Symbolic gestures, also called *emblems* by Efron, are gestural representations devoid of any morphological relationship with the visual or logical object represented. A common example of symbolic gesture is hand waving as a greeting device. Mentioned by most existing classifications, symbolic gestures have very strictly defined characteristics in nonverbal communication research. According to Ekman and Friesen (1972), they are verbal acts that (1) have a direct verbal translation consisting of one or two words, (2) have a precise meaning known by the group, class, or culture, and (3) are most often used intentionally to send a particular message to the receiver.

Conclusion

The list of hand gestures summarized in Table 7.1 covers the various hand gestures likely to be displayed by any speaking person in connection with some structural or content aspect of his or her speech. It would be a matter of convention to add to this list gestures like self-scratching, self-touching, hand-to-hand contact, or object manipulation. Such gestures are not integrated with speech, as are the classes of movements just considered. But they have been hypothesized as sometimes occurring coincidentally with significant points of the speech flow (see, e.g., Freedman, 1972).

The validity of this classificatory system is supported by the remarkable agreement among the classes of gesture considered by Efron and those proposed by later authors. Nevertheless, there has been no empirical assessment of exhaustiveness, independence of categories, interjudge agreement, and reliability in using them. But research in this direction, on classes of gesture close to those considered here, has now been initiated (Feyereisen, Van de Wiele, & Dubois, 1988).

Efron's classes suggest a number of processes that people use to express personal representations in words. Thus, speech markers evidence that while expressing the verbal message, the speaker keeps monitoring the potential ambiguities of the message content, the relative importance and novelty of introduced elements, and the successive steps of his or her own reasoning. Ideographs indicate that while speaking, the subject also keeps representing the logical track underlying the development of the message. Iconics and pantomimes show that when

Table 7.1. *The revised Efron system of speech-related hand gestures*

Gestures referring to the ideational process
1. Nondepictive gestures: speech markers
   • Stress some elements of the speech for the sake of clarity.
   • Parallel the introduction of some new element in the discourse.
   • Chunk the sentence following the steps of the underlying reasoning.
   Related classes: batonlike (Efron, 1941/1972), punctuating movements (Freedman, 1972), minor qualifiers (Freedman, 1972), batonic (McNeill, 1985; McNeill & Levy, 1982), batons (Ekman & Friesen, 1972), beats (McNeill, 1987a), paraverbals (Cosnier, 1985).

2. Depictive gestures: ideographs
   • Sketch in space the logical track followed by the speaker's thinking.
   • Parallel abstract thinking.
   Related classes: logicotopographic gestures (Efron, 1941/1972), metaphoric gestures (McNeill, 1985; McNeill & Levy, 1982).

Gestures referring to the object: depictive kinds
1. Iconographic or iconic gestures
   • Present some figural representation of the object evoked in speech.
   • Subclass: a. *pictographic:* represents the shape.
          b. *spatiographic:* represents some spatial relation.
          c. *kinetographic:* represents some action.
   Related classes: physiographic (Efron, 1942/1972), motor-primacy representational movements (Freedman, 1972), illustrative gestures (Cosnier, 1982), illustrators (Ekman & Friesen, 1972).

2. Pantomimic gestures
   • "Play" the role of the referent.

Gestures referring to the object: evocative kinds
1. Deitic gestures or pointing
   • Point toward some visually or symbolically present object.

2. Symbolic gestures or emblems
   • Are devoid of any morphological relation with visual or logical referent.
   • Have a direct translation into words.
   • Have a precise meaning known by the group, class, or culture.
   • Usually deliberately used to send a particular message.

---

displaying spatial or dynamic configurations, the speaker may use readily available bodily displays likely to parallel the speech (iconics) or to substitute for it (pantomimics). Deictics show that the speaker actively maintains a topographical relationship with the referent. Finally, symbolic gestures indicate that although involved in verbal coding, the speaker is likely to switch instantaneously to a quite different coding system when it becomes useful to his or her communicative purposes. In sum, then, the observation of speech-accompanying hand gestures suggests that the mental environment of a speaking person is still much more complex than what is suggested by considering speech alone. The next section of this chapter will review the major empirical findings regarding the relationship between speech and gestures.

Review of research data

The study of the relationships between speech and gestures, with a few exceptions, has practically no real empirical tradition and lacks any systematic exploration. The available studies are generally scattered across types of gestures as well as subdisciplines and journals in the behavioral sciences. Literature reviews are virtually nonexistent. We organized the available material into five groups, each of which covers a different dimension of the relationship between speech and gestures: (1) verbal development and verbal abilities, (2) speech content, (3) speech flow, (4) relative difficulty of verbal performance, and (5) effects of gestural activity on cognitive and verbal performance.

Gestures, verbal development, and verbal abilities

The prevailing ontogenetic view has been that gesture is an expressive system different from and independent of speech. According to Hewes (1973), early iconic gestural language was progressively transferred to vocalizations and then verbal expression. De Laguna (1927) and Werner and Kaplan (1963) also considered gestures to originate as a primitive mode of cognitive representation. Bates and her colleagues (Bates, Benigni, Bretherton, Camaioni, & Volterra, 1977; Bates, Shore, Bretherton, & McNew, 1983) suggested a continuity between preverbal and verbal signaling. Deictics, or pointing gestures, have been the object of special attention by authors sharing Bates's view. Thus, Murphy (1978) observed pointing gestures in infants aged 9, 14, 20, and 24 months who were looking at books. She found pointing to emerge at 9 months but not to be integrated with vocal activity until 14 months. Masur (1983) traced the emergence and development of three object-related gestures: pointing, extending objects, and open-hand reaching in infants aged 9 to 18 months. Pointing was the last among these gestures to emerge, at 12 to 14 months of age. In a careful ontogenetic observation of two children between the ages of 10 and 21 months, Zinober and Martlew (1985) confirmed this. They found that instrumental gestures such as offering objects and reaching were displayed before pointing and showing were.

Pointing was not firmly established until 14 months, and by this time, when used with vocalizations, such gestures fulfilled only the function of indicating. Once conventional words were coordinated with gestures, pointing began to serve a number of new functions: labeling, requesting, and asking for information. Pointing was also observed to be used with a variety of words, with verbal and nonverbal modes conveying either similar or complementary meanings.

The view that gesture is a primitive precursor to later verbalization might mean that it would gradually vanish from children's communication repertoire once their language begins to develop. However, many observations refute this prediction. When, comparing 2-year-old children with superior verbal competence with a group of children of the same age with normal verbal abilities, Dobrich and Scarborough (1984) found no significant difference in the frequency of use of deictic gestures. Emslie and Brooke (1982) observed pointing to be frequently used among 4-year-old children. In order to stimulate deictics among 2- to 9-year-old children, Pechman and Deutsch (1982) asked them to indicate among various objects the one that they would like to offer to some friend. The older children resorted to the verbal channel when the gestural one was likely to elicit ambiguity. But when confusion was unlikely, these children used gestures as often as the younger children did. Evans and Rubin (1979) observed gestural behavior among children of three different age groups who were instructed to explain the rules of games to an adult. No decrease with age was recorded, as both the younger (6 years old) and the older (10 years old) children in this study were the most likely to display speech-accompanying gestures.

Jancovic, Devoe, and Wiener (1975) addressed the question of an evolving amount of gesturing across stages of speech development. They recorded the occurrence of deictics, pantomimics, and more complex speech-accompanying hand movements (punctuations, ideographs, and iconographs; see Table 7.1) among children aged 8 to 18 years who answered questions about a cartoon they had just seen. The data evidenced no developmental change for deictics. But pantomimics showed a strong linear decrease with age, and a significant corresponding increase was recorded for more complex speech-accompanying gestures. Thus, rather than a disappearance of gesturing, the developmental data show a shift in the type of gestures displayed as age increases.

The emergence of more complex speech-accompanying hand gestures like ideographs or iconographs in children's repertoires of nonverbal behaviors has been documented by studies of the development of symbolic activities in expressive manifestations (e.g., Acredolo & Goodwyn, 1988). In studies by Overton and Jackson (1973) and Jackson (1974), gestural symbolic acts were elicited from 3- to 8-year-old children by instructing them to pretend using various objects in action sequences. The younger subjects had marked difficulties in performing such imaginary actions. Those in the intermediate age group were able to perform, but they had to use some of their body parts to represent objects in the sequence. Finally, the older children were perfectly able to represent objects through purely symbolic gestures. Not only is the capacity to produce symbolic gestures modified by developmental changes, but these changes also have been shown to affect temporal synchronization between gestures and speech. Van Meel (1984) observed 4- to 6-year-old children making gestures before the beginning of their verbal answer. Eight- to 10-year-olds tended to gesture at the beginning of their speech and to continue it throughout their utterance. Finally, the older children, aged 12 to 14 years, displayed their gestures in temporal correspondence with the part of the sentence comprising the symbolized element.

These developmental data may be added to observations of the relationships between mental or linguistic abilities and gestural behavior. Thus, in a sample of 8- to 16-year-old children with mental deficits, Duffy and Moore (1971) recorded moderate significant positive correlations between verbal performance and intelligence scores, on the one hand, and indices of proficiency and frequency of gestural usage, on the other hand. Similarly, in a study investigating performances of normal and mentally deficient children in various tasks of cognitive and verbal encoding, Van Meel and Van den Brink (quoted in Van Meel, 1984) demonstrated a positive relationship between the level of mental development and the use of gestural techniques. Finally, Rimé, Thomas, Laubin, and Richir (1983) observed the frequency of speech-accompanying movements in epileptic adolescents who were assessed for verbal expressive abilities. These adolescents, ranging from 11 to 20 years of age, were placed in two conversational situations, one with a peer subject of a comparable verbal level and one with the same peer and an adult. During both types of conversation, those subjects classified as high in verbal expressive abilities showed a much higher rate of speech-accompanying hand movements than did the subjects classified as low in expressive abilities, even though these two groups spoke for the same length of time.

Overall, then, the data suggest gestural behavior to precede verbal expression and to pave the way for the later emergence of communicative abilities. But this precursor does not seem to vanish once linguistic abilities show up. Rather, the evolution of symbolic thinking that parallels language development appears to elicit shifts in the gestural universe as well and to lead to the progressive emergence of more complex manifestations in gestural speech-accompanying activities.

Gestures and speech content

As we mentioned in the introduction of this chapter, Rimé and Gaussin (1982) observed many gestural behaviors and bodily movements among subjects engaged in verbal interactions of high communicative density (i.e., talking about one's recent life events), compared with those in an interaction of low density (i.e., repeating digits in a memory task). Bull and Brown (1977) had data suggesting that gestures occur more frequently in utterances in which the speaker introduces much information (e.g., declarative sentences) than in utterances with weaker informational value (e.g., questions).

Besides simple density of information, the type of information communicated seems also to be an important determinant of gestural behavior. Thus, "physiographic movements" (i.e., iconographic movements in our classification; see Table 7.1) were found by Riseborough (1982) to be abundantly elicited among children instructed to talk about pictures or to describe previously executed motor activities. However, when these children were asked to tell a story, almost no such gesture was observed. This was consistent with earlier observations by Hoffman (1968), showing that description tasks such as those involved in the classic Thematic Apperception Test produced more "representational hand movements" (i.e., again, iconographic movements in our proposed standardization) than storytelling tasks did. Hoffmann discovered that such gestures were most likely to occur when the idea seeking expression was in pictorial form in the mind. In a similar vein, Barroso, Freedman, Grand, and Van Meel (1978) and Van Meel (1982) showed that when children performed a verbal task involving mental images of actions or of objects, they displayed significantly more iconographic gestures than when the verbal task required less visual imagery. Observations of this kind led Riseborough (1982) to hypothesize that iconographic expression would be used when there was some discrepancy between units of thought and units of speech: "A discrepancy is assumed to exist when information of an essentially visual, spatial, or motoric nature has to be verbalized. Vice versa, the finding that stories produced very few gestures reflects closer correspondence between the units involved in thinking and speaking" (Riseborough, 1982, p. 502). This would explain why Shephard and Feng (1972) observed that subjects engaging in "mental paper folding tasks" used iconic gestures when requested to verbalize this task. A view similar to this one was also expressed by Freedman (1972) and by Rimé (1983).

Indeed, there is persuasive evidence that dense information in speech content leads to increased gesturing and that when speech involves verbalization of visual, spatial, or motoric information, iconographic gesturing would be most likely elicited.

Gesture and speech flow

Many data suggest that bodily movements and hand gestures tend to occur electively and in temporal coincidence with pauses and hesitations in the course of verbal utterances (Dittman, 1972; Dittman & Llewelyn, 1969; Marcos, 1977; Ragsdale & Silvia, 1982). De Long (1981) observed a similar relationship among 5-year-old children. Butterworth and Beattie (1978) obtained data showing that gestures illustrating speech content (i.e., iconic or iconographic, according to our standards) occurred more frequently with pausing in the course of fluid utterances, whereas rhythmic or punctuating gestures were associated with periods of phonation. In a related field, Hadar, Steiner, and Rose (1984a,b) observed head movements as also occurring with speech pauses and hesitation. This finding may be relevant to our topic, as in addition to the hands, the head is a body zone particularly actively associated with speech (Ragsdale & Silvia, 1982).

Although predominantly based on small samples of speech and case studies, other data on the temporal relationship between gesture and speech flow strongly suggest the temporal precedence of gestures with respect to related verbal events. Dittman and Llewellyn (1969) equipped subjects with accelerometers on their arms while holding a conversation. Hand movements were observed to be particularly concentrated around the first word of fluid verbal utterances, as well as around the first word following a hesitation. An analysis of a sample of speech led Kendon (1972) to conclude that when the form of the movement could be definitely matched to a lexical item, the movement in question had begun before the lexical item it was to mark. From similar analyses, Butterworth and Beattie (1978) concluded that the initiation of iconic gestures usually precedes and never follows the words with which they are associated, the mean delay being around 0.80 seconds, with a range of 0.10 to 2.5 seconds. Finally, Kendon (1980) had samples of conversations analyzed into tone units, each characterized by an accentuation mark in the utterer's tone of voice. He observed that each such tone tended to be accompanied by a gesture. In regard to temporal relationship between gestural and tonal events, Kendon surmised that the gesture always begins before and never after the accentuation point of the tone unit. Bull and Connelly (1985) had data confirming the temporal associations of nonverbal behavior with vocal accentuations by the utterer.

In summary, the data on the relationships between gesture and speech support the view that gestures usually precede speech. The recurrently observed association between gesture and pauses or hesitations also contributed to the view that speech-accompanying gestures pertained to launching the cognitive processes underlying speech, particularly in the case of cognitive complexity or cognitive difficulty. Studies specifically designed to test this hypothesis have been carried out.

Gestures and the relative difficulty of verbal performance

Cohen (1977) instructed subjects to describe a given geographical itinerary three times successively. The frequency of speech-accompanying hand gestures was shown to decrease linearly from the first to the third trial as the encoding process was facilitated by means of repetition. Moreover, a higher rate of gesture was associated with descriptions of more complex itineraries. This occurred despite the presence or absence of an addressee. Van Heugten and Van Meel (1980) observed that in children, more frequent and longer representational gestures accompanied the verbal encoding of more complex geometric figures. Verbal encoding is usually considered to be more difficult in a second language than in the mother tongue. Several studies have shown that when subjects speak in a second language, they use more gestures than they do with their usual language (Grand, Marcos, Freedman, & Barroso, 1977; Marcos, 1979a,b). Verbal encoding is also more difficult for people with neuropsychological handicaps, particularly aphasic subjects who display a higher frequency of speech-accompanying gestures than do nonimpaired control subjects (Feyereisen, 1983).

Although these data clearly suggest a positive relationship between the cognitive complexity of verbal performance and speech-accompanying hand movements, any simple conclusion in this regard is nevertheless precluded by other research findings. In line with what has been reviewed thus far, one might assume that more fluent subjects would gesticulate less, and less fluent ones would gesticulate more. Hoffman (1968) also posited this hypothesis, yet he actually found that less fluent subjects seldom gestured and that the relationship between gesture and fluency was complex, particularly for the most fluent subjects. Other confounding results were found by Baxter, Winters, and Hammer (1968), who compared subjects with high and low verbal competences instructed to talk about either a familiar or an unfamiliar topic. People with low verbal competence tended to display more gestures in the unfamiliar topic condition than in the familiar one, which is indeed consistent with the cognitive complexity hypothesis. But, subjects with high verbal competence displayed gestures at a maximal frequency level in the familiar topic condition, which contradicts this hypothesis.

The effect of gestural activity on cognitive or verbal performance

Some experimental data support the view that motor activity has some impact on coding or symbolic activity. Miller (1963) approached this question from the angle of semantic satiation, that is, the loss of meaning that occurs when a person repeats a word several times in rapid succession. Subjects had to repeat a word such as *push, pull, lower,* or *lift.* The delay for semantic satiation to set in was considerably lengthened when the repeated word was accompanied by the corresponding movement, whereas the delay was shortened when the movement opposed the meaning of the word. In a study of the tachistoscopic recognition of action words, Dowling (1962) found the level of recognition to be lower when the subjects had to carry on an activity corresponding to the meaning of the stimulus word. The opposite was observed when the activity was a discordant one. Rand and Wapner (1967) had their subjects assume different postures while learning a series of nonsense words. The subjects' performance was better when relearning the series of syllables if they did so in the learning posture. Saltz and Dixon (1982) investigated the effects of motoric enactment (pretend play) of sentences on the remembering of these sentences. Motoric enactment facilitated the remembering of sentences in both children and adults. But contrary to what would have been expected from Rand and Wapner's (1967) results, motoric enactment was not found to be an important cue for retrieval. This result – which clearly contradicts the hypothesis of speech-accompanying gesture as a cue to retrieval in the verbal encoding process – certainly deserves further experimental consideration.

Besides these studies in which semantic, perceptual, or memory aspects were taken as dependent variables, experimental studies have also considered the impact of variations in gestural activity on speech structure or content. For example, McNeill (1975) found that adults were unable to produce patterned speech when instructed to simultaneously verbalize and execute complex, unfamiliar movements. In another study, Rimé, Schiaratura, Hupet, and Ghysselinckx (1984) found no significant modifications in speech fluency among subjects physically restrained from performing bodily movements, as compared with subjects free to move. In this study, however, speech content was affected by immobilization, as the restrained subjects evidenced a lower level of imagery of speech than did the subjects free to move. Graham and Heywood (1975) had their subjects describe linear figures to a partner who then had to find the figure among a series of graphic reproductions. In one condition, the subjects were instructed to remain immobile while speaking. When compared with subjects free to move, immobility induced changes in the semantic content of utterances, increased time spent pausing while speaking, and caused a poorer performance by their partners (Graham & Argyle, 1975). Finally, Wolff and Gutstein (1972) had their subjects produce imaginary short stories while performing either circular or linear movements. A content analysis revealed that the type of gestures performed definitely affected the content of the produced stories.

Conclusion

The research findings can be summed up as follows. With movements like deictics – and perhaps also like pantomimics – gesture first emerges in development as a percursor of verbal expression, which then gradually coordinates with speech. Gesture is certainly not a substitute for verbal language. Indeed, early forms of gesturing continue to be displayed even when language is fully developed. Moreoover, the evolution of symbolic thinking parallels the emergence of new and more complex gestural forms like punctuations, ideographs, and iconographs, which suggests that speech-accompanying movements fulfill functions of their own in the expressive process. Data from studies of the relationships between gesture and speech content indicate that dense information leads to increased gesturing. Also, it seems that iconic gestures are elicited mainly when there is a discrepancy between units of thought and units of speech, as is the case when the verbalization of visual, spatial, or motoric information is involved. Various data support the view that gestures often precede in time the corresponding units in speech. They also seem to occur in association with pauses and hesitation and are displayed more frequently with more complex or more difficult verbal performances. Finally, some data show that gesticulation might have a causal impact on speech performance or speech content.

Theoretical views of gestures and speech

Several authors have constructed theories regarding speech-accompanying gestures in their relationships to the speech process (Freedman, 1972; Freedman & Hoffman, 1967; Kendon, 1984, 1986b; McNeill, 1985, 1987a; McNeill & Levy, 1982; Rimé, 1979, 1983, 1985). In this section, we shall review the various positions adopted by Freedman, by Kendon, and by McNeill.

Freedman: Gestures as instrumental to speech

Freedman's interest in gestures began with a study of movement behavior during clinical interviews (Freedman, 1972; Freedman & Hoffman, 1967). He regards movement and speech as two vehicles of a common symbolic process. Among bodily movements, those of the hands accompanying either the content or the rhythm of speech play a critical role in verbal encoding. Freedman believes that they define the structures underlying speech. With respect to this, two types of speech-accompanying gesture, ranging along a continuum, have been distinguished (Freedman, 1972). At one extreme, Freedman considers *speech-primacy* gestures (speech markers in the revised Efron system), which closely parallel the formal and rhythmic properties of speech, as the most integrated into the verbal content. At the other extreme of the continuum, *motor-primacy* gestures (iconics in the revised Efron system), which consist of movements that are representational in themselves, are only minimally integrated into the verbal content. The motor act itself becomes representational.

When speech-primacy movements (speech markers) predominate in the speaker's expression, speech is usually the primary vehicle of the message. The language forms tend to be strongly differentiated and characterized by a relatively complex syntactical structure. Hand gestures play only an ancillary role in such a context, being restricted to a self-monitoring and clarifying function similar to that ascribed by some authors to vocalization. Much more central in this respect are motor-primacy gestures (iconics), which represent a visible expression of the speaker's thought. Freedman's view is that motor-primacy responses indicate a failure to verbalize and to transform images into word representations. Each such movement manifests a surplus meaning, that is, something not fully verbalized, that seeks its immediate expression. Iconic gesturing, to use an analogy, serves the same function as taking a detour when in a traffic jam (Freedman, 1972). In a later work, however (e.g., Barroso, Freedman, Grand, & Van Meel, 1978), Freedman and his colleagues also specified an instrumental role played by these gestures with respect to the speech process. They stated that these gestures were intimately involved in activating connections between symbols (e.g., words) and their referents. Thus iconic hand movements could aid in the image–symbol linkage by reactivating a decaying image or enhancing an as-yet unclear visualization. Such gestures, then, play a crucial role in maintaining fluency, especially verbal descriptions.

Freedman's views of gesture and speech are summarized in Figure 7.1. Its major statements are as follows: First, gesture originates in the mental image that the speaker is attempting to translate into words. When the translation process proceeds without difficulty, no representational or iconic (motor-primacy) gesture is expected. Second, an inverse relationship is predicted between the level of speech sophistication and the patterning of gesture. The less articulated the speech is, the more the gesture will be patterned, and vice versa. Third, the gesture always fulfills some instrumental role with respect to the speech process, either through the self-monitoring function of speech-primacy gestures or through the reactivation of images and their link to words in the case of motor-primacy gestures.

Kendon: Gestures as substitutes for speech

Kendon's basic interests are anthropological and center on the origins of language (e.g., Kendon, 1983, 1984, 1986a,b; but see also Kendon, 1972, 1980). He therefore has made careful case studies of how expressive structures are modeled by communication circumstances.

Kendon insists that as conveyors of meaning, spoken utterances are

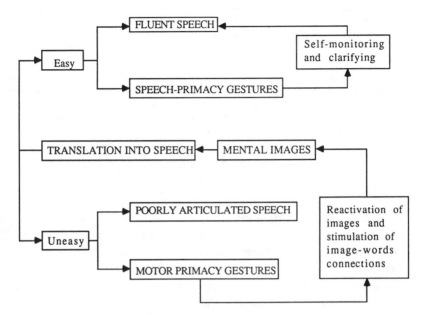

Figure 7.1. A summary of Freedman's view of the relationship between speech and gesture (based on Barosso et al., 1978; Freedman, 1972; Freedman & Hoffman, 1967).

subject to limitations that are not encountered by gestures. Indeed, spoken utterances must be primarily structured according to the rules of the language system (e.g., form of lexical elements, rules of syntax, sequential order of elements) and only indirectly to any aspect of the structure of what is being referred to. In contrast, with gestures, motions can be used that have a direct relationship to the action sequence: Pictorial diagrams may be produced; a spatial relationship may be directly portrayed; and parts of the body – or even the whole body – may be moved around as if they were actual objects. Therefore, there are more degrees of freedom for expression in gestures than in spoken utterances. In fact, from picturing to lexicalization, every mode of representation can be used in the gestural medium, whereas only the lexical mode is used in speech (Kendon, 1986b). Thus, we find the following:

• In the gesture phrase, which expresses a complex idea in a single unit of action and cannot be analyzed into constituents, the picturing possibilities of gesturing are at their maximum. Gesture phrases are fully part of the utterance plan, but they encode aspects of the meaning quite differently than do words. Furthermore, they encode aspects of the meaning that are not even alluded to in the words.
In speech-alternate gestures, which Kendon describes as occurring in alternation with speech, the spoken phrase is typically incomplete. Unless we take

into account the gesture phrase, we can make no sense of what is said. Although the speech-alternate gestures do the work of lexical items in a sentence, they are more complex. Gestures convey complex images that can be translated into words, but only by using extended phrases. They rarely replace single words.

- In autonomous gestures (i.e., symbolic or emblematic in the revised Efron system), which may be used as complex utterances of their own, gestures do not refer anymore to complex images. Although they are not fully lexicalized, they are, in some respect, more like words than anything considered so far.

- In gesture systems like the sign language of deaf–mute persons, there is a full lexicalization of gestures. Here, from a repertoire of gestural forms, organized sequences are chosen to convey meaning in much the same way as do words in spoken language.

This led Kendon to consider that overall, in speech-accompanying gestures we do not observe a representation of the same material that is also, perhaps later, represented in words. Rather, we observe components of the utterance content that are not represented in words but that the utterer nevertheless is striving to represent. In most cases, indeed, gestures allow for representing aspects of the experience that can be represented in words at best only indirectly and, in some respects, not at all. For instance, it is impossible to display the occurrence of an action except through some form of action, or to represent spatial arrangements without moving the hands and the body.

Speech-accompanying hand movements are thus characterized by Kendon as an integral part of an individual's communicative effort. This applies to all gesticulation, even to that comprising only rhythmic spatial patterning without informational content or any apparent communicative function. Such hand movements actually constitute part of a person's actions used to represent meaning to another. In this sense, gestures are employed not to meet the transmission conditions of the interactional event but, rather, to meet the requirements of representational activity. Thus, when gesticulation takes a beatlike form, it functions as a visual analogue of the phonological "chunking" carried out by stress intonation, and pause. With iconic gestures, the speaker appears to be visually representing aspects of content that are not referred to in the verbal component of the utterance. When gesticulation is emblematic or symbolic, the speaker uses gestures as an alternate to speech, letting them do the work of the utterance. Overall, then, utterers use gesture as one of the resources available to them for getting their meaning across. Speech-accompanying gestures do not constitute an externalization of the encoding of "thought" into spoken language.

Rather, they are a consequence of the translation of thought into utterance, of which speech is another consequence.

As we mentioned, part of Kendon's work focused on the various conditions under which individuals use the gestural expressive mode (e.g., Kendon, 1984):

1. To supplement speech when certain environmental factors, such as distance or ambient noise, make it difficult for speech to be received.
2. As a substitute for speech when the speech channel is already occupied by another speaker.
3. As a device for completing a sentence that, if spoken, might prove embarrassing to the speaker.
4. To clarify some potentially ambiguous word.
5. As a means of telescoping what one wants to say, when the available turn space is smaller than one would like.
6. As an additional component of the utterance, when the spoken account appears unlikely to approach the suitable representation of what the speaker intends.

From such examples, Kendon concluded that the speaker divides the task of conveying meaning between the two expressive modalities in such a way as to achieve either economy of expression or a particular effect on the recipient.

One can sum up Kendon's position on the relationship between speech and gesture as follows (Figure 7.2): The speaker is described as fundamentally impelled by the requirements of the representational activity in which he or she engages. Inherent limitations of the verbal channel as a conveyor of meaning, as well as constraints exerted on this channel by situational contingencies, contribute to the speaker's using the more flexible gestural channel as an alternative tool for expressing representations. Therefore, speech-accompanying gestures usually represent components of the utterance content that are not represented in enunciated words. In contrast with Freedman (1972), who assigned to gestures important functions in cognitive processes such as monitoring speech and transforming meaning into words, Kendon concentrated on the expressive aspects of gestures. Nevertheless, the two conceptions are largely compatible, as both see the primary role of speech-accompanying gestures as representing meanings not conveyed by words.

McNeill: The interaction of imagistic and syntactic thinking

Primarily psycholinguistic, McNeill's (1985, 1987a; McNeill & Levy, 1982) interest in gesture evolves from his approach to the temporal devel-

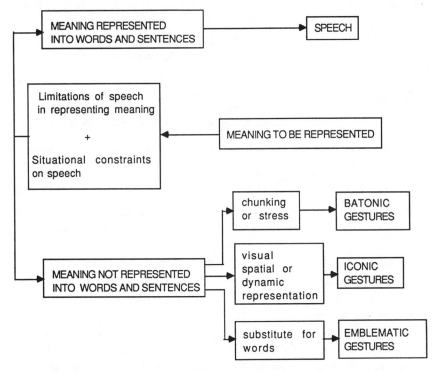

Figure 7.2. A summary of Kendon's view of the relationship between speech and gesture. Note that batonic and emblematic gestures are equivalent to speech markers and symbolic gestures, respectively, in the Revised Efron System (based on Kendon, 1983, 1984, 1986a,b).

opment of linguistic acts, with an emphasis on the processes taking place in "deep time," that is, the early stages of sentence elaboration. With this framework, McNeill sees speech-accompanying gestures as integral parts of sentences belonging to the early stages of language production.

McNeill's basic statement is that in speaking, a transformation of thinking from one type to another occurs, so that thinking and speaking have to be considered as lying on a continuum. "At one end of the continuum, thinking is more global and imagistic, and at the other end, more segmented and syntactic" (1987a, p. 1). From wordless thought, through inner speech, and then to outer speech, there is a certain continuity. As we pass along this continuum, our visual–imagistic cognition declines and our verbal elaboration increases. With thinking that is highly intense and concentrated, inner linguistic symbols may be completely replaced by images. Under these circumstances, the person may actually feel incapable of speaking, a phenomenon about which physicists and others engaged in sustained mathematical reasoning often complain. With verbal rehearsal just before emitting speech, on the other hand, images may disappear, to be replaced by fully developed sentences. Ordinary thinking occupies an intermediate place along this continuum and is characterized by the interplay of two forms of symbolization, that is, the phonological and the analogical. In this case, the symbols of inner speech appear in an environment of images.

The occurrence of gestures as a person speaks reveals that he or she is engaging in two types of thinking simultaneously: imagistic (i.e., thinking that is global and synthetic) and syntactic (i.e., thinking that is linear and segmented). Indeed, the linguistic act creates a synthesis, or mutual penetration, of both types of elements. Images are shaped by the system of linguistic values, and sentences are shaped by the images they unpack. A critical concept in McNeill's view is that the sentence is, at all stages, both imagistic and syntactic. There is no break between input and output in this situation, but only different developmental stages of a single process. Influencing one another, gesture and speech refer interactively to a single memory system in which complex configurational structures are stored.

Not only do gestures cooccur with their sentences and exhibit imagistic thinking, but gestures and sentences also are, to a degree, interchangeable. Complexity shifts between them. They exist in the same form at an early stage in deep time and can take each other's place in the developing sentence after this stage. The speaker's meaning can appear in either channel, depending on the tactical problem of expressing it in spoken rather than gestural form. Indeed, McNeill reported having observed subjects describing scenes with words containing information first presented only in gestural form and, conversely, subjects producing gestures containing information first presented only in spoken form. The balance, then, between imagistic and syntactic thinking changes progressively until thought achieves a form that can be spoken. The linguistic symbol and image emerge together. The image particularizes the symbol, and the symbol codifies the image (McNeill, 1987a).

To summarize, McNeill's view of the relationship between speech and gesture evolved from his conception of how knowledge is stored mentally. He views meanings as being stored in complex configurational structures, independent of language formats. In the speech process, meanings are transformed directly into either linguistic or gestural form, the choice between the two depending on the utterer's tactical decisions. A detailed discussion of McNeill's positions can be found in Feyereisen (1987) and in Butterworth and Hadar (1989), as well as in responses by the author (McNeill, 1987b, 1989).

Conclusions

All three theoretical positions that we have examined rest on the assumption that gestures originate somewhere in the process through which unarticulated mnemonic elements – imagistic representations for Freedman, global representations for Kendon, and complex configurational structures for McNeill – are translated into the articulated speech formats. The three views vary with respect to the reasons for the emergence of gestures.

According to Freedman, when representational material is easily transformed into sentences and words, only rhythmic, speech-marking gestures occur. Patterned, representational iconic gestures are displayed only when the translation process partially fails to accomplish its aim. Such gestures help restore this process, by further activating image–word connections. In Kendon's view, the verbal expression of global representation may be limited by the available verbal resources or by constraints exerted on the verbal channel by situational or social contingencies. This results in the use of the alternative channel, that is, the gestural one, which allows not only the expression of structural aspects of representations (stress, intonation, pauses, logical relationships, logical steps, etc.) but also the expression of the content aspects of these representations (shape of the referent, action, spatial arrangement, etc.). For both Freedman and Kendon, then, gestures manifest a surplus of meaning beyond what is temporarily permitted in the verbal expressive channel. Although both authors recognized the details of the representational material to be a major cause of such calls to gesticulation, Kendon also emphasized the effect of social and communication circumstances. Whereas Freedman attributed to gestures an instrumental role in restoring the prevalence of speech, Kendon sees them as substitutive expressive resources in the communication process. Finally, in McNeill's view, imagistic and syntactic thinking complement each other in elaborating unarticulated memory elements into speech. The occurrence of gestures depends on the tactic of expression temporarily preferred by the speaking person, either fully spoken or more imagistic. However, variables that could influence the speaker's choice in this respect are not specified by the theory, so that finally it fails to predict conditions under which gestures would be observed.

A cognitive-motor view of expression

The cognitive-motor view of expression (Rimé, 1979, 1983, 1985) was instigated by the puzzling occurrence of depictive gestures – pantomimes, iconics, ideographs – in speaking persons. To take an extreme case of this type of gesturing, consider the 7-year-old boy who has just come back from a fun fair and gives his parents a detailed account of his experiences. A child in this situation hardly limits himself to verbal description. Objects, scenes, and events are depicted bodily. The boy is again speeding up and down in the wagon of the spiraling train. He is the witch who has frightened him in the magic tunnel. He is the plastic duck against which he has been throwing balls. Bodily participation is typical of children's verbal expression, but this type of expression fades as the child's communication abilities improve. Yet, the frequent occurrence of depictive gestures accompanying adults' speech demonstrates that the phenomenon is still alive later in life. Moreover, it can dramatically reappear when the adult refers in speech to some animated or exciting event, for instance. According to the cognitive-motor view, such manifestations cannot be explained without considering the contribution of motor processes to shaping representations of reality.

Motor processes in perception

Motor processes contribute to perception in at least four different ways. First, the sense organs are far from operating independently of the rest of the organism: These organs' activities strongly depend on the motor tracking of stimuli by oculomotor movements, by movements of the head, and, in most instances, by movements of various other parts of the body. Feedback information from these motor processes should thus be assumed to be part of the sensory data. Second, the person involved in perception and reality processing is usually far from being passive. Responses generally are being adapted from moment to moment, and again, efferent and afferent data are necessarily associated in stored information. Thus, anticipatory head, hand, and leg movements by the baseball player ready to catch the ball, are blended with eye-tracking movements and with the picture of the ball crossing the sky. Third, as neutral stimuli are rare, most stimulations elicit in the perceiver the affective or emotional reactions manifested in the form of postural and facial changes. This constitutes another element to be added to the efferent data collected in perception. Finally, there is still a fourth way in which motor aspects contribute to mental representation. Virtually forgotten by modern psychology, this dimension was recognized by Aristotle, who considered that the "human being is the most mimetic of all animals, and it is by mimicking that he or she acquires all his or her knowledge" (quoted in Jousse, 1955/1974, p. 55). We do not limit ourselves in selecting verbal attitudes to qualify objects or events we meet. We also, tacitly, make abundant use of motor coding by means of motor attributes. Thus, the spiraling movement is latent in our representation of a spiraling staircase. A mouse may be motorically coded by its two mobile ears, its long pointing nose, its gnawing jaws, or the fast movement of its body when escaping. As with verbal attributes, several motor codes are usually selected for the same object, and they are hierarchically organized according to their perceived saliency. Often, when we fail to remember the name of an object, its attributes still are available in our conscious memory, and we are able to display gesturally our motor codes for it.

This perspective on the role of motor processes in perception cannot be reconciled with the widespread view that the psychological universe is split into a stimulus and a response side. Transactions between individual and external reality are such that in terms of collected information, "responses" generally cannot be dissociated from "stimuli." Represented stimuli would probably have no adaptive meaning if they were not made up of response elements that contributed to their being built up in the subject's mind.

Elements of representations

We come then to a consideration of our representations of reality as containing three types of element: (1) concepts and verbal attributes likely to be articulated into language propositions, (2) images, and (3) incipient somatotonic changes reminiscent of the various motor responses involved in the perception of the referent. This view is close to Lang's (1979) theory of emotional imagery and traces back to Jacobson's (1930a,b, 1931) studies, which revealed that low-level physiological changes usually accompany mental processes. Jacobson observed that when asked to think of certain events or to imagine certain actions, the subjects mental activity was invariably accompanied by electrical activity in the muscular groups associated with the imagined actions. Observations of this kind have now been replicated in the study of mental imagery of emotion (e.g., Ekman, Levenson, & Friesen, 1983; Sirota & Schwartz, 1982). Through their interactions, somatotonic elements of a representation form with imagery the active reminiscence of the apprehension process. Concepts and verbal forms associated with these elements are both a part and a consequence of their cognitive processing. Each of the three elements has the property of eliciting, or cueing, the two others. Thus, concepts, images, and motor changes are equally appropriate inputs to the network of elements that constitutes the representation.

Each element of a network is itself associated with elements of other networks or representations, because of either structural analogy or former evocation in spatiotemporal contiguity. Therefore, any new external or mental event is likely to elicit through its own representational components the activation of motoric, imagistic, or conceptual elements associated with other representational networks. Although motoric elements usually go unnoticed by the subject, the imagistic ones are perceived, and the conceptual elements accompanying them are articulated and rationalized through the sense-giving activity of silent language. This gives rise to the continuous flow of inner speech and imagery characteristic of mental life. Through this continuous activity, representations are processed. Images emerge under new variations; they simplify and present increasingly schematized forms. Simultaneously, they are transformed by the sense-giving activity of silent language. Accompanying labels and concepts become richer and more apt. Successive repetitions of this cognitive work may lead the network to the point that its linguistic formalization is completed. In this case, it is available to the subject in a well-integrated conceptual form, which is typically the stage at which a writer begins writing sentences on paper.

When processed as described here, the representational elements issued from the subject's perception of the world are progressively articulated into an *expressive structure*. In this new structure, the raw material of experience is organized in accordance with the rules of rationality and language and is ready for verbal expression. This structure evolves from the progressive differentiation or articulation (Werner & Kaplan, 1963) of the representation's *raw structure*, that is, the original motoric, imagistic, and raw conceptual material issuing from the experience of the world. The expressive structure may now be handled – in thinking and in communication – with relative independence with respect to the raw structure. Nevertheless, the raw structure itself is never reduced or erased but retains its position as the core of the representation.

Expressing representations

Verbal expression, or the attempt to share a representation with other persons, is a challenging task. A complex, multidimensional matrix of information has to be expressed as a one-dimensional string of verbal communication and has to follow rules of lexicon, syntax, and logic. The difficulties in these cognitive operations can be easily overcome if the representational network to be evoked in speech already possesses, because of former processing, a highly articulated expressive structure. In this case, the material likely is already organized into sequential forms; appropriate concepts have become part of the network; and schemata of sentences may already be available. In other words, the representation is stamped by the subject's linguistic–cognitive processes. One can expect, then, that the speech will be fluent, relatively devoid of hesitation, and characterized by abstract, objective expression and by the use of conventional, highly codified lexical forms and strongly articulated syntax. Because the raw structure of the representional network need not be very active to permit such communication, we can expect the speaker's muscular activity to be weak. Thus, he or she is likely to display predominantly the small, rhythmical head and hand gestures that generally accompany the melody of fluent verbal expression.

If the speaker's representation to be unfolded in speech has only a poorly articulated expressive structure or, for some reason, if this speaker has to refer directly to the raw structure, this raw structure will have to be activated during the communication process. This will allow the motoric elements of the representational network to prime the conceptual and linguistic forms likely to approximate the meanings they carry. In this case, then, verbal expression is properly the result of a dynamic interplay between the subject's visceromotor matrix of information and his or her general matrix of conceptual competences. This explains, in our view, the occurrence of the speaker's hand gestures that depict in some rough manner the referent of the speech. Such gestures are generally made completely out of the speaker's awareness, but by priming appropriately related conceptual forms, they help pave the way to verbal expression. In such instances, verbal expression is expected to be only partially fluent, with pauses, hesitations, and word searches. Lexical forms are more likely to have a relatively personal, idiomatic character. Syntax tends to be relatively poor, with weakly articulated linguistic connections. Finally, the vocal signal itself is likely to present colorful variations isomorphic to the referred representational events.

Speech styles

These considerations lead to a contrast of two types of speech style that can be conceived of as lying at two opposite ends of a continuum. One of them, poorly articulated and weakly codified, concrete, and subjective, develops when the speaker is relying mainly on the raw structure of its representation, and it thus is characteristically related to iconic hand gestures. We could call this the *direct* verbal–gestural style. The second one, highly articulated, distant from personal experience, conventional, abstract, and objective, occurs when the speech evolves from surface structures of representations, and it thus is expected to be paralleled by speech-marking hand gestures. This second style could be called the *mediated* or *elaborate* one. This contrast between two speech styles is hardly a new one. Authors like Wallon (1970), Jousse (1955/1974), Moscovici (1967), and Werner and Kaplan (1963) have already proposed distinctions close to this one (for a review, see Rimé, 1983).

The question now arises of the conditions influencing the type of verbal–gestural style adopted by a speaker in a given circumstance. Rimé (1983) has proposed the rule according to which a speaker's style is a function of his or her degree of differentiation from each of the elements in the communication process, that is, the referent, the representation, the addressee, and the medium of communication. For each of these four items, this rule may be specified as follows:

Referent. One expects a speaker to present a "direct" style when he or she is weakly differentiated from the referent of his or her speech. This happens when this referent (1) is new, unusual, or recently experienced; (2) is personally involving; (3) has marked perceptive–dynamic dimensions; or (4) comprises complex, wholistic structures. In all such instances, the raw structure of the speaker's representional activity tends to predominate, and iconic gestures accompanied by concrete and subjective, weakly articulated verbal expressions are expected. The reverse prediction also applies to opposite conditions.

Representations. A "direct" verbal–gestural style is expected when the speaker's personal characteristic (e.g., age, developmental level, sociocultural characteristics, mastery of language, cognitive style) makes him or her weakly differentiated from his or her representations, thus limiting his or her competence to develop articulated structures of expression.

Addressee. A "direct" style is predicted when the speaker feels weakly differentiated from his or her addressee. Vygotsky (1962) mentioned the impact of interpersonal intimacy on the communication style of adults, stating that the weak polarization of relations creates an expressive style very close to the forms of expression used when addressing oneself. As we go from the intimate relationship toward relationships that are more differentiated, we should observe the verbal–gestural style sliding toward forms that are more articulated, more conventional, and even close to protocol. This is the case to a certain degree when the speaker addresses someone whom he or she perceives as being dominant or hierarchically superior. On this continuum, the expressive style becomes progressively more codified, with its extreme being a style close to written language. As suggested by Moscovici and Plon (1966), in written language, the speaker–addressee differentiation is maximal, the addressee being anonymous as well as psychologically, spatially, and temporally distant.

Medium. The medium, or means of communication that the speaker uses encompasses both physical supports (e.g., telephone, interphone, loud speakers, video) and ecological conditions (e.g., spatial position, distance from partner). These aspects of the communication setting may be either familiar or new to the speaker. The more familiar the medium is, the less differentiated the speaker's relation to it will be, which leads us to predict the usage of a direct verbal style with iconic gestures. Conversely, when the speaker expresses himself or herself under unfamiliar conditions or settings, he or she is expected to use a strongly articulated, formal, expressive style.

Conclusions

The cognitive-motor view of gestural behavior stresses speech-accompanying gestures as emerging from the speaker's attempts to communicate what could be called an embodied matrix of data. This matrix, or system of information, is viewed as having evolved from patterns of sensory and motor components of the subject's apprehension of external objects and events. In his or her communication efforts, the speaker is trying to unpack the system into the sequential terms of vocal expression. The tools for this task are the socially shared elements of logic, syntax, and lexicon. By making a communicative effort, the speaker is most often led to reactivate the embodied elements or the raw structure of the representational matrix. The reactivated material is what he or she tries to signify in the social setting, and this reactivation materializes in gesturing. In some cases, the earlier cognitive processing leads the speaker to develop inner logical, syntactical, and lexical coverages of the matrix of data. Then, verbal expression is likely to induce only a low reactivation of this processing, and in this case, gestural behavior is only minimal. What the subject expresses verbally in this case is restricted to a schematic, simplified structure of data. The cost in density of information is compensated by the greater accuracy and communicability.

Social perception and the social impact of hand gestures

So far in this chapter, we have considered speech-accompanying hand gestures exclusively from the encoder side, that is, in their relationships with representational and expressive processes. Now, we shall switch to the decoder side and explore the role of these hand gestures with respect to the communication itself. Laypersons usually believe that a speaker's hand gestures carry meanings that complement and supplement his or her words and sentences, that hand gestures influence the addressee's decoding activity. But this view is contradicted by the following three facts: First, the addressee usually does not notice the speaker's hand gestures. Contrary to external observers, people who have been personally involved in a verbal interaction are, after the fact, usually unable to remember anything about the speaker's hand gestures. Do they process this information in an out-of-awareness mode? If this were the case, a second fact would refute the view of gestures as carriers of critical information in the communication process. Experimental data have shown that those communication situations in which the interactants cannot see each other are no different from face-to-face situations, from neither an interpersonal point of view nor that of message reception and understanding (Rimé, 1982; Williams, 1977). A third fact is that subjects are unable to guess the speech content to which gestures relate, which supports the view that hand gestures do not provide independent access to a meaning expressed in words (Feyereisen, Van de Wiele, & Dubois, 1988).

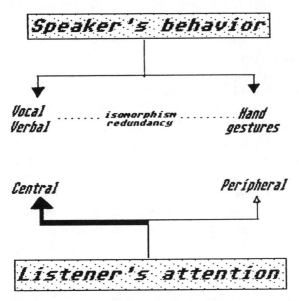

Figure 7.3. The figure–ground model of the listener's attention to the speaker's verbal and nonverbal behaviors.

A figure–ground model

The latter data open the way to understanding some of the reasons that the speaker's gestures usually have no impact on the decoding person. Consistent with the view that gestures are manifestations of the motor representations underlying speech, there is usually much redundancy in the verbal and gestural channels. An immediate consequence of this redundancy is that listeners often neglect one of these two sources of information. Naturally, the listeners' attention is much more likely to be directed to the complex, more exhaustive, and codified verbal message than to the simpler, allusive, and idiosyncratic hand gesture. This is the basis on which we developed a figure–ground model of the relationships between verbal and nonverbal materials with respect to decoding activities (Rimé, 1983).

According to this figure–ground model (Figure 7.3), a speaker's nonverbal behavior is usually only at the periphery of the listener's attention, whereas the center is focused on the heavy task of decoding the verbal message and encoding potential verbal answers. Nevertheless, the nonverbal data – elements of the ground – are always present as potential attention captors. Even when they do not retain central atten-

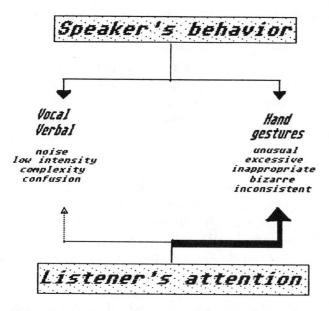

Figure 7.4. Major conditions for a figure–ground reversal in the listener's attention to the speaker's verbal and nonverbal behavior.

tion, they probably color the central verbal figure. But as important re- dundancies link verbal and nonverbal material, this coloring is probably negligible. The figure–ground model also implies that the relation may slip and reverse temporarily, so that nonverbal data take the role of the figure, thereby occupying the center of the perceiver's attention. Two types of situation are likely to induce such an effect: a rise in intensity in the nonverbal channel and a fall in intensity in the verbal channel (Figure 7.4).

The effects of an increase in the intensity of nonverbal materials

When unfamiliar, excessive, bizarre, or discordant with regard to the situation or context, nonverbal material may be said to rise in intensity in the observer's or partner's eyes, as in such circumstances it becomes noticeable. We assume that under such circumstances, nonverbal mate- rial becomes the figure, with a resulting heightened potential impact on the observer's or partner's reaction. Concomitantly, verbal data, slip- ping to the ground, lose importance. Data supporting this view can be found in a study in which the degree of concordance or discordance between the verbal message and the visible expression of a communicator were systematically varied (De Paulo, Rosenthal, Eisenstat, Rogers, & Finkelstein, 1978). When in the discordant condition, the receivers of these messages were found to switch their allocation of attention from the audible message to the visible expression of the communicator, as predicted by the figure–ground model. In regard to the impact of unfamiliar or excessive nonverbal behavior, an illustration of the effects described by the figure–ground model may be found in data from a study in which psychopathic and nonpsychopathic subjects were compared for nonverbal behaviors in interview situations. Rimé, Bouvy, Leborgne, and Rouillon (1978) observed marked differences between these two groups of subjects. As a group, psychopaths had a higher rate of gestures; they directed their gaze much longer at the interviewer; sat markedly closer to him; and smiled less frequently. Though unaware of the subject's psychopathic or control status in the study and even though he was instructed to maintain the same behavior throughout the interviews, the interviewer spoke for a shorter time when interacting with psychopaths, compared with the control subjects. Thus, the excessive nonverbal behavior of these psychopathic individuals appeared to have a marked correlative counterpart in their interviewer's reactions, as predicted by the figure–ground model.

The effects of a decrease in the intensity of nonverbal materials

The second prediction of the figure–ground model is that a decrease in the intensity of the sender's verbal channel can also induce the figure–ground reversal, thus bringing the sender's nonverbal behavior closer to the center of the receiver's attention. This would be the case when the intensity of the physical signal decreases, when a noise occurs in the communication, or when the intelligibility of speech content itself degrades. In regard to the effects of noise, supporting evidence may be found in data by Rogers (1979). The subjects received messages from a speaker according to three modalities: complete audiovisual signals (i.e., face, body, and voice), altered audiovisual signals (by eliminating face and lips), and audio signals alone. In all these modalities, the audio signal was altered according to one of four levels of noise intensity. The independent variable was the degree of the subject's comprehension. The results showed that for a weak noise level, the three modalities of sending produced levels of comprehension that varied very little from one another. But as the noise level increased, these three modalities produced increasingly different levels of comprehension, favoring complete audiovisual signals and not audio-only signals. It is clear that as the audio signal decreases in intelligibility, the need to use visible information, weakly present in normal conditions, becomes more important. Further evidence supporting this prediction of the figure–ground model can be found in a study in which the intelligibility of speech content was varied according to three conditions (Rimé, Boulanger, & d'Ydewalle, 1988). Flemish-speaking subjects were exposed to a videotape display of a female professional interpreter who was telling the same story either in the subjects' own language, or in a language they could understand more or less well (French), or in a language that none of them could understand (Russian). The interpreter's nonverbal behaviors (gaze, iconic gestures, and speech markers) were completely standardized across conditions. While watching this videorecording, the subjects' ocular activity was continuously monitored by means of an eye movement registration apparatus (using the corneal reflection-pupil center method and tracking eye movements with a resolution of 20 msec). The data demonstrated a very low level of attention ($\overline{X}$ = 6.66% of the time) to the speaker's hand gestures when she was speaking the subject's own language. This confirmed the view that the speaker's gestures generally have a weak saliency to the receiver's eyes. However, as predicted by the figure–ground model, this attention for gestures nearly doubled ($\overline{X}$ = 11.20%) when the speech was only partially understandable and tripled ($\overline{X}$ = 19.65%) for the Russian version. Nevertheless, despite this considerable rise in attention to gestures, no subject in the last condition was able to report anything coherent about the content of the speech. Here again, gestures seem not to have contributed to the understanding of the message.

General conclusions

To conclude this chapter, we shall consider the practical question of whether the speaker should or should not use gestures if he or she wants to achieve optimal communication.

Controlling one's gestures would probably require lengthy training, as this activity is automatic to a large extent. Nevertheless, the data collected on the decoder's point of view offer some interesting hints. In an unpublished study, Rimé, Boulanger, and Thomas showed subjects a videotape of speaking persons whose rate of speech-accompanying gestures was either low (10% of speaking time or less), moderate (11 to 20%), or high (more than 20%). Half of the subjects viewed the material while a mask covered the lower part of the screen so that only the face and not the hand gestures of the speaking person could be seen. The remaining subjects saw the full screen. All of the participants were then invited to rate the speaking person on two types of scale, one assessing qualities of the speech (clarity, fluidity, and accuracy) and the other, the qualities of the speaking person (warmth, presence, and relaxation). The data showed the speech quality ratings to be affected by both quantity and visibility of hand gestures. Indeed, the speech was perceived as less clear and less fluid when the speaking person used many gestures. The same happened when the gestures were visible, compared, with the masked screen condition. This suggests that the presence of gestures in the decoding person's perceptual field has some detrimental effect on his or her subjective appreciation of the verbal material to which this person is exposed. The figure–ground model would attribute it to an intrusion of nonverbal materials on focal attention, thus competing with the decoding of verbal information. However, the data on the qualities of the speaking person showed that displaying a relatively high rate of gestures is far from having only negative consequences on social perception. Indeed, higher gesturers were rated as much warmer and much more relaxed than were speakers making fewer gestures. Interestingly, this effect occurred independently of whether the gestures were visible or masked on the video screen. This led us to conclude that it had to be attributed not to gestures as such but, rather, to the global expressive style correlated with the display of a high rate of gesture. Therefore, according to our current knowledge, the person who intends to speak is faced with two contradictory alternatives: If he or she wants to be clearly understood, he or she should display as few gestures as possible. But if this person wants to be positively perceived and appreciated for interpersonal qualities, he or she should adopt a speech style using an abundance of gestures.

References

Acredelo, L., & Goodwyn, S. (1988). Symbolic gesturing in normal infants. *Child Development, 59,* 450–466.

Barroso, F., Freedman, N., Grand, S., & Van Meel, J. (1978). Evocation of two types of hand movements in information processing. *Journal of Experimental Psychology: Human Perception and Performance, 4*(2), 321–329.

Bates, E., Benigni, L., Bretherton, I., Camaioni, L., & Volterra, V. (1977). From gesture to the first word: On cognitive and social prerequisites. In M. Lewis & L. A. Rosenblum (Eds.), *Interaction, conversation and the development of language* (pp. 247–307). New York: Wiley.

Bates, E., Shore, C., Bretherton, I., & McNew, S. (1983). Names, gestures and objects: Symbolization in infancy and aphasia. In K. E. Nelson (Ed.), *Children's language* (Vol. 4, pp. 59–123). Hillsdale, NJ: Erlbaum.

Baxter, J. C., Winters, E. P., & Hammer, R. E. (1968). Gestural behavior during a brief interview as a function of cognitive variable. *Journal of Personality and Social Psychology, 8*(3), 303–307.

Bull, P. E., & Brown, R. (1977). The role of postural change in dyadic conversations. *British Journal of Social and Clinical Psychology, 16,* 23–33.

Bull, P. E., & Connelly, G. (1985). Body movement and emphasis in speech. *Journal of Nonverbal Behavior, 9*(3), 169–187.

Butterworth, B., & Beattie, G. (1978). Gesture and silence as indicators of planning in speech. In R. N. Campbell & P. T. Smith (Eds.), *Recent advances in the psychology of language* (pp. 347–360). New York: Plenum.

Butterworth, B., & Hadar, U. (1989). Gestures, speech, and computational stages: A reply to McNeill. *Psychological Review, 96*(1), 168–174.

Cohen, A. (1977). The communicative functions of hand illustrators. *Journal of Communication, 27,* 54–63.

Cosnier, J. (1982). Communications et langages gestuels. In J. Cosnier, J. Coulon, J. Berrendonner, & C. Orecchioni (Eds.), *Les Voies du langage: Communications verbales, gestuelles et animales* (pp. 255–303). Paris: Dunod.

De Laguna, G. A. (1927). *Speech, its function and development.* New Haven, CT: Yale University Press.

De Long (1981). Kinesic signals at utterance boundaries in preschool children. In A. Kendon (Ed.), *Nonverbal communication, interaction and gesture* (pp. 251–281). The Hague: Mouton.

DePaulo, B. M., Rosenthal, R., Eisenstat, R. A., Rogers, A. L., & Finkelstein, S. (1978). Decoding discrepant nonverbal cues. *Journal of Personality and Social Psychology, 36,* 313–323.

Dittman, A. T. (1972). The body movement–speech rhythm relationship as a cue to speech encoding. In A. R. Siegman & B. Pope (Eds.), *Studies in dyadic communication* (pp. 135–151). Elmsford, NY: Pergamon.

Dittman, A. T., & Llewellyn, L. C. (1969). Body movement and speech rhythm in social conversation. *Journal of Personality and Social Psychology, 11*(2), 98–106.

Dobrich, W., & Scarborough, H. S. (1984). Form and function in early communication: Language and pointing gestures. *Journal of Experimental Child Psychology, 38,* 475–490.

Dowling, R. (1962). *Effect of sensorimotor and conceptual activity on perceptual functioning.* Unpublished doctoral dissertation, Clark University, Worcester, MA.

Duffy, R. J., & Moore, M. (1971). The relationship between intelligence and gestural behavior in a mentally retarded population. *Journal of Genetic Psychology, 119,* 195–202.

Efron, D. (1941/1972). *Gesture, race and culture.* The Hague: Mouton.

Ekman, P., & Friesen, W. (1972). Hand movements. *Journal of Communication, 22,* 353–374.

Ekman, P., Levenson, R. W., & Friesen, W. V. (1983). Autonomic nervous system activity distinguishes among emotions. *Science, 221,* 1208–1210.

Elmslie, T. J., & Brooke, J. D. (1982). Communicative gestures of the hand and arm when 4-year-old sons and their mothers interact. *Journal of Experimental Child Psychology, 34,* 151–155.

Evans, M. A., & Rubin, K. (1979). Hand gestures as a communicative mode in school-aged children. *Journal of Genetic Psychology, 135,* 189–196.

Feyereisen, P. (1983). Manual activity during speaking in aphasic subjects. *International Journal of Psychology, 18,* 545–556.

(1987). Gestures and speech, interactions and separations: A reply to McNeill (1985). *Psychological Review, 94*(4), 493–498.

Feyereisen, P., Van de Wiele, M., & Dubois, F. (1988). The meaning of gestures: What can be understood without speech? *Cahiers de Psychologie Cognitive, 8*(1), 3–25.

Freedman, N. (1972). The analysis of movement behavior during the clinical interview. In A. R. Siegman & B. Pope (Eds.), *Studies in dyadic communication* (pp. 153–175). Elmsford, NY: Pergamon.

Freedman, N., & Hoffman, S. P. (1967). Kinetic behavior in altered clinical states: Approach to objective analysis of motor behavior during clinical interviews. *Perceptual and Motor Skills, 24,* 527–539.

Graham, J. A., & Argyle, M. (1975). A cross-cultural study of the communication of extra-verbal meaning by gestures. *International Journal of Psychology, 10*(1), 57–67.

Graham, J. A., & Heywood, S. (1975). The effects of elimination of hand gestures and of verbal codability on speech performance. *European Journal of Social Psychology, 5,* 189–195.

Grand, S., Marcos, L. R., Freedman, N., & Barroso, F. (1977). Relation of psychopathology and bilingualism to kinesic aspects of interview behavior in schizophrenia. *Journal of Abnormal Psychology, 86*(5), 492–500.

Gratiolet, (1865). *De la Physionomie et des mouvements d'expression.* Paris: Hetzel.

Hadar, U., Steiner, T. J., Grant, E. C., & Rose, F. (1983). Head movement correlates of juncture and stress at sentence level. *Language and Speech, 26*(2), 117–129.

Hadar, U., Steiner, T. J., & Rose, F. (1984a). Involvement of head movement in speech production and its implications for language pathology. In F. C. Rose (Ed.), *Advances in Neurology. Vol. 42: Progress in Aphasiology* (pp. 247–261). New York: Raven Press.

(1984a). The timing of shifts of head postures during conversation. *Human Movement Science, 3,* 237–245.

(1984b). The relationship between head movements and speech dysfluencies. *Language and Speech, 27*(4), 333–342.

Harper, R. G., Wiens, A. N., & Matarazzo, J. D. (1978). *Nonverbal communication: The state of the art.* New York: Wiley.

Hewes, G. W. (1973). Primate communication and the gestural origins of language. *Current Anthropology, 14,* 5–24.

Hoffman, J. P. (1968). *Empirical study of hand movements.* Unpublished doctoral dissertation, New York University, New York City.

Jackson, J. P. (1974). The relationship between the development of gestural imagery and the development of graphic imagery. *Child Development, 45,* 432–438.

Jacobson, E. (1930a). Electrical measurements of neuromuscular states during mental activities: Evidence of contraction of specific muscles during imagination. *American Journal of Physiology, 95,* 703–712.

(1930b). Electrical measurements of neuromuscular states during mental activities: Visual imagination and recollection. *American Journal of Physiology, 95,* 694–702.

(1931). Electrical measurements of neuromuscular states during mental activities: Variations of specific muscles contracting during imagination. *American Journal of Physiology, 96,* 115–121.

Jancovic, M., Devoe, S., & Wiener, M. (1975). Age-related changes in hand and arm movements as nonverbal communication: Some conceptualizations and an empirical exploration. *Child Development, 46,* 922–928.

Jousse, M. (1955/1974). *L'Anthropologie du geste.* Paris: Gallimard.

Kendon, A. (1972). Some relationships between body motion and speech. In A. W. Siegman & B. Pope (Eds.), *Studies in dyadic communication* (pp. 177–210). Elmsford, NY: Pergamon.

   (1980). Gesticulation and speech: Two aspects of the process of utterance. In M. R. Key (Ed.), *The relationship of verbal and nonverbal communication* (pp. 207–227). The Hague: Mouton.

   (1983). Gesture and speech: How they interact. In J. M. Wiemann & R. P. Harrison (Eds.), *Nonverbal interaction* (pp. 13–45). Beverly Hills, CA: Sage.

   (1984). Some uses of gestures. In D. Tannen & M. Saville-Troike (Eds.), *Perspectives on silence* (pp. 215–234). Norwood, NJ: Ablex.

   (1986a). Current issues in the study of gesture. In J. l. Nespoulous, P. Perron, & A. R. Lecours (Eds.), *The biological foundations of gestures, motor and semiotic aspects,* pp. 23–47. Hillsdale, NJ: Erlbaum.

   (1986b). Some reasons for studying gesture. *Semiotica, 62*(1/2), 3–28.

Lang, P. J. (1979). A bio-informational theory of emotional imagery. *Psychophysiology, 16,* 495–512.

McNeill, D. (1975). Semiotic extension. In L. R. Solso (Ed.), *Information processing and cognition. The Loyola symposium* (pp. 351–380). Hillsdale, NJ: Erlbaum.

   (1985). So you think gestures are nonverbal? *Psychological Review, 92*(3), 350–371.

   (1987a). *Psycholinguistics: A new approach.* New York: Harper & Row.

   (1987b). So you think gestures are nonverbal! Reply to Feyereisen. *Psychological Review, 94*(4), 499–504.

   (1989). A straight path – to where? Reply to Butterworth and Hadar. *Psychological Review, 96*(1), 175–179.

McNeill, D., & Levy, E. (1982). Conceptual representations in language activity and gesture. In R. Jarvella & W. Klein (Eds.), *Speech, place and action* (pp. 271–295). New York: Wiley.

Marcos, L. R. (1977). *Hand movements in relation to the encoding process in bilinguals.* Unpublished doctoral dissertation, Downstate Medical Center, State University of New York, Brooklyn.

   (1979a). Hand movements and nondominant fluency in bilinguals. *Perceptual and Motor Skills, 48,* 207–214.

   (1979b). Nonverbal behavior and thought processing. *Archives of General Psychiatry, 36,* 940–943.

Masur, E. F. (1983). Gestural development, dual-directional signaling, and the transition to words. *Journal of Psycholinguistic Research, 12*(2), 93–109.

Miller, A. (1963). Verbal satiation and the role of concurrent activity. *Journal of Abnormal and Social Psychology, 66*(3), 206–212.

Moscovici, S. (1967). Communication processes and the properties of language. In L. Berkowitz (Ed.), *Advances in experimental social psychology* (Vol. 3, pp. 225–270). New York: Academic Press.

Moscovici, S., & Plon, M. (1966). Les situations-colloques: Observations théoriques et expérimentales. *Bulletin de Psychologie, 19*(274), 702–722.

Murphy, C. M. (1978). Pointing in the context of a shared activity. *Child Development, 49,* 371–380.

Overton, W. F., & Jackson, J. P. (1973). The representation of imagined objects in action sequences: A development study. *Child Development, 44,* 309–314.

Pechman, T., & Deutsch, W. (1982). The development of verbal and nonverbal devices for reference. *Journal of Experimental Child Psychology, 34,* 330–341.

Ragsdale, J. D., & Silvia C. (1982). Distribution of kinesic hesitation phenomena in spontaneous speech. *Language and Speech, 25*(2), 185–190.

Rand, G., & Wapner, S. (1987). Postural status as a factor memory. *Journal of Verbal Learning and Verbal Behavior, 6,* 268–271.

Rimé, B. (1979). Communication non verbale ou comportements nonverbaux? Vers une théorie cognitivo-motrice des comportements non verbaux. Unpublished manuscript, University of Louvain, Department of Psychology, Louvain-la-Neuve, Belgium.

(1982). The elimination of visible behavior from social interactions: Effects on verbal, nonverbal and interpersonal variables. *European Journal of Social Psychology, 12,* 113–129.

(1983). Nonverbal communication or nonverbal behavior? Towards a cognitive-motor theory of nonverbal behavior. In W. Doise & S. Moscovici (Eds.), *Current issues in European social psychology* (Vol. 1, pp. 85–141). Cambridge: Cambridge University Press.

(1985). "Do you see what I mean?" The process of sharing representations in interpersonal communication. *Symposium on the Social Constitution of Meaning in Interpersonal Communication.* Bad Homburg, December 4–7.

Rimé, B., Boulanger, B., & d'Ydewalle, G. (1988). *Visual attention to the communicator's nonverbal behavior as a function of the intelligibity of the message.* Paper presented at the Symposium on TV Behavior, 24th International Congress of Psychology, Sydney, Australia, August 28–September 2.

Rimé, B., Bouvy, H., Leborgne, B., & Rouillon, F. (1978). Psychopathy and nonverbal behavior in an interpersonal situation. *Journal of Abnormal Psychology, 87,* 636–647.

Rimé, B., & Gaussin, J. (1982). Sensibilité des comportements non verbaux aux variations de la densité de communication. *L'Année Psychologique, 82,* 173–187.

Rimé, B., Schiaratura, L., Hupet, M., & Ghysselinckx, A. (1984). Effects of relative immobilization on the speaker's nonverbal behavior and on the dialogue imagery level. *Motivation and Emotion, 8,* 311–325.

Rimé, B., Thomas, D., Richir, M., & Laubin, P. (1983). *The nonverbal behavior of individuals with different levels of verbal deficit.* Unpublished manuscript, University of Louvain, Department of Psychology, Louvain-La-Neuve, Belgium.

Riseborough, M. G. (1982). Meaning in movement: An investigation into the interrelationship of physiographic gestures and speech in seven-year-olds. *British Journal of Psychology, 73,* 497–503.

Rogers, W. T. (1979). The relevance of body motion cues to both functional and dysfunctional communicative behavior. *Journal of Communication Disorders, 12,* 273–282.

Saltz, E., & Dixon, D. (1982). Let's pretend: The role of motoric imagery in memory for sentences and words. *Journal of Experimental Child Psychology, 34,* 77–92.

Schiaratura, L., & Rimé, B. (1990). *Les gestes des mains chez le locuteur: Catégories et classifications.* Unpublished manuscript. University of Louvain, Belgium.

Shepard, R. N., & Feng, C. A. (1972). A chronometric study of mental paper folding. *Cognitive Psychology, 3,* 228–243.

Sirota, A. D., & Schwartz, G. E. (1982). Facial muscle patterning and lateralization during elation and depression imagery. *Journal of Abnormal Psychology, 91,* 25–34.

Van Heugten, A. A. T., & Van Meel, J. M. (1980). Handbewegingen tijdens de opname van in benoembaarheid en moeilijkheidsgraas variënde informatie. *Nederlands Tijdschrift voor de Psychologie, 35,* 23–40.

Van Meel, J. M. (1982). The nature and development of the kinetic representational system. In B. de Gelder (Ed.), *Knowledge and representation.* London: Routledge & Kegan Paul.

(1984, March). *Kinesic strategies in representation and attention-deployment.* Paper presented at the Symposium on the Relation of Language, Thought and Gestures. Tilburg, the Netherlands.

Vygotsky, L. S. (1962). *Thought and language.* Cambridge, MA: MIT Press.

Wallon, H. (1970). *De l'Acte à la pensée.* Paris: Flammarion.

Werner, H., & Kaplan, B. (1963). *Symbol formation.* New York: Wiley.

Williams, E. (1977). Experimental comparisons of face-to-face and mediated communication: A review. *Psychological Bulletin, 84,* 963–976.

Wolff, P., & Gutstein, J. (1972). Effects of induced motor gestures on vocal output. *Journal of Communication, 22,* 277–288.

Wundt, W. (1900/1973). *The language of gestures.* The Hague: Mouton.

Zinober, B., & Martlew, M. (1985). Developmental changes in four types of gesture in relation to acts and vocalizations from 10 to 21 months. *British Journal of Developmental Psychology, 3,* 203–306.

PART IV

Individual differences and social adaptation

8. Expressiveness as an individual difference

ANTONY S. R. MANSTEAD

One of the most obvious facts about emotional expressiveness is its marked variation across individuals. Some persons are highly expressive, making their feelings apparent through facial expressions, gestures, tone of voice, and what they say, whereas others are much more reserved, making it difficult to infer their emotional states.

Clear-cut evidence of how much individuals differ in this respect comes from a study reported by Miller (1974), in which the subjects acted as either senders or receivers of facial expressions. The senders were required to solve a problem in order to gain a monetary prize. On each trial of this task, a light indicated whether it was a "penny," "quarter," or "jackpot" trial. The senders were led to believe that by pressing the appropriate button on a three-button response box, they could (on penny and quarter trials) release a coin into the "jackpot chamber," where successive rewards could accumulate into a respectable total. On jackpot trials, the "correct" response was rewarded by releasing these accumulated coins into a drawer that would be given to the sender at the end of the session. By contrast, "incorrect" responses on jackpot trials released the coins into a box where they would be lost to the sender. Although the scheduling of trials and reinforcements was actually predetermined, all the trappings of the task led the senders to believe that the reinforcements were contingent on their responses. Their facial expressions were covertly videotaped throughout the task. The receiver subjects were shown the apparatus and given a complete description of the task that had confronted the senders. They were then shown the senders' videotaped facial expressions and were asked to judge whether each trial from a 10-trial sequence of videotape was a penny, quarter, or jackpot trial.

Table 8.1 shows the number of correct judgments made, broken down by sender and receiver subjects. The total possible correct is 10, and 6

285

Table 8.1. *Number of correct responses[a] in ten trial sequences of each of eight videotaped stimulus subjects*

		Sender								
Receiver		1	2	3	4	5	6	7	8	Total
1		4	2	6	7	5	6	2	6	38
2		4	3	7	3	7	5	6	6	40
3		6	6	6	7	7	6	7	6	51
4		6	5	6	5	5	6	8	4	45
5		3	5	3	2	7	5	4	6	35
6		1	7	6	4	4	7	3	3	35
7		6	3	4	0[b]	5	4	4	3	29
8		2	4	4	1	1	4	2	4	22
9		3	2	5	2	5	4	3	2	26
10		6	4	4	1	5	8	6	3	37
11		5	4	3	2	6	5	5	2	37
12		2	2	4	1	4	3	2	5	23
13		6	3	5	2	4	5	3	3	31
	Total	54	50	63	37	65	68	55	52	

[a]With three possible responses on each trial, six or more correct choices is significant beyond the 0.06 point.
[b]Zero correct responses is significant beyond the 0.06 point, indicating a below-chance reception of nonverbal cues.
Source: Adapted from Miller (1974).

or more correct judgments represent significantly greater than chance accuracy. If one focuses on the column totals, it is readily apparent that some senders' facial expressions were much more accurately decoded than others' were; compare, for example, senders 5 and 6 with sender 4. Although sizable individual differences in receiving skill are also apparent in these data, it is the variation across senders with respect to how easy others found it to make correct inferences about the stimulus situation on the basis of facial expressions that will form the topic of this chapter. My focus will be on individual differences in facial expressiveness, rather than other nonverbal or verbal channels. My objective will be to review the literature on such individual differences in order to address the following questions. First, to what extent are differences among individuals in facial expressiveness reflections of group rather than individual differences? That is, how much of the variance in facial expressiveness can be explained by factors such as race, gender, and nationality? Second, what are the correlates of individual differences in

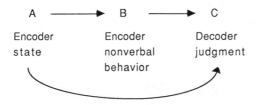

Figure 8.1. A simple model of judgment studies. (Reprinted by permission of Rosenthal, 1987)

facial expressiveness? In other words, are there other personal attributes (apart from race, gender, and nationality) that reliably covary with such individual differences? Third, what is the etiology of individual differences in facial expressiveness? Here I shall be concerned with the extent to which such differences are innate or acquired and more specifically with the processes establishing these differences. Finally, are there any consequences of individual differences in facial expressiveness? Here I shall concentrate on recent research suggesting that the inhibition of facial expressiveness is associated with certain physical disorders. Before addressing these three broad questions, however, I shall briefly review the principal methods used to measure facial expressiveness and comment on their relative advantages and disadvantages.

Methods of measuring facial expressiveness

There are three general types of measure of facial expressiveness. The first is the *judgment* measure, which was described in regard to Miller's (1974) findings. As Rosenthal (1987) pointed out, the essence of a judgment study in the realm of nonverbal behavior can be summarized in a simple model (Figure 8.1) in which the encoder (or sender) experiences certain states (A) that are manifested behaviorally in certain ways (B), such as facial expressions. Then these behavioral manifestations are presented to judges for decoding (C).

Probably the most widely used instance of a judgment measure of facial expressiveness is some variant of what has come to be known as the *slide-viewing paradigm* (Buck, 1979b), derived from Miller, Caul, and Mirsky's (1967) research on the effects of social isolation on emotional communication in rhesus monkeys. These investigators constructed a cooperative conditioning paradigm (Miller, Murphey, & Mirsky, 1959) in which monkeys were tested in pairs. Both monkeys were first taught to press a bar within a few seconds of a light coming on, in order to avoid receiving an electric shock. Then one monkey acted as the sender and the other as the receiver. The sender monkey could see the light but had no access to the bar; the receiver monkey could not see the light but could see the sender monkey's face via closed-circuit television and also had access to the bar. Thus the receiver could prevent the sender from being shocked by pressing the bar at the appropriate time on shock trials. Clearly, the only basis for the receiver's action was the sender's facial expression. If the sender learned the association between the shock signal and the shock and expressed fear (A) of the impending shock through facial expressions (B), then the receiver had the opportunity to decode those expressions as signals of fear (C) and to learn to make the appropriate response to prevent the shock from being delivered. Miller et al. (1967) found that pairs of normally reared monkeys were able to learn to avoid the shocks in this way quite rapidly but that 12-month-old monkeys who had been reared in isolation performed significantly less well on this task.

The general properties of the cooperative conditioning paradigm used by Miller et al. (1967) were later adapted for use with human subjects (Buck, Savin, Miller, & Caul, 1972). Affective states in the sender (A) were induced by emotionally loaded color slides, rather than by signaling impending shock, and the receiver's decoding task (C) was to infer from the sender's facial expressions (B) which of five types of slide (sexual, scenic, maternal, injury, or unusual photographic effects) the sender had viewed during a particular interval. The primary measure of "communication accuracy" in such research is usually the accuracy with which receivers make judgments about slide type. Because the judgments are categorical, this is sometimes known as the *categorization* measure. Senders who earn relatively high categorization scores are deemed to be more facially expressive than are those who earn relatively low scores. Other measures of expressiveness included (1) "pleasantness correlations," that is, a measure of the degree to which a sender's self-reported pleasantness of affective state while viewing a slide covaries with the judges' ratings of the pleasantness of the sender's affective response to the same slide, with these correlations being averaged across all slides; and (2) global ratings of facial expressiveness made by researchers or independent judges who view a videotape of the sender's facial reactions to the slides. Researchers may modify the general features of this slide-viewing paradigm, sometimes to induce affective states in the sender by using stimuli other than slides. As we saw earlier, Miller et al. (1974) used a problem-solving task involving monetary rewards for this purpose, and Zuckerman, Hall, DeFrank, and Rosenthal (1976) used videotapes depicting pleasant or unpleasant material. Another variation on this general theme that was used by Wagner, MacDonald, and Manstead (1986): Instead of asking receivers to judge what kind of slide the sender had seen during a specified interval, they asked both senders and receivers to name the emotion label that best described the sender's affective response to the slide. Accuracy of judgment was measured using the sender's nomination as the criterion, and expressiveness of the senders was assessed in terms of the accuracy scores they attracted.

The second general technique for measuring facial expressiveness is electromyography (EMG). EMG techniques for recording movement in the facial musculature typically entail the use of surface electrodes, sited over the muscle groups of interest. The electrodes detect the electrical discharges of contracting fibers in the muscles. These discharges are amplified, filtered, and integrated to provide a DC voltage that varies with the degree of contraction of the muscles at the recording site. A technical description of the procedures is provided by Fridlund and Fowler (1978).

Facial EMG has not been extensively used to address questions about individual differences in facial expressiveness, although the technique clearly has considerable potential for this purpose. The most relevant set of studies for our purposes are those examining EMG differences in the facial behavior of males and females. Other EMG studies focused on differences between persons diagnosed as suffering from an affective disorder (almost invariably depression) and normal control subjects. Such studies are founded on the observation that corrugator and zygomatic activity distinguish positive from negative affective states. The effect of the corrugator is to lower the brows and pull them together, as in frowning. The effect of the zygomatic muscle is to pull the corners of the lips back and upward, as in smiling. Corrugator-region activity, in particular, has been associated with the distinction between positive and negative affective states (see Fridlund & Izard, 1983, for a review). Unsurprisingly, corrugator activity is generally found to be greater in subjects engaging in negative imagery than in those engaging in positive imagery; also, corrugator activity has been found to covary with self-reported mood negativity. On this basis, researchers have used EMG techniques to study depressive symptomatology and how it responds to antidepressant drug therapy. In the course of such research, investigators have discovered relationships between the amount of facial activity (or expressiveness) and the state of clinical depression, suggesting that one source of individual differences in facial expressiveness might be dispositional differences in affective state. We cannot spend more time on this research on expressiveness and affective disorders, but the interested reader is referred to Fridlund and Izard (1983), for a review and commentary on this research.

A third technique for measuring individual differences in facial expressiveness is measuring facial movement using an objective, standardized system for coding type, degree, and duration of facial activity. Several such coding systems are available, the best known being the MAX and AFFEX systems developed by Izard and his associates (Izard, 1979; Izard & Dougherty, 1980) and the FAST and FACS systems developed by Ekman and his colleagues (Ekman & Friesen, 1978; Ekman, Friesen, & Tomkins, 1971). FACS is the most comprehensive and widely used of these systems, although MAX is popular among researchers studying facial expressions in infants and children (e.g., Malatesta, Culver, Tesman, & Shepard, 1989). FACS will be used as our example of coding systems. Ekman and Friesen's primary goals in developing FACS were for it to be comprehensive and to separate descriptions of facial actions from inferences about the meanings or significance of facial behaviors. The FACS system therefore measures all visible facial movements, with the emphasis on describing the movements and underlying muscular actions. Facial behaviors are scored in "action units" (AUs), which reflect which muscles have contracted to produce the observed movements. FACS consists of 44 AUs, one example of which is AU-12. In FACS this is called "lip corner puller," the muscular basis of which is contraction of the zygomatic major muscle. As we noted, the visible appearance of this AU corresponds to a smile, but by avoiding the name *smile* for this AU, Ekman and Friesen avoid equating AU-12 with other AUs that result in an upturned mouth shape but have a different anatomical basis. In addition to these 44 single AUs, the FACS manual describes in detail more than 44 combinations of 2 or more AUs. The coder's task is (1) to determine which AU or AUs are responsible for the observed facial movement, (2) to score the intensity of action of 5 of the 44 AUs (as low, medium, or high), (3) to score the AUs for asymmetry or unilaterality, and (4) to score the head and eye position during the facial movement. As with EMG, FACS and other coding systems have not been used very extensively to study individual differences in facial expressiveness, although they have considerable potential in this regard, as evidenced by the research reported by Malatesta et al. (1989). In the FACS system, expressiveness can be scored as *frequency* of facial actions, *duration* of facial actions, and *intensity* of (at least some) facial actions. Like the EMG technique, FACS has been used to investigate differences in the facial behavior of normal and clinically diagnosed groups, such as depressed patients. Again, this research will not be reviewed, but readers are referred to Ellgring (1989) for a recent study.

Of the three methods for measuring facial expressiveness, the judgment method has been used most often in research. This method has some advantages. First, it is easier to use than either of the other two methods, as it requires no special resources other than a video camera and recorder, and expressiveness can be measured in real time. By contrast, facial EMG requires relatively sophisticated and expensive amplification, filtering and integrating hardware, plus a computer and specialized software for signal processing, and FACS and other coding systems require extensive training and repeated reviewing of videotapes, using slow motion. Another virtue of the judgment technique is that it focuses on those aspects of expressiveness that are visible to untrained human observers who do not have the benefit of slow-motion replay. This means that individual differences in expressiveness measured using the judgment technique are closer to the individual differences that are noticeable in everyday social interaction. By contrast, with EMG techniques one can assess facial movements that cannot be detected by eye, even with the benefit of repeated slow-motion replay, whereas coding systems such as FACS enable one to measure facial movements that would pass unnoticed by observers in normal interaction. Both the judgment method and facial coding systems require the use of human observers, or judges, which of course raises questions about their reliability. In the case of judgment measures, researchers often use relatively large numbers of judges as a means of tackling this problem, whereas users of FACS and other coding systems try to ensure before they begin their research that coders are carefully trained in the use of the system. Both the judgment method and facial coding systems can be made to be very unobtrusive. Researchers often take care to hide video cameras, so that the subjects are not aware that their facial activity is being recorded. By contrast, the use of facial EMG makes it very difficult to record facial actions unobtrusively, although researchers try to persuade their subjects that facial electrodes are recording variables such as skin temperature (e.g., Manstead, Wagner, & MacDonald, 1984) or electrical activity in the brain (e.g., Vaughan & Lanzetta, 1980), rather than facial movement. The primary advantages of facial EMG are its immediacy, precision, sensitivity, and objectivity. FACS offers nearly the same precision and objectivity and adds the virtue of unobtrusiveness. Set against these considerations are FAC's nonimmediacy and lesser sensitivity. Finally, the primary advantages of the judgment measure are its straightforwardness, immediacy (relative to FACS), and unobtrusiveness (relative to EMG).

One other methodological issue warrants a comment before proceeding to the main review, and this is the issue of "posed" versus "spontaneous" measures of expressiveness. Posed measures of facial expressiveness are those taken when the subject is asked to create a facial expression of anger, sadness, happiness, or whatever. Spontaneous measures are those taken without the subject's awareness, during exposure to emotional stimuli. Some investigators have reported significant positive correlations between the two measures of expressiveness (e.g., Buck, 1975; Cunningham, 1977; Zuckerman, Hall, DeFrank, & Rosenthal, 1976), although the correlations have typically been rather small in magnitude. However, other researchers (e.g., Fujita, Harper, & Wiens, 1980; Morency & Krauss, 1982) have not found significant relationships between measures of spontaneous expressivity and the ability to pose emotional expressions. Moreover, there are neurological (Rinn, 1984), anatomical (Ekman, Hager, & Friesen, 1981), and theoretical (Buck, 1984) reasons for thinking that posed and spontaneous expressions differ in important respects. Because there is evidence (e.g., Fujita et al., 1980) that instructions to pose facial expressions attenuate differences in expressiveness that are apparent in spontaneous expressions, this chapter will concentrate on the evidence relating to individual differences in spontaneous facial expressions. This is not to say that individual differences in the ability to pose facial and other nonverbal expressions are without interest. For example, DePaulo (Chapter 10, this volume) discusses the ability to manage nonverbal behaviors as an important aspect of self-presentation.

Group differences in facial expressiveness

Race and socioeconomic status

The effects of race and socioeconomic status (SES) on facial expressiveness have not been the subject of systematic research attention. Rather, researchers who have examined race and SES effects have focused on other indices of nonverbal behavior, such as interpersonal distance and body orientation (*proxemics*), touch, and eye gaze. These studies have been reviewed by Halberstadt (1985) and therefore will not be discussed in detail here. For our purposes it is sufficient to summarize Halberstadt's main conclusions: First, the clearest proxemic difference between blacks and whites is the one relating to body orientation: Whites stand more "directly" than blacks. Second, blacks touch others more often than whites do. Third, blacks gaze at others less frequently than whites do. However, the extent to which these differences can be attributed to race per se is highly questionable. Halberstadt noted that very few investigators attempted to match their racial groups for SES and that of the 10 studies (out of 58) that controlled for SES in some fashion, however rudimentary, 7 reported no significant race differences. Thus these "race" differences may reflect the impact of social class instead of (or as well as) race. A similar point was made by Hanna (1984), who commented that "the state of the art of nonverbal communication similarities and differences between blacks and whites is beset with little research and the intertwining of color with social class" (p. 403).

A more general point about this literature is that investigators have not in the main been concerned with race or SES effects on facial expressiveness. This contrasts markedly with the literature on gender differences in nonverbal communication, for which there is quite a large body of research addressing this issue. It is tempting to conclude that the lack of research on race or SES effects on facial expressiveness reflects the fact that researchers in this field have failed to observe such differences in everyday interaction and have therefore not been stimulated to conduct formal research on this issue. However, the combination of possible ethnocentrism on the part of white, middle-class investigators and the relatively low number of blacks in the college student population from which subjects are typically recruited argue against too rapid a conclusion that race or SES effects on facial expressiveness are too weak or unsystematic to be of interest. Hanna (1984) observed that "a low-income black concerned with style, soul, and jockeying for position is characterized by higher energy, faster response, and less restrained emotion than what is found among whites (and middle-class blacks)" (p. 380), and she went on to discuss black–white differences in, for example, the expression of anger. Her own ethnographic study of race differences in nonverbal behavior in a school setting led her to believe that black children were more overtly expressive of anger than were whites, whose anger tended to be expressed in a "controlled" fashion.

However, the extent to which the greater expressiveness of black children reflected or included differences in facial expressiveness is unclear, for the examples cited by Hanna entail verbal behavior, body movements, or eye movements. It is evident that conclusions about the relationship between race or SES, on the one hand, and facial expressiveness, on the other, cannot be reached in the absence of further, systematic research.

Culture and nationality

The notion that individuals who differ in culture or nationality vary systematically in their facial expressiveness is closely related to the concept of *display rules*, a term coined by Ekman and Friesen (1969). Ekman (1978) defined display rules as "social norms regarding facial appearance, probably learned early in life and functioning on a habitual basis. They specify which one of four management techniques is to be applied by whom to which emotion in a given circumstance " (p. 111). The four management techniques referred to by Ekman are (1) intensifying an expression, (2) deintensifying that expression, (3) neutralizing the expression, and (4) masking it with an expression of another emotion. To the extent that these display rules do influence facial expressiveness and do vary across cultural or national contexts, we can expect differences in expressiveness in these contexts.

Somewhat surprisingly, there is very little systematic cross-cultural research examining the operation of display rules. The best-known study is one conducted by Ekman and Friesen (Ekman, 1972; Friesen, 1972), using Japanese and American students as subjects. The participants watched neutral and stressful films during which their facial reactions were covertly recorded. Using the FAST coding system, Ekman (1972) showed that the subjects' facial movements were very similar. As Ekman (1989) put it, "Virtually the same repertoire of facial movements occurred at the same points in time" (p. 151).

After seeing the film alone, each subject reviewed the film in the company of a white-coated "scientist" whose ethnicity was the same as the subject's. Now there were detectable differences in the facial displays of the two groups of subjects. The Japanese students masked their facial expressions of negative emotions to a greater extent than did the American students (Friesen, 1972). More specifically, the Japanese looked more polite and engaged in more "social" smiling than did the Americans. Ekman (1989) commented that a slow-motion analysis of the videotapes of Japanese subjects' facial behavior revealed how a smiling movement would be imposed on an earlier expression of disgust or fear. Here, then, is empirical evidence of the way in which culturally specified display rules can influence the expression of emotion. It would seem that in the Japanese culture people learn that it is impolite to express negative emotions openly; instead, one should "spare" others the signs of one's negative affect. Interesting anthropological evidence consistent with this interpretation of Japanese display rules relating to negative affect was reported by Hendry (1986), which helps explain the origin of the Western popular stereotype of Japanese "inscrutability."

In the Ekman and Friesen research just described, it is evident that social presence triggered or enhanced the operation of a display rule. If these rules are socially transmitted, it makes good sense for them to operate more powerfully under social surveillance. Indeed, in research on the North American culture there is a fair amount of evidence that the facial expressiveness of adults and children is reduced when others are known or thought to be present (e.g., Kilbride & Yarczower, 1980; Kleck et al., 1976; Kraut, 1982; Yarczower & Daruns, 1982; Yarczower, Kilbride, & Hill, 1979). This is not to say, however, that the effects of culturally specified display rules are apparent only in the presence of others. Rather, Ekman (1978) suggested that they are habitual, which raises the possibility that they are overlearned and therefore automatic in their operation. At the very least, one might expect that residual forms of the display rules would become internalized by adulthood, so that they would operate even when the person is alone. In this way, individuals who grow up in a culture that values the overt expression of emotion might be more facially expressive, on the average, than would individuals who are raised in a culture that values the inhibition of overt emotional expression.

There is no other systematic research on cultural differences in overt expression in which expressiveness has been measured by means other than self-report. Nevertheless, there are some studies in which self-report measures have been used and that bear on the general issue of cultural variation. Lambert, Hamers, and Frasure-Smith (1979) conducted a 10-nation study of parents' tolerance of anger expressions in their children and found, for example, that English and Italian parents were more tolerant of anger expressions than were French-Belgian or English-Canadian parents. Sommers (1984) reported a 4-nation study of students' tendencies to express or inhibit expressions of different emotions, in which she found that West Indians, Greeks, and Chinese were less concerned about inhibiting anger expressions than were Americans and that Greeks and Americans were less concerned about inhibiting feelings of love than were West Indians and Chinese. In an 8-nation study, Wallbott, Ricci Bitti, and Bänninger-Huber (1986) found that French and Belgian subjects reported high amounts of control over non-verbal reactions to joy, sadness, and anger and that British subjects also reported high control for sadness and anger. These three groups differed from the others in reporting relatively high amounts of control over nonverbal reactions in emotional episodes. Low control over joy and sadness expressions was reported by German subjects, as did Italian subjects in regard to sadness and anger. Finally, Swiss subjects were very low in control over anger reactions.

Although the patterns of findings reported by Lambert et al. (1979), Sommers (1984), and Wallbott et al. (1986) could be regarded as broadly consistent (in certain respects at least) with cultural stereotypes, it is difficult to know how much such self-reported differences in tolerance or control attempts are manifested in nonverbal behavior in general and facial expressiveness in particular. Here there is a clear need for further research on cultural–national differences in facial expressiveness and on how these differences relate to display rules, parents' beliefs about emotional expression, and social presence.

Gender

As I noted earlier, there is a reasonable body of research on gender differences in facial expressiveness. Researchers using EMG to assess facial responses to emotional stimuli have often found that females exhibit greater facial EMG than males do. In a series of studies, Schwartz and his associates (Schwartz, Ahern, & Brown, 1979; Schwartz, Brown & Ahern, 1980; Schwartz, Fair, Salt, Mandel, & Klerman, 1976a,b; Schwartz, Fair, Salt, Mandel, Mieske, & Klerman, 1978) found that females, compared with males, tend to produce greater facial EMG, relative to rest, during affective imagery; to exhibit somewhat higher levels of corrugator activity (possibly indicative of greater sadness or concern) and lower levels of masseter activity (possibly indicative of less anger) during rest; and to generate larger facial EMG patterns when asked to pose overt expressions corresponding to different emotions.

These findings are consistent with research examining gender differences in facial expressiveness using judgment measures. Consider first those studies of adult subjects. Here there is consistent evidence that females' spontaneous facial responses to emotional stimuli (typically color slides) are more accurately decoded by receiver subjects, compared with males' facial responses (Buck et al., 1972; Buck, Miller, & Caul, 1974; Fujita et al., 1980; Gallagher & Shuntich, 1981; Harper, Wiens, Fujita, & Kallgren, 1981; Sabatelli, Buck, & Dreyer, 1980). It is worth noting that when researchers have examined gender differences within type of emotional stimulus, they have tended to find that females are more expressive than males are in response to some stimuli but not others. But there is inconsistency across studies in this respect. Harper et al. (1981) found that the difference between female and male expressiveness was greater in response to positive (happy or novel) slides than to negative (sad or injury) ones. By contrast, Buck, Baron, Goodman, and Shapiro (1980) found that females were more expressive than males were in response to negative (injury) slides, whereas males were actually more expressive than females were in response to sexual slides. It seems likely that this discrepancy simply reflects differences in the contents of the slides used in different studies. Progress in our understanding would clearly be enhanced by using a standard set of eliciting slides.

The gender difference in spontaneous facial expressiveness typically observed in adults is not reliably found in infants and children. In two studies of preschoolers, Buck (1975, 1977) found a small gender difference in expressiveness, in that undergraduate receivers were more accurate in guessing the type of stimulus viewed by girls as compared with boys. However, there was no difference between girls' and boys' sending accuracy when the child's mother acted as the receiver. Moreover, Field (1982) found no reliable gender differences in the facial expressiveness of neonates. Similarly, Yarczower and Daruns (1982) found no gender differences in their study of children aged 6 or 12, and Morency and Krauss (1982) found no gender differences in facial expressiveness among 6- and 11-year-olds. These failures to find reliable gender differences among children suggest that the differences observed in adults are acquired relatively late in childhood and may therefore be mediated by sex role socialization. Consistent with such an interpretation is Buck's (1975, 1977) finding that sending accuracy tends to be inversely related to age among boys, but not girls – implying that spontaneous facial expressiveness in boys decreases as they get older.

In order to cast more light on the relationship between communication accuracy and gender differences in facial behavior, Buck and his associates (Buck et al., 1980; Buck et al., 1982) subjected videotapes of spontaneous facial expressions to *segmentation analysis,* a procedure in which observers are instructed to press a button whenever "something meaningful" occurs. The Buck et al. (1980) paper reports two such studies. In the first, student receivers were shown 32 video sequences of adult senders viewing one of four types of slide, and 18 sequences of child senders viewing one of three types of slide. Among the adult senders, the females elicited more "breakpoints" (i.e., button presses) than did the males, although this main effect was qualified by an interaction between sex of sender and type of slide. The injury slides provoked significantly fewer breakpoints in male senders than did any other type of slide. By contrast, the injury slides evoked significantly more breakpoints in female senders than did any other type of slide. The female senders also tended to elicit more breakpoints than did the males in regard to scenic slides, whereas the male senders tended to elicit more breakpoints than the females did in regard to sexual slides. The child senders elicited a much larger average number of breakpoints than did the adults. As with the adult senders, there was a significant interaction between sex of sender and slide type, but here the unpleasant slides resulted in more breakpoints for the male senders than for the females, whereas the unusual slides resulted in more breakpoints for the female senders than for the males. Receivers were also asked to determine what type of slide the senders had seen. For both adult and child senders, there was an interaction between sex of sender and slide type. As noted earlier, adult females were more accurately decoded than males in regard to unpleasant slides, and males were more accurately decoded than females in regard to sexual slides. Among children, boys were generally more accurately decoded than were girls, although this advantage was relatively greater in relation to the unpleasant slides. Sending accuracy was positively and significantly associated with the number of segmentation points noted by subjects in relation to the facial expressions of females, but this was not the case with males' expressions. This pattern applied to both adult and child senders. Thus the amount of "meaningful" facial/gestural activity exhibited by sender subjects was related to their sending accuracy in the case of females but not males. In the second study reported by Buck et al. (1980), student receivers were shown 40 video sequences, 10 each of four senders. These senders were those found to have been most expressive and least expressive in an earlier study (one male and one female of each type). As expected, the expressive senders were much more accurately decoded than were the inexpressive senders (33.9% vs. 17.7% accuracy, with chance being 20%), but the expressive female was decoded especially accurately. Segmentation scores again revealed a pattern that differed according to the sender's sex. Whereas the expressive female sender elicited more break-points than did her less expressive female counterpart, the opposite pattern was revealed for the male senders. Thus these two studies are consistent in showing that expressiveness as indexed by communication accuracy is related to the number of meaningful events segmented in the nonverbal displays of females but that these two variables are not related in males.

In the Buck et al. (1982) study, a more detailed analysis of segmentation points was performed, permitting the investigators to assess not just the number of segmentation points but also the number of *consensual segmentation points* (CPs), a CP being defined as a 1-second period that earned more than one standard deviation above the average number of segmentation points per second given to that video sequence. Obviously, the greater the number of CPs, the more observers had agreed in their judgment of the location of meaningful behaviors. Furthermore, a second group of observer subjects were shown the same videotape of facial expressions and told where the CPs occurred. For each CP, these subjects had to judge whether it was based on a facial expression of the sender or was related to some other behavior, such as head movement of postural change. The percentage of CPs judged to be facial expressions indicates the extent to which consensual judgments of meaningful behavior involve facial expressions. In this study it was found that the females' sending accuracy was significantly and positively correlated not only with the number of segmentation points (as in the earlier studies) but also with the number of CPs. Neither of these correlations was significant in the case of males. The percentage of CPs judged to be facial expressions was positively and significantly related to sending accuracy for males but not for females. These findings indicate that sending accuracy – as reflected in the degree to which spontaneous facial expressiveness permits observers to make accurace inferences about the sender's state – is based on different behaviors in males and females. It seems that among females, sending accuracy is related simply to the amount of meaningful activity but that among males, sending accuracy is related to the extent to which such activity involves facial expressions. As Buck (1984) observed, there appear to be qualitative as well as quantitative differences between males and females with regard to the communicativeness of their facial expressions. Why this should be so is as yet unknown, and there is an obvious need for more research on this topic.

Correlates of individual differences in facial expressiveness

The externalizer–internalizer distinction

The externalizer–internalizer distinction relates to the correlation between facial expressiveness and autonomic activity (cf. Buck, 1979a). Its intellectual roots can be traced to Freud's "hydraulic" conception of emotional energy. According to this position, because energy needs to be expressed, if one channel of expression is impeded or constrained, the energy will be expressed more forcibly through the other channels.

Theorists have drawn on this hydraulic conception of emotional expression to account for observed relationships between overt emotional expression and autonomic activity. Jones (e.g., 1950, 1960) found that infants exhibited high thresholds for electrodermal responses, as compared with older children, and that among older children consistent relationships between autonomic activity and overt expressiveness could be identified. He accounted for the threshold differences by arguing that "as the infant passes into early and later childhood, overt emotional expression tends to bring disapproval and punishment rather than succorance. The internal avenues of discharge are not disapproved or inhibited; to an increasing extent these hidden channels carry the efferent load of major as well as minor emotional changes" (1960, p. 15). Among older children, Jones claimed to be able to discriminate three types of relationship between overt expressiveness and covert responding: "The 'externalizer,' who displays a somewhat infantile pattern of marked overt but reduced or infrequent galvanic responses; the 'internalizer,' who reverses this relationship; and the 'generalizer,' who tends to respond with a total discharge both overt and internal" (1950, p. 163).

For several years Jones's theory and findings were generally ignored by emotion theorists. The revival of interest in the externalizer–internalizer distinction was stimulated mainly by unanticipated empirical findings. Lanzetta and Kleck (1970) were surprised to find that subjects whose facial expressions were accurately decoded by others (and who were therefore presumed to be expressive) tended also to exhibit low electrodermal activity during emotional stimulation. This finding was replicated under somewhat different conditions by other research groups (e.g., Buck, Savin, Miller, & Caul, 1972; Notarius & Levenson, 1979), and the apparent robustness of this inverse relationship served to reawaken interest in Jones's (1950) concepts of "externalizing" and "internalizing" response modes (the "generalizer" mode has typically been ignored in recent research).

Although all proponents of the E–I distinction would predict an inverse correlation between facial expressiveness and autonomic activity, they would differ in their preferred explanation for this prediction. There are three sorts of explanation for the E–I distinction. The first is the "discharge" model (Notarius & Levenson, 1979), which grew out of the hydraulic conceptions of the relationship between overt expression and physiological activity favored by early investigators, including Jones (1935). The second is referred to as the "innate arousability" model and has its origins in Eysenck's (1967) theory of the psychophysiological basis of individual differences in extroversion and introversion. The third is the "response conflict" model, proposed by Lanzetta and Kleck (1970).

The essence of the discharge model is described by Notarius, Wemple, Ingraham, Burns, and Kollan (1982) as follows: "Emotion is viewed as a form of energy and as such must follow the basic dynamics of energy conservation. As a person becomes emotionally aroused, this arousal must be discharged either directly through expression or indirectly through internal pathways" (p. 400). Jones's (1950, 1960) explanation of the E–I distinction in these terms is based on the notion of differential socialization. According to Jones, the "natural" inclination of infants is to externalize their affective states, but socialization tends to promote the inhibition of affective display. Those children exposed to especially strong inhibitory socialization become internalizers, whereas those for whom this socialization is relatively weak become externalizers.

The innate arousability model is similar in many respects to Jones's version of the discharge model. It, too, invokes differential socialization to account for the inverse relationship between overt expressiveness and physiological responding, but the presumed direction of causality is reversed. Instead of inhibitory socialization causing increased physiological responding, it is argued that greater innate arousability causes inhibitory socialization to be more effective. More specifically, Eysenck (1967) contended that individual differences in extroversion–introversion pertain to differences in the arousal threshold of the reticular activating system. Introverts are thought to have a lower arousal threshold and are therefore regarded as more susceptible to the impact of socialization. Extroverts, by contrast, are thought to have a higher arousal threshold and therefore are less easily conditioned. Because Eysenck (like Jones) assumes that socialization includes the inhibition of overt responding, differential sensitivity to socialization should result in an inverse relationship between autonomic activity and overt expressiveness.

Lanzetta and Kleck's (1970) response conflict model also accords an important role to socialization:

> It presumes that some individuals have, during the course of their socialization, been punished for engaging in overt displays of emotionality and have learned to inhibit such displays. However, since internal states of arousal continue to be generated by affect-related stimuli, the individual tends to experience response conflict in any emotional situation between tendencies to express his arousal and tendencies to inhibit overt expression of it. (p. 18)

Assuming that this response conflict increases autonomic activity, individuals who have been strongly socialized to inhibit expressive displays should be relatively low in overt expressiveness but high in autonomic reactivity.

These three theoretical accounts are similar in many ways, which makes them difficult to distinguish empirically. Nevertheless, they can be regarded as making different predictions in certain respects. For example, whereas the discharge and response conflict models lead one to expect that the E–I distinction is associated with gender, on the grounds that males are, on the average, more strongly encouraged than females are to refrain from overt emotional expression, the innate arousability model leads one to expect an association between the E–I distinction and introversion–extroversion.

There are 13 published studies in which correlations between facial expressiveness and autonomic activity are reported, which are listed in the first column of Table 8.2. The second column indicates how the senders' emotional state was manipulated. Note that although the same stimulus was used to evoke facial expressiveness and autonomic activity in 10 studies, this was not the case in the other 3. In Field's (1982) study, neonates' facial expressiveness was rated as they watched a model pose a series of emotional expressions, whereas their heart rate was recorded during sleep. Strictly speaking, this study does not yield evidence directly relevant to the E–I distinction, in that ANS (autonomic nervous system) activity was not recorded during emotional stimulation. But it is included in the present set because it has interesting implications for the role of socialization. In Newlin's (1981) study, relatively stressful tasks (RT and Stroop) were used to generate autonomic responses, but facial expressiveness was measured in the absence of emotional stimulation. The expressiveness index is therefore not a measure of emotional expressiveness. In Notarius and Levenson's (1979) study, the subjects were first shown a stressful film, during which expressiveness was assessed. The subjects (classified as high or low in expressiveness) were then exposed to an ostensibly high threat of receiving an electric shock, during which ANS measures were taken. Although expressiveness was also monitored during shock threat, the correlation between ANS activity and expressiveness during shock threat was not reported.

The third and fourth columns of Table 8.2 summarize how expressiveness was measured and which psychophysiological parameters were recorded. Several measurement procedures were used for each of these variables.

The relationship between expressiveness and ANS activity has been assessed (1) in terms of a correlation coefficient, (2) by dividing subjects into expressiveness categories and examining mean differences in ANS activity, or (3) by dividing subjects into ANS categories and examining mean differences in facial activity. Evidence of the inverse relationship expected on the basis of the E–I distinction is strongest in the studies reported by Lanzetta and Kleck (1970), Miller (1974), and Vaughan and Lanzetta (1980). The findings of Notarius and Levenson (1979) are also consistent with the E–I distinction, although here the inverse relationship failed to appear on the electrodermal measure.

The three studies by Buck and his associates all yield evidence of an inverse relationship, but there is inconsistency across the studies with respect to the sex of the subjects in which this evidence was apparent. The findings reported by Notarius et al. (1982) also are only partly supportive of the E–I distinction: Whereas subjects low in expressiveness (LEs) exhibited greater HR change than did those high in expressiveness (HEs), there was no difference on this measure between HEs and a small group of subjects classified as *nonexpressive*, in whom one might have expected the greatest HR change. Furthermore, even the supportive difference between LEs and HEs was confined to a high-threat condition (see Notarius, 1983, and Zuckerman, 1983a,b, for a critique and defense of this study).

Evidence from the remaining five studies is either less consistent or actually inconsistent with the E–I distinction. In Field's (1982) study, neonates classified as LEs were higher (and more variable) in HR than were neonates classified as HEs – but as I noted earlier, HR was recorded during sleep. The extent to which these findings support the

Table 8.2. *Summary of research on the externalizer–internalizer distinction*

Study	Emotional stimulus	Measures Expressiveness[b]	Measures ANS[c]	Subjects[a] Gender	Subjects[a] n	Relation between expressiveness and ANS
1. Buck (1977)	Slides (4 types)	C.A. (Id and Pl)	SCRch	M	13	Id-SCRch = −0.54 Pl-SCRch = −0.55* Id-SCRch = −0.41 Pl-SCRch = −0.01
				F	12	
2. Buck et al. (1972)	Slides (5 types)	C.A. (Pl)	SCRch SCRamp RHch	M	9	Pl-SCRch = −0.55 Pl-SCRamp = −0.15 Pl-HRch = −0.21 Pl-SCRamp = −0.91† Pl-SCRamp = −0.65* Pl-HRch = −0.60*
				F	10	
3. Buck et al. (1974)	Slides (5 types)	C.A. (Pl)	SCRch HRch	M	16	Pl-SCRch = −0.74† Pl-HRch = −0.27 Pl-SCRch = −0.17 Pl-HRch = −0.43
				F	16	
4. Eisenberg et al. (1988)	Film segments (3 types)	Rated expressiveness	HRch	M + F	82	HRacc < HRdec[d]
5. Field (1982)	Facial expressions (happy, sad, surp.)	Rated expressiveness	HR	M + F	74	Lo Es > Hi Es[e] during sleep (no means reported)
6. Lanzetta & Kleck (1970)	Shocks (shock vs. no shock)	C.A. (Id)	SRLch	M	12	Id-SRLch = −0.69†
7. Miller (1974)	Problem solving for reward	C.A. (Id)	HR	M	8	Id-HR = −0.71
8. Newlin (1981)	RT task Stroop task	Expressivity during questionnaire completion	HR, SBP, DBP, FPA, SCL, SSCR	M	49	Hi Es > Lo Es for SSCRs and DBP (no means reported)

Study[a]	Film (negative)	No. of exprs. and rated expressiveness[b]	ANS measure[c]	Sex	N	Results
9. Notarius & Levenson (1979)	Shock threat		HRch RRch SCLch	M	43	FRch: Hi Es < Lo Es RRch: Hi Es < Lo Es SCLch: Hi Es = Lo Es
10. Notarius et al. (1982)	Reprimand from experimenter	Rated activity	Hrch	F	31	Hi Es < Lo Es (but No Es = Hi Es)
11. Vaughan & Lanzetta (1980)	Witnessed pain	EMG brow, eye jaw	SCLdiff	M + F	19	Brow-SCLdiff = −0.41 Eye-SCLdiff = −0.21 Jaw-SCLdiff = −0.56
12. Winton et al. (1984)	Slides (5 types)	C.A. (PI)	SCRmag HR SCRch	M	20	Corrs. range from 0.06 to 0.30 (all n.s.)
13. Zuckerman et al. (1981)	Videos (pos., neutral, neg.)	C.A. (PIdiff and Id)	SCLdiff HRdiff	M + F	44	Id-BVdiff = 0.43† PI-BVdiff = 0.30* Id-SCLdiff = 0.43† PI-SCLdiff = 0.45† Id-HRdiff = 0.13 PI-HRdiff = 0.26

[a] Subjects in all studies except Buck (1977: preschoolers), Eisenberg et al. (1988: preschoolers and second graders), and Field (1982: neonates) were adults.

[b] Expressiveness abbreviations: C.A. = communication accuracy; PI = correlation between senders' self-reported pleasantness while watching stimulus and receivers' ratings of senders' pleasantness; Id = accuracy of judgments about type of stimulus seen by sender; EMG = electromyography; Pldiff = receivers' ratings of pleasantness of facial reactions to positive scenes minus equivalent ratings of facial reactions to negative scenes.

[c] ANS abbreviations: SCRch = change in number of skin conductance responses from baseline to stimulus; HRch = change in heart rate from baseline to stimulus; SRLch = change in skin resistance level from baseline to stimulus; SCRamp = median size of largest skin conductance response during stimulus; HR = heart rate; SBP = systolic blood pressure; DBP = diastolic blood pressure; FPA = finger pulse amplitude; SSCR = spontaneous skin conductance responses; RRch = change in respiration rate from baseline to stimulus; SCLmag = magnitude of skin conductance response on initial presentation of stimulus; BVdiff = blood volume during affective scenes minus blood volume during neutral scene; SCLdiff = skin conductance level during affective scenes minus skin conductance level during neutral scene; HRdiff = heart rate during affective scenes minus heart rate during neutral scene.

[d] HRacc = subjects who exhibited HR acceleration to film; HRdec = subjects who exhibited HR deceleration to film. Difference was significant only for facial sadness.

*p < .05, †p < .1.

[e] Hi Es = subjects high in expressiveness; Lo Es = subjects low in expressiveness; No Es = subjects who showed no facial activity during scoring period.

Source: Adapted from Manstead in Hugh L. Wagner (Ed.), Social psychophysiology: Theory and clinical applications. Copyright 1988 by John Wiley & Sons, Ltd., and reprinted with their permission.

E–I distinction seems questionable without knowing whether the ANS difference between HE and LE neonates would also be found under emotional stimulation. What Field's findings do show is that there is considerable variation in neonates' facial expressiveness, which implies that differential socialization cannot be exclusively responsible for producing individual differences in facial expressiveness. Similarly, Oster (personal communication, 1988; Rosenstein & Oster, 1988) has observed individual differences in facial expressiveness, as indexed by "Baby FACS," a version of FACS adapted for use with infants, in 2-hour-old neonates. It is apparent that such differences must be based on innate temperamental factors and that a theoretical analysis accounting for the E–I distinction purely in terms of differential inhibitory socialization is too simplistic. This is an issue that I shall address in more detail later in this chapter.

Although Newlin's (1981) findings appear to be inconsistent with the E–I distinction, there are several procedural differences between his study and those in which expressiveness and ANS activity were inversely related. The most important of these is that facial expressions were overtly videotaped while the subjects were completing their questionnaires in the presence of an experimenter who attended to the subjects' eye movements (as an index of hemisphericity). This contrasts markedly with the procedures adopted in the other studies in Table 8.2, most of which were designed to tap individual differences in spontaneous emotional expressiveness.

Less easily accommodated are the findings of Zuckerman et al. (1981), Winton, Putnam, and Krauss (1984), and Eisenberg et al. (1988). In the first of these studies ANS-expressiveness correlations were positive and mainly significant; in the second they were positive and nonsignificant; in the third, male subjects classified as HR decelerators during a sad film exhibited more facial sadness than did those who showed either small deceleration or acceleration, and there was also some evidence that those subjects whose HR accelerated during a happy film exhibited more facial happiness. There are several procedural and measurement differences between Eisenberg et al.'s study and those in which evidence supportive of the E–I distinction is reported. First, the subjects were divided into accelerators or decelerators on the basis of the difference between their mean HR while viewing one of four films and mean HR during a 10-second prefilm baseline period. Second, facial expressiveness was scored by experimenters on five-point scales for each of four emotions (happiness, sadness, fear, and anxiety–apprehension). The authors interpret their findings as inconsistent with the E–I distinction, arguing that during each film facial activity and HR activity both changed in ways that would be expected on the basis of earlier research and in this sense covaried positively; however, the fact that decelerators exhibited more facial sadness could, of course, be interpreted as supporting the E–I distinction. Furthermore, as the authors themselves noted the measures of facial expressiveness and HR were not exactly concurrent.

The two studies reported by Zuckerman et al. (1981) and by Winton et al. (1984) make it unlikely that Eisenberg et al.'s findings fail to support the E–I distinction simply because of procedural variations. Both Zuckerman et al. and Winton et al. used judgment procedures similar to those used by Buck and his associates; indeed, Winton et al. used the same types of slides as those Buck used, measured expressiveness using the same pleasantness index of communication accuracy, and computed change in number of SCRs in the same way. Thus the reason for the inconsistency across studies remains obscure, although it is possible that variations across studies in the strength and quality of emotional stimuli do play an important role. It is known, for example, that sexual slides induce HR acceleration and that unpleasant (injury) slides induce HR deceleration. It follows that if the subjects in a given study were more disposed to inhibit facial reactions to sexual slides than to other slides, the HR–expressiveness correlation would be more likely to be negative than if the subjects were more disposed to inhibit facial responses to unpleasant slides than to other slides. This line of reasoning may not fully account for the discrepancies among the findings reported by different investigators, but it does illustrate the way in which type of emotional stimulus can interact with facial and autonomic measures. Once again, the advantages of working with a standard set of emotional stimuli are apparent. Future research on the E–I distinction should examine the stability of expressiveness–ANS correlations across stimuli varying in strength and quality.

On balance, there is more supportive than nonsupportive evidence for the E–I distinction. But there is scant support for the view that socialization mediates the differentiation of individuals into externalizers and internalizers. Field's (1982) study shows that individual differences in expressiveness are present from a very early age. Furthermore, Buck (1977) found some evidence of a negative expressiveness–ANS relationship (in males, at least) among preschoolers. Together these findings call into question the notion that the E–I distinction is mediated simply by socialization processes.

On the other hand, there is some evidence that the E–I distinction is associated with gender. Buck et al. (1972, 1974) found a significant tendency for females to be externalizers (i.e., above the group median in communication accuracy and below the group median in change in electrodermal activity) and for males to be internalizers. The fact that Field (1982) and Buck (1977) found no sex differences could be interpreted as consistent with the discharge model, in that the association between gender and externalizing or internalizing response mode in adults presumably depends on sex role socialization during childhood and adolescence. On the other hand, Eisenberg et al. (1988) reported a pattern of gender differences that could be construed as related to the E–I distinction, and their subjects were aged between 5 and 7. Girls were more willing than boys were to express facial sadness, and boys' HR decelerations during the sad film were related to facial expressions of sadness, whereas the girls' HR activity was unrelated to facial sadness. The authors concluded that their findings "are consistent with Buck's (1984) view that males are more likely than females to express emotion internally" (p. 245). Unfortunately, most of the other studies in Table 8.2 did not include both male and female subjects; of the two that did, Vaughan and Lanzetta (1980) did not treat gender as an independent factor, and Zuckerman et al. (1981) partialed out the influence of gender in computing their correlations but noted that this procedure "had a minimal effect on the obtained correlations" (p. 939).

Finally, there is not much evidence to support the notion that the E–I distinction is consistently related to the extroversion–introversion dimension. Although Buck et al. (1972) found extroversion to be positively correlated with communication accuracy and Buck et al. (1974) found that the externalizers' extroversion scores tended to be higher than those of the internalizers, Notarius and Levenson (1979) found no difference in extroversion between their low- and high-expressive subjects. The relationship between extroversion and facial expressiveness will be considered in more detail in the following section.

To summarize, the 13 studies considered here provide little support for the three theoretical models of the E–I distinction described earlier. Extroversion appears to be of little importance in mediating the relationship between expressiveness and ANS activity, and the only evidence that socialization plays a significant role comes from research on the relationship between gender and the E–I distinction.

Extroversion

As already noted, some researchers have explored the relationship between facial expressiveness and extroversion. One of the earliest studies in which this relationship was examined is that reported by Buck et al. (1972), who discovered that the extroversion scores of female senders were positively related to expressiveness as indexed by the categorization measure of communication accuracy. Buck et al. (1974) found that subjects classified as externalizers tended to have higher extroversion scores than did subjects classified as internalizers. However, in each case, the relationship between expressiveness and extroversion was actually rather weak. In the Buck et al. (1972) study, the relationship was based on 12 female senders and fell short of significance; in the Buck et al. (1974) study, the difference was between 11 externalizers and 11 internalizers and was significant only when the experimenter's ratings of expressiveness were used to classify the subjects as externalizers or internalizers. A somewhat more robust relationship between extroversion and facial expressiveness was reported by Cunningham (1977), although in some of the sending conditions incorporated into this relationship, the type of facial expressiveness assessed was posed rather than spontaneous.

Some studies revealed no relationship between expressiveness and extroversion. In a study using methods very similar to those of Buck and his associates, Harper, Wiens, and Matarazzo (1979) failed to find a significant relationship between communication accuracy and extroversion, and as I noted, Notarius and Levenson (1979) failed to find a significant difference in the extroversion scores of their high- and low-expressive subjects.

In trying to account for the fact that later studies have tended not to find a significant relationship between expressiveness and extroversion, Buck (1984) suggested that the Eysenck Personality Inventory (EPI; Eysenck & Eysenck, 1968) may no longer tap those facets of extroversion that relate systematically to facial expressiveness. As we have seen, however, there is very little published research in which extroversion as measured by the EPI or related measures has been strongly correlated with facial expressiveness.

Self-report measures of expressiveness

Friedman and his associates devised a self-report measure of individual differences in expressiveness, known as the Affective Communication Test (ACT). Friedman, Prince, Riggio, and DiMatteo (1980) argued that individuals who are nonverbally expressive tend to have a "dramatic flair" that is healthy and readily recognized by others. They also are likely to be in occupations or positions that entail interacting with and influencing others. ACT scores correlate quite highly, but by no means perfectly, with extroversion (see Friedman et al., 1980).

The ACT has been validated in several ways (e.g., friends' ratings, social characteristics, nonverbal skills). Friedman et al. (1980) discovered that the ACT was related to females' (but not males') ability to pose expressions, but there is not a great deal of evidence that ACT scores relate to spontaneous, rather than posed, expressiveness. Friedman et al. (1980) found that the emotional "tone" of the sessions in which raters judged nonverbal behavior seemed to be set mainly by the most expressive person in the group, as indexed by his or her ACT score. In a follow-up study, Friedman and Riggio (1981) focused more directly on the relationship between expressiveness as measured by the ACT and what they called the "spread" of emotion. They assembled 27 groups of three persons, one of whom was always high in expressiveness and two were always low. The subjects were told that the study concerned mood change, and they were asked to complete measures of current mood twice, once before and once after a 2-minute period during which they were free to look at one another but not to engage in any discussion. The mood scores of the high-expressive subjects changed significantly less than did those of the low expressives, and at the end of the session the mood scores of the low expressives were more similar to those of the high expressives than they were at the start. The authors argued that this convergence of mood toward the relatively stable mood of the high expressives resulted from the greater "facial animation" of the high-expressive subjects, although they had no formal evidence to support this interpretation.

The Test of Emotional Styles (TES) devised by Allen and Hamsher (1974) was designed to measure three dimensions of emotionality: responsiveness (intensity and frequency of covert emotional experience), orientation (propensity to seek out and enjoy emotional experiences), and expressiveness (intensity and frequency of overt expressions of affect). Harper et al. (1981) reported two studies examining the relationship between TES scores and expressiveness. The first was a slide-viewing study, in which expressiveness was assessed by the usual categorization and pleasantness measures. No relationship between TES scores and either measure of expressiveness was found for females. For males, marginally reliable relationships were found between the TES orientation and the pleasantness measure of expressiveness and between the TES expressiveness and the pleasantness measure of expressiveness. In the second study, the subjects were asked to play the role of a suspect being interviewed in connection with a crime he or she had not committed. Here expressiveness was coded in terms of the frequency, rate, and duration of negative and positive facial expressions (although no details are given of how these expressions were identified). For females, the TES orientation correlated significantly with the frequency and duration of negative facial expressions, and the TES expressiveness correlated significantly with the rate of positive expressions. For males, the TES expressiveness and responsiveness correlated significantly with the duration of positive expressions. As the authors noted, the fact that the TES expressiveness was no more consistently or strongly related to overt expressiveness than were the other two TES scales raises doubts about the meaning of the scales. But the fact that different scales related to different indices of expressiveness in males and females may simply reflect the operation of sex-differentiated display rules that vary across emotional settings.

In summary, there is some reason to believe that the ACT and TES measure constructs that relate to individual differences in facial expressiveness. There is more evidence relating to the ACT than to the TES, and in this sense the ACT is better validated. However, to date there is (to my knowledge) no published evidence that the ACT is reliably correlated with individual differences in spontaneous facial expressiveness. By contrast, there is some evidence that the TES relates to spontaneous facial expressiveness, but the evidence comes from just one study. Although the TES would appear to be a potentially useful self-report measure of expressiveness that deserves to be used more widely, there is a clear need for further research examining its validity as a measure of facial expressiveness.

The Affect Expression Rating Scale

The Affect Expression Rating Scale (AERS; Buck, 1975, 1977, 1979a) differs from the ACT and TES in that it is completed by someone other than the subject whose expressive behavior is the focus of interest. Buck devised the AERS in his research on the externalizer–internalizer distinction. His objective was to see whether individual differences in facial expressiveness in young children are related to the attributes reported by Jones (1960) as differing between high and low electrodermal responders. The scale consists of 37 items, each describing a behavior (e.g., "often shows aggression," "plays alone much of the time," "is cooperative"). The scale is completed by the children's teachers, who rate each child on a five-point scale in terms of how characteristic the behavior in question is of that child. The reliability of the ratings can be enhanced by having more than one teacher rate every child and averaging across the ratings.

Buck (1975, Study 2) found that the preschool children's scores on the AERS items were correlated with their facial expressiveness scores. Items correlating significantly and positively with expressiveness (as indexed by the pleasantness correlation measure) in both boys and girls were "Has many friends at school" and "Expresses his/her hostilities directly." Another group of items tended to correlate negatively with expressiveness. Those items for which these correlations were significant for boys and girls were "Controls his/her emotions" and "Is quiet and reserved." There were several other items that were correlated significantly (positively or negatively) with expressiveness for one sex but not the other. Better insight into these findings is provided by the results of a factor analysis by Buck (1979a). In view of the small number of subjects he used, these results must be treated with caution, although the factor structure has been replicated (Buck, 1977; Goldman, 1989). The first three factors extracted were interpreted as expressive–inhibited, antagonistic–cooperative, and independent–dependent. The factor scores on these three factors were then correlated with the boys' and girls' expressiveness scores. The expressiveness factor scores tended to be significantly positively correlated with measures of facial expressiveness in boys and girls.

Buck (1977) conducted a second study using very similar methods. Here expressiveness factor scores were significantly positively correlated with facial expressiveness in boys but not girls, and antagonism factor scores were significantly positively correlated with facial expressiveness in girls but not boys. Also available in this second study were correlations between AERS factor scores and measures of the children's electrodermal response to the slides. The boys' expressiveness factor scores were inversely related to electrodermal response, whereas the girls' antagonism factor scores were inversely related to electrodermal response. Thus the personality differences manifested in children's overt behavior related not only to their facial expressiveness but also to their autonomic responses to emotional stimuli. The nature of these relationships suggests a distinction between externalizing children (high in facial expressiveness, described by teachers as expressive [boys] or antagonistic [girls], and low in electrodermal response to emotional slides) and internalizing children (low in facial expressiveness, described by teachers as inhibited [boys] or cooperative [girls], and high in electrodermal response to emotional slides).

Buck's two studies (1975, 1977) show that the AERS is a potentially useful measure of personality characteristics that relate to facial expressiveness in ways that make reasonable intuitive and theoretical sense. But the sample sizes were small, and there are several inconsistencies in the pattern of correlations observed in the two studies. Unfortunately, there is a dearth of follow-up research using the AERS. Goldman (1989) studied the relationships among kindergartner's AERS scores, spontaneous facial expressiveness, and peer popularity, and she found a significant positive correlation between the AERS expressiveness factor scores and spontaneous facial expressiveness as assessed by the categorization measure. The boys' AERS expressiveness factor scores were also significantly positively correlated with their peer popularity. Walden and Field (1990) used the AERS as an index of "spontaneous expressivity" and also found a significantly positive correlation between expressivity and peer popularity. Although these findings concerning popularity may appear superficially to conflict with the picture of the expressive, antagonistic child that emerges from Buck's research, teacher-rated "antagonism" should not be equated with low peer popularity. Further research is needed in which the factor structure of the AERS is examined in a large sample of children, and the relationships among AERS factor scores, measures of facial expressiveness, and measures of autonomic reactivity to emotional stimuli are assessed.

Etiology of individual differences in facial expressiveness

Thus far we have seen that there is some evidence that individual differences in facial expressiveness arise from socialization. Cultural differences and gender differences, in particular, appear to result primarily from acquired dispositions on the part of some individuals to inhibit the facial expression of at least some emotions. But the research on infants and young children has revealed individual differences in expressiveness that probably reflect more than just socialization. Innate factors such as temperament may also help establish individual differences in facial expressiveness. In this section I shall consider theory and evidence relating to temperamental differences and differential socialization and shall try to show how these two strands of influence might in combination produce the individual differences in facial expressiveness.

Temperament

Temperament may be defined (cf. Lamb, 1988) as a constitutionally determined style of behavior that exhibits some temporal stability. The fact that it is constitutionally determined is not generally taken to mean that it is genetically fixed and temporally invariant; rather, the view is that temperament can be influenced at least to some degree by environment and experience.

The dimensions of behavior that constitute temperament are generally regarded as including affect. This line of thinking is most explicit in the work of Goldsmith and Campos (1982, 1986), who proposed that temperament be defined as individual differences in the probability of experiencing and expressing arousal and the primary emotions (i.e., anger, sadness, fear, joy–pleasure, disgust, interest, and surprise). Goldsmith (in Goldsmith, Buss, Plomin, Rothbart, Thomas, & Chess, 1987) contends that "temperament is emotional in nature, . . . pertains to individual differences, . . . refers to behavioral tendencies rather than actual occurrences of emotional behavior (and thus is relatively stable), and . . . is indexed by the expressive aspect of emotion" (p. 511). Goldsmith and Campos (1982) argued that the majority of other theorists' dimensions of temperament (e.g., Buss & Plomin's [1984] "sociability" or Thomas & Chess's [1977] "approach/withdrawal") can readily be incorporated into their emotion-based framework. Especially compatible with the Goldsmith–Campos approach is the work of Rothbart (e.g, Rothbart, 1986; Rothbart & Derryberry, 1981), which focuses on positive reactivity, negative reactivity, behavioral inhibition to novel or intense stimuli, and capacity to focus and shift attention. Clearly, this general approach to temperament leads one to assume that genetically endowed temperamental differences among children are manifested (partly, at least) in individual differences in facial expressiveness. Unfortunately, there are few studies of temperament that have used formal measures of facial expressiveness as a core measure, so there is, to date, rather little evidence that directly addresses this prediction (but see Malatesta et al., 1989). Research by Goldsmith and Campos (1986) showed that maternal reports of infant behavior (assessed by Rothbart's [1981] Infant Behavior Questionnaire) correlate reasonably well with laboratory composite measures of behaviors such as smiling, laughing, and distress or avoidance in the stranger approach or visual cliff situations, so there is at least some evidence that questionnaire measures of infant temperament relate systematically to individual differences in overt emotional responses to situational demands.

Another approach that is compatible with the Goldsmith–Campos approach is that of Kagan (e.g., Kagan, Reznick, Clarke, Snidman, & Garcia-Coll, 1984; Kagan, Reznick, & Snidman, 1987), who concentrated on inhibition. In two longitudinal studies of children aged 21 or 31 months to 7.5 years, Kagan and his colleagues showed a preservation of inhibited and uninhibited behavioral styles, such that approximately three quarters of those classified as either inhibited or uninhibited at 21 or 31 months were similarly classified as such at 7.5 years. Moreover, children classified as inhibited were more likely than their uninhibited counterparts to exhibit certain peripheral physiological characteristics, such as higher HR, lower HR variability, and greater HR reactivity in the test setting.

The study of temperament clearly has considerable potential in the explication of individual differences in facial expressiveness. At the risk of greatly oversimplifying the complexities of research on this topic, converging lines of evidence suggest that there are at least two – and possibly more – basic temperaments: inhibited, restrained, quiet, and shy; and uninhibited, sociable, and affectively spontaneous. It seems likely – although there is as yet little formal evidence to support this – that these two types of temperament are associated with individual differences in facial expressiveness and with individual differences in autonomic reactivity. There is great scope and a pressing need for research measuring facial expressiveness (among other indices of emotional response), but the preliminary evidence suggests that there is an innate basis for individual differences in facial expressiveness and that this basis is related to the externalizer–internalizer distinction.

Socialization

As we have seen, there are empirical grounds for arguing that the gender difference in facial expressiveness observed in adults is acquired in the course of socialization. It is one thing to state that gender differences in facial expressiveness are acquired, but quite another to provide a plausible account of the processes by which they are acquired. Fortunately, some progress has been made in addressing this difficult issue. Using the MAX coding system, Malatesta and her colleagues (Malatesta, Grigoryev, Lamb, Albin, & Culver, 1986; Malatesta & Haviland, 1982; Malatesta & Lamb, 1987) explored the role played by mothers' modeling of facial expressions and the way in which mothers respond contingently to their infants' facial expressions during the first 2 years of life. In the Malatesta and Haviland (1982) study, 60 mothers and their 3- to 6-month-old infants were videotaped during a 16-minute play period. Although the male and female infants exhibited no significant difference in the type and rate of facial expression change, the mothers were found to respond differentially to males and females. The mothers of male infants tended to match their child's expressions with similar expressions of their own, whereas the mothers of female infants tended to follow their child's expressions with dissimilar expressions of their own. The mothers showed higher levels of contingent responding (especially contingent smiling) to the smiles of older versus younger male infants. This pattern was reversed for female infants, with mothers showing lower contingent responding to older versus younger females.

In the Malatesta and Lamb (1987) study, 58 mothers and their 2-year-olds were videotaped during a 9-minute play period and in the "strange situation" developed by Ainsworth (1973). The mothers of male infants showed significant matching of infant sadness, unlike the mothers of females. On the other hand, the mothers of females showed significant matching of a "pressed lip" expression (thought to relate to anger suppression), whereas the mothers of males tended to ignore this expression. Finally, when the infants displayed full anger expressions, the mothers of girls tended to ignore such expressions, whereas the mothers of boys did not.

The notion that such differential responding to male and female infants' expressions may have an impact on the infants' pattern of facial expressions is supported by evidence from the longitudinal study reported by Malatesta et al. (1986). This research, spanning the period from 2 to 7 months of age, not only found further evidence of differential patterns of contingent responding and modeling on the part of mothers as a function of their infant's gender, but it also discovered evidence that exposure to this differentiated pattern of stimulation in time results in different patterns of expressiveness. For example, modeling by mothers of joy and interest when the infant was 5 months old was predictive of increases in infant joy and interest expressions 2.5 months later.

The research conducted by Malatesta and her associates is in need of replication, but it does suggest that the ways in which males and females express emotion facially may elicit different reactions from caregivers even at a very early age. These differences may not in themselves be sufficient to confirm a clear-cut gender difference in children's facial expressiveness, for as we have seen, such a difference does not become reliable until adolescence. However, if this differentiated pattern of contingent responding is sufficient over time to point to subtle differences in infants' facial displays of emotion, consider how much more powerful the more overt socialization effected at later ages, via verbal instruction, is likely to be.

With regard to gender differences in expressiveness, it is likely that same-sex peer groups will be important agents of socialization from puberty onward, acting to reinforce behaviors consistent with culturally endorsed sex roles. Children as young as 2 to 3 years attribute to a male doll the characteristic that "he never cries" (Kuhn, Nash, & Bruchan, 1978), and by the time they are aged 5 to 8, children know many of the sex-steretyped personality traits, including the "feminine" traits of emotionality (Best et al., 1977). Given that overt socialization tends to incorporate cultural beliefs about the appropriateness of overt emotional displays by males and females, it is hardly surprising that by adulthood males are less expressive than females are in their spontaneous facial behaviors.

Considering the socialization of individual differences in facial expressiveness more generally, one important source of influence is the child's family environment. Halberstadt (1984, 1986) argued that the expressiveness of the family environment has an impact on the child's own expressiveness, by setting norms and establishing values that encourage emotional expression. There is a reasonable amount of empirical support for this proposition (see Halberstadt, Chapter 4, this volume), although it is of course difficult to determine the degree to which parent–child similarities in expressiveness result from socialization rather than shared temperamental characteristics.

Whether the agent of socialization is the child's mother, general family environment, or same-sex peer group and whether the process of socialization is observation or more direct tuition, the content of socialization can be thought of as display rules. Since 1980 there has been a marked upsurge of research interest in children's acquisition of display rules. Although some of this research has focused on what children say they would express facially under specified circumstances (e.g., Gnepp & Hess, 1986; Saarni, 1979), other studies have examined actual facial behavior under conditions that varied with respect to the applicability of culturally given display rules. For example, Saarni (1984) observed 6- to 10-year-old children's facial expressions under two conditions: In the first they received an attractive present in return for helping the researcher, and in the second, they received a disappointing gift in return for further help. In the first situation, children typically looked pleased and expressed gratitude; in the second, most avoided overtly expressing the disappointment they presumably felt. Interestingly, there was evidence of a gender difference in the management of negative affect, in that girls were more likely to mask their disappointment with a smile, whereas boys were more likely to deintensify their disappointment into a neutral facial display. Cole (1986) extended this research by expanding the age range of the children she studied and by using FACS to code the children's facial responses to the disappointing gift. In her first study she found that children as young as 4 controlled their display of negative affect, in that they tended to exhibit positive expressions when receiving the disappointing gift. As in Saarni's study, however, there were sex differences in the management of negative affect. Female children smiled more than boys did, especially when receiving the disappointing gift; indeed, girls smiled as much when receiving this gift as the attractive one. Male children, by contrast, smiled less when receiving the disappointing gift than the attractive one. In a follow-up study of 3- to 4-year-old girls, Cole varied the setting in which the disappointing gift was received. For half the children (social condition) the experimenter was present when the child looked at the gift, and for the other half (nonsocial condition) she was absent when the child looked at it. As expected, there were significantly more positive displays and fewer negative displays on receiving the disappointing gift in the social condition, compared with the nonsocial condition. Thus even children as young as 3 or 4 attempt to control the expression of negative emotion when the circumstances call for such control. Even when they are unable to articulate a display rule verbally, children may well have internalized it and act on it appropriately.

In summary, there is growing evidence that others respond to children's facial expressions differently, according to the child's gender and that this differential reaction is associated with later individual differences in facial expressions. There is also good reason to believe that young children are familiar with sex stereotypes relating to emotionality and affective displays, and this knowledge is likely to influence the child's own expressive behavior. The expressiveness of the child's family environment has also been shown to be related to how facially expressive that person is in early adulthood. These socializing influences on expressiveness are best thought of as operating through display rules that are absorbed and/or explicitly taught during infancy and childhood.

The joint influence of temperament and socialization

It should be apparent from the research I reviewed that a comprehensive understanding of the etiology of individual differences in facial expressiveness can develop only out of a theoretical and empirical approach that embraces both temperamental differences and socialization influences. Just such an approach was taken by Malatesta and her associates (1989), in an extension of their longitudinal study (Malatesta et al., 1986) referred to earlier. One of the prime objectives of this study was to examine the roles of constitutional factors and interaction with mothers during infancy in shaping subsequent expressive behavior. Three aspects of the findings of this study are worth noting. First, in analyzing the facial expressions of 2-year-olds, Malatesta et al. found that four individual difference variables, alone or in combination, influenced the type and prevalence of affect displays in stressful and non-stressful settings: *maternal contingency* (high, medium, or low) summed over the previous three waves of the study, in which contingency was defined as the proportion of the infant's expression changes to which the mother responded with an expression change of her own; *gender attachment* (secure or insecure); and *birth status* (preterm or full term). Although the details of these findings are too complex to be reported here, the fact that all four factors had significant effects on facial expressions is in itself an indication of the complexity of the causal influences involved.

Second, the expressive behavior in infants showed some continuity over the first 2 years of life, although the wave-to-wave correlations were stronger for mothers than for infants. Again, this pattern of results suggests that expressiveness is to some degree innate but is also flexible enough to vary during infancy, presumably as a function of experience. By adulthood, however, there is more temporal stability in facial behavior.

The third finding of particular interest concerns the contribution of different factors to the prediction of specific expressions, namely, anger and sadness, exhibited by the child during "reunion" (i.e., following separation from the mother). Mothers who had previously (waves 1 to 3) responded to their infants' distress expressions with interest expressions tended to have children who exhibited less sadness during reunion at wave 4, after partialing out the effects of birth status and child's sadness during waves 1 to 3. With respect to anger expressions during the wave 4 reunion, the interaction of gender and birth status emerged as an important predictor: Female preterms expressed the most anger, followed by the male and female full terms, and then the male preterms. Maternal expressions of surprise to infant sadness also emerged as a significant predictor. Again, these findings point to the importance of the combination of temperamental factors (in the shape of birth status) and socialization influences (maternal contingencies) together with gender and attachment, in determining facial expressive behavior.

Buck (1984, 1988) proposed a neural mechanism model that takes into account both temperament and social learning (see also Field & Walden, 1982). The basic argument encapsulated by the model is that expressiveness depends on excitatory and inhibitory neural systems that are jointly determined by temperament and social learning. It is assumed that early in life there are reasonably stable individual differences in the arousal and arousability of excitatory and inhibitory neural systems and that the levels of activity in these systems in specific circumstances can be altered by social learning. Thus an initially "externalizing" temperament, which according to Buck is more susceptible to the influence of reward than punishment, should result in relatively greater overt expression of emotion if such expression is rewarded (as it might be in females or in highly expressive family environments), together with relatively little arousal, whereas an initially internalizing temperament, which is posited to be more responsive to punishment than to reward, should result in relatively little overt expression of emotion if such expression is punished (as it might be in males or in families that are very low in emotional expressiveness), together with relatively greater arousal. Of course, social learning can also work "against" initial temperamental disposition, thereby weakening the influence of the disposition. Although this model has not been submitted to any direct test, it does seem to account for a large proportion of what is known about the developmental course of individual differences in expressiveness.

Consequences of individual differences in facial expressiveness

This chapter will conclude with a brief consideration of the consequences that individual differences in facial expressiveness – howsoever these come about – may have for the individual. Although there is evidence that expressive persons tend to be perceived more positively than their less-expressive counterparts (cf. Sabatelli & Rubin, 1986), the consequences I shall focus on here are physical rather than social.

An abiding problem in emotion research is the fact that different indices of emotion (psychophysiological, self-report, facial expression, behavioral) tend not to relate to one another straightforwardly; moreover, it seems that these relationships vary from individual to individual. For example, various investigators have contended that the repression of overt expression of emotion may result in increased psychophysiological activity. Thus Fowles (1980) showed that behavioral inhibition in humans is associated with increased electrodermal activity; Waid and Orne (1982) showed that highly "socialized" individuals, whose behavior is more inhibited, exhibit higher SC levels than do their less socialized counterparts. Similarly, Hare and his colleagues (see Hare, 1978) demonstrated that sociopaths, whose behavior is low in inhibition, tend to have lower SC levels than do normal individuals. As we have seen, investigators studying the relationship between spontaneous facial expressiveness and autonomic activity have often reported negative between-subjects correlations, and Pennebaker and Chew (1985) demonstrated that the suppression of expressive behavior that is associated with deception is correlated with an increase in electrodermal activity. There are grounds, then, for thinking that the inhibition of overt expression of emotion leads to increased psychophysiological activity and that individuals who chronically suppress emotional expression are more autonomically reactive than are those who do not. Here is a basis for an individual differences analysis of emotion that links two key components of emotion. Indeed, other components could be integrated into this analysis if the notion of expression were broadened to include any behavioral index of emotion, including self-report. Individuals who are willing to express emotion by communicating it to others in the form of uninhibited facial expression, self-report, or other behaviors should in theory be characterized by low psychophysiological activity relative to those who are inhibited in expression.

A number of researchers have argued that the suppression of emotion can play a causal role in somatic illness (see, e.g., Florin, Freudenberg,

& Hollaender, 1985; Malatesta, Jonas, & Izard, 1987; Watson, Pettingale, & Greer, 1984; Wirsching, Stierlin, Hoffman, Weber, & Wirsching, 1982). The fact that individual differences in style of emotional expression have been shown to be associated with illnesses as diverse as asthma, arthritis, eczema, and cancer lends further importance to the search for an understanding of the relationships among variables such as temperament, socialization, expressiveness, and physiological activity.

Concluding comment

As I noted at the outset of this chapter, the fact that there are individual differences in facial expressiveness is readily confirmed by the everyday observation of friends and acquaintances. The research I have reviewed indicates that these individual differences are associated with nationality and gender, that they are associated with different patterns of autonomic activity and personality, that they most likely originate in temperamental differences and socialization experiences, and that they may be associated with certain physical disorders. In each case, however, the evidence is less solid than one would ideally like. One of the most obvious conclusions to draw from this review is that further research is needed on the antecedents, correlates, and consequences of individual differences in facial expressiveness.

References

Ainsworth, M. D. S. (1973). The development of mother–infant attachment. In B. M. Caldwell & H. N. Ricciuti (Eds.), *Review of child development research* (Vol. 3, pp. 1–94). Chicago: University of Chicago Press.

Allen, J. G., & Hamsher, J. H. (1974). The development and validation of a test of emotional styles. *Journal of Consulting and Clinical Psychology, 42*, 663–668.

Best, D. L., Williams, J. E., Cloud, J. M., Davis, S. W., Robertson, L. S., Edwards, J. R., Giles, H., & Fowles, J. (1977). Development of sex-trait stereotypes among young children in the United States, England, and Ireland. *Child Development, 48*, 1375–1384.

Buck, R. (1975). Nonverbal communication of affect in children. *Journal of Personality and Social Psychology, 31*, 644–653.

(1977). Nonverbal communication of affect in preschool children: Relationships with personality and skin conductance. *Journal of Personality and Social Psychology, 35*, 225–236.

Buck, R. (1979a). Individual differences in nonverbal sending accuracy and electrodermal responding: The externalizing–internalizing dimension. In R. Rosenthal (Ed.), *Skill in nonverbal communication: Individual differences* (pp. 140–170). Cambridge, MA: Oelgeschlager, Gunn & Hain.

(1979b). Measuring individual differences in the nonverbal communication of affect: The slide-viewing paradigm. *Human Communication Research, 6,* 47–57.

(1984). *The communication of emotion.* New York: Guilford Press.

(1988). *Human motivation and emotion* (2nd ed.). New York: Wiley.

Buck, R., Baron, R., & Barrette, R. (1982). Temporal organization of spontaneous emotional expression: A segmentation analysis. *Journal of Personality and Social Psychology, 42,* 506–517.

Buck, R., Baron, R., Goodman, N., & Shapiro, B. (1980). Unitization of spontaneous nonverbal behavior in the study of emotion communication. *Journal of Personality and Social Psychology, 39,* 522–529.

Buck, R., Miller, R. E., & Caul, W. F. (1974). Sex, personality, and physiological variables in the communication of affect via facial expression. *Journal of Personality and Social Psychology, 30,* 587–596.

Buck, R., Savin, V. J., Miller, R. E., & Caul, W. F. (1972). Communication of affect through facial expressions in humans. *Journal of Personality and Social Psychology, 23,* 362–371.

Buss, A. H., & Plomin, R. (1984). *Temperament: Early developing personality traits.* Hillsdale, NJ: Erlbaum.

Cole, P. M. (1986). Children's spontaneous control of facial expression. *Child Development, 57,* 1309–1321.

Cunningham, M. R. (1977). Personality and the structure of the nonverbal communication of emotion. *Journal of Personality, 45,* 564–584.

Eisenberg, N., Fabes, R. A., Bustamente, D., Mathy, R. Q., Miller, P. A., & Lindholm, E. (1988). Differentiation of vicariously induced emotional reactions in children. *Developmental Psychology, 24,* 237–246.

Ekman, P. (1972). Universals and cultural differences in facial expression of emotion. In J. Cole (Ed.), *Nebraska Symposium on Motivation* (pp. 207–283). Lincoln: University of Nebraska Press.

(1989). The argument and evidence about universals in facial expressions of emotion. In H. L. Wagner & A. S. R. Manstead (Eds.), *Handbook of social psychophysiology* (pp. 143–164). Chichester: Wiley.

Ekman, P., & Friesen, W. V. (1969). The repertoire of nonverbal behavior: Categories, origins, usage, and coding. *Semiotica, 1,* 49–98.

(1978). *Facial affect coding system.* Palo Alto, CA: Consulting Psychologists Press.

Ekman, P., Friesen, W. V., & Tomkins, S. S. (1971). Facial affect scoring technique (FAST): A first validity study. *Semiotica, 3,* 37–58.

Ekman, P., Hager, J. C., & Friesen, W. V. (1981). The symmetry of emotional and deliberate facial actions. *Psychophysiology, 18,* 101–106.

Ellgring, H. (1989). *Nonverbal communication in depression.* Cambridge: Cambridge University Press.

Eysenck, H. J. (1967). *The biological basis of personality.* Springfield, IL: Thomas.

Eysenck, H. J., & Eysenck, S. B. G. (1968). *The manual of the Eysenck Personality Inventory.* San Diego: Educational and Industrial Testing Service.

Field, T. M. (1982). Individual differences in the expressivity of neonates and young infants. In R. S. Feldman (Ed.), *Development of nonverbal behavior in children* (pp. 279–298). New York: Springer-Verlag.

Field, T. M., & Walden, T. A. (1982). Perception and production of facial expressions in infancy and early childhood. In H. Reece & L. Lipsett (Eds.), *Advances in child development and behavior,* (Vol. 16, pp. 169–211). New York: Academic Press.

Florin, I., Freudenberg, G., & Hollaender, J. (1985). Facial expressions of emotion and physiologic reactions in children with bronchial asthma. *Psychosomatic Medicine, 47,* 382–393.

Fowles, D. C. (1980). The three arousal model: Implications of Gray's two-factor theory for heart rate, electrodermal activity, and psychopathy. *Psychophysiology, 17,* 87–104.

Fridlund, A. J., & Fowler, S. C. (1978). An eight-channel computer-controlled scanning electromyograph. *Behavior Research Methods and Instrumentation, 10,* 652–662.

Fridlund, A. J., & Izard, C. E. (1983). Electromyographic studies of facial expressions of emotions and patterns of emotions. In J. T. Cacioppo & R. E. Petty (Eds.), *Social psychophysiology: A sourcebook* (pp. 243–286). New York: Guilford Press.

Friedman, H. S., Prince, L. M., Riggio, R. E., & DiMatteo, M. R. (1980). Understanding and assessing nonverbal expressiveness: The affective communication test. *Journal of Personality and Social Psychology, 39,* 333–351.

Friedman, H. S., & Riggio, R. E. (1981). Effect of individual differences in nonverbal expressiveness on transmission of emotion. *Journal of Nonverbal Behavior, 6,* 96–104.

Friesen, W. V. (1972). *Cultural differences in facial expressions in a social situation: An experimental test of the concept of display rules.* Unpublished doctoral dissertation, University of California, San Francisco.

Fujita, B. N., Harper, R. G., & Wiens, A. N. (1980). Encoding–decoding of nonverbal emotional messages: Sex differences in spontaneous and enacted expressions. *Journal of Nonverbal Behavior, 4,* 131–145.

Gallagher, D., & Shuntich, R. J. (1981). Encoding and decoding of nonverbal behavior through facial expressions. *Journal of Research in Personality, 15,* 241–252.

Gnepp, J., & Hess, D. L. R. (1986). Children's understanding of verbal and facial display rules. *Developmental Psychology, 22,* 103–108.

Goldman, C. (1989). *The relationship of inhibited and expressive emotional behavior to sending accuracy and peer relationships in kindergarten children.* Unpublished master's thesis, University of Connecticut.

Goldsmith, H. H., Buss, A. H., Plomin, R., Rothbart, M. K., Thomas, A., & Chess, S. (1987). What is temperament? Four approaches. *Child Development, 58,* 505–529.

Goldsmith, H. H., & Campos, J. J. (1982). Toward a theory of infant temperament. In R. N. Emde & R. J. Harmon (Eds.) *The development of attachment and affiliative systems* (pp. 161–193). New York: Plenum.

(1986). Fundamental issues in the study of early temperament: The Denver Twin Temperament Study. In M. E. Lamb, A. L. Brown, & B. Rogoff (Eds.), *Advances in developmental psychology* (Vol. 4, pp. 231–283). Hillsdale, NJ: Erlbaum.

Halberstadt, A. G. (1984). Family expression of emotion. In C. Z. Malatesta & C. E. Izard (Eds.), *Emotion in human development* (pp. 235–252). Beverly Hills, CA: Sage.

(1985). Race, socioeconomic status, and nonverbal behavior. In A. W. Siegman & S. Feldstein (Eds.), *Multichannel integrations of nonverbal behavior* (pp. 227–266). Hillsdale, NJ: Erlbaum.

(1986). Family socialization of emotional expression and nonverbal communication styles and skills. *Journal of Personality and Social Psychology, 51,* 827–836.

Hanna, J. L. (1984). Black/white nonverbal differences, dance, and dissonance:

Implications for desegregation. In A. Wolfgang (Ed.), *Nonverbal behavior: Perspectives, applications, intercultural insights* (pp. 373–409). Lewiston, NY: Hogrefe.

Hare, R. D. (1978). Electrodermal and cardiovascular correlates of psychopathy. In R. D. Hare and D. Schalling (Eds.), *Psychopathic behavior: Approaches to research* (pp. 107–143). New York: Wiley.

Harper, R. G., Wiens, A. N., Fujita, B. N., & Kallgren, C. (1981). Affective-behavioral correlates of the test of emotional styles. *Journal of Nonverbal Behavior, 5,* 264–267.

Harper, R. G., Wiens, A. N., & Matarazzo, J. D. (1979). The relationship between encoding–decoding of visual nonverbal emotional cues. *Semiotica, 28,* 171–192.

Hendry, J. (1986). *Becoming Japanese: The world of the pre-school child.* Manchester: Manchester University Press.

Izard, C. E. (1979). *The maximally discriminative facial movement coding system (MAX).* Newark: University of Delaware Press.

Izard, C. E., & Dougherty, L. M. (1980). *A system for identifying affect expressions by holistic judgments (AFFEX).* Newark: University of Delaware Press.

Jones, H. E. (1935). The galvanic skin response as related to overt expression. *American Journal of Psychology, 47,* 241–251.

(1950). The study of patterns of emotional expression. In M. Reymert (Ed.), *Feelings and emotions* (pp. 161–168). New York: McGraw-Hill.

(1960). The longitudinal method in the study of personality. In I. Iscoe & H. W. Stevenson (Eds.), *Personality development in children* (pp. 3–27). Chicago: University of Chicago Press.

Kagan, J., Reznick, J. S., Clarke, C., Snidman, N., Garcia-Coll, C. (1984). Behavioral inhibition to the unfamiliar. *Child Development, 55,* 2212–2225.

Kagan, J., Reznick, J. S., & Snidman, N. (1987). The physiology and psychology of behavioral inhibition in children. *Child Development, 58,* 1459–1473.

Kilbride, J. E., & Yarczower, M. (1980). Recognition and imitation of facial expressions: A cross-cultural comparison between Zambia and the United States. *Journal of Cross-Cultural Psychology, 11,* 281–296.

Kleck, R. E., Vaughan, R. C., Cartwright-Smith, J., Vaughan, K. B., Colby, C., & Lanzetta, J. T. (1976). Effects of being observed on expressive, subjective, and physiological reactions to painful stimuli. *Journal of Personality and Social Psychology, 34,* 1121–1218.

Kraut, R. E. (1982). Social presence, facial feedback, and emotion. *Journal of Personality and Social Psychology, 42,* 853–863.

Kuhn, D., Nash, S. C., & Bruchan, L. (1978). Sex role concepts of two- and three-year-olds. *Child Development, 49,* 445–451.

Lamb, M. E. (1988). Social and emotional development in infancy. In M. H. Bornstein & M. E. Lamb (Eds.), *Developmental psychology* (pp. 359–410). Hillsdale, NJ: Erlbaum.

Lambert, W. E., Hamers, J. F., & Frasure-Smith, N. (1979). *Child-rearing values: A cross-national study.* New York: Praeger.

Lanzetta, J. T., & Kleck, R. E. (1970). Encoding and decoding of nonverbal affect in humans. *Journal of Personality and Social Psychology, 16,* 12–19.

Malatesta, C. Z., Culver, C., Tesman, J., & Shepard, B. (1989). The development of emotion expression during the first two years of life: Normative trends and patterns of individual differences. *Monographs of the Society for Research in Child Development, 54,* Nos. 1–2.

Malatesta, C. Z., Grigoryev, P., Lamb, C., Albin, M., & Culver, C. (1986). Emotion socialization and expressive development in preterm and full-term infants. *Child Development, 57,* 316–330.

Malatesta, C. Z., & Haviland, J. M. (1982). Learning display rules: The socialization of emotion expression in infancy. *Child Development, 53,* 991–1003.

Malatesta, C. Z., Jonas, R., & Izard, C. E. (1987). The relation between low facial expressivity during emotional arousal and somatic symptoms. *British Journal of Medical Psychology, 60,* 169–180.

Malatesta, C. Z., & Lamb, C. (1987, August). *Emotion socialization during the second year.* Paper presented at the Annual Meeting of the American Psychological Association, New York City.

Manstead, A. S. R., Wagner, H. L., & MacDonald, C. J. (1984, May). *Subjective and autonomic effects of attenuating facial response during emotional stimulation.* Paper presented at the General Meeting of the European Association of Experimental Social Psychology, University of Tilburg, The Netherlands.

Miller, R. E. (1974). Social and pharmacological influences on nonverbal communication in monkeys and man. In L. Krames, T. Alloway, & P. Pliner (Eds.), *Advances in the study of communication and affect: Nonverbal communication* (Vol. 1, pp. 77–100). New York: Plenum.

Miller, R. E., Caul, W. F., & Mirsky, I. A. (1967). Communication of affects betwen feral and socially isolated monkeys. *Journal of Personality and Social Psychology, 7,* 231–239.

Miller, R. E., Murphey, J. V., & Mirsky, I. A. (1959). Nonverbal communication of affect. *Journal of Clinical Psychology, 15,* 155–158.

Morency, N. L., & Krauss, R. M. (1982). Children's nonverbal encoding and decoding of affect. In R. S. Feldman (Eds.), *Development of nonverbal behavior in children* (pp. 181–199). New York: Springer-Verlag.

Newlin, D. B. (1981). Hemisphericity, expressivity, and autonomic arousal. *Biological Psychology, 12* 13–23.

Notarius, C. I. (1983). Support for the discharge model of emotion: A reply to Zuckerman. *Journal of Personality and Social Psychology, 45,* 1162–1164.

Notarius, C. I., & Levenson, R. W. (1979). Expressive tendencies and physiological response to stress. *Journal of Personality and Social Psychology, 37,* 1204–1210.

Notarius, C. I., Wemple, C., Ingraham, L. J., Burns, T. J., & Kollar, E. (1982). Multichannel responses to an interpersonal stressor: Interrelationships among facial display, heart rate, self-report of emotion, and threat appraisal. *Journal of Personality and Social Psychology, 43,* 400–408.

Pennebaker, J. W., & Chew, C. H. (1985). Behavioral inhibition and electrodermal activity during deception. *Journal of Personality and Social Psychology, 49,* 1427–1433.

Rinn, W. E. (1984). The neuropsychology of facial expression: A review of the neurological and psychological mechanisms for producing facial expressions. *Psychological Bulletin, 95,* 52–77.

Rosenstein, D., & Oster, H. (1988). Differential facial response to four basic tastes in newborns. *Child Development, 59,* 1555–1568.

Rosenthal, R. (1987). *Judgment studies: Design, analysis, and meta-analysis.* Cambridge: Cambridge University Press.

Rothbart, M. K. (1981). Measurement of temperament in infancy. *Child Development, 52,* 569–578.

(1986). Longitudinal home observation of infant temperament. *Developmental Psychology, 22,* 356–365.

Rothbart, M. K., & Derryberry, D. (1981). Development of individual differences in temperament. In M. E. Lamb & A. L. Brown (Eds.), *Advances in developmental psychology* (Vol. 1 pp. 37–86). Hillsdale, NJ: Erlbaum.

Saarni, C. (1979). Children's understanding of display rules for expressive behavior. *Developmental Psychology, 15,* 424–429.

——— (1984). Observing children's use of display rules: Age and sex differences. *Child Development, 55,* 1504–1513.

Sabatelli, R. M., Buck, R., & Dreyer, A. (1980). Communication via facial cues in intimate dyads. *Personality and Social Psychology Bulletin, 6,* 242–247.

Sabatelli, R. M., & Rubin, M. (1986). Nonverbal expressiveness and physical attractiveness as mediators of interpersonal perceptions. *Journal of Nonverbal Behavior, 10,* 120–133.

Schwartz, G. E., Ahern, G. L., & Brown, S. L. (1979). Lateralized facial muscle response to positive versus negative emotional stimuli. *Psychophysiology, 16,* 561–571.

Schwartz, G. E., Brown, S. L., & Ahern, G. L. (1980). Facial muscle patterning and subjective experience during affective imagery: Sex differences. *Psychophysiology, 17,* 75–82.

Schwartz, G. E., Fair, P. L., Mandel, M. R., Salt, P., Mieske, M., & Klerman, G. L. (1978). Facial electromyography in the assessment of improvement in depression. *Psychosomatic Medicine, 40,* 355–360.

Schwartz, G. E., Fair, P. L., Salt, P., Mandel, M. R., & Klerman, G. L. (1976a). Facial expression and imagery in depression: An electromyographic study. *Psychosomatic Medicine, 38,* 337–347.

——— (1976b). Facial muscle patterning to affective imagery in depressed and nondepressed subjects. *Science, 192,* 489–491.

Sommers, S. (1984). Adults evaluating their emotions: A cross-cultural perspective. In C. Z. Malatesta & C. E. Izard (Eds.), *Emotion in adult development* (pp. 319–338). Beverly Hills, CA: Sage.

Thomas, A., & Chess, S. (1977). *Temperament and development.* New York: Brunner/Mazel.

Vaughan, K. B., & Lanzetta, J. T. (1980). Vicarious instigation and conditioning of facial expressive and autonomic responses to a model's expressive display of pain. *Journal of Personality and Social Psychology, 38,* 909–923.

Wagner, H. L., MacDonald, C. J., & Manstead, A. S. R. (1986). Communication of individual emotions by spontaneous facial expressions. *Journal of Personality and Social Psychology, 50,* 737–743.

Waid, W. W., & Orne, M. T. (1982) Reduced electrodermal response to conflict, failure to inhibit dominant behaviors, and delinquent proneness. *Journal of Personality and Social Psychology, 43,* 769–774.

Walden, T. A., & Field, T. M. (1990). Preschooler children's social competence and production and discrimination of affective expressions. *British Journal of Developmental Psychology, 8,* 65–76.

Wallbott, H. G., Ricci Bitti, P., & Bänninger-Huber, E. (1986). Non-verbal reactions to emotional experiences. In K. Scherer, H. G. Wallbott, & A. B. Summerfield (Eds.), *Experiencing emotion: A cross-cultural study* (pp. 98–116). Cambridge: Cambridge University Press.

Watson, M., Pettingale, K. W., & Greer, S. (1984). Emotional control and autonomic arousal in breast cancer patients. *Journal of Psychosomatic Research, 28,* 467–474.

Winton, W. M., Putnam, L. E., & Krauss, R. M. (1984). Facial and autonomic manifestations of the dimensional structure of emotion. *Journal of Experimental Social Psychology, 20,* 195–216.

Wirsching, M., Stierlin, H., Hoffman, F., Weber, G., & Wirsching, B. (1982). Psychological identification of breast cancer patients before biopsy. *Journal of Psychosomatic Research, 26,* 1–10.

Yarczower, M., & Daruns, L. (1982). Social inhibition of spontaneous facial expressions in children. *Journal of Personality and Social Psychology, 43,* 831–837.

Yarczower, M., Kilbride, J. E., & Hill, L. A. (1979). Imitation and inhibition of facial expression. *Developmental Psychology, 15,* 453–454.

Zuckerman, M. (1983a). A comment on Notarius, Wemple, Ingraham, Burns, and Kollar's study of emotional responses to an interpersonal stressor. *Journal of Personality and Social Psychology, 45,* 1160–1161.

(1983b). A rejoinder to Notarius. *Journal of Personality and Social Psychology, 45,* 1165–1166.

Zuckerman, M., Hall, J. A., DeFrank, R. S., & Rosenthal, R. (1976). Encoding and decoding of spontaneous and posed expressions. *Journal of Personality and Social Psychology, 34,* 966–977.

Zuckerman, M., Klorman, R., Larrance, D. T., & Spiegel, N. H. (1981). Facial, autonomic, and subjective components of emotion: The facial feedback hypothesis versus the externalizer–internalizer distinction. *Journal of Personality and Social Psychology, 41,* 929–944.

9. Social competence and nonverbal behavior

ROBERT S. FELDMAN, PIERRE PHILIPPOT,
AND ROBERT J. CUSTRINI

Introduction

By now, the importance of nonverbal behavior, from both an intra-psychic and an interpersonal perspective, is unquestioned. Beginning with Darwin's consideration of how facial expressions convey emotions to observers, there is a long history showing that nonverbal behavior plays a central role in everyday social interaction. Our ability to understand others, and the responses that we make to them, is based in large part on our ability to use effectively the nonverbal behavior that is displayed in any interpersonal interaction.

Consider, for instance, the example of two students to whom a professor has just returned their corrected midterm examinations, with the grade at the top of the paper. The classmates, seated next to each other, have very different nonverbal reactions: One smiles broadly, leaving the paper displayed on her desk, but the other frowns, sighs, and quickly puts the paper away. The first student, seeing her classmate's reaction, then tries to make eye contact with the second and adopts a look of what she hopes is sympathy, despite the fact that she can barely contain her own feelings of delight at doing well on the exam.

Although this is fairly simple social interaction – no words have been spoken – the opportunities for miscommunication are many. The success of the interaction, at least in terms of the participants' conveying what they intend to communicate, is predicated on the abilities of the interactants to encode and decode nonverbal behavior appropriately. Suppose, for example, the first student misinterprets the second student's frown and is unaware that the second has done poorly on the exam. Instead of attempting to look sympathetic, she may try to share her joy – a most inappropriate response. Or suppose the first student is inept in conveying her sympathy nonverbally, and instead her happi-

329

ness at her own success "leaks" out. In either case, the social interaction will proceed with major shortcomings.

As this simple example illustrates, it is clear that a person's ability to communicate effectively on a nonverbal level is critical to the success of particular social interactions. Indeed, one could extend the argument further and suggest that a person's general ability to interact effectively across social situations is related to his or her general level of nonverbal behavioral competence – an argument that is central to this paper.

In this chapter, we shall consider the relationship between social competence and nonverbal behavior. The basic hypothesis underlying our work is that nonverbal behavior represents a social skill that socially competent people use in their everyday social interactions. We assume that those people who are the most effective in their social interactions are successful at decoding the nonverbal behavior of others and also are able to encode nonverbally in a manner that others can understand. Conversely, we hypothesize that those who are socially deficient might suffer from a lack of nonverbal decoding and encoding skills.

To examine this hypothesis, we first shall discuss social competence and nonverbal behavior from a theoretical perspective. Next, we shall consider the empirical evidence that supports this theory. Finally, we shall present research from our own laboratory that is congruent with the hypothesis.

Social competence and nonverbal behavior: Conceptual perspectives

Social competence

Although the construct of social competence is encountered frequently throughout the psychological literature, there is no definition or conception of social competence that most researchers and theoreticians accept. For instance, the concept has been used synonymously with the terms *social skill, impression management,* and *interpersonal competence.* Moreover, a bewildering array of specific aspects of social competence have been studied over the past several decades, varying in level of analysis from the molar (e.g., peer relations; Parker & Asher, 1987) to the molecular (e.g., individuals' ability to create a specific social impression; Riggio, Tucker, & Widaman, 1987). In addition, studies of social competence have variously focused on communicative competence, emotional competence, cognitive competence, and a considerable number of other competences, and such studies have ranged the theoretical spectrum from the strictly behavioral to the psychodynamic.

In this chapter, we shall take a broad approach, considering social competence as a hypothetical construct relating to evaluative judgments of the adequacy of a person's social performance. These evaluations may be based on normative data, judgments by knowledgeable observers (parents, teachers, or peers), or performance in relation to some specific criterion.

We assume that specific social skills, overt or cognitive behaviors that an individual performs, underlie social competence. Following this approach, social competence comprises a multidimensional domain that includes (but is not limited to) verbal and nonverbal skills.

By viewing social competence as a hypothetical construct that encompasses individual and discrete social skills, we achieve several theoretical and practical advantages. First, this approach makes explicit the notion that social competence is not a univariate entity, but a set of related dimensions having behavioral, cognitive, and emotional aspects. Although such an approach precludes a single operational definition of social competence, it does permit us to consider that there are varying degrees of independence and dependence among the various subdimensions of the construct. Furthermore, by conceptualizing social competence as a hypothetical construct, we can theorize in both general and specific terms, looking simultaneously at broad aspects of social competence and narrower, more specific ones.

In this chapter, we shall concentrate on what we conceive of as a primary aspect of the construct of social competence: nonverbal behavioral skills. We view the effective use and control of nonverbal behavior during social interaction as a critical social skill, one that is related to the maintenance and facilitation of social interaction. More specifically, we suggest that both decoding and encoding skills can be viewed as manifestations of social competence. The effective decoding of others' facial expressions aids in understanding the emotions being experienced by other social interactants and thus in producing a more accurate cognitive representation of the social situation as a whole, potentially leading to more effective social interaction.

Likewise, effective nonverbal encoding is manifested by cases in which an individual displays nonverbal behavior that accurately reflects the internal state being experienced or that creates an intended impression of an internal state. If such nonverbal behavior can be appropriately decoded by others, we would expect it to facilitate social interaction, as the other interactants would be able to understand more accurately an individual's actual or intended communication.

"Effective" or "appropriate" decoding and encoding are not necessarily the same as "accurate" decoding and encoding. For example, several studies by Rosenthal and colleagues demonstrated quite convincingly that in some cases effective decoding is expressed by ignoring or overlooking certain (unintended) parts of nonverbal messages (e.g., Rosenthal & DePaulo, 1979). In these instances, the socially competent use of nonverbal behaviorial cues is demonstrated by an apparent (but not actual) lack of decoding accuracy. It is arguable whether individuals who overlook certain nonverbal cues do so because they are insensitive to the cues in the first place or if they first accurately decode nonverbal information and then determine that the cues should be disregarded. Whatever the case, it is clear that the concept of nonverbal behavioral skill, and the broader concept of social competence, is a complex one. We take the position that "effective" and "appropriate" nonverbal behavioral skill is manifested when the use of nonverbal behavior enhances the course of a social interaction and the goals of the interaction are more likely to be achieved. This point of view is supported by several converging lines of theory and research.

Nonverbal behavior as a manifestation of social competence: Theoretical considerations

Research in at least three areas supports the contention that nonverbal behavioral skills are important to determining the success of specific social interactions and more generally the social competence and adaptation of an individual. First, nonverbal behavior has been shown to be a source of information about emotional states and attitudes that is reliable and readily available to social interactants (Cacioppo, Martzbe, Petty, & Jassinary, 1988; Hall, DiMatteo, Rogers, & Archer, 1979). As such, nonverbal behaviors constitute a primary medium for the communication of affect (Buck, 1984), and they play a role in emphatic processes (Englis, Vaughan, & Lanzetta, 1982) and more generally in affective binding (Bretherton, Fritz, Zahn-Waxler, & Ridgeway, 1986). It thus seems reasonable to conclude that the successful decoding of others' nonverbal behavior aids in understanding the affect being experienced by the other social interactants and thus in producing a more accurate understanding of the social and interpersonal situation as a whole. Ultimately, decoding abilities may lead to more effective social interaction and more appropriate emphatic responding to others' emotion – thereby leading to greater social competence.

Concomitantly, the ability of an individual to express affect in a way that is understandable to others would be expected to facilitate social interaction and enhance social competence. For example, other interactants who are able to understand an individual's affective state or communication accurately would, as a consequence, be more likely to respond appropriately to this state or communication.

A second point supporting the notion of an association between nonverbal behavioral skills and social competence is that nonverbal behavior acts to regulate social interaction and communication. For example, specific patterns of eye contact or voice intonation have been proved to regulate speech turns during conversation (Rosenfeld, 1987). Furthermore, nonverbal behavior is used to comment on, provide nuances for, or correct verbal and linguistic messages. Some researchers have even contended that in many conversations more information is transmitted nonverbally than verbally (Mehrabian & Weiner, 1967). Because the ability to produce and consider these nonverbal cues is fundamental to effective conversation, it might well be expected that they would be related to overall social competence.

Finally, nonverbal behavior is the focus of social regulation and control. Display rules determine which nonverbal response is appropriate to a particular social context and the interactants' relationship (Ekman, 1984; Saarni, 1982). Similarly, decoders must understand nonverbal responses in terms of the social display rules specific to the social and cultural context. Individuals failing to comply with these rules, voluntarily or through ignorance, are likely to be considered as deviants by the members of their cultural group. Conversely, people who are aware of the display rules of a social group are expected to have considerably less difficulty in deciphering the nonverbal messages of the people with whom they are interacting (Matsumoto, Walbott, & Scherer, 1989).

In sum, several lines of study in the area of nonverbal behavior support the notion that nonverbal behavioral skills are associated with general social competence. We shall turn now to the empirical evidence that supports this contention.

Nonverbal behavior as a manifestation of social competence: Empirical support

The argument that there is a relationship between social competence and nonverbal behavioral skills is substantiated by a variety of studies. We shall first consider research that compares subjects labeled in some way as "disturbed" with a typical group.

Disturbed versus nondisturbed populations. Several investigators have attempted to identify potential differences between the nonverbal skills of normal populations and those with psychological or psychiatric disturbances, with the bulk of these focusing primarily on the subjects' ability to decode various expressions of emotion. In one such study conducted by McCown, Johnson, and Austin (1986), a group of adolescent male delinquents (from a medium-security youth correctional facility) were compared with a group of same-aged males who were judged to be at high risk for delinquency but who had not yet engaged in such behavior. The subjects were presented with a series of 60 slides selected from Ekman and Friesen's (1975) Photographs of Facial Affect, in addition to 8 slides portraying individuals in a neutral emotional state. The authors found that the delinquent group was significantly less accurate in decoding facial expressions of the six primary emotions of interest (anger, disgust, fear, happiness, sadness, and surprise). They hypothesized that the ability to decode another's affective state may be a socially acquired ability that is influenced largely by the child's home environment and that delinquents may have come from families from which appropriate parental modeling was absent.

In a similar study of decoding ability, Zabel (1979) compared groups of elementary and junior high school–aged students from both regular schools and special schools for children with emotional problems judged "too severe to be accommodated or remediated in regular schools." Using an emotion recognition task similar to that used by McCown, Johnson, and Austin (1986), the subjects (aged 7 to 15) each were presented with a series of 42 photographs selected from Ekman and Friesen's (1975) Photographs of Facial Affect. To be sure the subjects understood what they were to do, examples were given for each category, such as "A person who is having fun would probably be happy" or "Someone who is going to throw away a rotten egg, but drops it and it smells really bad, would probably be disgusted." Zabel found the disturbed groups to be less adept for both overall decoding ability and several different emotions.

Additional evidence of a possible link between social competence and decoding ability was provided by Camras, Grow, and Ribordy (1983), who compared groups of physically abused and/or neglected children with a group that was not suspected to have suffered such abuse. The subjects were males and females ranging in age from 3 to 6 years. Measures of decoding ability – again, using a forced-choice picture identification procedure similar to those described in the previously mentioned studies – indicated that the abused children in their sample were less accurate than were those who did not have a history of abuse. Teacher ratings of the two groups also showed that the abused children were viewed by their instructors as less socially competent than the comparison group was.

In another decoding study (Walker, 1981), groups of schizophrenic, anxious-depressed, unsocialized-aggressive, and typical control children (aged 9 to 13) were given Izard's (1971) Cross-Cultural Test of Emotion Recognition. This test consists of 32 photographs of adult male and female faces, each depicting one of eight emotions – anger, disgust, fear, interest, joy, sadness, shame, or surprise – with 4 photos for each category. Eight index cards printed with a commonly recognized name for each emotion were placed in front of the subject, who was then asked to match one of the labels to each photograph as it was presented.

Walker's (1981) results were less clear-cut than those obtained in the previously mentioned studies. Those children diagnosed as schizophrenic were significantly less proficient at decoding than were the other three groups; differences between the control group and the other two experimental groups, however, were not statistically significant. Walker suggested that the poor performance of the schizophrenic children is best explained by the fact that they exhibited greater social impairment than did either the control or the less severely disturbed groups but also noted that it is unclear whether such decoding deficits preceded social withdrawal or were a result of the process.

An unfortunate oversight in each of the aforementioned investigations is the lack of attention paid to the subjects' encoding accuracy or ability. We are left to wonder whether, as one might expect, the relationship between encoding skills and impaired social competence is also significant and, if so, how the two are related. In an attempt to address this issue, Feldman, White, and Lobato (1982) used measures designed to assess both decoding and encoding proficiency. The authors compared groups of emotionally disturbed and normal adolescent males (aged 13 to 16) on their ability to recognize and produce generalized (i.e., nonspecific) affective states. Within these two populations, the subjects were further divided into "high" and "low" social competence groups based on teacher or therapist ratings. Film scenes designed to elicit positive, neutral, or negative emotional reactions were presented to all the subjects, who were asked to rate their response to each on a five-point scale ranging from "very unpleasant" to "very pleasant." During this rating procedure, the subjects' nonverbal responses were also recorded on videotape.

To assess encoding accuracy, the subjects' nonverbal responses to each scene were similarly rated by a group of undergraduates. Decoding accuracy was measured by presenting others' nonverbal responses and asking the subjects to rate them on the same scale. Results showed that the normal adolescents were significantly more accurate in encoding and decoding than were their emotionally disturbed peers. Within the two populations, a positive relationship was also identified between level of social competence and encoding accuracy; decoding ability, however, did not vary as a function of this factor within groups.

Differences within nonclinical populations. We have seen that there are clear differences between the nonverbal abilities of certain clinical and nonclinical populations, with disturbed, delinquent, and abused children demonstrating less skill in recognizing – and in some cases producing – various facial expressions of affect. But what about the normal population? Can similar differences be observed in nonverbal ability between those who are only marginally successful at managing their interpersonal life and those who excel in social situations? The evidence available thus far seems to indicate that the answer to this question is a tentative yes.

The most common methodological approach to this question has been the use of sociometric measures. In one such study aimed at identifying differences in decoding accuracy between elementary school children who were relatively more or less popular with their peers, Edwards, Manstead, and MacDonald (1984) used a self-report scale asking groups of 8- to 11-year-olds how friendly they were with each of their classmates. They then selected those scoring highest and lowest on this measure for assignment to one of two experimental groups. Subjects were shown a series of photographs depicting adults or children demonstrating facial expressions of six emotions: anger, disgust, fear, happiness, sadness, and surprise. The pictures were presented one at a time in the company of a list of emotional categories that was both read and displayed, and the subject was asked to indicate the emotion being portrayed by each. The authors found a significant main effect due to sociometric status, with the popular children demonstrating greater skill in identifying emotional expressions than their less socially successful peers.

In another sociometric study of 60 kindergartners (Spence, 1987), the subjects were shown a collection of photographs displaying all of the members of their class and asked to identify three classmates with whom they would most and least like "to work on a painting with, play a game with and sit with during story time." The total number of positive and negative nominations for each child was computed. Their affective decoding ability was then measured by having the children label a selection of 12 posed photographs depicting both adults and children experiencing the emotions of anger, disgust, fear, happiness, sadness, or surprise. Spence found a strong correlation between the number of positive peer nominations received by an individual and his or her accuracy in correctly identifying the emotions portrayed in the photographs. Similar results were obtained by Vosk, Forehand, and Figueroa (1983) who reported significant differences between popular and unpopular children in their ability to perceive and identify affective reactions in others.

In a study using adult subjects, Christenson, Farina, and Boudreau (1980) looked at the nonverbal perceptual abilities of females attaining high or low scores on the Greengrass–Jain Scale of Social Competency (a self-report measure). They found that although those with low scores on this scale were generally as able to recognize nonverbal messages as were those with high scores, low-scorers were less likely to adjust their behavior in a socially appropriate manner.

Finally, Reichenbach and Masters (1983) showed slides of children's facial expressions to groups of preschoolers and third graders. Though the population was essentially a nonclinical one, the authors found a significant positive correlation between family stability and the subjects' ability to identify the emotions portrayed in the slides. They further found that children from "disrupted" families were less likely to misapply the label *happiness* but more likely to misjudge a given expression as *anger*. The authors hypothesized that "significant experiences may thus influence social and personality processes in ways that are not immediately detectable but which might possibly lead to eventual adjustment problems" (p. 1003).

Within the general population, the connection between social competence and encoding ability is less clear, and this is due in part to the relative lack of scientific attention given to this relationship. Buck (1975) found children's encoding ability to be positively correlated with aggression, sociability, and bossiness and negatively correlated with shyness and inhibition. But in a sociometric study looking at college women identified by peers as possessing either excellent or poor social skills, Goldenthal (1985) discovered that the two groups did not differ significantly in encoding ability.

Summary. Taken as a whole, the findings obtained in these studies strongly suggest that a high degree of skill and understanding in the area of human facial expressiveness is closely associated with social competence in children and adults. But they raise a number of questions as well. We can safely assume that a high level of decoding accuracy is a skill that will likely prove valuable to all individuals. But what about encoding accuracy? Is the socially competent person one who consistently and accurately conveys his or her affective state to others? Or is it more adaptive to be selective about displaying cues that might reveal one's true feelings?

Furthermore, those studies examining subjects' ability to decode specific categories of emotion (e.g., happiness, sadness, fear) used posed rather than spontaneous, naturally occurring stimuli in attaining their measures. Because such stimuli are typically much clearer than those to which we are normally exposed, to what degree can these results be generalized to everyday situations?

Finally, the previous studies tell us little about the development of decoding and encoding skills and their relationship to social competence, nor do they indicate methods for remediating deficits in nonverbal behavioral skills. We shall turn now to a series of studies that we conducted, designed to begin to respond to some of the remaining questions.

Research on social competence and nonverbal behavior

Decoding facial expression of emotion: Social competence and age effects

We have argued that nonverbal behavioral skills might well be considered a central component of more general social competence, and the results of previous investigations support that notion. Surprisingly, though, almost none of this research has been carried out on children between 3 and 5 years of age, a period that is crucial to the development of nonverbal skills in general. Indeed, it is at this particular period that children's abilities to recognize and label facial expression are established and develop dramatically (Camras & Allison, 1985; Charlesworth & Kreutzer, 1973; Ekman & Oster, 1982). It seems pertinent, then, to examine the relationship between nonverbal behavioral and social competence in this age group. Furthermore, a link between some forms of early social skills and later adjustment is being established (e.g., Parker & Asher, 1987).

To explore the relationship between facial expression decoding skills and social competence in early childhood, we conducted an experiment using a group of 3- to 5-year-olds (Philippot & Feldman, 1990). In this study, male and female preschoolers were assigned (using a median split) to either a high or low social competence group on the basis of their score on the Social Competence scale of the Achenbach Child Behavior Checklist (Achenbach & Edelbrock, 1982). This scale, completed by the subjects' parents, assesses a child's performance in areas such as peer and family relations, participation in organized groups, and recreational activities. This well-standardized scale constitutes a reliable measure of social competence in normal populations. Furthermore, it is not correlated with intelligence.

Each subject was shown nine 10- to 20-second videotaped silent scenarios, with three for each of three emotion categories (happiness, sadness, and fear). Each scenario consisted of an adult character participating in a setting that typically evoked a specific emotion. The script of each scenario was designed so that preschoolers could readily understand the situation. For example, one of the happiness scenarios depicted a protagonist who was receiving a birthday present, and one of the fear clips showed an individual being menanced by an intruder.

In each of the scenes, the protagonist's face was blacked out electronically. After being trained in the procedure, the subjects were asked to choose a face appropriate to the scenario from among three photographs of an adult model who was displaying the emotion of happiness, sadness, or fear.

Results. The outcome of the study was clear: As expected, the higher social competence subjects, who averaged 80% correct responses, were more successful decoders of facial expression than were the lower social competence subjects, who scored an average of 69% correct responses.

These results largely confirmed the hypothesis that social competence is significantly related to skill in the recognition of facial expression of emotion. The results suggest that even before the acquisition of social display rules – which begin to be learned around 3 years of age (Saarni, 1979) – basic processes in the decoding of fundamental emotion displays may be impaired in poorly socially skilled children.

Several secondary findings are noteworthy. First, decoding abilities improved with age, with performance in the recognition of facial expression improving significantly between 3 and 5 years of age. No previous study that has investigated this particular age range found an improvement in decoding abilities, suggesting that the procedure used in this study is particularly sensitive. The developmental trends also support the notion that the recognition of facial expressions and the knowledge of their relationships to specific situations are learned during the early years of childhood.

The results of the experiment also provided information regarding the relative decodability of various emotions. Comparable to earlier research, happiness was the easiest facial expression to recognize. However, contrary to the findings of two previous studies (Camras & Allison, 1985; Kirouac & Dore, 1983) that investigated similar age groups, sadness appeared to be more difficult to recognize than fear was. The difference between our results and previous findings may be methodological: Our study used more naturalistic stimuli than did earlier experiments, which employed verbal descriptions of emotional scenarios, rather than the videotaped scenarios such as we used.

In conclusion, the experiment demonstrated a relationship in preschool-aged children between the recognition of facial expressions and social competence. The fact that this relationship was demonstrated in very young children further suggests that the decoding deficits of poorly socially skilled individuals may be acquired early in life. The results are also strengthened by the fact that the relationship with social competence was found in a normal population.

What the results do not tell us, however, is whether the relationship between social competence and nonverbal skills is relegated to nonverbal decoding skills alone or if it holds for encoding skills as well. Furthermore, the decoding stimuli used in the study were posed photographs of prototypical emotional expressions. Such a procedure provides little information regarding the decodability of spontaneous, naturally occurring facial expressions. To overcome these drawbacks, as well as to extend the findings to a different population, we carried out a second experiment.

Children's social competence and nonverbal encoding and decoding of emotion

In our subsequent study (Custrini & Feldman, 1989), we examined an older age group: children aged 9 to 12. In the same experiment we also examined both decoding and encoding skills.

In the study, groups of children demonstrating above- and below-average levels of social competence were compared on their accuracy in both decoding and encoding various facial expressions of emotion. A series of videotaped film clips (each tested and shown to evoke reliably a specific type of reaction) was used to assess each subject's spontaneous encoding accuracy, and scenes of others naturalistically reacting to the same clips were used to measure their skill in decoding naturally occurring facial expressions of emotion.

Based on our earlier research and the findings of others, we hypothesized that children with below-average levels of social competence would be less accurate in both decoding and encoding facial expressions related to emotional expressivity. We also examined the possibility that children's gender would play a significant role in determining their encoding and decoding accuracy. Specifically, because earlier work had found that females generally show greater skill than males do at both encoding and decoding (e.g., Buck, 1982; Buck, Baron, Goodman, & Shapiro, 1980; Fugita, Harper, & Wiens, 1980; Hall, 1984), we reasoned that the nonverbal behavioral skills assessed in the study might appear differentially in girls and boys.

Approximately 50 motion picture film clips, each 2 to 3 minutes in length, were previewed and tested as part of an initial evaluation and pilot testing. Each was chosen for its anticipated effectiveness in evoking one of five types of emotions: anger, disgust, fear–surprise, happiness, or sadness. From this initial group, 10 film clips (2 for each category of emotion) were selected as stimuli for the encoding task in the experiment. They were chosen for their relative purity (i.e., their effectiveness in evoking a single category of emotion) and their ability to elicit moderate levels of arousal in those who viewed them.

The decoding stimuli consisted of a set of 20 viewer reaction sequences showing adults reacting to the film clips. Four encoders (two males and two females) were videotaped, and their reactions to specific 3- to 5-second segments of the clips were rated by a group of undergraduates. All five emotional categories were represented by each of the four encoders.

Our subjects were males and females, aged 9 to 12, recruited from the classrooms of two public elementary schools. They were assigned to one of two experimental groups based on their level of interpersonal functioning as indicated by parental responses to items on the Social Competence scale of the Achenbach Child Behavior Checklist for this particular age group (Achenbach & Edelbrock, 1982). This scale assesses a child's performance in areas such as peer and family relationships, school functioning, and involvement in recreational activities.

In the encoding phase of the experiment, the subjects watched the 10 film clips and were asked to identify their own reactions by choosing between one of five categories of emotion: anger, disgust, a combination of fear and surprise, happiness, and sadness. Their reactions were videotaped during the screening and then shown to a group of undergraduate raters who tried to identify the category of emotion encoded by the subject. If a rating matched the emotional response reported by the subject at the time of encoding, then he or she was said to have encoded an accurate response to that clip.

In the decoding phase, subjects were told that they would see a series of people who had watched movie clips similar to the ones that they had just viewed. Each subject was shown a silent tape containing a selection of viewer reaction sequences and was asked to indicate which of the five emotional categories was being displayed.

Results. As we expected, the high–social competence children showed a greater overall level of accuracy than their less socially competent peers did, for both encoding and decoding. This finding, however, was modified by a significant interaction between group and sex. Whereas males in both the above- and below-average social competence groups attained mean scores that were virtually identical (57.0% and 57.4%, respectively), females showed relatively large differences: Those demonstrating above-average levels of social competence attained a mean score of 62.9%, whereas the mean for the below-average group was only 47.2%. The overall difference based on social competence level, then, is due largely to differences between the high- and low-competence groups of females.

Although predominately restricted to females, the demonstration of significantly different levels of encoding and decoding accuracy by our two social competence groups provides strong evidence for the relevance of facial expressions to communicating information to others. Results of the current investigation showed that children with above-average levels of social competence were in fact more accurate not only in decoding facial expressions of emotion (as previous studies have indicated) but also in encoding such expressions in response to affect-inducing stimuli. This finding is particularly noteworthy because of the nature of the stimuli used to identify these differences. Rather than showing that children with varying social capabilities differ in their ability to produce posed facial expressions and to identify such artificial expressions in others, this investigation has shown that such children differ in the degree of encoding and decoding accuracy demonstrated in response to naturally occurring stimuli.

As we noted earlier, the combined effects of gender and social competence level revealed significant differences among groups. Females showed marked disparities in their overall accuracy scores depending on their level of social effectiveness, whereas males did not. This finding suggests that success at encoding and decoding facial expressions contributes much more to the general social competence of females than to males. One possible explanation for this is that male children in our culture have traditionally been encouraged to refrain from providing any external cues when experiencing strong affect, for such behavior is often seen as a sign of weakness or vulnerability, especially as it relates to the expression of fear or sadness. Females, however, are expected to behave more "emotionally" and are therefore given freedom to reveal their feelings – both verbally and nonverbally.

An alternative explanation for this gender disparity is the fact that males are often taught to behave actively and aggressively when attempting to communicate their thoughts and needs to those around them (Brooks-Gunn & Matthews, 1979; Maccoby & Jacklin, 1974). Females, on the other hand, are expected to use more passive means to express themselves and may therefore rely more heavily on nonverbal communication channels such as facial expressions or body posture when interacting with others.

Of course, the gender differences found in this study must be replicated in future work before placing too much credence in them. For example, in the first study we discussed, the effect of social skills was not modified by the sex of the subjects. If it is replicated, though, this finding will be important from a theoretical perspective because it relates social competence and nonverbal capabilities to socialization processes.

The major findings of this study, coupled with those obtained in earlier investigations, clearly demonstrate that a high degree of skill and understanding in the area of human facial expressiveness is associated with general social competence in children. For females in particular, knowledge of (and the skill to convey successfully) such nonverbal cues may enhance the ability to interact effectively with one's social environment. And although a limited capability in this area does not appear to have a detrimental effect on males' ability to function interpersonally, giving children of both sexes a greater understanding of nonverbal communication channels in general (and facial expressions in particular) can only heighten their sensitivity to the thoughts and feelings of those around them.

Training nonverbal behavioral decoding skill

Our two initial studies clearly indicate a relationship between the level of social competence displayed by children and their nonverbal behavioral skills. They also show that there are wide individual differences in the success with which people are able to encode and decode nonverbally. Such findings raise an intriguing possibility: that it may be possible to increase the level of nonverbal behavioral deficiency through training procedures. Furthermore, although our previous results do not inform us about the direction of causality, it is possible that by raising a person's level of nonverbal proficiency we might bring about a resultant increase in his or her general social competence.

Although such a possibility seemed quite speculative, we pursued it by developing a strategy to enhance the decoding abilities of children. Although at least two studies have attempted to improve adults' decoding abilities (Rosenthal & Berkowitz, cited in Rosenthal et al., 1979, pp. 334–37; Zuckerman, Koestner, & Alton, 1984), they had only mixed success. Furthermore, no systematic efforts have been made to increase intentionally the level of nonverbal decoding in children. Such an issue has implications on both a theoretical level (for understanding the development of nonverbal behavioral skills in general) and an applied level (for introducing the possibility of remediating the nonverbal deficits of children with low social competence).

In the experiment, a group of fifth- and sixth-grade subjects were asked to identify three of the emotions represented in the video segments used in our second study – happiness, sadness, and fear. In the first phase of the experiment, each subject was shown a series of video segments of a stimulus person and then asked to choose which emotion the person in the segment appeared to be expressing. After viewing each clip, the subjects in the experimental group were told the appropriate answer and then shown the same segment a second time. The control subjects also watched the segment again after making a response but received no feedback.

The test phase of the experiment was conducted after a short break, when the subjects were again shown a set of video segments and asked to identify the emotion that they thought the person was experiencing. In this part of the experiment, none of the subjects received feedback, and each segment was shown only once.

As anticipated, the results showed that subjects who received training showed significantly greater decoding accuracy ($M = 77\%$, corrected for guessing) than did the subjects who did not receive training ($M = 68\%$, corrected for guessing). Overall, then, the training procedure improved our subjects' ability to interpret facial expressions. But the training also proved to be differentially effective according to the specific emotion being tested. Specifically, the subjects in the training group performed significantly better on fear stimuli than did the subjects in the control group, whereas differences between trained and control subjects were not statistically significant for happiness and sadness stimuli.

The results clearly indicate that nonverbal decoding can be improved through a simple training procedure, in which subjects are given feedback on the correct response. Yet it also demonstrates that the procedure is not universally effective, given the differential improvement according to the specific emotion being decoded.

These findings also do not give us information about the long-term generalization of improvements or if there were subsequent changes in social competence levels. It seems rather unlikely that a short experiment such as this, in which decoding skills are shown to be temporarily enhanced, would produce effects that lasted beyond the experimental situation. Nor is it likely that the improvement would be sufficient to change overall social competence – even if a causal relationship had been established. Clearly, a more powerful procedure for training nonverbal skills, one that requires more practice, would be desirable.

Still, the results are intriguing and provocative. They suggest that the procedure is reasonable and that future research might well use similar training strategies involving other emotions. Furthermore, it suggests a mechanism by which social competence might be enhanced: the improvement of nonverbal decoding abilities.

Implications and prospects

The empirical data that we reviewed, as well as the theoretical arguments that we presented, support the idea that there is a general relation between nonverbal behavioral skills and social competence. But this association has been established only correlationally. None of the studies we reviewed specifies the processes by which this relation occurs. Thus, many questions remain unanswered about the direction and mechanism of the relation between nonverbal skills and social competence.

We suggested earlier that nonverbal skills are an aspect of social competence, conceptualized as a hypothetical and multidimensional construct. This theoretical position implies that any change in nonverbal behavioral competence and performance should affect an individual's general social functioning. Thus, improving the capacity to decode or encode nonverbal behavior in people relatively unskilled in this domain should concurrently improve their social competence.

Although this statement implies that there is a direct causal and directional relation in which nonverbal skills produce social competence, we do not believe this to be the only plausible sequence of causality. The different components constituting social competence are probably interactive, and hence improvements in any of the several dimensions of social competence could affect nonverbal performance. For example, developing the capacity to affiliate is likely to increase the frequency of social interaction, which in turn would offer more opportunities to learn and develop sensitivity to nonverbal cues. Similarly, improving one's understanding of social situations would allow one to identify relevant social cues and thus would offer more occasions in which nonverbal behaviorial skills could be practiced. Therefore, it seems unreasonable to conclude that there is a one-way causal relation between nonverbal skills and social competence. Rather, we think that the different dimensions making up social competence are dependent on one another and that these various aspects are continually interacting.

The study of the relationship between nonverbal behavioral skills and social competence takes us in several promising directions. For example, one way to examine the mechanism of the relationship between social competence and nonverbal skills is to determine how this relationship appears and develops during childhood. Although the development of nonverbal decoding capacities is well documented, at least at the descriptive level (Ekman & Oster, 1982), less is understood about how the relation between nonverbal decoding and social competence changes over time. Furthermore, although the relation between social competence and nonverbal decoding has been well established in grade school–aged children, more experimental evidence is needed to trace this relationship in preschool-aged and younger children.

We also need a greater understanding of the ways in which gender interacts with nonverbal behavioral skills. As we found in our second study, there is a relationship between social skills and nonverbal skills for girls but not boys. Although such a finding is not entirely surprising in light of the broader nonverbal performance differences favoring females over males, we still expected that the more socially competent males would display better encoding and decoding skills than would the less socially competent males. The fact that they did not suggests that nonverbal behavior may be a less-central component of boys' social competence, and further research is needed to explore this possibility.

If we are correct in our assumption that nonverbal behavioral skills are a component of general social competence, we will need to demonstrate that the enhancement of nonverbal skills leads to improved social competence. Although our research suggests that improvement of nonverbal decoding skills is possible, we are a long way from showing that these improved decoding skills in fact enhance social competence.

We also need to use more precise measures of social competence and examine the subcomponents of the construct and their relationship to nonverbal behavior skills. It is possible that very general measures of social competence cannot establish precisely which aspects of social functioning and adaptation are related to specific nonverbal capacities or processes.

The study of the relationship between nonverbal behavioral skills and social competence holds important practical implications for therapy, education, and many other fields concerned with improving social adaptation and competence. Thus, we need training studies investigating (1) whether it is possible to establish socially appropriate nonverbal reponses and to teach them to individuals who are experiencing nonverbal deficits, and (2) whether, once trained to improve their nonverbal skills, the social competence of these individuals will improve.

Further research is also needed to understand the ontogeny and development of both social competence and nonverbal skills. Although it is clear that individuals show large individual differences, we know less about the source of such skills. One could hypothesize that the deficits in nonverbal skills and/or in social competence originate from a familial environment in which the parents themselves are lacking these skills. Still, without further research, these hypotheses remain speculative.

References

Achenbach, T. M., & Edelbrock, C. S. (1982). *Manual for the Child Behavior Checklist and Child Behavior Profile*. Burlington: Department of Child Psychiatry, University of Vermont.

Beck, L., & Feldman, R. S. (1989). Enhancing children's decoding of nonverbal behavior. *Journal of Nonverbal Behavior, 13*, 269–278.

Blanck, P. D., Buck, R., & Rosenthal, R. (1986). *Nonverbal communication in the clinical context*. University Park: Pennsylvania State University Press.

Bretherton, I., Fritz, J., Zahn-Waxler, C., and Ridgeway, D. (1986). Learning to talk about emotions: A functionalist perspective. *Child Development, 57*, 529–548.

Brooks-Gunn, J., & Matthews, W. (1979). *He and she: How children develop their sex-role identity*. Englewood Cliffs, NJ: Prentice-Hall.

Buck, R. (1975). Nonverbal communication of affect in children. *Journal of Personality and Social Psychology, 31*, 644–653.

(1982). Spontaneous and symbolic nonverbal behaviors and the ontogeny of communication. In R. S. Feldman (Ed.), *The development of nonverbal behavior in children* (pp. 29–62). New York. Springer-Verlag.

(1984) *The communication of emotion*. New York: Guilford Press.

Buck, R., Baron, R., Goodman, N., & Shapiro, N. (1980). The unitization of nonverbal behavior in the study of emotion communication. *Journal of Personality and Social Psychology, 39*, 522–529.

Cacioppo, J. T., Martzbe, J. S., Petty, R. E., & Tassinary, L. G. (1988). Specific forms of facial EMG response index emotion during an interview: From Darwin to the continous flow hypothesis of affect-laden information processing. *Journal of Personality and Social Psychology, 54*, 592–604.

Camras, L. A., & Allison, K. (1985). Children's understanding of emotional facial expressions and verbal labels. *Journal of Nonverbal Behavior, 9*, 84–94.

Camras, L. A., Grow, J. G., & Ribordy, S. C. (1983). Recognition of emotional expression by abused children. *Journal of Clinical Child Psychology, 12*, 325–328.

Charlesworth, W., & Kreutzer, M. (1973). Facial expressions of infants and children. In P. Ekman (Ed.), *Darwin and facial expression, a century of research in review* (pp. 91–168). New York: Academic Press.

Christenson, D., Farina, A., & Boudreau, L. (1980). Sensitivity to nonverbal cues as a function of social competence. *Journal of Nonverbal Behavior, 4*, 146–156.

Custrini, R., & Feldman, R. S. (1989). Children's social competence and nonverbal encoding and decoding of emotion. *Journal of Child Clinical Psychology, 18*, 336–342.

Darwin, C. (1872). *The expression of the emotions in man and animals*. London: John Murray.

Duncan, D. B. (1955). Multiple range and multiple *F* tests. *Biometrics, 11*, 1–42.

Edwards, R., Manstead, A. S. R., & MacDonald, C. J. (1984). The relationship between children's sociometric status and ability to recognize facial expressions of emotion. *European Journal of Social Psychology, 14,* 235–238.

Ekman, P. A. (Ed.). (1982). *Emotion in the human face* (2nd ed.). Cambridge: Cambridge University Press.

(1984). Expression and the nature of emotion. In K. Scherer (Ed.), *Approaches to emotion.* Hillsdale, NJ: Erlbaum.

Ekman, P. A., & Friesen, W. V. (1975). *Photographs of facial affect recognition test.* Palo Alto, CA: Consulting Psychologists Press.

Ekman, P. A., Friesen, W. V., & Ellsworth, P. (1982). What are the relative contributions of facial behavior and contextual information to the judgment of emotion? In P. Ekman (Ed.), *Emotion in the human face* (2nd ed., pp. 111–127). Cambridge: Cambridge University Press.

Ekman, P., & Oster, H. (1982). Review of research, 1970–1980. In P. Ekman (Ed.), *Emotion in the human face* (2nd ed., pp. 147–173). Cambridge: Cambridge University Press.

Englis, B. G., Vaughan, K. B., and Lanzetta, J. T. (1982). Conditioning of counter-empathic emotional responses. *Journal of Experimental Social Psychology, 18*(4), 375–391.

Feldman, R. S., White, J. B., & Lobato, D. (1982). Social skills and nonverbal behavior. In R. S. Feldman (Ed.), *Development of nonverbal behavior in children* (pp. 259–277). New York: Springer-Verlag.

Field, T. M., & Walden, T. A. (1982). Production and discrimination of facial expressions by preschool children. *Child Development, 53,* 1299–1301.

Fridlund, A. J., Ekman, P. A., & Oster, H. (1987). Facial expressions of emotion. In A. W. Seigman & S. Feldstein (Eds.), *Nonverbal behavior and communication* (pp. 143–224). Hillsdale, NJ: Erlbaum.

Fugita, B. N., Harper, R. G., & Wiens, A. N. (1980). Encoding–decoding of nonverbal emotional messages: Sex differences in spontaneous and enacted expressions. *Journal of Nonverbal Behavior, 4,* 131–145.

Goldenthal, P. (1985). Posing and judging facial expressions of emotion: The effects of social skills. *Journal of Social and Clinical Psychology, 3,* 325–338.

Gresham, F. M. (1986). Assessment of social skills. *Journal of School Psychology, 19,* 120–133.

Hall, J. A. (1984). *Nonverbal sex differences: Communication accuracy and expressive style.* Baltimore: Johns Hopkins University Press.

Hess, U., Kappas, A., and Scherer, K. R. (1988). Multichannel communication of emotion: Synthetic signal production. In K. R. Scherer (Ed.), *Facets of emotion.* Hillsdale, NJ: Erlbaum.

Izard, C. E. (1971). *The face of emotion.* New York: Appleton-Century-Crofts.

Kirouac, G., & Dore, F. Y. (1983). Accuracy and latency of judgment of facial expressions of emotions. *Perceptual and Motor Skills, 57,* 683–686.

Maccoby, E. E., & Jacklin, C. N. (1974). *The psychology of sex differences.* Stanford, CA: Stanford University Press.

McCown, W., Johnson, J., & Austin, S. (1986). Inability of delinquents to recognize facial affects. *Journal of Social Behavior and Personality, 1,* 489–496.

Matsumoto, D., Walbott, H., & Scherer, K. R. (1989). Emotion and intercultural communication. In W. Gudykunst and M. Asante (Eds.), *Handbook of intercultural communication* (pp. 225–246). Beverly Hills, CA: Sage.

Mehrabian, A., & Weiner, M. (1967). Decoding of inconsistent communications. *Journal of Personality and Social Psychology, 6,* 109–114.

Myers, J. (1979). *Fundamentals of experimental design.* Boston: Allyn & Bacon.

Parker, J. G., & Asher, S. R. (1987). Peer relations and later personal adjustment: Are low-accepted children at risk? *Psychological Bulletin, 102,* 357–389.

Philippot, P., & Feldman, R. S. (1990). Age and social competence in pre-schooler's decoding of facial expressions. *British Journal of Social Psychology, 29,* 43–54.

Posner, M. (1978). *Chronomatic explorations of mind.* Hillsdale, NJ: Erlbaum.

Reichenbach, L., & Masters, J. C. (1983). Children's use of expressive and contextual cues in judgments of emotion. *Child Development, 54,* 993–1004.

Riggio, R. E., Tucker, J., & Widaman, K. F. (1987). Verbal and nonverbal cues as mediators of deception ability. *Journal of Nonverbal Behavior, 11,* 126–145.

Rosenfeld, H. M. (1987). Conversational control functions of nonverbal behavior. In A. W. Siegman & S. Feldstein (Eds.), *Nonverbal behavior and communication* (2nd ed., pp. 563–601). Hillsdale, NJ: Erlbaum.

Rosenthal, R., Hall, J. A., DiMatteo, M. R., Rogers, P. L., & Archer, D. (1979). *Sensitivity to nonverbal communication: The PONS Test.* Baltimore: Johns Hopkins University Press.

Rosenthal, R., & DePaulo, B. M. (1979). Sex differences in eavesdropping on nonverbal cues. *Journal of Personality and Social Psychology, 37,* 273–285.

Saarni, C. (1979). Children's understanding of display rules for expressive behavior. *Developmental Psychology, 15,* 424–429.

     (1982). Social and affective functions of nonverbal behavior: Developmental concerns. In R. S. Feldman (Ed.), *Development of nonverbal behavior in children* (pp. 123–148). New York: Springer-Verlag.

Spence, S. H. (1987). The relationship between social–cognitive skills and peer sociometric status. *British Journal of Developmental Psychology, 5,* 347–356.

Vosk, B. N., Forehand, R., & Figueroa, R. (1983). Perception of emotions by accepted and rejected children. *Journal of Behavioural Assessment, 5,* 151–160.

Walden, T. A., & Field, T. M. (1982). Discrimination of facial expressions by preschool children. *Child Development, 53,* 1312–1319.

Walker, E. (1981). Emotion recognition in disturbed and nondisturbed children. *Psychology in the Schools, 16,* 119–126.

Zabel, R. H. (1979). Recognitions of emotions in facial expressions by emotionally disturbed children and nondisturbed children. *Psychology in the Schools, 16,* 119–126.

Zuckerman, M., Koestner, R., & Alton, A. O. (1984). Learning to detect deception. *Journal of Personality and Social Psychology, 46,* 519–528.

10. Nonverbal behavior and self-presentation: A developmental perspective

BELLA M. DePAULO

The development of voluntary control over nonverbal expressive behavior is a topic that has been of great interest to contemporary developmental and social psychologists (e.g., Buck, 1984; Cole, 1985; Lewis & Michalson, 1985; Malatesta & Haviland, 1985; Thelen, 1985; Zivin, 1982). This review differs from the others in its focus on one particular type of expressive control – the deliberate regulation of nonverbal expressive behaviors for self-presentational purposes. By controlling their nonverbal behaviors toward this end, people are contributing to the construction of their own identities (e.g., Baumeister, 1982; Jones & Pittman, 1982; Schlenker & Weigold, 1988). The little boy who wants to be seen as a good boy, the adolescent girl who wants to be seen as "tough" enough to fit into her swaggering peer group, and the balding and graying executive who would like to hold on to a more youthful appearance all are likely to try purposefully to regulate their nonverbal behaviors to serve their identity-relevant goals. People of all ages who try to appear unperturbed by the dentist's drill, who pretend to be enjoying a barely edible dinner cooked in their honor, or who try to suppress their expressions of delight upon trouncing a much-loathed competitor are also participating in the regulation of nonverbal behaviors for self-presentational purposes. By deliberately trying to control their nonverbal expressive behaviors, people are sometimes acting deceptively, in that they are trying to convey an impression of themselves that they know to be false. But deliberate control encompasses far more than deception. People often regulate their nonverbal behaviors in order to deintensify their genuine reactions, to exaggerate them, or to make their true feelings or attitudes even clearer than they would be if they were expressed spontaneously and unselfconsciously.

When people are alone, they are unlikely to try to regulate their nonverbal behavior for self-presentational purposes (DePaulo, 1990). But when

351

they are with others, they are unlikely not to be trying to do so. Even when nonverbal behaviors are being used very straightforwardly to communicate information (as when a father points to the person who is wanted on the telephone rather than trying to shout above the decibels of his wailing infant) or to perform a task (as when a chiropractor massages a patient's back), the ways in which these behaviors are performed can be of self-presentational significance (e.g., pointing sternly or massaging gently). Although it might appear at first that attempts to convey the impression of being a certain type of person would be limited to audiences who are relatively unfamiliar, in fact self-presentational efforts are unlikely to be limited in this way, either. Sometimes the impressions of themselves that people try deliberately to convey to those with whom they are most intimate are the most important of all. A dedicated spouse who is falsely accused of infidelity will probably not leave to chance the manifestations of her faithfulness; instead, she will purposefully control her nonverbal (and verbal) behaviors in order to convey her love more clearly. Similarly, the child whose parents have promised him a treat for good behavior will take pains to make his angelic nature readily apparent to them.

Nonverbal expressive behaviors include facial expressions; tone-of-voice cues; body movements, orientations, and postures; touching; and other ways of regulating interpersonal distances. Physical appearance cues, modes of attire, and even the arrangement and decoration of physical spaces are considered by some (e.g., Knapp, 1978) to be examples of nonverbal expressive cues. There are many reasons that nonverbal behaviors are of special importance to the study of the development of self-presentational strategies. First, nonverbal behaviors are salient and irrepressible. It is impossible to refrain from nonverbally conveying an impression of oneself. Second, nonverbal behaviors can sometimes be very difficult to control. Many scholars of nonverbal behavior are now convinced that there are hardwired links between emotions and nonverbal behaviors (especially facial expressions): When certain basic emotions such as happiness, sadness, fear, anger, and surprise are elicited, facial muscles controlling the expressions of those emotions are automatically triggered (e.g., Ekman, 1972; Izard, 1977). It is possible to attempt purposefully to override these direct and automatic links – and indeed, this is what the deliberate control of nonverbal behaviors for self-presentational purposes often is – but the task is difficult. Even when people are not working against their emotions – and in fact may not be experiencing any particular emotions – the deliberate control of nonverbal behavior can present quite a challenge. Some nonverbal behaviors are difficult to produce at will, even for adults (Ekman, 1985). Further, in attempting to regulate the impressions they convey with their nonverbal behaviors, people are stuck with an important and interesting obstacle: They can never see or hear their own nonverbal behavior exactly as others do. They do, of course, hear their own voices as they speak, but because the sound waves are transmitted differently to their own ears than to other people's, the sound they hear is not the same. Similarly, even if they were to look in a mirror while interacting with another person, the image of their own faces that they would see would of course be a mirror image and not the exact image seen by the other person. Thus, although in principle it would be very useful to people who are trying to control the impressions they convey to others to be able to see what their faces look like to others and to hear what their voices sound like, they will not be able to do so. With regard to the information conveyed by nonverbal behaviors, then, people can never know themselves as well as others can know them.

Those who dare to study the deliberate regulation of nonverbal behaviors for self-presentational purposes face challenges no less daunting than those encountered by the self-presenters themselves. One such challenge is the identification of deliberateness. Often it is difficult to ascertain whether particular nonverbal behaviors are enacted purposefully or whether, for example, they are behaviors that were once carefully practiced and deliberately conveyed but are currently overlearned and reeled off habitually. The traditional southern belle who throughout much of her childhood practiced smiling and "sitting like a lady," for example, may find herself assuming a faint smile and a ladylike posture even while engrossed in an intellectually challenging electronics exam at an East Coast university.

A second challenge to researchers is that of determining when nonverbal behaviors are motivated by self-presentational goals. Infants may learn rather early in their lives to use crying instrumentally to secure the attentions of their caregivers (e.g., Murray, 1979). However, it would be inappropriate to infer that the infants are deliberately trying to convey the impression of being needy babies. This second challenge points directly to the third. At what point developmentally is the self-system sufficiently sophisticated that children can be described as desiring certain identities and as actively trying to claim them during social interactions? Although much exciting work has been done on the development of self (e.g., Harter, 1983; Kagan, 1984), the answer to this question is still far from definitive.

Issues relevant to the definition of intentionality, the identification of motives, and the emergence of the self have challenged philosophers and psychologists for centuries. In this review, we shall acknowledge the thorniness of these issues but press onward, even though our sides may be stinging a bit. Our tack will be to be emboldened rather than cowed by the difficulties. We shall draw widely from the literature, citing evidence that may be relevant to our self-presentational theme in only an indirect or a suggestive way. We shall also review uses of nonverbal behaviors that may better be described as precursors to the deliberate use of expressive behaviors for self-presentational ends, than as good exemplars of such use. In opting for an expansive rather than a restrictive approach, we hope to point to the potential for, as well as to the difficulty of, this kind of research.

We shall begin by considering in detail the kinds of factors that can make it so difficult to regulate nonverbal behaviors for self-presentational purposes. These include the constraints imposed by the nonverbal behaviors themselves (i.e., inherent limits to their controllability), motivational and emotional impairments, and cultural and situational constraints. We shall also consider self-presentationally relevant individual difference factors, such as expressiveness and emotionality, in two different ways: as potential impediments to self-presentational success and as potential facilitators. We shall describe what we believe to be the components of the effective use of nonverbal behaviors for self-presentational purposes (such as fine-motor skills and knowledge of conventions regarding the regulation of expressive behavior) and review research detailing the growth of these component processes over the course of development. We last shall review research in which children and adults were instructed to try to convey particular impressions with their nonverbal behaviors or to try to dissemble nonverbally. Such studies are silent on the issue of whether people will try to regulate their nonverbal behaviors in such ways when left to their own devices; however, they do speak to the issue of whether people can, in principle, succeed at such regulation, should they attempt to do so.

Constraints on the use of nonverbal behaviors for self-presentational purposes

Constraints on the controllability of particular nonverbal behaviors

Physical characteristics. Many physical characteristics make striking impressions on others but are under little or no control. These include body build, height, head size and shape, facial morphology, skin color, and physical attractiveness. Because these kinds of characteristics are so salient, they can severely constrain the types of impressions that can be convincingly conveyed. Children who are tall and muscular, for example, can more realistically hope to create a commanding presence among their peers than can those who are short and flaccid.

Although there is generally little that can be done to alter the physical characteristics themselves, there are other ways that these characteristics can be used to serve self-presentational purposes. Some of these uses are quite creative and suggest resourcefulness in the face of challenges that might otherwise prove disheartening. For example, children whose physiques make them appear a bit nerdy relative to the norms of their peer group can use their nerdiness for comic effect in ways that endear them to their friends. Children with more socially desirable physical characteristics can also learn to work with those characteristics in order to maximize their self-presentational outcomes. Those whose faces are especially babyish, for example, can perhaps learn to assume a particularly moving facial expression of vulnerability or of hurt feelings when accused of misdeeds.

The capacity to work with one's static physical characteristics in order to facilitate interpersonal goals presupposes certain knowledge and skills. Most basically, perhaps, it assumes some awareness, if only rudimentary, of one's own physical characteristics. The beginnings of such awareness can be traced as far back as infancy (e.g., Harter, 1983). Yet the lesson of years of research on topics such as body image and self-perceptions of physical attractiveness is that the tremendous cognitive accomplishments that have been attained by adolescence and adulthood are no guarantee of accuracy in the awareness of one's physical self (e.g., Fisher, 1986). The task of maintaining an awareness of one's physical characteristics is in a way more challenging for children than for young adults, because the rate of change of their physical selves is likely to be much greater. In the later adult years, it is possible that awareness may again lag behind the actual rate of change when changes (e.g., in muscle tone) begin to occur in a different direction than what characterized all the earlier phases of development. Unexpected changes (e.g., the convergence in the physical appearance of spouses that occurs over the course of many years of cohabitation; Zajonc, Adelman, Murphy, & Niedenthal, 1987) may also register in awareness only dimly.

The ability to use physical characteristics effectively for self-presentational purposes requires an awareness not just of the characteristics themselves but also of their self-presentational significance. That a babyish countenance can be used effectively to protest innocence is the type of realization that may dawn gradually over the course of development.

Dynamic cues. Dynamic cues such as facial expressions and body movements and postures are much more amenable to deliberate control than are the more static physical characteristics. These are the kinds of nonverbal behaviors that typically show interesting developmental progressions, influenced by the myriad familiar factors such as socialization, temperament, and cognitive sophistication. There are, however, certain nonverbal behaviors that are quite difficult to control (e.g., Rinn, 1984) and even some that most people never learn to produce at will. One example of the latter is the raising and pulling together of the eyebrows that occurs spontaneously when people are afraid (Ekman, 1985). Because these movements typically cannot be produced deliberately, there are constraints on people's abilities to feign fear successfully, and most adults are just as disadvantaged in this respect as are children.

Occasionally people try to "control" their dynamic nonverbal cues by trying not to behave nonverbally at all, as if this might convey a neutral, inconspicuous, or innocent impression. However, passivity can instead be seen as indicative of dullness, withdrawal, uneasiness, snobbish aloofness, or even deceptiveness (cf. Davis & Holtgraves, 1984; DePaulo & Kirkendol, 1989; Hall, Roter, & Katz, 1987). Further, even when dynamic nonverbal cues are relatively still, the more permanent features are still available to perceivers. There is nothing people can do to prevent perceivers from drawing inferences, whether warranted or unwarranted, from their nonverbal cues. The best they can do is to try to control the nature of those inferences.

Emotional and motivational impairments

Emotional impairments. According to Ekman's (1972) neurocultural model of facial expressions of emotion, the elicitation of each of the basic emotions automatically triggers particular sets of facial muscles that produce overt expressions of the emotion. With age, children learn to try to mask or squelch these muscle movements when appropriate. However, the automaticity of the link between emotions and emotional expressions constrains the possible effectiveness of attempts at deliberate regulation of nonverbal expressions, even for adults. Particularly when the experience of an emotion is very intense, behaviors indicative of the emotion may "leak" through people's best efforts at control. Someone who is furious, for instance, will probably be unsuccessful at donning a calm countenance and a steady voice. Similarly, those who suffer from affective disorders, such as depression, are likely to be constrained in the types of nonverbal self-presentations that they can effectively convey (cf. Gerson & Perlman, 1979; Prkachin, Craig, Papageorgis, & Reith, 1977). In fact, they may also be constrained in the types of impressions that they will even attempt to convey, particularly if some impressions seem to require much more effort to convey than do others.

The ease with which various emotions can be elicited, and the kinds of factors that will elicit them, may change dramatically over the course of development. Some of these changes may have the paradoxical effect of making it more difficult for older children than for younger ones to succeed at their self-presentational attempts. For example, older children, largely by dint of their greater cognitive sophistication, are more sensitive than are younger children to potentially self-threatening implications of negative social comparisons (e.g., DePaulo, Tang, Webb, Hoover, Marsh, & Litowitz, 1989; Ruble, 1983). In many interpersonal situations, however, it is inappropriate to express one's disappointment and distress at another person's stellar performance. To the extent that older children feel even worse than younger ones do about the self-relevant implications of another person's performance, they may do less well at assuming an acceptable nonverbal expression upon learning of the other's success.

The links between emotions and nonverbal expressions are constraining when people are trying to suppress the expression of the emotion or to cover it with the expression of a different emotion, but they can instead be facilitative when people are attempting to work with the emotion, as when they are trying to make their true feelings perfectly clear or when they are trying to convey an exaggerated version of their genuine feelings. Children probably learn to work successfully with their genuine emotions in this way before they learn to work effectively against their emotions by neutralizing or concealing them.

When the unregulated expression of an emotion is likely to compromise self-presentational success, an alternative to attempting to control the expression is to try to control the experience of the emotion itself. In the preschool and early grade school years, children's thoughts about how to accomplish emotional self-regulation are rather limited; often, for example, they suggest that a change in situation might help (e.g., going out to play to get over a feeling of sadness). Within a few years, though, the possibilities that children entertain become more diverse and (literally) imaginative, as they begin to appreciate the potential of mental manipulations in controlling their emotions. For example, they may consider distracting themselves, thinking about other kinds of things, and becoming immersed in an absorbing task (Harris, 1989; McCoy & Masters, 1990). Another strategy sometimes mentioned by older children and adults is to try deliberately to experience the emotion they would like to be feeling, rather than the one they really are feeling (cf. Hochschild, 1983). This can be accomplished, for instance, by calling to mind actual experiences from the past in which that emotion was experienced rather intensely. Hochschild (1983) described this strategy as *deep acting*, to distinguish it from the *surface acting* that people use when trying to regulate only their outward expressions and not their underlying feelings. She found frequent references to both in her discussions with flight attendants who are under constant pressure to regulate their emotions when dealing with passengers. Among professional actors and actresses, the method of deep acting is now a well-established technique, called the Stanislavski method (Stanislavski, 1965).

Motivational impairments. The motivation to convey certain impressions of oneself can fuel the learning process and thereby accelerate the rate of socialization of nonverbal expression. We shall examine this facilitating effect of motivation later. Here, the ways in which motivation can be constraining will be addressed.

High motivation to convey a particular impression, when coupled with low expectations for success at doing so, results in the debilitating state of social anxiety (Schlenker & Leary, 1982, 1985). Socially anxious individuals speak less fluently, show more nervous gestures, and distance themselves from the process of social interaction by initiating fewer conversations and having less to say in the conversations in which they are involved. They also seem partial to a protective style of interacting, characterized by such innocuous behaviors as nodding, smiling, and refraining from interrupting. In these ways, socially anxious individuals can perhaps cut their anticipated losses in social exchanges; however, at the same time they are compromising their ability to convey particularly positive impressions. Although even kindergartners are aware of the potentially energizing effects of high motivation, only much later, toward the end of the grade school years, do children also appreciate that there can be debilitative aspects of motivation to succeed interpersonally (Darby & Schlenker, 1986).

One realm in which the disruptive effect of high motivation has been particularly well documented is that of the communication of deception. People who are highly motivated to succeed at deceiving, particularly those who also are insecure about their chances for success, tell lies that are, paradoxically, more easily distinguished from their truths than are the lies told by less highly motivated communicators (DePaulo & Kirkendol, 1989; DePaulo, Lanier, & Davis, 1983; DePaulo, LeMay, & Epstein, 1991; DePaulo, Stone, & Lassiter, 1985b). High levels of motivation are particularly disruptive to the nonverbal aspects of performance. When people are motivated to get away with their lies, they appear to try hard to control all of their verbal and nonverbal behaviors (DePaulo, Kirkendol, Tang, & O'Brien, 1988). But because nonverbal behaviors are not so amenable to willful control (cf. Polanyi, 1962), people's attempts at regulating such behaviors can backfire, making them appear especially deceptive when lying, as compared with when they are telling the truth. When emotions are involved in deception, either because people are lying about an emotion (e.g., pretending not to feel angry) or because they feel emotional (e.g., guilty, apprehensive) about the fact that they are telling a lie, they may try to control the emotional cues by attempting to suppress or inhibit their expression. This strategy, too, is likely to be counterproductive, in that people who appear inhibited and unexpressive sometimes convey the impression that they have something to hide; this is, of course, exactly the impression that they are trying to avoid.

With age, as children master more of the lessons of socialization and internalize them more thoroughly, they may become more motivated to live up to societal ideals. One example of this is that they may become more painfully aware of the self-relevant implications of being caught in their lies. Unlike younger children, whose concerns may focus primarily on the fear of punishment, older children begin to care about the shame of being perceived as a "bad" person (cf. Ekman, 1989). If, as a result, they feel more guilty when lying, their attempts to deceive can be compromised, in that they will then need to try to conceal not just the content of the lie but also the guilt that they feel about telling the lie.

Individual differences

Level and range of expressive cues. Although most dynamic nonverbal cues, such as voice pitch, can be controlled to some degree, there are constraints on the extent of regulation that can be achieved. These constraints are imposed by an individual's mean level of such cues and, perhaps more importantly, by the range of cues that the individual can command. Children with particularly high pitched voices, for example, may have difficulty trying to come across as adultlike and authoritative. The self-presentational issues are similar to those for the more static physical characteristics discussed earlier. In order to realize their expressive potential, individuals need to be aware of the level and range of their expressive behaviors (including the ways in which they change over the course of development) and of the self-presentational implications of those aspects of their nonverbal expressive profiles. Learning to turn expressive limitations into advantages, by working with them in creative ways, is a kind of developmental milestone that, for many people, may never be attained. In fact, people who become settled into a stable social network may find it especially difficult to make nontrivial identity-relevant changes in their nonverbal self-presentations. It may take a dramatic change in the settings of one's social life, such as with moves to new cities or the adolescent's entry into an out-of-town college, for a person to muster the courage to work with expressive behaviors in new ways.

Spontaneous expressiveness. Starting in infancy (Field, 1982), there are reliable individual differences in the degree to which people spontaneously express their internal states. Most of the research has concentrated on facial expressions, but spontaneous expressiveness is probably an important dimension of other nonverbal behaviors as well. Spontaneous expressiveness can be measured directly in paradigms in which people watch affect-laden slides while being videotaped surreptitiously, or indirectly by self-report or other-report measures designed to tap expressiveness (as Manstead has noted in Chapter 8 of this volume). Individuals who are characteristically spontaneously expressive enjoy many interpersonal advantages. Yet, there are also important constraints imposed by this expressive style, particularly when people wish to hide their feelings or cover them with expressions of different feelings. For people who habitually express their feelings spontaneously, the links between internal states and overt expressions of those states seem to be especially strong; hence, they often fail in their attempts to work against their internal states by expressing something at odds with those states.

A very creative demonstration of the self-presentational impediments imposed by spontaneous expressiveness was reported by Friedman and Miller-Herringer (1989). Their subjects, who were either expressive or unexpressive, learned that they had just defeated two other competitors. This information was delivered either in the presence of the two other people or in their absence. Most of these college student subjects managed to look less excited about their success when their rivals were present than when they were absent. But this was more difficult for the expressive people, who conveyed much more of their delight when their competitors were present than did the unexpressive people.

Affect intensity. One of the four fundamental temperaments described by Buss and Plomin (1975) is *emotionality*, which is the tendency to respond to stimuli intensely and to experience emotions deeply. Like spontaneous expressiveness, emotionality is likely to disrupt attempts at self-presentation, when such attempts involve efforts to work against the emotion that is being experienced, by neutralizing it or covering it with an expression of some other state. (Also like spontaneous expressiveness, emotionality can facilitate self-presentational success when the individual's goal is to work with the emotion by expressing it clearly and accurately or even more intensely than it is felt.)

Stable individual differences in emotionality are present from infancy and have been documented and discussed in detail (e.g., Goldsmith et al., 1987). More recently, the measurement of affect intensity in adults has received research attention, particularly in the work of Larsen and Diener (1987). From this research program, it is possible to trace the development of affect intensity. Individual differences in affect intensity have been shown to be reliable in adulthood, and the general level of affect intensity has been found to decrease systematically between the ages of 16 and 68, particularly between the young adult and middle-age years (Diener, Sandvik, & Larsen, 1985). There are also interesting data on the ways in which people varying in affect intensity process attend to affective information differently. For example, when watching emotionally laden slides, people high in affect intensity focus more on the affective aspects of the slides and think about them in a more personal way than do people who are low in affect intensity. They are also less likely to think about things that are totally unrelated to the slides. That older adults are less likely than younger ones to process emotional information in this intense way suggests that they will often be less hampered in their attempts at suppressing, neutralizing, or masking their emotional expressions.

Demeanor effects. Adults have a well-documented "demeanor bias" in their nonverbal expressions: They have faces and voices that characteristically appear pleasant or unpleasant, honest or dishonest (Kraut, 1982; Wallbott & Scherer, 1986; Zuckerman, DeFrank, Hall, Larrance, & Rosenthal, 1979; Zuckerman, Larrance, Hall, DeFrank, & Rosenthal, 1979). People with a pleasant face, for example, appear to be watching something pleasant both when they really are watching pleasant slides and when they actually are watching unpleasant slides. Similarly, people who characteristically look dishonest appear to be lying both when they are lying and when they are telling the truth (Riggio, Tucker, & Throckmorton, 1987). The demeanor bias is a constraint in that it limits the kinds of impressions that can be readily and effectively conveyed. People with angelic faces and voices are unlikely to be successful in assuming the role of a mean and nasty intimidator.

The demeanor bias is stronger for vocal expressions than for facial expressions (Zuckerman, Larrance, Spiegel, & Klorman, 1981), a result that Zuckerman and his colleagues explained by pointing to the fact that tone-of-voice cues are harder to control than are facial expressions. If this explanation is indeed the correct one, then it suggests that the demeanor bias may generally be stronger in younger children than in older ones, because younger children are less skilled at controlling their nonverbal behaviors.

Personal style. *Personal style* is the term used by Gordon Allport (Allport, 1937; Allport & Vernon, 1933) to refer to all of a person's expressive behaviors, considered together. Allport believed that "style . . . develops gradually from within; it cannot for long be simulated or feigned" (1937, p. 493). According to this viewpoint, a person's expressive behaviors are a coherent constellation that are not amenable to deliberate regulation or control, except perhaps for very brief periods of time. Personal style is a constraint on the possibilities for nonverbal self-presentation, because expressions that are inconsistent with one's personal style should be more difficult to produce in a convincing fashion. If, as Allport suggested, personal style does indeed develop gradually, then children should be less constrained by personal style than adults are, in that their styles are presumably less developed and less crystallized.

Situational and cultural constraints

Situational constraints. Certain situations constrain the full range of nonverbal expressions because the norms for conveying only certain expressions are so strong. Children should not weep at their own birthday parties, nor should their guests. Laughing uproariously during solemn religious services is likewise generally considered to be highly inappropriate behavior. In these kinds of situations, display rules (Ekman, 1972) govern the regulation of nonverbal behaviors. The dictates of display rules are not absolute; even in situations as highly ritualized as religious services, there is room for individual variability in expressiveness. Still, the range of expressions will generally be much less impressive. Most people conform to expectations, thereby revealing little about themselves as individuals (Jones & Davis, 1965).

Younger children, who have not yet mastered all of the intricacies of display rules, may accordingly be less constrained in their nonverbal expressions by situational considerations than are older children and adults. They are likely not only to comment verbally on the emperor's new clothes but also to look at him as if he were naked.

Cultural constraints. In addition to variations in the situational norms for expressiveness that govern behavior within cultures, there are also important differences in the tolerance and encouragement of expressiveness across cultures (e.g., Ekman, 1972). These norms are often age graded, in that there are striking regularities in just how early, developmentally, the young of the culture are expected to comply with the norms (e.g., Hess, Kashiwagi, Azuma, Price, & Dickson, 1980). By the time the members of a particular culture have completely internalized the relevant norms for expressiveness, the potential for variety in their nonverbal self-presentations has become constrained, for several reasons. One is motivational: Those who have internalized the norm of stoicism, for example, feel uncomfortable behaving in other than a subdued way. Another reason is skill related: Those who have long practiced stoicism may find that it is difficult to produce animated gestures and expressions; after years of practice in nonverbal inhibition and suppression, the unexpressive style has become habitual. These cultural constraints on expressiveness are likely to be cumulative; thus, older people, who have more fully mastered the relevant cultural mores, may actually be more constrained in the kinds of nonverbal self-presentations that are available to them than will younger people.

Strategic and interpretive shortcomings. For most of the constraints that we have discussed so far, it was assumed that people know generally what nonverbal behaviors they would like to produce and what kinds of impressions those nonverbal behaviors are likely to convey, but they simply cannot produce those behaviors or know that they should not even try. Sometimes, however, people are not sure of the kind of impression they want to convey, or even when they are sure, they may not know how to behave nonverbally in order to convey it. Eventually, they will attempt to implement a nonverbal expressive strategy. But once they do, they may be constrained by interpretive limitations. For example, they may not realize how their nonverbal behaviors appear to others or how others judge those behaviors.

In one-on-one interactions among adults, accuracy at understanding the impression that is being conveyed to the other person is far from impressive (e.g., DePaulo, Kenny, Hoover, Webb, & Oliver, 1987; Kenny & DePaulo, 1989; see also Zuckerman, Koestner, & Driver, 1981). Although the relevant research has not yet been conducted, it is likely that children are even less successful than are adults at realizing how others view them. From the research on verbal communication, it appears that younger grade school children are less sensitive than are older grade school children and beginning high school students to the kinds of remarks that might prove offensive to others (Johnson, Greenspan, & Brown, 1984). They may be similarly insensitive to the kinds of facial and vocal expressions that could irritate, anger, or hurt others.

Predictors of individual differences in self-presentational uses of nonverbal behaviors

Individuals vary systematically across a set of dimensions relevant to their potential success in regulating nonverbal behaviors for self-presentational purposes. These dimensions include (1) their knowledge and cognitive sophistication regarding expressive behavior, intrapersonal experiences, and social life; (2) their abilities relevant to the expressive domain and their practice and experience in that domain; (3) their motivation to achieve desired self-presentational outcomes; (4) their confidence; (5) their spontaneous expressiveness; and (6) their emotionality or affect intensity. Although these factors do not, of course, constitute an exhaustive list of self-presentationally relevant individual differences, when considered together, they should increase appreciably the predictability of self-presentational success for different categories of people. Ideally, it should be possible to use these factors to predict variations in self-presentational outcomes for people who differ in physical attractiveness, need for approval, self-consciousness, and other dimensions as well (see DePaulo, 1990). Here, however, the focus is on the relevance of these factors to predicting differences in self-presentational outcomes across the life span.

Knowledge and cognitive sophistication

What kinds of knowledge or cognitive abilities might it take for a person to convey, effectively and nonverbally, the impression that she is a certain kind of person (e.g., that she is older than she really is or that she is a good kid) or that she is experiencing a certain affect or emotion (e.g., gratitude) or a certain mental state (e.g., comprehension)? Some understanding of the nature of the internal state to be conveyed, of expressive behavior and conventions regulating expressive behavior, and of the impact of expressive behavior on others may be necessary in order for children and adults to attempt to convey certain impressions and to do so successfully.

Understanding of nonverbal behaviors. One fundamental lesson that children learn about nonverbal behaviors is that they reveal internal states. Over the course of their development, children (and perhaps even adults) acquire an increasingly sophisticated understanding of the kinds of internal states that can and cannot be conveyed nonverbally. Also growing is their realization of what these states look like and sound like when conveyed by others (e.g., DePaulo & Rosenthal, 1982) and what it feels like to produce such nonverbal behaviors oneself.

In addition to learning that there are links between internal states and expressive behaviors, children also need to realize that these links can be deliberately severed. By the age of 6, and perhaps even earlier, children do show some insight into the fact that people's expressive behaviors do not always correspond to their internal states (e.g., Harris, Donnelly, Guz, & Pitt-Watson, 1986) and that one of the reasons for the dissociation is that people can deliberately control their expressive behavior so as to convey a misleading impression (e.g., Gnepp & Hess, 1986; Harris, Olthof, & Terwogt, 1981; Saarni, 1988; see also Carroll & Steward, 1984). Understanding of the intricacies of expressive control becomes increasingly sophisticated between the ages of 6 and 11 but then appears to level off (Gnepp & Hess, 1986; Harris et al., 1981; Saarni, 1979).

Still another lesson to be learned is that one's efforts at expressive control are not always successful. One can, of course, try to act cool or even tough when the school principal asks the true identity of the child who set off the fire alarm, but it is possible that the principal will see through the veneer of false bravado. When asking second, fifth, and eighth graders about this hypothetical situation, Saarni (1988) found that the penetrating eye of the authority figure is exactly what they expected. In other situations, though, such as feigning liking for a disappointing present from an aunt, the children were more likely to expect to be believed. The older children, however, were less optimistic about the probable success of their expressive dissembling than were the younger children (Cole, 1986).

There is a kind of knowledge about nonverbal behavior that is likely to be fairly slow to develop. This is the appreciation of the subtleties of nonverbal behaviors, such as the fact that nonverbal behaviors are in many instances more ambiguous than verbal behaviors are, and also more deniable (DePaulo, 1990). The adolescent who can constrain his exasperation at his parents' hopeless squareness to a nonverbal manifestation can more readily disavow any such impatience (when challenged by his equally exasperated parents) than can the adolescent who puts his feelings into words.

Understanding of expressive conventions. Children need to understand not only the nature of nonverbal behavior and the links between nonverbal behavior and internal states but also the links between nonverbal behaviors and external events. Among the most important of these links are the norms or display rules (Ekman, 1972) governing the use of nonverbal behaviors by different categories of people in different cultures, families, and contexts. Children's understanding of the use of other-oriented display rules, designed to protect the feelings of others, develops earlier than does their understanding of the use of self-oriented display rules, which are used to protect their own feelings or identities (e.g., pretending not to be upset when being teased by one's peers). Perhaps mastery occurs in this sequence because the socialization of other-oriented rules is even more direct than the socialization of self-oriented rules (Gnepp & Hess, 1986). Differences in the overtness of socialization pressures may also account for the fact that children's understanding of verbal display rules (e.g., "Thank your grandmother for the present") appears earlier developmentally than does their understanding of nonverbal display rules (Gnepp & Hess, 1986).

Although examples of display rules often involve children or adults, there may be expressive conventions that refer even to the behaviors of infants. Harkness and Super (1985) argued, for example, that cultures differ systematically in their attitudes toward crying and the responses to crying that they deem appropriate. Children raised in cultures in which intense expressions of emotions are tolerated or even encouraged during infancy and throughout the early childhood years should, in order to succeed in conveying desired impressions, adopt very different self-presentational strategies than should children raised in cultures in which emotionality is shunned.

The success of children's self-presentational efforts also depends on their skill at reading the expressive conventions within their own families. Halberstadt (chapter 4 in this volume) has documented that families, like cultures, vary in the degree to which they encourage expressiveness. Perceptive children can use their insights into family norms to regulate more effectively their own nonverbal behaviors. It also is useful to them to understand and anticipate the emotional reactions of specific family members. There is evidence for the development of this type of understanding as early as the end of the second year of life, when, for example, toddlers become increasingly adept at tormenting their siblings (Dunn & Munn, 1985; see also Harris, 1989).

Appreciation of situational norms for expressive behaviors is also important to self-presentational success. Children probably learn rather quickly, for example, that in formal situations, relative to informal ones, one should be more guarded in one's expressive behaviors. An understanding of the relationship between situations and emotional experiences should also be useful to people who are concerned with conveying a particular impression. Some situations are quite unequivocal with regard to the kinds of emotions they are likely to engender in others. Children ranging in age from kindergartners to third graders show some understanding of the links between these unequivocal situations and the emotions they elicit (Gnepp, McKee, & Domanic, 1987). The understanding of the more variable emotional implications of equivocal situations deepens over those childhood years, though even the oldest children have difficulty appreciating that the same person can experience, in one situation, a variety of emotions simultaneously (Gnepp et al., 1987; see also Donaldson & Westerman, 1986; Harris, 1983; Harter & Buddin, 1987; Harter & Whitesell, 1989; Stein & Trabasso, 1989). To the extent that children are confused about the ways in which others might be reacting in particular situations, it should be correspondingly more difficult for them to tailor successfully their expressive behaviors so as to convey particular impressions to those persons.

Understanding people. The more psychologically sophisticated that children are about other people (e.g., what pleases and displeases them, how they are likely to react to different situations and different people), the more adept they should be at regulating their expressive behaviors in ways that are interpersonally effective (cf. Weiner & Handel, 1985). There is some evidence, for example, that extroverts are generally liked better than are introverts (e.g., Toris & DePaulo, 1984). Children (and adults) who realize this may also recognize that in the absence of any other information about a new acquaintance, they have a better chance of making a favorable impression on that person if they act extroverted than if they act introverted.

It is also important to perceive differences among varying categories of people. The kinds of expressive behaviors that might engender acceptance and positive regard among parents and teachers may be very different from those that would be effective with an adolescent peer group (cf. Miller & Sperry, 1987). First, fourth, and sixth graders do have different expectations for different categories of people. For example, they expect more positive reactions to their expressions of sadness from their mothers than from their fathers, and they also expect their mothers to react more positively to their expressions of sadness than to their expressions of anger (Fuchs & Thelen, 1988). They also expect more accepting responses from both of their parents when they are expressing negative feelings in situations in which they are themselves vulnerable (as when getting an injection) than in situations in which others are vulnerable (as when their expressions of negativity might hurt another person's feelings) (Saarni, 1989, 1990). Although these studies did not directly assess the accuracy of these expectations, it is likely that at least some of the insights are on target. Still, even by the adult years, there are misperceptions (Zelko, Duncan, Barden, Garber, & Masters, 1986).

Even more challenging than understanding the differences among categories of persons is understanding the differences among individual persons (e.g., that one sibling likes quiet interactions more than does the other) (e.g., Gnepp, 1989a,b). It is also important, though probably not easy, to be alert to variations within a given individual in moods and behaviors across different times and different situations. Kindergartners, for example, have difficulty appreciating that a person's current feelings can be affected not just by the situation they are in at the moment (e.g., getting a new kitten), but also by their previous experiences (e.g., learning the day before that their old cat had died). By the fifth grade, they are much more sensitive, though still not unerringly so, to the personal emotions brought on by previous experiences (Gnepp & Gould, 1985). This ability to see things from another person's perspective is likely to be predictive of effectiveness across a variety of self-presentational tasks. There is already evidence that it is predictive of skill at deceiving throughout the childhood years (Feldman, White, & Lobato, 1982; Shennum & Bugental, 1982).

Ability, practice, and experience

Social knowledge is indispensable to nonverbal self-presentational success. Children and adults need to know what kinds of nonverbal expressions are likely to create particular impressions on particular other people in particular situations. However, simple understanding is not enough. Once people know, in principle, which nonverbal behaviors they want to enact, they must be able to produce those behaviors.

At birth, infants' facial musculature is already completely formed and fully functional (Fridlund, Ekman, & Oster, 1987). Within the first few months, babies can produce facial expressions that resemble many adult expressions of emotions (Camras, Malatesta, & Izard, this volume). By 6 months, they also appear to imitate spontaneously mouth movements of other people, and those imitations increasingly resemble those of the model (Kaye & Marcus, 1978).

It is, of course, possible to ask preschoolers and older children to try directly to imitate the facial expressions shown in a photograph or by a live model. The ability to do so improves from the preschool through the adolescent years (Hamilton, 1973; Kwint, 1934; Odom & Lemond, 1972; Yarczower, Kilbride, & Hill, 1979). In a study of 5-, 9-, and 13-year-olds, Ekman and his colleagues (Ekman, Roper, & Hager, 1980) found that the children did especially well at imitating specific facial movements if they could look in a mirror and practice. Still, even the oldest children had difficulty producing some of the movements associated with fear, sadness, and anger.

Experience at attempting to regulate expressive behaviors should also facilitate success at so doing. We have no research on the role of experience in children's expressive control, but we do have some suggestive data from studies of adults. For example, observational studies of successful poker players show that they may be especially skilled at controlling their nonverbal behaviors (Hayano, 1980). And in a study of sales pitches made by experienced salespersons (DePaulo & DePaulo, 1989), it was found that observers were completely unable to distinguish, along a dimension of deceptiveness, the pitches for products that the salespersons really did like (the honest pitches) from the pitches for products that the salespersons did not like at all (the dishonest pitches). The salespersons appeared to be particularly adept at controlling their expressive behaviors so as not to reveal that they were dissembling.

Motivation

A prerequisite to self-presentational success is some minimal motivation to achieve desired interpersonal outcomes. Those who are indifferent to their outcomes in particular social interactions or who are confident to the point of complacency may not invest sufficient effort to be successful (Schlenker & Leary, 1985), except, perhaps, fortuitously.

Motivation is important at all phases of the self-presentational process. It fuels the pursuit of knowledge about the identity-relevant aspects of social life; it inspires the practice and refinement of nonverbal strategies and abilities; and it nudges people to attend more carefully to the intricacies of interpersonal interactions, in order to understand better the impact of their own nonverbal behaviors on others. To the extent that people's motivation to convey appropriate impressions in interpersonal interactions is apparent to others and is seen as indicative of sensitivity and concern (rather than, say, manipulativeness and self-aggrandizement), the mere fact of being motivated can be interpersonally advantageous.

Still, as we noted, motivation can have costs. People who care too much about creating just the right impression are at risk for adopting counterproductive strategies, particularly if they also feel insecure about their ability to convey those impressions that are so important to them (e.g., DePaulo, LeMay, & Epstein, 1991; Schlenker & Leary, 1985; see also Baumeister & Scher, 1988).

As young children first begin to become aware of the many cultural display rules, family norms, and other conventions governing nonverbal expressions, and especially as they develop some sense of the degree to which social outcomes are contingent on adhering to these conventions, their motivation to learn more about these matters and to practice their nonverbal self-presentational skills probably increases. Children's growing sensitivity to the importance of regulating their expressive behaviors probably occurs with, and is influenced by, the fact that others hold them more and more responsible for controlling their nonverbal behaviors in ways that are deemed socially appropriate.

Beyond the point at which the most important expressive conventions have been mastered, the developmental course of level of self-presentational motivation is not clear. Adolescence has long been viewed as a time when identity-relevant concerns become focal. But so far we have no research linking these hypothesized concerns with specific self-presentational expressive behaviors. Do adolescents spend more time than do preadolescents or young adults trying out different facial expressions in the mirror and reading popular pieces on how to make people like you? The research would be both theoretically interesting and fun to do.

The course of motivation throughout the adulthood years might also be examined. One hypothesis is that the motivation to learn more about expressive behaviors and their impact on others, and to practice those behaviors, wanes, especially for adults who have developed life-styles that are highly routinized and who have stable social networks. Alternatively, however, major life changes, such as the empty nest phenomenon or the death of a spouse, could provide the impetus to learn and try out new expressive styles.

Confidence

People who have confidence in their understanding of expressive conventions and in their ability to convey particular impressions, succeed at conveying those impressions more often than do those who are insecure about these matters. The facilitating effect of confidence on the effectiveness of interpersonal communications has been demonstrated both for people who are dispositionally self-confident (e.g., Leary, 1983; Schlenker & Leary, 1982, 1985) and for those in whom high expectations for success have been experimentally induced (e.g., DePaulo, LeMay, & Epstein, 1991). Confidence is especially important in situations in which motivation to convey a particular impression is high, for it seems to neutralize the potentially debilitating effects of excessive concern (e.g., DePaulo, LeMay, & Epstein, 1991).

Confidence may be an active element in a cycle of increasingly sophisticated self-presentational strategies and skills. Confident people are likely to experience more interpersonal successes, which may motivate them to learn even more about the self-presentational aspects of social life and to practice their skills even more diligently, which further adds to their refinement of those skills. Alternatively, people who are insecure about how to behave nonverbally and who show that insecurity on their faces and in their voices may invite more direct feedback from others about how best to proceed. That feedback could help them improve their abilities, and perhaps ultimately their confidence in their abilities.

Like motivation, confidence can also undermine self-presentational effectiveness when it reaches levels that are too high. Whereas the result of excessively high motivation is that people try too hard to create a particular impression, the result of overconfidence is that they do not try hard enough.

If confidence were perfectly correlated with self-presentationally relevant knowledge and abilities, then confidence should increase throughout the childhood years. However, young children may be more confident than is warranted by their knowledge and skills, because they are relatively unaware of what they do and do not know and what they can and cannot do. Older children, who are more attuned to the potential hazards of interpersonal life and who are also more sensitive to potentially threatening social comparison information (e.g., that their closest friends are much better than they are at controlling their facial expressions), may often feel less confident than their abilities warrant. Over the course of development, people may find themselves in interpretive ruts, in which they feel quite confident of their reading of the expressive guidelines that are in force in particular situations and fail to attend sufficiently to cues that might indicate that the guidelines have changed. All of this, though, is mere speculation; there is as yet scant empirical foundation for these predictions.

Spontaneous expressiveness

For some people, expressive behaviors do seem to be a window to their hearts and souls; for even when they are not deliberately trying to make their feelings known to others (and in fact, even when they think that no one else is present), those feelings, attitudes, and other internal states are immediately evident from their nonverbal behaviors. Earlier we noted that people who are spontaneously expressive are disadvantaged in situations in which they would like to mask or suppress the expression of their internal states. This inhibition truly "goes against the grain" for such people, and they are likely to be less successful than others who are not generally so spontaneously expressive. Next we shall consider the developmental course of spontaneous expressiveness and the considerable advantages of the spontaneously expressive style.

Developmental changes in spontaneous expressiveness. Individual differences in expressiveness are apparent in infancy (e.g., Buck, 1984; Field & Walden, 1982) and also appear to be stable developmentally. For example, Kagan and his colleagues (e.g., Kagan, Reznick, Snidman, Gibbons, & Johnson, 1988; see also Bronson, 1966) investigated inhibited and uninhibited styles, construed as entire constellations of behaviors, not specific to nonverbal expressions. They found evidence of consistencies in this style from age 2 until at least age 7. The stability of spontaneous expressiveness is also suggested indirectly by the fact that the personality correlates of expressiveness are strikingly similar for children (Buck, 1975, 1977) as for adults (Buck, Miller, & Caul, 1974; Cunningham, 1977; Friedman, DiMatteo, & Taranta, 1980; Friedman, Prince, Riggio, & DiMatteo, 1980; Friedman, Riggio, & Segall, 1980) and by the fact that these correlates are consistent across rather different measures of expressiveness and personality.

In the infancy studies, expressiveness was conceptualized as an uninhibited style of behaving. In research involving preschoolers and older children and adults, however, expressiveness has often been defined more specifically as the accuracy with which internal states are communicated nonverbally when the communicators are not deliberately trying to make their inner experiences known to others. Often the methodology used is Buck's slide-viewing paradigm (e.g., Buck, 1975) in which participants sit alone in a room watching different kinds of emotion-laden slides, unaware that their facial expressions are being videotaped. In other paradigms, participants might, for example, talk about events that have made them feel particular emotions (e.g., Bugental & Moore, 1979; Malatesta & Izard, 1984). Although it is possible that the participants in those kinds of studies were deliberately making some effort to control their nonverbal cues, they were not specifically instructed to do so.

For preschoolers, there are striking individual differences in the accuracy of their spontaneous expressions of affect (Buck, 1975, 1977). As a group, preschoolers' spontaneous facial expressions typically convey the relevant affect at a level that is just slightly better than chance (Buck, 1975, 1977). Occasionally, accuracy is above chance only for certain subgroups of the children, certain affects, or certain kinds of observers. For example, Feinman and Feldman (1982) found that mothers (but not non-mothers) could decipher preschoolers' spontaneous expressions of happiness, but not their expressions of sadness, fear, or anger. In Buck's studies (1975, 1977), boys (but not girls) consistently showed some decline in the legibility of their facial expressions during the preschool years.

By first grade, the accuracy with which emotions can be read from children's spontaneous facial expressions is solidly above chance, and by fifth grade, these emotional expressions become clearer still (Morency & Krauss, 1982). Children in first, third, and fifth grade sound especially happy when talking about happy things that have happened to them, even to adults who can only hear the tone of the children's voices and not any of their words; only the first graders, though, sound noticeably sadder when discussing sad events from their lives, relative to neutral ones (Bugental & Moore, 1979). Certain internal states other than the basic emotions can also be read accurately from children's spontaneous expressions; for example, adults observing fourth graders can tell just from looking at their faces whether the children are listening to a very easy lesson or a very difficult one (Allen & Atkinson, 1978, 1981).

In late adolescence and early adulthood, spontaneous facial expressions are generally quite accurate reflections of internal emotional states (e.g., Buck, Miller, & Caul, 1974; Kraut, 1982; Zuckerman, Hall, DeFrank, & Rosenthal, 1976; Zuckerman, Larrance, Hall, DeFrank, & Rosenthal, 1979). These findings are quite robust across studies in which observers are asked simply to report their impressions of the overall degree of pleasantness or unpleasantness. But when observers are asked to identify the particular emotion that the person is experiencing (Wagner, MacDonald, & Manstead, 1986), then the facial expressions seem to be a little less clear to them. Observers' readings of internal emotional states are also accurate when they are based solely on adults' tone-of-voice cues (e.g., Cunningham, 1977; Scherer, 1986; Zuckerman, Larrance, Hall, DeFrank, & Rosenthal, 1979). Little is known about the spontaneous expressiveness of body movements and postures, but when these cues are combined with facial expressions, observers can distinguish adults who are feeling embarrassed from those who are not (Edelman & Hampson, 1981).

There is suggestive evidence that spontaneous facial expressions may become less clearly communicative during the later adulthood years. In a study in which women, whose average ages were 33, 55, and 69, discussed emotional events from their lives, the older women's faces were more likely than the younger women's to be characterized by miniaturization, fragmentation, and blending of expressions, rather than by full-blown expressions of single emotions (Malatesta & Izard, 1984).

Over the life span, then, spontaneous expressiveness may follow a curvilinear path. The clarity of spontaneous expressions of internal states is probably greatest in the late childhood, adolescent, and early adulthood years. In the preschool years, and then again in the later adulthood years, the correspondence between internal states and their spontaneous nonverbal expression may be somewhat muted and confused. The reasons for these ambiguities, however, are likely to be very different for the preschoolers than for the older adults. Preschoolers may be less attentive to the emotional inductions, and they may therefore actually experience the emotions less deeply. In addition, there may also be a process whereby after years of experience at deliberately regulating one's facial expressions so as to make particular expressions abundantly clear to others, even one's spontaneous expressions become more clearly communicative. Preschoolers' expressions are less likely than older children's and adults' to have been molded by such a process. In contrast, the ambiguities in older adults' spontaneous expressions may be the product of habitual attempts at muting the clarity of their expressions so as to maintain privacy and regulate affect and arousal (Malatesta & Izard, 1984).

Interpersonal advantages of spontaneous expressiveness. Although the personality profile of spontaneously expressive children and adults includes a number of traits, such as dominance and impulsiveness, that might be regarded as negative, the impact that expressive people have on others is generally quite positive. For in addition to being somewhat bossy, they are also extroverted, playful, and socially skilled. In study after study, people say that they like expressive children and adults more than they like their more subdued counterparts (DePaulo, 1990).

In interpersonal interactions, expressive people make things happen. In group situations, expressive people influence other people's moods more than unexpressive people do (Friedman & Riggio, 1981), and they may also elicit more reciprocal openness and expressiveness from others (Buck, 1989). Even infants are responsive to variations in expressiveness; when mothers are more facially expressive, their 4-month-olds are more expressive, too (Kaye & Fogel, 1980).

Because their nonverbal expressions are so clear to others, expressive people – more so than unexpressive people – may find that others are inclined to comment on those expressions and on the internal states that they might reflect (Buck, 1988). This feedback may prove useful to them in further refining their nonverbal expressions and in understanding the impact that those expressions have on others.

Perhaps in part because of the greater amounts of feedback that they receive from others, spontaneously expressive people – both children (Buck, 1975) and adults (Cunningham, 1977; Zuckerman et al., 1976; Zuckerman, Larrance, Hall, DeFrank, & Rosenthal, 1979) – are more skillful at conveying the impression nonverbally that they are experiencing a particular affect or emotion when in fact they are not experiencing any particular emotion. Only when they are trying to convey an expression of an internal state different from the one they are actually experiencing are expressive people likely to be less successful at regulating their nonverbal expressions than unexpressive people are. That is, spontaneously expressive people are less successful liars, a finding that again holds true for both children (Morency & Krauss, 1982) and adults (Kraut, 1982; see also Friedman & Miller-Herringer, 1989).

Because expressive people are liked more than unexpressive people, are more influential in certain interpersonal ways, and are more skilled at manipulating their nonverbal expressions to simulate particular emotions when they are not feeling especially emotional, it should follow that they are more apt to be successful in attaining their self-presentational goals. Indirect evidence supporting this hypothesis comes from research with athletes showing that more expressive athletes are perceived as trying harder than less expressive athletes are, and that after they have failed, expressive athletes are seen as more able and less responsible for their failure than are unexpressive athletes (Rejeski & Lowe, 1980). Physicians, too, seem to benefit from expressiveness: Those who are more skilled at posing affects nonverbally have more satisfied patients (DiMatteo, 1979; Friedman, DiMatteo, & Taranta, 1980).

Affect intensity

People who react to stimuli intensely and who experience emotions deeply (Larsen & Diener, 1987) are likely to have self-presentational profiles very similar to those of people who are spontaneously expressive. When they are trying to convey their true feelings and internal states accurately and to convey their internal states in an exaggerated way, they should be more successful than are people who are less affectively intense. However, when attempting to work against their internal states, by either suppressing the nonverbal expression of those states or covering the expressions that might otherwise occur spontaneously with expressions of very different states, they are likely to be markedly less successful. Their difficulties with deceiving should be particularly pronounced when the deception concerns an emotion (e.g., they are trying to feign joy in another's accomplishment when they actually feel bitter resentment), when they feel emotional about the emotion that they are trying to hide (e.g., ashamed of their resentment), or when they feel emotional (e.g., guilty, apprehensive) about the fact that they are deceiving (cf. Ekman, 1985).

The correlates of affect intensity are similar to the correlates of spontaneous expressiveness. For example, people who experience emotions intensely tend to be more sociable, arousable, active, and extroverted than are people who are less intensely emotional. In most situations, then, people high in affect intensity are likely to have an advantage in creating a favorable impression on others. They may, though, find certain situations treacherous, as when they must try to mute or hide their own feelings to spare the feelings of others.

The development of skill at conveying impressions nonverbally

In the previous sections, we discussed separate components of skill at conveying impressions nonverbally. In the following sections, we shall review several kinds of nonverbal self-presentational performances to which the individual components contribute. First, we shall examine the ability to assume a convincing nonverbal expression of an internal state when neither that state nor its opposite is present, as well as the ability to communicate clearly an internal state that is present. Following this discussion of nonverbal "posing" skill will be a related discussion of skill at deceiving – that is, at conveying a nonverbal expression of a state that is quite different from the one actually experienced. The studies of posing and deceiving are those in which participants were directly instructed to try to convey particular impressions. In the last section, we shall cover the uninstructed use of nonverbal behaviors for self-presentational purposes. In all the sections, our emphasis will be on the development of these skills across the life span.

Nonverbal posing skill

Can children, in the perfectly safe and dogless environment of a university laboratory, convey a convincing expression of fear when asked to make a face like the one they would if they were being chased by a mean dog (Odom & Lemond, 1972)? Can adults watch a murder scene from the movie *Psycho* and make it quite clear to others viewing only their faces or listening only to the tone of their voices that they are watching something quite unpleasant (Zuckerman et al., 1976)? In these studies and dozens of others, people ranging in age from preschoolers to young adults have been asked to pose a wide variety of affects and states that they are not really experiencing, or to make clear to others the internal states that they are experiencing. The paradigms are similar to those used to study the accuracy of spontaneous expressions, except that in the posing studies, participants are instructed to try deliberately to convey convincing nonverbal expressions.

Although intuitively it may seem reasonable to expect natural and spontaneous expressions of internal states to be much clearer to others than are simulated expressions of those same states, in fact the results are quite the contrary. Posed expressions of internal states are strikingly more legible than are the unregulated spontaneous expressions of those states. Adults, then, can pose emotions more convincingly than they can express them naturally (e.g., Zuckerman et al., 1976; Zuckerman, Larrance, Hall, DeFrank, & Rosenthal, 1979), and in most studies, so can children (Feinman & Feldman, 1982; Morency & Krauss, 1982; however, see also Felleman, Barden, Carlson, Rosenberg, & Masters, 1983).

To simulate an expression of an emotion or other internal state without actually experiencing that state probably requires some knowledge of what such an expression should look or sound like (or how it should feel to produce it), the ability to control the relevant muscles in order to produce the appropriate expression, and practice and experience at so doing. Confidence should help, too, as should motivation (within the nondebilitating range). In paradigms in which there are no emotion-evoking external stimuli (e.g., those in which children are asked to imagine the mean dog), affect intensity should not be particularly important. However, when people are exposed to some stimulus such as an affect-laden slide and are asked to convey nonverbally to others information about what they are experiencing, people who experience emotions more deeply will probably be at an advantage. In that people who are spontaneously expressive are also better at conveying emotions deliberately, spontaneous expressiveness is a facilitating factor, too. Most of these predictor factors increase with age; therefore, skill at posing should also improve, at least throughout the childhood years.

The youngest children asked to pose facial expressions of the basic emotions were the 3- and 4-year-olds studied by Zuckerman and Przewuzman (1979). These preschoolers were successful at the task, as were the 4-, 5-, and 6-year-olds studied by Feinman and Feldman (1982). Zuckerman and Przewuzman (1979) found, as had Buck (1975, 1977) for spontaneous communications, that boys' facial expressions became less legible with age, whereas the girls' posed expressions became more readable. Two other studies compared fifth graders' facial posing skill with that of either kindergartners (Odom & Lemond, 1972) or first graders (Morency & Krauss, 1982). In both cases, even the youngest children were successful at making facial expressions that were accurately read by others, although the fifth graders were noticeably more successful at doing so than were the younger children (see also Fulcher, 1942).

Unsurprisingly, the many studies of adults' nonverbal posing skill have consistently shown that young adults can quite successfully convey to others – using only nonverbal cues – the impression that they are experiencing a particular internal state. As is customary, the research on facial posing is most abundant (e.g., Jaeger, Borod, & Peselow, 1986; Kraut, 1982; Wallbott & Scherer, 1986; Zaidel, & Mehrabian, 1969; Zuckerman et al., 1976; Zuckerman, Larrance, Hall, DeFrank, & Rosenthal, 1979; Zuckerman et al., 1975), but adults' success at posing also has been documented for tone-of-voice cues (e.g., Apple & Hecht, 1982; Scherer, 1986; Wallbott & Scherer, 1986; Zaidel & Mehrabian, 1969; Zuckerman et al., 1975; Zuckerman, Larrance, Hall, DeFrank, & Rosenthal, 1979), body movements and postures (Cunningham, 1977), and gait (Montepare, Goldstein, & Clausen, 1987).

Nonverbal deceiving skill

Studies of people's abilities to use their nonverbal behaviors to deceive others are similar in some ways to studies of nonverbal posing skill, except that in the deception studies, people try to convince others that they are experiencing something very different – often just the opposite – from what they really are experiencing. Observers then try to determine the nature of the people's true internal state, or they indicate the degree to which the people seemed to be deceptive.

When people try to deceive, some of the attributes that serve them well in nondeceptive contexts can instead become disruptive to self-presentational success. Those who experience emotions more deeply, for example, as well as those who express them more spontaneously, are likely to have more difficulty than do other less-emotional and less-expressive people when trying to use their nonverbal behaviors to convince others that they feel very different than they really do. Motivation, too, can be disruptive of nonverbal deceptive success, as has been amply documented for adults (e.g., DePaulo & Kirkendol, 1989). Confidence, though, should help people deceive more successfully, just as it helps them pose more effectively. Ability, practice, and experience should also facilitate deceptive success. Knowledge should be especially helpful, as deceivers need to understand their interpersonal worlds from both their own perspectives and the point of view of others (Feldman, White, & Lobato, 1982; Shennum & Bugental, 1982).

The methodology that has been used across the widest span of ages is Feldman's drink-tasting paradigm (e.g., Feldman, Jenkins, & Popoola, 1979; Feldman & White, 1980). In the first such study, first graders, seventh graders, and college students sipped a sweetened and an unsweetened drink while trying to convey the impression that they really liked both drinks (Feldman et al., 1979). First graders were totally unsuccessful in hiding their true feelings about the drinks. Undergraduates watching only their facial expressions on a videotape could tell that they liked the unsweetened drink much less than the sweetened drink. The first graders' actual distaste for the bad-tasting drink, then, "leaked" from their facial expressions. The seventh graders used a strategy of "naturalistic reproduction": Facially, they appeared just as happy with the unsweetened as with the sweetened beverages. The college students assumed a dramatic style of "hamming": They actually appeared more pleased with the unsweetened than with the sweetened beverages.

First graders have been unsuccessful at using their nonverbal behaviors to deceive in other paradigms, too. In a study in which first and fifth graders watched very pleasant and very unpleasant slides and tried to convey the impression that they really were watching just the opposite kinds of slides, adults who watched videotapes of the children's facial expressions could tell that the first graders were more deceptive when they were trying to convey false impressions than when they were trying to convey truthful ones (Morency & Krauss, 1982). In fact, when the tapes were shown to other children, even the first graders could tell that the first graders on the tape were acting deceptively when they were watching a pleasant slide but pretending that it was unpleasant.

Even by the third grade, children still have trouble controlling their facial expressions so as to convey a false impression. In one study (Feldman, Devin-Sheehan, & Allen, 1978), third graders tutored other children who performed well or poorly. The tutors were instructed to try always to provide encouraging and supportive feedback, regardless of the children's performance. Yet other third graders who viewed the tutors' facial expressions could tell that the tutors were less pleased with the children who performed poorly than they were with those who performed well. Objective analyses revealed that when the children gave an incorrect answer, compared with when they gave a correct answer, the tutors paused more, smiled less, and showed more mouth displeasure.

By the fourth and fifth grades, children become markedly more successful in their deceptive attempts. The fifth graders in the Morency and Krauss (1982) study who were pretending to be watching slides that were pleasant while actually watching quite unpleasant slides could convince not only other children but even adults (including their own parents) of their truthfulness. When pretending to be watching unpleasant slides while actually watching pleasant ones, though, they appeared truthful only to the other children.

Fourth and fifth graders can also successfully fake understanding a lesson that they actually find totally incomprehensible, and being baffled by a lesson that they actually find quite easy (Allen & Atkinson, 1978). Adults watching only their faces think that the children feigning comprehension really do understand the lesson better than do the children feigning noncomprehension.

The strategy of hamming used by the college students in Feldman's drink-tasting paradigm has also been documented in other kinds of studies involving adults. For example, when faking extroversion, adults speak even more quickly than do genuine extroverts, and when faking introversion, they speak even more slowly than do genuine introverts (Feldstein & Sloan, 1984). The hamming strategy, though, is not the modal strategy used by adults (see DePaulo, Stone, & Lassiter, 1985a, for a review). For example, when adults are truthfully describing people they really do like, they convey more liking than when just pretending to like people whom they actually dislike (DePaulo & Rosenthal, 1979). Similarly, they convey more disliking for the genuinely disliked persons than for people they are only pretending to dislike (DePaulo & Rosenthal, 1979). If they were hamming, they would convey more disliking for the people they were only pretending to dislike than for the disliked people they were describing honestly. A subset of adults, however (mostly males), do use the hamming strategy, and they are quite successful at getting away with their lies when they do so (DePaulo & Rosenthal, 1979).

The hamming strategy is of special interest because one study reported quite a lot of use of just such a strategy by children as young as 6 years old (Shennum & Bugental, 1982). Children ranging in age from 6 to 12 years old first talked honestly with the experimenters about their likes and dislikes. Then they were asked to try to act like famous actors and actresses and to pretend to like the things they just said that they actually disliked and to pretend to dislike the things that they said they actually liked. They were also asked to pretend to feel neutrally about those things. Using adults as judges, Shennum and Bugental studied the degree of positivity and the degree of deceptiveness conveyed by both the children's faces and the tone of their voices. When pretending to like things that they actually disliked and when pretending to feel neutrally about things that they disliked, children across all ages hammed with their faces and their voices. They looked and sounded even more positively than they did when truthfully describing things that they really did like. Perhaps they adopted this hamming style in response to the instructions to act like movie stars on talk shows. What is especially interesting about the strategy is that even though it is an adultlike strategy that often works for adults, it did not work for these children. The adult observers who watched their faces and listened to their voices thought that the children sounded quite deceptive. The exaggerated positivity simply was not convincing. Apparently, a less dramatic style may have worked better, and in fact it did work better for some of the children. The older children's facial hamming was less extreme than that of the younger children, and they also were rated as less facially deceptive.

As in the Morency and Krauss (1982) study, the children in the Shennum and Bugental (1982) study had much more difficulty pretending to dislike something that they actually liked than they did pretending to like something that they actually disliked. This trouble that children (and sometimes even adults) have with expressing negativity is one that appears in many different kinds of studies: In the Shennum and Bugental (1982) study, the children of all ages adopted the very immature strategy (or nonstrategy) of "leaking" their actual positivity when trying to pretend to dislike the things that they actually liked. Their faces looked no more unpleasant in these fake-negative conditions than they did when they were honestly discussing things that they really did like. Their voices did sound just as negative when they were faking negativity as they did when they were honestly describing things that they really did dislike, suggesting a mature strategy of naturalistic reproduction. However, once again, the strategy was not successful. When they were faking negativity, the children sounded more deceptive than they did when honestly describing their dislikes. Perhaps the most striking aspect of these fake-negative findings is that there were no age trends; the 10- to 12-year-olds were just as unsuccessful, and were unsuccessful in the same ways, as were the 6- to 8-year-olds.

In their daily lives, children and adults are likely to face many more situations in which they are tempted to lie by pretending to feel more positively than they actually do than those in which they are tempted to feign greater negativity than they actually feel. And for the former kind of situation, the developmental trends are fairly clear: With age, children become more and more successful at manipulating their nonverbal behaviors so as to deceive others effectively. Research on the nonverbal communication of deception among young adults is voluminous and indicates quite convincingly that they are not entirely successful in their deceptive attempts. Observers can typically see at least some slight difference in deceptiveness when young adults are lying compared with when they are telling the truth (see DePaulo et al., 1985a, for a review). Research on the years beyond early adulthood is sorely lacking, but the one study in the literature indicates that nonverbal deceiving is a skill that continues to develop across the life span. Adults who were (on the average) 79 years old were more successful at using their faces to deceive others in the drink-tasting paradigm than were 19-year-olds (Parham, Feldman, Oster, & Popoola, 1981).

Regulation of nonverbal behaviors under self-presentational instructions

In a study of adults (Rosenfeld, 1966), skill at attaining what may be one of the most pervasive of all self-presentational goals – gaining the approval of another person – was examined. Subjects directly instructed to endear themselves to their interaction partners regulated their nonverbal behaviors in ways that differed systematically from those of subjects who were not seeking approval. For example, the men more frequently nodded their heads in agreement; the women gestured more; and both the men and the women indicated their attentiveness to the other person by "backchanneling" (e.g., saying "mm-hmm") while that person spoke. Adults are also adept at deliberately using nonverbal behaviors such as seating position to convey impressions of warmth and friendliness, coolness and aloofness, and leadership ability (Riess & Rosenfeld, 1980). These kinds of studies have not been conducted with children, but they should be.

Spontaneous use of nonverbal behaviors for self-presentational purposes

Nonverbal behaviors in self-presentationally relevant situations. In the studies of nonverbal posing and deceiving reviewed so far, the subjects were told to try to convey certain impressions. Perhaps even more interesting are those studies in which the subjects are observed in situations in which it might be advantageous for them to try deliberately to regulate their nonverbal behaviors for self-presentational purposes, but they are not actually told to do so. In these situations, most of the components (skill, knowledge, confidence, and so forth) necessary to achieve success at the instructed-posing and instructed-deceiving tasks are again necessary, but they are no longer enough. The subjects must figure out for themselves that the situation is one in which they should call upon their knowledge and abilities and deliberately try to regulate their nonverbal behaviors. The motivation to come across as a particular kind of person becomes especially important.

One of the first and most creative attempts to study children's spontaneous use of nonverbal behaviors for self-presentational purposes was Saarni's (1984) investigation of children's reactions to receiving a disappointing gift. The children were 9-, 10-, and 11-year-olds who, in the first phase of the study, had received attractive gifts as thanks for helping a market researcher evaluate workbooks. In the second phase, they again helped the researcher and received a wrapped gift for their efforts, but this time the gift was a drab and disappointing baby toy. Children's positive and negative facial and vocal (and verbal) behaviors were coded both times. Of central interest, of course, was the question of whether the children would be willing and able to conceal their disappointment and perhaps even look pleased upon receiving the unappealing present. The older children (especially the girls) were most adept at so doing – they showed more positive behaviors (e.g., smiling and looking at the researcher) and fewer negative behaviors (e.g., lowered brows, wrinkled nose) upon receiving the disappointing gift than did the younger children. In an extension of Saarni's research, Cole (1986) found that even 4-year-olds could manage to convey a seemingly positive reaction to a disappointing gift. Saarni's work, though, showed that even the oldest children were not entirely successful at hiding their disappointment, in that they reacted more positively to the gift that they really did like than to the one that they were just pretending to like.

In a study of deception among 3-year-olds (Lewis, Stanger, & Sullivan, 1989), the children were left alone in a room with an attractive toy behind them and were told not to look at it. Twenty-nine of the 33 children did take a peek. When asked subsequently if they had peeked, 38% told outright lies – they denied it. Another 24% gave no verbal response, and the other 38% fessed up. The outright liars acted very differently nonverbally than did the nonresponders – interestingly, they were much more positive (e.g., they smiled more). It would probably be a mistake to conclude from this study that the 3-year-olds were deliberately regulating their nonverbal behaviors for self-presentational purposes. However, the findings do suggest that the nonverbal behavior of preschoolers varies systematically with important dimensions of interpersonal communications, such as whether the communications are overtly deceptive versus merely evasive or unresponsive.

Somewhat more direct evidence for deliberate regulation of nonverbal behavior was reported in a study of children only a year or two older than those in the Lewis et al. (1989) study. Cummings (1987) studied the reactions of 4- and 5-year olds to "background anger" by staging in the lab a verbal altercation between two research assistants over who would clean up the room. Some of the children said they were angry about the conflict but that they wanted to try to ignore it. These children were successful at suppressing their affective reactions: Their facial expressions were neither positive nor negative.

Nonverbal behaviors in private and in public. If people act differently nonverbally when other people are present than they do when they are alone, it is likely that they are deliberately regulating their expressive behaviors for self-presentational purposes. This sort of evidence would not be definitive (cf. Tetlock & Manstead, 1985). For example, the nonverbal behaviors that occur in private may not be totally spontaneous and unregulated expressions of internal states but instead may be overlearned responses that have become habitual (e.g., when people use hand gestures while talking on the telephone) (Zivin, 1982). Even when alone, people may regulate their nonverbal behavior for their own benefit (such as to convince themselves that they are as intense as they want to think they are) or for the benefit of an imaginary audience (Schlenker & Weigold, 1988). Nonetheless, differences between nonverbal behavior in public and in private are interesting enough in a suggestive way to be worth considering.

A rather minimal social presence manipulation is one in which another person is present while the subject performs some task (such as trying to imitate the expressions shown in photographs or watching slides and trying to form impressions of them), but the subject's performance is in no way relevant to the other person. Typically, the other person is not performing the task but is simply sitting next to the subject. These kinds of studies have been conducted with first graders, sixth graders, and college students. The results are fairly consistent in showing that the subjects' facial expressions are more ambiguous, less intense, and less legible when the other person is present than when the subject is alone (e.g., Kilbride & Yarczower, 1980; Yarczower & Daruns, 1982; Yarczower, Kilbride, & Hill, 1979; see also Kraut, 1982).

When the other person is the target of the subject's communications, the psychological dynamics should be, and are, quite different. For example, in one variation of Feldman's drink-tasting paradigm, the subjects interacted with an interviewer either face to face or by speaking into a tape recorder (Feldman et al., 1979). All of the subjects were instructed to convey the impression that they liked both the sweetened and the unsweetened drinks. Their facial expressions were especially positive while tasting the sweetened drinks when the interviewer was right there with them. Similarly, in a variation of the disappointing gift paradigm, 4-year-olds reacted more positively when the person who gave them the gift remained there while they looked at it than when she left immediately (Cole, 1986). And in observations of children at play, it has been noted that 3- and 4-year-olds who get hurt are more likely to cry if they think someone is looking at them than if they think they are not being observed (Blurton-Jones, 1967).

Facial expressions also change in conflict situations. Camras (1982) videotaped pairs of children sitting across from each other at a table as they battled for possession of a box with a gerbil inside that only one of the children could play with at a time. The box could be pushed back and forth between the children on a rail. For some of the children, the views of each other were obstructed by a partition, whereas for the others, their views remained unobstructed. Children who "won" a given episode (i.e., retained possession of the gerbil box when the other child tried to claim it) tended to show a winning "plus" face, characterized by features such as medially raised brows and a slightly raised chin (Zivin, 1982). This winning facial expression was far less likely to be in evidence in the conditions in which the children could not see each other (Zivin, 1982).

Zivin (1982) found that the donning of the plus face predicted winning in conflict situations for people ranging in age from 4 to 45. After the age of 7, however, the plus face no longer appeared predominantly in conflict situations. Instead, it appeared on the faces of dominant children (those rated by their peers as "tough" or as "getting their way a lot") in competence-relevant situations that did not involve conflict (e.g., while the child was reading). Zivin suggested that these children had learned to carry with them their aura of competence and winningness, even into nonconflict situations. Girls who are high academic achievers seem to have mastered a similar expressive strategy: While listening to a lesson, they look like they understand it, even when in fact they are totally bewildered (Allen & Atkinson, 1978).

There is suggestive evidence, then, across a variety of situations, that children do attempt to control their nonverbal expressive behaviors for self-presentational purposes, though with varying degrees of success. Further studies of the development of the spontaneous regulation of nonverbal behaviors in self-presentationally relevant situations will be one of the most rewarding directions for future research.

Summary

As children learn to control their nonverbal behaviors during interpersonal interactions, they increase their opportunities to try out new identities and to claim those that fit most comfortably. Success at regulating nonverbal behaviors in the service of identity-relevant goals is born of knowledge, skill, practice, experience, motivation, and confidence. Most of these components change in ways that facilitate expressive control during the childhood and adolescent years. For instance, as they grow older, children become cognitively sophisticated in ways that are not at all specific to the expressive domain but that are as important in that domain as elsewhere. Their knowledge of their interpersonal world grows rapidly, and their ability to use that knowledge also improves, as does their skill at integrating different kinds of information. Knowledge more specific to the expressive domain also grows in quantity and complexity. For example, children become more sophisticated in their understanding of emotions and other internal states (how they are elicited, how they are regulated, and how they affect personal psyches and interpersonal outcomes), of expressive behaviors (what they look, sound, and feel like and what the norms are that govern their use), and of people (how they react to different kinds of situations and different kinds of emotions and how these reactions differ for different categories of people and different individuals).

Most of the factors that in most ways enhance nonverbal self-presentational success can in other ways undermine it. For example, children's growing knowledge enables them to discern more accurately the kinds of self-presentations that are likely to be most effective. But knowledge can also be daunting and perhaps even immobilizing, as when children and adolescents become painfully aware of the potential costs of failing to realize societal (and personal) ideals. Up to a point, the motivation to live up to such ideals and to embody them in one's own expressive behaviors augments self-presentational efforts and sharpens skills, but beyond that point, motivation can instead be debilitating. Emotions, too, are double-edged. When people are experiencing emotions more deeply, they can communicate those emotions more readily; but if they instead want to suppress those emotions or cover them with a facade of different emotions, then more intensely felt emotions are more disruptive of self-presentational success than are less intense ones. Even physical growth is both advantageous and treacherous. With physical maturation comes the development and refinement of fine-motor skills, which are essential to expressive control. Yet such growth can be quite rapid during many of the childhood years, thereby making it difficult for children's awareness of their physical characteristics and their self-presentational significance to keep pace with the rate of change of those characteristics.

Research on expressive control beyond the early adulthood years is scant, but the possibilities for such work are not. Throughout the chapter, we have offered various speculations about the course of expressive development across the life span. For example, we suggested that adults' mastery of cultural and situational norms for expressiveness can facilitate their smooth integration into the social life of their communities; however, it can also restrict the kinds of expressive performances they will think to try. If there are expressive skills that atrophy with lack of practice, then the underuse of undervalued expressive styles can erode not just motivation but also ability. It is also possible that over a long period of time, the enactment of certain roles, even very prestigious ones, can undermine expressive adeptness. The powerful executive, for example, who thinks that she does not need to hide how she feels may eventually find that she is not able to hide how she feels, even if she does want to.

Some nonverbal self-presentational skills, such as the ability to control deliberately certain hard-to-control facial muscles, may never develop very much without special training. For other skills, there is much room for continued refinement during the childhood, adolescent, and adult years, but that potential may or may not be realized. An example of such a skill is the ability to see oneself as others do. Though people can never see or hear their own nonverbal behaviors exactly as others do, they can try to remain ever alert to the ways in which their expressive behaviors seem to affect other people.

References

Allen, V. L., & Atkinson, M. L. (1978). Encoding of nonverbal behavior by high-achieving and low-achieving children. *Journal of Educational Psychology, 70,* 298–305.

    (1981). Identification of spontaneous and deliberate behavior. *Journal of Nonverbal Behavior, 5,* 224–237.

Allport, G. W. (1937). *Personality.* New York: Holt.

Allport, G. W., & Vernon, P. E. (1933). *Studies in expressive movement.* New York: Hafner.

Apple, W., & Hecht, K. (1982). Speaking emotionally: The relation between verbal and vocal communication of affect. *Journal of Personality and Social Psychology, 42,* 864–875.

Baumeister, R. F. (1982). A self-presentational view of social phenomena. *Psychological Bulletin, 91,* 3–26.

Baumeister, R. F., & Scher, S. J. (1988). Self-defeating behavior patterns among normal individuals: Review and analysis of common self-destructive tendencies. *Psychological Bulletin, 104,* 3–22.

Blurton, J. N. (1967). An ethological study of some aspects of social behaviour of children in nursery school. In D. Morris (Ed.), *Primate ethology* (pp. 347–368). London: Weidenfeld & Nicholson.

Bronson, W. C. (1966). Central orientations: A study of behavior organization from childhood to adolescence. *Child Development, 37,* 125–155.

Buck, R. (1975). Nonverbal communication of affect in children. *Journal of Personality and Social Psychology, 31,* 644–653.

    (1977). Nonverbal communication accuracy in preschool children: Relationships with personality and skin conductance. *Journal of Personality and Social Psychology, 33,* 225–236.

    (1984). *The communication of emotion.* New York: Guilford Press.

    (1988). Emotional education and mass media: A new view of the global village. In R. P. Hawkins, J. M. Weimann, & S. Pingree (Eds.), *Advancing communication science: Merging mass and interpersonal perspectives* (pp. 44–76). Beverly Hills, CA: Sage.

    (1989). Emotional communication in personal relationships: A developmental–interactionist view. In C. D. Hendrick (Ed.), *Review of personality and social psychology: Vol. 10. Close relationships* (pp. 84–96). Newbury Park, CA: Sage.

Buck, R., Miller, R. E., & Caul, W. F. (1974). Sex, personality, and physiological variables in the communication of affect via facial expression. *Journal of Personality and Social Psychology, 30,* 587–596.

Bugental, D. B., & Moore, B. S. (1979). Effects of induced moods on voice affect. *Developmental Psychology, 15,* 664–665.

Buss, A. H., & Plomin, R. (1975). *A temperament theory of personality development.* New York: Wiley.

Camras, L. A. (1977). Facial expressions used by children in a conflict situation. *Child Development, 48,* 1431–1435.

(1982). Ethological approaches to nonverbal communication. In R. S. Feldman (Ed.), *Development of nonverbal behavior in children* (pp. 3–28). New York: Springer-Verlag.

Carroll, J. J., & Steward, M. S. (1984). The role of cognitive development in children's understanding of their own feelings. *Child Development, 55,* 1486–1492.

Cole, P. M. (1985). Display rules and the socialization of affective displays. In G. Zivin (Ed.), *The development of expressive behavior* (pp. 269–290). New York: Academic Press.

(1986). Children's spontaneous control of facial expression. *Child Development, 57,* 1309–1321.

Cummings, E. M. (1987). Coping with background anger in early childhood. *Child Development, 58,* 976–984.

Cunningham, M. R. (1977). Personality and the structure of the nonverbal communication of emotion. *Journal of Personality, 45,* 564–584.

Darby, B. W., & Schlenker, B. R. (1982). Children's reactions to apologies. *Journal of Personality and Social Psychology, 43,* 742–753.

(1986). Children's understanding of social anxiety. *Developmental Psychology, 22,* 633–639.

Davis, D., & Holtgraves, T. (1984). Perceptions of unresponsive others. *Journal of Experimental Social Psychology, 20,* 383–408.

Demos, V. (1982). Facial expressions of infants and toddlers. In T. Field & A. Fogel (Eds.), *Emotion and early interaction* (pp. 127–160). Hillsdale, NJ: Erlbaum.

DePaulo, B. M. (1990). *Nonverbal behavior and self-presentation.* Manuscript submitted for publication.

DePaulo, B. M., Kenny, D. A., Hoover, C., Webb, W., & Oliver, P. (1987). Accuracy of person perception: Do people know what kinds of impressions they convey? *Journal of Personality and Social Psychology, 52,* 303–315.

DePaulo, B. M., & Kirkendol, S. E. (1989). The motivational impairment effect in the communication of deception. In J. Yuille (Ed.), *Credibility assessment* (pp. 51–70). Dordrecht: Kluwer Academic Publishers.

DePaulo, B. M., Kirkendol, S. E., Tang, J., & O'Brien, T. (1988). The motivational impairment effect in the communication of deception: Replications and extensions. *Journal of Nonverbal Behavior, 12,* 177–202.

DePaulo, B. M., Lanier, K., & Davis. T. (1983). Detecting the deceit of the motivated liar. *Journal of Personality and Social Psychology, 45,* 1096–1103.

DePaulo, B. M., LeMay, C. S., & Epstein, J. (1991). Effects of importance of success and expectations for success on effectiveness at deceiving. *Personality and Social Psychology Bulletin, 17,* 14–24.

DePaulo, B. M., & Rosenthal, R. (1979). Telling lies. *Journal of Personality and Social Psychology, 37,* 1713–1722.

(1982). Measuring the development of nonverbal sensitivity. In C. E. Izard (Ed.), *Measuring emotions in infants and children* (pp. 208–247). Cambridge: Cambridge University Press.

DePaulo, B. M., Stone, J. I., & Lassiter, G. D. (1985a). Deceiving and detecting deceit. In B. R. Schlenker (Ed.), *The self and social life* (pp. 323–370). New York: McGraw-Hill.

(1985b). Telling ingratiating lies: Effects of target sex and target attractiveness on verbal and nonverbal deceptive success. *Journal of Personality and Social Psychology, 48,* 1191–1203.

DePaulo, B. M., Tang, J., Webb, W., Hoover, C., Marsh, K., & Litowitz, C. (1989). Age differences in reactions to receiving help in a peer-tutoring context. *Child Development, 60,* 423–439.

DePaulo, P. J., & DePaulo, B. M. (1989). Can attempted deception by salespersons and customers be detected through nonverbal behavioral cues? *Journal of Applied Social Psychology, 19,* 1552–1577.

Diener, E., Sandvik, E., & Larsen, R. J. (1985). Age and sex effects for emotional intensity. *Developmental Psychology, 21,* 542–546.

DiMatteo, M. R. (1979). Nonverbal skill and the physician–patient relationship. In R. Rosenthal (Ed,), *Skill in nonverbal communication* (pp. 104–134). Cambridge, MA: Oelgeschlager, Gunn, & Hain.

Donaldson, S. K., & Westerman, M. A. (1986). Development of children's understanding of ambivalence and causal theories of emotions. *Developmental Psychology, 22,* 655–662.

Dunn, J., & Munn, P. (1985). Becoming a family member: Family conflict and the development of social understanding in the second year. *Child Development, 56,* 480–492.

Edelmann, R. J., & Hampson, S. E. (1981). The recognition of embarrassment. *Personality and Social Psychology Bulletin, 7,* 109–116.

Eisenberg, N., Fabes, R. A., Bustamante, D., Mathy, R. M., Miller, P. A., & Lindholm, E. (1988). Differentiation of vicariously induced emotional reactions to children. *Developmental Psychology, 24,* 237–246.

Ekman, P. (1972). Universals and cultural differences in facial expressions of emotion. In J. K. Cole (Ed.), *Nebraska Symposium on Motivation* (pp. 207–283). Lincoln: University of Nebraska Press.

(1985). *Telling lies.* New York: Norton.

(1989). *Why kids lie.* New York: Scribner.

Ekman, P., Roper, G., & Hager, J. C. (1980). Deliberate facial movement. *Child Development, 51,* 886–891.

Feinman, J. A., & Feldman, R. S. (1982). Decoding children's expressions of affect. *Child Development, 53,* 710–716.

Feldman, R. S., Devin-Sheehan, L., & Allen, V. L. (1978). Nonverbal cues as indicators of verbal dissembling. *American Educational Research Journal, 15,* 217–231.

Feldman, R. S., Jenkins, L., & Popoola, O. (1979). Detection of deception in adults and children via facial expressions. *Child Development, 50,* 350–355.

Feldman, R. S., & White, J. B. (1980). Detecting deception in children. *Journal of Communication, 30,* 121–129.

Feldman, R. S., White, J. B., & Lobato, D. (1982). Social skills and nonverbal behavior. In R. S. Feldman (Ed.), *Development of nonverbal behavior in children* (pp. 259–278). New York: Springer-Verlag.

Feldstein, S., & Sloan, B. (1984). Actual and stereotyped speech tempos of extroverts and introverts. *Journal of Personality, 52,* 188–204.

Felleman, E. S., Barden, R. C., Carlson, C. R., Rosenberg, L., & Masters, J. C. (1983). Children's and adults' recognition of spontaneous and posed emotional expressions in young children. *Developmental Psychology, 19,* 405–413.

Field, T. (1982). Individual differences in the expressivity of neonates and young infants. In R. S. Feldman (Ed.), *Development of nonverbal behavior in children* (pp. 279–298). New York: Springer-Verlag.

Field, T., & Walden, T. (1982). Production and perception of facial expressions in infancy and early childhood. In H. Reese & L. Lipsitt (Eds.), *Advances in child development* (Vol. 16, pp. 169–211). New York: Academic Press.

Fisher, S. (1986). *Development and structure of the body image* (Vol. 1). Hillsdale, NJ: Erlbaum.

Fridlund, A. J., Ekman, P., & Oster, H. (1987). Facial expressions of emotion. In A. W. Siegman & S. Feldstein (Eds.), *Nonverbal behavior and communication* (2nd ed., pp. 143–224). Hillsdale, NJ: Erlbaum.

Friedman, H. S., DiMatteo, M. R., & Taranta, A. (1980). A study of the relationship between individual differences in nonverbal expressiveness and factors of personality and social interaction. *Journal of Research in Personality, 14,* 351–364.

Friedman, H. S., & Miller-Herringer, T. (1989). *The nonverbal display of emotion in private and in public: Self-monitoring, personality, and expressive cues.* Manuscript submitted for publication.

Friedman, H. S., Prince, L. M., Riggio, R. E., & DiMatteo, M. R. (1980). Understanding and assessing nonverbal expressiveness: The affective communication test. *Journal of Personality and Social Psychology, 39,* 333–351.

Friedman, H. S., & Riggio, R. E. (1981). Effect of individual differences in nonverbal expressiveness on transmission of emotion. *Journal of Nonverbal Behavior, 6,* 96–104.

Friedman, H. W., Riggio, R. E., & Segall, D. O. (1980). Personality and the enactment of emotion. *Journal of Nonverbal Behavior, 5,* 35–48.

Fuchs, D., & Thelen, M. H. (1988). Children's expected interpersonal consequences of communicating their affective state and reported likelihood of expression. *Child Development, 59,* 1314–1322.

Fulcher, J. S. (1942). "Voluntary" facial expression in blind and seeing children. *Archives of Psychology, 272,* 5–49.

Gerson, A. C., & Perlman, D. (1979). Loneliness and expressive communication. *Journal of Abnormal Psychology, 88,* 258–261.

Gnepp, J. (1989a). Children's use of personal information to understand other people's feelings. In C. Saarni & P. L. Harris (Eds.), *Children's understanding of emotion* (pp. 151–177). Cambridge: Cambridge University Press.

(1989b). Personalized inferences of emotions and appraisals: Component processes and correlates. *Developmental Psychology, 25,* 277–288.

Gnepp, J., & Gould, M. E. (1985). The development of personalized inferences: Understanding other people's emotional reactions to light to their prior experiences. *Child Development, 56,* 1455–1464.

Gnepp, J., & Hess, D. L. R. (1986). Children's understanding of verbal and facial display rules. *Developmental Psychology, 22,* 103–108.

Gnepp, J., McKee, E., & Domanic, J. A. (1987). Children's use of situational information to infer emotion: Understanding emotionally equivocal situations. *Developmental Psychology, 23,* 114–123.

Goldsmith, H. H., Buss, A. H., Plomin, R., Rothbart, M. K., Thomas, A., Chess,

S., Hinde, R. A., & McCall, R. B. (1987). Roundtable: What is temperament? Four approaches. *Child Development, 58,* 505–529.

Goldsmith, H. H., & Campos. J. J. (1986). Fundamental issues in the study of early temperament: The Denver twin temperament study. In M. E. Lamb, A. L. Brown, & B. Rogoff (Eds.), *Advances in developmental psychology* (Vol. 4, pp. 231–283). Hillsdale, NJ: Erlbaum.

Hall, J. A., Roter, D. L., & Katz, N. R. (1987). Task versus socioemotional behaviors in physicians. *Medical Care, 25,* 399–412.

Hamilton, M. L. (1973). Imitative behavior and expressive ability in facial expression of emotion. *Development Psychology, 8,* 138.

Harkness, S., & Super, C. M. (1985). Child–environment interactions in the socialization of affect. In M. Lewis & C. Saarni (Eds.), *The socialization of emotions* (pp. 21–36). New York: Plenum.

Harper, R. G., Wiens, A. N., & Matarazzo, J. D. (1978). *Nonverbal communication.* New York: Wiley.

Harris, P. L. (1983). Children's understanding of the link between situation and emotion. *Journal of Experimental Child Psychology, 36,* 490–509.

(1989). *Children and emotion.* Oxford: Blackwell Publisher.

Harris, P. L., Donnelly, K., Guz, G. R., & Pitt-Watson, R. (1986). Children's understanding of the distinction between real and apparent emotion. *Child Development, 57,* 895–909.

Harris, P. L., Olthof, T., & Terwogt, M. M. (1981). Children's knowledge of emotion. *Journal of Child Psychology and Psychiatry, 22,* 247–261.

Harter, S. (1983). Developmental perspectives on the self-system. In E. M. Hetherington (Ed.) & P. H. Mussen (Series Ed.), *Handbook of child psychology: Vol. 4. Socialization, personality, and social development* (4th ed., pp. 275–385). New York: Wiley.

Harter, S., & Buddin, B. J. (1987). Children's understanding of the simultaneity of two emotions: A five-stage developmental acquisition sequence. *Developmental Psychology, 23,* 388–399.

Harter, S., & Whitesell, N. R. (1989). Developmental changes in children's understanding of single, multiple, and blended emotion concepts. In C. Saarni & P. L. Harris (Eds.), *Children's understanding of emotion* (pp. 81–116). Cambridge: Cambridge University Press.

Hayano, D. M. (1980). Communicative competency among poker players. *Journal of Communication, 30,* 113–120.

Hess, R. D., Kashiwagi, K., Azuma, H., Price, G. G., & Dickson, W. P. (1980). Maternal expectations for mastery of developmental tasks in Japan and the United States. *International Journal of Psychology, 15,* 259–271.

Hochschild, A. R. (1983). *The managed heart.* Berkeley and Los Angeles: University of California Press.

Izard, C. E. (1977). *Human emotions.* New York: Plenum.

Jaeger, J., Borod, J. C., & Peselow, E. (1986). Facial expression of positive and negative emotions in patients with unipolar depression. *Journal of Affective Disorders, 11,* 43–50.

Johnson, R. R., Greenspan, S., & Brown, G. M. (1984). Children's ability to recognize and improve upon socially inept communications. *Journal of Genetic Psychology, 144,* 255–264.

Jones, E. E., & Davis, K. E. (1965). From acts to dispositions: The attribution process in person perception. In L. Berkowitz (Ed.), *Advances in experimental social psychology* (Vol. 2, pp. 219–266). New York: Academic Press.

Jones, E. E., & Pittman, T. S. (1982). Toward a general theory of strategic self-presentation. In J. Suls (Ed.), *Psychological perspectives on the self* (Vol. 1, pp. 231–262). Hillsdale, NJ: Erlbaum.

Kagan, J. (1984). Continuity and change in the opening years of life. In R. N. Emde & R. J. Harmon (Eds.), *Continuities and discontinuities in development* (pp. 15–39). New York: Plenum.

Kagan, J., Reznick, J. S., Snidman, N., Gibbons, J., & Johnson, M. O. (1988). Childhood derivatives of inhibition and lack of inhibition to the unfamiliar. *Child Development, 59,* 1580–1589.

Kaye, K., & Fogel, A. (1980). The temporal structure of face-to-face communication between mothers and infants. *Developmental Psychology, 16,* 454–464.

Kaye, K., & Marcus, J. (1978). Imitation over a series of trials without feedback: Age six months. *Infant Behavior and Development, 1,* 141–155.

Kenny, D. A., & DePaulo, B. M. (1989). *Do we know how others view us? An empirical and theoretical account.* Manuscript submitted for review.

Kilbride, J. E., & Yarczower, M. (1980). Recognition and imitation of facial expressions: A cross-cultural comparison between Zambia and the United States. *Journal of Cross-Cultural Psychology, 11,* 281–296.

Knapp, M. L. (1978). *Nonverbal communication in human interaction* (2nd ed.). New York: Holt, Rinehart and Winston.

Kraut, R. E. (1982). Social presence, facial feedback, and emotion. *Journal of Personality and Social Psychology, 42,* 853–863.

Kwint, L. (1934). Ontogeny of mobility of the face. *Child Development, 5,* 1–12.

Larsen, R. J., & Diener, E. (1987). Affect intensity as an individual difference characteristic: A review. *Journal of Research in Personality, 21,* 1–39.

Leary, M. R. (1983). *Understanding social anxiety.* Beverly Hills, CA: Sage.

Lewis, M., & Michalson, L. (1985). Faces as signs and symbols. In G. Zivin (Ed.), *The development of expressive behavior* (pp. 153–180). New York: Academic Press.

Lewis, M., Stanger, C., & Sullivan, M. W. (1989). Deception in 3-year-olds. *Developmental Psychology, 25,* 439–443.

McCoy, C. L., & Masters, J. C. (1990). Children's strategies for the control of emotion in themselves and others. In B. S. Moore & A. M. Isen (Eds.), *Affect and social behavior.* Cambridge: Cambridge University Press.

Malatesta, C. Z., & Haviland, J. M. (1982). Learning display rules: The socialization of emotion expression in infancy. *Child Development, 53,* 991–1003.

(1985). Signals, symbols, and socialization: The modification of emotional expression in human development. In M. Lewis & C. Saarni (Eds.), *The socialization of emotions* (pp. 89–116). New York: Plenum.

Malatesta, C. Z., & Izard, C. E. (1984). The facial expression of emotion: Young, middle-aged, and other adult expressions. In C. Z. Malatesta & C. E. Izard (Eds.), *Emotion in adult development* (pp. 253–273). Beverly Hills, CA: Sage.

Miller, P., & Sperry, L. L. (1987). The socialization of anger and aggression. *Merrill-Palmer Quarterly, 33,* 1–31.

Montepare, J. M., Goldstein, S. B., & Clausen, A. (1987). The identification of emotions from gait information. *Journal of Nonverbal Behavior, 11,* 33–42.

Morency, N. L., & Krauss, R. M. (1982). Children's nonverbal encoding and decoding of affect. In R. S. Feldman (Ed.), *Development of nonverbal behavior in children* (pp. 181–199). New York: Springer-Verlag.

Murray, A. D. (1979). Infant crying as an elicitor of parental behavior: An examination of two models. *Psychological Bulletin, 86,* 191–215.

Odom, R. D., & Lemond, C. M. (1972). Developmental differences in the perception and production of facial expressions. *Child Development, 43,* 359–369.

Parham, I. A., Feldman, R. S., Oster, G. D., & Popoola, O. (1981). Intergenerational differences in nonverbal disclosure of deception. *Journal of Social Psychology, 113*, 261–269.

Polanyi, M. (1962). *Personal knowledge*. Chicago: University of Chicago Press.

Prkachin, K. M., Craig, K. D., Papageorgis, D., & Reith, G. (1977). Nonverbal communication deficits and response to performance feedback in depression. *Journal of Abnormal Psychology, 86*, 224–234.

Rejeski, W. J., & Lowe, C. A. (1980). Nonverbal expression of effort as casually relevant information. *Personality and Social Psychology Bulletin, 6*, 436–440.

Riess, M., & Rosenfeld, P. (1980). Seating preferences as nonverbal communications: A self-presentational analysis. *Journal of Applied Communication Research, 8*, 22–30.

Riggio, R. E., Tucker, J., & Throckmorton, B. (1987). Social skills and deception ability. *Personality and Social Psychology Bulletin, 13*, 568–577.

Rinn, W. E. (1984). The neuropsychology of facial expression: A review of neurological and psychological mechanisms for producing facial expressions. *Psychological Bulletin, 95*, 52–77.

Rosenfeld, H. M. (1966). Approval-seeking and approval-avoiding functions of verbal and nonverbal responses in the dyad. *Journal of Personality and Social Psychology, 4*, 597–605.

Ruble, D. N. (1983). The development of social comparison processes and their role in achievement-related self-socialization. In E. T. Higgins, D. N. Ruble, & W. W. Hartup (Eds.), *Social cognition and social development* (pp. 134–157). Cambridge: Cambridge University Press.

Saarni, C. (1979). Children's understanding of display rules for expressive behavior. *Developmental Psychology, 15*, 424–429.

(1984). An observational study of children's attempts to monitor their expressive behavior. *Child Development, 55*, 1504–1513.

(1988). Children's understanding of the interpersonal consequences of dissemblance of nonverbal emotional–expressive behavior. *Journal of Nonverbal Behavior, 12*, 275–294.

(1989). Children's understanding of strategic control of emotional expression in social transactions. In C. Saarni & P. Harris (Eds.), *Children's understanding of emotion* (pp. 181–208). Cambridge: Cambridge University Press.

(1991). Emotional competence: How emotions and relationships become integrated. In R. Thompson (Ed.), Socioemotional development. *Nebraska Symposium on Motivation* (Vol. 36, pp. 115–182). Lincoln: University of Nebraska Press.

Scherer, K. R. (1986). Vocal affect expression: A review and a model for future research. *Psychological Bulletin, 99*, 143–165.

Schlenker, B. R., & Leary, M. R. (1982). Social anxiety and self-presentation: A conceptualization and model. *Psychological Bulletin, 92*, 641–669.

(1985). Social anxiety and communication about the self. *Journal of Language and Social Psychology, 4*, 171–192.

Schlenker, B. R., & Weigold, M. F. (1988). Goals and the self-identification process: Constructing desire identities. In L. Pervin (Ed.), *Goal concepts in personality and social psychology* (pp. 243–290). Hillsdale, NJ: Erlbaum.

Shennum, W. A., & Bugental, D. B. (1982). The development of control over affective expression in nonverbal behavior. In R. S. Feldman (Ed.), *Development of nonverbal behavior in children* (pp. 101–121). New York: Springer-Verlag.

Stanislavski, C. (1965). *An actor prepares*. New York: Theatre Arts Books. (Original work published 1948)

Stein, N. L., & Trabasso, T. (1989). Children's understanding of changing emotional states. In C. Saarni & P. L. Harris (Eds.), *Children's understanding of emotion* (pp. 50–80). Cambridge: Cambridge University Press.

Strayer, J. (1988). Children's attributions regarding the situational determinants of emotion in self and others. *Developmental Psychology, 22*, 649–654.

Tetlock, P. E., & Manstead, A. S. R. (1985). Impression management versus intrapsychic explanations in social psychology: A useful dichotomy? *Psychological Review, 92*, 59–77.

Thelen, E. (1985). Expression as action: A motor perspective of the transition from spontaneous to instrumental behaviors. In G. Zivin (Ed.), *The development of expressive behavior* (pp. 221–248). New York: Academic Press.

Thompson, R. A. (1987). Development of children's inferences of the emotions of others. *Developmental Psychology, 23*, 124–131.

Toris, C., & DePaulo, B. M. (1984). Effects of actual deception and suspiciousness of deception on interpersonal perceptions. *Journal of Personality and Social Psychology, 47*, 1063–1073.

Wagner, H. L., MacDonald, C. J., & Manstead, A. S. R. (1986). Communication of individual emotions by spontaneous facial expressions. *Journal of Personality and Social Psychology, 50*, 737–743.

Wallbott, H. G., & Scherer, K. R. (1986). Cues and channels in emotion recognition. *Journal of Personality and Social Psychology, 51*, 690–699.

Weiner, B., & Handel, S. J. (1985). A cognition–emotion–action sequence: Anticipated emotional consequences of causal attributions and reported communication strategy. *Developmental Psychology, 21*, 102–107.

Yarczower, M., & Daruns, L. (1982). Social inhibition of spontaneous facial expressions in children. *Journal of Personality and Social Psychology, 43*, 831–837.

Yarczower, M., Kilbride, J. E., & Hill, L. A. (1979). Imitation and inhibition of facial expression. *Developmental Psychology, 15*, 453–454.

Zaidel, S. F., & Mehrabian, A. (1969). The ability to communicate and infer positive and negative attitudes facially and vocally. *Journal of Experimental Research in Personality, 3*, 233–241.

Zajonc, R. B., Addelmann, P. K., Murphy, S. T., & Niedenthal, P. M. (1987). Convergence in the physical appearance of spouses. *Motivation and Emotion, 11*, 335–346.

Zelko, F. A., Duncan, S. W., Barden, R. C., Garber, J., & Masters, J. C. (1986). Adults' expectancies about children's emotional responsiveness: Implications for the development of implicit theories of affect. *Developmental Psychology, 22*, 109–114.

Zivin, G. (1982). Watching the sands shift: Conceptualizing development of nonverbal mastery. In R. S. Feldman (Ed.), *Development of nonverbal behavior in children* (pp. 63–98). New York: Springer-Verlag.

Zuckerman, M., DeFrank R. S., Hall, J. A., Larrance, D. T., & Rosenthal, T. (1979). Facial and vocal cues of deception and honesty. *Journal of Experimental Social Psychology, 15*, 378–396.

Zuckerman, M., Hall, J. A., DeFrank, R. S., & Rosenthal, R. (1976). Encoding and decoding of spontaneous and posed facial expressions. *Journal of Personality and Social Psychology, 34*, 966–977.

Zuckerman, M., Koestner, R., & Driver, R. (1981). Beliefs about cues associated with deception. *Journal of Nonverbal Behavior, 6*, 105–114.

Zuckerman, M., Larrance, D. T., Hall, J. A., DeFrank, R. S., & Rosenthal, R. (1979). Posed and spontaneous communication of emotion via facial and vocal cues. *Journal of Personality, 47*, 712–733.

Zuckerman, M., Larrance, D. T., Spiegel, N. H., & Klorman, R. (1981). Controlling nonverbal displays: Facial expressions and tone of voice. *Journal of Experimental Social Psychology, 17,* 506–524.

Zuckerman, M., Lipets, M. S., Koivumaki, J. H., & Rosenthal R. (1975). Encoding and decoding nonverbal cues of emotion. *Journal of Personality and Social Psychology, 32,* 1068–1076.

Zuckerman, M., & Przewuzman, S. J. (1979). Decoding and encoding facial expressions in preschool-age children. *Environmental Psychology and Nonverbal Psychology, 3,* 147–163.

PART V

Interpersonal processes

11. Interpersonal coordination: Behavior matching and interactional synchrony

FRANK J. BERNIERI AND ROBERT ROSENTHAL

Observing a train station at rush hour or a busy street corner in a large city provides a striking example of how smoothly individuals can mesh their flow of behaviors with one another. If we did not have this skill of coordinating our movement with others, imagine what driving an automobile through a busy intersection or on a highway would be like. Interpersonal coordination is present in nearly all aspects of our social lives, helping us negotiate our daily face-to-face encounters. When conversing with another, the ability to coordinate the alternating flows of speech allows for the smooth, efficient exchange of verbal information. We also coordinate our nonverbal behavior with others to communicate that we are listening to them and want to hear more. There is further evidence to suggest that we coordinate our behavior to a greater degree when interacting with others whom we like, suggesting that the degree of rapport between interactants is reflected by the behavioral coordination between them. Although interpersonal coordination is an ever-present aspect of all our social and professional encounters, we rarely regard it as a target of our concern or study.

It is becoming apparent that many, if not all, of life's various processes are intimately linked to the external environment. Biologists have long known, for instance, that our body temperature and brain activity are in sync with the motions of the sun in the sky. We sleep at night and are active during the day. Although our "free running" cycles are actually 25 hours long, our body is endowed with various systems that constantly resynchronize its physiological processes with the natural 24-hour solar day. The environment acts like a timekeeper or conductor who sets the pace of life. The function and benefit of synchronizing with the environment has not been precisely determined, but it is believed

The research reported in this chapter was supported in part by a National Science Foundation grant.

to help optimize an organism's efficiency in interacting with its environment. It is not surprising, then, that social scientists in many fields are discovering that various aspects of interpersonal behavior show synchronizing characteristics that similarly may enhance the efficiency with which humans interact with one another.

Consider what takes place during a conversation. Normally, we are unaware of how well we are coordinating ourselves until something disrupts the normal process. A slight time delay in a long-distance phone call, for instance, can result in more frequent interruptions and mutual silences. When this occurs, it often can lead to the phrase "You go first," which illustrates a need to resort to verbal directives to compensate for some breakdown in the communication process. Or consider the awkwardness that often occurs when a native New Yorker interacts with someone from the West Coast or Deep South. The rates of speech and activity common to both areas differ, and this discrepancy can often play havoc with normal conversation. The New Yorker, who is used to relatively short, quick bursts of speech, tends to become impatient and interrupt the native southerner, who speaks in longer, less hurried phrases. Although both parties may have a strong command of the English language, a failure to coordinate temporally their verbal and nonverbal behavior can lead to feelings of frustration and estrangement.

In this chapter we shall review the work on interpersonal coordination and explore its possible function and importance in social interaction. We shall describe four conceptualizations of the phenomenon that emphasize slightly different aspects of interpersonal coordination. The variety in approaches to understanding interpersonal coordination has led to the development of a number of measurement techniques. Therefore, we shall discuss these methodologies used to study interpersonal coordination and some of the results found with them. These methods all use some type of behavior coding and analysis, and are distinguished on the basis of whether they code specific behaviors related to synchrony or direct perceptions of synchrony collected from naive judges. A new method of synchrony measurement based on synchrony ratings will be presented along with some initial findings. Finally, we shall discuss briefly the practical implications that behavioral coordination may have for our social and professional encounters.

Interpersonal coordination

The study of interpersonal coordination is the study of how people "get it together" and synchronize with one another. Defined loosely, *inter-*

personal coordination is the degree to which the behaviors in an interaction are nonrandom, patterned, or synchronized in both timing and form. The behavioral coordination that has been observed can be categorized into two basic types: *behavior matching* or similarity and *interactional synchrony*. Interactional synchrony, in turn, is composed of three components: rhythm, simultaneous movement, and the smooth meshing of interaction. For an example of these forms of interpersonal coordination, consider the behavior among members of a jazz band while playing an improvisation.

The particular piece of music being produced by the individual musicians of a band may be spontaneous and unrehearsed, and yet obviously it is patterned and highly synchronized. In this respect it is similar to a social interaction. One element present in jazz is a musical theme, a melody that is echoed or repeated throughout the piece. A melody initiated by a guitar, for instance, may be mimicked later by a saxophone. The two musicians may even opt to play the melody together. Likewise, in a nonmusical social interaction, people may mimic behavior patterns by adopting similar postures. Two people conversing may be leaning forward, or they both may have their arms or legs crossed in the same way. In some instances they may appear to be mirrored reflections of each other. This similarity of behavior patterns is one type of interpersonal coordination.

At the core of any jazz piece is the rhythm, whose importance cannot be overstated. A particular rhythm, once adopted by a group of musicians, becomes the supporting structure of the music. The rhythm sets the tempo and style in which the others must play. As in jazz, interpersonal behavior has tempo and style. Some interactions occur in a rapid, staccatolike fashion, whereas others are slower and more fluid. Interaction rhythm is the first of three aspects of interactional synchrony, the second type of interpersonal coordination.

In jazz, the elements of the music are highly synchronized in that individual notes from the different instruments tend to occur precisely at the same instant. There is a downbeat with which all instruments synchronize. Notes from individual musicians tend to begin and end simultaneously. In fact, a band's ability to hit a note simultaneously, sometimes referred to as *tightness*, is an important criterion of their quality and skill. As in jazz, interpersonal behavior may have identifiable downbeats, precise moments at which two people interacting change movements simultaneously. Simultaneous movement is the second aspect of interactional synchrony.

A jazz band is composed of separate entities generating different sounds that fit together to create the perception of a single piece of music. Thus another element in jazz is the ability to mesh and interweave smoothly the various components of the total piece of music. As with simultaneous movement, this means synchronizing with the others. The musicians must be playing at the same tempo. They must increase and decrease their loudness together. The music played by each instrument sometimes complements and intertwines with the others. A band thus becomes a unit playing one song; it "grooves." When people interact, their behaviors intertwine as do the sounds from different instruments in a band. They may mesh smoothly, as does a surgical team that has worked together for many years, or their behaviors may clash, as when one interactant feels awkward or clumsy in the presence of another. This process of smooth meshing is the third component of interactional synchrony, which when added to behavior matching constitute the four main manifestations of interpersonal coordination.

Developmental, cognitive, and social significance

The infant synchronizer

Evidence is slowly accumulating to suggest that some forms of interpersonal coordination involving interactional synchrony may be closely associated with many important developmental and social phenomena.[1] The synchronization of one's behaviors with those of another may be one of the earliest forms of human communication to develop and may even be present at birth. Condon and Sander (1974) observed in a hospital nursery infants only a few days old and found that infants synchronized their movements to human speech, even when it was tape recorded or in a language not native to the child's parents. This ability to coordinate movements to auditory stimuli may be specific to human speech as the infants did not synchronize with nonspeech-related sounds (i.e., street noises or rhythmic tapping). These findings were replicated in Japan by a group of researchers using a computerized grid system designed to detect even the slightest movements (Kato et al., 1983).

It has been suggested that interactional synchrony between adults communicates interest and approval. To synchronize with another is to show that one is "with" that person in one's attentions and expectancies (Kendon, 1970). When a listener is coordinating his or her movements with the speech and movements of another, it is as if the listener is continually saying "Go ahead, I'm right with you." For infants, this synchronization may be a means of regulating their involvement in social interactions. Infants consistently match (in timing and duration) their own vocalizations and speech-related behaviors to those of their mothers (Cappella, 1982, p. 121). When interacting with nonresponsive adults, infants intensify their coordinating activity, presumably to obtain greater involvement from the inactive adult (Tronick, Als, Adamson, & Wise, 1978). Tronick, Als, and Brazelton (1977) speculated that synchrony may be a way for a child to communicate "continue" and that "dissynchrony" may communicate "stop." When interacting with adults with whom they were unacquainted, in one study the movements of infants became less coordinated with those of their partner over the course of an interaction (Bernieri, Reznick, & Rosenthal, 1988). This loss of synchronization was found to be associated with an increase in the negative emotional affect of the infant.

Facilitating communication

The ability to coordinate or synchronize with another's speech rhythms may facilitate the learning of language and may be a necessary precursor to it. Rhythm and synchrony are believed by some to be essential to communication and language learning, as Laurence Wylie pointed out:

> Forty years ago such linguists as Stetson, Pike, Delattre, and Denkinger stressed the learning of rhythm in language classes but apparently the lesson did not sink in. We are prone to forget that speech is essentially music and that rhythm is its basis. (Wylie, 1985, p. 780)

Wylie reminded us that we communicate with every means at our disposal and not just with the parts that produce speech. Studies have shown that our body movements are, in fact, intimately linked to the rhythms of speech. Head and hand movements have been determined to coincide with stress points and hesitations in the speech itself.

Movement transducers affixed to the various parts of the body have enabled investigators to detect, record, and track over time the precise nature of all body movements generated while conversing. Dittman and Llewellyn (1969) recorded the movement of speakers' hands, head, and feet and found that during speech, movements were more likely to occur early in phonemic clauses and in speech hesitations. That is, the movements were not distributed randomly throughout the course of a conversation but were much more likely to correspond to the rhythm of speech. It was as if the physical movements of the body were tracking the articulatory structure of the speech.

William Condon (Condon, 1970; Condon & Ogston, 1966, 1967) observed this physical tracking to one's own speech at a microlevel of analysis, at which many individual instances of body-to-speech synchronization can occur within a mere fraction of a second. More importantly, he observed an apparent breakdown in this process in certain abnormal samples. Children suffering from dyslexia and other learning disabilities, for example, show deficiencies in the ability to synchronize their movements with speech rhythms (Condon, 1982), as do schizophrenics (Condon & Ogston, 1966). It seems, then, that normally we do invoke our entire body when communicating with others and that the patterns we generate in our speech are found in the movements we concurrently produce.

The astonishing finding in this literature, however, is not that our body is synchronized with our own verbal utterances but that our body tends also to coordinate with the verbal utterances of anyone we happen to be listening to at the time. In one study examining head movements in listeners (Hadar, Steiner, & Rose, 1985), approximately one fourth of all head movements were found to occur synchronously with the speaker's speech. The synchronization of head nods to the vocalizations of the speaker has also been found by others (Dittman & Llewellyn, 1968) and can be found to occur in our micromovements as well (Condon & Ogston, 1967). Furthermore, the coordination of body movements may continue even after the verbal–verbal coordination between interactants deteriorates. Rutter and Stephenson (1977) found that although the flow of conversation was sometimes disrupted with various types of speech disturbances (interruptions, simultaneous speech, and pauses), the degree of interpersonal coordination apparent in the nonverbal behaviors of the interactants continued unabated.

The exact function of the body's tendency to move synchronously with speech has been unclear. One possibility is that the coordination of body movement to speech is a fundamental skill that facilitates the initial acquisition and development of language (Condon & Sander, 1974). In other words, the body may learn the physical manifestations and patterns of speech long before the mind is developed enough to insert the words. Thus it could be a biological predeterminant of language. Another possibility is that synchrony facilitates interpersonal communication by allowing for the smooth and fluent exchange of verbal utterances (Dittman & Llewellyn, 1968, 1969). By coordinating ourselves with a speaker's movements we can anticipate more accurately the termination of their vocalizations and hasten the promptness with which we respond without prematurely cutting them off, thus enhancing the efficiency of the communication. Finally, Kendon (1970) hypothesized that synchrony serves a communicative function in itself. The level of synchrony manifested at any given moment may communicate the degree of understanding, agreement, or support that a listener is currently experiencing. Whatever the function, it is clear that interactional synchrony is closely related to communication processes.

Involvement and rapport

In one review of the literature, interpersonal coordination was theoretically linked to rapport (Tickle-Degnen & Rosenthal, 1987). Although rapport may be more commonly associated with positive affect or attitude, descriptive references to coordinated aspects of behavior are common in our everyday descriptions of social events. High states of rapport are often associated with descriptive terms such as harmonious, smooth, "in tune," or "on the same wavelength." Similarly, states of low rapport are often associated with terms such as awkward, "out of sync," or "not getting it together." In their review of the literature, Tickle-Degnen and Rosenthal posited three distinct components of rapport that, though they can vary independently, together constitute rapport. Interpersonal coordination, along with emotional positivity and attentional focus, make up the total experience of rapport.

Behavioral or postural similarity may provide a common backdrop to the ongoing interaction. Scheflen (1964) suggested that people in a group often mirror one another's posture and that this reflects a shared viewpoint. The importance of similarity to interpersonal attraction is well documented in social psychology (Byrne, 1971). Smooth meshing of interpersonal behavior may enhance feelings of togetherness or similarity. That is, people perceive others as being more similar to them to the extent that their behaviors (postures and posture shifts) are congruent (Dabbs, 1969). In some instances we may mimic another's behavior to show we sympathize or understand what that person is feeling. In one study, a victim of an apparently painful injury was either within eye contact of observers or was oriented in such a way that observers knew the victim was not looking at them. Then when the confederate victim "accidentally" reinjured an already splintered and bandaged finger, observers were more likely to wince and mimic the pained expression of the confederate if they had eye contact with him (Bavelas, Black, Lemery, & Mullett, 1986). Mimicry or behavior congruence may not necessarily be purposeful, but it clearly has interpersonal consequences.

The empirical evidence supporting the link between social rapport and interpersonal coordination comes mainly from the work on posture mirroring. Marriane LaFrance observed systematically the extent of posture mirroring in both natural settings and the lab (LaFrance, 1982). In a typical study, trained coders scanned a classroom and counted the number of students simultaneously displaying the same postural configuration as that of the teacher (LaFrance & Broadbent, 1976). Coders made these observations at specific points in time during the classroom session and returned to repeat the process many times over a period of a week. LaFrance found that the extent of posture similarity measured in this fashion correlated positively with the students' ratings of rapport, involvement, and togetherness made after each session.

In all but one study, posture similarity was positively associated with rapport between interactants. The one reversal (LaFrance & Ickes, 1981) was unusual in that the interactants were not acquainted with each other. All of the previous studies involving posture similarity and rapport included interactants who were familiar with each other and were involved in an ongoing interaction (such as a therapeutic dyad or classroom). LaFrance and Ickes suggested that posture similarity by itself does not constitute rapport but instead reflects an attempt to reach a state of rapport. In their study, posture mirroring was related to (1) feelings that the interaction was forced and strained, (2) heightened feelings of self-consciousness, and (3) an increase of reported attempts to influence the other to behave in particular ways. The authors cited evidence from a previous study indicating that early posture mirroring may be predictive of increased rapport 6 weeks later (LaFrance, 1979). If posture similarity is more reflective of attempts at reaching rapport than it is of the rapport itself, it could mean that the positive relationship between rapport and posture similarity in ongoing interactions is better interpreted as reflecting an attempt at sustaining rapport.

Posture similarity is a form of behavior matching and is only one of the four aspects of interpersonal coordination hypothesized to exist. Unfortunately, the relationship between rapport and the other three aspects of behavior coordination has generated little research. In order to validate this hypothesized relationship, convergent findings must be obtained for the other forms of synchrony as well.

A close examination of the literature reveals that investigators differ widely in how they conceptualize interpersonal coordination. The researchers' different assumptions about behavior coordination have invariably led to different methods employed to define and measure it. We shall next describe the various approaches to the study and measurement of interpersonal coordination.

Conceptual definitions of interpersonal coordination

Matching

Researchers interested in the matching-of-behavior aspect of interpersonal coordination are primarily concerned with the correspondence of the interactants' internal states and attitudes. It is believed that the congruence of mental states between interactants is reflected in their physical behaviors toward each other (Scheflen, 1964). By determining the congruence of physical behavior between two people, one can estimate the "togetherness" or similarity of their internal states. Studies have shown that people who assume like postures are judged to have a higher rapport with each other than do those whose postures are not similar (Dabbs, 1969; Trout & Rosenfeld, 1980). But no study has yet attempted to compare the actual internal states of interactants to determine whether the external similarity–internal similarity hypothesis holds true.

Psychotherapists have been the most concerned with this kind of interpersonal coordination, hoping that an understanding of behavior matching would aid in identifying a patient's current mental state and in building rapport during the therapeutic interaction (Charney, 1966; Scheflen, 1964). Researchers studying interactants' "togetherness" in this fashion emphasize all aspects of the interactants' similarity (both physical and mental). The interactants are considered more "together" and, hence, coordinated to the extent that their mental states and external behaviors are more alike and matched.

Interactional synchrony

Interaction rhythms. Many biological processes are known to be cyclical or rhythmical in nature and driven by the central nervous system, and there is evidence to suggest that human interactions may have rhythms as well (see Davis, 1982 for a review). It is likely that these, too, are driven by some neural mechanism as yet unknown, but one notion of interpersonal coordination is the synchronization of endogenous behavioral rhythms.

The environment in which we live is strikingly periodic. From the motions of the earth, moon, and sun we can derive naturally occurring cycles with periods of a day, month, and year. Not surprisingly, many biological and physiological processes have evolved to be cyclical, oscillating in a manner corresponding to the environment surrounding them. Humans display a wide spectrum of frequencies in their rhythmic process, with periods ranging in length from a fraction of a second (the electrical activity of the brain) to many weeks (the menstrual cycle in women).

The best-researched rhythmic processes are those that have periods roughly equal to a day. There is clear evidence that skin temperature, body-core temperature, arousal level, activity level, and a host of metabolic functions show cyclical patterns roughly corresponding to a 24-hour day. These are called *circadian* (Latin: *circa* = about; *dies* = day) *rhythms*. When humans are removed from all external time cues, these processes are allowed to be "free running": The cycles continue, but their period increases to a length greater than a day. Aschoff and Wever (1962)[2] isolated individuals in a cellar of a hospital for over a week, and Siffre (1964) lived alone in a cave for 2 months. In both instances, the activity–rest cycle was observed to be approximately 25 hours.

Our biological rhythms do not just incidentally "match" the solar day, they actively entrain to it. The term *entrainment* is used to describe the process whereby our body is "captured" (i.e., modified in periodicity and phase) by an external cycle with a rhythm near the one the body rhythm would have had, had it not been affected by any external force. McGrath and Kelly (1986) demonstrated the concept with an analogy to the action of a tuning fork:

> If a tuning fork is set in motion by an outside force and then held near another tuning fork of approximately the same frequency (or a multiple or submultiple of that frequency), it will set that second tuning fork into motion as well. We can say that the latter fork is entrained by (set in motion by) that first tuning fork. (p. 43)

The environment works as a "time giver" or *zeitgeber*, with which the physiological processes synchronize. Under normal conditions the human body entrains to the daylight cycle; however, there is some evidence that humans can entrain to social cues as well, such as mealtimes

(Vernikos-Danellis & Winget, 1979). In fact, it is becoming apparent that there may be many distinct "entrainment systems" operating in humans. At least two distinct entrainment systems have been found that synchronize with the 24-hour cycle (Moore-Ede, Sulzman, & Fuller, 1982). One seems to be organized around body-core temperature and rapid-eye-movement (REM) sleep, and the other is organized around the rest–activity cycle.

From this perspective, social behavior is assumed to have certain cyclical and rhythmic properties. Behavioral rhythms, like other biological processes, have entrainment systems that allow them to synchronize with some *zeitgeber;* in some instances this can be another human being. According to this conceptualization, interactional synchrony is defined as the degree of congruence between the behavioral cycles of two or more people. In fact, if any aspect of an interaction were found to have rhythmic or cyclical characteristics, it would imply that the interactants themselves were in sync; otherwise their combined behavior (i.e., their interaction) would not show any temporal pattern.

Many instances of interaction rhythms have already been discovered. Hayes and Cobb (1982) for example, recorded the conversational behavior of a couple who lived together in isolation for 30 days. They found that verbal activity was not randomly distributed throughout the day; rather, the level of conversation activity varied cyclically every 90 to 100 minutes, suggesting that the man and woman were entrained to the same verbal activity behavioral cycle. Even after this rhythm was disrupted by an unplanned set of natural events, the same stable rhythm reemerged. Hayes and Cobb argued that because of the predictability of the participants' cycles, conversational behavior does not occur solely as a function of conscious decision. They hypothesized that endogenous oscillators must, to some extent, guide conversational behavior and must somehow adapt or entrain to certain aspects of the social and physical environment (Hayes & Cobb, 1982, pp. 333–334).

Other interaction cycles have been observed with much shorter time frames. Interactions between mothers and infants have been found to have periods of engagement and disassociation (i.e., particular combinations of body orientation, gaze, vocal activity, and facial expression) repeating every few seconds (Stern, 1971, 1974). In one study, the levels of engagement of both mother and child were measured individually. A frame-by-frame film analysis found cycles of engagement and disengagement lasting roughly 10 seconds. Furthermore, these cycles were such that the mother–infant interaction was marked by periods of mutual engagement and disengagement that prevailed throughout the filmed session (Tronick et al., 1977).

One interesting implication arising from the rhythms approach to interpersonal coordination pertains to the location of a *zeitgeber* within a given interaction unit. In biology, a *zeitgeber* is usually some naturally occurring cyclical process in the physical universe, such as the day–night cycle of the sun that entrains some biological process in a living organism. In interactional synchrony, it is quite likely that the *zeitgeber* is one of the interactants, although this is not a necessity. For instance, when a couple dances across the dance floor, they both may be entraining to the beat of the music external to their interaction. Or, one can imagine the difference between a conversation between two friends who meet accidentally on a New York City street during rush hour and the same two friends meeting on a golf course later that weekend. In these instances, the ambient rhythm and tempo of the two situations would likely affect the resulting rhythm and tempo of the interactive behavior.

In interactions largely devoid of rhythmic stimuli external to the dyad, the time giver is one (or both) of the interactants. In this case, the location of the *zeitgeber* in the dyad may have some implications for its social composition. For example, the stability of a *zeitgeber* within one individual throughout an interaction may be a physical manifestation or consequence of the dominance relationship between the interactants. Baron and Boudreau (1987) speculated that dominance can be defined as the discrepancy between the proportion of time that Person A serves as the time giver for an interaction relative to the time that Person B serves as time giver.

Similarly, the psychological concept of personal charisma may also be related to the asymmetric *zeitgeber* strengths of individuals in interactions. Good public speakers, such as politicians and television evangelists, are probably very effective time givers. The often-heard phrase "had the audience in the palm of his hand" may be an attempt to indicate that a speaker was effectively entraining a mass of individuals listening to him. Although there is yet no empirical evidence regarding this subject, the potential for synchrony to be implicated in these concepts of interpersonal influence is highly promising.

Simultaneous movement. One of the more remarkable manifestations of interactional synchrony is simultaneous movement. By simultaneous we mean only the cooccurrence of two or more behaviors. The term *behaviors* is used here in the broadest sense. It may refer to specific muscle movements, nonverbal gestures, vocalizations, body positions, and even mental states. The defining quality is the timing of the movements, and the criterion of cooccurrence varies depending on the behavior being studied. Postures, for example, may be considered simultaneous (congruent) within the time frame of an entire interaction or interaction segment. When observing micromovement changes, the time frame for determining simultaneity may be less than $\frac{5}{100}$ of a second.

William Condon was the first to employ a "microanalysis" of filmed behavior in the study of coordinated movement (Condon & Ogston, 1966). In his work he emphasized the importance of the articulatory structure of speech, which he feels is ultimately responsible for the synchronization of the listener's body movements with those of the speaker. He was interested in the simultaneity and timing of body movements, irrespective of their nature, that occur within a single motion picture frame. He described this kind of interactional synchrony as the simultaneous movement of body and speech:

> These diverse body parts – eyes, mouth, trunk, head, arms, fingers, etc. – tend to change and sustain direction of movement together. If one body part moves or changes direction of movement, it does so concomitantly and in concert with the other body parts moving at that time. . . . What is being described is an ongoing flow of "moments-of-sustaining together" of body parts. (Condon & Ogston, 1967, p. 224)

Behavioral meshing. The fundamental feature common to all conceptualizations of interactional synchrony is the apparent unification of two potentially random, unpatterned behavioral elements into a meaningfully described "whole" or synchronous event. The elements of this event may be simultaneous within a fixed time period, identical in their appearance or oscillating with the same frequency. The essential feature is that when the elements are put together, they "come together." That is, it is the extent to which the events are not entirely independent but become interrelated. What is important is the apparent degree of unification of two otherwise independent phenomena.

Interactional synchrony relates directly to the degree of interrelatedness of interpersonal behaviors. The goal in setting synchrony in motion is to establish specific objective criteria by which events can be deemed nonindependent or patterned. A difficulty arises, however, in that the criteria become more difficult to meet as the fixed time frame (i.e., unit of measurement) becomes shorter. In other words, what may

be synchronized to the second may not be synchronized to the milli-
second. The temporal criteria used so far have been determined by the
practical constraints of the recording instruments rather than by any
theoretically derived definition of synchrony. At present it is unclear as
to what the proper time criterion for synchrony should be.

A perceptual approach to the study of interactional synchrony begins
with the assumption that the perception of patterned stimuli comes naturally to humans. The defining criterion for a pattern or unity is its phenomenological perception. Interpersonal behavior is synchronous to the
extent that it "appears" synchronous to a group of observers. To study
interpersonal coordination one need not rely only on advanced technology or microanalysis but also on human perception. Our appreciation
of music, dance, and team sports (e.g., certain preplanned plays in basketball, football, soccer, and volleyball) seem largely dependent on our
perception of the coordinated aspects of these activities. Although there
may be individual differences in this skill, the utility of human measuring instruments for many such complex perceptual phenomena should
not be underestimated (Scherer & Ekman, 1982).

Measuring interpersonal coordination: Behavior coding

The basic methodology used to detect and calculate the degree of interpersonal coordination is to code behaviors for synchrony using objective
criteria. We shall next survey the various methods used to study synchrony and discuss the implications of each.

Microanalysis

In microanalysis, films of social interactions are analyzed frame by
frame. Individual body parts are scrutinized until the precise point
(frame of film) of a change in movement (i.e., initiation, termination,
change in speed, or change in direction) can be identified. These "movement boundaries" are then analyzed for their cooccurrence with movement boundaries from other individuals. Interactional synchrony is the
extent of cooccurrence of movement boundaries between individuals.

The kind of measurement used in a microanalysis of behavior is a
painstaking process in which the motion of every observable joint is
independently transcribed. Phonetic boundaries of speech are transcribed as well. Indeed, an interaction lasting just a minute may generate a transcription many feet in length. William Condon found that mo-

tion changes within a person do not occur at random but, instead, cluster as simultaneous events called *process units* (Condon & Ogston, 1966). These process units invariably occur at various types of speech junctures. Condon observed very early in his research that the process units of the listener were often synchronized with the process units of the speaker (Condon & Ogston, 1966).

The study of interactional synchrony as established by Condon (Condon, 1970; Condon & Ogston, 1966, 1967) has not gone without controversy (Rosenfeld, 1981). In a review of the microsynchrony literature Cappella noted the excessive generality inherent in Condon's working definition (Cappella, 1981). Specifically, Cappella took issue with the notion that any change in any part of a person's physical motions occurring at the same instant as a change in any part of the other's motion would be evidence of synchrony. Cappella claimed that with so many possible discrete events, there is a certain baseline of coordinated (simultaneous) movements that would be expected by chance. Without a statistical control for this baseline of chance synchrony, the microanalysis method makes observations appear synchronous (Cappella, 1981, p. 119).

McDowall (1978) provided the only study in which a baseline level of synchronous events expected by chance was calculated and statistically compared with observed levels (McDowall, 1978). In his study, McDowall found no evidence to indicate that the observed levels of synchrony could not be explained by chance occurrences. However, Gatewood and Rosenwein (1981) claimed that McDowall's results should not be interpreted as a failure to replicate Condon's findings. They cited various methodological inconsistencies between McDowall's method and Condon's (Condon, 1970). The most significant difference was that McDowall did not code speech boundaries, which Condon claims are essential to the detection of microsynchrony. Gatewood and Rosenwein concluded that McDowall's results are therefore inconclusive.

Only one investigator was able to replicate Condon's work exactly (Kendon, 1970), although others have used related methods (Beebe et al., 1982; Berghout-Austin & Peery, 1983). Technological developments introduced into this field of research are enabling more rigorous tests of this phenomenon. With the aid of a computer-generated grid, a group of Japanese researchers observed synchronization of body movements beyond levels explainable by chance (Kato et al., 1983). Future improvements in computer-aided vision may greatly enhance the study of microsynchrony.

Spectral analysis

Spectral analysis is a statistical technique used to detect rhythms or cycles. It is usually applied to data representing behaviors that were coded over many points in time. The general purpose of spectral analysis is to break down the total power (variance) in a time series into a sum of independent periodic components. The components are sine waves of different frequencies. The "power spectrum" of a time series shows the power attributed to each periodic component in a fashion analogous to the way in which an analysis of variance partitions the variance of a variable into independent effects (Bloomfield, 1976). In truly random temporal data, the power of the various periodic components would be distributed randomly. Data are considered to be cyclical at a given frequency when a periodic component of that frequency accounts for a significant amount of the data's variability.

Researchers use spectral analysis to determine whether behavior is rhythmic or cyclical. First, the behavior of an individual (or interaction) is coded within a large number of discrete time periods. In one study of mother–infant interactions, behaviors indicating attention and involvement were coded for both the mother and child every $\frac{1}{24}$ of a second (Beebe et al., 1982) for 2 minutes. In another, Hayes and Cobb (1982) recorded the amount of conversation between a man and women in 6-minute intervals for a period of 30 days. These temporal data were then analyzed via a spectral analysis to determine the extent to which it was cyclical. Beebe and her colleagues found maternal behavior cycles occurring in time periods as short as one-fourth second, whereas the rhythms of conversation described by Hayes and Cobb were on the order of an hour and a half.

This research investigated the interaction dyad. That is, the investigators did not specifically measure the degree of entrainment or coupling of rhythms between individuals but, instead, measured the degree to which the interaction dyad as a unit displayed any periodicity in behavior over time. The implicit assumption was that if any dyadic rhythms were found, both individuals in the dyad must be contributing to it by coordinating their behavior.

In a series of studies completed by Newtson and his colleagues, spectral analysis was used to measure directly the degree of coupling between the behavior rhythms of two people performing a number of tasks (Newtson, Hairfield, Bloomingdale, & Cutino, 1987). Interactants were filmed while performing activities such as unloading boxes from a truck and putting together a tent. The behavior of each individual in an interaction was coded at 1-second intervals. A *cross-spectral analysis* was then performed to determine the relation between the two series (Gottman, 1981). This analysis generates a "coherence index" that indicates the proportion of variance at each frequency in a series from one individual that can be predicted by the series from another. In all activities, significant coherence between the rhythms of the interactants was found.

Interestingly, the nature of the interaction activity was found to have an effect on the frequencies showing the strongest coherence. For example, in the truck-unloading sequence, there was a significant coherence of a 25-second behavior cycle and no coherence of behavior cycles with periods of less than 10 seconds. For the basketball sequence, the coherence of behavior rhythms between individuals occurred only for behavior cycles with periods of less than 2 seconds. Apparently the nature of the activity can affect or even determine the length of the predominant behavior rhythms for a given interaction.

The impact of spectral analysis in the study of interpersonal coordination could be very great, as it can objectively quantify the degree of at least one aspect of synchrony, namely, the entrainment of behavior rhythms. Unfortunately, the data sets required for such detailed time series analyses are often so massive that studies of even a moderate number of interactions are prohibitive. In the work just described, the results for a given type of setting are reported for only one interaction dyad. The full utility and validity of this measurement technique thus cannot be fully determined until larger studies replicate past work and thus ensure the generality and robustness of these results.

Speech analysis

The flow of speech during normal conversation is as complicated a phenomenon as is the flow of any other motor behavior. Consider that in a rapid arpeggio, a pianist may play as many as 16 notes in a second. In contrast, the rate of motor commands in the speech musculature has been calculated as high as 1,400 per second (Lenneberg, 1967). With such an abundance of behavior occurring at such speeds, it is not surprising that a great deal of organization has been observed.

When examining verbal behavior for synchrony, the flow of speech is first segmented into its components. The level of analysis may vary from the phonetic boundaries measured in milliseconds to complete sentence clauses lasting for seconds. Once these boundaries are determined, synchrony can be measured in one of two ways: the degree to which one's body movement synchronizes with another's speech patterns or the smoothness of the interweaving of speech during conversation.

Synchrony. Spontaneous speech is composed of discernible *chunks*, or sequences of syllables, usually a few seconds in length, that are held together by an internal rhythm and form a single speech act. Trager and Smith (1951) first described these speech units and called them *phonemic clauses*. Patterns of pitch, rhythm, and loudness define phonemic clauses as individual units. Phonemic clauses end with a *terminal juncture*, a barely perceptible slowing of speech in which the changes of pitch, rhythm, and loudness end and level off, leading into the next phonemic clause. This abrupt leveling off is one of the defining characteristics of a phonemic clause. Although actual pauses in speech may accompany terminal junctures, they are not a necessary feature and are absent in about half of the time.

Conversational speech is made up of a series of phonemic clauses strung together. Consequently, patterns of rhythm, pitch, and loudness are repeated during the flow of speech. These rhythms are not limited to the articulatory structure of speech but are apparent also in the body movements of the speaker. It has been observed that a speaker's body movements do not occur randomly but instead accentuate phonemic clauses. Dittman and Llewellyn (1969) affixed movement transducers to the heads, hands, and feet of college students and recorded their movements during a brief interview. They segmented their subjects' speech into phonemic clauses and found significantly more body movements at the start of phonemic clauses than anywhere else.

Turn taking. Some investigators are interested primarily in the smoothness of turn taking within conversations. For practical reasons, measuring *dis*-synchrony turns out to be easier than measuring synchrony. Examples of turn-taking dissynchrony include things like simultaneous speech, mutual silences, and interruptions. Turn taking is considered smoother and more synchronous to the extent that turn-taking breakdowns are less frequent and shorter in duration.

Surprisingly, it has been found that conversations tend to be more synchronous when the interactants cannot see each other than when they are face to face. Rutter and Stephenson (1977) recorded the speech conversations of subjects sitting face to face and compared them with recorded conversations that took place over an audio intercom link. Simultaneous speech was more frequent and lasted longer when the conversants could see each other than when they could not. The authors' explanation for this result invokes a compensation hypothesis: They suggested that in face-to-face interactions the synchronizing of nonverbal behavior compensates and allows for temporary breakdowns in the smoothness of turn taking. Their explanation is intriguing, for it implies the presence of distinct synchrony channels that may engage and disengage independently. It is as if there must be a minimum level of synchrony between the interactants to keep the interaction running smoothly. By maintaining this minimum level requirement, one would be free to execute a limited number of intentionally dissynchronous behaviors.

Dissynchronous behavior has been hypothesized to be a means of communicating a desire to terminate an interaction (Tronick et al., 1977). As long as synchrony is being maintained on one channel of communication (i.e., the nonverbal channel), another channel may be used intentionally to "cut off" another's train of thought or to "cut in" with one's own thoughts. In other words, it allows one to maintain the synchrony needed to keep an interaction going but allows for the use of selective dissynchrony as a communication technique. It would be interesting to examine best friends involved in an impassioned debate to see whether they could be, at the same time, exhibiting high levels of both synchrony and dissynchrony.

Behavior matching

The writings on behavior mirroring and mimicry go back as far as McDougall (1908) and predate any systematic investigations of interpersonal coordination. Although no one equates behavior matching with interactional synchrony, it is believed to be at least one manifestation or consequence of interpersonal coordination.

Behavior matching occurs when two or more people show similar body configurations. For example, if both members of an interacting dyad were sitting back in their chairs with their right leg crossed over their left knee, their behavior would be congruent. If they sat facing each other and one had his left leg crossed and the other had her right leg crossed, they would be mirroring each other. In either case, there would be some degree of behavior matching.

The work on posture congruence is a prime example of behavior matching. As described earlier, posture congruence has been measured in classrooms, therapy sessions, and in getting-acquainted situations. The perception of rapport and similarity by outside observers has been found to be positively influenced by the degree of behavior matching recorded (Trout & Rosenfeld, 1980). For the interactants themselves, studies have found a relationship between behavior matching and self-reported rapport and involvement (Charney, 1966; LaFrance, 1982), but as mentioned earlier, behavior matching may reflect only an attempt to achieve a state of rapport.

Behavior rating: A new method for the measurement of interpersonal coordination

Although most methods of studying synchrony include an analysis of synchrony (i.e., breakdown or segmentation of behavior into its atomistic components), an alternative is to take a gestalt approach. The rating method starts with the assumption that humans can directly perceive real stimulus properties in the environment. Gibson (1979) referred to these properties as *affordances* and claimed that they constrain the appearance as well as the movement–action properties of entities. As a consequence of their effect on appearance, affordances can be directly perceived rather than inferred.

Baron and Boudreau (1987) described *social affordance* as a property that defines the social environment and does not reside in any single object or entity. They concluded that this property exists only in the reciprocal, coordinated action of two or more individuals. Furthermore, they stated:

> Relational behavior provides direct input for social perception in the sense that there is information in the stimulus array for different types of social properties that can be perceived as opposed to being constructed, providing that the observer can see the joint action over time. (Baron & Boudreau, 1987, p. 1223)

A series of studies reported by Newtson, Hairfield, Bloomingdale, and Cutino (1987) directly addressed and supported the validity of this assumption. Their subjects viewed a series of relational tasks (e.g., a man and a woman putting up a tent) and completed a perceptual rating task. This rating task was shown to be sensitive to the coordinated movement between the interactants. When the subjects were given a perceptual interference task while making their ratings, the relationship between their ratings and the coordinated movement in the interactions they viewed weakened, whereas a standard cognitive interference task showed no such effects. The results from the two interference tasks suggest that subjects were not cognitively deriving or inferring their ratings of the interaction but were perceiving them directly.

Given the potential of human perception, it may be just as easy to perceive synchrony as it is to measure synchrony with mechanical or electronic instruments. It should be noted that with the exception of the computer-aided vision technique introduced in Japan (Kato et al., 1983), all of the methods described earlier have had, at some point in their execution, a time at which a human perceptual judgment is required. A method that directly asks raters for their perceptions of synchronous behavior differs from other methods only in the degree to which human perceptual judgments are used.

In order to establish the validity of perceived synchrony, two issues must be addressed: Does synchrony truly exist beyond some baseline level attributable to chance movement, or is the level of perceived synchrony merely projected onto the stimulus by the perceiver? And is synchrony being directly observed, or is it being inferred from directly observable characteristics other than synchrony, such as the apparent emotional affect of the interactants? A new experimental paradigm has been developed to address just these issues.

The pseudosynchrony experimental paradigm

The crux of the pseudosynchrony experimental paradigm is the generation of a perceived synchrony control stimulus (i.e., an interaction stimulus) that is known, by definition, to be lacking true synchronous movement yet contains all the properties of the interaction for which a true perceived synchrony rating is desired. The idea is to generate two measures of perceived synchrony for an interaction: the level of synchrony perceived for that interaction and a baseline level of synchrony, called *pseudosynchrony*, for that interaction with which the level of perceived synchrony can be compared.

Consider the following example: Person A is recorded while interacting with Person B. The level of perceived synchrony can be measured by asking the subjects to look at interaction AB and to rate the amount of synchrony they can see. Suppose now that Person A was also recorded in a separate interaction with Person C (interaction AC) and that Person B was recorded in another interaction with Person D (interaction BD) (Figure 11.1). From videotapes of interactions AC and BD, a *pseudo-*

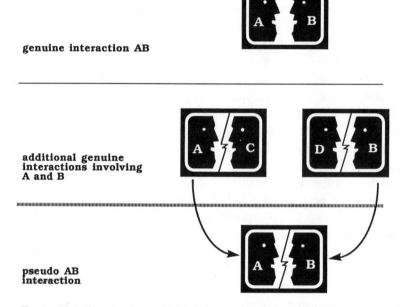

genuine interaction AB

additional genuine
interactions involving
A and B

pseudo AB
interaction

Figure 11.1. Construction of pseudointeraction video clip of Person A with Person B from two separate interactions involving Persons C and D.

interaction AB could be constructed to appear as though it were a genuine recording of an interaction between Person A and Person B. In other words, the behavior sequences of two people in different interactions are combined at random. The subjects who rated the amount of synchrony in this pseudointeraction would be rating pseudosynchrony, thus providing a baseline against which the synchrony from the genuine interaction between Person A and Person B could be compared.

An important point is that an asymmetry in the conversational stream is necessary to form a pseudointeraction. An essential quality of a proper pseudointeraction control is that the judges believe it to be a genuine interaction. If a clip showed interactants frequently talking simultaneously and taking conversational turns out of sequence, it would become obvious to a viewer (even with the sound turned off) that the clip was not of a genuine interaction. In such case, the value of the pseudointeraction clip as a control is diminished, as any decrease in synchrony could be explained by a rating bias of these obviously artificial pseudointeraction clips. In order to use the pseudointeraction paradigm effectively, great care must be taken when choosing the interaction to be investigated. Not all types of social interaction are amenable to this analysis. Next we shall describe two types of interactions that have been studied successfully with this method.

Mother–infant synchrony study (Bernieri, Reznick, & Rosenthal, 1988). In the mother–infant synchrony study, untrained judges were used to rate directly the amount of synchrony they perceived between mothers and 14-month-old infants in short, silent (sound removed), videotaped interaction segments. The mothers and their babies sat facing each other, separated by a table making them too far apart to touch each other. The mothers were instructed to talk to their child in a way to maximize the child's engagement in the interaction. The mothers also interacted with a child belonging to another mother whom they had just met. The entire procedure for an experimental session involved two mothers (Mother A and Mother B) and their respective children (Child A and Child B), from which four genuine mother–child interactions of about 5 minutes each were recorded: (1) Mother A with Child A, (2) Mother B with Child B, (3) Mother A with Child B, and (4) Mother B with Child A. All the interactions were recorded with a split-screen generator, allowing us to isolate and treat independently the images of each interactant.

For each of these four interactions, a pseudointeraction stimulus clip similar to the one described earlier was constructed. For example, a pseudointeraction control clip for Mother A with Child A was constructed from the interactions of Mother A with Child B and Mother B with Child A. A second type of pseudointeraction control clip that *desynchronized* the interactants was also constructed. For example, the video image of Mother A recorded in the third minute of her interaction with Child A was paired with the video image of Child A recorded in the first minute of their interaction. This type of psuedointeraction differed from the first in that the original genuine interaction provided the video images that were recombined to form the pseudointeraction.

To summarize, three interaction stimulus clips of Mother A interacting with Child A were formed. The first was the genuine interaction of Mother A with her own Child A. The second was an *external* pseudointeraction clip of Mother A and Child A, constructed from two interactions external to the genuine Mother A with Child A interaction. The third was an *internal* pseudointeraction clip of Mother A and Child A that was constructed from the original genuine interaction but had desynchronized the time frame of the interactants. Although it is obvious that the two pseudointeraction clips differed it was unclear whether one was any more appropriate to use as a pseudosynchrony control than the other was.

A total of eight mothers with their children were videotaped. The raters viewed all the interaction clips over a period of 4 days and were not told of the pseudointeraction nature of the clips. The judges were given a brief description of three kinds of synchronous behavior patterns to look for: (1) *simultaneous movement* reflecting the quantity or degree of movement that appears to begin or end at the same moment, (2) *tempo similarity* reflecting the degree to which the two people seem to be "marching to the beat of the same drummer" (much like the tempo an orchestra follows at a concert), and (3) *coordination and smoothness* reflecting the degree to which the interactants' behavior intertwine, mesh, and flow smoothly and evenly. The three ratings of synchrony were highly correlated (med $r = .76$), suggesting that judges did not distinguish among them. Because of this, the three ratings were combined and were considered a global measure of perceived movement synchrony.

The judges were given the pseudointeraction clips mixed in with the true interaction clips. With the sound turned off, the judges did not realize they were seeing pseudointeractions. If they were perceiving directly some kind of genuine coordination in the interactions, we would expect them to perceive more synchrony in the true interaction video clips than in the pseudointeraction video clips. As can be seen in Table 11.1, for mothers interacting with their own children, the judges rated synchrony significantly higher in the true interaction clips, thus demonstrating that the synchrony between a mother and her child can be directly perceived. The results also showed that synchrony increased with time. A somewhat unexpected (but not surprising) result was the fact that interactions between unacquainted women and children showed no evidence of perceivable synchrony. That is, for an unrelated mother and child, synchrony ratings from genuine interactions, not shown here, were no different from the pseudosynchrony ratings than from the corresponding pseudointeractions.

A second study collected observer ratings of the emotional affect of each mother and child separately in all of the recorded video segments comprising the genuine and pseudointeraction video clips. We wanted to determine whether the raters were inferring an amount of synchrony from other more obvious aspects of the recorded interaction, namely, the apparent emotional affect of the interactants (e.g., warmth, enthusiasm). If raters were not perceiving synchrony directly but were inferring it instead from the emotional state of the interactants, then the syn-

Table 11.1. *Mean ratings of movement synchrony for a mother with her own child*

Type of stimulus clips	First	Third	Mean	Difference (third – first)
External pseudointeraction	5.17	4.69	4.93	−0.48
Internal pseudointeraction	5.43	5.66	5.55	0.23
Genuine interaction	5.48	5.97	5.73	0.49
Mean of pseudointeraction	5.30	5.18	5.24	−0.12
Genuine – mean pseudo-difference	0.18	0.79^b	0.49^a	0.61^a

Note: Values in the table are means computed across eight dyads.
$^a p < .025$, $^b p < .005$.

chrony ratings (including pseudosynchrony) should correlate with the emotional affect of the interactants. However, the correlations between the mean affect rating of the mother and child in an interaction clip and the perceived synchrony in that clip were not significant. The failure of any variable to correlate significantly with the pseudosynchrony ratings indicated that the judges were not relying on the mere emotional or motivational state of the interactants to infer synchrony. Thus, they must have perceived it directly.

Although the results from this study validate synchrony as a directly perceivable phenomenon, other questions remained. For instance, the *internal* or *desynchronized* pseudointeraction control generated weaker results than did the *external* pseudointeraction control. It could be argued that the internal pseudointeraction clip is a more stringent type of control and that if the pseudosynchrony it generated did not differ significantly from true synchrony, the perceivable synchrony hypothesis would be severely limited. Another test of this type of pseudointeraction control was needed to establish the robustness of perceived synchrony.

The first study also showed some signs that synchrony was related to interactant rapport. In the true interaction clips, observed interactant warmth and happiness were correlated with synchrony. A stronger test of the synchrony–rapport relationship was designed that used the interactants' self-reports. Finally, with the validity of perceived synchrony established, its relationship with the fourth hypothesized aspect of synchrony (behavior matching) needed to be investigated. Specifically, the similarity of the interactants' postures was measured and examined for its relationship to movement synchrony.

High school student synchrony, posture similarity, and rapport study (Bernieri, 1988). In the next study, 38 high school students were videotaped while teaching one another a series of make-believe words. This type of interaction was chosen because the act of teaching lends itself nicely to the pseudointeraction paradigm. While the teacher talks continually throughout the interaction, the student listens and speaks rarely if at all. The asymmetric quality of verbal behavior makes the resulting pseudointeractions difficult for the unsuspecting rater to detect.

The judges identified and rated two types of dyadic coordination: the degree of movement synchrony (i.e., a composite variable made from ratings of simultaneous movement, tempo similarity, and gestaltlike coordination) and the degree of posture congruence (behavior matching). In this study, only the internal pseudointeraction control was employed.

Movement synchrony in true interactions was judged significantly greater than in the internal pseudointeraction control clips, thus replicating the earlier results using this method and further validating the judges' ability to perceive synchrony. A metaanalysis of the two studies comparing internal pseudosynchrony and genuine synchrony found that the magnitude of the difference between synchrony and pseudosynchrony was relatively constant across studies, even though the significance associated with the size of each effect differed. In the study by Bernieri et al. (1988) the effect that failed to reach significance was caused by the small n of that study.

Our next item of interest was the relationship between posture similarity and synchrony. Because past research has implied that the two are interchangeable, it was important to determine their exact relationship. Although posture similarity was highly correlated with movement synchrony ($r = .58$, $p < .05$), the ratings of posture similarity did not differ significantly between true and pseudointeraction clips.

Further discrepancies between posture similarity and synchrony became apparent when measures of dyadic rapport were correlated with synchrony and posture similarity. The interactants' self-ratings made on various social and emotional adjectives indicated a strong relationship between movement synchrony and dyadic rapport, but posture similarity showed no relationship with rapport. Table 11.2 shows that positive affect and talkativeness correlated strongly with movement synchrony,

Table 11.2. *Correlations between coordinated movement and mean dyadic rapport*

Self-rating	Movement synchrony	Posture similarity
1. Positivity[a]	.74[†]	−.04
2. Negativity[b]	−.20	.01
3. Anxiety[c]	.00	.50*
4. Control[d]	.22	−.25
5. Talkative	.48*	−.21
6. Tiredness	−.40	−.24
7. Sexuality	.23	−.04

Note: N = 18 dyads.
[a]Mean of enjoyment, enjoyment of role (i.e., student or teacher), liking of partner, happiness, satisfaction, friendliness, excitement, interest, enthusiasm, motivation, attentiveness, "easygoingness," cooperation, and humor.
[b]Mean of anger, disgust, frustration, and boredom.
[c]Mean of tension, nervousness, and self-consciousness.
[d]Mean of control, dominance, and forcefulness.
*$p < .05$, [†] $< .001$.

although neither correlated significantly with posture similarity. Only anxiety correlated substantially with posture similarity, a finding also reported by LaFrance and Ickes (1981).

The results from this second study were important in three ways: (1) They help validate perceived synchrony by replicating the fact that genuine synchrony is greater than pseudosynchrony, even when employing the more stringent internal pseudointeraction control. (2) They provide strong empirical support for the synchrony–rapport relationship. (3) They suggest that although the two are correlated, behavior matching as measured by posture similarity should be distinguished from the other aspects of synchrony. Also, because posture similarity was correlated with anxiety, behavior matching could reflect an interactional process different from the other measures of synchrony.

The results from this research demonstrate the utility and validity of synchrony ratings. Of all the methods mentioned, the use of observers to generate synchrony ratings seems the most straightforward and easy to collect. This technique has been used to study mother–infant interactions and teacher–student interactions and is currently being used to measure the synchrony between college students in cooperative and competitive situations (Bernieri, Davis, Knee, & Rosenthal, 1990; Davis, 1988). Unlike some of the more sophisticated microsynchrony analyses requiring computerized video equipment or filmed recordings, this technique has the valuable asset of allowing investigators to analyze standard videotape-recorded interactions for synchrony.

The main disadvantage of synchrony ratings is that until now, the method has been used only on silent recordings. It is not known whether the validity of synchrony judgments can generalize to recordings that contain speech. Because some synchrony researchers have strongly emphasized speech, it is important for us to know what effect the presence of speech has on synchrony perceptions. Given the possibility of a synchrony channel compensation process mentioned earlier, we should be able to measure both the verbal and nonverbal channels of communication for synchrony.

Conclusion

Interpersonal coordination (especially synchrony) is associated with many important social, cognitive, and developmental phenomena. It is an integral aspect of communication, present at birth, and may be an important mediator of conversational turn taking and perhaps even of comprehension itself. Developmentally, the bonding between a mother and child may be affected by the extent to which they coordinate and synchronize with each other. By being "in sync" with her child, a mother may moderate more effectively the child's arousal level and thereby ensure an optimal level of stimulation and communication without overtaxing the child's cognitive or emotional capabilities. In this manner, synchrony could have a profound impact in moderating a child's cognitive, emotional, and social development.

The most empirically demonstrated result involving interpersonal coordination has been its relationship with social rapport. People seem to get along better when their behavior is well coordinated (in both matching and synchrony). The reason for this relationship is unclear. It is conceivable that not synchronizing with the person with whom you are interacting may be an inherently negative experience, in which case synchrony would directly affect rapport. In fact, as some have suggested (Tickle-Degnen & Rosenthal, 1987), synchrony may be a major component of rapport. Indirectly, a coordinated interaction may only heighten feelings of similarity, in which case the increased mutual feelings of similarity would mediate the coordination–rapport relationship. In either case, the implication is that social and emotional relationships are closely linked to a physical aspect of human interaction of which we are usually unaware.

One important issue that needs to be addressed in the future is the person-to-person variability in synchrony. Do some people have an easier time synchronizing their interactions than others do? Are there some stable individual differences among people that would permit us to predict which dyads were more likely to synchronize? Baron and Boudreau (1987) hypothesized that the ability to coordinate with others should be related to one's social competence. Unfortunately, there are virtually no data available that address this question. Only one study has any relevant data at all. Preliminary findings reported by Penman, Meares, Baker, and Milgram-Friedman (1983) suggested that mothers with hypersensitive neurophysiology (inferred from GSR response to an auditory stimuli habituation task) are less able to synchronize with their children than are mothers with more normally responding neurophysiology. The authors interpreted their findings as meaning that synchrony can be inhibited by concurrent distracting stimuli. Hypersensitive mothers have a more difficult time habituating to, or screening out, unimportant stimuli, and this may distract their attention to and involvement in their interactions, which could interfere with the synchrony process.

Interpersonal coordination and synchrony may eventually explain how it is that we can "hit it off" immediately with some people and never "get it together" with others. This aspect of rapport certainly would be of concern to professions dealing with intimate personal relations. The success of psychotherapists, physicians, counselors, and teachers all depend to some extent on the degree of rapport they can achieve in their professional interactions. Their ability to coordinate and synchronize with different people under various circumstances may have a significant effect on their professional competence and effectiveness. An understanding of the impact that interpersonal coordination can have on an interaction may eventually lead to the development of new synchronizing strategies or techniques that will aid the entrainment process. For instance, it may be useful to investigate the question of whether certain types of music facilitate interpersonal coordination. For schoolteachers, an understanding of interpersonal coordination could help identify teaching styles or rhythms to which children may be differentially receptive. Teachers then could be assigned students who are more likely to coordinate with their particular teaching behavior.

The theoretical and methodological diversity in synchrony research so far has inhibited the development of a robust unifying construct of synchrony. This is unfortunate, as the potential value of the investigation of interpersonal coordination for our understanding of social interaction and communication is considerable. It is surprising that a phenomenon potentially so important can have been so seldom investigated. One reason for this lack of research may be that researchers have not had available reasonable and accepted methods of measuring the coordination and synchrony between people. Perhaps with the development of new techniques for measuring interpersonal coordination, such as the rating method described here, there will be an additional impetus for research on this distinctively social psychological topic, a topic of great basic importance, especially for applied areas of social interaction such as medicine, psychotherapy, education, management, and social relations generally.

Notes

1. For more complete reviews of the possible developmental, social, and cultural implications of interpersonal coordination the reader is referred to Davis (1982) and Kendon, Harris, and Key (1975).
2. Reported in Moore-Ede, Sulzman, and Fuller (1982).

References

Baron, R. M., & Boudreau, L. A. (1987). An ecological perspective on integrating personality and social psychology. *Journal of Personality and Social Psychology, 53*, 1222–1228.

Bavelas, J. B., Black, A., Lemery, C. R., & Mullett, J. (1986). "I *show* how you feel": Motor mimicry as a communicative act. *Journal of Personal and Social Psychology, 50*, 322–329.

Beebe, B., Gerstman, L., Carson, B., Dolins, M., Zigman, A., Rosensweig, H., Faughey, K., & Korman, M. (1982). Rhythmic communication in the mother–infant dyad. In M. Davis (Ed.), *Interaction rhythms: Periodicity in communicative behavior* (pp. 13–22). New York: Human Sciences Press.

Berghout-Austin, A. M., & Peery, J. C. (1983). Analysis of adult–neonate synchrony during speech and non speech. *Perceptual Motor Skills, 57*, 455–459.

Bernieri, F. (1988). Coordinated movement and rapport in teacher–student interactions. *Journal of Nonverbal Behavior, 12*, 120–138.

Bernieri, F., Davis, J., Knee, C., & Rosenthal, R. (1990). *Validating synchrony judgments of cooperative and competitive interactions.* Unpublished manuscript.

Bernieri, F., Reznick, J. S., & Rosenthal, R. (1988). Synchrony, pseudo synchrony, and dissynchrony: Measuring the entrainment process in mother–infant interactions. *Journal of Personality and Social Psychology, 54*(2), 243–253.

Bloomfield, P. (1976). *Fourier analysis of time series: An introduction.* New York: Wiley.

Byrne, D. (1971). *The attraction paradigm.* New York: Academic Press.

Cappella, J. N. (1981). Mutual influence in expressive behavior: Adult–adult and infant–adult dyadic interaction. *Psychological Bulletin, 89,* 101–132.

Charney, J. E. (1966). Psychosomatic manifestations of rapport in psychotherapy. *Psychosomatic Medicine. 28,* 305–315.

Condon, W. S. (1970). Method of micro-analysis of sound films of behavior. *Behavior Research Methods and Instrumentation, 2,* 51–54.

(1982). Cultural microrhythms. In M. Davis (Ed.), *Interaction rhythms: Periodicity in communicative behavior* (pp. 53–76). New York: Human Sciences Press.

Condon, W. S., & Ogston, W. D. (1966). Sound film analysis of normal and pathological behavior patterns. *Journal of Nervous and Mental Diseases, 143,* 338–457.

(1967). A segmentation of behavior. *Journal of Psychiatric Research, 5,* 221–235.

Condon, W. S., & Sander, L. W. (1974). Synchrony demonstrated between movements of the neonate and adult speech. *Child Development, 45,* 456–462.

Dabbs, J. M. (1969). Similarity of gestures and interpersonal influence. *Proceedings, 77th Annual Convention, 4,* 337–338 (Summary).

Davis, J. (1988). *Psychological sex role, rapport, and synchrony.* Unpublished manuscript.

Davis, M. (1982). Introduction. In M. Davis (Ed.), *Interaction rhythms: Periodicity in communicative behavior* (pp. 23–29). New York: Human Sciences Press.

Dittman, A. T., & Llewellyn, L. G. (1968). Relationship between vocalizations and head nods as listener responses. *Journal of Personality and Social Psychology, 9,* 79–84.

(1969). Body movement and speech rhythm in social conversation. *Journal of Personality and Social Psychology, 11,* 98–106.

Gatewood, J. B., & Rosenwein, R. (1981). Interactional synchrony: Genuine or spurious? A critique of recent research. *Journal of Nonverbal Behavior, 6,* 12–29.

Gibson, J. J. (1979). *The ecological approach to visual perception.* Boston: Houghton Mifflin.

Gottman, J. M. (1981). *Time-series analysis: A comprehensive introduction for social scientists.* Cambridge: Cambridge University Press.

Hadar, U., Steiner, T. J., & Rose, F. C. (1985). Head movement during listening turns in conversation. *Journal of Nonverbal Behavior, 9,* 214–228.

Hayes, D. P., & Cobb, L. (1982). Cycles of spontaneous conversation under longterm isolation. In M. Davis (Ed.), *Interaction rhythms: Periodicity in communicative behavior* (pp. 319–340). New York: Human Sciences Press.

Kato, T., Takahashi, E., Sawada, K., Kobayashi, N., Watanabe, T., & Ishii, T. (1983). A computer analysis of infant movements synchronized with adult speech. *Pediatric Research, 17,* 625–628.

Kendon, A. (1970). Movement coordination in social interaction: Some examples described. *Acta Psychologica, 32,* 1–25.

Kendon, A., Harris, R. M., & Key, M. R. (Eds.). (1975). *Organization of behavior in face-to-face interactions.* The Hague: Mouton.

LaFrance, M. (1979). Nonverbal synchrony and rapport: Analysis by the cross-lag panel technique. *Social Psychology Quarterly, 42,* 66–70.

(1982). Posture mirroring and rapport. In M. Davis (Ed.), *Interaction rhythms: Periodicity in communicative behavior* (pp. 279–298). New York: Human Sciences Press.

LaFrance, M., & Broadbent, M. (1976). Group rapport: Posture sharing as a nonverbal indicator. *Group and Organization Studies, 1,* 328–333.

LaFrance, M., & Ickes, W. (1981). Posture mirroring and interactional involvement: Sex and sex typing effects. *Journal of Nonverbal Behavior, 5,* 139–154.

Lenneberg, E. H. (1967). *Biological foundations of language.* New York: Wiley.

McDougall, W. (1908). *Introduction to social psychology.* London: Methuen.

McDowall, J. J. (1978). Interactional synchrony: A reappraisal. *Journal of Personality and Social Psychology, 36,* 963–975.

McGrath, J. E., & Kelly, J. R. (1986). *Time and human interaction: Toward a social psychology of time* (pp. 79–104). New York: Guilford Press.

Moore-Ede, M. C., Sulzman, F. M., & Fuller, C. A. (1982). *The clocks that time us.* Cambridge, MA: Harvard University Press.

Newtson, D., Hairfield, J., Bloomingdale, J., & Cutino, S. (1987). The structure of action and interaction. *Social Cognition, 5,* 191–237.

Penman, R., Meares, R., Baker, K., & Milgram-Friedman, L. (1983). Synchrony in mother–infant interaction: A possible neurophysiological base. *British Journal of Medical Psychology, 56,* 1–7.

Rosenfeld, H. M. (1981). Whither interactional synchrony? In K. Bloom (Ed.), *Prospective issues in infancy research* (pp. 71–97). Hillsdale, NJ: Erlbaum.

Rutter, D. R., & Stephenson, G. M. (1977). The role of visual communication in synchronizing conversation. *European Journal of Social Psychology, 7,* 29–37.

Scheflen, A. E. (1964). The significance of posture in communication systems. *Psychiatry, 27,* 316–331.

Scherer, K. R., & Ekman, P. (1982). Methodological issues in studying nonverbal behavior. In K. R. Scherer and P. Ekman (Eds.), *Handbook of methods in nonverbal behavior research* (pp. 287–361). Cambridge: Cambridge University Press.

Siffre, M. (1964). *Beyond time.* New York: McGraw-Hill.

Stern, D. N. (1971). A micro-analysis of mother–infant interaction. *Journal of the Academy of Child Psychiatry, 10,* 501–517.

(1974). Mother and infant at play. In M. Lewis and L. Rosenblum (Eds.), *Origins of behavior, Vol. 1: The effect of the infant on its caregiver* (pp. 187–213). New York: Wiley.

Tickle-Degnen, L., & Rosenthal, R. (1987). Group rapport and nonverbal behavior. *Review of Personality and Social Psychology, 9,* 113–136.

Trager, G. L., & Smith, H. L. (1951). An outline of English structure. *Studies in linguistics: Occasional papers, 3.* Norman, OK: Battenberg Press.

Tronick, E. D., Als, H., Adamson, L., & Wise, S. (1978). The infant's response to entrapment between contradictory messages in face-to-face interaction. *Journal of the American Academy of Child Psychiatry, 17,* 1–13.

Tronick, E. D., Als, H., & Brazelton, T. B. (1977). Mutuality in mother–infant interaction. *Journal of Communication, 27,* 74–79.

Trout, D., & Rosenfeld, H. M. (1980). The effect of postural lean and body congruence on the judgment of psychotherapeutic rapport. *Journal of Nonverbal Communication, 4,* 176–190.

Vernikos-Danellis, J., & Winget, C. M. (1979). The importance of light, postural and social cues in the regulation of plasma cortisol rhythms in man. In A. Reinberg and F. Halbert (Eds.), *Chronopharmacology* (pp. 101–106). Elmsford, NY: Pergamon.

Wylie, L. (1985). Language learning and communication. *The French Review, 53,* 777–785.

12. Symbolic nonverbal behavior: Talking through gestures

PIO ENRICO RICCI BITTI AND ISABELLA POGGI

Introduction

Gestures are one of the most interesting aspects of kinetic behavior and, as such, have been the subject of many studies. The criteria used to aggregate or distinguish gestures are diverse, and so systematic, comparative analysis of the various classifications is rather difficult, because several gesture classifications have been constructed. We can group gestures into two major categories according to Kendon (1983): *semiotic*, which mainly consider what modalities gestures have in relation to their meaning, and *functional*, which primarily consider the ways in which gestures are used in relation to the accompanying discourse.

The semiotic classifications discriminate among gestures that convey their meaning through indication, gestures that in some way describe or indirectly explain their meaning, and gestures in which the relationship between the form of movement and the expressed meaning is purely conventional. For the most part, the functional classifications distinguish gestures playing a direct role in the conversation, that is, that are inseparable from concomitant discourse; gestures that, despite their importance to the interaction, are not linked to the conversation but possess their own functional autonomy; and, finally, gestures whose significance expresses either the psychological conditions or the mental processes of the encoder and that, according to some authors (Kendon, 1983), should not, strictly speaking, even be considered as gestures.

Among the various classifications, we feel it useful to recall the one suggested by Ekman and Friesen (1969, 1972) that links single gestures to the conditions in which they are used, to their origins, and to their codification, thus adopting a mixed criterion for classification (though it is predominantly functional in type). Ekman and Friesen defined five

433

categories of nonverbal signals: emblems, illustrators, regulators, affect displays, and adaptors.

Emblems or *symbolic gestures* are distinguished from the others in that they are intentionally emitted signals with a specific meaning that can be directly translated into words. This meaning is known and shared by the members of a certain social group, class, or subculture, and so such gestures are deliberately produced to transmit a certain message to someone else who knows the meaning of the gesture and understands why it is being used. Typical emblematic gestures are shaking hands in greeting, calling by signs, and indicating. They can repeat or substitute the contents of verbal communication, be used when oral communication is hindered, and emphasize the ritualized aspects of verbal exchange (salutation, leave taking).

There are, however, other gestures belonging to other classes or categories that, in certain cases, can assume symbolic characteristics and functions, for example, gestures that display affects. This category includes those gestures that, along with the face – the main channel for manifesting emotions – express an individual's interior emotional state. To this category of signals belong movements such as shaking a fist or stamping one or both feet in anger and covering one's face with the hand to indicate shame. Hinde (1974), for example, identified a series of gestures in several cultures that consist of placing one's hands over one's face, mouth, or eyes. These gestures are connected with shyness and embarrassment and seem, in some way, to be derived from the act of hiding. This might be a case in which emotional expression has been transformed into a true symbolic gesture that is produced not so much because a person is experiencing that particular emotion but because he or she is talking about it.

In this chapter we shall analyze the characteristics and functions of symbolic gestures used in social interactions, paying particular attention to those problems in gesture research that seem to be most relevant and, in a certain sense, still unresolved.

We shall begin by describing symbolic gestures and reviewing some of the research on them. We shall also consider the case in which symbolic gestures, when organized and combined in particular ways, become formal gestural systems or sign languages.

The next section will examine the difference between iconic gestures, which are similar to their referents and produced according to simple rules of inference, and symbolic gestures, which share a code and are governed by rules of correspondence between signal and meaning. We shall analyze four different types of communicative system (pantomime, articulated lexicon, holophrastic lexicon, and language).

Then we shall look at two major categories of symbolic gestures: the word gesture (in which the gesture carries only a part of the communication) and the sentence gesture (in which the gesture corresponds to an entire communicative action). We shall compare symbolic gestures (the lexicon of gestures) and words (the lexicon of words), pointing out the differences and also some interesting analogies. Finally, in the last two sections, we shall describe two of our own studies. The first investigated the cognitive and expressive mechanisms that operate when a speaker has to explain gesturally the meaning of a common noun, and the second examined the importance of the facial component in symbolic gestures in order to understand the meaning of the gesture itself.

Symbolic gestures, gestural systems, and sign language

As we have seen, although a large part of gesturing forms an integral element of discourse and, therefore, requires a verbal context in order to carry out its function and also to be understood by the recipient, *symbolic gestures* can exist independently of the conversation. In some situations it is not possible during social interaction to use verbal language (e.g., in the case of external restrictions or serious sensorial deficiencies). In such cases gesturing is used as a substitute for the spoken word, resulting in *gestural systems* and *sign languages*.

As we have seen, symbolic gestures operate as complete expressions requiring no other expressive elements to perform their communicative function. Precisely because of this, Kendon (1983) defined them as *autonomous gestures*, to distinguish them from all those that are produced in the verbal interaction of which they are a part and are defined as gesticulations in the strict sense.

There are several types of symbolic gestures: gestures regulating and controlling the interlocutor's behavior (salutations, orders, requests, or threats), gestures commenting on the interlocutor's actions or on objects of the outside world, gestures with a performative function that represents an actual action, and gestures that represent the interior states of the communicator.

Ample space has already been dedicated elsewhere to symbolic gestures: in studies carried out by researchers in linguistics, psychology, cultural anthropology, human ethology, and so on. These studies have generally shared certain basic objectives: to draw up complete lists of the symbolic gestures or emblems used by particular social groups or linguistic communities; to define differences in the repertory and use of symbolic gestures in different cultural groups in order to identify the various meanings attributed to the same gesture in different groups or to discover different gestures that have the same meaning; to analyze the relationship among the origin, historical evolution, and geographic distribution of gestures; or to carry out a semantic analysis of specific symbolic gestures.

In regard to preparing dictionaries of the symbolic gestures typical of a particular cultural group, the best-known and most satisfactory method from a procedural point of view is the one proposed by Johnson, Ekman, and Friesen (1975; see also Ekman, 1976).

Among the attempts to analyze the repertoire of symbolic gestures and to draw up a complete list of symbolic gestures typical of specific cultural groups or linguistic communities, one can cite, for example, the works of Efron (1941), Green (1968), Saitz and Cervenka (1972), Barakat (1973), Creider (1977), Wylie (1977), and Sparhawk (1978). Efron (1941), for example, observed that Italian and Jewish immigrants to America used gestures differently. This is a historically important study, as it led to the distinctions between emblems and other kinds of gesture.

Saitz and Cervenka (1972) studied the gestures used in Colombia and the United States: Some gestures were used with the same meanings in both cultures, whereas others were used differently. Some of the more common ones are shown in Table 12.1.

The research by Morris, Collett, Marsh, and O'Shaughnessy (1979) is one of the more recent examples of intercultural analysis of symbolic gestures. The authors selected a list of 20 symbolic gestures on the basis of a preliminary investigation and submitted the graphic representation of these gestures to "judges" in 40 different localities of Western Europe and the Mediterranean area, to check on the meaning attributed to each gesture in each of the various places. The investigation brought out important differences in the use of these gestures, as well as in the meanings attributed to them in each locality. These results have been affected, however, by methodological choices. The most important of these is the fact that the graphic representation proposed to the judges, besides not expressing the typical movement of each gesture, was limited to presenting one component (i.e., the hand configuration) of the gesture. This meant that for certain gestures, such as the *hand purse* (Figure 12.1, gesture 1), the *vertical horn-sign* (gesture 2), the *horizontal horn-sign* (gesture 3), the *ring* (gesture 4), and the *thumb up* (gesture 5), in

Table 12.1. *Gestures commonly used in Colombia and the United States*

Gesture	Meaning
head-nod	agreement
shake fist	anger
rub palms	anticipation
clapping	approval
raise hand	attention
yawn	boredom
rub hands	cold
beckon	come
extend hand	invite to dance
point	give direction
thumb down	disapproval
shrug shoulder	disinterest
pat on back	encouragement
action of shooting self	*faux pas*
outline female body	attractive female
rub stomach	hungry
wave hands	goodbye
shake hands	greetings

Source: Saitz & Cervenka (1972).

which nonverbal components other than the hand configuration are important (e.g., facial expression), the attribution of meaning became rather difficult.

For some gestures, the Morris et al. (1979) research also brought out the relationship between geographic distribution and origin of the gesture. For example, the gesture defined as the *head toss* (Figure 12.1, gesture 6), which signifies negation, is used – among the various Italian localities considered in the research – only in a southern part of Italy with clearly definable boundaries. This area coincides with the location where the Greeks settled in the first millennium B.C., which took the name Magna Grecia. The gesture is still used not only in Greece but in other Mediterranean regions as well. Furthermore, Collett and Contarello (1987), in an investigation on the origin, evolution, and geographic distribution of certain affirmative and negative gestures, confirmed that the geographic distribution of the head toss in south Italy conforms closely to the Greek settlements established 3000 years ago, thus showing the tendency to preserve this symbolic gesture. Finally, Poggi's

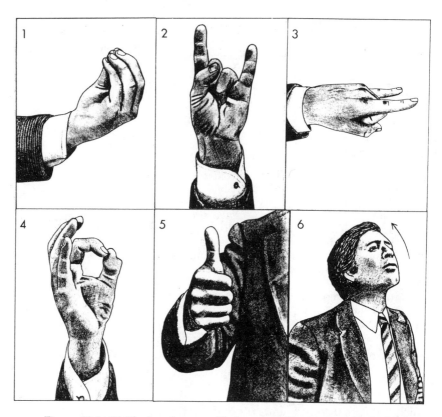

Figure 12.1. (1) The hand purse, (2) the vertical horn-sign, (3) the horizontal horn-sign, (4) the ring, (5) the thumb up, (6) the head toss. (From Morris et al., 1979.)

(1983b) research is an example of semantic analysis of a symbolic gesture: the hand purse (gesture 1). This contribution points to the importance of facial expression in codifying this symbolic gesture.

When, as we mentioned, the use of verbal language is not possible for a variety of reasons, gestures are organized into *gestural systems* that replace verbal language. Examples of this are the signs used in airports and TV studios and by referees in sporting events. In certain cases these gestural systems become so complex and articulated as to assume the characteristics of a language proper. We then find ourselves faced with so-called sign languages containing a collection of signs that provide an extremely large number of possible combinations organized according to precise syntactical rules. The several existing sign languages are determined by social or cultural causes. For instance, they are often considered as "alternative" languages like that of the Australian aborigines, some Trappist orders, and native Americans. But the sign language used by the deaf is the one in which the greatest interest has been shown (see, e.g., work on American Sign Language [ASL] by Stokoe, 1960, or Baker & Cokeley, 1980; and on the sign languages used by the deaf in other linguistic communities, e.g., Volterra, 1987, for the Italian sign language). All of these studies have shown that the systemization of gestural forms and the corresponding systemization of ways of combining these gestural forms within a discourse lead to structural and syntactical characteristics quite similar to those of the spoken language.

The lexicon of symbolic gestures

We shall turn now to the symbolic gestures used by hearing people and shall define the features of these gestures from a cognitive point of view. In order to do this, we need to describe the system of symbolic gestures found in different communication systems.

Communication may be defined (Castelfranchi & Poggi, 1987) as a process in which knowledge held by a sender's mind is transmitted to an addressee's mind. When Sender A wants Addressee B to know some new information, some new meaning, he or she must link this abstract meaning to some perceivable signal, that is, some object or event that can be heard, seen, smelled, or otherwise perceived by the addressee. There may be various rules through which abstract meanings and perceivable signals are linked to one another. A communication system may be defined as a particular set of rules for linking meanings to signals.

There are two basic types of communication system: pantomimic and lexical. And there are three types of lexical system, according to which the lexical items have the meaning of sentences or of words or in addition to the lexical rules, they include syntactic rules, too. In sum, we have four types of communication system:

1. pantomime
2.a. holophrastic lexicon
2.b. articulated lexicon
2.c. lexicon + syntax = language

We shall describe these four types of communication system according to their increasing cognitive complexity and therefore also according to their earlier or later onset through philogenetic and ontogenetic evolution (Parisi, 1983; Poggi & Zomparelli, 1987).

From pantomime to lexicon

The first type of human communication system is *pantomime*, that is, the natural human capacity for using one's own body to imitate objects, actions, or events in order to communicate. For instance, the system we use to try to communicate gesturally with strangers is pantomime. In such cases, we sketch forms of objects in the air or imitate their movements with our hands or body.

Let us trace this type of communication system from its onset: Two persons, A and B, are watching animals in a forest, now and then showing each other the animals they see, but without speaking, so as not to scare them. Person A wants to communicate silently to Person B that she has seen a squirrel: She thus might draw in the air an imaginary tail, from which Person B, thanks to his ability to draw inferences (i.e., creating new knowledge from previous knowledge), can understand that Person A has discovered a squirrel. If Person A later shakes her arms to mimic wings, Person B may infer that Person A has sighted a bird. In such cases, for retrieving a signal – meaning a link – an inferential process is sufficient and is usually based on some physical likeness between the gesture and its referent (the object to which Person A is referring). Even a passerby, Person C, who does not know what Persons A and B are doing, could understand that Person A is "talking" about a squirrel and a bird.

Now let us follow Persons A and B in the forest, sighting more birds and squirrels. By this time, the gestures meaning the two animals may become more sketchy and stylized and less and less resembling true tails or wings: "Bird" might be conveyed by a single wing – just one hand, closer to the trunk, or even a shaking finger. Person A can perform the gesture in this way because by now in Person B's memory a link has been set between each gesture and its meaning: A rotating gesture = "squirrel," and a shaking gesture = "bird." In this case, if a passerby could see Person A's gestures, he might not understand them. Earlier they were iconic gestures; that is, they resembled their referent, but now they are less and less so. Thus, there has been a shift from a pantomime communication system to a lexical system.

We can say that Persons A and B formed a lexicon, a set of *correspondence rules*, quite stable and stored in their memories, linking signals to meanings. Whereas pantomime adhered to only a few generative *inference rules*, a lexicon requires coding and storing a greater number of *correspondence rules*, and therefore it calls for a memory in which such rules may be firmly stored. The rules in a lexicon are coded in that each "speaker" uses "words" while assuming that the other gives them the same meaning that she does: Person A assumes that in Person B's mind the same correspondence holds between a gesture and a meaning as it does in her own mind.

These, then, are the features of the two types of communication systems, pantomime and lexicon:

1. Pantomime is a communication system formed by a few generative inference rules, typically based on the resemblance between a signal's physical aspects and its meaning. By definition, then, a pantomimic system tends to be iconic.
2. A lexicon is a list of lexical items – correspondence rules between signals and meanings – coded and stored in memory.

Where and when the shift exactly occurs from a pantomimic to a lexical system is an open question. It also is difficult to define a lexical gesture, as it might depend on a number of different criteria, like how large the community is that shares it, how frequently it is used, how long it takes to plan and produce it and how widely shared or idiosyncratically it is produced.

Word gestures and sentence gestures

Symbolic gestures form a lexicon whose signals are gestures. According to Ekman and Friesen (1969), a symbolic gesture is a gesture that in a given culture has a largely shared meaning and therefore can be translated into words quite easily and unequivocally. In Figure 12.2, gestures 7, 8, 9, and 10 are examples of Italian symbolic gestures. Respectively, they mean "I," "a lot," "what are you doing?" and "to eat." Gestures 11 (Figure 12.2) and 5 (Figure 12.1) are both Italian and American symbolic gestures, meaning "afterwards," "tomorrow," and "OK."

We can distinguish two types of communication system based on a lexicon: a holophrastic lexicon, and an articulated lexicon. The two lexical systems differ in the kinds of information they convey. A *holophrastic lexicon* is a whole speech act carried in one signal. Each item in such a lexicon may be paraphrased by a whole sentence, and therefore it might be called a *sentence item*. Items of this kind exist in all languages as interjections, like "say!" "oh!" and "help!" These words have the meaning of a complete sentence. For example, "say!" might be paraphrased as "I am surprised at this"; "help!" as "please help me!" and the like (James, 1974; Poggi, 1981).

A complete sentence (Poggi, 1987) is a sequence of sounds that communicates four kinds of information:

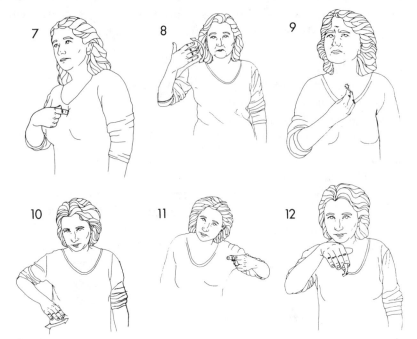

Figure 12.2. (7) I, me; (8) a lot; (9) What are you doing/saying? (10) to eat; (11) afterwards, tomorrow; (12) Come here. (From I. Poggi & M. Zomparelli, 1987.)

1. Arguments (persons, objects, places, times, or events one is discussing).
2. Predicate (some feature or relationship referring to the arguments).
3. Tense (the time to which the predicate refers).
4. The speaker's attitude, including the speech act performed by the sentence (to put a question, to request action, to provide information) and the speaker's degree of certainty (whether she is sure of what she is saying, denies it, or just considers it likely).

In this definition, for a sentence to be complete, it is not sufficient or necessary that it be composed of more than one word. For example, "Listening to you!" contains three words but is not a complete sentence. On the other hand, "Say!" is only one word but is a sentence nonetheless, as it contains all four kinds of information:

1. There is somebody surprised at something (predicate).
2. The surprised one is the speaker, and the cause of the surprise is some fact to be retrieved from the utterance context (argument).
3. The speaker's speech act is information, and he or she is quite sure of it (attitude).
4. The speaker is surprised in the present (tense), that is, at the same time when the speaker speaks.

Every verbal language contains a few *sentence items* that form a holophrastic lexicon, that is, a communication system of type 2a. All other words in a language form an articulated lexicon, type 2b, in which each item conveys only the meaning of a part of a sentence and needs a whole sentence made up of two or more words. This leads, therefore, to the necessity of syntactic *combination rules* that, added to an articulated lexicon (type 2b) make a lexical plus a syntactic system (type 2c), or a language.

In a verbal or sign language of normal native adults we can observe only two types of lexical system, type 2a and type 2c, because after an articulated lexicon has evolved from a holophrastic one, the next step to a lexical–syntactic system is a logical one. We can find systems of type 2b only in developmental or impaired states of language, namely, child language, pidgin languages (those deriving from the mixture of two different languages), and some cases of aphasia, like agrammatism (Parisi, 1981).

In contrast with verbal and sign languages proper (which always have precise and complex syntactic rules), hearing people's symbolic gestures do not seem to include a system of type 2c. The reason is that they include no rules for combining word items into sentences (Volterra & Caselli, 1985).

The so-called gestural systems (Kendon, 1983), which have a rudimentary combinatory structure, might be located conceptually between symbolic gestures and the language proper. But instead, such symbolic gestures are only of types 2a and 2b; that is, we may distinguish *sentence gestures* and *word gestures*. For instance, gesture 12 (Figure 12.2), which means "Come here," is a sentence gesture, as it always refers to some person coming to some place, the person being the hearer and the place being near the speaker. Therefore we have a predicate, two arguments, a present tense, and a request attitude. All of this information is, so to speak, incorporated in the gesture meaning. In contrast, in Figure 12.3, gesture 14 (which means "to eat"), gesture 13 (which means "you"), and, in Figure 12.2, gesture 11 (which means "afterwards") are word gestures. Besides corresponding to words in verbal language, they have the meaning of just a predicate or an argument, not of a whole sentence.

In conclusion, the symbolic gestures used by hearing people, in contrast with verbal and sign languages, form only a lexicon, partly of the holophrastic and partly of the articulated type. But, they do not form a language, as they are not governed by syntactic rules.

A lexicon of words and a lexicon of gestures

As we have argued, the symbolic gestures of hearing people form a lexicon, that is, a set of signal–meaning correspondence rules coded and

Figure 12.3. (13) You; (14) to eat; (15) Victory! (16) What are you doing/ saying? (17) cigarette, I want to smoke, He smokes a lot; (18) behind me, I hitchhike. (From I. Poggi & M. Zomparelli, 1987.)

stored in long-term memory. In addition, verbal languages and sign languages differ from the gestures of hearing people in that the former also contain combination rules, whereas the latter do not. Apart from this difference, the two kinds of lexicon – that of a language and that of a system lacking syntactic rules – are largely similar.

We shall next compare the lexicon of a verbal language with one of symbolic gestures. Our examples are drawn from English and the lexicons of gestures used by hearing people in the United States and Italy.

In a verbal language we can observe the phenomenon of *synonymy*. Pairs of words, like *speech* and *language, to say* and *to tell,* or *sweater* and *pullover,* are synonymous; that is, they have more or less the same meaning. Two words can be only "more or less" synonymous, because a language is an economical system and so would not contain different words with exactly the same meaning. Thus *sweater* and *pullover* have some different nuances, in terms of their frequency, their meaning, or the physical images to which they are linked. Nonetheless, we can say that they are synonymous with each other.

There are synonyms among symbolic gestures as well. For example, the American gestures 15 (Figure 12.3) and 5 (Figure 12.1) both have a meaning of "victory" or "succeeding in some enterprise." But in this case, too, the meaning of the two gestures is not exactly the same.

The Italian gestures 9 (Figure 12.2) and 16 (Figure 12.3) both mean "What are you doing?" or "What are you saying?" but gesture 16 is somewhat ironically imploring, whereas gesture 9 is not.

Another important feature of words is their *ambiguity*. A simple glance through a dictionary shows that each word has a number of different meanings, or "readings." A word's different meanings may be semantically linked wih one another; that is, they may or may not share a part of their meaning. We call the former case *polysemy*, and the latter *omophony*. An example of omophony is the word *watch*, which has completely unrelated meanings that we can paraphrase as either "look" or "clock."

A case of polysemy is *ring*, meaning both a "circular object that people put on their fingers" and a "place where boxing and wrestling matches are held." These two apparently different concepts share, however, a semantic core, as both refer to a closed boundary around some object or place.

Ambiguity and the distinction between omophonic and polysemic items can be found also in symbolic gestures. A case of gestural omophony (we could call it *omochery*) is gesture 15 in Figure 12.3, which in Italy means both "Victory!" and "May I go to the bathroom?"

A polysemic Italian gesture is gesture 17 in Figure 12.3, which may mean "cigarette," "I want to smoke," "Give me a cigarette," "He smokes a lot," and so on.

At first sight, then, one could say that the same ambiguity of a vocal lexicon can be found in gestures. Yet, gestures seem to be ambiguous much more seldom than words are, as there is always something, in the nonmanual components of the gesture (trunk and shoulder posture, facial expression, etc.) or in the kind of movement by which the gesture is performed, that clarifies the gesture. For example, gesture 15 in Italy means "Victory!" only if the hand is held quite high and if the facial expression and hand movement are quite firm and assertive. In contrast, in the other meaning the hand is lower and the expression is of shyness.

We might say that this is analogous to verbal language, in which the ambiguity of words is minimized by their context. If the word *watch* in a sentence is followed by the words *is broken*, one immediately will know

Table 12.2. *Articulated (A) and holophrastic (H) readings in ambiguous words and gestures*

	Words			Gestures	
	"look"	A		"eat"	
watch			(14)		
	"clock"	A		"blockhead"	
	"I'm surprised"	H		"what . . . ?"	
oh			(9)		
	"I see"	H		"I don't agree"	
	"tell"	A		"behind me"	
say			(18)		
	"I'm surprised"	H		"I hitchhike"	

that it is the "clock" meaning and not the "look" meaning. In the same way, we might claim that facial expression or body posture are communicative signals that are separate from the gesture but that interact with it, thus forming its context. Thus a single gesture, just like a word, may have two or more different meanings that are clarified by the context.

An opposing view could contend that nonmanual components are an intrinsic part of the gesture and not simply its context. According to this view, a gesture can never be ambiguous, simply because its nonmanual components convey a great amount of information. This leads to the conclusion that a lexicon of gestures is inherently different from a lexicon of words in that gestures are never really ambiguous.

We shall not take sides in these opposing viewpoints, but arrive at another, less doubtful analogy between gestures and words. As we mentioned, both words and symbolic gestures may be either holophrastic or articulated. On the one hand, some words and gestures form sentences, for example, the word *oh* and gesture 12 ("Come here," in Figure 12.2). On the other hand, some words and gestures mean only a part of a sentence (the word *afterwards* and its corresponding gesture 11, in Figure 12.2). Now, if we accept the first view, that gestures are ambiguous in the same way as words are, we can distinguish the different readings of an ambiguous gesture as holophrastic or articulated. Thus, we could have three different cases, for both words and gestures (Poggi, 1983a): (1) both readings articulated, (2) both readings holophrastic, or (3) an articulated reading and a holophrastic reading. Let us consider some verbal and gestural examples (Table 12.2).

Among words, both *clock* and *look* are articulated readings for "watch." *Oh* has two holophrastic readings, one as an expression of surprise ("I'm surprised") and one for saying that one has just acquired new information ("I understand," "I see"). Finally, *say* has an articulated reading (similar to "tell") and a holophrastic one ("I'm surprised").

Among gestures, gesture 14 in Figure 12.3, as it is used in Rome, has two articulated readings: one meaning "to eat" and one meaning "blockhead." Gesture 9 (Figure 12.2) has two holophrastic readings: In the first it can be paraphrased as any open question (an open, or *wh*-question, is a question asking some who, when, where, or how, as opposed to a yes–no question); it is a sincere question, by which one is actually asking something that he does not know and wants to know. The other reading is strongly distinguished from the first by facial expression and partly by the gesture movement itself; it is not a true but a rhetorical question, one that in fact criticizes the addressee, expresses disagreement, and can be paraphrased as "What are you doing/saying?" or "I don't agree" (Poggi, 1983b; Ricci Bitti, Boggi Cavallo, Brighetti, & Garotti, 1987).

Finally, gesture 18 (Figure 12.3) in Italy has an articulated reading, paraphrased as "here, behind me," and a holophrastic one, "I hitchhike." However, in this gesture, as well as in gesture 9, the so-called nonmanual components are very important to choosing the reading; that is, the holophrastic meaning is triggered by a clearly inquiring facial expression.

Naming through pantomime

Pantomime is a gestural system of communication that hearing people may happen to use any time they need to "invent" a new language. Specifically, if you have to communicate with a stranger with whom you do not share a language, you may have to invent gestures that she can understand. Such gestures often are iconic.

The onset of a pantomimic system was investigated in a study of how people name through pantomime (Zomparelli & Poggi, 1987). The research sought to find out what cognitive mechanisms are at work when people try to express the meaning of nouns through gestures.

From a cognitive point of view, what is a noun? Suppose I call some object a *table*. In doing this, I am using a signal whose meaning includes the definition of a table, whose features allow me to see a particular table as similar to all other objects we call *tables* and also to distinguish it from other objects such as chairs and shelves. In constructing the meaning that I will link to the signal "table," I have to sort out some distinctive features, mainly its function (people use it for eating or working) and sometimes its form or the material from which it is made. Naming thus implies summarizing all the distinctive features of an object and linking them to a verbal or gestural signal.

But suppose I have to create a name by means of gestures alone. How could I construct the meaning, and what gestures would I most likely link to it? The hypothesis of the Zomparelli and Poggi study was the following: If one names an object, one must first sort out the features that distinguish it best and then represent these features through the communicative means at hand. It follows that the features that one selects for representation will differ according to whether a visual–body or an audio–vocal channel is available. The question addressed in the study was what kind of information people are likely to choose as the most distinctive when referring to a certain object. People tend to select particular kinds of information. For example, if one is to name pantomimically things like salt or telephone, one is likely to represent the most typical uses of such things. In comparison, when naming a double bass or a cloud, one is more likely to depict its form by means of one's hands.

The working hypothesis of the experiment was that in naming things through pantomime one tends to represent the most characteristic features of one's referent and, among them, the easiest ones to be mimed. In the experiment each subject was presented with a noun and was asked to convey this noun to another person by means of pantomime. Each pantomime was analyzed to discover which features of each noun were most likely selected and represented through gestures. The results allowed us to draw up a typology of six types of pantomimic noun, according to that feature of its meaning most frequently selected for representation.

Form

For some concrete objects the most distinctive and thus the most often selected feature is form. A typical case is that of a double bass, whose outline the subjects often sketched.

Referent's typical actions

When miming persons, other living beings, or moving things, like teacher, dog, or fire, people often mimic their actions or movements.

Sometimes they show the referent's prototypical action, that is, the one that first comes to mind in thinking of that – for instance, wings shaking for the meaning of bird.

Speaker's typical actions

In other cases the most typical actions linked to the referent are not those performed by the referent itself but those the speaker would perform in its connection. For instance, the speaker's typical actions were performed when miming salt or telephone. Sometimes the subjects mimed a whole "script" (according to Schank & Abelson, 1977) – a series of actions that people usually perform in the context of some object. For example, in the pantomime for streetcar, the subjects would pretend to be waiting at a bus stop, getting on, and rocking while holding onto the strap.

The strategy of describing a whole script was used to represent not only visible objects but also some referents that are concrete but do not have form or prompt actions, like "light," and abstract concepts like "loyalty." For "light," the subjects switched a lamp on and off; for "loyalty," one subject mimed the actions of hugging a person and then defending him or her from aggression.

If the referents are concrete objects, a pantomime of them is not so difficult. Rather, the problems are with abstract nouns, such as "democracy," or with concrete things that cannot be directly perceived, like "wind." In this case, one has to find a feature that is both linked to the referent and can be seen.

Perceivable effects

If some referent cannot be seen, one can mime its effects. For the meaning "wind," the subjects mimed flying leaves or hats.

Cultural representations

When it was particularly difficult to find perceivable elements linked to the referent, the subjects often took a shortcut and used symbolic gestures already lexicalized, that is, culturally linked to the referent, sometimes metaphorically. For example, to represent "lie," an abstract concept and not so easy to link to a visual representation, the subjects often mimicked Pinocchio's long nose.

Negating the opposite concept

An interesting possibility had not been predicted by the hypothesis even though the subjects used this mechanism surprisingly often. The subjects never gave up miming even very abstract and semantically complex concepts such as "democracy" or "loyalty," which might seem impossible to represent by means of visual–body language. All the subjects found a way to make them understood. One trick they used was to represent the opposite of the noun and then to negate it through a cultural representation, the symbolic gesture for "not." For example, to represent "democracy," a subject mimed Mussolini as a symbol of dictatorship and then negated that concept.

Facial component of symbolic gestures

Few of the studies of symbolic gestures have given enough credit to their structure. Conversely, scholars of sign languages have made the most of the various structural components of signs, which have been helpful, as well, to those interested in the symbolic gestures used by those able to hear.

As we saw when analyzing sign languages, several structural components of the sign have been considered: the hand configuration, the movement made by the hand, the place where the movement is executed with respect to the body's axes, and the hand position (orientation of the palm, direction of the metacarpus, bend of the wrist) (Battison, 1974; Radutsky & Santarelli, 1987; Stokoe, 1960). The need to consider other expressive elements used in communicating the meaning of many signs has also been demonstrated, such as the nonmanual components, that is, facial expressions and body movements (Baker & Padden, 1977; Franchi, 1987; Liddell, 1977).

Baker-Shenk (1985) showed that the accompanying facial expression may have semantic and syntactical as well as regulatory functions in the discourse, with one of the most apparent functions of the facial expression being the use of the face to express adverbs (Baker & Cokely, 1980).

Transferring these considerations to the symbolic gestures used by hearing people, we can then consider the same structural elements of both manual (configuration, movements, place, symmetry, palm orientation, dominance of one hand over the other) and facial components. Indeed, the insufficient attention paid to those elements making up the structure of a symbolic gesture may lead to inexact and unsatisfactory

Figure 12.4. (19) The hand extended and perpendicular to the forearm (From Ricci Bitti, 1983–1984).

results, especially in intercultural research on particular symbolic gestures. We have reason to believe for example, that the results obtained in the research by Morris, Collett, Marsh, and O'Shaughnessy (1979) can in part be attributed to the fact that several of the structural elements in some of the gestures they considered were neglected, particularly in facial expressions. The principal aim of the Morris et al. (1979) research was to check the spread of 20 symbolic gestures in 40 European and Mediterranean localities and the different meaning attributed to them in the various places.

The fact that the static graphic images of these symbolic gestures were used as a visual stimulus for the investigation automatically eliminated some important sources of information such as movement and facial expression. In particular, for some gestures to which facial expression is crucial, the results obtained in relation to both the distribution of the gestures and the meaning attributed to them leave us somewhat perplexed.

Starting from these considerations, we have studied four symbolic gestures used in Italy by hearing people (Ricci Bitti et al., 1987). Each pair of gestures has the same manual component. The common manual component in the first two gestures is the hand purse (gesture 1, Figure 12.1) and that common to the second pair is the hand extended and perpendicular to the forearm, which moves up and down in a frontal position at chest height (gesture 19, Figure 12.4).

The first gesture of the first pair (presenting the hand purse as the common manual component) signifies a real question and is accompanied by a questioning face with a fixed, severe expression. The second

Figure 12.5. The two facial expressions accompanying the hand purse.

gesture of the first pair signifies a rhetorical question with an ironic component, criticism, and is accompanied by a facial expression showing skepticism and/or sarcasm (Figure 12.5).

The gestures of the second pair signify "much" or "so much" when the hand movement is accompanied by a facial expression with lowered lip angles and a raised chin. When puffed-out cheeks accompany the hand movement, it means "too much" or "how boring" (Figure 12.6).

The four facial expressions accompanying the gesture's manual components were analyzed by means of FACS (Ekman & Friesen, 1978). This enabled us to determine the facial actions or combinations of them characterizing each gesture of each pair, differentiating one gesture from the other. In regard to the gestures of the first pair, the first is a combination of facial actions 4 and 5, which lower the eyebrows and bring them closer, produce vertical furrows between the eyebrows, open the eyes wider, and affect the frontal and eyebrow zone without any particular involvement of the lower face. In contrast, the second gesture of the first pair is a combination of facial actions 12 and 14 (the latter only in semiface) in the lower face, which stretch the lip angles, thereby increasing the distance between them (a typical smile), and produce a dimple at the angle of the lips, thereby signifying irony, sarcasm, or skepticism.

In regard to the gestures of the second pair, the first is the appearance in the lower face of a combination of facial actions 15 and 17, which

Figure 12.6. The two facial expressions accompanying the hand extended and perpendicular to the forearm.

lower the lip angles and raise the point of the chin, pushing the lower lip upward. In comparison, the other gesture is essentially puffed-out cheeks (AD 34, according to FACS).

Our research hypotheses predicted that the facial expression accompanying the hand movement would represent the element that differentiates between the two gestures of each pair.

We used an approach based on recognition. Two actors were videotaped going through the four gestures studied (they both were given beforehand the meaning of each gesture and its manual configuration).

The eight videotapes of the gestures were presented to two groups of 16 judges each. Only the manual component of each gesture was shown to the first group, whereas the complete gesture (including both the manual component and the accompanying facial expression) was presented to the second group. The judges' task was to transcribe on a sheet of paper the meaning attributed to each gesture.

Two people independently analyzed the judges' answers, matching the meanings attributed to the gestures with the actors' intentions. The research showed that in three cases out of four, the facial component of the symbolic gestures was indispensable to understanding the gestures themselves and that this facial component was specifically expressed in the mimed facial actions of each gesture.

We should emphasize, however, that the research also demonstrated

the need for clearer definitions of the reciprocal functions of the gestures' various elements. As we have seen, the relationship between the
manual and the facial components is not consistent. In some cases they
both are important and carry out a complementary role in representing
the meaning. But in other cases, a component may be only a secondary
accessory. Thus it would be useful to be able to apply a semantic analysis of the symbolic gestures to the methods used in this research. An
example is Poggi's (1983b) study of the hand purse.

Finally, we note that in the first pair of gestures (with the hand purse
as the common manual component), the meaning of the real question
may not require the accompanying facial expression in order to be understood, whereas in the ironic meaning the facial expression is indispensable to understanding. This might shine some light on the evolution of the two gestures: The manual component might have been, at
one time, a gesture complete in itself with univocal meaning (the meaning still acknowledged even without the help of the facial expression)
and that from it a second gesture was generated that, however, requires
a specific accompanying facial expression in order to be understood.
Moreover, it seems to us that in regard to the two gestures making up
the second pair, it is the face that is crucial to understanding. In comparison, the manual component carries out an essentially adverbial function with respect to the meaning manifested by the mimicked expression.

Conclusion

Our chapter presented a partial picture of the research on symbolic gestures. Although we chose to confine our reflections to that research
most relevant to our own point of view, we also brought into focus the
most significant areas of study.

Perhaps the most interesting aspect of symbolic gestures is that areas
of research whose origins might initially have seemed a long way from
one another have ended up approaching and influencing one another.
For example, whereas social psychologists and anthropologists have
been interested primarily in problems concerning the use and functions
of gestures in social interactions, linguists and psycholinguists have
concentrated on the mechanisms binding the form and meaning of gestures. Hence, it seems to us that an analysis of symbolic gestures that
considers different perspectives would be more useful, permitting, as it
does, the establishment of complementary criteria to analyze their many

aspects. Based on this conviction, we have brought together our knowledge and our disciplinary "idiosyncracies" in an effort to understand symbolic gestures that pass over the frontiers between different sectors of study and to assume new meaning.

As for the prospects for future research, two directions, contradictory in appearance, seem important. On the one hand, it will certainly be necessary to go beyond the rigid distinctions outlined here and elsewhere between symbolic and all other types of gesture. In fact, it is already possible from some examples to see how a gesture that sometimes can be classified as symbolic may not only assume the function of illustrator in certain contexts but may actually, at the same time, be part of an illustrator's vocabulary.

An example of this may, once again, be represented by the Italian gesture of the hand purse which, besides being used with the two meanings already seen, symbolic in type, is often used accompanied by language, especially when the speaker argues with particular enthusiasm and conviction. In such a case, the gesture can be paraphrased as "That's it; it can only be that!" In our opinion this meaning can be plausibly drawn from an ironic reading of this gesture. If I say to you, "But what are you saying?" I am implying – through my denial of what you believe – my equally strong conviction.

This gesture, used with this meaning, however, can no longer replace speech: It is acceptable only if produced along with the spoken word. Therefore it ceases to be part of the category of symbolic gestures, which was, among other things, defined as being capable of expression without words. Hence, certain categories of gesture may be able to shade into one another.

On the other hand, we feel that it is at the same time necessary to distinguish in more detail among the symbolic gestures themselves. In this chapter we made only some first attempts to distinguish among different kinds of symbolic gestures, separating holophrastic from articulated gestures. The criterion we used was the amount and type of semantic information a gesture conveys. But this is not the only possible criterion. One could, for instance, distinguish gestures according to their iconicity, that is, according to how closely the signal imitates physical aspects of the meaning. Or even more than one criterion could be adopted at a time.

In conclusion, to deepen the analysis of gestures is, in our opinion, an important way to attain a further understanding of the mechanisms of human social interaction and the functioning of the human mind.

456   Pio Enrico Ricci Bitti and Isabella Poggi

References

Baker, C., & Cokeley, D. (1980). *American Sign Language: A teacher's resource text on grammar and culture.* Silver Spring, MD: T. J. Publishers.
Baker, C. L., & Padden, C. (1978). Focusing on the nonmanual components of ASL. In P. Siple (Ed.), *Understanding language through sign language research* (pp. 27–58). New York: Academic Press.
Baker-Shenk, C. (1985). Nonmanual behaviors in sign languages: Methodological concerns and recent finding. In W. Stokoe & V. Volterra (Eds.), *SRL '83, sign language research* (pp. 175–184). Silver Spring, MD: Linstock Press.
Barakat, R. (1973). Arabic gestures. *Journal of Popular Culture, 6,* 749–792.
Battison, E. (1974). Phonological deletion in American Sign Language. *Sign Language Studies, 5,* 1–19.
Castelfranchi, C., & Poggi, I. (1987). Communication: Beyond the cognitive approach and speech act theory. In J. Verschueren & M. Bertuccelli-Papi (Eds.), *The pragmatic perspective* (pp. 239–254). Amsterdam: John Benjamins.
Collett, P., & Contarello, A. (1987). Gesti di assenso e di dissenso. In P. E. Ricci Bitti (Ed.), *Comunicazione e gestualità* (pp. 69–85). Milan: Franco Angeli.
Creider, C. (1977). Towards a description of East African gestures. *Sign Language Studies, 14,* 1–20.
Efron, D. (1941). *Gesture and environment.* New York: Kings Crown Press.
Ekman, P. (1976). Movements with precise meaning. *Journal of Communication, 26,* 14–26.
Ekman, P., & Friesen, W. V. (1969). The repertoire of nonverbal behavior. *Semiotica, 1,* 49–98.
(1972). Hand movements. *Journal of Communication, 22,* 353–374.
(1978). *Manual for the Facial Action Coding System.* Palo Alto, CA: Consulting Psychologists Press.
Franchi, M. L. (1987). Componenti non manuali. In V. Volterra (Ed.), *La lingua italiana dei segni* (pp. 159–177). Bologna: Il Mulino.
Green, J. R. (1968). *A gesture inventory for teaching Spanish.* New York: Clinton Books.
Hinde, R. (1974). *Biological bases of human social behaviour.* London: McGraw-Hill.
James, D. (1974). *The syntax and semantics of some English interjections: Papers in linguistics.* Ann Arbor: University of Michigan Press.
Johnson, H. G., Ekman, P., & Friesen, W. V. (1975). Communicative body movements: American emblems. *Semiotica, 15,* 335–353.
Kendon, A. (1983). Gesture and speech. In J. M. Wiemann & R. P. Harrison (Eds.), *Nonverbal interaction* (pp. 13–45). London: Sage.
Liddell, S. K. (1978). Nonmanual signals and relative clauses in ASL. In P. Siple (Ed.), *Understanding language through sign language research,* (pp. 59–90). New York: Academic Press.
Morris, D., Collett, P., Marsh, P., & O'Shaughnessy, M. (1979). *Gestures: Their origins and distribution.* Briarcliff Manor, NY: Stein & Day.
Parisi, D. (1981). Sintassi solo umana? In V. Volterra (Ed.), *I segni come parole,* (pp. 100–111). Turin: Boringhieri.
(1983). A three-stage model of language evolution: From pantomime to syntax. In E. De Grobier (Ed.), *Glossogenetics: The origins and the evolution of language* (pp. 419–434). Paris: Harwood Academic Publishers.
Poggi, I. (1981). *Le interiezioni.* Turin: Boringhieri.

(1983a). Le analogie fra gesti e interiezioni: Alcune ossevazioni preliminari. In F. Orletti (Ed.), *Comunicare nella vita quotidiana* (pp. 117–133). Bologna: Il Mulino.

(1983b). La mano a borsa: Analisi semantica di un gesto emblematico olofrastico. In G. Attili & P. E. Ricci Bitti (Eds.), *Comunicare senza parole* (pp. 219–238). Rome: Bulzoni.

(1987). Frasi e parole con la voce e con le mani. In I. Poggi (Ed.), *Le parole nella testa* (pp. 329–337). Bologna: Il Mulino.

Poggi, I., & Zomparelli, M. (1987). Lessico e grammatica nei gesti e nelle parole. In I. Poggi (Ed.), *Le parole nella testa* (pp. 291–327). Bologna: Il Mulino.

Poyatos, F. (1975). Gesture inventories: Fieldwork methodology and problems. *Semiotica, 13,* 199–227.

Radutzky, E., & Santarelli, B. (1987). Movimenti e orientamenti. In V. Volterra (Ed.), *La lingua italiana dei segni* (pp. 109–158). Bologna: Il Mulino.

Ricci Bitti, P. E. (1983–1984). Communication et gestualité. *Bulletin de Psychologie, 37,* 365, 559–564.

(1987). Comunicazione e gestualità. In P. E. Ricci Bitti (Ed.), *Comunicazione e gestualità* (pp. 13–32). Milan: Angeli.

Ricci Bitti, P. E., Boggi Cavallo, P., Brighetti, G., & Garotti, P. L. (1987). Componenti facciali e manuali di gesti simbolici. In P. E. Ricci Bitti (Ed.), *Comunicazione e gestualità* (pp. 171–178). Milan: Angeli.

Saitz, R. L., & Cervenka, E. J. (1972). *Handbook of gestures: Columbia and the United States.* The Hague: Mouton.

Schank, R. C., & Abelson, R. P. (1977). *Scripts, plans, goals and understanding: An inquiry into human knowledge structures.* Hillsdale, NJ: Erlbaum.

Sparhawk, C. M. (1978). Contrastive identificational features of Persian gesture, *Semiotica, 24,* 49–86.

Stokoe, W. (1960). *Sign language structure.* Silver Spring, MD: Linstock Press.

Volterra, V. (Ed.). (1981). *I segni come parole.* Turin: Boringhieri.

(1987). *La lingua italiana dei segni.* Bologna: Il Mulino.

Volterra, V., & Caselli, M. C. (1985). From gestures and vocalizations to signs and words. In W. Stokoe & V. Volterra (Eds.), *Sign language research* (pp. 1–9). Silver Spring, MD & Rome: Linstock Press & Istituto di Psicologia CNR.

Wylie, L. (1977). *Beaux gestes: A guide to French body talk.* Cambridge, MA: Undergraduate Press.

Zomparelli, M., & Poggi, I. (1987). Dare nomi con i gesti. In I. Poggi (Ed.), *Le parole nella testa* (pp. 257–290). Bologna: Il Mulino.

13. A functional approach to nonverbal exchange

MILES L. PATTERSON

In this chapter I shall present a functional perspective on the role of nonverbal behavior in social interaction, specifically, a functional model of interactive behavior or nonverbal exchange. This model represents a revision and elaboration of an earlier one (Patterson, 1982, 1983), with new linkages among background variables, additional functions, and a sampling of more recent research. Because this functional approach evolved as a response to earlier trends in research, I first shall review the theoretical and empirical work that preceded it.

A historical view

Early trends

The systematic study of nonverbal behavior in interaction began in earnest around 1960. Among the earliest empirical research were the studies by Sommer (1959, 1961, 1962, 1965) on "personal space." Since that time, the research on spatial behavior accelerated, so much that Aiello's (1987) review was able to identify over 700 studies on the topic. Around the same time as Sommer's work, Exline and his colleagues (Exline, 1963; Exline, Gray, & Schuette, 1965; Exline & Winters, 1965) were investigating patterns of gaze in interaction.

Complementing Sommer's and Exline's detailed empirical approaches was the anthropologist E. T. Hall's descriptive and comparative approach (1959, 1963, 1966). Hall also offered a classification system that related variable distances to both different nonverbal cues and different types of interactions (1966, 1968). For example, Hall proposed that as

The preparation of this chapter was facilitated by grant no. MH41793 from the National Institute of Mental Health.

interactions become more formal and less intimate, the distances between the interactants increase. In addition, because of the greater distance, the interactants rely less on tactile and olfactory cues and more on verbal and visual cues.

Throughout the 1960s and into the early 1970s, most of the research on nonverbal behavior consisted of relatively narrow empirical studies. During this period of research, the dependent measures focused on a single behavior or "channel" at a time, and the studies were often correlational, designed to identify potential individual or group differences in nonverbal behavior. In the latter case, the research often concentrated on the influence of culture, personality, and gender on nonverbal behavior.

The groundwork for a new approach to the study of nonverbal behavior was established relatively early, even though it was not widely accepted until many years later. Specifically, similar multivariate constructs such as intimacy (Argyle & Dean, 1965), proxemics (Hall, 1963, 1966), and immediacy (Mehrabian, 1969) were offered that challenged the adequacy of the channel approach to nonverbal behavior. Although these constructs differ somewhat from one another, they share the assumption that it is important to focus on the patterns of behavior across different channels and not on one channel at a time. For the remainder of this chapter, I shall use the term *involvement* to refer to those behaviors (distance, gaze, touch, body orientation, lean, facial expressiveness, talking duration, postural openness, head nods, and paralinguistic cues) that together determine the level of interactive intensity (Patterson, 1982).

Theoretical developments

Through the 1960s and the first half of the 1970s, with the exception of Argyle and Dean's (1965) equilibrium model of interpersonal intimacy, little attention had been paid to theoretical explanations of nonverbal exchange. Perhaps this was the case because equilibrium theory, a simple yet elegant model, had received substantial empirical support for a number of years (Cappella, 1981; Patterson, 1973a). Equilibrium theory posits that in any given interaction, an appropriate level of behavioral intimacy can be specified.[1] Furthermore, if the behavioral intimacy – expressed in terms of distance, gaze, smiling, and verbal intimacy – deviates too far from the appropriate level, behavioral adjustments by one or both interactants are predicted. For example, if one person approaches another at an inappropriately close distance, the latter person may decrease both gaze and smiling toward the first person. Presumably, this compensatory response helps restore the behavioral intimacy to its appropriate level. That is, an equilibrium in intimacy can be maintained.

Equilibrium theory suffers from one important deficiency, however: It cannot explain those instances in which people respond to others with a behavioral pattern of matching or reciprocation. This inadequacy prompted the development of alternative theoretical models that attempt to explain both compensation and reciprocation (Andersen & Andersen, 1984; Burgoon, 1978; Cappella & Greene, 1982; Patterson, 1976). All of these models assign to arousal an important mediating role. Furthermore, the models assume a consistency between the cognitive–affective reactions and an individual's behavior. In particular, compensation for increased involvement is related to negative affect and/or less favorable perceptions of the partner, whereas the reciprocation of increased involvement is related to positive affect and/or more favorable perceptions of the partner.

There is evidence, however, that interactive behavior is not always consistent with the actor's underlying affect. Specifically in two studies, those subjects who had negative expectations of an interaction partner behaved in a more friendly or "warmer" fashion than did subjects who had positive expectations (Bond, 1972; Ickes, Patterson, Rajecki, & Tanford, 1982). Further evidence for the independence of affect and behavior may be seen in the general case of deceptive behavior. Deception, of course, is the expression of behavior inconsistent with a person's thoughts or feelings (see Ekman, 1985).

Another characteristic is common to all of the arousal-based models: They all are reactive. That is, any behavior at a given time is viewed as a product of the partner's preceding behavior. In addition, this emphasis on the reactive development of interactive behavior ignores the possibility that individuals may have goals or motives that direct their behavior somewhat independently of their partner's specific behavior. Finally, reactive explanations fail to recognize that some coordinated patterns of behavior, such as greetings or farewells, may be both parties' responses to a common script (Abelson, 1981) and not just to the specific behavior of their partners.

A functional model of nonverbal exchange

The functional model of nonverbal exchange (Patterson, 1982, 1983) attempts to provide a more comprehensive explanation of nonverbal exchange than that offered by earlier theories. In contrast with the arousal-based models, the functional model assumes that an individual's naive perception of the purpose or function of a given interaction is a more important determinant of interactive behavior than is arousal. Furthermore, the functional model assumes that behavior and affect can be independent of each other. For example, one might "act" very friendly (e.g., stand close, smile a great deal, and hold a high level of gaze) toward a disliked partner, if that served a useful purpose in the interaction.

A variety of different purposes or functions may be served by interactive behavior, including (1) providing information, (2) regulating interaction, (3) expressing intimacy, (4) managing affect, (5) exercising social control, (6) presenting identities or images, and (7) facilitating service and task goals. These functions will be discussed in detail later in the chapter. At this point we should note only that they are part of the functional model. The model itself contains a series of related, sequential processes that determine the patterns of behavior in interactions. In the next section, I shall examine the basic processes and linkages that comprise the functional model.

Overview

The functional model identifies discrete stages that relate to one another in affecting interactive behavior. Figure 13.1 shows the relationships among the various stages. The basic determinants are the genetic and environmental factors. Each person's genetic makeup reflects some characteristics that are representative of the species in general and others that are unique to that individual. The influence of the genetic factors is, of course, constrained by that of the environmental factors. In other words, over time, it is the interaction of the genetic and environmental factors that shapes the new gene pool, that is, the process of natural selection.

The basic determinants influence the nature of the remote antecedents, the most important of which are culture, gender, and personality. These, in turn, contribute both directly and indirectly to the development of the preinteraction mediators (behavioral predispositions, arousal, and cognitive–affective reactions), through the selection of situations and relationships.

The preinteraction mediators set the stage for the interaction. People enter social situations with habitual ways of behaving toward others (i.e., behavioral predispositions), specific arousal reactions, and cognitive–

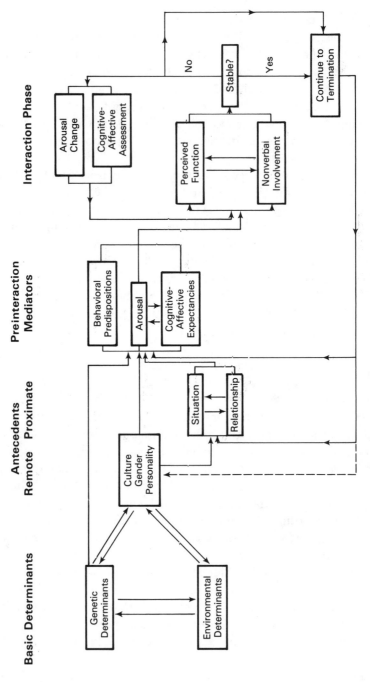

Figure 13.1. An illustration of the functional model of nonverbal exchange.

affective expectancies. These responses help constrain both the perceptions of the interaction and the levels of behavioral involvement initiated by each person. To the extent that the initial involvement levels are similar and the perceived functions are complementary, the interaction tends to be stable.

Stability refers to the extent to which interactions are smooth, predictable, and synchronous. As long as the exchanges remain stable, the behavior patterns evolve with relatively little awareness or reflection. But when one or both parties detect some instability, an arousal change and a cognitive–affective assessment are likely, leading to adjustments in involvement levels and possibly even a change in the perceived function of the interaction. The dynamics of the interaction phase are guided by a type of negative feedback mechanism. That is, arousal change, assessment, and eventually behavioral adjustments are triggered by instability. In turn, the assessment and behavioral changes tend to increase stability. In the absence of instability, however, little attention is paid to the exchange process.

Finally, the residue from a completed interaction influences the next round of antecedents and preinteraction mediators. In Figure 13.1, the arrow back to the remote antecedents is a broken line, because the effects are limited primarily to personality and even those are likely to have an impact only with repeated occurrences. The particular choice of the next interaction, defined in terms of the situation and relationship, may well be affected by the outcome of an earlier interaction. In addition, the residual arousal patterns and cognitive–affective reactions are likely to color the next interaction.

At this level, the model is a very general one, describing the dynamics that are assumed to underlie the process of nonverbal exchange. The specific patterns that are likely to evolve are the product of different combinations of the antecedent factors and preinteraction mediators. The meshing of these factors for two (or more) individuals in an interaction shapes the expression of different functions of the nonverbal exchange. In the remainder of the chapter, I shall examine the specific stages of the model and their linkages to one another.

Background processes

Basic determinants

Genetic influences. Perhaps the most elementary and consistent genetic influence on social behavior can be found in the structure of the human body and its sensory and motor capabilities. This may seem like a trivial and unimportant point, but the form and capabilities of the human body set very real limits on the variability in interactive behavior. An obvious example is that two people cannot reach out and touch each other if they are separated by 10 or more feet – despite the repeated claims of AT&T. In a similar fashion, visual, auditory, and olfactory sensations are limited by the distance and orientation between the interactants (Hall, 1966, 1968). Very close distances (e.g., 1 foot or less) provide the opportunity for increased tactile, thermal, olfactory, and auditory information, but at the same time, visual input is distorted. In contrast, at 4 or 5 feet, neither thermal input nor all but the strongest scents can be detected. At the same time, a distance of 4 to 5 feet permits easy visual focusing of one's partner.

A second aspect of the genetic determinants pertains to common processes and behaviors, not just to the structural capabilities and limitations of the human body. The genetic influence on social behavior is not absolute but, rather, is complemented by adaptive learning (Fridlund, in press). Thus, genetic control might be the ability to learn a particular behavior pattern that also must be activated by the appropriate circumstances. Cross-cultural commonalities in behavior suggest the presence of a shared genetic factor, but it is also possible that such commonalities are merely the product of shared learning experiences (Fridlund, in press). Perhaps the clearest example here is the similar facial expressions of emotion seen across a variety of different cultures. Fridlund, Ekman, and Oster (1987) reported that there is clear evidence that the expressions of happiness, anger, disgust, sadness, and combined fear and surprise are universally encoded and decoded across cultures.

This universality in facial expressions of emotion is also in line with Darwin's (1872/1955) notions of natural selection. An oversimplified explanation that appeals to natural selection is the following: Greater clarity and consistency in the expression of emotion permit other members of the species to understand better the encoder's internal state. In turn, these observers are more likely to respond appropriately, whether it is an instance of happiness, anger, or fear. If this is the case, then the encoder's survival will be facilitated, and so the underlying genetic characteristics will be favored. A complementary explanation of the selection of better decoders is that the survival of the decoders is facilitated by a more accurate reading of the expressions of others.

It seems likely that infants also have a universal need for tactile comfort and stimulation. Such contact not only promotes the infant's psychological well-being, but it also contributes to the attachment between the mother (or caregiver) and the child (Bowlby, 1969; Montagu, 1971). Both of these consequences should have survival value for the species. That does not mean that all cultures are similar in promoting or fulfilling such a need but merely that a minimum level of tactile involvement seems critical to the well-being of all infants (see also Spitz, 1945).

Another process common to humans, other primates, and probably to a variety of other species even lower on the phylogenetic scale is the attention to and interest in conspecifics. One can make a clear case for the survival value of attention to other members of one's species, in terms of the advantage of imitation or observational learning. That is, not all members of a group have to repeat the same trial-and-error sequence before achieving some desired goal. They just have to copy the one who did it right. At an even more basic level, association with and attention to other group members help ensure protection from external dangers. Thus, in group-living animals, the startle reaction of the first animal to notice a threat serves to alert the rest of the group to the danger. At the human level, there is evidence for both a basic affiliative motive (Schachter, 1959) and a need for social comparison (Festinger, 1954).

What does all this have to do with nonverbal behavior? These basic biological and psychological needs offer powerful motives for increased contact among conspecifics, a "contact" that is expressed in closer distances, touch, and greater visual attention. In general, then, in those situations in which such motives are activated, some minimal level of involvement is simply the fulfillment of these basic needs. In all of these instances, the genetic influence is reflected in the direct link between the genetic determinants and the behavioral predispositions.

The indirect genetic influence on social behavior is mediated through the remote antecedents, including the group and individual difference factors, such as culture, gender, and personality. I shall not attempt to describe this linkage further, except to suggest that some of the behavioral differences among cultures (especially those that are relatively isolated), between males and females, and among different types of personalities may be partially a product of genetic determinants. Again, even here, the genetic components may not determine the specific behavior pattern but, instead, be just the ability to learn an adaptive response (Fridlund, in press).

Environmental influences. Evolutionary theory suggests a very close relationship between genetic and environmental determinants. That is, in the long term, the environment selects those characteristics that promote survival.

The influence of the environment may also be seen in the way that the ecology affects the development of different cultural practices. For example, factors such as climate, terrain, and the ease of obtaining food can influence cultural norms regarding family structure, social roles, and child-rearing practices (Altman & Chemers, 1980, chap. 1). In turn, the combined effects of the environment and culture can affect both sex roles and personality. I shall not attempt to analyze the complicated relationship between the environment and culture, but discussions of the linkages between the two may be found elsewhere (see Berry, 1975, 1976; Vayda, 1969). One element of the environment – the setting of an interaction or the situation – merits special attention as a proximate antecedent in this model and will be treated separately later. Finally, I should emphasize that the linkages between the environment and genetics and between the environment and remote antecedents are recursive; that is, the environment affects these other factors, but it is also shaped by them.

Remote antecedents

Culture. The term *culture* typically refers to the consensus of beliefs and perception, values and norms, customs, and behavior that is transmitted from one generation to the next in a particular group or society (Altman & Chemers, 1980, pp. 3–4). Given the breadth of this definition of culture, it is not surprising that its effects can be seen in patterns of nonverbal behavior. There are two main areas of influence. The first is differences in expressive behavior, specifically in facial expressions of emotion. At first glance, this might appear to be inconsistent with the earlier judgment of uniformity in the facial expressions of emotion across cultures. The critical determinant here, however, is whether the expression of affect is spontaneous or managed.

The spontaneous expression of basic emotional states does seem to be uniform across cultures. On the other hand, there are cultural differences in the display rules for specific emotions (Ekman, 1972, 1978). For example, Ekman (1972) reported that when they were seated alone, college students in both Japan and the United States exhibited very similar expressions to stressful films. In the presence of a research assistant, however, the Japanese students masked their facial reactions much more than the U.S. students did. In this case, the apparent display rule for the Japanese students was to control their expression of negative affect in the presence of others.

There also are substantial differences among cultures in the ways in which they manage involvement levels in interaction. The work of E. T. Hall (1963, 1966, 1968) focused on the pervasive influence of culture on the use of space. Hall proposed that cultures may be categorized along a continuum from high to low involvement. Specifically, his observations suggested that Arabs, southern Mediterranean people, and Latin Americans were on the high-involvement end of the continuum, whereas the British and northern Europeans were on the low-involvement end.

Hall (1968) proposed that these cultural differences in styles of interaction are based on the selective programming of sensory capacities of individuals in different cultures. Specifically, people in contact cultures tend to emphasize tactile and olfactory information, whereas those in the noncontact cultures are more likely to emphasize visual cues. Thus, the preferred modes of obtaining sensory information prompt people from different cultures to initiate interactions at different distances. According to Hall, close interaction distances are the result of a general tendency to obtain tactile and olfactory information about the environment (including people in the environment). In cultures in which visual information is emphasized, people have to stand farther apart to permit the easy focusing of their partners.

Hall's suggestion of cultural differences in nonverbal involvement has been supported by several different studies, including comparisons among (1) Arab and American students (Watson & Graves, 1966); (2) North American and Latin American students (Forston & Larson, 1968); (3) Costa Rican, Panamanian, and Colombian subjects (Shuter, 1976); (4) Indonesian and Australian subjects (Noesjirwan, 1977, 1978); and (5) Venezuelan and Japanese subjects (Sussman & Rosenfeld, 1982). The last study is particularly interesting because it bears directly on the dynamics that Hall proposed to account for cultural differences.

Sussman and Rosenfeld (1982) found that pairs of Venezuelan foreign students sat relatively close and that pairs of Japanese foreign students sat relatively far apart when they were speaking their own languages. The difference between the two cultural groups faded, however, when both groups spoke English. Furthermore, American subjects speaking English sat at a distance comparable to that of the Venezuelan and Japanese subjects speaking English. Thus, the Venezuelan and Japanese subjects closely approximated the American conversational distance when they spoke English, but not when they spoke their native language.

If the Venezuelan and Japanese spacing patterns are primarily a function of their experiencing different sensory inputs, then simply changing the language spoken should not affect those sensory experiences. In contrast with Hall's proposal, the differences in the Sussman and Rosenfeld study suggest that the spacing preferences may be situationally determined. In this case, the use of a particular spoken language may, in itself, constrain the behavior initiated in interactions.

Gender. An extensive amount of research has shown that males and females differ in their nonverbal behavior. In interactions, especially those with same-sex partners, females prefer higher levels of nonverbal involvement with one another than males do. This pattern may be seen in the following behaviors:

1. closer interaction distances (Aiello & Jones, 1971; Evans & Cherulnik, 1980; Pellegrini & Empey, 1970);
2. higher levels of gaze (Dabbs, Evans, Hopper, & Purvis, 1980; Exline, 1963; Exline, Gray, & Schuette, 1965; Libby, 1970); and
3. more frequent use of touch and/or a more positive reaction to touch (Fisher, Rytting, & Heslin, 1976; Jourard, 1966; Whitcher & Fisher, 1979).

An additional concern when evaluating the sex differences in interactive behavior is whether the sex of the actor or that of the partner is more important (Dabbs, 1977). When comparing same-sex groups, the sex of the actor and that of the partner are necessarily confounded. Nevertheless, according to studies that examined both the sex of the actor and that of the partner, the sex-of-partner effects are similar in direction to and possibly are slightly larger than the sex-of-actor effects (Hall, 1985). Thus females appear to initiate and receive higher levels of involvement than males do.

It is generally assumed that the sex differences reported here are the product of learning (Hall, 1985). Such an interpretation may be viewed as differences in sex role orientation (Ickes, 1981). In contrast, a sociobiological view would link the sex differences in nonverbal behavior more closely to a genetic basis. That is, the behavior of males and females differs because of the selective advantage such differences offer to the survival of the species. Although most researchers support the learning interpretation of sex differences in nonverbal behavior, some genetic component may also be contributing to the contrasting patterns.

Personality. Because there is such an extensive literature on personality and nonverbal behavior, only a brief overview is possible here. Some of the research explored the broad contrast between normal and psychiatric groups. A few studies showed that psychiatric patients typically prefer greater distances from others (Horowitz, Duff, & Stratton, 1964; Sommer, 1959) and reduced gaze (Rutter & Stephenson, 1972; Waxer, 1974; Williams, 1974), compared with normal subjects. Rutter (1977, 1978) suggested, however, that the schizophrenics' higher levels of gaze avoidance, in particular, may simply be a product of talking about their problems and not reflect a stable individual style.

Several studies have reported that in order to be comfortable, violent individuals require a much greater interpersonal distance from others, compared with nonviolent controls (Curran, Blatchley, & Hanlon, 1978; Gilmore & Walkey, 1981; Kinzel, 1970; Roger & Schalekamp, 1976; Rubinstein, 1975).

Within a more normal range of personality differences, patterns of nonverbal involvement have been related to a variety of dimensions, including (1) locus of control (Duke & Nowicki, 1972; Heckel & Hiers, 1977; Rajecki, Ickes, & Tanford, 1981), (2) field dependence (Greene, 1976; Konstadt & Forman, 1965; Nevill, 1974), (3) self-monitoring (Ickes & Barnes, 1977), (4) self-esteem (Frankel & Barnett, 1971; Kissell, 1974), and (5) dominance (Fromme & Beam, 1974).

A number of studies looked at dimensions such as introversion–extroversion (Cook, 1970; Patterson & Holmes, 1966; Pedersen, 1973; Williams, 1971), social anxiety (Daly, 1978; Patterson, 1973b, 1977), and affiliation (Clore, 1969; Mehrabian & Diamond, 1971; Mehrabian & Ksionzky, 1972). Because these dimensions are highly correlated with one another (Patterson & Strauss, 1972), it may be best to consider them as representing a general *social approach–avoidance* factor. Across these studies, individuals who were classified as social-approach types (i.e., extroverted, low social anxious, and affiliative) showed higher levels of involvement, in terms of closer distances, more gaze, and increased talking, than did social-avoidant types (i.e., introverted, high social anxious, and nonaffiliative).

Summary. The discussion in this section emphasized the linkages among the antecedents of culture, gender, and personality and habitual patterns of nonverbal behavior. These habitual patterns are represented in the behavioral predispositions mediator in the model. Culture, gender, and personality also are important because of their influences on the choice of different situations and the development of relationships. These two proximate antecedents will be addressed in the next section.

Proximate antecedents

Situation. All social behavior happens in a context, whether it is a living room, a restaurant, or a space capsule. This is an obvious, but not a trivial, statement, because a given setting exercises considerable influence over the behavioral options available. The behavior-setting approach of ecological psychology (Barker, 1968; Wicker, 1979) asserts that the physical design and the social norms of a given setting produce pressure toward a greater homogeneity of behavior across individuals. Selection pressures also work to increase homogeneity in behavior. That is, individuals with similar interests and abilities are likely to choose similar situations. Snyder (1981, 1983) suggested that the choice of different situations actually reflects aspects of one's personality. In the functional model, this sort of influence can be found in the link between personality and situation. Furthermore, the situation itself may also limit access to specific types of person. In this case, the setting's direct or indirect selection by age, income, attitudes, or ability complements the self-selection process. The result of these converging influences is a decreased variability in behavior among people in any particular setting than would be found in random sampling of people across settings.

Situations vary in their norms for appropriate involvement levels. Hall's (1966) classification of distance zones may be applied to basic differences in the interaction's formality. For example, close distances with high levels of gaze and occasional touch are more likely in casual, social exchanges than in formal, business exchanges.

Relationships. Both the type and the intimacy of a relationship have a substantial effect on the social behavior of the partners. In general, the greater the intimacy of the relationship is between the partners, the higher the level of mutual involvement will be. Nevertheless, the effects of relationship intimacy also are qualified by culture, gender, and personality. For example, studies of North American subjects have shown that greater relationship intimacy in opposite-sex pairs is related to patterns of greater nonverbal involvement (Allgeier & Byrne, 1973; Goldstein, Kilroy, & Van de Voort, 1976; Jourard, 1966; Rubin, 1970).

Similar trends are characteristic of female–female relationships, but males interacting with other males tend to exhibit lower levels of involvement (Greenbaum & Rosenfeld, 1980; Heshka & Nelson, 1972; Heslin & Boss, 1980). Thus, in comparably intimate relationships, male partners tend to exhibit less involvement with each other than do either males or females with a female partner.

Hall's (1966) observations of people from southern European countries, the Middle East, and Latin America suggest that males in close relationships are comfortable with high levels of involvement, including frequent touch. Consistent with Hall's reports, Vaksman and Ellyson (1979) found that male American students maintained a greater distance and lower levels of gaze than did male foreign students from a variety of countries, including Argentina, Guatemala, Houduras, Iran, Libya, Saudi Arabia, and Venezuela (cited in Aiello, 1987). Furthermore, cultures differ in their norms regarding appropriate behavior in public for opposite-sex pairs. In most Western countries, it is acceptable for couples to hold hands, walk arm in arm, and even share a brief hug or kiss in public. But in some fundamentalist Islamic societies, such intimacy between males and females in public would be judged as clearly inappropriate and might even result in harsh punishment.

Personality and situation also help determine the role of the relationship in nonverbal involvement. First, the effect of personality is present, even before an interaction begins, in the selection of specific situations and relationships (Snyder 1981, 1983). Extroverts differ from introverts not only in the way in which they behave in comparable settings but also in their preferences for different settings and relationships. Extroverts tend to choose those settings in which there is greater social stimulation and activity, whereas introverts, if they can, generally avoid such settings. Similarly, socially anxious individuals, concerned about others' evaluations of them (Leary, 1983; Schenker & Leary, 1982), tend to avoid social settings in which those evaluations are likely.

A final concern that merits attention here is the specific effect of situation in determining a relationship. The same individuals may interact in different kinds of situations, but their relationships may vary according to their different roles in those situations. For example, a husband and wife who work in the same office have a different relationship there (i.e., as coworkers) than they do at home. Alexander and Rudd (1981) proposed that people strive to project different roles or situated identities in different settings. As a result, their relationships with other people are considerably affected by the situations in which they interact.

Mediating mechanisms

The remote and proximate antecedents described in the last two sections combine to influence the manner in which interactions develop, but their effects are mediated by specific underlying or covert mechanisms. That is, simply being a male or a female, living in a Western or an Eastern culture, or being an extrovert or an introvert, does not in itself directly determine how a person will interact with a given partner. Neither do the situational constraints nor the relationships directly determine interaction patterns. Rather, it is assumed that in combination these various factors exercise their influence on underlying or covert mechanisms that determine the initiation and development of interaction. These mechanisms are the behavioral, physiological, and cognitive–affective states of the individual immediately before and during an interaction. In other words, factors such as culture, gender, personality, the situational context, and the relationship between interactants affect behavioral habits, physiological arousal, and thoughts and feelings about the interaction. It is this latter set of factors that determines how an interaction will be perceived (i.e., its function) and how the behavioral exchange will develop.

Behavioral predispositions. An individual carries with him or her general, habitual ways of interacting with others. The differences in involvement preferences described under the remote antecedents as a product of culture, gender, or personality are representative of these predispositions. Although a behavioral predisposition might be viewed as an average, there is a considerable range of involvement possible on each side of this average, depending on other factors such as the situation and the relationship to the partner. Because they represent habitual ways of relating to others, developed over a long period of time, it is assumed that the behavioral predispositions are activated automatically and unconsciously. Even when there is reason to reflect on one's own behavior, it is likely that attributions about the cause of this behavior will relate to the situation or one's partner (Jones & Nisbett, 1971).

Arousal. The importance of a given exchange, its affective quality (e.g., friendly vs. disagreeable), the attractiveness of or interest in one's partner, and various other factors can affect arousal at the start of an interaction. The role of arousal or activation is a common concern when analyzing a variety of different kinds of behavior. One of the more reliable principles in psychology is that activation level is curvilinearly related to performance (Yerkes & Dodson, 1908). That is, as activation increases up to some moderate level, performance generally also increases. Then as activation continues to increase, performance begins to decrease.

Whether we are looking at test performance, assembling a complicated piece of equipment, or effectively interacting with a new boss, arousal level can affect how well we manage. In such instances, some moderate level of arousal is likely to be motivating without being disruptive.

Arousal or, more generally, arousal change also is important because it can signal changing circumstances in the environment (Mandler, 1975). That is, an increase in arousal (or perhaps even a decrease) can alert an individual to attend to important changes in his or her immediate environment. Once alerted, a person is likely to conduct a meaning analysis in order to understand and act on the relevant changes. For example, suppose an acquaintance simply stops smiling in the middle of a friendly conversation. That change may be enough to trigger a change in arousal without the meaning of the change registering in one's awareness. But this change in arousal is a signal to figure out what is happening. By attending more carefully and reflecting on the recent conversation, you may surmise that your friend is upset by something you said.

Sometimes the meaning of a behavior pattern is obvious, and in such a case, the meaning of the event is the cause of the increased arousal, not the effect of it. An example is the close and rapid approach of a large, angry-looking man with clenched fists. The meaning is clear: trouble! One does not need to notice a change in arousal first in order to determine the significance of such an occurrence.

In summary, arousal is an important mediator of social behavior because, first, arousal level affects the quality and intensity of a person's behavior. Second, variations in arousal can also alert an individual to a changing environment and stimulate a search to interpret those changes. The cognitive activity that results from such a search is one form of the third mediator: cognitive and affective expectancies.

Cognitive and affective expectancies. Thoughts and feelings before and during interactions are major determinants of how we relate to other people. In the last section, I stated that cognitions may develop out of a need to interpret changes in arousal. Cognitive and affective judgments also occur routinely as we are about to meet someone, anticipate an interaction, or evaluate our partner's reaction to what we have said in a conversation. Simple affective reactions in the form of a vague feeling of liking or disliking frequently occur as we notice an approaching stranger. Such judgments may be made even before the person has a chance to say a word. In fact, Zajonc (1980) claimed that these primary responses can develop in just a fraction of a second.

Whatever the source of this evaluation, such initial judgments can set the tone for the interaction. In fact, first impressions or, more generally, expectancies about another person can often take the form of self-fulfilling prophecies (Merton, 1948, 1957; Rosenthal, 1966, 1974; Swann & Snyder, 1980). Thus, a given expectancy can lead to self-confirming behavior, or what might be described as a *reciprocation strategy*. That is, the perceiver reciprocates the behavior anticipated from the partner, thereby increasing the likelihood that the expected behavior will indeed occur.

There is also evidence for a *compensation strategy* (Bond, 1972; Ickes, Patterson, Rajecki, & Tanford, 1982). In this case, the expectancy leads to behavior that should compensate for the anticipated behavior of the partner. In the two experiments conducted by Ickes et al. (1982), those subjects receiving a negative expectancy about a partner initiated higher levels of nonverbal involvement than did those receiving a positive expectancy. The higher involvement by subjects in the negative expectancy condition occurred even though these subjects rated their partners more negatively than did the positive expectancy subjects. Apparently, the negative expectancy subjects tried to make the interaction more pleasant by increasing their nonverbal involvement.

Scripts are another type of cognitive expectancy that can influence interaction. Scripts are activity or situation-specific expectancies that give us a guide for our subsequent interactive behavior (Abelson, 1981; Schank & Abelson, 1977). In addition, to the extent that a script is well known and generally followed, people who deviate from it may be evaluated negatively (Jones & Davis, 1965).

According to the functional model, cognitive and affective expectancies are especially important because they can reflect a person's view of an interaction's function. In turn, an individual's behavior in an interaction is guided substantially by the perceived function. Thus if we assume that a meeting with an acquaintance will be a pleasant, friendly exchange, we are likely to be relaxed. Sensitivity to and awareness of how we ought to act in such a case is probably minimal. If we are meeting the same person in order to gain her support for an important project at work, we will be very sensitive to our style of presenting our case and to monitoring her reactions to our appeal. The functions of the two interactions, both with the same person and in the same setting, are very different and have different implications for our behavior. Consequently, our cognitions about the interaction before anything is even said are pertinent determinants of how the interaction will start and develop.

Functions of nonverbal involvement

Our discussion thus far has indicated that each person brings a variety of influences to bear on the course of an interaction. According to the functional model, the cumulative effect of the various antecedent factors is concentrated in the preinteraction mediators. In turn, these mediating effects are expressed in both the initial involvement levels and the expectancies regarding the function of the interaction.

The range of potential involvement expressed by an individual is a product of that person's behavioral predispositions. For example, extroverts, females, and people from high-contact cultures generally initiate and prefer higher levels of involvement. These baseline preferences, however, provide only a rough estimate of how a person is likely to behave in a specific interaction. Cognitive and affective expectancies regarding the interaction further specify social behavior. For example, the anticipation of meeting a friend is likely to include some positive affect and a minimum of deliberation regarding how one ought to behave. In contrast, the anticipation of meeting one's boss about a raise is likely to include some apprehension and considerable deliberation about one's behavior.

Providing information

From a decoding perspective, it is obvious that nonverbal behavior can provide information about a person's states, traits, or motives. For example, the facial expressions of basic emotions (happiness, sadness, fear, disgust, anger, and fear–surprise) seem to be universally decoded (Ekman, 1972, 1973; Ekman et al., 1987). In addition, the moderately high levels of involvement (e.g., closer approaches, increased gaze, touch) by an actor generally result in more favorable impressions (see Andersen, 1985; Kleinke, 1986, chaps. 6 & 7; Patterson & Edinger, 1987; Thayer, 1986, for reviews of some of this research). Of course, the upper limit of the positive reaction to increased involvement depends on antecedent factors such as culture, gender, personality, situation, and relationship.

There is another sense in which interactive behavior can be informative. Specifically, the actor's own behavior may help inform him or her about feelings and reactions. For example, facial feedback theory proposes that feedback from the facial muscles helps inform an individual about specific emotional states (Tomkins, 1982). More generally, self-perception theory (Bem, 1967, 1972) states that actors use their own behavior to make inferences about attitudes. Thus, the recognition that one smiled or gazed a great deal at a partner might, in itself, lead to an inference of greater liking.

The function of providing information is a pervasive one and thus cannot help us distinguish among different kinds of interactions. Nevertheless, it is important to recognize the role of interactive behavior in providing information about others and oneself.

Interaction regulation

Nonverbal behavior also serves to facilitate the orderly give-and-take of interactions. Typically, behaviors serving this function occur more or less spontaneously and are initiated outside awareness. For example, most interactions take place in arrangements in which the individuals are, at least, partially facing one another (Kendon, 1976, 1977). Facing arrangements permit easy visual monitoring among the interactants and offer a boundary between the group and the surrounding environment (Ciolek & Kendon, 1980).

The physical arrangement of individuals in a group provides a relatively fixed structure in which more variable behaviors affect conversational exchange. In a conversation, the speaker's movements and gestures help segment the verbal comments (Boomer, 1978; Boomer & Dittmann, 1962; Dittmann & Llewellyn, 1969). The scope or range of movement may also be related to the size of the spoken segment: It has been suggested that smaller, briefer movements are related to smaller speech segments, whereas larger postural shifts are related to more general changes in content or topic (Scheflen, 1964; Thomas & Bull, 1981).

Overall, speakers gaze less at listeners than listeners do at speakers, and this difference may grow when there are hesitations and nonfluent speech and when judgmental evaluations take place (Allen & Guy, 1977; Kendon, 1967). Apparently, gaze avoidance by speakers during periods of hesitation or nonfluency helps speakers limit the distraction and potential stimulus overload produced by gazing at the listeners.

Around the transition point at which the speaker's and the listener's roles are switched, distinct behavioral patterns are revealed. The speaker offers a variety of cues, primarily paralinguistic, as his or her turn is about to end, such as changes in the pitch and a drawl or stretching out of the last word or syllable (Duncan, 1972). A speaker is also more likely to gaze at the listener at the end of a turn than at other points in the turn (Harrigan & Steffen, 1983; Kendon, 1967). Apparently the intensified gaze at the end of a turn gives the speaker an opportunity to evaluate the listener's reactions to the completed comment.

There is an extensive literature on turn taking and a number of excellent reviews of this topic (e.g., Cappella, 1985; Duncan & Fiske, 1977; Feldstein & Welkowitz, 1987; Wiemann, 1985). The maintenance of relatively smooth and comfortable interactions requires some minimal level of nonverbal involvement throughout an interaction. Variations from such a baseline may be attributed to one or more other functions, prominent among which is expressing intimacy.

Expressing intimacy

Intimacy may be considered as reflecting the degree of union with or openness toward another person, and it is represented in one's affective attachment (e.g., liking or love) to a person. McAdams (1988) drew a contrast between intimacy, as a communal motive, and power, as an agentic motive (see also Bakan, 1966). This contrast is similar to that between the intimacy and social control functions. In general, it is assumed that the strength and valence of the intimacy felt toward a partner is spontaneously reflected in the actor's nonverbal involvement, although this is qualified by the social norms operating in different settings.

Numerous studies, most of cross-sex pairs, show that as the relationship between individuals becomes more intimate, the level of nonverbal involvement increases. This may be seen in the smaller interpersonal distances (Aiello & Cooper, 1972; Heshka & Nelson, 1972; Willis, 1966), increased frequency and intimacy of touch (Greenbaum & Rosenfeld, 1980; Heslin & Boss, 1980), and increased mutual gaze (Goldstein, Kilroy, & Van de Voort, 1976; Rubin, 1970).

The pattern of increased involvement with increased intimacy of relationship is most typical of interactions involving at least one female.

That is, involvement patterns reflect relationship intimacy more clearly in male–female pairs and in female–female pairs than in male–male pairs (e.g., Foot, Chapman, & Smith, 1977; Greenbaum & Rosenfeld, 1980; Heshka & Nelson, 1972; Heslin & Boss, 1980). For the subjects in the majority of the studies (North American and British people), the social norms regarding the expression of same-sex intimacy are undoubtedly more restrictive for males than for females. Given that the norms for same-sex intimacy vary as a function of culture, different patterns of male–male interactions might be expected in other cultures.

In general, there seems to be a greater pull for the intimacy function when (1) interpersonal evaluations are clear and strong; (2) social norms permit variable levels of nonverbal involvement; and (3) task constraints and attempted influence are not salient to the interaction (Patterson, 1983, p. 86).

Managing affect

Adjustments in nonverbal involvement occasionally can serve to modulate affect, especially when it is strong. For example, the experience of embarrassment usually leads to avoidance behaviors such as decreased gaze toward others and increased movement (Edelmann & Hampson, 1979, 1981; Modigliani, 1971). Such behavior may lessen the negative affect and vulnerability of the embarrassed person. Grief and fear often lead to greater involvement with others, which serves to comfort the distressed individual.

In the case of positive affect, such as success in an important venture or good fortune (e.g., winning the lottery), the excitement may often result in hugs, kisses, and smiling and laughter shared among friends and relatives. The intense affect triggers momentary increases in involvement among partners. Typically, these adjustments are relatively spontaneous in nature, but some forms become rituals. For example, in many athletic contests one might see "high-fives" or a pat on the buttocks following a successful play. This form of touch between players might be seen as a form of congratulations, but it is not likely to be as spontaneous as it is in other instances of intense affect.

Exercising social control

The social control function is manifested in the purposeful use of nonverbal behavior to influence an interaction partner. By "purposeful" I mean that an individual has some awareness of trying to influence his or her partner. Thus, a person need not be aware of using a particular behavior pattern (e.g., a smile or touch) to influence another person, although he or she may sometimes be aware of it. In addition, a person initiating such influence attempts is more likely to monitor his or her own behavior and its consequences than is someone behaving more spontaneously.

There are a number of circumstances in which the social control function may be seen. For example, status usually permits greater flexibility in nonverbal involvement, including the initiation of touch (Henley, 1973) and high (or low) levels of gaze (Exline, 1972; Exline, Ellyson, & Long, 1975). Compliance with simple requests (e.g., signing a petition, taking a leaflet, donating to charity) may be greater when a close approach, increased gaze, or touch accompanies the request (Baron, 1978; Baron & Bell, 1976; Brockner, Pressman, Cabitt, & Morgan, 1982; Bull & Gibson-Robinson, 1981; Kleinke, 1977; Kleinke & Singer, 1979; Patterson, Powell, & Lenihan, 1986; Valentine & Ehrlichman, 1979).

Another example of the social control function may be seen in the exercise of impression management. Studies of employment interviews show that applicants who initiate higher levels of involvement are usually evaluated more positively than are those initiating lower levels of involvement (Forbes & Jackson, 1980; Imada & Hakel, 1977; McGovern, 1977; Young & Beier, 1977). Impression management techniques may also be activated when an unfriendly or unpleasant interaction is anticipated. Some research shows that the expectation of a cold or unfriendly interaction leads the actor to behave in a more friendly fashion in order to compensate for the partner's behavior (Bond, 1972; Coutts, Schneider, & Montgomery, 1980; Ickes, Patterson, Rajecki, & Tanford, 1982). In the Ickes et al. (1982) study, this was manifested in the negative expectancy subjects smiling more at their partners than did the positive expectancy subjects, even though the negative expectancy subjects rated their partners more negatively than did the positive expectancy subjects. In general, smiling at a partner is an important part of being polite (Bugenthal, 1986), covering negative affect (Ekman & Friesen, 1982), ingratiating someone (Lefebvre, 1975), and signaling interest in meeting another person (Walsh & Hewitt, 1985).

Presenting images and identities

The presentational function, like the social control function, is characterized by the managed use of nonverbal behavior to influence others.

In contrast with the social control patterns, however, presentational patterns are designed to influence third-party observers, not the immediate-interaction partner (Patterson, 1987). These behavior patterns may be considered as "performances" (e.g., Goffman, 1959, 1963, 1967) that are enacted to create an image or identity for a surrounding audience. Because these patterns are interactional, they necessarily involve a partner, but the actor's performance is directed toward the audience. An example is a parent's close interaction with a young son or daughter in front of the family-oriented boss.

Some behavioral patterns may be seen as self-presentations, but others are designed to create a relationship or pair identity. In the latter instance, couples might stand close, hold hands, and touch. Goffman (1972) used the term *tie-signs*, and Scheflen (1974; Scheflen & Ashcraft, 1976) used *withness* cues to describe such patterns. These patterns may also be initiated when there is a potential threat to the relationship (Fine, Stitt, & Finch, 1984).

In general, presentational patterns are precipitated by the evaluation apprehension that results from being in front of a valued audience. These patterns may be the product of one person's playing off an unsuspecting partner, or they may be collaborative in nature (e.g., the feuding husband and wife who act the parts of a loving husband and wife in front of acquaintances). Finally, presentational patterns can lead to either exaggerated increases or decreases in involvement, depending on the audience's expectations.

Facilitating service and task goals

Patterns of interactive behavior may also be determined by the service or task goals in a particular setting. For example, professional service exchanges such as those with physicians, dentists, and tailors typically involve close distances, touch, and careful visual scrutiny. Thus the particular service relationship, independent of any affective reactions to the client, may require a high level of involvement by the practitioner. In such cases, the interactive behavior in a service encounter often follows a predictable, scripted routine (Abelson, 1981).

Task goals may also affect patterns of interactive behavior in a variety of settings. Some types of work, such as complex or confidential tasks, are typically completed in relative isolation; and so decreased involvement with others is a necessary consequence. For example, when students use libraries for serious studying, they usually choose a location to avoid distractions and noise from other people, rather than to have easy access to desired reference material (Schaeffer & Patterson, 1977; Sommer, 1986, 1968). In contrast, in many work settings, such as retail selling and assembly-line work, a task's demands may force persons into very close arrangements.

The nature of the setting is obviously important to shaping service-task behavior. Behavior-setting analysis (Barker, 1968; Wicker, 1979) suggested that because particular roles are well defined and their related behaviors more or less scripted, people can be interchanged or substituted. Thus, physician–client exchanges tend to be relatively similar regardless of the particular physician and client. In addition to the setting's norms controlling interactive behavior, self-selection is also a factor in producing similar patterns in different individuals. That is, people usually choose careers or jobs that are consistent with their personal preferences for involvement with others. Thus, extroverted and dominant individuals are more likely than are introverted and submissive individuals to choose those professions that offer frequent and highly involving interactions with others.

Interaction phase

Setting the stage

Now that we have completed the description of the functions, it might be useful to review briefly the various influences that converge at the time of an interaction. In one way, their cumulative effect may be seen as "setting the stage" for the interaction itself. That is, much of what happens in an interaction is constrained by factors set in motion long before two people meet. The genetic determinants, environmental constraints, and remote antecedents (culture, gender, and personality) reciprocally influence one another. These influences promote within-group (culture or ethnic identity) similarity while, at the same time, allow for extensive differences among groups. Culture, personality, and gender help determine the habitual patterns of behavior, arousal, and cognitive–affective reactions represented in the preinteraction mediators. Differences in personality, gender (and sex roles), and other factors indirectly affect the preinteraction mediators by influencing the choice of interaction settings and the specific relationships with others. The particular functional expectancies in an interaction are a complex product of relationship, setting, and motivational factors.

Exchange process

A basic consideration in assessing the course of an interaction is the stability of the exchange. Stability refers to the interaction's being smooth, predictable, and orderly. That is, the give-and-take between two people proceeds without hitches, surprises, or awkward moments. Instability usually results from violations of some norm or expectancy, such as too much gaze from the partner or the unexpected initiation of touch. But these violations may sometimes be viewed positively (see Burgoon, 1983). For example, an overture of friendliness from an attractive acquaintance, not previously considered to be a close friend, may be especially welcome. Whether negative or positive in nature, instability is manifested in the recognition of discontinuity in the smooth flow of interactive behavior.

In contrast, stability is likely to result when preferred levels of involvement between partners are relatively similar and the perceived functions are complementary. Thus, individuals who share preferences for involvement (because of similarity in culture, gender, or personality) find it easier to maintain a stable interaction than do those who do not. Stability is also likely to result when partners share a script for their behavior. In such cases, interactive behavior is primarily a result of knowing and following the relevant script. Examples of such scripted routines are greetings and departures, interviews, and formal receptions.

In general, to the extent that exchanges are stable, partners do not have to reflect on, evaluate, or adjust their behavior. Stable exchanges end because the agenda of the interaction is completed, the partners run out of time, or some conflicting activity requires their attention. But unstable interactions may end prematurely because the partners are uncomfortable. Unless an interaction is extremely uncomfortable right from the start, there usually is some attempt to make adjustments and rescue it.

Making adjustments

The circumstance of instability in an interaction is depicted in the upper right-hand corner of Figure 13.1. The recognition of an unexpected change in involvement (i.e., instability) precipitates a cognitive or affective assessment and/or a change in arousal. In many cases, the meaning quickly becomes apparent, and the person does not have to spend much effort analyzing what is happening.

The sequence of events in reacting to instability is variable. If the meaning of the instability is immediate and obvious, then the cognitive–affective component is likely to be primary, with arousal possibly affected later. But if the instability is ambiguous, then the arousal may be primary, followed by a cognitive search for the meaning of events. Cappella and Greene (1982) proposed a cognition–arousal linkage that fits very well with the dynamics in the interaction phase of the functional model. They believe that the cognitive aspect refers to an evaluation of the discrepancy between the expected and actual behavior of the partner. As the discrepancy (i.e., instability) widens, the arousal also is heightened. According to Cappella and Greene, to the extent that a partner's greater involvement triggers moderate arousal, that involvement will be matched or reciprocated. When still greater involvement triggers high arousal, that involvement will produce compensation.

The result of the cognitive–affective assessment and arousal change is a reevaluation of the interaction's function and/or an adjustment in one's involvement level. This development is shown in Figure 13.1 by the loop from arousal change and cognitive–affective reassessment to perceived function and nonverbal involvement. Adjustments in one or both of these factors should lead to greater stability in the interaction. If the precipitating instability is minimal, resulting in only a slight feeling of unease (without any cognitive elaboration), a simple change in involvement may resolve it. For example, if an acquaintance initiates a slightly closer than usual approach or an increase in gaze, you may feel just uncomfortable enough to turn away slightly and reduce your gaze level. Such adjustments might well occur outside your awareness. A more extreme difference between expected and actual behavior increases the likelihood that thoughts, feelings, and arousal change all come into play in guiding your reaction. In such cases, a change in your behavior and a reevaluation of the function of the interaction are likely.

If the behavioral adjustments and any related change in the perceived function lead to more stability, then the exchange will be back on track again. If there is still considerable instability, then the individual will recycle back through the negative feedback loop. That is, additional cognitive–affective assessment and/or arousal change are triggered, leading to new behavioral adjustments and a possible change in the perceived function. In principle, the existence of continued instability should lead to repeated assessments and adjustments. In reality, however, the discomfort of such a circumstance usually leads to an early end of the interaction.

Residual effects

There is an old song with the lyric "The song is over, but the melody lingers on." It is much the same way with interactions, both pleasant and unpleasant ones. The consequences identified in Figure 13.1 include the residual impact on both the proximate antecedents and the preinteraction mediators. Obviously, preferences for one or another situation might be intensified. Similarly, feelings or judgments about a particular relationship partner might be affected. In turn, these residual effects influence future relationships and setting choices. Although no single interaction is likely to have a substantial effect on a person's habitual behavior patterns (behavioral predispositions), the consequences of a particular interaction may affect how the next interaction is anticipated. In principle, changes in personality are also possible, as reflected in the weaker link (the broken line in Figure 13.1) with the personality factor. Such a pervasive change, however, occurs only in extreme incidents or repeated exchanges of a particular type over time.

Recent research

The functional model has provided a convenient framework for reviewing the extensive research on interactive behavior. Most of the existing research, however, is not directly relevant to the critical distinctions proposed among the functions. Three studies discussed earlier in the chapter suggest that people who have negative expectancies about an interaction partner deliberately increase their involvement with the partner in order to make the interaction more comfortable (Bond, 1972; Coutts, Schneider, & Montgomery, 1980; Ickes et al., 1982). Although the results of these studies are consistent with the operation of a social control function, the studies were not designed as specific tests of the social control function.

A recent study by Honeycutt (1989), however, does provide clearer support for the social control function. Honeycutt manipulated partner expectations (unfriendly, friendly, no expectancy) in one member of a pair of unacquainted subjects. The unfriendly expectancy subjects initiated conversation more frequently than did the subjects in the other conditions. In addition, the unfriendly expectancy subjects reported that they compensated more for their partner's failure to initiate conversation than did the friendly expectancy subjects. Furthermore, a later analysis of the expectancy subjects who initiated and those who did not initiate conversation showed an expectancy–initiate interaction effect. That is, the unfriendly expectancy subjects who initiated conversation reported higher levels of attempted compensation than did the subjects in any of the other conditions. This last finding is consistent with the kind of motivated change in involvement predicted in the social control function.

One contrast hypothesized between the intimacy and social control functions pertains to the amount of attention required of an actor to manage his or her own behavior and monitor its consequences. Intimacy behavior is relatively spontaneous and, consequently, minimizes the cognitive demands surrounding the actor's behavior. In contrast, if a person initiates a social control pattern, greater cognitive demands should result from managing one's behavior and evaluating its consequences. Two studies of self-presentation and social inference offer evidence that the initiation of a specific self-presentation exacts a cognitive toll on interpersonal judgments. In one study, when the subjects were asked to ingratiate a dislikable (versus a likable) confederate by "making eye contact, smiling, nedding, and so forth," the accuracy of inferences about the confederate suffered (Gilbert, Krull, & Pelham, 1988). In this case, behaving in a friendly manner toward a dislikable partner was clearly a more demanding social control task than was behaving in a friendly manner toward a likable other. Presumably, judgments about the partner suffered in the dislikable condition because a greater cognitive effort was required to manage one's own behavior.

In the second study, the subjects were required to present themselves very favorably or very modestly to a naive partner (Baumeister, Hutton, & Tice, 1989). Both the favorable and the modest subjects saw their presentations as unrepresentative of their real selves. That is, these subjects were quite aware of managing their own behavior. Like the subjects in the Gilbert et al. (1988) study, the subjects in this study did not accurately judge the dispositions underlying their partner's behavior. Furthermore, the subjects in the modest presentation condition (judged as more difficult to enact than the favorable presentation condition) showed more errors in memory for the interaction than did the subjects in the favorable presentation condition.

The results of these two studies indicate that the purposeful patterns of behavior, like those enacted in the social control function and presentational functions, require a cognitive expenditure that may have negative interpersonal consequences. That is, individuals who manage their behavior so as to influence others may be less accurate in judging the behavior of their partners and may even remember less of the interaction. In the long run, such "side effects" might prove detrimental to effectively influencing others. To the extent that such managed routines are highly practiced, the negative side effects might be reduced or even eliminated. In effect, such managed behavior patterns require only a little more attention than do the spontaneous ones. In any case, the cognitive consequences of spontaneous versus managed behavior provide an interesting focus for expanding the application of the functional model.

Summary

The functional model described in this chapter emphasizes patterns of nonverbal involvement. That is, people do not behave in one channel at a time, but rather, their actions are coordinated and their behaviors interdependent. In addition, understanding the patterns of nonverbal exchange requires the analysis of various factors present long before people even meet in an interaction. Genetic and environmental determinants shape the antecedent factors of culture, gender, and personality. In turn, these antecedents affect the kinds of relationship that individuals develop and the situations they choose. The converging effects of all of these components may be seen in habitual preferences for nonverbal involvement, arousal change, and cognitive–affective reactions.

Consequently, as two people meet and start to interact, the way in which they behave has already, in large part, been structured. Their initial behavior is a product of their preferences for involvement and their expectancies regarding each other and the interaction. When people have similar (or complementary) behavioral preferences and functional expectancies, their exchange tends to be smoother and more stable. In contrast, partners who have discrepant behavioral styles and functional expectancies are more likely to have an unstable exchange. This instability typically leads to a reassessment of the interaction, resulting in behavioral adjustments and/or a change in perceived function. Over time, the exchange will move toward greater stability or, failing that, a faster-than-normal termination.

Because the functional model attempts to describe interactive behavior more comprehensively, it is necessarily broader and more complex than is a model such as equilibrium theory. Consequently, it is more difficult to devise specific and critical tests of the model. We hope that this weakness of the model will be outweighed by its advantage of linking together a variety of factors and processes into a kind of systems approach to nonverbal exchange.

Note

1. *Intimacy* is the term by Argyle and Dean (1965), and that term is used here also. It is similar to *involvement* in being a multivariate construct.

References

Abelson, R. P. (1981). Psychological status of the script concept. *American Psychologist, 36*, 715–729.

Aiello, J. R. (1987). Human spatial behavior. In D. Stokols & I. Altman (Eds.), *Handbook of environmental psychology* (Vol. 1, pp. 389–504). New York: Wiley.

Aiello, J. R., & Cooper, R. E. (1972). Use of personal space as a function of social affect. *Proceedings of the 80th Annual Convention of the American Psychological Association, 7*, 207–208.

Aiello, J. R., & Jones, S. E. (1971). Field study of the proxemic behavior of young school children in three subcultural groups. *Journal of Personality and Social Psychology, 19*, 351–356.

Alexander, C. N., Jr., & Rudd, J. (1981). Situated identities and response variables. In J. T. Tedeschi (Ed.), *Impression management theory and social psychological research* (pp. 83–103). New York: Academic Press.

Allen, D. E., & Guy, R. F. (1977). Ocular breaks and verbal output. *Sociometry, 40*, 90–96.

Allgeier, A. R., & Byrne, D. (1973). Attraction toward the opposite sex as a determinant of physical proximity. *Journal of Social Psychology, 90*, 213–219.

Altman, I. (1975). *The environment and social behavior*. Monterey, CA: Brooks/Cole.

Altman, I., & Chemers, M. M. (1980). *Culture and environment*. Monterey, CA: Brooks/Cole.

Andersen, P. A. (1985). Nonverbal immediacy in interpersonal communication. In A. W. Siegman & S. Feldstein (Eds.), *Multichannel integrations of nonverbal behavior* (pp. 1–36). Hillsdale, NJ: Erlbaum.

Andersen, P. A., & Andersen, J. F. (1984). The exchange of nonverbal intimacy: A critical review of dyadic models. *Journal of Nonverbal Behavior, 8*, 327–349.

Argyle, M., & Dean, J. (1965). Eye-contact, distance and affiliation. *Sociometry, 28*, 289–304.

Bakan, D. (1966). *The duality of human existence*. Chicago: Rand McNally.

Barker, R. G. (1968). *Ecological psychology: Concepts and methods for studying the environment of human behavior*. Stanford, CA: Stanford University Press.

Baron, R. A. (1978). Invasions of personal space and helping: Mediating effects of invader's apparent need. *Journal of Experimental Social Psychology, 14*, 304–312.

Baron, R. A., & Bell, P. A. (1976). Physical distance and helping: Some unexpected benefits of "crowding in" on others. *Journal of Applied Social Psychology. 6*, 95–104.

Baumeister, R. F., Hutton, D. G., & Tice, D. M. (1989). Cognitive processes during deliberate self-presentation: How self-presenters alter and misinterpret the behavior of their interaction partners. *Journal of Experimental Social Psychology, 25* 59–78.

Bem, D. J. (1967). Self perception: An alternative interpretation of cognitive dissonance phenomena. *Psychological Review, 74*, 183–200.

(1972). Self perception theory. In L. Berkowitz (Ed.), *Advances in experimental social psychology* (Vol. 6, pp. 1–62). New York: Academic Press.

Berry, J. W. (1975). An ecological approach to cross-cultural psychology. *Netherlands Journal of Psychology, 30*, 51–84.

(1976). *Ecology of cognitive style: Comparative studies in cultural and psychological adaptation.* New York: Sage/Halstead.

Bond, M. H. (1972). Effect of an impression set on subsequent behavior. *Journal of Personality and Social Psychology, 24*, 302–305.

Boomer, D. S. (1978). The phonemic clause: Speech unit in human communication. In A. W. Siegman & S. Feldstein (Eds.), *Nonverbal behavior and communication* (pp. 245–262). Hillsdale, NJ: Erlbaum.

Boomer, D. S., & Dittman, A. T. (1962). Hesitation pauses and juncture pauses in speech. *Language and Speech, 5*, 215–220.

Bowlby, J. (1969). *Attachment and loss* (Vol. 1). New York: Basic Books.

Brockner, J., Pressman, B., Cabitt, J., & Moran, P. (1982). Nonverbal immediacy, sex and compliance: A field study. *Journal of Nonverbal Behavior, 6*, 253–258.

Bugental, D. B. (1986). Unmasking the "polite smile": Situational and personal determinants of managed affect in adult–child interaction. *Personality and Social Psychology Bulletin, 12*, 7–16.

Bull, R., & Gibson-Robinson, E. (1981). The influences of eye-gaze, style of dress, and locality on the amounts of money donated to a charity. *Human Relations, 34*, 895–905.

Burgoon, J. K. (1978). A communication model of personal space violations: Explication and an initial test. *Human Communication Research, 4*, 129–142.

(1983). Nonverbal violations of expectations. In J. M. Wiemann & R. P. Harrison (Eds.), *Nonverbal interaction* (pp. 77–111). Beverly Hills, CA: Sage.

Cappella, J. N. (1981). Mutual influence in expressive behavior: Adult–adult and infant–adult dyadic interaction. *Psychological Bulletin, 89*, 101–132.

(1985). Controlling the floor in conversation. In A. W. Siegman & S. Feldstein (Eds.), *Multichannel integrations of nonverbal behavior* (pp. 69–103). Hillsdale, NJ: Erlbaum.

Cappella, J. N., & Greene, J. O. (1982). A discrepancy–arousal explanation of mutual influence in expressive behavior for adult and infant–adult interaction. *Communication Monographs, 49*, 89–114.

Ciolek, T. M., & Kendon, A. (1980). Environment and the spatial arrangement of conversational encounters. *Sociological Inquiry, 50*, 3–4.

Clore, G. (1969). *Attraction and interpersonal behavior.* Paper presented at the annual meeting of the Southwestern Psychological Association, Austin, TX.

Cook, M. (1970). Experiments on orientation and proxemics. *Human Relations, 23*, 61–76.

Coutts, L. M., Schneider, F. W., & Montgomery, S. (1980). An investigation of the arousal model of interpersonal intimacy. *Journal of Experimental Social Psychology, 16*, 545–561.

Curran, S. F., Blatchley, R. J., & Hanlon, T. E. (1978). The relationship between body buffer zone and violence as assessed by subjective and objective techniques. *Criminal Justice and Behavior, 5*, 53–62.

Dabbs, J. M., Jr. (1977). Does reaction to crowding depend upon the sex of subject or sex of subject's partners? *Journal of Personality and Social Psychology, 35*, 343–344.

Dabbs, J. M., Jr., Evans, M. S., Hopper, C. H., & Purvis, J. A. (1980). Self-monitors in conversation: What do they monitor? *Journal of Personality and Social Psychology, 39,* 278–284.

Daly, S. (1978). Behavioral correlates of social anxiety. *British Journal of Social and Clinical Psychology, 17,* 117–120.

Darwin, C. (1955). *The expression of the emotions in man and animals.* New York: Philosophical Library. (Originally published, 1872)

Dittman, A. T., & Llewellyn, L. G. (1969). Body movement and speech rhythm in social conversation. *Journal of Personality and Social Psychology, 11,* 98–106.

Duke, M. P., & Nowicki, S., Jr. (1972). A new measure and social-learning model for interpersonal distance. *Journal of Experimental Research in Personality, 6,* 119–132.

Duncan, S. D., Jr. (1972). Some signals and rules for taking speaking turns in conversations. *Journal of Personality and Social Psychology, 23,* 283–292.

Duncan, S. D., Jr., & Fiske, D. W. (1977). *Face to face interaction: Research, methods, and theory.* Hillsdale, NJ: Erlbaum.

Edelmann, R. J., & Hampson, S. E. (1979). Changes in nonverbal behavior during embarrassment. *British Journal of Social and Clinical Psychology, 18,* 385–390.

  (1981). Embarrassment in dyadic interaction. *Social Behavior and Personality, 9,* 171–177.

Ekman, P. (1972). Universals and cultural differences in facial expressions of emotion. In J. Cole (Ed.), *Nebraska Symposium on Motivation* (Vol. 19, pp. 207–283). Lincoln: University of Nebraska Press.

  (1973). Cross-cultural studies of facial expressions. In P. Ekman (Ed.), *Darwin and facial expression* (pp. 169–229). New York: Academic Press.

  (1978). Facial expression. In A. W. Siegman & S. Feldstein (Eds.), *Nonverbal behavior and communication* (pp. 97–116). Hillsdale, NJ: Erlbaum.

  (1985). *Telling lies: Clues to deceit in the marketplace, politics, and marriage.* New York: Norton.

Ekman, P., & Friesen, W. (1982). Felt, false, and miserable smiles. *Journal of Nonverbal Behavior, 4,* 238–252.

Ekman, P., Friesen, W. V., O'Sullivan, M., Chan, A., Diacoyanni-Tarlatzis, I., Heider, K., Krause, R., Le Compte, W. A., Pitcairn, T., Ricci Bitti, P. E., Scherer, K., Tomita, M., & Tzavaras, A. (1987). Universals and cultural differences in the judgments of facial expression of emotion. *Journal of Personality and Social Psychology, 52,* 712–717.

Evans, R. M., & Cherulnik, P. D. (1980). Sex composition and intimacy in dyads: A field study. *Journal of Social Psychology, 110,* 139–140.

Exline, R. V. (1963). Explorations in the process of person perception: Visual interaction in relation to competition, sex, and need for affiliation. *Journal of Personality, 31,* 1–20.

  (1972). Visual interaction: The glances of power and preference. In J. K. Cole (Ed.), *Nebraska Symposium on Motivation* (Vol. 19, pp. 163–206). Lincoln: University of Nebraska Press.

Exline, R. V., Ellyson, S. L., & Long, B. (1975). Visual behavior as an aspect of power role relationships. In P. Pliner, L. Krames, & T. Alloway (Eds.), *Advances in the study of communication and affect* (Vol. 2, pp. 21–51). New York: Plenum.

Exline, R. V., Gray, D., & Schuette, D. (1985). Visual behavior in a dyad as affected by interview content and sex of respondent. *Journal of Personality and Social Psychology, 1,* 201–209.

Exline, R. V., & Winters, L. C. (1965). Affective relations and mutual glances in dyads. In S. Tomkins & C. Izard (Eds.), *Affect, cognition, and personality* (pp. 319–350). New York: Springer-Verlag.

Feldstein, S., & Welkowitz, J. (1987). A chronography of conversation: In defense of an objective approach. In A. W. Siegman & S. Feldstein (Eds.), *Nonverbal behavior and communication* (pp. 435–500). Hillsdale, NJ: Erlbaum.

Festinger, L. A. (1954). A theory of social comparison processes. *Human Relations, 7*, 117–140.

Fine, G. A., Stitt, J. L., & Finch, M. (1984). Couple tie-signs and interpersonal threat: A field experiment. *Social Psychology Quarterly, 47*, 282–286.

Fisher, J. D., Rytting, M., & Heslin, R. (1976). Hands touching hands: Affective and evaluative effects of an interpersonal touch. *Sociometry, 39*, 416–421.

Foot, H. C., Chapman, A. J., & Smith, J. R. (1977). Friendship and social responsiveness in boys and girls. *Journal of Personality and Social Psychology, 35*, 401–411.

Forbes, R. J., & Jackson, P. R. (1980). Non-verbal behavior and the outcome of selection interviews. *Journal of Occupational Psychology, 53*, 65–72.

Forston, R. F., & Larson, C. V. (1968). The dynamics of space: An experimental study in proxemic behavior among Latin Americans and North Americans. *Journal of Communication, 18*, 109–116.

Frankel, S. A., & Barrett, J. (1971). Variations in personal space as a function of authoritarianism, self esteem and racial characteristics of a stimulus situation. *Journal of Consulting and Clinical Psychology, 37*, 95–98.

Fridlund, A. J. (in press). Evolution and facial action in reflex, social motive, and paralanguage. In P. K. Ackles, J. R. Jennings, & M. G. H. Coles (Eds.), *Advances in psychophysiology* (Vol. 4). Greenwich, CT: JAI Press.

Fridlund, A. J., Ekman, P., & Oster, H. (1987). Facial expression. In A. W. Siegman & S. Feldstein (Eds.), *Nonverbal behavior and communication* (pp. 143–224). Hillsdale, NJ: Erlbaum.

Fromme, D. K., & Beam, D. C. (1974). Dominance and sex differences in nonverbal responses to differential eye contact. *Journal of Research in Personality, 8*, 76–87.

Gilbert, D. T., Krull, D. S., & Pelham, B. W. (1988). Of thoughts unspoken: Social inference and the self-regulation of behavior. *Journal of Personality and Social Psychology, 55*, 658–694.

Gilmour, D. R., & Walkey, F. H. (1981). Identifying violent offenders using a video measure of interpersonal distance. *Journal of Consulting and Clinical Psychology, 49*, 287–291.

Goffman, E. (1959). *Presentation of self in everyday life.* New York: Doubleday.
   (1963). *Behavior in public places.* New York: Free Press.
   (1967). *Interaction ritual.* Garden City, NY: Doubleday.
   (1972). *Relations in public.* New York: Harper & Row.

Goldstein, M., Kilroy, M., & Van de Voort, D. (1976). Gaze as a function of conversation and degree of love. *Journal of Psychology, 92*, 227–234.

Greenbaum, P. E., & Rosenfeld, H. M. (1978). Patterns of avoidance in response to interpersonal staring and proximity: Effects of bystanders on drivers at a traffic intersection. *Journal of Personality and Social Psychology, 36*, 575–587.
   (1980). Varieties of touching in greetings: Sequential structure and sex-related differences. *Journal of Nonverbal Behavior, 5*, 13–25.

Greene, L. R. (1976). Effects of field dependence on affective reactions and compliance in dyadic interactions. *Journal of Personality and Social Psychology, 34*, 569–577.

Hall, E. T. (1959). *The silent language.* Garden City, NY: Doubleday.

(1963). A system for the notation of proxemic behavior. *American Anthropologist, 65,* 1003–1026.

(1966). *The hidden dimension.* New York: Doubleday.

(1968). Proxemics. *Current Anthropology, 9,* 83–108.

Hall, J. A. (1985). Male and female nonverbal behavior. In A. W. Siegman & S. Feldstein (Eds.), *Multichannel integrations of nonverbal behavior* (pp. 195–225). Hillsdale, NJ: Erlbaum.

Harrigan, J. A., & Steffen, J. J. (1983). Gaze as a turn-exchange signal in group conversations. *British Journal of Social Psychology, 22,* 167–168.

Heckel, R. V., & Hiers, J. M. (1977). Social distance and locus of control. *Journal of Clinical Psychology, 33,* 469–471.

Henley, N. M. (1973). Status and sex: Some touching observations. *Bulletin of the Psychonomic Society, 2,* 91–93.

Heshka, S., & Nelson, Y. (1972). Interpersonal speaking distance as a function of age, sex, and relationship. *Sociometry, 35,* 491–498.

Heslin, R., & Boss, D. (1980). Nonverbal intimacy in airport arrival and departure. *Personality and Social Psychology Bulletin, 6,* 248–252.

Honeycutt, J. M. (1989). Effect of preinteraction expectancies on interaction involvement and behavioral responses in initial interaction. *Journal of Nonverbal Behavior, 13,* 25–36.

Horowitz, M. J., Duff, D. F., & Stratton, L. O. (1964). Body-buffer zone. *Archives of General Psychiatry, 11,* 651–656.

Ickes, W. (1981). Sex role influences in dyadic interaction: A theoretical model. In C. Mayo & N. Henley (Eds.), *Gender and nonverbal behavior* (pp. 95–128). New York: Springer-Verlag.

Ickes, W., & Barnes, R. D. (1977). The role of sex and self-monitoring in unstructured dyadic settings. *Journal of Personality and Social Psychology, 35,* 315–330.

Ickes, W., Patterson, M. L., Rajecki, D. W., & Tanford, S. (1982). Behavioral and cognitive consequences of reciprocal versus compensatory responses to pre-interaction expectancies. *Social Cognition, 1,* 160–190.

Imada, A. S., & Hakel, M. D. (1977). Influence of nonverbal communication and rater proximity on impressions and decisions in simulated employment interviews. *Journal of Applied Psychology, 62,* 295–300.

Jones, E. E., & Davis, K. E. (1965). From acts to dispositions: The attribution process in person perception. In L. Berkowitz (Ed.), *Advances in experimental social psychology* (Vol. 2, pp. 219–266). New York: Academic Press.

Jones, E. E., & Nisbett, R. E. (1971). *The actor and the observer: Divergent perspectives of the causes of behavior.* Morristown, NJ: General Learning Press.

Jourard, S. M. (1966). An exploratory study of body-accessibility. *British Journal of Social and Clinical Psychology, 5,* 221–231.

Kendon, A. (1967). Some functions of gaze-direction in social interaction. *Acta Psychologica, 26,* 22–63.

(1976). The F-formation system: The spatial organization of social encounters. *Man–Environment Systems, 6,* 291–296.

(1977). Spatial organization in social encounters: The F-formation system. In A. Kendon (Ed.), *Studies in the behavior of social interaction.* Lisse: Peter de Ridder Press.

Kinzel, A. F. (1970). Body-buffer zone in violent prisoners. *American Journal of Psychiatry, 127,* 59–64.

Kissell, P. D. (1974). The relationship of self-esteem, programmed music, and time of day to preferred conversational distance among female college students. *Dissertation Abstracts International, 35,* 2280B. (University Microfilms No. 74–25,001)

Kleinke, C. L. (1977). Compliance to requests made by gazing, and touching experimenters in field settings. *Journal of Experimental Social Psychology, 13,* 218–223.

(1986). *Meeting and understanding people.* New York: Freeman.

Kleinke, C. L., & Singer, D. A. (1979). Influence of gaze on compliance with demanding and conciliatory requests in a field setting. *Personality and Social Psychology Bulletin, 5,* 386–390.

Konstadt, N., & Forman, E. (1965). Field dependence and external directedness. *Journal of Personality and Social Psychology, 1,* 490–493.

Leary, M. R. (1983). *Understanding social anxiety: Social, personality and clinical perspectives.* Beverly Hills, CA: Sage.

Lefebvre, L. M. (1975). Encoding and decoding of ingratiation in modes of smiling and gaze. *British Journal of Social and Clinical Psychology, 14,* 33–42.

Libby, W. L., Jr. (1970). Eye contact and direction of looking as stable individual differences. *Journal of Experimental Research in Personality, 4,* 303–312.

McAdams, D. P. (1988). Personal needs and personal relationships. In S. W. Duck (Ed.), *Handbook of personal relationships* (pp. 7–22). Chichester: Wiley.

McGovern, T. V. (1977). The making of a job interviewee: The effect of nonverbal behavior on an interviewer's evaluations during a selection interview. *Dissertation Abstracts International, 37,* 4740B–4741B. (University Microfilms No. 77–6239)

Mandler, G. (1975). *Mind and emotion.* New York: Wiley.

Mehrabian, A. (1969). Some referents and measures of nonverbal behavior. *Behavior Research Methods and Instrumentation, 1,* 203–207.

Mehrabian, A., & Diamond, S. G. (1971). Effects of furniture arrangement, props, and personality on social interaction. *Journal of Personality and Social Psychology, 20,* 18–30.

Mehrabian, A., & Ksionzky, S. (1972). Categories of social behavior. *Comparative Group Studies, 3,* 425–436.

Merton, R. K. (1948). The self-fulfilling prophecy. *Antioch Review 8,* 193–210.

(1957). *Social theory and social structure.* Glencoe, IL: Free Press.

Modigliani, A. (1971). Embarrassment, facework, and eye contact: Testing a theory of embarrassment. *Journal of Personality and Social Psychology, 17,* 15–24.

Montagu, A. (1971). *Touching: The human significance of the skin.* New York: Columbia University Press.

Nevill, D. (1974). Experimental manipulation of dependency motivation and its effects on eye contact and measures of field dependency. *Journal of Personality and Social Psychology, 29,* 72–79.

Noesjirwan, J. (1977). Contrasting cultural patterns of interpersonal closeness in doctors' waiting rooms in Sydney and Jakarta. *Journal of Cross-Cultural Psychology, 8,* 357–368.

(1978). A laboratory study of proxemic patterns of Indonesians and Australians. *British Journal of Social and Clinical Psychology, 17,* 333–334.

Patterson, M. L. (1973a). Compensation in nonverbal immediacy behaviors: A review. *Sociometry, 36,* 237–252.

(1973b). Stability of nonverbal immediacy behaviors. *Journal of Experimental Social Psychology, 9,* 97–109.

(1976). An arousal model of interpersonal intimacy. *Psychological Review, 83,* 235–245.

(1977). Interpersonal distance, affect, and equilibrium theory. *Journal of Social Psychology, 101*, 205–214.

(1982). A sequential functional model of nonverbal exchange. *Psychological Review, 89*, 231–249.

(1983). *Nonverbal behavior: A functional perspective.* New York: Springer-Verlag.

(1987). Presentational and affect management functions of nonverbal involvement. *Journal of Nonverbal Behavior, 11*, 110–122.

Patterson, M. L., & Edinger, J. A. (1987). A functional analysis of space in social interaction. In A. W. Siegman & S. Feldstein (Eds.), *Nonverbal behavior and communication* (pp. 523–562). Hillsdale, NJ: Erlbaum.

Patterson, M. L., & Holmes, D. S. (1966, September). *Social interaction correlates of the MPI extraversion–introversion scale.* Paper presented at the annual meeting of the American Psychological Association, New York City.

Patterson, M. L., Powell, J. L., & Lenihan, M. G. (1986). Touch, compliance, and interpersonal affect. *Journal of Nonverbal Behavior, 10*, 41–50.

Patterson, M. L., & Strauss, M. E. (1972). An examination of the discriminant validity of the social-avoidance and distress scale. *Journal of Consulting and Clinical Psychology, 39*, 169.

Pedersen, D. M. (1973). Relations among sensation seeking and simulated and behavioral personal space. *Journal of Psychology, 83*, 79–88.

Pellegrini, R. J., & Empey, J. (1970). Interpersonal spatial orientation in dyads. *Journal of Psychology, 76*, 67–70.

Rajecki, D. W., Ickes, W., & Tanford, S. (1981). Locus of control and reactions to strangers. *Personality and Social Psychology Bulletin, 7*, 282–289.

Roger, D. B., & Schalekamp, E. E. (1976). Body-buffer zone and violence: A cross-cultural study. *Journal of Social Psychology, 98*, 153–158.

Rosenthal, R. (1966). *Experimenter effects in behavioral research.* New York: Appleton-Century-Crofts.

Rosenthal, R. (1974). *On the social psychology of the self-fulfilling prophecy: Further evidence for pygmalion effects and their meditating mechanisms.* New York: M.S.S. Information Corporation Modular Publication.

Rubin, Z. (1970). Measurement of romantic love. *Journal of Personality and Social Psychology, 16*, 265–273.

Rubinstein, E. S. (1975). Body buffer zones in female prisoners. *Dissertation Abstracts International, 36*, 1456B–1457B. (University Microfilms No. 75-20, 30)

Rutter, D. R. (1977). Visual interaction and speech patterning in remitted and acute schizophrenic patients. *British Journal of Social and Clinical Psychology, 16*, 357–361.

(1978). Visual interaction in schizophrenic patients: The timing of looks. *British Journal of Social and Clinical Psychology, 17*, 281–282.

Rutter, D. R., & Stephenson, G. M. (1972). Visual interaction in a group of schizophrenic and depressive patients. *British Journal of Social and Clinical Psychology, 11*, 57–65.

Schachter, S. (1959). *The psychology of affiliation.* Stanford, CA: Stanford University Press.

Schaeffer, G. R., & Patterson, M. L. (1977). Studying preferences, behavior, and design influences in a university library. In P. Suedfeld, J. A. Russell, L. M. Ward, F. Szigeti, & G. Davis (Eds.), *The behavioral basis of design* (Book 2, pp. 301–305). Stroudsberg, PA: Dowden, Hutchinson, & Ross.

Schank, R. C., & Abelson, R. P. (1977). *Scripts, plans, goals and understanding.* Hillsdale, NJ: Erlbaum.

Scheflen, A. E. (1964). The significance of posture in communication systems. *Psychiatry, 27,* 316–331.

(1974). *How behavior means.* Garden City, NY: Doubleday.

Scheflen, A. E., & Ashcraft, N. (1976). *Human territories: How we behave in space-time.* Englewood Cliffs, NJ: Prentice-Hall.

Schlenker, B. R., & Leary, M. R. (1982). Social anxiety and self-presentation: A conceptualization and model. *Psychological Bulletin, 92,* 641–669.

Shuter, R. (1976). Proxemics and tactility in Latin America. *Journal of Communication, 26,* 46–52.

Snyder, M. (1981). On the influence of individuals on situations. In N. Cantor & J. Kihlstrom (Eds.), *Cognition, social interaction, and personality* (pp. 309–329). Hillsdale, NJ: Erlbaum.

(1983). The influence of individuals on situations: Implications for understanding the links between personality and social behavior. *Journal of Personality, 51,* 497–516.

Sommer, R. (1959). Studies in personal space. *Sociometry, 22,* 247–260.

(1961). Leadership and group geography. *Sociometry, 24,* 99–110.

(1962). The distance for comfortable conversation: A further study. *Sociometry, 23,* 111–116.

(1965). Further studies of small group ecology. *Sociometry, 28,* 337–348.

(1966). The ecology of privacy. *Library Quarterly, 36,* 234–248.

(1968). Reading areas in college libraries. *Library Quarterly, 38,* 249–260.

Spitz, R. A. (1945). Hospitalism: An inquiry into the genesis of psychiatric conditions in early childhood. *Psychoanalytic Study of the Child, 1,* 53–74.

Sussman, N. M., & Rosenfeld, H. M. (1982). Influence of culture, language, and sex on conversational distance. *Journal of Personality and Social Psychology, 42,* 66–74.

Swann, W., & Snyder, M. (1980). On translating beliefs into action: Theories of ability and their application in an instructional setting. *Journal of Personality and Social Psychology, 38,* 879–888.

Thayer, S. (1986). History and strategies of research on social touch. *Journal of Nonverbal Behavior, 10,* 12–28.

Thomas, A. P., & Bull, P. (1981). The role of pre-speech posture change in dyadic interaction. *British Journal of Social Psychology, 20,* 105–111.

Tomkins, S. S. (1982). *Affect, imagery, consciousness* (Vol. 3). New York: Springer-Verlag.

Vaksman, E., & Ellyson, S. L. (1979). *Visual and spatial behavior among U.S. and foreign males: A cross-cultural test of equilibrium theory.* Paper presented at the Eastern Psychological Association Convention, Philadelphia.

Valentine, M. E., & Ehrlichman, H. (1979). Interpersonal gaze and helping behavior. *Journal of Social Psychology, 107,* 193–198.

Vayda, A. P. (Ed.). (1969). *Environment and cultural behavior.* New York: Natural History Press.

Walsh, D. G., & Hewitt, J. (1985). Giving men the come-on: Effect of eye contact and smiling in a bar environment. *Perceptual and Motor Skills, 61,* 873–874.

Watson, O. M., & Graves, T. D. (1966). Quantitative research in proxemic behavior. *American Anthropologist, 68,* 971–985.

Waxer, P. (1974). Nonverbal cues for depression. *Journal of Abnormal Psychology, 56,* 319–322.

Whitcher, S. J., & Fisher, J. D. (1979). Multidimensional reaction to therapeutic touch in a hospital setting. *Journal of Personality and Social Psychology, 37,* 87–96.

Wicker, A. W. (1979). *An introduction to ecological psychology*. Monterey, CA.: Brooks/Cole.

Wiemann, J. M. (1985). Interpersonal control and regulation in conversation. In R. L. Street & J. N. Cappella (Eds.), *Sequence and pattern in communication behavior* (pp. 85–102). London: Arnold.

Williams, E. (1974). Analysis of gaze in schizophrenics. *British Journal of Social and Clinical Psychology, 13*, 1–8.

Williams, J. L. (1971). Personal space and its relation to extraversion–introversion. *Canadian Journal of Behavioral Sciences, 3*, 156–160.

Willis, F. N. (1966). Initial speaking distance as a function of the speakers' relationship. *Psychonomic Science, 5*, 221–222.

Yerkes, R. M., & Dodson, J. D. (1908). The relation of strength of stimulus to rapidity of habit-formation. *Journal of Comparative Neurology and Psychology, 18*, 459–482.

Young, D. M., & Beier, E. G. (1977). The role of applicant nonverbal communication in the employment interview. *Journal of Employment Counseling, 14*, 154–165.

Zajonc, R. B. (1965). Social facilitation. *Science, 149*, 269–274.

(1980). Feeling and thinking: Preferences need no inferences. *American Psychologist, 35*, 151–175.

Author index

Subject index

Achenbach Child Behavior Checklist, 339
action
  gestural use of, 449
  imagined, and electrical activity in muscle, 267
adolescent, 371, 374; *see also* student
adult
  affect of: vs. infant, 100; intensity, 361
  interest expression, 84
affect
  vs. expectation and behavior, 460
  infant, 100, 129
  intensity of, 361, 377
  modulation, 478
  negative, and gender, 318
  parameters, 203
  positive, and reciprocation, 460
  and synchrony, 425
  and voice, 211, 220
  see also emotion
Affect Expression Rating Scale (AERS), 310, 312, 313
Affective Communication Test (ACT), 310–11
AFFEX, 83 87, 90–4, 100, 167–8
affordance, 420
age
  and expressiveness, 111, 135, 297
  see also specific age class
ambiguity, and gesture, 445–6
anger, expression of, 94, 97, 98
  child, 113
  cold vs. hot, 213
  cross-cultural comparison, 130, 295

vs. distress-pain, 93, 96, 99
and family expressiveness, 115
infant, 94–5
vs. sadness, 97, 99–100
in Utku society, 128
animal
  emotional expression in, 287
  vocal communication of, 208
anthropological data, and individual's expressiveness, 129
anxiety, behaviors described, 358
aphasia, 37, 42, 48, 56
approach–avoidance factor, 469
arousal, 428, 473
  and expressiveness, 136
  vs. functionalism, 460–1
  and gesture, 240
articulated gesture, vs. holophrastic, 455
articulation, 208; *see also* voice, production
asymmetry
  brain, *see* brain, lateralization
  facial, 47–8
  left-ear advantage, 50
attribution model, 229
auditory comprehension, *see* aphasia
autonomic nervous system (ANS), and expressiveness, 302–9

batonic movement, 243
beat, hand movement, 243
behavior, *see specific behavior*; nonverbal behavior; verbal behavior
bidirectionality, 116, 132
blacks, expressiveness of, 130